SOCIAL AND POLITICAL PHILOSOPHY

Social and Political Philosophy: Contemporary Perspectives introduces and explores the central questions of social and political philosophy from opposing perspectives. Each essay has been accessibly written by a philosopher at the forefront of the field, advancing the discussion in ways that are of interest to professional philosophers and students alike. Traditional perspectives are balanced with new challenges that have emerged. The book concludes with an attempt to respond to and reconcile a number of the arguments presented in the essays.

Social and Political Philosophy: Contemporary Perspectives is an excellent collection that focuses and reinvigorates discussion on the central questions of social and political philosophy.

James P. Sterba is Professor of Philosophy at the University of Notre Dame. He is the author of numerous books, including *How to Make People Just*, *Feminist Philosophies* (2nd edn), *Morality in Practice* (6th edn), *Earth Ethics* (2nd edn), *Justice for Here and Now* and *Three Challenges to Ethics*.

SOCIAL AND POLITICAL PHILOSOPHY

Contemporary perspectives

Edited by
James P. Sterba

ROUTLEDGE
Taylor & Francis Group

London and New York

First published 2001
by Routledge
11 New Fetter Lane, London EC4P 4EE

Simultaneously published in the USA and Canada
by Routledge
29 West 35th Street, New York, NY 10001

Routledge is an imprint of the Taylor & Francis Group

Typeset in Times by Taylor & Francis Books Ltd
Printed and bound in Great Britain by
St Edmundsbury Press, Bury St Edmunds, Suffolk

British Library Cataloguing in Publication Data
A catalogue record for this book is available from the British Library

Library of Congress Cataloging in Publication Data
Sterba, James P.
Social and political philosophy: contemporary perspectives / James P. Sterba.
Includes bibliographical references and index.
1. Social justice. 2. Justice (Philosophy). 3. Social ethics.
4. Political science–Philosophy. 5. Sociology–Philosophy. I. Title
HM671 .S74 2001
303.372–dc21   00-062761

ISBN 0–415–21795–4 (hbk)
ISBN 0–415–21796–2 (pbk)

CONTENTS

CONTENTS

CONTENTS

CONTRIBUTORS

Eve Browning Cole is an associate professor in the philosophy department at the University of Minnesota Duluth. She earned a Ph.D. at U.C. San Diego, where she first learned that the expression "go to the mats" (as in philosophical argument) doesn't refer to yoga or transcendental meditation. She works on ancient Greek philosophy, feminist philosophy, and ethics. She has published two books, *Explorations in Feminist Ethics* (1992) and *Philosophy and Feminist Criticism* (1993).

Alan Gewirth began his teaching career at the University of Chicago in 1947, where he is now an emeritus professor of philosophy. He has received many grants and awards. He has been a Rockefeller Fellow, a Guggenheim Fellow, and a Fellow of the American Academy of Arts and Sciences. He is also past president of the American Philosophical Association's Western Division and past president of the American Society for Political and Legal Philosophy. His books include: *Reason and Morality* (1978), *Human Rights: Essays on Justification and Application* (1982), *The Community of Rights* (1996) and *Self-Fulfillment* (1998).

Bernard Gert is Stone Professor of Intellectual and Moral Philosophy and Chair of the Philosophy Department at Dartmouth College and Adjunct Professor of Psychiatry at Dartmouth Medical School. He has also taught at the Johns Hopkins University, the University of Edinburgh, the Hebrew University of Jerusalem, the Nacional Universidad de La Plata and the Universidad de Buenos Aires. He was the Principal Investigator on a Grant from National Institutes of Health, "Ethical Issues Arising from the Human Genome Project" (1990–93), which resulted in the book *Morality and the New Genetics* (1996). He is editor of *Man and Citizen* (1991) (Thomas Hobbes's *De Homine* and *De Cive*); first author of *Bioethics: A Return to Fundamentals* (1997); and author of *Morality: Its Nature and Justification* (1998).

Tibor R. Machan is a Freedom Communications Professor at the Argyros School of Business and Economics, Chapman University, California, Research Fellow at the Hoover Institution, Stanford University, and political adviser to

Freedom Communications, Inc. He is a widely published columnist, author of 20 books, most recently *Ayn Rand* (Peter Lang, 2000) and *Initiative: Human Agency and Society* (Hoover Institution Press, 2000), editor of another 15 and has written a couple of hundred scholarly papers. He is also editor of the series *Philosophical Reflections on a Free Society* at the Hoover Institution Press. He publishes and edits *Reason Papers*, an annual journal of interdisciplinary normative studies.

Jan Narveson was educated at the University of Chicago and at Harvard, and is Professor of Philosophy at the University of Waterloo in Ontario, Canada, where he has taught since 1963. He also taught at the University of New Hampshire, 1961–3, and as Visiting Professor at Johns Hopkins (1967), Stanford (1968), and Calgary (1976), and was Visiting Research Scholar at the Centre for Philosophy and Social Policy, Bowling Green State University, Ohio (1990). His publications include over two hundred papers and reviews in philosophical periodicals and anthologies, mainly on ethical theory and practice. His published books include *Morality and Utility* (Johns Hopkins Press, 1967), *The Libertarian Idea* (Temple University Press, 1989), *Moral Matters* (Broadview Press, 1993), *Political Correctness* (co-authored with Marilyn Friedman, 1994); and two anthologies: *Moral Issues* (Oxford U.P. 1983) and *For and Against the State*, co-edited with J. T. Sanders (Rowman & Littlefield, 1996).

Eva Feder Kittay is Professor of Philosophy at SUNY at Stony Brook. In addition to numerous articles, she has published the following books: *Metaphor: Its Linguistic Structure and Its Cognitive Force* (Oxford University Press, 1987), *Women and Moral Theory* (Rowman & Littlefield, 1987), *Frames, Fields and Contrasts: New Essays in Semantics and Lexical Organization* (Lawrence Erlbaum Associates, 1992), *Love's Labor: Essays on Equality and Dependency* (Routledge, 1999).

John Deigh teaches moral and political philosophy at Northwestern University. He is the author of *The Sources of Moral Agency*, a collection of essays in moral psychology. He is the editor of *Ethics: An International Journal of Social, Political and Legal Philosophy*.

Robert C. Solomon is Quincy Lee Centennial Professor of Business and Philosophy and Distinguished Teaching Professor at the University of Texas at Austin. He is the author of *Above the Bottom Line, It's Good Business, Ethics and Excellence* and *New World of Business* as well as *The Passions, In the Spirit of Hegel, About Love, A Passion for Justice, Up the University* and (with Kathleen M. Higgins) *A Short History of Philosophy, A Passion for Wisdom, The Joy of Philosophy*, and (most recently) *What Nietzsche Really Said*.

Michael Boylan is Professor of Philosophy at Marymount University. He is the author of *Basic Ethics*, an essay in normative and applied ethics. He has also written or edited seven other books in philosophy. Along with being a philosopher he has also published five works in fiction and poetry and has directed a poetry series in the Washington, DC, area since 1990. Boylan has over sixty published articles ranging from ethics to the history of science to critical studies of contemporary fiction.

Kai Nielsen received his Ph.D. from Duke University, Durham, NC. He is currently Emeritus Professor of Philosophy at the University of Calgary and adjunct Professor of Philosophy at Concordia University. He specializes in metaphilosophy, contemporary ethical and political theory, and Marxism. He is the author of some 22 books and 415 articles. His most recent books are *Transforming Philosophy* (1995), and *Naturalism Without Foundations* (1996).

Carol C. Gould is Professor of Philosophy at Stevens Institute of Technology, Research Associate at the Centre de Recherche en Epistemologie Appliquée, Ecole Polytechnique, C.N.R.S., Paris, and Adjunct Professor of International and Public Affairs at Columbia University. In 2000–01, she is Fulbright Florence Chair of Political and Social Science at the European University Institute in Fiesole, Italy. She is the author of *Marx's Social Ontology* (MIT Press, 1978) and of *Rethinking Democracy* (Cambridge University Press, 1988), editor or co-editor of six books, including *Women and Philosophy* (with M. W. Wartofksy); *Beyond Domination: New Perspectives on Women and Philosophy*; *The Information Web: Ethical and Social Implications of Computer Networking*; *Gender*; and most recently, *Cultural Identity and the Nation-State* (with Pasquale Pasquino, Rowman & Littlefield, 2001), and has published over forty articles. She is currently Co-Executive Director of the Society for Philosophy and Public Affairs and President of the American Society of Value Inquiry.

Alison M. Jaggar is Professor of Philosophy and Women Studies at the University of Colorado at Boulder. Her books include *Feminist Frameworks* (3rd edn 1993); *Feminist Politics and Human Nature* (1983); *Gender/Body/Knowledge: Feminist Reconstructions of Being and Knowing* (1989); *Living with Contradictions: Controversies in Feminist Social Ethics* (Westview, 1994), *Morality and Social Justice* (1995); *The Blackwell Companion to Feminist Philosophy* (1998). Presently, she is working on *Sex, Truth and Power: A Feminist Theory of Moral Reason* and a book of essays on sexual equality. Jaggar was a founder member of the Society for Women in Philosophy, past chair of the American Philosophical Association Committee on the Status of Women, and past co-president of the North American Society for Social Philosophy.

Rosemarie Tong is Distinguished Professor in Health Care Ethics in the Department of Philosophy at the University of North Carolina at Charlotte. An award-winning teacher and prolific writer and lecturer, she is the author of *Women, Sex, and the Law* (1984), *Feminine and Feminist Ethics* (1993),

Feminist Approaches to Bioethics: Theoretical Reflections and Practical Applications (1997), and *Feminist Thought: A More Comprehensive Introduction* (1998). Tong currently serves as co-coordinator of the International Network on Feminist Approaches to Bioethics, and she is co-editor of an anthology tentatively entitled *Globalizing Feminist Bioethics: Women's Health Concerns Worldwide* and scheduled for publication in 2000.

Claudia Card is a Fully Revolting Hag at the University of Wisconsin with tenure in the Department of Philosophy and teaching affiliations in Women's Studies and Environmental Studies. She is the author of *Lesbian Choices* (1995) and *The Unnatural Lottery: Character and Moral Luck* (1996) and editor of *Feminist Ethics* (1991), *Adventures in Lesbian Philosophy* (1994), and *On Feminist Ethics and Politics* (1998). In 1996 she was honored as Distinguished Woman Philosopher of the Year by the Society of Women in Philosophy. She chairs the American Philosophical Association's Committee on the Status of Lesbian, Gay, Bisexual, and Transgendered People in the Profession. She is currently at work on a book on the concept of evil, for which she has received an American Council of Learned Societies Senior Fellowship and a Resident Fellowship at the Institute for Research in the Humanities at the University of Wisconsin.

John Corvino is Senior Lecturer in the philosophy department at Wayne State University, Detroit. He is the editor of *Same Sex: Debating the Ethics, Science, and Culture of Homosexuality* (Rowman & Littlefield, 1997). In addition to sexual ethics, his research interests include business ethics and Hume's metaethics.

Charles W. Mills is Professor of Philosophy at the University of Illinois at Chicago. He received his Ph.D. from the University of Toronto. His main research interests are in oppositional political theory, particularly around issues of class, gender and race. He has published two books from Cornell University Press: *The Racial Contract* and *Blackness Visible: Essays on Philosophy and Race*.

Chung-Ying Cheng has been a member of the Philosophy Department at the University of Hawaii at Monoa since 1963. He received his doctorate from Harvard University in the field of analytical philosophy and logic. He has received fellowships and grants from the National Science Foundation, the Pacific Cultural Foundation and the Stanford Institute in the Philosophy of Science. He is the founder and a past president of the International Society of Chinese Philosophy. He also founded and serves as president of the International Society for Yijing Studies. Cheng has edited the *Journal of Chinese Philosophy* since its founding in 1972 and has received an Honorary Doctorate from the Far Eastern Institute of the Russian Academy of Sciences. Cheng has authored and edited 15 books and over 150 articles in Western,

Chinese, and comparative philosophy. He is currently working on a book on onto-hermeneutics and a book on contemporary Chinese philosophy.

Holmes Rolston III is Professor of Philosophy and University Distinguished Professor at Colorado State University, Fort Collins. He is the author of *Environmental Ethics: Duties to and Values in the Natural World, Philosophy Gone Wild, Conserving Natural Value*, and *Science and Religion: A Critical Survey*. His Gifford Lectures at the University of Edinburgh are published as *Genes, Genesis and God*. He is Associate Editor of the journal *Environmental Ethics* and past president of the International Society for Environmental Ethics.

Mary Anne Warren is Professor of Philosophy at San Francisco State University. She writes on a range of issues in biomedical and applied ethics, including abortion, affirmative action, sex segregation in education, medical means of pre-selecting the sex of children, in vitro fertilization and embryo research, animal rights, and environmental ethics. She has published three books, *The Nature of Woman: An Encyclopedia and Guide to the Literature* (Edgepress, 1980); *Gendercide: The Implications of Sex Selection* (Littlefield Adams, 1985); and *Moral Status: Obligations to Persons and Other Living Things* (Oxford University Press, 1997).

Robert L. Holmes is Professor of Philosophy at the University of Rochester, NY, and author of *On War and Morality* (1989) and *Basic Moral Philosophy*, 2nd edn (1998). Former editor of *Public Affairs Quarterly*, he has been Fulbright Lecturer to the Soviet Union and has held the Rajiv Gandhi Chair in Peace and Disarmament at Jawharlal Nehru University, New Delhi, India.

Laurence Thomas is professor in the departments of political science and philosophy at Syracuse, where he also teaches in the Jewish Studies program. He is the author of numerous articles and three books *Living Morally, Vessels of Evil* and *Sexual Orientation and Human Rights*.

James P. Sterba is Professor of Philosophy at the University of Notre Dame, IN, where he teaches moral and political philosophy. He has written more than 150 articles and published 23 books, including *How to Make People Just* (1988), *Contemporary Social and Political Philosophy* (1995), *Social and Political Philosophy: Classical Texts in Feminist and Multicultural Perspectives*, 2nd edn (1998), *Feminist Philosophies*, 2nd edn (1999), *Earth Ethics* 2nd edn (2000), *Morality in Practice*, 6th edn (2000), and *Three Challenges To Ethics* (2000). His book, *Justice for Here and Now*, published with Cambridge University Press, was awarded the 1998 Book of the Year Award of the North American Society for Social Philosophy. He is past president of the International Society for Social and Legal Philosophy, the American Section, past president of Concerned Philosophers for Peace, and past president of the North American Society for Social Philosophy. He has lectured widely – in Europe, Asia, and Africa, as well as in the United States.

PREFACE

This is a ground-breaking work in social and political philosophy. Twenty-one well-known philosophers have written new and substantial essays exploring the central questions of social and political philosophy. Each essay has been accessibly written by a philosopher at the forefront of the field. The contributors have also written essays in which they can develop their own views, and advance the discussion of social and political philosophy in ways that would interest professional philosophers as well as students. The themes of the essays are initially introduced in the Introduction, and draw on my book, *Justice for Here and Now*. Different essays in the volume discuss the foundations of social and political philosophy, alternative social and political perspectives, challenges to social and political philosophy, and the application of social and political philosophy under nonideal conditions. The Conclusion attempts to respond to and reconcile a number of the arguments presented in the essays. The book is ideal for all ranges of courses in social and political philosophy. It is designed to enable students to build their own social and political philosophy by moving them through the various steps required for its construction. The uniqueness of the collection, the list of well-known contributors, and the fact that the book has the worthy pedagogical goal of offering students the tools necessary to build their own social and political philosophy, should make this anthology a welcome addition to the market.

I wish to especially thank Tony Bruce at Routledge for encouraging me in this project from the very beginning; and also the University of Notre Dame for funding the conference on "Alternative Conceptions of Justice", 14–16 April 2000, at which at number of the contributions to this volume were first presented and profitably discussed.

James P. Sterba

Part I

INTRODUCTION

JUSTICE FOR
HERE AND NOW

James P. Sterba

Too often, doing philosophy is modeled after fighting a battle or making war. Arguments are attacked, shot down (like a plane) or sunk (like a ship). Theses are defended, defeated, or demolished (like the walls of a city). Ideas (like people) are killed and destroyed.[1] There are clearly problems with doing philosophy in this way. There is unfairness inherent in the practice, along with its tendency to undercut the possibility of reaching truly justified views. Fortunately, there is a peacemaking alternative. This way of doing philosophy that, while seeking to determine what are the most justified philosophical views, is committed to

1 a fair-mindedness that, among other things, puts the most favorable interpretation on the views of one's philosophical opponents,
2 an openness that reaches out to understand challenging new philosophical views, and
3 a self-criticalness that requires modifying or abandoning one's philosophical views should the weight of available evidence require it.

From rationality to morality

Now a *first step* to implementing a peacemaking way of doing philosophy with respect to social and political philosophy is to examine carefully the possibility of grounding morality on the widely shared norms of rationality. This requires not simply showing that morality is rationally permissible, because that would imply that egoism and immorality were rationally permissible as well. Rather, what needs to be shown is that morality is rationally required, thus excluding egoism and immorality as rationally permissible.

In his recent book, *The Rational and the Moral Order*, Kurt Baier attempts to overcome this gap between egoism and morality by interpreting morality as a system of reasons of mutual benefit that are appropriate for contexts in which everyone's following self-interested reasons would have suboptimal results for everyone.[2] So interpreted, moral reasons apply only

3

when there exists an adequate enforcement system that makes acting against those reasons unprofitable. Morality so construed never requires any degree of altruism or self-sacrifice; it only requires that people act upon reasons of mutual benefit. According to Baier,

> [The] Limited Good Will [of morality] is not a straightforward other-regarding or benevolent, let alone an altruistic ... pattern. ... Persons of limited conditional goodwill may thus be motivated primarily by concern for their own good life and their conforming with [moral] guidelines is a contribution to the concerns of others, which (since they may not care about these others) is made mainly or only because the realization of their own ends is seen to depend on the contributions made by others, and because they are prepared to recognize the reasonableness of reciprocity in this matter.[3]

Given this interpretation of morality, it is not possible for the egoist to do better by acting against morality. So construed, morality and egoism do not conflict.

Unfortunately, this does not seem to be the defense of morality for which we were hoping. It succeeds only by redefining morality in a question-begging way so that it no longer demands any degree of altruism or self-sacrifice, e.g. for those who are poor and misfortunate, and in that way is rendered compatible with egoism.

Searching for such a non-question-begging justification of morality, Alan Gewirth has proposed a quite different argument.[4] The central premises of his argument can be summarized as follows:

1 All agents regard their purposes as good according to whatever criteria are involved in their actions to fulfill them.
2 Therefore, all agents must affirm a right to the freedom and well-being necessary to achieve their purposes.
3 All agents must affirm such a right on the basis of simply being prospective, purposive agents.
4 Hence, all agents must affirm that every prospective, purposive agent has a right to freedom and well-being.

Gewirth claims that the universalized right affirmed in the conclusion of his argument is a moral right, that is, a right that is action-guiding for the rightholder and for others as well, a right that implies at least that others ought not to interfere with the exercise of that right. Such rights are symmetrically action-guiding because they are action-guiding both for the rightholder and for others as well.

Nevertheless, the success of Gewirth's argument depends on the impossibility of interpreting the universalized right in his conclusion as anything

4

other than a moral right. Unfortunately for Gewirth's argument, another interpretation is possible. According to this interpretation, a universalized right can be deduced from the premises of his argument, but it is a prudential right, not a moral right. This interpretation is plausible because Gewirth maintains that the right referred to in premise 3 is prudential,[5] and the universalization of a prudential right can be understood to be a prudential right, albeit a universal one.[6]

Now, what distinguishes a prudential right from a moral right is that a prudential right is action-guiding for the rightholder only, and not for others, and so it does not imply that others ought not to interfere with the exercise of that right. Such rights are asymmetrically action-guiding because they are action-guiding only for the rightholder and not for others. Prudential rights are also analogous to the oughts found in most ordinary cases of competitive games – cases that we otherwise would have thought conform to the requirements of practical reason. For example, in football a defensive player may think that the opposing team's quarterback ought to pass on a third down with five yards to go, while not wanting the quarterback to do so and indeed hoping to foil any such attempt the quarterback makes. Or, to adapt an example of Jesse Kalin's, if you and I are playing chess, at a certain point in the game I may judge that you ought to move your bishop and put my king in check, but this judgment is not action-guiding for me. What I in fact should do is sit quietly and hope that you do not move as you ought. If you fail to make the appropriate move and, later in the game, I judge that I ought to put your king in check, that judgment, by contrast, would be action-guiding for me. So prudential rights are asymmetrically action-guiding in just the same way as these oughts of competitive games are asymmetrically action-guiding.

Given that the universal right to freedom and well-being in the conclusion of Gewirth's argument can thus plausibly be interpreted to be a prudential right, Gewirth's justification of morality cannot succeed, because it depends on the impossibility of interpreting the universal right in the conclusion of his argument as anything other than a moral right. Still, we can take from Gewirth's work the view that if morality is to be rationally required, it must be given a non-question-begging justification.

My own defense of morality employs the same general strategy as those offered by Baier and Gewirth. It differs from theirs primarily in that it introduces the perspective of altruism in constructing a non-question-begging argument to show that egoism is contrary to reason. But I claim that this is just the missing ingredient that is needed to make the argument work.

To see this, let us begin by imagining that each of us is capable of entertaining and acting upon both self-interested and moral reasons, and that the question we are seeking to answer is what sort of reasons for action it would be rational for us to accept.[7] This question is not about what sort of reasons we should publicly affirm, since people will sometimes publicly affirm reasons that are quite different from those they are prepared to act upon. Rather it is a question about what reasons it would be rational for us to accept at the deepest level – in our heart of hearts.

Of course, there are people who are incapable of acting upon moral reasons. For such people, there is no question about their being required to act morally or altruistically. Yet the interesting philosophical question is not about such people but about people, like ourselves, who are capable of acting self-interestedly or morally and are seeking a rational justification for following a particular course of action.

In trying to determine how we should act, let us assume that we would like to be able to construct a *good* argument favoring morality over egoism, and given that good arguments are non-question-begging, we accordingly would like to construct an argument that does not beg the question as far as possible. The question at issue here is what reasons each of us should take as supreme, and this question would be begged against egoism if we propose to answer it simply by assuming from the start that moral reasons are the reasons that each of us should take as supreme. But the question would be begged against morality as well if we proposed to answer the question simply by assuming from the start that self-interested reasons are the reasons that each of us should take as supreme. This means, of course, that we cannot answer the question of what reasons we should take as supreme simply by assuming the general principle of egoism:

Each person ought to do what best serves his or her overall self-interest.

We can no more argue for egoism simply by denying the relevance of moral reasons to rational choice, than we can argue for pure altruism simply by denying the relevance of self-interested reasons to rational choice and assuming the following general principle of pure altruism:

Each person ought to do what best serves the overall interest of others.[8]

Consequently, in order not to beg the question, we have no other alternative but to grant the *prima facie* relevance of both self-interested and moral reasons to rational choice, and then try to determine which reasons we would be rationally required to act upon, all things considered. Notice that in order not to beg the question, it is necessary to back off from both the general principle of egoism and the general principle of pure altruism, thus granting the *prima facie* relevance of both self-interested and moral reasons to rational choice. From this standpoint, it is still an open question whether either egoism or pure altruism will be rationally preferable, all things considered.

In this regard, there are two kinds of case that must be considered. First, there are cases in which there is a conflict between the relevant self-interested and moral reasons. Second, there are cases in which there is no such conflict.

It seems obvious that where there is no conflict and both reasons are conclusive reasons of their kind, both reasons should be acted upon. In such contexts, we should do what is favored both by morality and by self-interest.

When we rationally assess the relevant reasons in conflict cases, it is best to cast the conflict not as a conflict between self-interested reasons and moral reasons, but instead as a conflict between self-interested reasons and altruistic reasons.[9] Viewed in this way, three solutions are possible. First, we could say that self-interested reasons always have priority over conflicting altruistic reasons. Second, we could say just the opposite, that altruistic reasons always have priority over conflicting self-interested reasons. Third, we could say that some kind of compromise is rationally required. In this compromise, sometimes self-interested reasons would have priority over altruistic reasons, and sometimes altruistic reasons would have priority over self-interested reasons.

Once the conflict is described in this manner, the third solution can be seen to be the one that is rationally required. This is because the first and second solutions give exclusive priority to one class of relevant reasons over the other, and only a completely question-begging justification can be given for such an exclusive priority. Only by employing the third solution, and sometimes giving priority to self-interested reasons, and sometimes giving priority to altruistic reasons, can we avoid a completely question-begging resolution.

Notice also that this standard of rationality will not support just any compromise between the relevant self-interested and altruistic reasons. The compromise must be a nonarbitrary one, for otherwise it would beg the question with respect to the opposing egoistic and altruistic perspectives.[10] Such a compromise would have to respect the rankings of self-interested and altruistic reasons imposed by the egoistic and altruistic perspectives, respectively. Since for each individual there is a separate ranking of that individual's relevant self-interested and altruistic reasons (which will vary, of course, depending on the individual's capabilities and circumstances), we can represent these rankings from the most important reasons to the least important reasons, as shown in the table.

Individual A		Individual B	
Self-interested reasons	Altruistic reasons	Self-interested reasons	Altruistic reasons
1	1	1	1
2	2	2	2
3	3	3	3
.	.	.	.
.	.	.	.
.	.	.	.
N	N	N	N

Accordingly, any nonarbitrary compromise among such reasons in seeking not to beg the question against either egoism or pure altruism, will have to give priority to those reasons that rank highest in each category. Failure to give priority to the highest-ranking altruistic or self-interested reasons would, other things being equal, be contrary to reason.

Of course, there will be cases in which the only way to avoid being required to do what is contrary to your highest-ranking reasons is by requiring someone else to do what is contrary to her highest-ranking reasons. Some of these cases will be "lifeboat cases," as, for example, where you and two others are stranded on a lifeboat which has only enough resources for two of you to survive before you will be rescued. But although such cases are surely difficult to resolve (maybe only a chance mechanism can offer a reasonable resolution), they surely do not reflect the typical conflict between the relevant self-interested and altruistic reasons that we are or were able to acquire. Typically, one or the other of the conflicting reasons will rank significantly higher on its respective scale, thus permitting a clear resolution.

Now we can see how morality can be viewed as just such a nonarbitrary compromise between self-interested and altruistic reasons. First, a certain amount of self-regard is morally required or at least morally acceptable. Where this is the case, high-ranking self-interested reasons have priority over low-ranking altruistic reasons. Second, morality obviously places limits on the extent to which people should pursue their own self-interest. Where this is the case, high-ranking altruistic reasons have priority over low-ranking self-interested reasons. In this way, morality can be seen to be a nonarbitrary compromise between self-interested and altruistic reasons, and the "moral reasons" that constitute that compromise can be seen as having an absolute priority over the self-interested or altruistic reasons that conflict with them.[11]

Of course, exactly how this compromise is to be worked out is a matter of considerable debate. Yet however this debate is resolved, it is clear that some sort of a compromise moral solution is rationally preferable to either egoism or pure altruism when judged from a non-question-begging standpoint. In this way, it is possible to argue from rationality to morality.

Nevertheless, most contemporary philosophers do not try to justify morality by appealing to norms of rationality alone. Rather, they claim that morality must be grounded in the acceptance of moral values like liberty, fairness, equality, or the common good, and the only question is what these moral values require in practice. At this juncture, some philosophers have taken a more pessimistic turn while others have taken a more optimistic one. Those who have taken the more pessimistic turn contend that because the moral values that people hold are incommensurable they lead to radically different practical requirements.[12] Those who have taken the more optimistic turn contend that while people do hold some incommensurable values, it is still possible to achieve at least a partial agreement on practical requirements.[13]

One strategy for determining which of these views is correct is to examine social and political philosophical perspectives that appear to have minimal practical requirements, like libertarianism, to determine what practical requirements actually do follow from them. If it turns out that the practical requirements of such social and political philosophical perspectives can be shown to be more extensive than their advocates maintain, it may be possible to reconcile them at the practical level with other social and political philosophical perspectives. For example, if the libertarian's ideal of liberty could be shown to have the same practical requirements as the welfare liberal's ideal of fairness and the socialist's ideal of equality, then, at least at the practical level, it would be possible to reconcile libertarianism with welfare liberalism and socialism. Since our peacemaking model of doing philosophy is committed to providing the strongest possible justification for practical requirements, a *second step* required by this model is to examine carefully the possibility of achieving a practical reconciliation of alternative social and political philosophical perspectives by arguing in this fashion.[14]

From liberty to equality

Thus, suppose we interpret the ideal of liberty in the manner favored by libertarians.[15] So understood, liberty is the absence of interference by other people from doing what one wants or is able to do. Interpreting their ideal in this way, libertarians claim to derive a number of more specific requirements, in particular a right to life, a right to freedom of speech, press and assembly, and a right to property. Here it is important to observe that the libertarian's right to life is not a right to receive from others the goods and resources necessary for preserving one's life; it is simply a right not to be killed unjustly. Correspondingly, the libertarian's right to property is not a right to receive from others the goods and resources necessary for one's welfare, but rather a right to acquire goods and resources either by initial acquisition or by voluntary agreement.

Of course, libertarians would allow that it would be nice of the rich to share their surplus resources with the poor. Nevertheless, according to libertarians, such acts of charity should not be coercively required. For this reason, libertarians are opposed to coercively supported welfare programs.

Now, in order to see why libertarians are mistaken about what their ideal requires, consider a typical conflict situation between the rich and the poor. In this conflict situation, the rich, of course, have more than enough resources to satisfy their basic needs. By contrast, the poor lack the resources to meet their most basic needs even though they have tried all the means available to them that libertarians regard as legitimate for acquiring such resources. Under circumstances like these, libertarians usually maintain that the rich should have the liberty to use their resources to satisfy their luxury needs if they so wish. Libertarians recognize that this liberty might well be enjoyed at the expense of the satisfaction of the most basic needs of the poor; they just think that liberty always has priority over other political ideals, and since they assume that the liberty of the poor is not at stake in such conflict situations, it is easy for them to conclude that the rich should not be required to sacrifice their liberty so that the basic needs of the poor may be met.

Of course, libertarians would allow that it would be nice of the rich to share their surplus resources with the poor. Nevertheless, according to libertarians, such acts of charity are not required because the liberty of the poor is not thought to be at stake in such conflict situations.

In fact, however, the liberty of the poor is at stake in such conflict situations. What is at stake is the liberty of the poor not to be interfered with in taking from the surplus possessions of the rich what is necessary to satisfy their basic needs. When libertarians are brought to see that this is the case, they are genuinely surprised, one might even say rudely awakened, for they had not previously seen the conflict between the rich and the poor as a conflict of liberties.[16]

When the conflict between the rich and the poor is viewed as a conflict of liberties, we can either say that the rich should have the liberty not to be interfered with in using their surplus resources for luxury purposes, or we can say that the poor should have the liberty not to be interfered with in taking from the rich what they require to meet their basic needs. If we choose one liberty, we must reject the other. What needs to be determined, therefore, is which liberty is morally preferable: the liberty of the rich or the liberty of the poor.

I submit that the liberty of the poor, which is the liberty not to be interfered with in taking from the surplus resources of others what is required to meet one's basic needs, is morally preferable to the liberty of the rich, which is the liberty not to be interfered with in using one's surplus resources for luxury purposes. To see that this is the case, we need only appeal to one of the most fundamental principles of morality, one that is common to all social and political perspectives, namely, the "ought" implies "can" principle. According to this principle, people are not morally required to do what they lack the power to do or what would involve so great a sacrifice that it would be unreasonable to ask, and/or in cases of severe conflict of interest, unreasonable to require them to abide by.

For example, suppose I promised to attend a departmental meeting on Friday, but on Thursday I am involved in a serious car accident which puts me into a coma. Surely it is no longer the case that I ought to attend the meeting now that I lack the power to do so. Or suppose instead that on Thursday I develop a severe case of pneumonia for which I am hospitalized. Surely I could legitimately claim that I cannot attend the meeting on the grounds that the risk to my health involved in attending is a sacrifice that it would be unreasonable to ask me to bear. Or suppose the risk to my health from having pneumonia is not so serious that it would be unreasonable to ask me to attend the meeting (a supererogatory request), it might still be serious enough to be unreasonable to require my attendance at the meeting (a demand that is backed up by blame or coercion).

What is distinctive about this formulation of the "ought" implies "can" principle is that it claims that the requirements of morality cannot, all things considered, be unreasonable to ask, and/or in cases of severe conflict of interest, unreasonable to require people to abide by. The principle claims that reason and morality must be linked in an appropriate way, especially if we are going to be able to justifiably use blame or coercion to get people to abide by the requirements of morality. It should be noted, however, that while major figures in the history of philosophy, and most philosophers today, including virtually all libertarian philosophers, accept this link between reason and morality, the link is not usually conceived to be part of the "ought" implies "can" principle. Nevertheless, I claim that there are good reasons for associating this link between reason and morality with the "ought" implies "can" principle, namely, our use of the word "can" as in the example just given, and the natural progression from logical, physical and psychological possibility found in the traditional "ought" implies "can" principle to the notion of moral possibility found in this formulation of the "ought" implies "can" principle. In any case, the acceptability of this formulation of the "ought" implies "can" principle is determined by the virtual universal acceptance of its components, and not by the manner in which I have proposed to join those components together.[17]

Applying the "ought" implies "can" principle to the case at hand, it seems clear that the poor have it within their power willingly to relinquish such an important liberty as the liberty to take from the rich what they require to meet their basic needs. Nevertheless, it would be unreasonable to ask or require them to make so great a sacrifice. In the extreme case, it would involve asking or requiring the poor to sit back and starve to death. Of course, the poor may have no real alternative to relinquishing this liberty. To do anything else may involve worse consequences for themselves and their loved ones and may invite a painful death. Accordingly, we may expect that the poor would acquiesce, albeit unwillingly, to a political system that denied them the right to welfare supported by such a liberty, at the same time that we recognize that such a system imposed an unreasonable sacrifice upon the poor – a sacrifice that we could not morally blame the poor for trying to evade.[18] Analogously, we might expect that a woman whose life was threatened would submit to a rapist's demands, at the same time that we recognize the utter unreasonableness of those demands.

By contrast, it would not be unreasonable to ask and require the rich to sacrifice the liberty to meet some of their luxury needs so that the poor can have the liberty to meet their basic needs.[19] Naturally, we might expect that the rich, for reasons of self-interest and past contributions, might be disinclined to make such a sacrifice. We might even suppose that the past contribution of the rich provides a good reason for not sacrificing their liberty to use their surplus for luxury purposes. Yet, unlike the poor, the rich could not claim that relinquishing such a liberty involved so great a sacrifice that it would be unreasonable to ask and require them to make it; unlike the poor, the rich could be morally blameworthy for failing to make such a sacrifice.

Consequently, if we assume that however else we specify the requirements of morality, they cannot violate the "ought" implies "can" principle, it follows that, despite what libertarians claim, the right to liberty endorsed by them actually favors the liberty of the poor over the liberty of the rich.

Yet couldn't libertarians object to this conclusion, claiming that it would be unreasonable to ask the rich to sacrifice the liberty to meet some of their luxury needs so that the poor could have the liberty to meet their basic needs? As I have pointed out, libertarians don't usually see the situation as a conflict of liberties, but suppose they did. How plausible would such an objection be? Not very plausible at all, I think.

For consider: what are libertarians going to say about the poor? Isn't it clearly unreasonable to require the poor to sacrifice the liberty to meet their basic needs so that the rich can have the liberty to meet their luxury needs? Isn't it clearly unreasonable to require the poor to sit back and starve to death? If it is, then, there is no resolution of this conflict that would be reasonable to require both the rich and the poor to accept. But that would mean that libertarians could not be putting forth a moral ideal, because a moral ideal resolves severe conflicts of interest in ways that it would be reasonable to ask and require everyone affected to accept. Therefore, as long as libertarians think of themselves as putting forth a moral ideal, they cannot allow that it would be unreasonable in cases of severe conflict of interest *both* to require the rich to sacrifice the liberty to meet some of their luxury needs in order to benefit the poor, and to require the poor to sacrifice the liberty to meet their basic needs in order to benefit the rich. But I submit that if one of these requirements is to be judged reasonable, then, by any neutral assessment, it must be the requirement that the rich sacrifice the liberty to meet some of their luxury needs so that the poor can have the liberty to meet their basic needs; there is no other plausible resolution, if libertarians intend to be putting forth a moral ideal.

In brief, I have argued that a libertarian ideal of liberty can be seen to support a right to welfare through an application of the "ought" implies "can" principle to conflicts between the rich and the poor. In the interpretation I have used, the principle supports such rights by favoring the liberty of the poor over the liberty of the rich. In another interpretation (developed elsewhere), the principle supports such rights by favoring a conditional right to property over an unconditional right to property.[20] In either interpretation, what is crucial to the derivation of these rights is the claim that it would be unreasonable to require the poor to deny their basic needs and accept anything less than these rights as the condition for their willing cooperation.

In his book, *Individuals and their Rights*, Tibor Machan criticizes my argument that a libertarian ideal of liberty leads to welfare rights, accepting its theoretical thrust but denying its practical significance.[21] He appreciates the force of the argument enough to grant that if the type of conflict cases I describe between the rich and the poor actually obtained, the poor would have welfare rights. But he denies that such cases – in which the poor have done all that they legitimately can to satisfy their basic needs in a libertarian society – actually obtain. "Normally," he writes, "persons do not lack the opportunities and resources to satisfy their basic needs."[22]

But this response virtually concedes everything that defenders of welfare rights had hoped to establish. For the poor's right to welfare is not unconditional. It is conditional principally upon the poor doing all that they legitimately can to meet their own basic needs. So it is only when the poor lack sufficient opportunity to satisfy their own basic needs that a right to welfare has moral force. Accordingly, on libertarian grounds, Machan has conceded the legitimacy of just the kind of right to welfare that defenders of welfare had hoped to establish.

It is possible that libertarians convinced to some extent by the above arguments might want to accept a right to welfare but deny that there is a right to equal opportunity. Such a stance, however, is only plausible if we unjustifiably restrict the class of morally legitimate claimants to those within a given (affluent) society, for only then would a right to equal opportunity require something different from a right not to be discriminated against in filling roles and positions in society that follows from a right to welfare.[23] To see why this is the case, consider what is required by a right to welfare when the class of morally legitimate claimants is not unjustifiably restricted, but is taken to include both distant peoples and future generations.

At present there is probably a sufficient worldwide supply of goods and resources to meet the normal costs of satisfying the basic nutritional needs of all existing persons. According to former US Secretary of Agriculture, Bob Bergland,

> For the past 20 years, if the available world food supply had been evenly divided and distributed, each person would have received more than the minimum number of calories.[24]

Other authorities have made similar assessments of the available world food supply.[25]

Accordingly, the adoption of a policy of supporting a right to welfare for all existing persons would necessitate significant changes, especially in developed countries. For example, the large percentage of the US population whose food consumption clearly exceeds even an adequately adjusted poverty index might have to alter their eating habits substantially. In particular, they might have to reduce their consumption of beef and pork in order to make more grain available for direct human consumption. (Currently, 37% of worldwide production of grain and 70% of US production is fed to animals.[26]) Thus at least the satisfaction of at least some of the nonbasic needs of the more advantaged in developed countries will have to be forgone, if the basic nutritional needs of all those in developing and underdeveloped countries are to be met. Of course, meeting the long-term basic nutritional needs of these societies will require other kinds of aid, including appropriate technology and training and the removal of trade barriers favoring developed societies.[27] In addition, raising the standard of living in developing and underdeveloped countries will require a substantial increase in the consumption of energy and other resources. But such an increase will have to be matched by a substantial decrease in the consumption of these goods in developed countries; otherwise, global ecological disaster will result from increased global warming, ozone depletion and acid rain, lowering virtually everyone's standard of living.[28] For example, some type of mutually beneficial arrangement needs to be negotiated with China, which, with 50% of the world's coal resources, plans to double its use of coal within the next two decades, yet is currently burning 85% of its coal without any pollution controls whatsoever.[29]

Furthermore, once the basic nutritional needs of future generations are also taken into account, the satisfaction of the nonbasic needs of the more advantaged in developed countries would have to be further restricted, in order to preserve the fertility of cropland and other food-related natural resources for the use of future generations. Obviously, the only assured way to guarantee the energy and resources necessary for the satisfaction of the basic needs of future generations is to set aside resources that would otherwise be used to satisfy the nonbasic needs of existing generations. And once basic needs other than nutritional ones are taken into account as well, still further restrictions will be required. For example, it has been estimated that presently a North American uses about fifty times more goods and resources than a person living in India. This means that in terms of resource consumption the North American continent's population alone consumes as much as 12.5 billion people living in India would consume.[30] So, unless we assume that basic goods and resources, such as arable land, iron, coal, oil, and so forth, are in unlimited supply, this unequal consumption would have to be radically altered in order for the basic needs of distant peoples and future generations to be met.[31] Accordingly, recognizing a right to welfare applicable both to distant peoples and to future generations would lead to a state of affairs in which few resources would be available for directly meeting nonbasic needs, and this would significantly affect the right to equal opportunity that people can be guaranteed.

The form of equal opportunity that John Rawls defends in *A Theory of Justice* requires that persons who have the same natural assets and the same willingness to use them have an equal chance to occupy roles and positions in society commensurate with their natural assets.[32] So construed, equal opportunity provides two sorts of benefit. It benefits society as a whole by helping to ensure that the most talented people will fill the most responsible roles and positions in society; it benefits individuals by ensuring that they will not be discriminated against with respect to filling the roles and positions in society for which they are qualified, thereby giving them a fair chance of securing whatever benefits attach to those roles and positions.

I have argued, however, that once it is recognized that the class of morally legitimate claimants includes distant peoples and future generations, then guaranteeing a right to welfare to all morally legitimate claimants would lead to a state of affairs in which few resources would be available for directly meeting nonbasic needs, although such needs might still be met indirectly through the satisfaction of basic needs. As a consequence, there normally would not be greater benefits attaching to certain roles and positions in society, since people can expect only to have their basic needs directly met in whatever roles and positions they happened to occupy. Of course, we would still want the most talented people to occupy the most responsible roles and positions in society, it is just that occupying those roles and positions would normally not secure greater benefits to those who occupy them. Therefore, to ensure that the most talented people occupy roles and positions commensurate with their abilities, we will need to do something like the following. First, borrowing an idea from socialist justice, we will need to make the roles and positions people occupy as intrinsically rewarding as possible. Second, we will need to convince the more talented that they have a moral responsibility to the less talented and to society as a whole to use their talents to the fullest. Consequently, the equal opportunity that will be guaranteed to everyone in society will, for the most part, be a fair means of ensuring that everyone's basic needs are met, rather than a means of providing differential rewards or of serving directly to meet nonbasic needs.

Accordingly, my practical reconciliation argument fails to guarantee a right to equal opportunity that provides greater benefits to the talented, enabling them directly to meet nonbasic as well as basic needs. But this failure is no objection to my argument, given that having this sort of equal opportunity is incompatible with the more fundamental requirement of meeting everyone's basic needs. On this account, both libertarians and welfare liberals would come to endorse the same right to equal opportunity – an equal right not to be discriminated against in filling roles and positions in society that is compatible with a right to welfare.

What these arguments show, therefore, is that libertarianism or a libertarian conception of justice supports the same practical requirements as welfare liberalism or a welfare liberal conception of justice: both favor a right to welfare and a right to equal opportunity.

Still, one might want to press Machan's objection to this argument from liberty to equality, which is that the argument has no practical significance because "persons do not lack the opportunities and resources to satisfy their basic needs." However, this objection is particularly easy to refute once the libertarian ideal is seen to ground a universal right to welfare. This is because there is simply no denying that most of the 1.2 billion people who are living today in conditions of absolute poverty "lack the opportunities and resources to satisfy their basic needs."[33] Yet the objection also fails when we look closely at the poor within our own society. It is estimated that some 32 million Americans live below the official poverty index, and that one fifth of American children are growing up in poverty.[34] Surely many of these Americans also "lack the opportunities and resources to satisfy their basic needs."

It might also be objected that this argument falls victim to its own success. If a universal right to welfare requires an equal sharing of resources, wouldn't talented people simply lack the incentive to produce according to their ability when such a right is enforced? But what sort of incentive is needed? Surely there would be moral incentive for the talented to make the necessary sacrifices if the ideal of liberty requires such a right to welfare. Yet, except for those who closely identify with such moral incentives, there would not be sufficient self-interested incentive to accept the equality of resources required by a universal right to welfare. Even so, if it can be shown, as I claim, that morality has priority over self-interested prudence, there is no question of what ought to be done.

So in brief, a libertarian conception of justice supports the same rights to welfare and equal opportunity as those endorsed by a welfare liberal conception of justice. In this way, it is possible to argue from liberty to equality.

From equality to feminism

Now a welfare liberal conception of justice, in virtue of its right to equal opportunity, has been appealed to by contemporary feminists in support of a conception of feminist justice that accords with the ideal of a gender-free or androgynous society. But how is this ideal of a gender-free or androgynous society to be interpreted? It is a society where basic rights and duties are not assigned on the basis of a person's biological sex. Being male or female is not the grounds for determining what basic rights and duties a person has in a gender-free society. But this is to characterize the feminist ideal only negatively. It tells us what we need to get rid of, not what we need

16

to put in its place. A more positive characterization is provided by the ideal of androgyny. Putting the ideal of feminist justice more positively in terms of the ideal of androgyny also helps to bring out why men should be attracted to feminist justice.

In a well known article, Joyce Trebilcot distinguishes two forms of androgyny.[35] The first postulates the same ideal for everyone. According to this form of androgyny, the ideal person "combines characteristics usually attributed to men with characteristics usually attributed to women." Thus we should expect both nurturance and mastery, openness and objectivity, compassion and competitiveness, from each and every person who has the capacities for these traits.

By contrast, the second form of androgyny does not advocate the same ideal for everyone, but rather a variety of options from "pure" femininity to "pure" masculinity. As Trebilcot points out, this form of androgyny shares with the first the view that biological sex should not be the basis for determining the appropriateness of gender characterization. It differs in that it holds that "all alternatives with respect to gender should be equally available to and equally approved for everyone, regardless of sex."

It would be a mistake, however, to distinguish sharply between these two forms of androgyny. Properly understood, they are simply two different facets of a single ideal. For, as Mary Anne Warren has argued, the second form of androgyny is appropriate only "with respect to feminine and masculine traits which are largely matters of personal style and preference and which have little direct moral significance."[36] However, when we consider so-called feminine and masculine virtues, it is the first form of androgyny that is required, because then, other things being equal, the same virtues are appropriate for everyone.

We can even formulate the ideal of androgyny more abstractly so that it is no longer specified in terms of so-called feminine and masculine traits. We can specify the ideal as requiring no more than that the traits that are truly desirable in society be equally open to both women and men or, in the case of virtues, equally expected of both women and men, other things being equal.

Most contemporary defenses of the ideal of androgyny attempt to derive it from various conceptions of equality. Some feminists have tried to derive the ideal from a welfare liberal conception of equal opportunity, and others from a socialist conception of equal self-development. Let me briefly consider each of these defenses in turn.

Obviously, a right to equal opportunity could be interpreted, minimally, as providing people only with the same legal rights of access to all advantaged positions in society for which they are qualified. But this is not the interpretation that should be given this right, either by welfare liberals or by libertarians. Rather, it was argued that a right to equal opportunity should be interpreted as a right not to be discriminated against in filling the roles and positions in society, and it is this right to equal opportunity that feminists have tended to focus on in attempting to justify the ideal of androgyny.[37] The point feminists have been making is simply that failure to achieve the ideal of androgyny translates into a failure to guarantee equal opportunity to both women and men.

As it turns out, support for the ideal of androgyny provided by a socialist conception of equal self-development is as direct as that provided by a welfare liberal conception of equal opportunity.[38] Just as the ideal of androgyny can be seen to be required by a welfare liberal or libertarian right to equal opportunity, so too can it be seen to be required by a socialist right of equal self-development. In fact, once the socialist right to equal self-development is correctly understood to be an equal right to the provision of resources for self-development, it can be seen to be equivalent to the welfare liberal's right to equal opportunity.[39] What remains distinctive about the socialist defense of androgyny, however, is its claim that in contemporary capitalist societies, the ideal of androgyny is best achieved by socializing the means of production, which is to say that a cure for capitalist exploitation will also be a cure for women's oppression.[40]

Now one locus for the radical restructuring required by the ideal of a gender-free or androgynous society is the family. Here two fundamental changes are needed. First, all children, irrespective of their sex, must be given the same type of upbringing consistent with their native capabilities. Second, normally mothers and fathers must also have the same opportunities for education and employment consistent with their native capabilities.[41]

Yet, at least in the United States, this need radically to modify traditional family structures to guarantee equal opportunity confronts a serious problem. Given that a significant proportion of the available jobs are at least 9 to 5, families with preschool children require day-care facilities if their adult members are to pursue their careers. Unfortunately, for many families such facilities are simply unavailable.[42] In New York City, for example, more than 144,000 children under the age of six are competing for 46,000 full-time slots in day-care centers. In Seattle, there is licensed day-care space for 8,800 of the 23,000 children who need it. In Los Angeles, there is no licensed childcare available for 135,000 children who need such programs. In Miami, two children, three and four years old, were left unattended at home while their parent worked. They climbed into a clothes dryer while the timer was on, closed the door, and burned to death.[43]

Moreover, even the available day-care facilities are frequently inadequate, either because their staffs are poorly trained or because the child/adult ratio in such facilities is too high. At best, many such facilities provide little more than custodial care; at worst, they actually retard the development of those children under their care.[44] What this suggests is that at least under present conditions, if preschool children are to be adequately cared for, frequently one of the adult members of the family has to remain at home to provide

18

that care. But because most jobs are at least 9 to 5, this requires that the adult members who stay at home temporarily give up pursuing a career. However, such sacrifice appears to conflict with the equal opportunity requirement of feminist justice.

Families might try to meet this equal opportunity requirement by having one parent relinquish a career for a certain period of time and the other give up pursuing a career for a subsequent (equal) period of time. But there are problems here too. Some careers are difficult to interrupt for any significant period of time, while others never adequately reward latecomers. In addition, given the high rate of divorce and the inadequacies of most legally mandated child support, those who first sacrifice their careers may find themselves later faced with the impossible task of trying to begin or revive them while continuing to be the primary caretaker of their children.[45] Furthermore, there is considerable evidence that children will benefit more from equal rearing from both parents.[46] So the option of having just one parent doing the child rearing for any length of time is, other things being equal, not optimal.

It would seem therefore, that to truly share child-rearing within the family what is needed are flexible (typically part-time) work schedules that allow both parents to be together with their children for a significant period every day. Some flexible work schedules have already been tried by various corporations.[47] But if equal opportunity is to be a reality in our society, the option of flexible work schedules must be guaranteed to all those with preschool children. A recent estimate shows that married full-time career women still do almost as much of the housework chores – 70% – as the average full-time housewife, who does 83% of the housework.[48] Obviously this will have to change if we are to achieve the ideal of a gender-free or androgynous society.

A second locus of change required by the ideal of a gender-free or androgynous society is the distribution of economic power in the society. In the United States, the percentage of women in the labor force has risen steadily for three decades, from 35% (of those aged sixteen or more) in 1960 to 59% in 1995. Roughly 70% of women with children at home were employed in 1995, including more than 63% of mothers with children under the age of six and 59% of mothers with children under the age of one.[49]

Yet in 1995 women employed full-time still earned $.72 for every $1 men earned, up from the $.60 for every $1 that held from the 1960s through the 1980s. Earnings do increase with education for all workers, but all women, as well as men of color, earn less than white men at every level of education. For example, women with four years of college education earn less on average than men who have not completed high school.[50]

Sometimes women and men working in the same job category have different incomes. For example, while female clerical workers earned a median wage of $384 per week in 1995, the median wage for male clerical workers was $489.[51] More frequently, however, women and men tend to be employed in different job categories that are paid differently. According to one study done a few years ago in the state of Washington, women employed as clerk-typists earned less than men employed as truck drivers or warehouse workers. In another study done in Denver, women employed as nurses earned less than men employed as tree cutters. While in each of these cases the women earned about 20% less than the men, the women's jobs, when evaluated in terms of skill, responsibility, effort, and working conditions, were given equal or higher scores than the men's jobs with which they were compared. Clearly, denying women the opportunity to earn the same as men do for equal or comparable work is a basic injustice in our society, and it will be a very costly one to correct.[52]

To remedy these inequalities suffered by women in the economic sphere will require programs of affirmative action and comparable worth. Affirmative action is needed to place qualified women in positions they deserve to occupy because of past discrimination. Without affirmative action, the structural violence of past discrimination will not be rectified. Only with affirmative action can the competition for desirable jobs and positions be made fair again, given our past history of discrimination. There are even cases where affirmative action candidates are clearly the most qualified, but where those in charge of hiring, because of their prejudice, can only see the candidates as simply qualified but not as the *most* qualified candidates.[53]

Comparable worth is also needed because, without it, women will not receive the salaries they deserve. They will do work that is judged equal or comparable to the work that men are doing in male-dominated occupations, but without comparable worth they will be paid less than the men. Paying for comparable worth programs will not be easy, but it can be done. The state of Washington spent $115 million over seven years on a comparable worth program, and the state of Iowa spent almost 9% of its payroll over a three-year period to achieve comparable worth.[54]

A third locus of change required by the ideal of a gender-free or androgynous society is the overt violence perpetrated against women in our society. According to former Surgeon General Antonia Novello, "The home is actually a more dangerous place for the American woman than the city streets." "One-third of the women slain in the U.S.," she continues, "die at the hands of husbands and boyfriends."[55] In addition, women in the United States live in fear of rape. Twenty percent of women are raped at some time during their lives, according to one national study; 44% of women are subjected either to rape or attempted rape at some point during their lives, according to another study done in the San Francisco area, and almost 50% of male college students say they would commit rape if they were certain that they could get away with it.[56] Not infrequently, women are beaten by their own husbands and lovers (between one quarter and one third of women are battered in their homes by husbands and lovers).[57] One third of all women who require emergency-room hospital treatment are there as a result of domestic violence.[58] Thirty-eight percent of little girls are sexually molested inside or outside the family.[59] Since most of these crimes are minimally prosecuted in our society, women in our society can be raped, battered, or sexually abused as children, and little, if anything, will be done about it. What this shows is that the condition of women in our society is actually that of being subordinate to men by force.[60]

Feminist justice demands that we put an end to the overt violence against women, which takes the distinctive form of rape, battery, and sexual abuse. This overt violence is in every way as destructive as the other forms of violence we oppose, so we cannot in consistency fail to oppose it. According to one cross-cultural study of ninety-five societies, 47% of them were free of rape.[61] This shows that it is possible to eliminate, or at least drastically reduce, overt violence against women.

One way to help bring about this result is to ban hard-core pornography that celebrates and legitimizes rape, battery, and the sexual abuse of children, as the Supreme Court of Canada has recently done.[62] Catharine MacKinnon has argued that pornography of this sort goes beyond mere speech in constituting a practice of sex discrimination that is a violation of women's civil rights.[63] According to MacKinnon, men who participate in the practice learn through the pleasures of masturbation to enjoy the forceful subordination of women, and they seek to find ways to impose that same subordination on the women who come into their lives. Because of the severity of these impositions, MacKinnon and other anti-pornography feminists claim that the practice of hard-core pornography violates women's civil rights by denying their equal status as citizens.[64]

Another locus of change required by the ideal of a gender-free or androgynous society overlaps the previous two. It is rooted in the distribution of economic power in society and it frequently takes the form of overt violence against women. It is the problem of sexual harassment. Actually, sexual harassment was not recognized as an offense by US trial courts until the late 1970s, and it was only affirmed by the US Supreme Court as an offense in the 1980s. The term "sexual harassment" was not even coined until the 1970s. So the moral problem of sexual harassment is one that many people have only recently come to recognize. The Senate Judiciary Committee hearings on Anita Hill's charge that Clarence Thomas had sexually harassed her obviously heightened people's awareness of this problem.

In 1986, the US Supreme Court, in Meritor Savings Bank v. Vinson, ruled that there could be two types of sexual harassment: harassment that conditions concrete employment benefits on granting sexual favors (often called the *quid pro quo* type), and harassment that creates a hostile or offensive work environment without affecting economic benefits (the hostile environment type).[65]

Nevertheless, the Supreme Court made it difficult for a plaintiff to establish that either of these types of sexual harassment had occurred. For example, a polite verbal "no" does not suffice to show that sexual advances are unwelcome; a woman's entire conduct both inside and outside the workplace is subject to appraisal in order to determine whether or not she welcomed the advances. For example, in the Vinson case, there was "voluminous testimony regarding Vinson's dress and personal fantasies," and in the Senate Judiciary Committee hearings, Anita Hill was not able to prevent intensive examination of her private life, although Clarence Thomas was able to declare key areas of his private life as off-limits, such as his practice of viewing and discussing pornographic films.

The Supreme Court also made it difficult to classify work environments as hostile to women unless the harassment is sufficiently severe or pervasive. Applying the Supreme Court's standard, a lower court, in Christoforou v. Ryder Truck Rental, judged a supervisor's actions of fondling a plaintiff's rear end and breasts, propositioning her, and trying to force a kiss at a Christmas party, to be "too sporadic and innocuous" to support a finding of a hostile work environment.[66] Similarly, in Rabidue v. Osceola Refining Co., a workplace where pictures of nude and scantily clad women abounded (including one, which hung on a wall for eight years, of a woman with a golf ball on her breasts and a man with his golf club standing over her and yelling "Fore!") and where a co-worker, never disciplined despite repeated complaints, routinely referred to women as "whores," "cunts," "pussies," and "tits," was judged by a lower court not to be a sufficiently hostile environment to constitute sexual harassment.[67] Notice, by contrast, that the Senate Arms Services Committee, in its recent hearings, regarded an environment in which known homosexuals are simply doing their duty in the military to be too hostile an environment in which to ask male heterosexuals to serve.

Yet why should we accept the Supreme Court's characterization of sexual harassment, especially given its unwelcomeness and pervasiveness requirements? As the Supreme Court interprets sexual harassment, a person's behavior must be unwelcome in a fairly strong sense before it constitutes sexual harassment. But why should a woman have to prove that the offer "If you don't sleep with me, you will be fired" is unwelcome before it constitutes sexual harassment?[68] Isn't such an offer objectively unwelcome? Isn't it just the kind of offer that those in positions of power should not be making to their subordinates, an offer that purports to make their continuing employment conditional upon providing sexual favors? Surely, unless we are dealing with some form of legalized prostitution, and maybe not even then, such offers are objectively unwelcome.[69] Given, then, that such offers are objectively unwelcome, why is there any need to show that they are also subjectively unwelcome before regarding them as violations of Title VII of the Civil Rights Act? The requirement of subjective unwelcomeness is simply a gratuitous obstacle that makes the plaintiff's case far more difficult to prove than it should be.[70]

In addition, if the plaintiff is fired after refusing such an offer, the Supreme Court requires her to prove that the firing occurred because the offer was refused, which is very difficult to do unless one is a perfect employee. Wouldn't it be fairer to require the employer to prove that the plaintiff would have been fired even if she had said "yes" to the offer? Of course, employers could avoid this burden of proof simply by not making any such offers in the first place.[71] But when they do make objectively unwelcome offers, why shouldn't the burden of proof be on them to show that any subsequent firing was clearly unrelated to the plaintiff's refusal of the offer? Fairness is particularly relevant in this context because we are committed to equal opportunity in the workplace, which requires employing women and men on equal terms. Accordingly, we must guard against imposing special burdens on women in the workplace, when there are no comparable burdens imposed on men. Feminist justice, with its ideal of a gender-free or androgynous society, will be satisfied with nothing less.[72]

The demand for equal opportunity in the workplace also appears to conflict with the Supreme Court's pervasiveness requirement for establishing a hostile environment. Citing a lower court, the Supreme Court contends that, to be actionable, sexual harassment "must be sufficiently severe or pervasive 'to alter the conditions of the [victim's] employment and create an abusive working environment.' "[73] But as this standard has been interpreted by lower courts, the pervasiveness of certain forms of harassment in the workplace has become grounds for tolerating them. In Rabidue, the majority argued:

> [I]t cannot seriously be disputed that in some work environments, humor and language are rough hewn and vulgar. Sexual jokes, sexual conversations and girlie magazines abound. Title VII was not meant to or can change this. Title VII is the federal court mainstay in the struggle for equal employment opportunity for the female workers of America. But it is quite different to claim that Title VII was designed to bring about a magical transformation in the social mores of American workers.[74]

The Supreme Court itself seems to sound a similar theme by emphasizing the application of Title VII to only extreme cases of sexual harassment as found in Vinson.

However, as the EEOC (Equal Employment Opportunity Commission) interprets Title VII, the law has a broader scope. It affords employees the right to work in an environment free from discriminatory intimidation, ridicule, and insult. According to the EEOC, sexual harassment violates

Title VII where conduct creates an intimidating, hostile, or offensive environment or where it unreasonably interferes with work performance.[75]

But how are we to determine what unreasonably interferes with work performance? In Rabidue, the majority looked to prevailing standards in the workplace to determine what was reasonable or unreasonable. Yet Justice Keith, in dissent, questioned this endorsement of the status quo, arguing that just as a Jewish employee can rightfully demand a change in her working environment if her employer maintains an anti-Semitic work force and tolerates a workplace in which "kike" jokes, displays of Nazi literature, and anti-Jewish conversation "may abound," surely women can rightfully demand a change in the sexist practices that prevail in their working environments.[76] In Henson v. Dundee, the majority also drew an analogy between sexual harassment and racial harassment:

> Sexual harassment which creates a hostile or offensive environment for members of one sex is every bit the arbitrary barrier to sexual equality at the workplace that racial harassment is to racial equality. Surely, a requirement that a man or woman run a gauntlet of sexual abuse in return for the privilege of being allowed to work and make a living can be as demeaning and disconcerting as the harshest of racial epithets.

And this passage is also quoted approvingly by the Supreme Court in Vinson.

Moved by such arguments, the majority in Ellison v. Brady proposed that, rather than looking to prevailing standards to determine what is reasonable, we should look to the standard of a reasonable victim, or given that most victims of sexual harassment are women – the standard of a reasonable woman.[77] They contend that this standard may be different from the standard of a "reasonable man." For example, what male superiors may think is "harmless social interaction" may be experienced by female subordinates as offensive and threatening.[78]

Nevertheless, if we are concerned to establish the equal opportunity in the workplace that feminist justice with its ideal of a gender-free or androgynous society demands, there should be no question about what standard of reasonableness to use here. It is not that of a reasonable woman, nor that of a reasonable man for that matter, but the standard of what is reasonable for everyone to accept. For equal opportunity is a moral requirement, and moral requirements are those which are reasonable for everyone to accept. This assumes that apparent conflicts over what is reasonable to accept – for example, conflicts between the standard of a reasonable woman and that of a reasonable man – are conflicts that can and should be resolved by showing that one of these perspectives is more reasonable than the other, or that some still other perspective is even more reasonable. However, at least in the context of sexual harassment, this standard of what is reasonable for everyone to accept will accord closely with the standard of a reasonable woman, given that once women's perspectives are adequately taken into account, the contrasting perspective of a reasonable man will be seen as not so reasonable after all.

In sum, the achievement of feminist justice requires a number of important changes in our society. It requires changes in traditional family structures so that children, irrespective of their sex, will have the same type of upbringing, and mothers and fathers have the same opportunities for education and employment. It requires changes in the distribution of economic power in our society through programs of affirmative action and equal pay for comparable work that remove the structural violence against women. It requires the changes that are necessary to put an end to overt violence against women in the form of rape, battery, and sexual abuse. Last, it requires changes to implement new programs against sexual harassment in the workplace in order to achieve the equal opportunity that feminist justice promises to everyone. All of these changes, and more, are required by feminist justice's ideal of a gender-free or androgynous society.

From feminism to multiculturalism

Despite its obvious importance, it would be a mistake to pursue feminist justice alone, given that it is both theoretically and practically connected to other forms of justice. Moreover, a peacemaking way of doing philosophy demands that we work out just such connections in order to build as broad a political consensus as possible. Accordingly, we need to focus on both the theoretical and the practical connections of feminist justice to three other forms of justice: racial justice, homosexual justice, and multicultural justice.

While feminist justice seeks to remedy the injustice of sexism, racial justice seeks to remedy the injustice of racism, homosexual justice seeks to remedy the injustice of heterosexism, and multicultural justice seeks to remedy the injustice of Eurocentrism. As it turns out, each of these injustices is supported by similar theoretical arguments. The more blatant argument begins by noting certain differences among either individuals, groups or cultures. It then claims that these differences are grounds for regarding some individuals, groups, or cultures as superior to other individuals, groups, or cultures. This superiority is then claimed to legitimate the domination of some individuals, groups and cultures by other individuals, groups and cultures.[79] In each case, the theoretical argument moves from a claim of difference to a claim of superiority and then to a claim of domination. In the case of sexism, the biological differences between men and women, or other differences claimed to be linked to these biological differences, are said to be grounds for regarding men as superior to women; this superiority is then claimed to legitimate the domination of women by men. In the case of racism, specifically the principal form of racism in the United States,[80] the biological differences between whites and blacks, or other differences that are claimed to be linked to these biological differences, are said to be grounds for regarding whites as superior to blacks; this superiority is then claimed to legitimate the domination of blacks by whites. In the case of heterosexism, the biological or acquired differences between heterosexuals and homosexuals are said to be grounds for regarding heterosexuals as superior to homosexuals; this superiority is then claimed to legitimate the domination of homosexuals by heterosexuals. In the case of Eurocentrism, the cultural differences between Western culture and non-Western cultures are said to be grounds for regarding Western culture as superior to non-Western cultures; this superiority is then claimed to legitimate the domination of non-Western cultures by Western culture. In response, feminist justice, racial justice, homosexual justice and multicultural justice claim that none of these forms of domination can be justified.

Sometimes, however, the theoretical argument for sexism, racism, heterosexism or Eurocentrism takes a less blatant form. This argument begins by renouncing forms of domination adopted in the past as unjustified. Simply to deny people equal opportunity on the basis of their sex, race, sexual orientation, or culture is claimed to be wrong by this version of the argument.[81] But the argument further claims that people now, for the most part, are no longer being denied equal opportunity on the basis of sex, race, sexual orientation, or culture. Accordingly, it is claimed that the ways in which men are still favored over women, whites over blacks, heterosexuals over homosexuals, or Western culture over non-Western cultures, must either be grounded in a legitimate superiority of one over the other or be a residue of past injustices that cannot be removed without doing additional injustice.

Of course, whether the more blatant or less blatant argument for sexism, racism, heterosexism or Eurocentrism is employed, depends on how plausible it is to claim that people now are no longer denied equal opportunity by one or another of these forms of domination. Clearly, only with respect to men and women or blacks and whites does the claim seem even remotely plausible. So, as would be expected, it is only in these two contexts that the less blatant argument tends to be used, maintaining as it does that the ways in which men are still favored over women, and whites over blacks, must either be grounded in a legitimate superiority of one over the other, or be a residue of past injustices that cannot be removed without doing additional injustice. Still, it is difficult to defend even this argument because data such as we noted above make it difficult to maintain that equal opportunity currently exists, either between men and women or between whites and blacks. As a consequence, those who employ this form of the argument usually try to show that most of the inequality that does exist is a residue of past injustices that cannot be removed without doing additional injustice. Specifically, they attack both affirmative action and comparable worth as attempts to correct for past injustices that produce new injustice.

By contrast, neither heterosexists nor Eurocentrists argue in this round-about way for their view. Instead, they endorse the more blatant argument for heterosexism or Eurocentrism and maintain that there are certain differences between heterosexuals and homosexuals, or between Western culture and non-Western cultures, that ground the superiority of the former over the latter. This superiority is then further claimed to legitimate the domination of homosexuals by heterosexuals, or of non-Western cultures by Western culture.

In view of this theoretical connection between feminist justice, racial justice, homosexual justice, and multicultural justice, the practical connection between these forms of justice is quite straightforward: it is that these forms of justice should be pursued together, as much as possible, because given the theoretical connection between these forms of justice, failure to pursue them together will be looked upon with suspicion and distrust by anyone whose cause is excluded.

Of course, it can be difficult to pursue all these forms of justice together. To build a political movement strong enough to effect the necessary changes, it may be necessary to focus attention on the pursuit of just one of these forms of justice. Yet even when this is necessary, it is possible to recognize the need for the other forms of justice while still focussing primarily on only one form of justice. For example, advocates of feminist justice can recognize the need to achieve racial, homosexual and multicultural justice as well as feminist justice. Similarly, advocates of racial, homosexual and multicultural justice can also recognize the need to achieve feminist justice. Thus being as inclusive as possible can serve to bring together as many people as possible in support of one's cause, and also to signal to supporters and nonsupporters alike the uncompromising justice of that cause. Surely, given the theoretical and practical connections between these forms of justice, a peacemaking way of doing philosophy concerned to fashion a conception of justice for here and now can be satisfied with nothing less.

From anthropocentrism to nonanthropocentrism

A central debate, if not the most central debate, in contemporary environmental ethics, is between those who defend an anthropocentric ethics and those who defend a nonanthropocentric ethics. This debate pits deep ecologists like George Sessions against reform or shallow ecologists like John Passmore.[82] It divides biocentric egalitarians like Paul Taylor from social ecologists like Murray Bookchin.[83] Fortunately, we can go some way toward resolving this debate in accord with a peacemaking model of doing philosophy by showing that, when the most morally defensible versions of each of these perspectives are laid out, they will lead to the same set of principles for achieving environmental justice.[84] In this context, our peacemaking model for doing philosophy will lead to peacemaking of a different sort by significantly restricting the violence that humans can legitimately do to nature.

Consider first the nonanthropocentric perspective. In support of this perspective, it can be argued that we have no non-question-begging grounds for regarding the members of any living species as superior to the members of any other. It allows that the members of species differ in myriad ways, but argues that these differences do not provide grounds for thinking that the members of any one species are superior to the members of any other. In particular, it denies that the differences between species provide grounds for thinking that humans are superior to the members of other species. Of course, the nonanthropocentric perspective recognizes that humans have distinctive traits, which the members of other species lack, like rationality and moral agency. It just points out that the members of nonhuman species also have distinctive traits that humans lack, like the homing ability of pigeons, the speed of the cheetah, and the ruminative ability of sheep and cattle.

Nor will it do to claim that the distinctive traits that humans have are more valuable than the distinctive traits that members of other species possess, because there is no non-question-begging standpoint from which to justify that claim. From a human standpoint, rationality and moral agency are more valuable than any of the distinctive traits found in nonhuman species, since, as humans, we would not be better off if we were to trade in those traits for the distinctive traits found in nonhuman species. Yet the same holds true of nonhuman species. Generally, pigeons, cheetahs, sheep and cattle would not be better off if they were to trade in their distinctive traits for the distinctive traits of other species.[85]

Of course, the members of some species might be better off if they could retain the distinctive traits of their species while acquiring one or another of the distinctive traits possessed by some other species. For example, we humans might be better off if we could retain our distinctive traits while acquiring the ruminative ability of sheep and cattle.[86] But many of the distinctive traits of species cannot be, even imaginatively, added to the members of other species without substantially altering the original species. For example, in order for the cheetah to acquire the distinctive traits possessed by humans, presumably it would have to be so transformed that its paws became something like hands to accommodate its humanlike mental capabilities; thereby it would lose its distinctive speed and cease to be a cheetah. So possessing distinctively human traits would not be good for the cheetah.[87] And, with the possible exception of our nearest evolutionary relatives, the same holds true for the members of other species: they would not be better off having distinctively human traits. Only in fairy tales and in the world of Disney can the members of nonhuman species enjoy a full array of distinctively human traits. So there would appear to be no non-question-begging perspective from which to judge that distinctively human traits are more valuable than the distinctive traits possessed by other species. Judged from a non-question-begging perspective, we would seemingly have to regard the members of all species as equals.

Nevertheless, I want to go on to claim that regarding the members of all species as equals still allows for human preference, in the same way that regarding all humans as equals still allows for self-preference.

First of all, human preference can be justified on grounds of defense. Thus we have

> *A Principle of Human Defense*: Actions that defend oneself and other human beings against harmful aggression are permissible even when they necessitate killing or harming individual animals and plants, or even destroying whole species or ecosystems.[88]

This Principle of Human Defense allows us to defend ourselves and other human beings from harmful aggression, first, against our persons and the persons of other human beings to whom we are committed or happen to care about, and second, against our justifiably held property and the justifiably held property of other human beings to whom we are committed or happen to care about.[89]

This principle is analogous to the principle of self-defense that applies in human ethics[90] permitting actions in defense of oneself or other human beings against harmful human aggression.[91] In the case of human aggression, however, it will sometimes be possible to effectively defend oneself and other human beings by first suffering the aggression and then securing adequate compensation later. Since in the case of nonhuman aggression this is unlikely to obtain, more harmful preventive actions, such as killing a rabid dog or swatting a mosquito, will be justified. There are simply more ways to effectively stop aggressive humans than there are to stop aggressive nonhumans.

Second, human preference can also be justified on grounds of preservation. Accordingly, we have

> *A Principle of Human Preservation*: Actions that are necessary for meeting one's basic needs or the basic needs of other human beings are permissible even when they require aggressing against the basic needs of individual animals and plants, or even of whole species or ecosystems.[92]

Now needs, in general, if not satisfied, lead to lacks or deficiencies with respect to various standards. The basic needs of humans, if not satisfied, lead to lacks or deficiencies with respect to a standard of a decent life. The basic needs of animals and plants, if not satisfied, lead to lacks or deficiencies with respect to a standard of a healthy life. The means necessary for meeting the basic needs of humans can vary widely from society to society. By contrast, the means necessary for meeting the basic needs of particular species of animals and plants are more invariant.[93] Of course, while only some needs can be clearly classified as basic, and others clearly classified as nonbasic, there still are other needs that are more or less difficult to classify. Yet the fact that not every need can be clearly classified as either basic or nonbasic, as is true of a whole range of dichotomous concepts like moral/immoral, legal/illegal, living/nonliving, human/nonhuman, should not immobilize us from acting at least with respect to clear cases.[94]

In human ethics, there is no principle that is strictly analogous to this Principle of Human Preservation.[95] There is a principle of self-preservation in human ethics that permits actions that are necessary for meeting one's own basic needs or the basic needs of other people, even if this requires *failing to meet* (through an act of omission) the basic needs of still other people. For example, we can use our resources to feed ourselves and our family even if this necessitates failing to meet the basic needs of people in Third World countries. But, in general, we don't have a principle that allows us to *aggress against* (through an act of commission) the basic needs of some people in order to meet our own basic needs or the basic needs of other people to whom we are committed or happen to care about. Actually, the closest we come to permitting aggressing against the basic needs of other people in order to meet our own basic needs or the basic needs of people to whom we are committed or happen to care about, is our acceptance of the outcome of life-and-death struggles in lifeboat cases, where no one has an antecedent right to the available resources. For example, if you had to fight off others in order to secure the last place in a lifeboat for yourself or for a member of your family, we might say that you justifiably aggressed against the basic needs of those whom you fought to meet your own basic needs or the basic needs of the member of your family.[96]

Nevertheless, our survival requires a principle of preservation that permits aggressing against the basic needs of at least some other living things whenever this is necessary to meet our own basic needs or the basic needs of other human beings. Here there are two possibilities. The first is a principle of preservation that allows us to aggress against the basic needs of both humans and nonhumans whenever it would serve our own basic needs or the basic needs of other human beings. The second is the principle, stated above, that allows us to aggress against the basic needs of only nonhumans whenever it would serve our own basic needs or the basic needs of other human beings. The first principle does not express any general preference for the members of the human species, and thus it permits even cannibalism, provided that it serves to meet our own basic needs or the basic needs of other human beings. In contrast, the second principle does express a degree of preference for the members of the human species in cases where their basic needs are at stake. Of course, it would be theoretically possible to interact with the members of one's own species on the basis of the first principle of preservation considered above – the one that permits even cannibalism as a means for meeting basic needs. In the case of humans, adopting such a principle would clearly reduce the degree of predation of humans on other species, and so would be of some benefit to other species. Yet implicit nonaggression pacts based on a reasonable expectation of a comparable degree of altruistic forbearance from fellow humans have been enormously beneficial and probably were necessary for the survival of the human species. So it is difficult to see how humans could be justifiably required to forgo such benefits. Moreover, to require humans to extend these benefits to the members of all species would, in effect, be to require humans to be saints, and surely morality is not in the business of requiring anyone to be a saint. Given, then, that this greater altruism cannot be morally required, the degree of preference for the members of our own species sanctioned by the above Principle of Human Preservation is justified, even if we were to adopt a nonanthropocentric perspective.[97]

Nevertheless, preference for humans can go beyond bounds, and the bounds that are compatible with a nonanthropocentric perspective are expressed by the following:

> *A Principle of Disproportionality*: Actions that meet nonbasic or luxury needs of humans are prohibited when they aggress against the basic needs of individual animals and plants, or even of whole species or ecosystems.

This principle is strictly analogous to the principle in human ethics mentioned previously that prohibits meeting some people's nonbasic or luxury needs by aggressing against the basic needs of other people.[98] Without a doubt, the adoption of such a principle with respect to non-human nature would significantly change the way we live our lives. Such a principle is required, however, if there is to be any substance to the claim that the members of all species are equal. We can no more consistently claim that the members of all species are equal and yet aggress against the basic needs of some animals or plants whenever this serves our own nonbasic or luxury needs, than we can consistently claim that all humans are equal and aggress against the basic needs of some other human beings whenever this serves our nonbasic or luxury needs.[99] Consequently, if species equality is to mean anything, it must be the case that the basic needs of the members of nonhuman species are protected against aggressive actions, which only serve to meet the nonbasic needs of humans, as required by the Principle of Disproportionality.[100] So while a nonanthropocentric perspective allows for a degree of preference for the members of the human species, it also significantly limits that preference.[101]

To see why these limits on preference for the members of the human species are all that is required for recognizing the equality of species, we need to understand the equality of species by analogy with the equality of humans. We need to see that, just as we claim that humans are equal yet justifiably treat them differently, so too we can claim that all species are equal yet justifiably treat them differently. In human ethics, various interpretations are given to human equality that allow for different treatment of humans. In ethical egoism, everyone is *equally at liberty* to pursue his or her own interests, but this allows us always to prefer ourselves to others, who are understood to be like opponents in a competitive game. In libertarianism, everyone has an *equal right to liberty*, but although this imposes some limits on the pursuit of self-interest, it is said to allow us to refrain from helping others in severe need. In welfare liberalism, everyone has an *equal right to welfare and opportunity*, but this need not commit us to providing everyone with exactly the same resources. In socialism, everyone has an *equal right to self-development*, and although this may commit us to providing everyone with something like the same resources, it still sanctions some degree of self-preference. So just as there are these various ways to interpret human equality that still allow us to treat humans differently, there are various ways that we can interpret species equality that allow us to treat species differently.

Now one might interpret species equality in a very strong sense, analogous to the interpretation of equality found in socialism. But the kind of species equality that I have defended is more akin to the equality found in welfare liberalism or in libertarianism than it is to the equality found in socialism. In brief, this form of equality requires that we not aggress against the basic needs of members of other species for the sake of the nonbasic needs of members of our own species (the Principle of Disproportionality), but it permits us to aggress against the basic needs of members of other species for the sake of the basic needs of members of our own species (the Principle of Human Preservation), and it also permits us to defend the basic and even the nonbasic needs of members of our own species against harmful aggression by members of other species (the Principle of Human Defense). In this way, I have argued that we can accept the claim of species equality while avoiding imposing an unreasonable sacrifice on oneself or the members of our own species.[102]

But suppose we were to reject the central contention of the nonanthropocentric perspective, and deny that the members of all species are equal. We might claim, for example, that humans are superior because, through culture, they "realize a greater range of values" than members of nonhuman species, or we might claim that humans are superior in virtue of their "unprecedented capacity to create ethical systems that impart worth to other life-forms."[103] Or we might offer some other grounds for human superiority.[104] Suppose, then, we adopt this anthropocentric perspective. What follows?

First of all, we shall still need a principle of human defense. However, there is no need to adopt a different principle of human defense from the principle favored by a nonanthropocentric perspective. Whether we judge humans to be equal or superior to the members of other species, we shall still want a principle that allows us to defend ourselves and other human beings from harmful aggression, even when this necessitates killing or harming animals or plants.

Second, we will also need a principle of human preservation. But here too there is no need to adopt a different principle from the principle of human preservation favored by a nonanthropocentric perspective. Whether we judge humans to be equal or superior to the members of other species, we will still want a principle that permits actions that are necessary for meeting our own basic needs or the basic needs of other human beings, even when this requires aggressing against the basic needs of animals and plants.

The crucial question is whether we will need a different principle of disproportionality. If we judge humans to be superior to the members of other species, will we still have grounds for protecting the basic needs of animals and plants against aggressive action to meet the nonbasic or luxury needs of humans?

Here it is important to distinguish between two degrees of preference that we noted earlier. First, we could prefer the basic needs of animals and plants over the nonbasic or luxury needs of humans when to do otherwise would involve *aggressing against* (by an act of commission) the basic needs of animals and plants. Second, we could prefer the basic needs of animals and plants over the nonbasic or luxury needs of humans when to do otherwise would involve simply *failing to meet* (by an act of omission) the basic needs of animals and plants.

In human ethics, when the basic needs of some people are in conflict with the nonbasic or luxury needs of others, the distinction between failing to meet and aggressing against basic needs seems to have little moral force. In such conflict cases, both ways of not meeting basic needs are objectionable.[105] But in environmental ethics, whether we adopt an anthropocentric or a nonanthropocentric perspective, we would seem to have grounds for morally distinguishing between the two cases, favoring the basic needs of animals and plants when to do otherwise would involve *aggressing against* those needs in order to meet our own nonbasic or luxury needs, but not when it would involve simply *failing to meet* those needs in order to meet our own nonbasic or luxury needs. This degree of preference for members of the human species would be compatible with the equality of species, because humans can reasonably expect this degree of altruistic forbearance from their fellow members but not from members of other species.

Even so, this theoretical distinction would have little practical force, since most of the ways we have of preferring our own nonbasic needs over the basic needs of animals and plants actually involve aggressing against their basic needs to meet our own nonbasic or luxury needs, rather than simply failing to meet their basic needs.[106]

Yet even if most of the ways we have of preferring our own nonbasic or luxury needs do involve aggressing against the basic needs of animals and plants, wouldn't human superiority provide grounds for preferring ourselves or other human beings in these ways? Or, put another way, shouldn't human superiority have more theoretical and practical significance than I am allowing? Not, I claim, if we are looking for the most morally defensible position to take.

For consider: given that we have shown that nonhumans have excellences of their own, the claim that humans are superior to the members of other species, if it can be justified at all, is something like the claim that a person came in first in a race where others came in second, third, fourth, and so on. It would not imply that the members of other species are without intrinsic value, because they do have excellences of their own. In fact, it would imply just the opposite – that the members of other species are also intrinsically valuable, although not as intrinsically valuable as humans, just as the claim that a person came in first in a race implies that the persons who came in second, third, fourth, and so on are also meritorious, although not as meritorious as the person who came in first.

This line of argument draws further support once we consider the fact that many animals and plants are superior to humans in one respect or another, e.g. the sense of smell of the wolf, or the acuity of sight of the eagle, or the survivability of the cockroach, or the photosynthetic power of plants.[107] So any claim of human superiority must allow for the recognition of excellences in nonhuman species, even for some excellences that are superior to their corresponding human excellences. In fact, it demands that recognition.

Moreover, if the claim of human superiority is to have any moral force, it must rest on non-question-begging grounds. Accordingly, we must be able to give a non-question-begging response to the nonanthropocentric argument for the equality of species. Yet for any such argument to be successful, it would have to recognize the intrinsic value of the members of nonhuman species. Even if it could be established that human beings have greater intrinsic value, we would still have to recognize that nonhuman nature has intrinsic value as well. So the relevant question is: how are we going to recognize the presumably lesser intrinsic value of nonhuman nature?

Now if human needs, even nonbasic or luxury ones, are always preferred to even the basic needs of the members of nonhuman species, we would not be giving any recognition to the intrinsic value of nonhuman nature. But what if we allowed the nonbasic or luxury needs of humans to trump the basic needs of nonhuman nature half the time, and half the time allowed the basic needs of nonhuman nature to trump the nonbasic or luxury needs of humans? Would that be enough? Certainly, it would be a significant advance over what we are presently doing. For what we are presently doing is meeting the basic needs of nonhuman nature, at best, only when it serves our own needs or the needs of those we are committed to or happen to care about, and that does not recognize the intrinsic value of nonhuman nature at all.[108] A fifty-fifty arrangement indeed would be an advance; but it would not be enough.

The reason why it would not be enough is that the claim that humans are superior to nonhuman nature no more supports the practice of aggressing against the basic needs of nonhuman nature to satisfy our own nonbasic or luxury needs, than does the claim that a person who came in first in a race would support the practice of aggressing against the basic needs of those who came in second, third, fourth, and so on, to satisfy the nonbasic or luxury needs of the person who came in first. A higher degree of merit does not translate into a right of domination, and to claim a right to aggress against the basic needs of nonhuman nature in order to meet our own nonbasic or luxury needs is clearly to claim a right of domination.[109] All that our superiority as humans would justify is not meeting the basic needs of nonhuman nature when this conflicts with our nonbasic or luxury needs. What it does *not* justify is aggressing against the basic needs of nonhuman nature when this conflicts with our nonbasic or luxury needs.

In sum, I have argued that whether we endorse an anthropocentric or a nonanthropocentric environmental ethics, we should favor a Principle of Human Defense, a Principle of Human Preservation, and a Principle of Disproportionality, as I have interpreted them. In the past, failure to recognize the importance of a Principle of Human Defense and a Principle of Human Preservation has led philosophers to overestimate the amount of sacrifice required of humans.[110] By contrast, failure to recognize the importance of a Principle of Disproportionality has led philosophers to underestimate the amount of sacrifice required of humans.[111] I claim that taken together, these three principles strike the right balance between concerns of human welfare and the welfare of nonhuman nature.

From just war theory to pacifism

Traditionally, pacifism and just war theory have represented radically opposed responses to aggression. Pacifism has been interpreted to rule out any use of violence in response to aggression. Just war theory has been interpreted to permit a measured use of violence in response to aggression.[112] It has been thought that the two views might sometimes agree in particular cases, for example, that pacifists and just war theorists might unconditionally oppose nuclear war, but beyond that it has been generally held that the two views lead to radically opposed recommendations. By applying a peacemaking model of doing philosophy to the analysis of these two views, I hope to show that this is not the case. Specifically, I will argue that pacifism and just war theory, in their most morally defensible interpretations, can be substantially reconciled both in theory and practice.

In traditional just war theory there are two basic elements: an account of just cause and an account of just means. Just cause is usually specified as follows:

1   There must be substantial aggression.
2   Nonbelligerent correctives must be either hopeless or too costly.
3   Belligerent correctives must be neither hopeless nor too costly.

Needless to say, the notion of substantial aggression is a bit fuzzy, but it is generally understood to be the type of aggression that violates people's most fundamental rights. To suggest some specific examples of what is and is not substantial aggression, usually the taking of hostages is regarded as substantial aggression, while the nationalization of particular firms owned by foreigners is not so regarded. But even when substantial aggression occurs, frequently nonbelligerent correctives are neither hopeless nor too costly. And even when nonbelligerent correctives are either hopeless or too costly, in order for there to be a just cause, belligerent correctives must be neither hopeless nor too costly.

Traditional just war theory assumes, however, that there are just causes, and goes on to specify just means as imposing two requirements:

1   Harm to innocents should not be directly intended as an end or a means.
2   The harm resulting from the belligerent means should not be disproportionate to the particular defensive objective to be attained.

While the just means conditions apply to each defensive action, the just cause conditions must be met by the conflict as a whole.

It is important to note that these requirements of just cause and just means are not essentially about war at all. Essentially, they constitute a theory of just defense that can apply to war, but can also apply to a wide range of defensive actions short of war. Of course, what needs to be determined is whether these requirements can be justified. Since just war theory is usually opposed to pacifism, to secure a non-question-begging justification for the theory and its requirements, we need to proceed as much as possible from premises that are common to pacifists and just war theorists alike. The difficulty here is that there is not just one form of pacifism but many. So we need to determine which form of pacifism is most morally defensible.

When most people think of pacifism they tend to identify it with a theory of nonviolence. We can call this view "nonviolent pacifism." It maintains that

> Any use of violence against other human beings is morally prohibited.

It has been plausibly argued, however, that this form of pacifism is incoherent. In a well known article, Jan Narveson rejects nonviolent pacifism as incoherent because it recognizes a right to life yet rules out any use of force in defense of that right.[113] The view is incoherent, Narveson claims, because having a right entails the legitimacy of using force in defense of that right at least on some occasions.

Given the cogency of objections of this sort, some have opted for a form of pacifism that does not rule out all violence but only lethal violence. We can call this view "nonlethal pacifism." It maintains that

> Any lethal use of force against other human beings is morally prohibited.

In defense of nonlethal pacifism, Cheyney Ryan has argued that there is a substantial issue between the pacifist and the nonpacifist concerning whether we can or should create the necessary distance between ourselves and other human beings in order to make the act of killing possible.[114] To illustrate, Ryan cites George Orwell's reluctance to shoot at an enemy soldier who jumped out of a trench and ran along the top of a parapet half-dressed and holding up his trousers with both hands. Ryan contends that what kept Orwell from shooting was that he couldn't think of the soldier as a thing rather than a fellow human being.

However, it is not clear that Orwell's encounter supports nonlethal pacifism. For it may be that what kept Orwell from shooting the enemy soldier was not his inability to think of the soldier as a thing rather than a fellow human being, but rather his inability to think of the soldier who was holding up his trousers with both hands as a threat or a combatant. Under this interpretation, Orwell's decision not to shoot would accord well with the requirements of just war theory.

Let us suppose, however, that someone is attempting to take your life. Why does that permit you, the defender of nonlethal pacifism might ask, to kill the person making the attempt? The most cogent response, it seems to me, is that killing in such a case is not evil, or at least not morally evil, because anyone who is wrongfully engaged in an attempt upon your life has already forfeited his or her right to life by engaging in such aggression.[115] So, provided that you are reasonably certain that the aggressor is wrongfully engaged in an attempt upon your life, you would be morally justified in killing, assuming that it is the only way of saving your own life.

There is, however, a form of pacifism that remains untouched by the criticisms I have raised against both nonviolent pacifism and nonlethal pacifism. This form of pacifism neither prohibits all violence nor even all uses of lethal force. We can call the view "anti-war pacifism" because it holds that

> Any participation in the massive use of lethal force in warfare is morally prohibited.[116]

In defense of anti-war pacifism, it is undeniable that wars have brought enormous amounts of death and destruction in their wake and that many of those who have perished in them are noncombatants or innocents. In fact, the tendency of modern wars has been to produce higher and higher proportions of noncombatant casualties, making it more and more difficult to justify participation in such wars. At the same time, strategies for nonbelligerent conflict resolution are rarely intensively developed and explored before nations choose to go to war, making it all but impossible to justify participation in such wars.[117]

To determine whether the requirements of just war theory can be reconciled with those of anti-war pacifism, however, we need to consider whether we should distinguish between harm intentionally inflicted upon innocents, and harm whose infliction on innocents is merely foreseen. On the one hand, we could favor a uniform restriction against the infliction of harm upon innocents that ignores the intended/foreseen distinction. On the other hand, we could favor a differential restriction that is more severe against the intentional infliction of harm upon innocents, but is less severe against the infliction of harm that is merely foreseen. What needs to be determined, therefore, is whether there is any rationale for favoring this differential restriction on harm over a uniform restriction.

Let us first examine the question from the perspective of those suffering the harm. Initially, it might appear to matter little whether the harm would be intended or merely foreseen by those who cause it. From the perspective of those suffering harm, it might appear that what matters is simply that the overall amount of harm be restricted, irrespective of whether it is foreseen or intended. But consider. Don't those who suffer harm have more reason to protest when the harm is done to them by agents who are directly engaged in causing harm to them, than when the harm is done incidentally by agents whose ends and means are good? Don't we have more reason to protest when we are being used by others than when we are affected by them only incidentally?

Moreover, if we examine the question from the perspective of those causing harm, additional support for this line of reasoning can be found.

For it would seem that we have more reason to protest a restriction against foreseen harm than we have reason to protest a comparable restriction against intended harm. This is because a restriction against foreseen harm limits our actions when our ends and means are good, whereas a restriction against intended harm only limits our actions when our ends or means are evil or harmful, and it would seem that we have greater grounds for acting when both our ends and means are good than when they are not. Consequently, because we have more reason to protest when we are being used by others than when we are being affected by them only incidentally, and because we have more reason to act when both our ends and means are good than when they are not, we should favor the foreseen/intended distinction that is incorporated into just means.

It might be objected, however, that at least sometimes we could produce greater good overall by violating the foreseen/intended distinction of just means and acting with the evil means of intentionally harming innocents. On this account, it might be argued that it should be permissible at least sometimes to intentionally harm innocents in order to achieve greater good overall.

Now it seems to me that this objection is well taken insofar as it is directed against an absolute restriction upon intentional harm to innocents. It seems clear that there are exceptions to such a restriction when intentional harm to innocents is

1   trivial (e.g. as in the case of stepping on someone's foot to get out of a crowded subway)
2   easily repairable (e.g. as in the case of lying to a temporarily depressed friend to keep her from committing suicide), or
3   greatly outweighed by the consequences of the action, especially to innocent people (e.g. as in the case of shooting one of two hundred civilian hostages to prevent in the only way possible the execution of all two hundred).

Yet while we need to recognize these exceptions to an absolute restriction upon intentional harm to innocents, there is good reason not to permit simply maximizing good consequences overall, because that would place unacceptable burdens upon particular individuals. More specifically, it would be an unacceptable burden on innocents to allow them to be intentionally harmed in cases other than the exceptions we have just enumerated. And, allowing for these exceptions, we would still have reason to favor a differential restriction against harming innocents that is more severe against the intentional infliction of harm upon innocents but is less severe against the infliction of harm upon innocents that is merely foreseen. Again, the main grounds for this preference is that we would have more reason to protest when we are being used by others than when we are being affected by them only incidentally, and more reason to act when both our ends and means are good than when they are not.

So far, I have argued that there are grounds for favoring a differential restriction on harm to innocents that is more severe against intended harm and less severe against foreseen harm. I have further argued that this restriction is not absolute, so that when the evil intended is trivial, easily repairable or greatly outweighed by the consequences, intentional harm to innocents can be justified. Moreover, there is no reason to think that anti-war pacifists would reject either of these conclusions. Anti-war pacifists are opposed to any participation in the massive use of lethal force in warfare, yet this need not conflict with the commitment of just war theorists to a differential but nonabsolute restriction on harm to innocents as a requirement of just means.[118] Where just war theory goes wrong, according to anti-war pacifists, is not in its restriction on harming innocents, but rather in its failure to adequately determine when belligerent correctives are too costly to constitute a just cause, or lacking in the proportionality required by just means. According to anti-war pacifists, just war theory provides insufficient restraint in both of these areas. Now to evaluate this criticism, we need to consider a wide range of cases where killing or inflicting serious harm on others in defense of oneself or others might be thought to be justified, beginning with the easiest cases to assess from the perspectives of anti-war pacifism and the just war theory, and then moving on to cases that are more difficult to assess from those perspectives.

Case 1, where only the intentional or foreseen killing of an unjust aggressor would prevent one's own death.[119] This case clearly presents no problems. In the first place, anti-war pacifists adopted their view because they were convinced that there were instances of justified killing. And, in this case, the only person killed is an unjust aggressor. So surely anti-war pacifists would have to agree with just war theorists that one can justifiably kill an unjust aggressor if it is the only way to save one's life.

Case 2, where only the intentional or foreseen killing of an unjust aggressor and the foreseen killing of one innocent bystander would prevent one's own death and that of five other innocent people.[120] In this case, we have the foreseen killing of an innocent person as well as the killing of the unjust aggressor, but since it is the only way to save one's own life and the lives of five other innocent people, anti-war pacifists and just war theorists alike would have reason to judge it morally permissible. In this case, the intended life-saving benefits to six innocent people are judged to outweigh the foreseen death of one innocent person and the intended or foreseen death of the unjust aggressor.

Case 3, where only the intentional or foreseen killing of an unjust aggressor and the foreseen killing of one innocent bystander would prevent the death of many innocent people. In this case, despite the fact that we lack the justification of self-defense, saving the lives of five innocent people in the only way possible should still provide anti-war pacifists and just war theorists with sufficient grounds for granting the moral permissibility of killing an unjust aggressor, even when the killing of an innocent bystander is a foreseen consequence. In this case, the intended life-saving benefits to five innocent people would still outweigh the foreseen death of one innocent person and the intended or foreseen death of the unjust aggressor.

Case 4, where only the intentional or foreseen killing of an unjust aggressor and the foreseen killing of five innocent people would prevent the death of two innocent people. In this case, neither anti-war pacifists nor just war theorists would find the cost and proportionality requirements of just war theory to be met. Too many innocent people would have to be killed to save too few. Here the fact that the deaths of the innocents would be merely foreseen does not outweigh the fact that we would have to accept the deaths of five innocents and the death of the unjust aggressor in order to be able to save two innocents.

Notice that up to this point in interpreting these cases, we have simply been counting the number of innocent deaths involved in each case and opting for the solution that minimized the loss of innocent lives that would result. Suppose, however, that an unjust aggressor is not threatening the lives of innocents but only their welfare or property. Would the taking of the unjust aggressor's life in defense of the welfare and property of innocents be judged proportionate? Consider the following case.

Case 5, where only the intentional or foreseen killing of an unjust aggressor would prevent serious injury to oneself and/or five other innocent people. Since in this case the intentional or foreseen killing of the unjust aggressor is the only way of preventing serious injury to oneself and/or five other innocent people, then, by analogy with cases 1–3, both anti-war pacifists and just war theorists alike would have reason to affirm its moral permissibility. Of course, if there were any other way of stopping unjust aggressors in such cases short of killing them, that course of action would clearly be required. Yet if there is no alternative, the intentional or foreseen killing of the unjust aggressor to prevent serious injury to oneself and/or five other innocent people would be justified.

In such cases, the serious injury could be bodily injury, as when an aggressor threatens to break one's limbs, or it could be serious psychological injury, as when an aggressor threatens to inject mind-altering drugs, or it could be a serious threat to property. Of course, in most cases where serious injury is threatened, there will be ways of stopping aggressors short of killing them. Unfortunately, this is not always possible.

In still other kinds of case, stopping an unjust aggressor would require indirectly inflicting serious harm, but not death, upon innocent bystanders. Consider the following cases.

Case 6, where only the intentional or foreseen infliction of serious harm upon an unjust aggressor and the foreseen infliction of serious harm upon one innocent bystander would prevent serious harm to oneself and five other innocent people.

Case 7, where only the intentional or foreseen infliction of serious harm upon an unjust aggressor and the foreseen infliction of serious harm upon one innocent bystander would prevent serious harm to five other innocent people.

In both of these cases, serious harm is indirectly inflicted upon one innocent bystander in order to prevent greater harm from being inflicted by an unjust aggressor upon other innocent people. In case 6, we also have the justification of self-defense, which is lacking in case 7. Nevertheless, with regard to both cases, anti-war pacifists and just war theorists should agree that preventing serious injury to five or six innocent people in the only way possible renders it morally permissible to inflict serious injury upon an unjust aggressor, even when the serious injury of one innocent person is a foreseen consequence. In these cases, by analogy with cases 2 and 3, the foreseen serious injury of one innocent person and the intended or foreseen injury of the unjust aggressor should be judged proportionate, given the intended injury-preventing benefits to five or six other innocent people.

Up to this point there has been the basis for general agreement among anti-war pacifists and just war theorists as to how to interpret the proportionality requirement of just means, but in the following case this no longer obtains.

Case 8, where only the intentional or foreseen killing of an unjust aggressor and the foreseen killing of one innocent bystander would prevent serious injuries to the members of a much larger group of people. The interpretation of this case is crucial. In this case, we are asked to sanction the loss of an innocent life in order to prevent serious injuries to the members of a much larger group of people. Unfortunately, neither anti-war pacifists nor just war theorists have explicitly considered this case. Both anti-war pacifists and just war theorists agree that we can inflict serious injury upon an unjust aggressor and an innocent bystander to prevent greater injury to other innocent people, as in cases 6 and 7, and that one can even intentionally or indirectly kill an unjust aggressor to prevent serious injury to oneself or other innocent people, as in case 5. Yet neither anti-war pacifists nor just war theorists have explicitly addressed the question of whether we can indirectly kill an innocent bystander in order to prevent serious injuries to the members of a much larger group of innocent people. Rather they have tended to confuse case 8 with case 5 where it is agreed that one can justifiably kill an unjust aggressor in order to prevent serious injury to oneself or five other innocent people. In case 8, however, one is doing something quite different: one is killing an innocent bystander in order to prevent serious injury to oneself and five other innocent people.

This kind of trade-off is not accepted in standard police practice. Police officers are regularly instructed not to risk innocent lives simply to prevent serious injury to other innocents. Nor is there any reason to think that a trade-off that is unacceptable in standard police practice would be acceptable in larger-scale conflicts. Thus, for example, even if the Baltic republics could have effectively freed themselves from the Soviet Union by infiltrating into Moscow several bands of saboteurs who would then attack several military and government installations in Moscow, causing an enormous loss of innocent lives, such trade-offs would not have been justified. Accordingly, it follows that if the proportionality requirement of just war theory is to be met, we must save more innocent lives than we cause to be lost, we must prevent more injuries than we bring about, and we must not kill innocents, even indirectly, simply to prevent serious injuries to ourselves and others.

Of course, sometimes our lives and well-being are threatened together. Or better, if we are unwilling to sacrifice our well-being then our lives are threatened as well. Nevertheless, if we are justified in our use of lethal force to defend ourselves in cases where we will indirectly kill innocents, it is because our lives are also threatened, not simply our well-being. And the same holds for when we are defending others.

What this shows is that the constraints imposed by just war theory on the use of belligerent correctives are actually much more severe than anti-war pacifists have tended to recognize.[121] In determining when belligerent correctives are too costly to constitute a just cause, or lacking in the proportionality required by just means, just war theory under its most morally defensible interpretation:

1   allows the use of belligerent means against unjust aggressors only when such means minimize the loss and injury to innocent lives overall;
2   allows the use of belligerent means against unjust aggressors to indirectly threaten innocent lives only to prevent the loss of innocent lives, not simply to prevent injury to innocents;
3   allows the use of belligerent means to directly or indirectly threaten or even take the lives of unjust aggressors when it is the only way to prevent serious injury to innocents.

It might be objected that all that I have shown through the analysis of the above eight cases is that killing in defense of oneself or others is morally permissible, not that it is morally required or morally obligatory. That is true. I have not established any obligation to respond to aggression with lethal force in these cases, but only that it is morally permissible to do so. For one thing, it is difficult to ground an obligation to use lethal force on self-defense alone, as would be required in case 1 or in one version of case 5. Obligations to oneself appear to have an optional quality that is absent from obligations to others. In cases 2–3 and 5–7, however, the use of force would prevent serious harm or death to innocents, and here I contend it would be morally obligatory if either the proposed use of force required only a relatively small personal sacrifice from us, or if we were fairly bound by convention or by a mutual defense agreement to come to the aid of others. In such cases, I think we can justifiably speak of a moral obligation to kill or seriously harm in defense of others.

Another aspect of cases 1–3 and 5–7 to which someone might object, is that it is the wrongful actions of others that put us into situations where I am claiming that we are morally justified in seriously harming or killing others.[122] But for the actions of unjust aggressors, we would not be in situations where I am claiming that we are morally permitted or required to seriously harm or kill.

Yet doesn't something like this happen in a wide range of cases when wrongful actions are performed? Suppose I am on the way to the bank to deposit money from a fundraiser, and someone accosts me and threatens to shoot if I don't hand over the money. If I do hand over the money, I would be forced to do something I don't want to do, something that involves a loss to myself and others. But surely it is morally permissible for me to hand over the money in this case. And it may even be morally required for me to do so if resistance would lead to the shooting of others in addition to myself. So it does seem that bad people, by altering the consequences of our actions, can alter our obligations as well. What our obligations are under nonideal conditions are different from what they would be under ideal conditions. If a group of thugs comes into a classroom where I am lecturing and make it very clear that they intend to shoot me if each of my students doesn't give them one dollar, I think, and I would hope that my students would also think, that each of them now has an obligation to give the thugs one dollar when before they had no such obligation. Likewise, I think that the actions of unjust aggressors can put us into situations where it is morally permissible or even morally required for us to seriously harm or kill, when before it was not.

Now it might be contended that anti-war pacifists would concede the moral permissibility of cases 1–3 and 5–7, but still maintain that any participation in the massive use of lethal force in warfare is morally prohibited. The scale of the conflict, anti-war pacifists might contend, makes all the difference. Of course, if this simply means that many large-scale conflicts will have effects that bear no resemblance to cases 1–3 or 5–7, this can hardly be denied. Still, it is possible for some large-scale conflicts to bear a proportionate resemblance to the above cases. For example, it can plausibly be argued that India's military action against Pakistan in Bangladesh, and the Tanzanian incursion into Uganda during the rule of Idi Amin, resemble cases 3, 5 or 7 in their effects upon innocents.[123] What this shows is that anti-war pacifists are not justified in regarding every participation in the massive use of lethal force in warfare as morally prohibited. Instead, anti-war pacifists must allow that at least in some real-life cases, wars and other large-scale military operations both have been and will be morally permissible.

This concession from anti-war pacifists, however, needs to be matched by a comparable concession from just war theorists themselves, because too frequently they have interpreted their theory in morally indefensible ways.[124] When just war theory is given a morally defensible interpretation, I have argued that the theory favors a strong just means prohibition against intentionally harming innocents. I have also argued that the theory favors the use of belligerent means only when such means

1   minimize the loss and injury to innocent lives overall,
2   threaten innocent lives only to prevent the loss of innocent lives, not simply to prevent injury to innocents, and
3   threaten or even take the lives of unjust aggressors when it is the only way to prevent serious injury to innocents.

Obviously, just war theory, so understood, is going to place severe restrictions on the use of belligerent means in warfare. In fact, most of the actual uses of belligerent means in warfare that have occurred turn out to be unjustified. For example, the US involvement in Nicaragua, El Salvador and Panama, the Soviet Union's involvement in Afghanistan, and Israeli involvement in the West Bank and the Gaza Strip, all violate the just cause and just means provisions of just war theory as I have defended them. Even the recent US-led war against Iraq violated both the just cause and just means provisions of just war theory.[125] In fact, one strains to find examples of justified applications of just war theory in recent history. Two examples I have already referred to are India's military action against Pakistan in Bangladesh, and the Tanzanian incursion into Uganda during the rule of Idi Amin. But after mentioning these two examples it is difficult to go on. What this shows is that when just war theory and anti-war pacifism are given their most morally defensible interpretations, both views can be reconciled. In this reconciliation, the few wars and large-scale conflicts that meet the stringent requirements of just war theory are the only wars and large-scale conflicts to which anti-war pacifists cannot justifiably object.[126] We can call the view that emerges from this reconciliation "just war pacifism."[127] It is a view with which a peacemaking model of doing philosophy with its goal of reconciling alternative moral and political perspectives can rest content.

Conclusion

Pursuing peacemaking as a model for doing philosophy, I have argued that not only does rationality require morality, but that even a minimal morality like libertarianism requires rights to welfare and equal opportunity that lead to socialist equality and feminist androgyny. In this way, I have brought together the moral ideals of libertarianism, welfare liberalism, socialism and feminism into what could be called a reconciliationist conception of justice. In addition, I have argued that the pursuit of this reconciliationist conception of justice, especially in its feminist dimensions, is theoretically and practically connected to the pursuit of racial justice, homosexual justice and multicultural justice, and is further constrained by specific principles of environmental justice and just war pacifism.

Unfortunately, many countries with adequate resources have yet to secure a right to welfare for all their citizens, nor has a reasonable effort been made to extend this right to people in other countries, let alone to future generations. There are also the significant injustices suffered by women, blacks, homosexuals and members of non-Western cultures.

It goes without saying that victims of injustice and their allies should consider changing or removing existing injustices, first by normal politics, then by legal protest, then by civil disobedience, and only then by revolutionary action. But what if all of these means have been tried and are reasonably judged ineffective; or, alternatively, what if these means are reasonably judged too costly for those whom they are intended to benefit? If either of these conditions obtain, what is permissible for the victims of injustice to do? Is it permissible for them to engage in private illegal acts to secure those goods and resources to which they are morally entitled? If we assume that normal politics, legal protest, civil disobedience, and revolutionary action have all been tried and reasonably judged ineffective, or that such means are reasonably judged too costly for those whom they are intended to benefit, then it would seem that criminally disobedient acts would be morally permissible, provided that they are directed at appropriating surplus goods from people who have more than a fair share of opportunities to lead a good life, and at appropriating such goods with a minimum of physical force. In addition, there would be no moral justification for punishing this sort of criminal activity. For those who dislike this limit on the moral justification for punishment in societies like our own, there is an appropriate remedy: guarantee the basic human rights required by this reconciliationist conception of justice, and more punishment for crimes will then be morally justified.

NOTES

1 For a discussion of the similarities between argument and war, see George Lakoff and Mark Johnson, *Metaphors We Live By* (Chicago: University of Chicago Press, 1980) pp. 4–6, 77–86; and Edwin Burtt, "Philosophers as Warriors," in *The Critique of War*, edited by Robert Ginsberg (Chicago: Henry Regnery Co., 1969) pp. 30–42. Lakoff and Johnson argue that these similarities between argument and war are constitutive features of the nature of argument.

2 Baier, *The Rational and the Moral Order* (La Salle: Open Court, 1995). Baier's most recent defense of morality is quite similar to David Gauthier's in *Morals*

by Agreement (Cambridge: Cambridge University Press, 1986). I discuss Gauthier's view later in this chapter.

3 Baier, *The Rational and the Moral Order*, p. 188.

4 Alan Gewirth, *Reason and Morality* (Chicago: University of Chicago Press, 1978) chapters 1 and 2; "The Rationality of Reasonableness," *Synthese*, vol. 57 (1983) pp. 225–47; "From the Prudential to the Moral," *Ethics*, vol. 95 (1985) pp. 302–4; "Why There Are Human Rights," *Social Theory and Practice*, vol. 11 (1985) pp. 235–48; "Ethics and the Pain of Contradiction," *Philosophical Forum*, vol. 23 (1992) pp. 259–77.

5 For Gewirth's claim that the right in premise 3 is prudential, see "Replies to My Critics," in *Gewirth's Ethical Rationalism*, edited by Edward Regis (Chicago: University of Chicago Press, 1984) pp. 205–12.

6 No doubt some will find Gewirth's notion of a "prudential right" to be something of an oxymoron, but in his account the notion is clearly defined to be the equivalent of a prudential as opposed to a moral ought. So if it would help, barring a little awkwardness, it is possible to restate Gewirth's argument, as well as my response, by simply replacing every occurrence of "right" with one of "ought."

7 "Ought" presupposes "can" here. So unless people have the capacity to entertain and follow both self-interested and moral reasons for acting, it does not make any sense asking whether they ought or ought not to do so. Moreover, moral reasons here are understood to necessarily include (some) altruistic reasons, but not necessarily to exclude (all) self-interested reasons. So the question of whether it would be rational for us to follow self-interested reasons rather than moral reasons should be understood as the question of whether it would be rational for us to follow self-interested reasons exclusively, rather than some appropriate set of self-interested reasons and altruistic reasons which constitutes the class of moral reasons.

8 I understand the pure altruist to be the mirror image of the pure egoist. Whereas the pure egoist thinks that the interests of others count for them but not for herself except instrumentally, the pure altruist thinks that her own interests count for others but not for herself except instrumentally.

9 This is because morality itself already represents a compromise between egoism and altruism. So to ask that moral reasons be weighed against self-interested reasons is, in effect, to count self-interested reasons twice – once in the compromise between egoism and altruism and then again when moral reasons are weighed against self-interested reasons. But to count self-interested reasons twice is clearly objectionable.

10 Notice that by "egoistic perspective" here I mean the view that grants the *prima facie* relevance of both egoistic and altruistic reasons to rational choice and then tries to argue for the superiority of egoistic reasons. Similarly, by "altruistic perspective" I mean the view that grants the *prima facie* relevance of both egoistic and altruistic reasons to rational choice and then tries to argue for the superiority of altruistic reasons.

11 For further discussion, see my *Justice for Here and Now* (New York: Cambridge University Press, 1998), chapter 2.

12 For example, Alasdair MacIntyre, *After Virtue* (Notre Dame: University of Notre Dame Press, 1981).

13 For example, John Rawls, *Political Liberalism* (New York: Columbia University Press, 1993). For Rawls, justified agreement on practical requirements necessitates an overlapping consensus on political values, but unfortunately Rawls never establishes that there is any such overlapping consensus on political values. My approach is different. I argue that there are grounds for justified agree-

ment on practical requirements even in the absence of a consensus on political values.

14 Good examples of philosophers who have taken this approach are Will Kymlicka, *Contemporary Political Philosophy* (New York: Oxford University Press, 1990) and Seyla Benhabib, *Situating the Self* (New York: Routledge, 1992).

15 See John Hospers, *Libertarianism* (Los Angeles: Nash Press, 1971).

16 *Ibid.*, chapter 7.

17 I am indebted to Alasdair MacIntyre for helping me make this point clearer.

18 See James P. Sterba, "Is There a Rationale for Punishment?", *The American Journal of Jurisprudence* (1984).

19 By the liberty of the rich to meet their luxury needs, I continue to mean the liberty of the rich not to be interfered with when using their surplus possessions for luxury purposes. Similarly, by the liberty of the poor to meet their basic needs, I continue to mean the liberty of the poor not to be interfered with when taking what they require to meet their basic needs from the surplus possessions of the rich.

20 For this other interpretation, see my *How To Make People Just* (Totowa: Rowman & Littlefield, 1988) chapter 5.

21 Tibor Machan, *Individuals and Their Rights* (La Salle: Open Court, 1989) pp. 100–11.

22 *Ibid.*, p. 107.

23 Moreover, libertarians have not restricted the class of morally legitimate claimants in this fashion. After all, the fundamental rights recognized by libertarians are universal rights, that is, rights possessed by all people, not just those who live in certain places or at certain times. Of course, to claim that these rights are universal rights does not mean that they are universally recognized; obviously the fundamental rights that flow from the libertarian ideal have not been universally recognized. Rather to claim that they are universal rights, despite their spotty recognition, implies only that they ought to be recognized at all times and places by people who have or could have had good reasons to recognize these rights, whether or not they actually did or do so. Nor need these universal rights be unconditional. This is particularly true in the case of the right to welfare, which, I have argued, is conditional on people doing all that they legitimately can to provide for themselves. In addition, this right is conditional on there being sufficient goods and resources available so that everyone's welfare needs can be met. So, where people do not do all that they can to provide for themselves, or where there are not sufficient goods and resources available, people simply do not have a right to welfare.

Yet even though libertarians have claimed that the rights they defend are universal rights in the manner I have just explained, it may be that they are simply mistaken in this regard. Even when universal rights are stripped of any claim to being universally recognized or unconditional, still it might be argued that there are no such rights, that is, that there are no rights that all people ought to recognize. But how would one argue for such a view? One couldn't argue from the failure of people to recognize such rights, because we have already said that such recognition is not necessary. Nor could one argue that not everyone ought to recognize such rights because some lack the capacity to do so. This is because "ought" does imply "can" here, so that the obligation to recognize certain rights only applies to those who actually have or at some point have had the capacity to do so. Thus, the existence of universal rights is not ruled out by the existence of individuals who have never had the capacity to recognize such rights. It would be ruled out only by the existence of individuals who could recognize these

rights but for whom it would be correct to say that they ought, all things considered, not to do so. But we have just seen that even a minimal libertarian moral
ideal supports a universal right to welfare. And as I have argued in chapter 2,
when "ought" is understood prudentially rather than morally, a non-question-
begging conception to rationality favors morality over prudence (see chapter 2).
So for those capable of recognizing universal rights, it simply is not possible to
argue that they, all things considered, ought not to do so.

24 Bob Bergland, "Attacking the Problem of World Hunger," *The National Forum*
(1979) vol. 69, p. 4.

25 *Hunger 1995: Fifth Annual Report on the State of World Hunger* (Silver Springs
MD: Bread for the World Institute, 1994) p. 10; Ruth Sivard, *World Military and
Social Expenditures* (Washington DC: World Priorities, 1993) p. 28; Frances
Moore Lappe, *World Hunger* (New York: Grove Press, 1986) p. 9.

26 Lester Brown, Christopher Flavin and Hal Kane, *Vital Signs 1996* (New York:
Norton, 1996) pp. 34–5; Jeremy Rifkin, *Beyond Beef* (New York: Penguin, 1992)
p. 1.

27 Henry Shue, *Basic Rights* (Princeton: Princeton University Press, 1980) chapter 7.

28 For a discussion of these causal connections, see Cheryl Silver, *One Earth, One
Future* (Washington DC: National Academy Press, 1990); Bill McKibben, *The
End of Nature* (New York: Anchor Books, 1989); Jeremy Leggett (ed.) *Global
Warming* (New York: Oxford University Press, 1990); and Lester Brown (ed.)
The World Watch Reader (New York: Nelson, 1991).

29 Charles Park Jr (ed.) *Earth Resources* (Washington DC: Voice of America,
1980) chapter 13; Lester Brown, *State of the World 1995* (New York: Norton,
1997) chapter 7; Lester Brown (ed.) *The World Watch Reader* p. 268. China
currently uses more coal than the US. See Lester Brown, *State of the World
1995* (New York: Norton, 1997), p. 9.

30 G. Tyler Miller Jr, *Living with the Environment* (Belmont: Wadsworth Publishing
Co., 1990) p. 20. See also Janet Besecker and Phil Elder, "Lifeboat Ethics: A
Reply to Hardin," in *Readings in Ecology, Energy and Human Society*, edited by
William Burch (New York: Harper & Row, 1977) p. 229. For higher and lower
estimates of the impact of North Americans, see Holmes Rolston III, "Feeding
People versus Saving Nature?" in *World Hunger and Morality*, 2nd edn
(Englewood Cliffs: Prentice-Hall, 1996) pp. 259–60; Paul Ehrlich, Anne Ehrlich
and Gretchen Daily, *The Stork and the Plow* (New York: Grosset/Putnam, 1995)
p. 26.

31 Successes in meeting the most basic needs of the poor in particular regions of
developing countries (e.g. the Indian state of Kerala) should not blind us to the
growing numbers of people living in conditions of absolute poverty (1.2 billion
by a recent estimate) and how difficult it will be to meet the basic needs of all
these people in a sustainable way that will allow future generations to have their
basic needs met as well, especially when we reflect on the fact that the way we in
the developed world are living is not sustainable at all!

32 John Rawls, *A Theory of Justice* (Cambridge MA: Harvard University Press,
1971) chapter 2.

33 Alan Durning, "Life on the Brink," *World Watch*, vol. 3 no. 2 (1990) p. 24.

34 *Ibid.*, p. 29.

35 Joyce Trebilcot, "Two Forms of Androgynism," reprinted in *Feminism and
Philosophy*, edited by Mary Vetterling-Braggin, Frederick Ellison and Jane
English (Totowa: Rowman & Littlefield, 1977) pp. 70–8.

36 Mary Anne Warren, "Is Androgyny the Answer to Sexual Stereotyping?", in
"Femininity," "Masculinity," and "Androgyny", ed. Mary Vetterling-Braggin
(Totowa: Rowman & Littlefield, 1982) pp. 178–9.

37 See, for example, Virginia Held, *Rights and Goods* (New York: Free Press, 1984) especially chapter 11; and Gloria Steinem "What it Would be Like if Women Win," *Time*, 31 August 1970, pp. 22–3; Mary Jeanne Larrabee, "Feminism and Parental Roles: Possibilities for Changes," *Journal of Social Philosophy*, vol. 14 (1983) p. 18. See also National Organization for Women (NOW) Bill of Rights, and *Statement on the Equal Rights Amendment*, United States Commission on Civil Rights (1978).

38 See, for example, Ann Ferguson, "Androgyny as an Ideal for Human Development," in *Feminism and Philosophy*, pp. 45–69; and Evelyn Reed, "Women: Caste, Class or Oppressed Sex?" in *Morality in Practice*, 2nd edn, ed. James P. Sterba (Belmont: Wadsworth Publishing Co., 1983) pp. 222–8.

39 James P. Sterba, *How To Make People Just* (Totowa: Rowman & Littlefield, 1988) pp. 125–6.

40 Unfortunately, it is doubtful whether this distinctive aspect of a socialist defense of androgyny can be maintained. See Heidi Hartmann, "The Unhappy Marriage of Marxism and Feminism: Toward a More Progressive Union," in *Feminist Philosophies*, ed. Janet Kourany, James P. Sterba and Rosemarie Tong (Englewood Cliffs: Prentice-Hall, 1992) pp. 343–55.

41 The reason for qualifying this claim is that mothers and fathers, unlike children, may legitimately waive their right to equal opportunity when the reasons are compelling enough.

42 Childcare expenses consume about a fifth of the budgets of low-income families that pay for childcare. See Cynthis Costello and Anne Stone, *The American Woman, 1994–95* (New York: Norton, 1994), p. 306.

43 *New York Times*, 25 November 1987; Ruth Sidel, "Day Care: Do We Really Care?" in *Issues in Feminism*, ed. Sheila Ruth (Mountain View CA: Mayfield Publishing Co., 1990) p. 342. One explanation of this lack of day care in the US is that at present 99% of private US employers still do not offer it to their employees. See Susan Faludi, *Backlash* (New York: Crown Publishing Co., 1988) p. xiii.

44 *New York Times*, 25 November 1987; Ruth Sidel, "Day Care: Do We Really Care?"; see also Phyllis Moen, *Woman's Two Roles* (New York: Auburn House, 1992). According to one nationwide study by an agency of the US Department of Labor, 1% of day care facilities were "superior," 15% were "good," 35% were essential "custodial" or "fair," and nearly half were considered "poor." See Sidel, p. 341. See also Cost, Quality and Child Outcomes Study Team, *Cost, Quality and Child Outcomes in Child Care Centers*, 2nd edn (Denver: University of Colorado, 1995).

45 See Lenore Weitzman, *The Divorce Revolution: The Unexpected Social and Economic Consequences for Women and Children in America* (New York: Free Press, 1985).

46 Dorothy Dinnerstein, *The Mermaid and the Minotaur* (New York: Harper & Row, 1977); Nancy Chodorow, *Mothering: Psychoanalysis and the Sociology of Gender* (Berkeley: University of California Press, 1978); Vivian Gornick, "Here's News: Fathers Matter as Much as Mothers," *Village Voice*, 13 October 1975.

47 *New York Times*, 27 November 1987.

48 Women's Action Coalition, *WAC Stats: the Facts About Women* (New York: The New Press, 1993) p. 60.

49 *Statistical Abstracts of the United States 1996* (Washington DC: US Government Printing Office, 1996) pp. 393, 400.

50 See *Statistical Abstracts of the United States 1996*, p. 469. *New York Times*, 6, 18, and 19 October 1992; see also Moen, *Women's Roles*; Elaine Sorenson, "The

Comparable Worth Debate," in *Morality in Practice*, 4th edn, ed. James P. Sterba (Belmont: Wadsworth Publishing Co., 1994) pp. 293–4.

51 See *Statistical Abstracts of the United States 1996*, p. 426.

52 See Jerry Jacobs and Ronnie Steinberg, "Compensating Differentials and the Male-Female Wage Gap," *Social Forces*, vol. 69 (December 1990) pp. 439–68.

53 Gertrude Ezorsky, *Racism and Justice* (Ithaca: Cornell University Press, 1991).

54 Elaine Sorensen, *Comparable Worth* (Princeton: Princeton University Press, 1994) pp. 88–9. See also Ellen Paul, *Equity and Gender* (New Brunswick: Transaction, 1989); and Mary Ann Mason, "Beyond Equal Opportunity: A New Vision for Women Workers," *Notre Dame Journal of Law, Ethics and Public Policy*, vol. 6 (1992) pp. 359–92.

55 *New York Times*, 17 October 1991. See also Elizabeth Schneider, "The Violence of Privacy," *The Connecticut Law Review*, vol. 23 (1991) pp. 973–99.

56 See Mary Koss, *I Never Called It Rape* (New York: Harper and Row, 1988). Originally Koss' study indicated a 25% incidence of rape, but responding to criticism of one of her survey questions, Koss revised her findings and came up with a 20% incidence of rape.

57 Committee on the Judiciary, United States Senate, *Violence Against Women, A Majority Staff Report* (US Government Printing Office, 1992); Ron Thorne-Finch, *Ending the Silence: The Origins and Treatment of Male Violence Against Women* (Toronto: University of Toronto Press, 1992) chapter 1; Albert Roberts, *Helping Battered Women* (New York: Oxford University Press, 1996) part I.

58 Deirdre English, "Through the Glass Ceiling," *Mother Jones*, November 1992.

59 Diana Russell, *The Secret Trauma* (New York: Basic Books, 1986) p. 61; Diana Russell, "The Incidence and Prevalence of Intrafamilial and Extrafamilial Sexual Abuse of Female Children," *Child Abuse and Neglect: The International Journal*, vol. 7 (1983) pp. 133–46.

60 On this point, see Catharine MacKinnon, *Feminism Unmodified* (Cambridge MA: Harvard University Press, 1987) pp. 169–71.

61 Myriam Miedzian, *Boys Will Be Boys* (New York: Doubleday, 1991) p. 74.

62 Donald Victor Butler v. Her Majesty The Queen (1992).

63 Catharine MacKinnon, *Feminism Unmodified* (Cambridge MA: Harvard University Press, 1987) chapter 14; *Only Words* (Cambridge MA: Harvard University Press, 1993) chapter 1. According to MacKinnon, the materials used in the practice of hard-core pornography are sexually explicit, violent, and sexist, and they are contrasted with the materials used in the practice of erotica which are sexually explicit and premised on equality. But obviously it is not always easy to properly classify sexually explicit materials.

64 See MacKinnon, *Feminism Unmodified*, chapter 14. See also Andrea Dworkin, *Pornography: Men Possessing Women* (New York: Plume, 1989); Susan Cole, *Pornography and the Sex Crisis* (Toronto: Amanita, 1989) and *Pornography and Sexual Violence: Evidence of the Links* (London: Everywoman Ltd, 1988).

65 Meritor Savings Bank. 477 U.S. 57, 106 S. Ct. 2399, 91 L.Ed. 49 (1983).

66 Christoforou v. Ryder Truck Rental. 668 F. Supp.294 (S.D.N.Y. 1987).

67 Rabidue v. Osceola Refining Co. 805 F.2d 611, 620 (6th Cir. 1986).

68 Obviously most offers of this sort will be more subtle, but if they are going to serve their purpose their message must still be relatively easy to discern.

69 Even where there is legalized prostitution, such offers may still be objectively unwelcome.

70 There is an analogous requirement of subjective consent in the law concerning rape that is similarly indefensible. See Susan Estrich, "Sex at Work," *Stanford Law Review*, vol. 43 (1991) pp. 813–61.

71 Or they could simply not fire those to whom they make the offers.

72 Barbara Gutek contends that sexual harassment is caused by the fact that women are stereotypically identified as sexual objects in ways that men are not. She notes that women are stereotypically characterized as sexy, affectionate and attractive, whereas men are stereotypically characterized as competent and active. These stereotypes, Gutek claims, spill over into the workplace, making it difficult for women to be perceived as fellow workers rather than sex objects, and it is these perceptions that foster sexual harassment. See Gutek, "Understanding Sexual Harassment at Work," *Notre Dame Journal of Law, Ethics and Public Policy* (1992) pp. 335–8. It would seem, therefore, that eliminating the problem of sexual harassment from our society will require breaking down these stereotypes. But this, of course, is just what the ideal of a gender-free or androgynous society hopes to do.

73 Meritor Savings Bank v. Vinson.

74 Rabidue v. Osceola Refining Co. 805 F.2d 611, 620 (6th Cir. 1986).

75 "EEOC 1980 Guidelines on Sexual Harassment," in *Fair Employment Practices, Labor Relations Reporter*, The Bureau of National Affairs, Inc.

76 Rabidue v. Osceola Refining Co. 805 F.2d 611, 620 (6th Cir. 1986).

77 Ellison v. Brady, 924 f.2d 872 (9th Cir. 1991).

78 As one of Gutek's studies shows, reasonable men and reasonable women can disagree over what constitutes sexual harassment in the workplace. In this study, 67.2% of men as compared to 16.8% of women would be flattered if asked to have sex, while 15% of the men and 62.8% of the women said they would be insulted by such an offer. Gutek, "Understanding Sexual Harassment at Work."

79 For a discussion of this form of argument, see Karen Warren, "The Power and Promise of EcoFeminism," *Environmental Ethics*, vol. 12 (1990) pp. 121–46.

80 Although I will be focussing on racism directed at African Americans, the argument I will be developing applies to all forms of racism.

81 Denying people equal opportunity on the basis of culture is a way of showing disrespect to them and their culture. Accordingly, it is possible to conceive of multicultural justice as requiring respect for cultural diversity. See my *Contemporary Social and Political Philosophy* (Belmont: Wadsworth Publishing Co., 1995) chapter 7.

82 See John Passmore, *Man's Responsibility for Nature* (London: Charles Scribner's Sons, 1974); and George Sessions and Bill Devall, *Deep Ecology* (Salt Lake City: Gibbs Smith Publisher, 1985).

83 See Paul Taylor, *Respect for Nature* (Princeton: Princeton University Press, 1987); and Murray Bookchin, *The Ecology of Freedom* (Montreal: Black Rose Books, 1991). It is also possible to view Passmore as pitted against Taylor, and Bookchin as pitted against Sessions, but however one casts the debate, those who defend an anthropocentric ethics are still opposed to those who defend a nonanthropocentric ethics.

84 My reconciliation project contrasts with Bryan Norton's in *Toward Unity Among Environmentalists* (Oxford: Oxford University Press, 1991). While Norton's reconciliation project seeks to achieve a reconciliation at the level of practical policies, mine seeks a reconciliation at the level of general principles as well. While Norton's reconciliation project tends to exclude deep ecologists like George Sessions, and biocentric egalitarians like Paul Taylor, from the class of environmentalists that he is seeking to reconcile, my reconciliation project explicitly includes them.

85 See Taylor, *Respect for Nature*, pp. 129–35; and R. and V. Routley, "Against the Inevitability of Human Chauvinism," in *Ethics and Problems of the 21st Century*, ed. K. E. Goodpaster and K. M. Sayre (Notre Dame: University of Notre Dame Press, 1979) pp. 36–59.

86 Assuming God exists, humans might also be better off if they could retain their distinctive traits while acquiring one or another of God's qualities, but consideration of this possibility would take us too far afield. Nonhuman animals might also be better off if they could retain their distinctive traits and acquire one or another of the distinctive traits possessed by other nonhuman animals.

87 This assumes that there is an environmental niche that cheetahs can fill.

88 For my purposes here, I will follow the convention of excluding humans from the class denoted by "animals."

89 For an account of what constitutes justifiably held property within human ethics, see *Justice for Here and Now*, chapter 3.

90 By human ethics, I simply mean those forms of ethics that assume, without argument, that only human beings count morally.

91 Of course, one might contend that no principle of human defense applies in human ethics because either "nonviolent pacifism" or "nonlethal pacifism" is the most morally defensible view. However, I will argue in the next section that this is not the case, and that still other forms of pacifism more compatible with just war theory are also more morally defensible than either of these forms of pacifism.

92 The Principle of Human Preservation also imposes a limit on when we can defend nonhuman living beings against human aggression. Defense of nonhumans against human aggression is only justified when the humans who are aggressing are not doing so to meet their basic needs as permitted by the Principle of Human Preservation.

93 The difference between a standard of a decent life and a standard of a healthy life is, however, only one of degree. A standard of a decent life emphasizes the cultural and social dimensions of basic needs, while a standard of a healthy life emphasizes their physical and biological dimensions. For further discussion of basic needs, see James P. Sterba, *How To Make People Just* (Totowa: Rowman & Littlefield, 1988) pp. 45–50.

94 Moreover, this kind of fuzziness in the application of the distinction between basic and nonbasic needs is characteristic of the application of virtually all our classificatory concepts, and so is not an objection to its usefulness.

95 It should be pointed out that the Principle of Human Preservation must be implemented in a way that causes the least harm possible, which means that, other things being equal, basic needs should be met by aggressing against non-sentient rather than sentient living beings, so as to avoid the pain and suffering that would otherwise be inflicted on sentient beings.

96 It is important to recognize here that we also have a strong obligation to prevent lifeboat cases from arising in the first place.

97 It should also be pointed out that the Principle of Human Preservation does not support an unlimited right of procreation. In fact, the theory of justice presupposed here gives priority to the basic needs of existing beings over the basic needs of possible future beings, and this should effectively limit (human) procreation. Nor does the Principle of Human Preservation allow humans to aggress against the basic needs of animals and plants, even to meet their own basic needs, when those needs could effectively be met by utilizing available human surplus resources.

98 This principle is clearly acceptable to welfare liberals, socialists, and even libertarians. For arguments to that effect, see chapter 3. See also *How To Make People Just*, and the special issue of the *Journal of Social Philosophy*, vol. 22, no. 3, devoted to *How To Make People Just*, including my "Nine Commentators: A Brief Response."

99 Of course, libertarians have claimed that we can recognize that people have equal basic rights while, in fact, failing to meet, but not aggressing against, the basic needs of other human beings. However, I have argued in chapter 3 that this claim is mistaken.

100 It should be pointed out that although the Principle of Disproportionality prohibits aggressing against the basic needs of animals and plants to serve the nonbasic needs of humans, the Principle of Human Defense permits defending oneself and other human beings against harmful aggression of animals and plants, even when this only serves the nonbasic needs of humans. The underlying idea is that we can legitimately serve our nonbasic needs *by defending* our persons and our property against the aggression of nonhuman others but *not by aggressing against* them. In the case of human aggression, a slightly weaker principle of defense holds: we can legitmately serve our nonbasic needs by defending our persons and property *except* when humans are engaged in aggression against our nonbasic needs because it is the only way to meet their basic needs. This exception is grounded in the altruistic forbearance that we can reasonably expect of humans. In addition, in the case of human aggression, even when that aggression is illegitimate, it will sometimes be possible to effectively defend oneself and other human beings by first suffering the aggression and then securing adequate compensation later. Since in the case of nonhuman aggression this is unlikely to obtain, more harmful preventive actions against nonhuman aggression will be justified. There are simply more ways to effectively stop aggressive humans than there are to stop aggressive nonhumans.

101 It might be objected here that this argument is still speciesist in that it permits humans to aggress against nonhuman nature whenever it is necessary for meeting our own basic needs or the basic needs of humans we happen to care about. But this objection surely loses some of its force once it is recognized that it is also permissible for us to aggress against the nonbasic needs of humans, whenever it is necessary for meeting our own basic needs or the basic needs of humans we happen to care about. Actually, the differences in our moral requirements with respect to humans and nonhumans are grounded in altruistic forbearance that we can reasonably expect of humans but not of nonhumans, and in the additional ways we have of effectively stopping human aggression but not nonhuman aggression.

102 Another way to put the central claim here is to say that species equality rules out domination, where domination is taken to mean aggressing against the basic needs of other living beings for the sake of satisfying nonbasic needs. So understood, species equality does not rule out treating species differently, even preferring one's basic needs, or the basic needs of one's species to the basic needs of nonhuman individuals, species, and whole ecosystems.

103 Holmes Rolston III, *Environmental Ethics* (Philadelphia: Temple University Press, 1988) pp. 66–8; Bookchin, *The Ecology of Freedom*, p. xxxvi.

104 See the discussion of possible grounds of human superiority in Taylor, *Respect for Nature*, pp. 135–52; and in Bryan Norton, *Why Preserve Natural Variety?* (Princeton: Princeton University Press, 1987) pp. 135–50.

105 This is clearly true for welfare liberals and socialists, and it can even be shown to be true for libertarians, because most failings to meet the basic needs of others really turn out to be acts of aggressing against the basic needs of others, and so the earlier argument from liberty to equality applies.

106 The same holds true in human ethics where most of the ways we have of preferring our own nonbasic needs over the basic needs of other humans actually involve aggressing against those needs to meet our own nonbasic or luxury needs rather than simply failing to meet them, as I have argued earlier.

107 Cockroaches have been known to survive even inside nuclear reactors.

108 Actually, what we are presently doing may be only meeting our short-term and not even our long-term needs, and almost certainly not meeting the long-term needs of future generations of human beings. Accordingly, a policy that took our long-term needs as well as the needs of future generations of human beings into account would most likely be a policy that was more in coincidence with the needs of nonhuman nature. Nevertheless, it would be odd to expect a complete coincidence of interest here any more than we would expect a complete coincidence of interest (*pace* Adam Smith) among all human beings. In addition, any coincidence of interest between humans and nonhuman nature would only provide further support for the requirements of my principles of environmental justice. (For further discussion of the degree of coincidence of interests between humans and nonhuman nature, see Norton, *Toward Unity Among Environmentalists.*)

109 Assuming God exists, even she would *not* have a right to dominate her creatures. In truth, no one can have such a right because no one is superior to another living being in such a way that he or she would have a right to dominate it.

110 For example, in "Animal Liberation: A Triangular Affair," Baird Callicott had defended Edward Abbey's assertion that he would sooner shoot a man than a snake.

111 For example, Eugene Hargrove argues that from a traditional wildlife perspective, the lives of individual specimens of quite plentiful nonhuman species count for almost nothing at all. See chapter 4 of his *Foundations of Environmental Ethics* (Englewood Cliffs: Prentice Hall, 1989).

112 Some would say with too generous a measure.

113 Jan Narveson, "Pacifism: A Philosophical Analysis," *Ethics*, vol. 75 (1965) pp. 259–71.

114 Cheyney Ryan, "Self-Defense, Pacifism and the Possibility of Killing," in *The Ethics of War and Nuclear Deterrence*, ed. James P. Sterba (Belmont: Wadsworth Publishing Co., 1985) pp. 45–9.

115 Alternatively, one might concede that even in this case killing is morally evil, but still contend that it is morally justified because it is the lesser of two evils.

116 For two challenging defenses of this view, see Duane L. Cady, *From Warism to Pacifism* (Philadelphia: Temple University Press, 1989) and Robert L. Holmes, *On War and Morality* (Princeton: Princeton University Press, 1989). Among the members of Concerned Philosophers for Peace, anti-war pacifism seems to be the most widely endorsed pacifist view.

117 See Cady, *From Warism to Pacifism*, pp. 51, 89ff; and Holmes, *On War and Morality*, p. 278.

118 This is because the just means restrictions protect innocents quite well against the infliction of intentional harm.

119 By an "unjust aggressor" I mean someone whom the defender is reasonably certain is wrongfully engaged in an attempt upon her life or the lives of other innocent people.

120 What is relevant in this case is that the foreseen deaths are a relatively small number (one in this case) compared to the number of innocents whose lives are saved (six in this case). The primary reason for using particular numbers in this case and those that follow, is to make it clear that at this stage of the argument no attempt is being make to justify the large-scale killing that occurs in warfare.

121 And more severe than some just war theorists have tended to recognize.

122 See Holmes, *On War and Morality*, pp. 208–11.

123 Although there is a strong case for India's military action against Pakistan in Bangladesh, and the Tanzanian incursion into Uganda during the rule of Idi

Amin, there are questions that can be raised about the behavior of Indian troops in Bangladesh following the defeat of the Pakistani forces, and about the regime Tanzania put in power in Uganda.

124 See, for example, William V. O'Brien, *The Conduct of Just and Limited War* (New York: Praeger, 1981) and John Courtney Murray, *Morality and Modern War* (New York: Council on Religion and International Affairs, 1959).

125 The just cause provision was violated because the extremely effective economic sanctions were not given enough time to work. It was estimated at the time that when compared to past economic blockades, the blockade against Iraq had a near-100% chance of success if given about a year to work (see the *New York Times*, 14 January 1991). The just means provision was violated because the number of combatant and noncombatant deaths was disproportionate. As many as 120,000 Iraqi soldiers were killed, according to US intelligence sources. Moreover, what we have learned about Iraq's resistance to the less stringent economic blockade that followed the war does not undercut the reasonableness of pursuing a more stringent economic blockade on the basis of the available information we had before the war. Moreover, the humiliating defeat of Iraqi forces in the Gulf War may have contributed to the hardened Iraqi resistance to the less stringent post-war economic blockage.

126 Of course, anti-war pacifists are right to point out that virtually all wars have been fought with less and less discrimination and have led to unforeseen harms. These are considerations that in just war theory must weigh heavily against going to war.

127 For another use of this term, see Kenneth H. Wenker, "Just War Pacifism," *Proceedings of the American Catholic Philosophical Association*, vol. 57 (1983) pp. 135–41. For a defense of a similar view to my own, which is considered by the author to be a defense of pacifism, see Richard Norman, "The Case for Pacifism," *Journal of Applied Philosophy*, vol. 2 (1988) pp. 197–210.

Part II

FOUNDATIONS OF SOCIAL AND POLITICAL PHILOSOPHY

Moral methodology

1

ON THE HISTORY, NATURE AND DISADVANTAGES OF WARMAKING PHILOSOPHY

Eve Browning Cole

War is the father of all and the king of all, and some he shows as gods, others as men; some he makes slaves, others full.

(Heraclitus, fr. 80)[1]

Whether or not Heraclitus' point is true of the cosmos, it has certainly been true of the recent history of philosophy. "War," *polemos*, finds its contemporary philosophical counterpart in polemic, the lifeblood of most academic philosophical careers today and the mainstay of most philosophy journal articles as well.

Philosophical warfare is supposed to be genteel, "sparring" or "scrimmaging" rather than out-and-out bloodshed. Yet it too shows "some ... as gods, others as men"; to the victors go the spoils – whether these are a silenced student, an impressed lecture audience, a "downed" opponent, or an appreciative reader who enjoys the spectacle of intellectual carnage.

Philosophical combat, at least in its Anglo-American manifestations, is gladiatorial rather than modeling the pitched battles of, for example, the ancient Romans, in which organized groups of soldiers fought in regular unison. Philosophers don't join shields and creep along in the "testudo" or tortoise formation which the legionnaires found so effective at subduing baffled barbarians; they sally forth alone packing a few footnotes like day rations. We don't go in for attacks on schools so much as wrangling between individuals.[2]

Philosophy's particular brand of *polemos* has its critics. Among the most insistent critics of philosophizing-as-warfare is James P. Sterba, whose 1998 book *Justice for Here and Now* presents both the case for a "peacemaking way of doing philosophy" and a case-study in this method applied to some of the liveliest theoretical debates of our times in moral and political philosophy. The book also provides discussion of practical applications for each issue, which is treated along peacemaking lines: once truce is declared, one can think and talk concretely about what constitutes just action within our world here and now, and what kind of world we should be working toward.

The ground rules for philosophizing in a peacemaking way are simple and few. They include:

1   a principle of charity, or placing "the most favorable interpretation on the views of one's philosophical opponents";
2   open-mindedness, or the willingness to consider new views which are challenging to one's own; and
3   intellectual "mobility" as it were, the willingness to abandon views in light of decisive evidence against them.[3]

When stated thus, the peacemaking philosophical method seems indistinguishable from certain basics philosophy instructors expect, or perhaps even demand, of all intro-level students. Prejudicial reading or listening, dogmatism, and mental bullheadedness without rationale are a recipe for a poor grade in most philosophy classes I know of. Yet Sterba convincingly shows that just such attitudes define business as usual in large sectors of the academy, including much of academic philosophy. This is a paradox.

Sterba's book also presents a deeper paradox. When he recounts having used the peacemaking method to reconcile his views with those who have thought themselves in disagreement with him, attempting to resolve substantive theoretical differences and showing that both sides can commit to the same practical agenda, he encounters resistance. Such refusals of truce are often recounted in the footnotes, and they make a poignant undercurrent to the main arguments of the text itself.

Why are the basic prerequisites for philosophical integrity, which are widely taught in undergraduate classes, often honored only in the breach at research levels of academic philosophical activity? Why is it so easy to get acclimatized to the aggressive questioning style of the colloquium "discussion period," which usually somewhat shocks and unnerves the novice observer? Why are verbal fisticuffs ever effective as a substitute for careful and considerate conversation? (As an aside: why does the *Monty Python* skit about the argument shop, in which silly arguments such as "No it isn't!" "Yes it is!" "This isn't an argument!" "Is too!" bring such laughter from philosophy students?) Why are so many journal articles (and the books which grow out of them) rooted in a warmongering rather than a peacemaking method of philosophizing? And when it comes to evaluating the polemical and the pacific methods for addressing moral and political issues, which (if either) is the more *moral* moral methodology?

In this essay I will reflect on the answers to the above questions, which fall into two classes:

1   Psychological and historical questions about the appeal and the origins of the polemical method; and
2   Evaluative questions about the moral status of the polemical and the peacemaking methods respectively.

In a final section I will return to Sterba's specific application of the peacemaking method and its potential practical implications.

I Philosophical warfare: whence and why

The pervasiveness of the polemical model for philosophizing, at least in the dominant culture of the Anglo-American university and its products (both people and research), would argue for a complex answer to the questions of its origin and its appeal. Pointing to a historical source may be worthwhile even though it does not give a full explanation, since the question why any particular philosopher philosophized polemically would still remain.

Western philosophy in its earliest manifestations does display a predilection for the antithetical. Heraclitus in the quote at the heading of this paper is a famous case in point. One might also think of the at least *prima facie* contradictory parts of Parmenides' poem, the "Way of Truth" and the "Way of Seeming". And Empedocles, with his alternations of cosmic epochs ruled at one time by Strife and at another by Love, also made binary oppositions central to the workings of the universe.

But these early philosophers were advancing theses about a binary conflict or tension or duality at the heart of nature, or at the center of our experience of nature; they were not advocating nor (as far as we can tell from the paucity of our historical evidence) themselves exemplifying a polemical method of philosophizing. Both Parmenides and Empedocles wrote poems which may have been sung; it is hard to picture the contemporary pugnacious philosopher singing his refutations and counter-examples to the accompaniment of his own lyre-playing.

No; for the first undeniable instance of polemical philosophy we must wait for Plato. And in Plato's dialogues I think we come to one of the fountainheads of what Sterba deplores in contemporary philosophy: one-on-one philosophical skirmishing, in a formal semi-public setting, designed to kill off competing lines of argument, and often resulting in a clear victor/vanquished scenario. The ingredients of the contemporary APA convention are all provided here. It may be true (as I believe) that Plato had complex intentions in writing philosophy the way he did, and that nowhere among these was the intention to advocate verbal sparring as a means of achieving enlightenment. Nevertheless, the model he created, especially in the early "Socratic" dialogues, had such power that it continues to fascinate, invigorate, and inspire emulation among the philosophy students who are still often introduced to the subject by reading one of Plato's earlier dialogues.

In this connection, it is interesting to compare Plato's star student Aristotle on the subject of method and specifically of polemicizing. In Aristotle's works we find both straightforward polemic, sometimes against "the Friends of the Forms" which probably included Plato himself, and also what I would consider "appropriative peacemaking". By the latter I mean texts such as Aristotle's *Metaphysics* I.3–10, in which earlier thinkers are taken up and fitted (or in some cases shoehorned) into Aristotle's own schema of the four causes. Here Aristotle's intention is to show that the early thinkers' contributions do not present any type of cause which falls outside his schema – and also that his list of four is more comprehensive than any previous analysis of causality in nature.[4]

No doubt Plato's depictions of a refutation-oriented Socrates cast a long shadow over subsequent Western philosophy and still do so. But what is the appeal? To cite a precedent is not to explain the mechanism by which the precedent attracted a subsequent mind to emulate it. Why is polemical philosophy so appealing?

Polemical philosophy is combative; it stakes out territory, defends that territory, meets challengers with counter-attack, anticipates hostile incursions and develops counter-strategies for demolishing them. It is intellectual battle.

And battle is appealing. J. Glenn Gray has written persuasively, with much documentation from war journals and veterans' interviews, of the specific ways in which real combat experiences can be regarded as enjoyable, beneficial, fulfilling.[5] Gray isolates three components of the combat experience which mark it as positive for combatants:

1   "delight in seeing": the *spectacle* of battle is surprisingly beautiful to (at least some) participants.
2   "delight in comradeship": a particular form of solidarity is constructed by the battle conditions. And
3   "delight in destruction": lamentable though it may seem, the experience of blowing things up, blasting heads off, causing mayhem, etc., is in some deep way pleasurable and even exhilarating.[6]

Although Gray is far from celebrating these positive aspects of combat experience, he does argue that they contribute to the persistence of war as a problem-solving strategy in human history, and that they make pacifism a far more difficult project. Can these "enduring appeals of battle" shed any light on philosophy's penchant for the warmaking rather than peacemaking mode of operation?

The activity of aggressively defending a position, in writing or in person, and so also the passive experience of observing such an aggressive defense when well executed, can certainly be pleasurable. These pleasure responses are probably related to the more harmless pleasures of playing or watching a competitive sport. There are "good moves," "volleys," "quick recoveries," and points are scored or conceded and lost. This captures the strategic side of combat pleasure, philosophical and military. On the purely visual or aesthetic side, the grace or (mental or physical) athleticism of the combatants can be pleasing, as can the symmetry of a well constructed attack or defense (argument, phalanx, or soccer squad).

As for comradeship or solidarity, the individualism of the philosophical polemic in the Anglo-American academic community would seem to run counter to this. However, advancing a successful polemic means winning an audience – whether of invisible readers or visible symposium attendees. It may also mean attracting disciples, in the form of students. The footnotes of philosophy journal articles often display a kind of solidarity-group construction project: "On this point I agree with X as against Y ..." which is analogous to team-choosing or club-joining, surrogate comradeship if you will. So the loneliness of the philosophical gladiator may be more apparent than real; his/her rhetorical situation is one of aggressive team- or herd-building via exclusion of the competitor.

Finally, "delight in destruction" seems all too easy to detect in the intensity with which many philosophers inclined toward the warmaking method leap into the fray. Readers and audiences too may participate in the (perverse?) pleasure of seeing a position, even a position represented by a present person, appear to fall to pieces under enemy fire. The explanation for the pleasure of witnessing or perpetrating mayhem would lie deep in the wellsprings of human psychological energy I am sure; but the evidence for such a pleasure seems undeniable, whether one is considering the child demolishing her own carefully constructed sandcastle or the philosopher deploying her devastating counter-argument.[7]

So it would appear that some similarities exist between the attractions of real combat and those of intellectual combat as found in the academic philosophical community. So much for some possible sources and attractions of the warmaking method of philosophizing. What about its moral status, especially as contrasted with the peacemaking method advocated and exemplified by Sterba?

II Evaluating moral methodologies

Moral evaluation of philosophical methodologies is an infrequent practice in the current literature. One important contribution which Sterba's *Justice for Here and Now* will certainly make to current philosophy is the encouragement of more self-critical thinking, speaking and writing in current philosophical circles.[8] Sterba argues that approaching philosophical questions in the polemical spirit produces less good philosophy, because it encourages misreading, deflects good criticisms, and rewards intransigence. In addition, it can be wasteful of human time and resources, since it leads to overlooking good solutions and favoring poor ones simply because they are one's own. Such considerations, if valid, would lead to a higher moral valuation of peacemaking philosophical method(s) on consequentialist grounds if on no other, provided it could be shown that peacemaking philosophical methods have the virtues which correspond to these faults attributed to the polemical methods. That is, if it can be shown that peacemaking philosophy encourages careful reading of extant positions, considers good criticisms with the care they deserve, and discourages dogmatism, then (absent other optimizing considerations) the greater philosophical good is clearly served by peacemaking methods.

Against this point one might argue either, first, that warlike philosophical methods do have other optimizing consequences overlooked by Sterba; or second, that Sterba has misconstrued the nature of philosophy and its goals. I will pursue these potential counter-arguments separately.

While it is true that combative, position-defending, rear-guarding, point-scoring philosophical methods have the potential for the above noted shortcomings, they also have some assets. The first we may call the *calisthenic* benefit. It is great mental exercise to aggressively defend a position. The thrill of the combat calls forth mental energy which quiet and reflective mulling of a problem may not be able to evoke. The intellectual athleticism of the successful skirmish, and the palm of victory or ignominy of defeat, are effective inducements to the very activity of philosophizing and improvement thereof.[9] The second we may call the *winnowing* benefit. A vigorous logical drubbing gets rid of the dust and fleas which may have clung to any philosophical position. In light of the fact that human time is a limited resource, it must at least sometimes be the case that the best way to use limited time is to subject a position to strenuous criticism and see what is left over at the end, i.e. to approach it combatively rather than pacifically. It is possible that the warlike approach will be the most efficient approach for a philosophical position which just is untenable, and which peacemaking methods would take much longer to expose as such. Finally we should consider the *recruitment* effect of polemical methods. Philosophy has sought adherents, "converts" if you will, since its inception. Socrates is known to us only because he was an effective philosophical recruiter. Academic philosophy departments continue to exist only as long as they can emulate Socrates to some degree. And polemical methods bring in majors.[10] The "appeals of battle" are seductive in this sphere.

Are the calisthenic, winnowing and recruitment factors sufficient to morally justify a preference for polemical philosophy? Or to put it differently, is the choice between warlike and peacemaking philosophical methods a morally neutral choice?

I believe it is not. To see why, we need to consider the goals of this activity "philosophizing." If philosophizing were construed as itself a morally neutral activity, then the benefits of aggressive mental calisthenics, the winnowings of philosophical triage, and the "enduring appeals of battle" in attracting young minds would be redeeming (outcome-optimizing) features of polemical philosophy. However, philosophizing, especially as understood by Sterba, is not a morally neutral activity. At least as practiced within the halls of academe, it is the use of scarce resources available to a privileged few, and it should be directed toward the improvement of the human condition. Within these parameters, warmaking philosophical methods are irresponsible. The polemical philosopher is too inclined to substitute gamesmanship for social responsibility. She is also too inclined to destroy before sympathetically understanding. And each fresh "victory" renders her less amenable to fundamental changes in her own convictions. None of these is a morally deleterious consequence *unless* philosophizing is itself a morally charged activity which generates moral responsibilities for those who pursue it in an organized fashion. That it is so morally charged is clearly a presupposition of Sterba's entire project, and one which I completely endorse. Crucial issues of human welfare are at stake in the debates into which Sterba enters with his peacemaking method: oppressions of various forms, poverty, environmental degradation, and the very possibility of a viable future for the human race. As long as philosophers feel justified in conducting sandbox wars amongst themselves, rather than finding common ground and making strong cases for good policy, philosophers are making morally defective methodological choices which render their hard-won conclusions impractical and therefore functionally irrelevant.

Thus, on Sterba's grounds, we can argue that peacemaking philosophical methods are morally preferable to polemical ones, and that the choice between them is not a morally neutral one to be viewed as merely preference-driven. Instead, a strong imperative toward peacemaking methods can be justified, given the moral parameters in which philosophy exists "here and now."

Conclusion

I find Sterba's case for the method of conciliation or peacemaking, and also his practical applications in many areas, both compelling and refreshing. Perform this thought-experiment: imagine that from this moment forward, all the philosophical conversations in which you become involved, all the philosophical articles and books you read, and all the philosophy classes being conducted worldwide, suddenly adhere to Sterba's recommendations. First, everyone listens or reads with the utmost care and fairness of mind. Then, everyone charitably puts the best possible construction on every claim and argument. If objections occur to us as we listen or read, we attempt to respond to these objections ourselves, either from within the position being presented or by introducing additional considerations compatible with it. And if the position presented is compelling, everyone is willing to adopt it.

In such a philosophical Utopia, it is hard for me not to believe that better philosophy would be the result. In addition, the consolidation of practical implications at the outcome of the reconciliations which Sterba proposes would allow philosophy to have an efficacy which it now lacks, in being a recognizable and credible voice for social change.

NOTES

1 G. S. Kirk, M. E. Raven and M. Schofield, *The Presocratic Philosophers* (Cambridge: Cambridge University Press, 1983) p. 193.
2 This individualism seems much less frequent in Continental philosophy, Russian philosophy, and Chinese philosophy of our time; for these, most philosophical controversies seem to take place between or among schools, or groups identified by their affiliation with one particular leader.
3 James P. Sterba, *Justice for Here and Now* (Cambridge: Cambridge University Press, 1998) p. 10.
4 Sterba also engages in what I am calling "appropriative peacemaking" at several points in his book, most notably with his account of an ongoing exchange with Jan Narveson, *Justice for Here and Now*, chapter 3, pp. 72ff, although in Narveson's case, the appropriation and the peacemaking are apparently both resisted. Sterba's appropriative peacemaking with Narveson does not appear to be of the "shoehorning" variety; but, like Aristotle, Sterba intends to strengthen the justification of his own account by demonstrating that it is not incompatible with other accounts.
5 J. Glenn Gray, *The Warriors: Reflections on Men in Battle* (New York: Harcourt Brace, 1959). A selection, "The Enduring Appeals of Battle," is reprinted in Larry May, Robert Strikwerda, and Patrick D. Hopkins (eds) *Rethinking Masculinity: Philosophical Explorations in Light of Feminism* (Lanham MD: Rowman & Littlefield, 1996) pp. 45–62.
6 Gray, as reprinted in May *et al.*, *op. cit.*, pp. 47ff.
7 This phenomenon is also apparent when respondents to papers presented at APA meetings simply cannot be restrained from making yet another critical point, time limits notwithstanding.
8 As I was reading Sterba's book I found my teaching and ways of responding to students in the classroom undergoing some changes, even though I have never considered myself to be a particularly combative philosophical personality. I also found myself more actively and explicitly encouraging students to bring the attitudes Sterba advocates at the end of his introduction (p. 13) to their readings of assigned texts. I believe the class was the better and more philosophical because of these changes.
9 Any philosophy instructor who has used staged classroom debates, in which one side of the classroom must argue X, the other not-X, can attest to the awakening effect of sheer turf-defense responsibility as against a visible "enemy".
10 It is of course possible that the majors who are drawn in by polemical methods are those, and only those, who are predisposed to take pleasure in combat, and that other students choose more pacific avenues for their educational pursuits.

Rationality

2

THE RATIONAL
JUSTIFICATION OF
MORALITY REVISITED

Alan Gewirth

In this paper, I shall first comment on the discussion of the argument I have presented for the rational justification of morality in *Reason and Morality*. Then I shall comment on the argument for the same general purpose that James P. Sterba sets forth in *Justice for Here and Now*.

I

My argument has been very widely discussed in the two decades since the publication of *Reason and Morality*, and I and others have replied extensively to the various criticisms that have been made.[1] So I'm afraid I shall not say much that is new here, but I shall focus on the specific emphasis Sterba gives in his criticism. He holds that "the norms of rationality ... imply a commitment to consistency and non-question-beggingness" (p. 184; see p. 6). I agree with this, but I would add that consistency involves, among other things, the use of conceptual analysis, which I construe on the model of deductive logic, in that when a complex concept A is analysed as containing concepts B, C, and D, these concepts belong to A with logical necessity, so that it is contradictory to hold that A applies while denying that B, C, or D applies. In my argument I obtain and use the concepts of action and agent by such conceptual analysis; at the same time these concepts represent actual phenomena of human conduct. My argument proceeds by analysing what any agent logically must accept on the basis of her engaging in voluntary and purposive behavior. This gives the argument a kind of material necessity as well as formal necessity, for it involves that the content of agency has certain necessary features.[2]

Sterba questions a crucial step in my argument (I use his numbering as given on p. 20, but I rephrase the respective sentences). The argument depends on the interpretation of the transition from (3) "I have a right to freedom and well-being because I am a prospective purposive agent" to (4) "All prospective purposive agents have rights to freedom and well-being." I have held that the "right" in (3) is a prudential right, while the "right" in (4) is a moral right.

It is important to be clear about the meaning of these respective characterizations of rights. The right in (3) is prudential in that its aim is to support the interests of the agent or speaker. The right in (4), on the other hand, is moral in that, in affirming that all prospective purposive agents have these rights, the original agent or speaker takes favorable account of the interests of at least some persons other than or in addition to himself. So "moral" has here the traditional meaning of supporting the interests of other persons.

The contrast between "prudential" and "moral" is one that goes back at least to Kant. It is a matter of final causes: whose interests are supported or upheld. The transition from the prudential to the moral is accomplished through the logical principle of universalizability: if some subject S has predicate P because S has the quality Q (where this "because" is one of sufficient condition or reason), then every other subject $S_1, S_2 \ldots S_N$ that has Q must also have P.

As Sterba correctly points out, "the success of [my] argument depends on the impossibility of interpreting the universalized right in [my] conclusion as anything other than a moral right" (p. 20). This impossibility derives from the universalizability principle just stated, together with the social meaning of "moral" indicated above. But Sterba declares that "another interpretation is possible." According to this interpretation, the universalized right that can be deduced from my premises "is a prudential right, not a moral one" (p. 21). And "a prudential right is action-guiding for the right-holder only and not for others, and so it does not imply that others ought not to interfere with the exercise of that right" (p. 21).

There is a serious difficulty with Sterba's interpretation. It will have been noted that where I distinguish prudential and moral rights in terms of whose interests the rights are intended to support – either the agent's own interests or the interests also of other persons – Sterba puts the distinction in terms of whether the right is "action-guiding" only for the agent or right-holder or also "for others as well" (p. 20; see also p. 21). But these two distinctions do not coincide. A right can be action-guiding for some person A without being only for his own interests. For A may guide his action with the aim of supporting the interests of other persons as well as or in addition to his own interests. So Sterba's reformulation does not quite capture the meaning of my argument as I intended it. Hence, I cannot accept his contention that my argument can be correctly interpreted as establishing only a prudential right, not a moral one. His reinterpretation may indeed be "plausible," as he says, but only if "prudential" is construed in a way that is different from the one I intended. As I've said, my interpretation of "prudential" has a long lineage, going back at least to Kant.

Where I hold that the universalization of the agent's prudential right-claim entails a moral right, Sterba says that "the universalization of a prudential right can be understood to be another prudential right, albeit a universal one" (p. 21). But this understanding is incorrect on the final-cause interpretation of "prudential" and "moral." For when the agent has to accept, on the basis of universalization, that all prospective purposive agents have rights to freedom and well-being, she is thereby upholding the interests of other persons as well as herself – of "all prospective purposive agents." This is not a prudential right, precisely because she thereby takes positive, favorable account of the interests of other persons in their own freedom and well-being.

It must be recognized that universalization alone does not accomplish the transition to *universalist* morality that figures in my argument, whereby it is the interests of "*all* prospective purposive agents" that are upheld by the concluding rights-judgment. For this universalism to be attained, what is required besides the formal aspect of logical universalization is the material or contentual aspect whereby it is prospective purposive agents as such who are held to have the rights. If the content is not thus universalist – as when one says, for example, that "all Americans have certain legal rights" – what this gives us is only what I have elsewhere called "particularist morality," as against universalist morality.[3] In *Reason and Morality* I have given my reasons for holding that the content to which every agent is logically committed – the relevant similarity on which the argument is based – is the universal trait of being a prospective purposive agent.[4]

How is my interest-based conception of a moral right in my conclusion related to Sterba's thesis that, because "a prudential right is action-guiding for the right-holder and not for others ... it does not imply that others ought not to interfere with the exercise of that right" (p. 21)? To begin with, the moral right does imply that "others ought not to interfere." This is entailed by the correlativity of claim-rights and duties: if A has a right to have or do X, it logically follows that all other persons ought at least to refrain from interfering with A's having or doing X, and in some cases ought also to help A to have or do X. So the having of a moral right entails correlative duties at least of non-interference on the part of other persons.

What of Sterba's idea that the rights-judgment with which my argument concludes "is action-guiding for the right-holder only and not for others" (p. 21)? This is indeed an important point. We can elaborate it as follows: The agent right-holder may well conclude that all other prospective purposive agents have the generic rights, but this commits only him to respecting the rights or interests of other persons – it does not commit other persons to act accordingly. So here, "action-guiding for other persons" would mean something like: imposing obligations on other persons which *they* are committed to recognizing and accepting. Let us call this the *interpersonal-recognition objection*.

What must be stressed in reply is the personal-dialectical character of my argument. The argument establishes that, from within the standpoint of the individual agent who is going through the argument, he must recognize that all other agents have the generic rights, so that he has correlative obligations toward them. But he also recognizes that all other agents can, at least in principle, go through the same argument, with the same necessary conclusion about universal rights, so that they must recognize one another's generic rights. Hence the other agents are as logically committed to acknowledging one another's rights as he is to recognizing their rights. This, I submit, is how the interpersonal-recognition objection is to be answered.[5]

II

Let us now turn to Sterba's own argument as given in *Justice for Here and Now*, pp. 14–40. He presents as his goal "to show that morality is grounded in rationality ... that morality is rationally required, thus excluding egoism and immorality as rationally permissible" (p. 14). This passage suggests that Sterba views morality in the usual way as opposed simply to egoism. But, on the contrary, he uses "morality" in a way that may include both egoistic and altruistic reasons: "moral reasons here are understood necessarily to include (some) altruistic reasons but not necessarily to exclude all self-interested reasons" (p. 188); indeed, "morality itself already represents a compromise between egoism and altruism" (p. 190).

It is not anomalous to hold that the sphere of morality includes some version of self-interest together with a concern for others' interests. This is epitomized, for example, in Kant's second version of the categorical imperative: "Act so that you always treat humanity, whether *in your own person* or in that of another, always as an end and never as a means only."[6] A similar inclusion is found in the Principle of Generic Consistency: "Act in accord with the generic rights of your recipients *as well as of yourself*."[7]

It will be noted that in these versions of what may be called "moderate altruism,"[8] the self-concern that is upheld is subjected to basic moral limitations: it involves treating oneself as an end in oneself, as having generic rights. Because of these common moral limitations, there is ultimately no conflict between self-concern and concern for others: the rights of all must be equally protected. To deal with conflicts that may arise requires a consideration of degrees of needfulness for action,[9] and, in the political sphere, a constitutional order that includes the rule of law and other institutions that uphold equal and dignity-respecting rights.

Is any comparable moral limitation provided by Sterba's view of morality as a "compromise" between altruism and egoism? The question becomes especially significant in cases where there is conflict between self-interested and altruistic reasons. Sterba answers this question by an appeal to "rankings": "Such a compromise would have to respect the rankings of self-interested and altruistic reasons imposed by the egoistic and altruistic views, respectively" (p. 26). Reasons may rank higher or lower, but in every case those reasons that rank highest must have priority:

> Any nonarbitrary compromise among such reasons in seeking not to beg the question against egoism or altruism will have to give priority to those reasons that rank highest in each category. Failure to give priority to the highest-ranking altruistic or self-interested reasons would, other things being equal, be contrary to reason.
>
> (p. 26)

To evaluate the soundness of this conception of morality as a compromise between self-interested and altruistic reasons, we must ask how the relevant rankings are determined. Sterba's main answer to this question seems to make the rankings relative to the individual agent as chooser: "for each individual there is a separate ranking of that individual's relevant self-interested and altruistic reasons" (p. 26). But if this is so, it may seem that the moral limitations on self-concern to which I referred above may be dispensed with. Thus Sterba writes: "a certain amount of self-regard is morally required, or at least morally acceptable. Where this is the case, high-ranking self-interested reasons have priority over low-ranking altruistic reasons" (p. 27).

If I understand him correctly, Sterba seems not to have realized the morally injurious conduct which this commits him to upholding as "rational." His examples of self-interested reasons include marketing a harmful baby formula (p. 24) and harmful disposal of toxic wastes (p. 25). In each of these cases he argues that altruistic reasons are to be given priority.

But what if for some individual certain reasons of self-interest that are very harmful to others rank so high that they outweigh any altruistic reasons? Suppose Smith's highest-ranking desire is to dominate other people, while his desire to help other people ranks very low for him. On Sterba's account, the moral "compromise" here gives priority to Smith's self-centered "reason" of dominance. But this then puts morality on the side of moral evil.

At one point Sterba takes up the question of "reasons significantly opposed to the relevant moral reasons" (p. 24). He gives as an example "*malevolent* reasons seeking to bring about the suffering and death of other human beings" (p. 24; original emphasis). His response is as follows: "assuming that such malevolent reasons are ultimately rooted in some conception of what is good for oneself or others, these reasons would have already been taken into account, and by assumption outweighed by the other relevant reasons in this case" (p. 24). The context in which he addresses this consideration is one where there is no "conflict between the relevant self-interested and moral reasons" (pp. 23–4). He says, "it seems obvious that where there is no conflict and both reasons are conclusive reasons of their kind, both reasons should be acted upon. In such contexts, we should do what is favored by both morality and self-interest" (p. 24). So Sterba's point about the "malevolent" reasons is that even though they are self-interested, they will have been summed into the "conclusive reasons" which, *ex hypothesi*, do not conflict with morality.

I find this a rather dubious way of dealing with malevolent reasons. At the very least it should have been shown how they are "taken into account" in arriving at a lack of conflict with morality. As I have already indicated, Sterba's subsequent appeal to "rankings" does not help matters.

At some points Sterba seems to suggest a more objective criterion of rankings of reasons. He says, for example, that his "defense of morality presupposes that we can establish a conception of the good, at least to the degree that we can determine high- and low-ranking self-interested and altruistic reasons for each agent" (p. 190). This might be interpreted as meaning that reasons rank higher or lower according to some "conception of the good." On this interpretation the self-interested reason of the malevolent person who wants to dominate others might rank lower than an altruistic reason because of its opposition to "a conception of the good."

This might be a promising line of approach, although Sterba does not develop it. The conclusion we are left with, in any case, is that, like compromise in the political sphere, there are limits to the compromise Sterba envisages in his interesting idea of Morality as Compromise. Until he sets out these limits much more fully, he can hardly be held to have established a rational justification of morality.

NOTES

1 See especially Edward Regis Jr (ed.) *Gewirth's Ethical Rationalism: Critical Essays with a Reply by Alan Gewirth* (Chicago: University of Chicago Press, 1984); and Deryck Beyleveld, *The Dialectical Necessity of Morality: An Analysis and Defense of Alan Gewirth's Argument to the Principle of Generic Consistency* (Chicago: University of Chicago Press, 1991).

2 See A. Gewirth, *Reason and Morality* (Chicago: University of Chicago Press, 1978) pp. 161–71.

3 See Gewirth, *Self-Fulfillment* (Princeton: Princeton University Press, 1998) p. 52.

4 *Reason and Morality*, pp. 104–28.

5 For extensive discussion of this point, see Beyleveld, *Dialectical Necessity*, pp. 201–31, 455–7, 464–6, 468–9.

6 *Foundations of the Metaphysics of Morals*, chapter 2 (Akad. edn, p. 429; trans. L. W. Beck [Indianapolis: Bobbs-Merrill, 1959] p. 47; emphasis added).

7 *Reason and Morality*, p. 135.

8 See *Self-Fulfillment*, p. 88.

9 See Gewirth, *The Community of Rights* (Chicago: University of Chicago Press, 1996) pp. 45–54.

3

THEORETICAL VERSUS PRACTICAL RATIONALITY

Bernard Gert

There is a long-standing dispute among philosophers concerning the relationship between rationality and morality. Philosophers disagree about whether rationality supports morality in any significant way. Some philosophers hold that rationality requires all rational persons to put forward morality as a guide to behavior that governs all of them. Others go even further and claim that rationality requires everyone to act morally. James P. Sterba in his book, *Justice for Here and Now*, is one of the latter philosophers. Others, like myself, claim that rationality clearly does not require acting morally, and that it requires all rational persons to put forward morality as a guide to behavior that governs all of them, only with some significant qualifications. The disagreement between Sterba and myself involves both our accounts of rationality and our accounts of morality, but it also involves something else. We disagree about whether what needs to be shown is if it is practical rationality or theoretical rationality that requires acting morally.

When I claim that rationality clearly does not require acting morally, I am talking about practical rationality, that is, rationality with regard to action. Practical rationality is concerned with harms and benefits, both with regard to oneself and with regard to others. It is the relationship between practical rationality and morality that I regard as crucial. Sterba, on the contrary, seems to be concerned with the relationship between theoretical rationality and morality. As I understand theoretical rationality, it is primarily concerned with beliefs and arguments, that is, it requires that one use only true beliefs, valid arguments, and acceptable modes of argumentation. Of course, since the desired conclusion is that rationality requires *acting* morally, the conclusions of theoretical reason are supposed to entail conclusions with regard to practical reason. Among those philosophers who claim that reason requires acting morally, there are two groups. Some, like Thomas Hobbes, and some contemporary followers of Hobbes such as Kurt Baier and David Gauthier, do try to show directly that practical rationality requires acting morally. Others, like James P. Sterba and Alan Gewirth, claim that it is theoretical reason that requires acting morally. Both Sterba and Gewirth claim that practical judgments can be true or false, and so they accept that theoretical reason, which is concerned with truth, can entail conclusions about how a rational person should act. Sterba does not think that practical reason – by itself, that is, simply a concern about harms and benefits – can require acting morally. He holds that in order to show that reason requires acting morally, one must use the concept of theoretical reason.

In our e-mail conversations about this matter, he says, "If what is required by reason is simply not acting irrationally, as you define it, then, as you put it, only crazy people would not want to do what is required by reason." I understand Sterba's remark to acknowledge that practical reason does not require acting morally, but that he is concerned with a different sense of rationality, theoretical reason, which is more demanding in what it requires. He says,

> But I think that what is required by reason is a bit more demanding than this. Specifically, I think that reason also requires that we support our views with good arguments, and, since good arguments must be non-question-begging, I think that reason requires that we not beg the question. Now I agree with you that, given this more demanding definition of what reason requires, noncrazy people, that is, people who are not irrational in your sense of the term, may want to support or defend views for which they know they cannot give good arguments, that is, arguments which are non-question-begging, but, of course, we can understand and explain how this can be the case, that is, we can understand and explain how, for example, it can be in people's self-interest to support or defend such views.

It is important to note that Sterba's remarks make it clear that he thinks that reason sometimes *requires* one to act against one's self-interest. Although it is quite clear that morality sometimes *requires* one to act against one's self-interest, it is not at all clear that practical reason ever *requires* this. On the normal understanding of rationality, it allows one to act against one's self-interest, but it never requires one to. It is perfectly rational for a person to sacrifice his own interests for the greater interests of others, but on the ordinary concept of rationality, it is also perfectly rational for one to refuse to do so. On the ordinary concept of practical rationality it is perfectly rational either to be selfish or to be unselfish. On Sterba's account of rationality it is contrary to reason to be selfish when this involves the sacrifice of the greater interests of others. Sterba can claim that reason requires not being selfish because he is not primarily concerned with practical rationality, rather he is concerned with theoretical rationality. He is certainly correct that theoretical reason does not allow one to tailor one's arguments because of reasons of self-interest. The goal of theoretical reason is truth, and so theoretical reason requires that one not distort the reasoning process for reasons of self-interest.

Alan Gewirth agrees with Sterba that theoretical reason requires one not to act selfishly or immorally. He also agrees with Sterba that if theoretical reason requires this, then practical reason must also do so, for both hold that theoretical reason is more basic than practical rationality. What I mean by taking theoretical reason as more basic than practical reason, is taking rationality to be more concerned with truth than with benefits and harms. If one is concerned to show that reason supports morality over egoism, it is extremely tempting to take theoretical reason as basic, for in seeking the truth there is no place for egoism. Truth is determined in a completely impartial manner; whether an argument is valid or a statement is true is not affected at all by whether I, or anyone else, will benefit or be harmed. Thus it is not surprising that those who regard theoretical reason as basic try to show that acting immorally involves using an invalid argument, unacceptable method of argumentation, or a false statement. Showing this is, for them, sufficient to show that it is contrary to reason to act immorally.

As a matter of fact, no philosopher has ever shown that acting immorally always involves using an invalid argument, an unacceptable method of argumentation, or a false statement; but even were some philosopher to do so, it would not show that practical reason requires acting morally. All that it would show is that acting immorally involves acting contrary to theoretical reason; it would not show that acting immorally involves acting contrary to practical reason. Although, in general, acting contrary to theoretical reason involves acting contrary to practical reason, it is not necessarily so. Granted that employing invalid arguments, etc., will generally lead to more harms and less benefits than employing valid arguments, etc., it does not always do so. Rational persons who knew the truth about Oedipus' parents, and also knew what harms and benefits would result from his finding out this truth, would have advised him not to seek the truth. Although generally one will avoid more harms or gain greater benefits by employing valid arguments and true statements, on those occasions where theoretical reason and practical reason conflict, rational persons advise acting on practical reason.

Unless one could show that employing invalid arguments and false statements always, perhaps necessarily, involves suffering greater harms and gaining lesser goods than employing valid arguments and true statements, one would not have shown that practical reason always requires avoiding invalid arguments and false statements. But invalid arguments and false statements do not always lead to suffering greater harms and gaining lesser goods than employing valid arguments and true statements. This is clearly the case if acting immorally necessarily involves employing invalid arguments or false statements, for some cases of immoral action do not result in anyone suffering greater harms and gaining lesser goods.

Sterba tries to show that Gewirth's attempt to show that reason requires acting morally is faulty. I shall not discuss whether his criticism of Gewirth is correct, for Gewirth's primary objective is to show that acting immorally involves contradicting oneself. Sterba's objections to Gewirth's arguments are in a long line of objections raised to Gewirth's arguments, but I am not concerned with whether any of these are valid objections. My concern is with the power of Gewirth's conclusion. Suppose, contrary to fact, that Gewirth actually did show that if one acted immorally one necessarily contradicted oneself. What should we conclude from this, that it is irrational to act immorally? That is the conclusion that Gewirth wants us to draw, but if we draw this conclusion, then the following question makes perfectly good sense: "Why should I avoid acting irrationally?" But if this question makes sense, that is, if a person who would and should be held responsible for his actions can sensibly ask this question, then irrationality has lost its force.

Thus, even if Gewirth had actually shown that acting immorally involves contradicting oneself, nothing of practical significance would follow from this about how one should act. Unless one had an overpowering phobia concerning self-contradiction, it would still be an open question whether it would be rational to act immorally. Especially if it turned out that acting immorally and thus contradicting oneself resulted in less harms and greater goods for oneself and all one's friends. That is, showing that theoretical rationality requires acting morally is of extremely limited practical importance except to those, such as some philosophers, who are deeply committed to theoretical rationality. To these people, it is important to show that acting immorally involves violating theoretical rationality. However, if, as seems quite likely, theoretical rationality requires impartiality, then one does not need much more of an argument to show that theoretical rationality requires acting morally. But, although it is clear that practical rationality does not require acting impartially, it certainly allows one to act impartially, at least in those respects in which morality requires impartiality, and with regard to that group toward which morality requires impartiality,

Hobbes, the moral and political philosopher from whom I have learned the most, tries to show that breaking a promise involves contradicting oneself. However, Hobbes realizes that showing this is not sufficient to motivate all rational persons to avoid breaking promises. Hobbes is aware that it is far more important to rational persons to avoid harm to themselves and those whom they love, than to avoid self-contradictions. Thus Hobbes offers other considerations in favor of keeping promises, and these other considerations involve avoiding harm to oneself and others. It is acting against these other considerations that Hobbes correctly regards as being more important in showing that it is irrational to break valid promises. Like Hobbes, I realize that if irrationality is to have the normative force that makes it worthwhile to show that it is irrational to act immorally, then no person who is held responsible for her actions can ever want to act irrationally.

Sterba's attempt to ground morality in rationality is, as he admits, in the same tradition as Gewirth's. However, instead of trying to show that acting immorally involves contradicting oneself, Sterba tries to show that acting immorally involves begging the question. More precisely, Sterba tries to show that if a pure egoist is arguing with a pure altruist, then the only non-question-begging argument will be one in which both agree to act in a way that Sterba defines as acting morally. Sterba criticizes Kurt Baier's most recent attempt to ground morality in rationality by claiming that it results in a distorted account of morality. Ironically, the same criticism can be made of Sterba's attempt. His non-question-begging justification of morality results in a morality that has only a slight resemblance to our ordinary concept of morality. His account of morality only rules out immoral acts done for self-interest. But the most important immoral acts are not those done from self-interest, but for the sake of some cause, one's country, religion, race, ethnic group, colleagues, etc. Many of these actions actually involve some sacrifice of self-interest in order to benefit these other people. Further, unless he begs the question by incorporating moral reasons into his account of high-ranking altruistic reasons, Sterba has to count as morally acceptable those unjustified paternalistic actions that are genuinely motivated by the desire to help the person toward whom one is acting paternalistically.

Further, Sterba makes no distinction between hurting someone to avoid a lesser harm to oneself and not helping someone because doing so would result in a harm to oneself, even though it is a lesser harm. That is, his account of morality makes no distinction between violating a moral rule, e.g. Do not kill and Do not cause pain, and not acting on a moral ideal, e.g. Prevent death and Prevent pain. Indeed, Sterba's compromise account of morality seems to count cheating on one's income tax when the gain to oneself from cheating is greater than the loss to the government, as acting morally. Of course, if everyone were allowed to cheat on their income tax, this would cause significant harm, but Sterba's account of morality only considers the ranking of reasons for and against the particular act. Many immoral acts do not cause any direct harm to others, or only very little harm; and they benefit the person acting quite a bit. A student who can safely cheat on an exam may suffer serious harm if he fails, whereas, even if the course is graded on a curve, no one else suffers serious harm at all. Thus on Sterba's account, cheating is moral because the cheater has a high-ranking reason for cheating that requires little or no sacrifice from others to fulfill (p. 27).

A more direct objection to Sterba's account of rationality as avoiding question-begging derives from the fact that whether a way of arguing is question-begging is to be determined by the participants in the discussion. What is question-begging when arguing with one group of discussants would not necessarily be question-begging when arguing with another group. Sterba envisions the participants in the discussion to be a pure egoist and a pure altruist. A pure egoist is one who assumes: 1') All high-ranking self-interested reasons have priority over conflicting lower-ranking altruistic reasons, and 2') All low-ranking self-interested reasons have priority over conflicting higher-ranking altruistic reasons (p. 28). A pure altruist assumes: 1) All high-ranking altruistic reasons have priority over conflicting lower-ranking self-interested reasons, and 2) All low-ranking altruistic reasons have priority over conflicting higher-ranking self-interested reasons (pp. 27–8). The compromise view of morality accepts both 1 and 1'. It is not clear why Sterba has chosen these two participants, but it seems clear that it is not a good choice, for the pure altruist seems to be irrational. Anyone who chooses his own total ruin to prevent the least uneasiness to an Indian, or person wholly unknown to him, contrary to Hume, is acting irrationally. But according to Sterba's account of the pure altruist, that is what the pure altruist would choose. Granted that the pure egoist is also not the kind of person one would want to have around, he is at least rational. Why would he even enter into a discussion with such an irrational person as the pure altruist? And why should anyone else care about any non-question-begging solution to their dispute? Sterba does not provide us with any answers to these important questions.

But even if Sterba were to have shown that morality provides the only non-question-begging response to any dispute about how to act, why should one take that to be important? If one has a choice between begging the question and avoiding serious harm for oneself and one's friends, would any rational person have any doubt about which he would choose? Of course, if the alternative action avoided even greater harm to others, then a rational person might choose not to avoid harm to himself and his friends. But the relevant point is that if a rational person chose to suffer harm himself, it would be to avoid greater harm to others, not to avoid begging the question. I do not want to deny that many people, especially philosophers, do want to avoid begging the question, just as many people, especially philosophers, do want to avoid contradicting themselves. However, given the choice between begging the question or contradicting oneself, and suffering serious harm, only an obsessive philosopher would choose to suffer the serious harm. To think otherwise is to rank theoretical reason as more basic and more important than practical reason. If anyone were actually to act on this ranking, that is, to suffer significant harms simply to avoid contradicting oneself or to avoid begging the question, that person would be acting irrationally.

I can understand why Sterba and others have wanted to show that reason requires acting morally. They want to motivate people to act morally. Given this goal, it seems quite a natural strategy to try to show that acting immorally is acting contrary to reason. This seems a natural strategy because one assumes that no rational person wants to act contrary to reason. But this assumption holds only if acting contrary to reason is something that rational persons in the ordinary sense all want to avoid more than they want to avoid anything else. But not all rational persons want to avoid self-contradiction or begging the question more than they want to avoid anything else. As pointed out in the previous paragraph, rational persons forced to choose between self-contradiction or begging the question, and suffering significant harm, will choose to contradict themselves or to beg the question. Thus if acting immorally is necessary to avoid suffering significant harm, showing that acting immorally involves either self-contradiction or begging the question will not have the motivational force that one might have initially thought.

It may be thought that Sterba and others are not really concerned with motivating ordinary people to act morally. Philosophers are not preachers. Further, Sterba knows that few, if any, people will decide to act morally on the basis of having read his book. Indeed, Sterba knows that relatively few people will even read his book, let alone understand it and accept it. This is not intended as a disparaging remark about his book. As far as I know, no serious philosophy book has ever made it on to any best-seller list. Philosophy books are not big sellers. Further, Sterba is aware that no argument purporting to show that reason requires acting morally has ever been accepted by any significant percentage of philosophers. Thus it seems that, contrary to what he explicitly claims to be doing, Sterba is not attempting to provide an argument that will serve the practical purpose of motivating ordinary rational people to act morally.

Rather, the most plausible account of what Sterba is doing is that he is engaged in a purely philosophical task, namely, showing that defending egoism involves begging the question. He might be trying to show that no non-question-begging argument can be given in defense of egoism. And following Kurt Baier's position in *The Moral Point of View*, he might also want to show that no non-question-begging argument can be given in defense of altruism. Baier's insight was to see that altruism is not the same as morality, that as a matter of fact, a world of pure egoists would probably be a better world than that of pure altruists. Nonetheless. Baier correctly contends that a world of people acting morally would be better than either. Although Sterba criticizes Baier's attempt to ground morality in rationality, he does accept Baier's distinctions between egoism, altruism, and morality, and uses these distinctions in his argument. If Sterba is taken as attempting to demonstrate to philosophers that they cannot give any non-question-begging argument in favor of adopting either egoism or altruism, he has a better chance of being successful. Of course, his argument may still not be successful. Nonetheless, considering Sterba's argument as directed to philosophers, which it certainly seems to be, then pointing out to them that they will be acting contrary to theoretical reason by defending egoism may have considerable force.

As indicated earlier in this paper, I believe rationality clearly does not require acting morally, and that it requires all rational persons to put forward morality as a guide to behavior that governs all of them, only with some significant qualifications. These qualifications involve limiting themselves to beliefs that are shared by all other rational persons, together with one further qualification. This further qualification can be that they are trying to reach agreement among all rational persons. By a rational person, I mean a person insofar as he is acting rationally, and I provide the following definition of a rational action.

> An action is irrational in the basic sense if and only if it is an intentional action of a person with sufficient knowledge and intelligence to be fully informed, and who, if fully informed, would (1) believe that the action involves significantly increased risk of his suffering death, non-trivial pain, loss of ability, loss of freedom, or loss of pleasure, and (2) not have an adequate reason for the action. A reason for acting is a conscious rational belief that one's action will increase the probability of someone's avoiding any of the harms listed above or gaining greater consciousness, ability, freedom, or pleasure. A reason is adequate if any significant group of moral agents regard the harm avoided or benefit gained to compensate for the harm suffered. Any intentional action that is not irrational is rational.
>
> (*Morality: Its Nature and Justification*, p. 84)

This is an account of practical rationality, not of theoretical rationality. I do not provide an explicit account of theoretical rationality, even though I do provide an explicit account of a rational belief. Contradicting oneself or begging the question may indeed be contrary to theoretical reason, but acceptance of my account of a rational action requires accepting that practical rationality is more basic and more important than theoretical rationality. As pointed out above, in any conflict between theoretical rationality and practical rationality, practical rationality wins; that is, it is irrational to act according to theoretical rationality when doing so conflicts with practical rationality.

My account of rationality has a number of features that distinguish it from almost all other philosophical accounts of rationality. However, it is the only account which correctly describes the ordinary concept of rationality. These two features are not accidentally related. I developed my account of rationality so that it would correctly describe the ordinary concept of rationality. This meant that I had to abandon much of what was taken for granted in most philosophical accounts of rationality. Thus, contrary to most philosophical accounts, my account of rationality starts with irrationality, and simply defines a rational action as one that is not irrational. This has the significant result that there can be several incompatible rational actions. Starting with a definition of a rational action and defining an irrational action as one that is not rational almost inevitably leads to the view that no action is rationally allowed, that is, that no action is neither rational to do nor irrational not to do. But in ordinary life, most of the actions we do are of this kind. It is rationally allowed to go to a given movie or not to go to it, to order a given meal or not to order it. By starting with a definition of an irrational action, my account of rationality explains this feature of the ordinary concept of rationality.

Most philosophical accounts of rationality relate rationality very closely to acting on reasons; indeed, some philosophical accounts of rationality define acting rationally as acting on reasons, or acting on the best reasons. This is an example of providing a positive definition of rationality. On my account of rationality, in which acting rationally only requires not acting irrationally, one can act rationally without acting on any reasons at all. As long as one is not acting irrationally, that is, not doing anything that involves significantly increasing one's risk of suffering death, non-trivial pain, loss of ability, loss of freedom, or loss of pleasure, then anything one does counts as a rational action, whether or not one has any reasons for acting in that way. Thus, as long as one knows that one is not risking suffering any harm, one can act on a whim and still be acting rationally. This accords with the normal use of the concept of rationality, for innocent and trivial acts are not normally regarded as irrational. It is only philosophers, those who think about every action they take, who claim that a rational action has to be based on reasons.

Most philosophers do not even have a clear account of a reason. They generally relate reasons very closely to motives, either motives that one actually has, or motives that one would have if one were fully informed. But reasons, insofar as they are related to rationality, are related to justification, not to explanation, and they need not motivate at all.

My account of rationality also has a feature that philosophers, as well as ordinary people, regard as essential, namely that no one ever wants to act irrationally. Whereas on all other accounts of rationality, including all those which take theoretical rationality as basic, one can describe situations in which a person would want to act irrationally herself, or to advise those she loves to act irrationally, on my account no one would do so. However, the cost of having this feature is that it is clearly false that rationality requires acting morally. Some philosophers, Sterba for example, find this too high a cost. However, if the account of rationality does not have this feature, then it is of relatively little value to show that rationality requires acting morally. It is of relatively little value because then one can ask "Why should I act rationally?" If one can sensibly ask this question, then what is gained by showing that rationality requires acting morally?

As far as I know, my account of reasons for actions is the only account which provides a limit to the beliefs or facts that can count as basic reasons for acting. In the definition of a rational action provided above, I presented an account of basic reasons in terms of their content. But one can also define reasons for acting in a formal way. *Reasons for acting are conscious rational beliefs that can make some otherwise irrational actions, rational* (p. 56). Note that this definition of reasons depends on having an account of what "an otherwise irrational action" would be. Without such an account, it is impossible to provide an accurate account of reasons. But in addition to this formal account of a reason, one also needs a corresponding account of an adequate reason, for not all reasons are adequate reasons for all actions. *An adequate reason for acting is a conscious rational belief that can make the otherwise irrational action for which it is a reason, rational* (p. 57, modified on the basis of a criticism by Robert Audi). This account of reasons and adequate reasons allows for one to distinguish between beliefs (or facts) that are good (adequate) reasons, those that are bad (inadequate) reasons, and those that are not reasons at all. No other account does this.

Further, this account of reasons allows one to rank reasons. That is, it provides an objective way of measuring the strength of reasons. *If reason A would be an adequate reason for every otherwise irrational act that reason B would be an adequate reason for, and for some otherwise irrational acts as well, then reason A is a stronger or better reason than reason B* (pp. 77–8). The strength of a reason does not depend on who is benefited or harmed, simply on the amount of the benefit or harm. This account of the strength of reasons may provide an explanation of Sterba's view that reason requires acting morally. For Sterba, acting morally involves acting on the stronger reasons. This yields Sterba's compromise view of morality, where all high-ranking self-interested reasons have priority over conflicting lower-ranking altruistic reasons, and all high-ranking altruistic reasons have priority over conflicting lower-ranking self-interested reasons. Indeed, my account is even more general than Sterba's, and so allows one to rank reasons related to country, religion or race, as well as egoistic and altruistic reasons.

Sterba accepts this plausible sounding account of morality, and he probably also accepts the common philosophical view that rationality requires acting on the best or strongest reasons. If he does accept both of these views, he does not even need to bring in anything about begging the question. His view that rationality requires acting morally simply follows from these two very plausible views. However, though these views are plausible, they are not correct. It is not always true that there are better or stronger reasons for acting morally than for acting immorally. It is true that there are never better or stronger reasons for acting immorally than for acting morally, but that is a different claim. This latter claim has to be true or else it would sometimes be irrational to act morally. This would happen if one's self-interest conflicted with acting morally and the reasons for acting in one's self-interest were stronger than the reasons for acting morally. Reasons for acting immorally can never be stronger than the reasons for acting morally, but the reverse need not be true either. It may be that neither set of reasons is stronger than the other.

Somewhat more troubling to those who want rationality to require acting morally, is the hybrid character of rationality. Although the strength of reasons is determined impartially, no preference being given to reasons of self-interest or altruistic reasons, irrationality is not similarly impartial. The only irrational actions are those in which one is acting in a way that one knows or should know will cause or significantly increase the probability of one suffering harm oneself, either directly or because someone for whom one is concerned will suffer harm or have a significantly increased probability of suffering harm. Those who hurt others for whom they are not concerned when they know that neither they nor those for whom they are concerned will suffer any harm or increased risk of suffering harm, are not acting irrationally even if they are acting contrary to the best reasons. The ordinary concept of rationality does not view clever burglars as acting irrationally. They are acting immorally, but that is a different matter. Indeed, it is because they are acting both rationally (rationally allowed) and immorally that the ordinary concept of rationality does not hold that rationality requires acting on the best or strongest reasons.

Failure to recognize the hybrid character of rationality is what leads philosophers to hold the view that rationality requires acting morally. These philosophers take all of rationality to be like the concept of a reason, that is, they take all of rationality to be determined impartially. The opposite mistake is held by those who hold to rational egoism. They take all of rationality to be determined in the way irrationality is determined, that is, egoistically. But rationality is a hybrid concept; the only irrational actions are those that go against one's self-interest, or the interests of those about whom one is concerned, even though reasons related to the interests of others about whom one is not concerned can make it rational to go against one's self-interest or the interests of friends. This makes the concept of a rationally allowed action even more important. Given the hybrid character of rationality, it turns out that in almost all conflicts between acting morally and acting in one's self-interest, it is rationally allowed to act in either way. Indeed, even in conflicts between morality and the interests of one's country, race or religion, it is almost always rationally allowed to act in either way. Surprisingly, even in conflicts between self-interest and the interests of one's country, race or religion, it is also almost always rationally allowed to act in either way.

Rationality does not require acting in any way that any significant number of people normally regarded as rational would not act. Only if this feature of rationality is accepted can it be important to show that rationality requires acting in a particular way. A significant number of people normally regarded as rational knowingly act immorally; thus rationality cannot require acting morally. If any philosopher does show that rationality requires acting morally, then the sense of rationality that he is using is not the basic sense. It is a sense of rationality such that people normally regarded as rational can sensibly ask "Why act rationally?" I prefer to use the basic sense of rationality in which no person normally regarded as rational would ever ask "Why act rationally?" Unfortunately, for those like Sterba who want rationality to require acting morally, rationality in this basic sense does not and cannot require this.

Part III

ALTERNATIVE SOCIAL AND POLITICAL PERSPECTIVES

Libertarianism

4

LIBERTARIAN JUSTICE

Tibor R. Machan[1]

The nature of justice

By libertarian justice one would have in mind the account of justice advanced in libertarian political theory. Since what justice is has been and remains in serious, often deep-seated dispute, there are widely different conceptions of it emanating from different schools of political thought, each aiming to be the true or right one. Libertarianism proposes one, as do socialism, fascism, welfare-statism, and so forth.[1]

As to which conception of justice is right or what justice really is, there is a great deal to be said on how that might be determined. In this discussion I shall not be aiming to find a fixed, final, perfect ideal of justice, along lines suggested in some of Plato's dialogues. Nor am I convinced that some consensus is what is wanted, nor that no determination is possible. Instead, it seems to me that a conception that arises from justified and thus most reasonable propositions in various branches of human inquiry, starting with metaphysics and including psychology, economics and ethics, will constitute the right idea of what justice is. Why this should be so is a story that is too long to tell here, even though a great deal depends on it.[2]

To do justice is to treat something appropriate to its nature or as it deserves or ought to be treated. Only certain kinds of beings can be said to deserve or be owed justice. (There is no problem about doing justice to a rock or the moon, although some environmentalists argue that the issue does arise *vis-à-vis* trees, and even mountains.[3])

When we want to learn what it is to do justice to human beings, we must first learn what is due them. That, in turn, depends on what kind of beings they are.

As an analogous case in point, when defenders of animal rights lay out their reasons for why animals have rights, they tell us about the nature of animals. They focus on what kind of beings they are, on what in their nature warrants our ascribing to them and respecting their rights.[4] Justice for the

93

animals consists of treating them in accordance with standards derived from a consideration of their nature.[5]

Libertarian justice

Libertarians take it that justice consists in establishing and maintaining a political system in which the respect and protection of the right to life, liberty and property of the human individual are of primary legal significance.[6] They maintain that human beings are essentially creative, inventive, and choosing beings. To be human is then, primarily, to take the initiative via one's thinking mind, which then issues in intentions, deliberations, wants, omissions, and so forth, for all of which one can be responsible.

In particular, the thinking mind of a human being is not a passive, reflexive or reactive but an active faculty. Individual human beings are distinguished by virtue of their capacity to activate their conceptual form of awareness, their thinking, so as to learn how to live and flourish.[7]

We, then, regard and treat human beings appropriately by acknowledging that they do such thinking. We do them *justice* if we don't thwart their rational capacity for creativity, inventiveness, and initiative.

Justice as liberty

Justice as liberty, in contrast to justice as fairness, order, harmony or welfare,[8] rests on the above view. Human beings are in possession of free will, and need to guide their own lives to excellence or flourishing. The decisive issue about justice, as a guiding principle of a community, has to be human nature.

Before turning to human nature, I wish to spell out the most basic tenets of libertarianism. If these tenets are wrong, then so is libertarianism.

1 Adult human beings (and children derivatively and with proper adjustments) are sovereign over their lives, actions and belongings. They have the rights to life, liberty and property.
2 They have the responsibility in their communities to acknowledge and act in terms of this fact (namely 1 above) *vis-à-vis* all others.
3 They ought to develop institutions that assure the protection of their sovereignty, delegating the required powers to agents (governments, private defense agencies, legal authorities or some such special group) for this purpose.
4 Such delegation of powers must itself occur without the violation of sovereignty or individual rights.
5 The agencies to which the power of protecting rights is delegated must exercise this power for the sole purpose of protecting these rights.[9]

6   All concerns apart from the protection of individual rights must be acted on by members of communities without the violation of those rights.

As with all normative theories, libertarianism has several versions, even though the above tenets are not very complicated. Most libertarian political theorists would not find serious objections against them although their exact terminology may differ.[10]

Libertarianism and individual sovereignty

Libertarians uphold the sovereignty of each adult individual in social life. They hold that persons ought to be self-governing and ought not to be ruled by others without their consent.

Libertarians distinguish themselves in the political arena in most Western countries from both the left and the right, both of which enlist government for the purpose of regimenting certain aspects of the individual's life, thus conflicting with the libertarian concern with individual sovereignty or self-rule. This is because, on the one hand, the left is concerned with arranging community life so as to protect the materially worst off from the best off, taking the interests of the two to be in unavoidable conflict. So they regiment economic life and thus undermine the sovereignty with which libertarians are concerned. The right does the same when it comes to their spiritual or mental life, since it sees those elements of human community life as having primary importance. The libertarian, in contrast, sees justification for only those laws that aim at protecting everyone's sovereignty.

Since, however, body and soul aren't ever sharply divided, both the left's and right's administration of justice involves regulating both people's spiritual and their economic activities (e.g. when advertisers are regulated in what they may say in their commercials, and when Sunday blue laws prohibit commerce in liquor, respectively).[11]

So, in the particular areas of their philosophical focus, the left and right both want government to wield powers far beyond what is consistent with libertarianism.[12]

Protecting rights the highest public good

The libertarian sees the just function of the legal system and authorities as, first and foremost, to protect individual rights. In this respect the libertarian is more loyal to the (original) vision of the American republic than are republicans, democrats, socialists, conservatives, liberals, communitarians, as well as Islamic, Christian, Hindu or other religious fundamentalists with powerful political agendas. These all seek to impose ways of private conduct, often claiming that there does not even exist a sphere of legitimate privacy in human life.[13]

Libertarians believe that they flesh out the US Declaration of Independence more accurately, consistently and completely than do all others. Why? Because if we really do have the right to our lives, for example, then we may and even ought to establish a legal system that protects us against all efforts on the part of either criminals, foreign aggressors or the legal authorities themselves to force us to live our lives in any way other than how we choose to.[14] No official paternalistic intervention, even for the sake of improving some aspect of our lives, is tolerable – be it bans on drug abuse and smoking in private places, or regulation of employment. Adults are off-limits as far as regimenting their lives, actions and goals is concerned. That is what having an *unalienable right* to life, liberty and the pursuit of happiness comes to, nothing less. A proper legal order has as its primary goal to protect these rights.[15]

Cases in point

Consider the particularly controversial libertarian position that no one has the authority to prevent a sovereign adult citizen from committing or seeking assisted suicide, unless it is demonstrably evident that one is deranged. Or consider the view that adults may not be prohibited from using harmful, debilitating drugs, even ones that may be addictive for someone. Or again that risky activities such as mountain climbing, race car driving, sexual promiscuity, and so forth, should not be prohibited.

In all these cases the libertarian holds the position that adults have the basic right to make the choice to pursue the course they want to pursue, provided they are not "dumping" the damaging results on other persons by violating their rights.

Putting it plainly, libertarians hold that one's right to life implies the final, unqualified authority to decide what happens to one's life. So that if, for example, someone who can assist with suicide is freely, voluntarily invited to help, prohibiting it is wrong and ought to be unlawful.

The right to life, according to libertarianism, means that the individual agent, not other people, should be the one who makes decisions about his or her life, including whether to delegate to someone else who is willing the authority to help with ending it, whether to ruin it with drugs, and so forth.

Rights are principles identified in the field of political theory that spell out "borders" around us, or an individual's sphere of personal authority. This so that the sovereignty of the individual as a moral agent is acknowledged and can be protected in the midst of social life wherein others can choose to encroach upon it. In order to cross those borders, those inside must provide those outside with permission, an action that can then be evaluated as right or wrong for the agent to have carried out.

So if there are basic individual rights then they may not be violated. To have the authority to make someone act as one would want, that person's permission is required. The simplest example is sexual intercourse. Only if someone consents to such interaction may the intercourse commence. But even less drastic instances apply: no public authority may forcibly make one person provide services for another, however vital these services may be.[16] And if the service consists of supplying the person with resources wanted or needed, those too must be obtained with the permission of the owner. Since what is owned, even in great abundance, can be what a person creates or produces, to hold that others in dire need own these resources is to believe that others are due involuntary servitude and even own the agent's life and efforts which create the resources. (We will see shortly that rarely there may be justification for someone to expropriate someone else's resources, though this would not justify claiming that they have a right to them.)

Rights and sovereignty

A way to appreciate this issue of individual rights is to focus on the right to private property, as we normally understand it. Rights identify borders for all persons or citizens within which actions may be taken free of others' interference, regardless of the moral quality of those actions. Those actions need not be equal in their moral quality, yet none may stop or regulate them against the agent's will.

In the case of universal private property rights, the borders around one's actions are most clearly apprehensible because they often consist of actions *vis-à-vis* objects with clear physical limits. If it is your car, you have the authority to use it, provided no third parties are unavoidably affected.[17] Norman Malcolm tells the following illustrative story about Wittgenstein which makes the above point quite clear:

> When in very good spirits he would jest in a delightful manner. This took the form of deliberately absurd or extravagant remarks uttered in a tone, and with the mien, of affected seriousness. On one walk he "gave" me each tree that we passed, with the reservation that I was not to cut it down or do anything to it, or prevent the previous owners from doing anything to it: with those reservations they were henceforth *mine*.[18]

Ownership without the authority to decide to what use the owned item will be put is meaningless, absurd.

Similarly, if it is your life, somebody who wants to do something to it must gain your permission – as when you authorize a physician to perform a risky operation or a cabby to drive you to the airport. On the other hand if, for example, you don't want to go into the ring with a world champion boxer who wants to fight you, that, too, is properly up to you, not somebody else. If you want to smoke, drink, take drugs, climb mountains or go skiing, provided no one's rights are violated by such actions, you need no one's permission.

What, then, is so fundamental about libertarianism is that it proposes that individuals are the ones who are sovereign[19] over themselves and their belongings, not the legal authorities and not even the majority of the people.

Sovereignty in the present context is that condition under which somebody has the fundamental right to governance and others must ask permission before they intrude on the sphere being governed. Personal or individual sovereignty, which is what is at issue here, concerns self-governance.

Accordingly, in cases wherein some are being governed by others – for example, legal adjudication or a medical procedure – the consent of those who are to be governed is necessary before the government by others than oneself can commence. That is because the lives of those whose governance is at issue are their own, not someone else's – the family's, society's, nation's, race's, ethnic group's, gender's or humanity's – even if one misgoverns oneself, even if one wastes one's life away.

People may offer others advice, write editorials directed at them, send them letters, try to talk with them – in short, they may approach others in peaceful ways. But they have no authority to take over the governance of another's life.[20] Arguably, this is the very idea of civilized life, one catering to persons as citizens and not as subjects.

Libertarianism versus democracy

Even arguments for democracy – meaning for the rule of many, indeed, the bulk of the people – do not void this individual sovereignty. Why should they? After all, the majority is composed of individuals, and if alone they aren't authorized to intrude on your life, together they aren't either.

Democracy is a method, mainly, of selecting administrators of various, including governmental, tasks. Confined in line with sound moral principles, it may be deployed for the limited purpose of selecting administrators of a legal order that respects and protects individual rights in ways that do not violate those rights. Or it is a method which can be used to reach decisions on a great many issues, provided all those affected have agreed to its use, as in the Rotary or Lions Club.

One must authorize – delegate authority to – legal administrators to do certain things. Only then do they acquire proper authority – as opposed to mere power – to do them. If the authority was not given, then the officials lack it and must stay out of one's life (educational, commercial, scientific, religious, or anything else) as well as one's actions – that is what having the right to liberty means.

I am free in the political sense if I can take various actions without interference from other people. (There are other senses of "freedom" but they are not relevant here.[21]) If I want to pursue a life of productivity, creativity, art, science or education, I may embark on those pursuits and no one may prohibit me from doing so. If one requires the cooperation of others for success with these pursuits, their consent is morally necessary. And if one chooses not to embark upon such pursuits but, instead, chooses to be idle, lazy, imprudent, neglectful toward oneself and one's best interests, including making contributions to one's fellow human beings in need, this, though often morally reprehensible, is also something one has a right to do. No one is to be placed into involuntary servitude to others or even to oneself. Voluntary association is morally and politically essential to free men and women.[22]

The risks of liberty

An oft repeated reason for rejecting the libertarian position is that when one is wrong in what one chooses to do, then one has no right to act freely. This is why some kinds of forcible interference, including and especially by government, is thought to be justified. So that, for example, if one chooses to pursue a life of laziness, drug addiction or debauchery, then this may be forcibly prevented.[23]

A good example of this kind of objection is laid out by Robert Speamann, in connection with his support for an idea articulated by Socrates against Thrasymachus, to the effect that government must be the shepherd of the people so that the people act rightly rather than merely to please one another for profit:

> Socrates had used the image of the shepherd to characterize the ruler in a state. Thrasymachus points out that the shepherd delivers the sheep to the butcher and therefore doesn't have the well-being of the sheep in view. Socrates replies that this end is accidental to the shepherd's art. As shepherd the shepherd provides for the well-being of the sheep. At the bottom of this is the fact that the best sheep for people are the ones that have also best been able to develop as sheep during their lives. The art of the butcher does not define the art of the shepherd. Precisely this changes in the modern world. Here, the market dictates to the breeder how he is to keep the animals, and in no way is the keeping attuned to the animals' well-being. The viewpoints of the animal protector are external to those of the animal keeper and must be asserted "from without."[24]

In answer to this, the libertarian claims that we must accept the risk that goes with being free, including in the marketplace. Yes, some professionals, for example, will not pursue excellence but merely cater to whatever consumers demand. With the authority to run one's life, including one's profession, goes the risk that one may mismanage these.

But malpractice by no means needs to be the consequence of self-government. The shepherd, for example, ought to act in line with his own integrity. This will not occur as a result of regimentation by government. The consumer ought also to act with integrity and influence the "shepherd" accordingly. They all need to *choose to* do what is right, not made to behave correctly, for example, by dint of government regimentation. That is how the libertarian system accords with nature, that is, with the moral – i.e. choice making – nature of the citizens of a country.

Just because no guarantee exists that people will use their liberty so as to do the right thing, it does not follow that none will do it or that making them do it is a valid substitute. And it is unjustifiably cynical to think that those in a free market would not freely choose to pursue excellence while attempting to prepare their wares and services for purchase in the market. The market is viewed as much too demand-driven by the likes of Speamann. In fact, however, more often it is because of the desire for excellence that the market provides one with what is desirable. The mutual pursuit of excellence by producer and consumer is more likely what markets amount to, instead of the mutual pursuit of sheer and meager satisfaction.

There are other risks of the protection of individual rights to liberty that have been held to be intolerable by some critics of libertarianism. James P. Sterba has argued in many fora that the risk posed to the innocent poor or helpless who cannot find help in society based on voluntary contributions is morally and ought to be legally intolerable. It asks of these individuals to accept something that is unreasonable to ask anyone to accept, namely, to respect the private property of the very rich even while they are threatened with devastation.[25]

Sterba says that because of this unacceptable situation, the innocent poor or helpless have a right to welfare, namely, to portions of the wealth of those who have enough for themselves not to miss it.[26]

Yet Sterba's case is not a good one because there is no justification for even a good person to deprive another from what belongs to another merely because he may need sustenance. No one has a right to my second kidney, even though I may not need it, or my second eye, even though I could see well enough without it. If indeed I own my wealth, there is no justification for another to take it from me, even if I have plenty or am not making good use of it (as indeed many do with their talents or other assets).

Sterba has argued, also, that whether one owns something is to be established by reference to certain distributive principles, not by reference to whether the person has obtained it without doing violence to others. I assume that he would consider it doing violence to others not to help them when one has the capacity to do so without excessive harm to oneself. But this omits from consideration that not helping others is not doing violence to them because even if one were not alive, those others would be in need. One then cannot be said to have caused the neediness and thus has no obligation to repair it.[27]

Under certain circumstances, however, it would be unreasonable to demand of a desperately needy innocent person that he respect everyone's property rights. Such an emergency can make it reasonable for that person to steal. Yet that would remain stealing, only forgivable or excusable stealing.

To change the legal system in light of this fact falls under the well known edict that hard cases make bad law. The idea is that when extraordinary circumstances are met with extraordinary choices – for example, cannibalism in the Donner Party or murder in an overloaded lifeboat – the evaluation of that behavior ought not to be generalized to similar behavior in normal circumstances. Indeed, the legal systems of many societies respond to such cases with the instrument of judicial discretion. (Courts sometimes convict rare cases of cannibalism performed under extreme duress, only to later pardon the convict.[28])

Moreover, there are systemic ways for the innocent poor or helpless to obtain support without the violation of any individual's right to private property. They may not be guarantees, but then neither could welfare from state sources be guaranteed, either in a democracy or any other system. Michael Otsuka has argued that wealth might be obtained for the innocent poor or helpless from punishment of rich criminals.[29] And earlier he maintained that such help could be obtained from resources not owned by anyone.[30]

So not only would it be wrong to adjust a just human community to help the innocent poor or helpless by instituting systematic breaches of private property rights, but it would be unnecessary in order to help such persons.[31]

One reason that Sterba may be tempted to derive welfare rights from libertarianism is that many libertarians have not postulated a prior ethical theory from which they derive libertarianism. However, natural rights libertarianism, which is the richest in normative content, does not see the universal basic rights of human beings as normatively primary.

First, as in Locke, it is necessary to identify a sound ethics by which human beings ought to conduct themselves before one can identify principles of community life. Second, I have argued that the ethics of ethical egoism, in terms of which each person ought to (choose to) strive to live his or her life so as to aspire to the fullest development of one's humanity, are the basis for the natural right to one's life, liberty and property. Furthermore, since a moral life is a matter of achievement, something one reaches by a long series of choices, praiseworthy adherence to principles of ethics *per se* may not be coerced. No one may forcibly make another behave the right way – for example, to be generous, charitable, kind, or helpful. It matters not that these are indeed the ways one ought at times to act – for example, generously, charitably, kindly. The primary goal of the ethical life is self-perfection, self-development as a good human being, and so coercively to bring about the generous or helpful behavior of the rich or anyone else is morally and ought to be legally wrong.[32]

The integrity of law

The legal authority within a given jurisdiction is a kind of referee whose integrity – whose nature as the referee – would be sacrificed by intruding on the peaceful choices made by the citizenry. The legal authority is only concerned with maintaining peace and the maximum absence of violence against individual rights, and with no-one abridging those rights with impunity. That means that if someone's rights are violated, the culprit at least gets punished for the deed.

Neither the legal authorities nor anyone else can always prevent the violation of rights. Just like a referee in a basketball court who cannot always prevent the players from misbehaving. But once they have misbehaved, adverse consequences follow – they must get penalized for it. So similarly, the function of the legal authority, as the libertarian sees it, is to protect against and penalize violators of individual rights.

As adults we all have equal status – not economically, not in terms of our beauty, our background or how nice our parents are but in terms of our rights. "All men are created equal" does not mean that we are created equally wise, smart, wealthy, lucky or beautiful. It means that we are all equally in charge of our lives.

In the case of the US Declaration of Independence, wherein the Lockean libertarian political stance is clearly sketched out, we have an example of how the ideals of the right to negative liberty function. The Declaration could be used by Abraham Lincoln, for example, so as to criticize the Constitution of the United States, which tolerated slavery. Because in the Declaration there was no tolerance of slavery. The Declaration was not a political instrument as the Constitution was and still is, wherein a lot of compromises were and are still being made. The Declaration articulated an unblemished vision of a free society. It made reference to unalienable rights to life, liberty and the pursuit of happiness, and the function of government to secure these rights.

What governments are for

The libertarian theory of justice is laid out in the Declaration. Such justice consists of respecting the basic rights to life, liberty and the pursuit of happiness. And government aims to maintaining such justice when it secures those rights, protects them and acts in terms of them. Government is not established to do anything else. Not to manage a post office, build monuments, run Amtrak, conduct AIDS prevention programs, maintain parks, forests and beaches or undertake the education of children. Rather, the distinctive task of government or the legal authorities is to secure the basic rights that individuals have. This arises from the imperative to have one's rights protected, something that most likely requires expertise – due process, for example, is required in the administration of laws.

Libertarianism sees the rule of law secured via the system of constitutional negative rights that function as a system of consistent standards of justice. In contrast to a system of negative and positive rights, which conflict and thus require democratic or some alternative arbitration among basic rights, libertarian justice relies on this system of rights to serve as standards for adjudicating conflicting claims of legality.

We can grasp this distinctiveness of the libertarian polity by recalling that, in contrast, many conservatives and social democrats or modern liberals endorse such public policies as establishing minimum wages, social security systems, licensing of professions, regulations of industry, the "war on drugs", closer unity between government and church, and bans on prostitution, gambling, pornography and other vices. Each of these policies champions an unjustified paternalism and prior restraint. They also risk abandoning the rule of law in favor of what will often involve, in the end, arbitrariness and lack of objectivity (because of the frequent resistance to such paternalism and prior restraint that must be met with sanctions that are by their nature unjust).

The libertarian view of justice stresses consistency and integrity, and functions to diminish the role of the will of the legal authorities. This is achieved by laying down and maintaining a system of internally consistent, compossible negative individual rights as the standards for legal administration and adjudication. (Thus when some case comes to the highest court, the most basic question is whether the various parties have engaged in the violation of such rights, and not which of various basic rights ought to be protected.[33])

The question can be raised of course, do people really have these rights? That is the most controversial political question about the libertarian position on justice. Once we have correctly identified these rights it pretty much follows that the only time someone may use force against another person – which is what the legal authorities such as the courts, police, military, and bureaucracy are professionally trained to do – is in the protection of those rights.

But what if those basic, natural rights are all a fiction, a myth? What if they are – as has been claimed by philosophical luminaries from Jeremy Bentham and Karl Marx to Richard Rorty – nonsense, an ideological invention and just plainly untenable, respectively? Bentham thought very little of them because he distrusted the reasoning found in John Locke in support for basic individual rights. Marx thought they were thinly disguised ideological tools for maintaining the rule of the bourgeoisie. And Rorty just thinks they are culture-bound fictions having no foundations at all.

Rights and relativism

So, clearly it is prominently maintained, in opposition to libertarian political theory, that the rights spoken of in the Declaration of Independence are contrivances. Indeed, almost all intellectuals with access to prominent fora construe basic individual rights to life, liberty and property as eighteenth-century myths.

This view of rights is close to a similar position on political principles in general, namely, relativism. When one hears it said, for instance, that for the people of Cuba socialism may be a sound system, while for those in the USA it may well not be, one is hearing political relativism. It says that for certain people, related to their special historical situation or particular economic or technological development, it is okay for one party or a dictator to basically run their lives.

Some government officials at the 1996 Vienna conference on human rights, from Africa and Asia, protested the United Nations' endorsement of the very idea of basic individual rights because, they said, that those ideas do not apply to their society. And there is widespread agreement with this idea on the part of many people in university philosophy, political science and history departments. We can cite Richard Rorty again here, who maintains that "Non-metaphysicians [of whom Rorty and, by his account, all other wise men are members] cannot say that democratic institutions reflect a moral reality and that tyrannical regimes do not reflect one, that tyrannies get something wrong that democratic societies get right."[34]

Is there an answer to that? Yes there is, as the libertarian sees it.

Apart from metaphysical issues, there could well be certain facts that remain stable or steady in human affairs as long as the species exists as a distinctive kind of entity. If those in the fifth century BC were members of the human species, as were those in the nineteenth, are those in the twenty-first and will be those in the twenty-third century, that fact, of our mutual humanity, could have certain ethical and political implications. Some principles of ethics and politics could then be universalizable, apply throughout the human species, including the idea that each individual is a sovereign over his or her life. It is no easy task to demonstrate that the kind of being we humans are implies certain normative principles, but there is ample evidence that such an inference can be drawn from what we know of humans. If we do indeed have a distinctive nature involving the capacity for creative thought and self-government, a suitable community life would require that these basic facts about us be as fully accommodated as possible.[35]

Of course, not all thinkers through all historical periods have stressed the importance of individual sovereignty. But this does not mean that individual sovereignty was not right back then or is unimportant, only that many thinkers paid little attention to it. There may be many reasons for that.

For example, given that these thinkers were part of a class of people who benefited from treating many others as if those others could be used against – and thus not permitted to follow – their own will, this is not surprising. Pointing out to the world that every individual is equally important is not always in one's vested interest. Leaders of tribes, countries, nations, states and other political units would very likely lose their standing if it were to become widely known that they are not entitled to their special positions. Individualism, a vital component of libertarianism, would most likely be suppressed even if it came to light philosophically. It is, thus, no argument against the universal validity of the position that in many societies it is not prominently embraced and, rather, anti-individualist positions are the dominant traditions.

But, given the fact of some permanent features of human nature, it is true, among other things, that no human being should be made to serve the will of another human being against his or her choice. In other words, that slavery, whether it is full-scale, partial or even minimal, has always been and will always be wrong when it comes to human beings. It is no excuse that in the 1900s or in Athenian Greece, science, economics, sociology or politics were different. Slavery was wrong then and it was wrong 150 years ago and will always be so, as long as those slaves are human beings or have the characteristics of human beings, free will and moral responsibility over their lives. Such a principle could be correct even if not widely embraced – agreement with it isn't what makes it true.

Universalism and libertarianism

The anti-slavery stance is an example of a universal position that the libertarian embraces. Not that all principles are comparably widely universalizable. For example, how you should dress or keep clean or even rear your kids will change, based on technological, agricultural and other developments. The answers to various particular, special questions are not the same as they were 200 or 3,200 years ago. These answers depend a great deal on the vehicles we drive, the kind of dwellings in which we live. Given these changes, it would be silly to maintain that there is a fundamental principle concerning those details – how we should furnish our apartments and so forth. Those matters depend too much on certain variable aspects of human life. They include a great deal of what makes up various different and equally valid human cultures.

But there are basic principles to which people allude when they say that certain values or principles of conduct do not change. The reason for the libertarian thinking this is right, is that human beings do remain fundamentally the same throughout all those technological and related changes. No matter what the changes may be, our humanity remains intact.

Human nature and human rights

It is this idea of our universal humanity and that certain norms of human interaction follow from it for community life that is implicitly accepted by human rights watch groups going from country to country, examining whether such practices as slavery, forced labor and suppression of dissent exist. It does not matter whether it exists in China, Burundi, the USA or Canada. These human rights watch groups consider certain practices and policies to be inexcusable because of the fundamental humanity of the inhabitants of all these communities.

Underlying the idea of these rights to life, liberty and the pursuit of happiness – or property – is the fact of our human nature. And this nature is understood to be distinctive by virtue of the basic fact of our creative potential and our life-sustaining need to take the initiative in life, as well as the corresponding moral responsibility we have for living our lives properly (whatever that comes to).

For us, unlike for the rest of the animal world, there are very few instincts on which we can rely to guide us in our lives. We must discover how to live and flourish. That's why we need education – we are not born with sufficiently detailed genetically built-in programs that guide us through life the way in which geese, cats or even the higher mammals are, who do the right thing nearly automatically. We must learn that we have very few built-in measures that sustain our lives. We have to learn everything – how to eat, talk, walk, drive and the many, many far more complex tasks that amount to living human lives.

Nearly everything we do to live reasonably successfully has to be learned. So we either make good use of our minds or we don't. Human beings have the capacity to get themselves going or to fail to do so. This is fundamental to them all. Unless they are thwarted in this task by governments, criminals or invading armies, they are free either to pay heed to what their lives require or not to do so and then to act accordingly. And the right condition for their human lives is when others do not prevent them from doing so.

The wilds and the rest of non-human world – viruses, mad dogs, earthquakes, floods, and so forth – do not always leave us in peace, undisturbed and unharmed, so that we do often face terrible hardship caused by them. However, other persons can and ought to refrain from imposing themselves on us when we do not give our permission for them to do so, namely by consistently respecting our rights. In other words, it is right for us all not to be intruded upon, by those who have a choice about how they will act. This will enhance our chances to make the effort to think through the problems that face us and to act so as to reach solutions to those problems. Instead of interacting with others coercively, we will then enjoy the fruits of voluntary cooperative interactions, including competing with others, trading with them and so forth. It is only such a community of others that is suitable to us all, one in which we as adult human beings interact on a voluntary basis.

Libertarianism and community

By no means does this mean, as some critics of classical liberalism and libertarianism have suggested,[36] that community life is alien to us, quite the contrary. People flourish best among other people. But only if these other people do not thwart their freedom. We not only have the right to but definitely should form clubs, churches, associations, corporations and thus embark on the solutions of all of our problems and the attainment of our aspirations in the company of other persons. But only if this does not involve coercion, compulsion, or some other violation of these other persons' sovereignty.

Conservatives like George Will and modern liberals and communitarians unite against the libertarian, however, on grounds that his view of human beings is too narrow. Will joins Michael Sandel, claiming that

> much damage is done when we define human beings not as social beings – not in terms of morally serious roles (citizen, marriage partner, parent, etc.) – but only with reference to the watery idea of a single, morally empty capacity of "choice." Politics becomes empty; citizenship, too.[37]

But this is a bogus criticism, repeated since Hegel and Marx advanced it in more or less formidable ways, by all those who would forcibly twist the lives of people to follow a vision that they have not freely embraced. Of course, human beings are "social beings." But this does not mean what Marx meant by it, namely, "The human essence is the true collectivity of man."[38] Rather it means that human beings live and flourish most in the company of others. Yet this is something as human beings they must do by choice when they reach maturity, otherwise it isn't a fully human community in which they live. For the social options available to them are numerous, some suitable, some not. And they are responsible for making the right choice about the kind of social unions in which they will partake. And when they are prevented from exercising this choice, as in a totalitarian state, violence is done to them even while those perpetrating the violence claim they are merely reforming the victims by sending them to insane asylums or jailing them for counter-revolutionary conduct.

The condition of freely choosing how to live their own lives is a quintessentially human requirement based on the fact that moral choice cannot be secured from men and women who are coerced to live even in ways that may be best for them. F. A. Hayek made this point as follows:

> That freedom is the matrix required for the growth of moral values – indeed not merely one value among many but the source of all values – is almost self-evident. It is only where the individual has choice, and its inherent responsibility, that he has occasion to affirm existing values, to contribute to their further growth, and then earn moral merit.[39]

Hayek also argued that

> The growth of what we call civilization is due to this principle of a person's responsibility for his own actions and their consequences, and the freedom to pursue his own ends without having to obey the leader of the band to which he belongs.[40]

Human beings are properly held responsible for assuming various social roles in life – in their marriages, families, polities, etc. – but this responsibility is empty if not chosen by them but imposed on them coercively by, for example, an elite. What Will so cavalierly and callously regards as a "morally empty capacity of 'choice'," is, in fact, the absolutely indispensable prerequisite of the moral life.

In the making of these and other choices in our lives, we may or may not win the prize of success. There is no guarantee. That is one of the reasons that a libertarian proposes a non-utopian form of community. Such an arrangement does not promise to solve all of our problems. It rests on the recognition that free men and women might not solve their problems or might do so inadequately, incompletely. They may just decide to sit and fiddle their thumbs and watch TV talk shows all day long. There is plenty of evidence and common sense to support this view. There is no guarantee that people will do the right thing when they are free.

Yet it is more likely that they will discover the right thing to do if they are free, than if they are regimented around by others who have their own lives to attend to and, in any case, ought to mind their own business. Free men and women are more likely than those who aren't free to detect the consequences of their own chosen actions and learn from them. Their own lives are more familiar to them than to others; they will experience the adverse consequences of irresponsible conduct, whether via failures within their own lives or from adverse reactions from others who have been injured by them. If a legal system concentrates on retaliation rather than prevention, the lessons it can teach will not only follow the principles of justice but also have a better chance of registering and producing lessons for those who live within its framework. Prior restraint is not only morally and politically objectionable because it does violence to individual sovereignty and involves paternalism, but also because it contributes to what I have dubbed the moral tragedy of the commons. Therein the results of irresponsibility are not tied to those who perpetrate it but are dumped on the community at large, including many who are completely innocent of any wrongdoing.[41]

When government agents force us to pay a minimum wage, tell us how to run our business, and to meet various requirements so as to become doctors, psychologists, or chiropractors, they address an area that we ought to be left to address in our voluntary cooperative groups. These matters are not properly and fruitfully addressed by means of regimentation by others. They are not to be dealt with by petty or major tyrannical policies – that is, by people who wield guns even if they mean well.

That is the most fundamental notion concerning public policy, according to the libertarian. Based on this notion and various details we learn from all fields of knowledge, we can figure out, also, various peaceful ways of dealing with, for example, cloning, education, drug abuse, child raising, mental health, diseases and all kinds of issues with which life confronts us. These are some of the issues not directly dealt with in libertarian theory and must be left for other fields than politics to address. But there is at least one point implied by libertarianism for all areas of social life: coercion – which is to say rights violation – is not suited for any part of it. It is the right to freedom of association for all persons who are not crucially incapacitated that generates this point.

Liberty in context

As one must fill in a lot of details in order to learn the implications of the fundamental principles of physics for dealing with a particular area of the physical world, similarly, in politics the basic principles do not tell us everything. They provide a basic framework within which we are required to solve our problems. That means that if we are to solve problems in society, the only thing strictly forbidden in law is the violation of anyone's rights.[42] It is this that constitutes the central tenet of a libertarian theory of justice and must guide any legal order whose goal is to establish, maintain and further justice in human community life.

When important ends other than justice are attainable via the use of coercive force, using such force offsets any gains that might be reaped, be it order, cultural integrity, spiritual development, ecological harmony or any other end proposed.[43] As we have already recalled with F. A. Hayek's observation, "freedom is the matrix required for the growth of moral values."[44, 45]

NOTES

1 In recent years James P. Sterba has argued, however, that nearly all supposedly different theories of justice have basic elements from which only his welfare statist conception would follow. I will address some of Sterba's points later in this paper.

2 In the main I am convinced that a natural law method for identifying principles of right and justice is correct. See Tibor R. Machan, "Law, Justice and Natural Rights," *Western Ontario Law Review*, vol. 14 (1975) pp. 119–30; "Essentialism sans Inner Natures," *Philosophy of the Social Sciences*, vol. 10 (1980) pp. 195–200; "A Reconsideration of Natural Rights Theory," *American Philosophical Quarterly*, vol. 19 (1982) pp. 61–72; "Another Look at Naturalist Ethics and Politics," *Cogito*, vol. 3 (1985) pp. 75–114; "Metaphysics, Epistemology and Natural Law Theory," *American Journal of Jurisprudence*, vol. 31 (1986) pp. 65–77; and "Towards a Theory of Natural Individual Human Rights," *New Scholasticism*, vol. 61, no. 1 (winter 1987) pp. 33–78. See also Tibor R. Machan, *Individuals and Their Rights* (Chicago: Open Court Publishing Co., 1989), where I consider several of the central methodological issues of normative political

3 See for example Christopher Stone, *Should Trees Have Standing?*, 25th edn (Dobbs Ferry NY: Oceana Publications, 1996).

4 See Tom Regan, *The Case for Animal Rights* (Berkeley CA: University of California Press, 1984).

5 For example, they contend, among other things, that animals have interests or a certain type of consciousness and because of this they must not be used against their will. See, however, Tibor R. Machan, "Rights, Liberation and Interests: Is there a Sound Case for Animal Rights or Liberation?" (forthcoming). See also Tibor R. Machan, "Do Animals have Rights?", *Public Affairs Quarterly*, vol. 5 (April 1991) pp. 163–73.

6 The exceptions are libertarians who are pure positivists and have no account of rights. It should also be noted that normative libertarians would first establish that such rights exist and deserve respect. Then they would go on, as a matter of their political science, to show why such rights ought to be protected and how – some defending an anarchist, others a limited government approach. See John T. Sanders and Jan Narveson (eds) *For and Against the State* (Lanham MD: Rowman & Littlefield Publishers Inc., 1996).

7 Among philosophers who share crucial elements of this view we can list Socrates, Aristotle, Augustine, Aquinas, Descartes, Spinoza, Kant, Wittgeinstein, and, of course, Ayn Rand, who has spawned perhaps the most philosophically potent arguments for libertarian justice. (To be sure, Rand did not call herself a libertarian but, more fundamentally, an objectivist. Yet the conclusions she reached in the sphere of politics are libertarian ones.)

8 For how much in law and public policy is prompted by these and related (mis)conceptions of justice, see Thomas Sowell, *The Quest for Cosmic Justice* (New York: The Free Press, 1999). But see also Amartya Sen and Martha Craven Nussbaum (eds) *The Quality of Life: Studies in Development Economics* (London: Oxford University Press, 1993) where justice as fairness or equality is championed by the contributors and editors. Interestingly, many overlook the fact that John Rawls, in his *A Theory of Justice* (Cambridge MA: Harvard University Press, 1971), while endorsing justice as fairness, also supports certain basic rights as primary over distributive justice. And he allows, also, that unfairness is acceptable when it results in overall betterment. Some libertarians even invoke Rawls because they claim the free market system, for example, produces just that result.

9 For how this applies to a community's military policy, see Tibor R. Machan, "Defending a Free Society," *Journal of Value Inquiry*, vol. 33, no. 4 (December 1999) pp. 451–5.

10 This may be overstating the point a bit. As with other schools of thought, especially in normative disciplines, there are distinct sub-schools in libertarianism. While their conclusions regarding politics and public policy tend to be nearly identical, the paths they take to arrive at them differ. Mine will be the natural law, natural rights path, if one wishes to put a succinct label to it (see note 2 for more on this).

11 Conservatives aren't united so much on doctrine as on ways to think about normative matters. They hold that how we decide our institutions, laws and practices should be grounded in tradition: what has worked in the past, what has been tried and found true.

12 Ayn Rand noted this a long time ago – she suggested, thereby, that metaphysics has a good deal of impact on public policy. (The right's idealism and the left's materialism tend to dictate what is to be controlled.) See Ayn Rand, *Philosophy: Who Needs It?* (Indianapolis: Bobbs-Merrill, 1982), where she notes on pages 228–9:

> Yet it is the conservatives ... who proclaim the superiority of the soul over the body ... and the liberals who are predominantly materialist, who regard man as an aggregate of meat. ... This is merely a paradox, not a contradiction: *each camp wants to control the realm it regards as metaphysically important; each grants freedom only to the activities it despises.*

Some other libertarian or capitalist political economists and theorists do not share the view that metaphysics matters much in political theory. I disagree with this but leave the matter untreated for now.

13 Much ink has been used in debating whether the US Constitution prizes privacy, but the claim that only if the exact term is used explicitly would it do so can be rejected by reference to the counsel of the Ninth Amendment to the US Constitution and the use of "private property" in the Fifth. One who draws back into his private property enjoys privacy thereby.

14 Of course, what constitutes our lives is controversial. Some communitarians such as Charles Taylor would insist that we belong to our communities and thus the lives we have are not actually ours. See Charles Taylor, *Philosophy and the Human Sciences*, vol. 2 (Cambridge: Cambridge University Press, 1985), p. 188. Here Taylor speaks approvingly of "a principle which states our obligation as men to belong to or sustain society, or a society of a certain type, or to obey authority or an authority of a certain type." I address this issue in detail in Tibor R. Machan, *Classical Individualism* (London: Routledge, 1998), chapter 14.

15 I wish to note here that *pace* Taylor and others, it is not the case with all classical liberal or libertarian political positions that basic rights are normatively fundamental. Even for Locke, whom Taylor accuses of holding this idea, certain natural laws, ethical principles, are prior to any individual rights, ones that arise from these laws once we become concerned with our social relations.

16 In some drastic cases private individuals may gain moral justification to disregard those borders. For more on this, see Tibor R. Machan, "Prima Facie v. Natural (Human) Rights," *Journal of Value Inquiry*, vol. 10, no. 1 (1976) pp. 119–31. See also Eric Mack, "Egoism and Rights," *The Personalist*, vol. 54 (1971) pp. 5–33; and "Egoism and Rights Revisited," *The Personalist*, vol. 58 (1977) pp. 282–8. When Sterba claims it is unreasonable to require those in dire straits to respect the private property rights of those who could bail them out of their

trouble, he is implicitly endorsing a form of ethical egoism. Yet if he universalizes this ethical position, as he surely must, those with the capacity to help also ought to strive to advance their own interest and do so as a matter of choice. This may include helping those in dire straits, as I argue in Tibor R. Machan, *Generosity: Virtue in Civil Society* (Washington DC: Cato Institute, 1998). But if such generosity is to have moral significance, it must be voluntary, not coerced, as Sterba proposes via his theory of positive rights (i.e. proposes that the rights of the needy be provided for by those who are able to do this – which would, via taxation, involve coercing the latter to make the provisions).

17 This is a problematic concept. When I sell my car for a very low price, this may lead other persons to lower theirs. But not unavoidably. They are not forced to do so but choose to do this of their own free will. If I become drunk or otherwise alter myself with drugs, others may choose not to associate with me nor follow my lead. But again, this is not unavoidable – they are free agents in the process. Being influenced and being forced are significantly different from the moral point of view.

18 Norman Malcolm, *Ludwig Wittgenstein: A Memoir* (London: Van Nostrand Rinehold Co., 1970) pp. 31–2.

19 The concept "sovereign" relates, historically, to supreme rule over some realm, including those attached to that realm. Only with the emergence of individualism would it be applied to self-rule or self-governance. See J. D. P. Bolton, *Glory, Jest, and Riddle: A Study of the Growth of Individualism from Homer to Christianity* (New York: Barnes & Noble, 1973).

20 Some exceptions include when a person has become crucially incapacitated. Even in the case of punishing criminals, it is arguable from the libertarian position that the criminals have chosen or implicitly consented to be punished, given the rational implication of their criminal conduct.

21 I discuss those in Tibor R. Machan, *Initiative: Human Agency and Society* (Stanford CA: Hoover Institution Press, 2000) chapter 2. There is, briefly, freedom of the will, freedom from natural impediments to development, freedom from intrusions by other persons, and so forth.

22 See, for more on this, Tibor R. Machan, "Is There A Right to Be Wrong?" *International Journal of Applied Philosophy*, vol. 2 (1985) pp. 105–9.

23 For a statement of the view that one has no right to be wrong, see Tal Scriven, "Utility, Autonomy and Drug Regulation," *The International Journal of Applied Philosophy*, vol. 2 (1984) pp. 27–42.

24 Robert Speamann, "The Ontology of 'Right' and 'Left'," in Reiner Schuermann (ed.) *The Public Realm* (Albany NY: SUNY Press, 1990) p. 148.

25 Sterba has advanced his views in many forums, including his introduction to a book he edited, *Justice: Alternative Perspectives* (Belmont CA: Wadsworth Publishing Co., 1991); several papers for scholarly journals such as *The Journal of Social Philosophy*, *Social Theory and Practice* and *Ethics*; his contribution to the volume he organized, *Morality and Social Justice* (Lanham MD: Rowman & Littlefield, 1995); another volume he edited, *Social and Political Philosophy* (Belmont CA: Wadsworth Publishing Co., 1995); and his single-author volume on political philosophy, *Contemporary Political and Social Philosophy* (Belmont CA: Wadsworth Publishing Co., 1995). For some reactions to Sterba other than those coming from libertarian political theorists such as Douglas B. Rasmussen, Eric Mack and Jan Narveson, see, for example, Ruth Sample, "Libertarian Rights and Welfare Rights," *Social Theory and Practice*, vol. 24, no. 3 (1998) pp. 393–418.

26 Sterba calls this "surplus wealth" but he drops the crucial context of that concept, namely, Marxian economic analysis.

27 Lester H. Hunt, "An Argument Against a Legal Duty to Rescue," *Journal of Social Philosophy*, vol. 36 (1994); and Eric Mack, "Bad Samaritarianism and the Causation of Harm," *Philosophy and Public Affairs*, vol. 9 (Spring 1980) pp. 230–59.

28 I am told, however, that in some parts of France when a person in dire straits steals so as to obtain food, there is a defense to the effect of necessity that exculpates the accused. I am not familiar with the details and can only assume that this is for extraordinary cases and has not generated a general right to take from those who have by those who lack. In any case, it should not.

29 Michael Otsuka, "Making the Unjust Provide from the Least Well Off," *The Journal of Ethics*, vol. 2 (1998) pp. 247–59.

30 Michael Otsuka, "Self-Ownership and Equality," *Philosophy and Public Affairs*, vol. 27 (1998) pp. 65–92.

31 The only serious exception would be orphaned or severely neglected children, although with the considerable demand for adoptions and the general compassion most people have for children, it doesn't seem likely that unfortunate children would fail to find sufficient support for their flourishing in a free society. (I thank Randall R. Dipert for raising this issue to me.)

32 For a development of the case for the kind of robust ethical egoism or individualism that supports a political system of natural rights, see Machan, *Classical Individualism*.

33 In contrast, the United Nations Declaration of Human Rights is a system of mutually exclusive basic rights. The right to freedom of choice, for example, competes with such measures as the right to health care, where the one or the other must be selected as superior, requiring the authorities to select which.

34 Richard Rorty, "The Seer of Prague," *The New Republic*, 1 July 1991, pp. 35–40. For Rorty, non-metaphysics or anti-foundationalism is the correct position to take on any philosophical issue, including morality and politics. The gist of this position is that what guides sound thinking is not some argument that is sound independently of some perspective or community, but one's community's framework. And no-one can escape his or her community's framework so as to get at the ultimate truth of things. Ergo, no judgment as to which community's framework is better is possible, except as an expression of community preference. See Richard Rorty, *Objectivity, Relativism, and Truth* (London: Cambridge University Press, 1991), especially the essays "Solidarity versus Objectivity" and "The Priority of Democracy over Philosophy."

35 For my development of these elements of a version of libertarianism, see Tibor R. Machan, *Individuals and Their Rights* (LaSalle IL: Open Court Publishing Co., 1989).

36 See for example Thomas S. Spragens, "The Limitations of Libertarianism," *The Responsive Community* (1992). See also Amitai Etzioni, *The Spirit of Community* (New York: Morrow, 1995). But see Aeon Skoble, "Another Caricature of Libertarianism," *Reason Papers*, no. 17 (1992).

37 George Will, "What Courts Are Teaching," *Newsweek*, 7 December 1998, p. 98.

38 Karl Marx, "On the Jewish Question," in D. McLellan (ed.) *Selected Writings* (London: Oxford University Press, 1977) p. 126.

39 F. A. Hayek, "The Moral Element in Free Enterprise," in Mark W. Hendrickson (ed.) *The Morality of Capitalism* (Irvington-on-Hudson NY: The Foundation for Economic Education, 1992) (originally written for *The Freeman*, 1962).

40 F. A. Hayek, "Socialism and Science," in Chiaki Nishiyama and Kurt R. Leube (eds) *The Essence of Hayek* (Stanford CA: Hoover Institution Press, 1984) p. 118.

41 See Machan, *Classical Individualism*, where I discuss what I have dubbed "the moral tragedy of the commons," a circumstance

in which we have no way to differentiate between the good and evil deeds of different individuals; they all get mixed up with one another and thus lead to the perpetuation of the process of wrongdoing. Neither blame nor credit can be taken in the case of such dumping. The good that people do will not be a source of self-esteem, nor the evil a source of guilt.

(p. 49)

42 And because people often resist these implications and even deny them, the drawing of them becomes much more controversial than drawing out the implications of a sound theory of the physical universe.

43 At this stage of our discussion it will be useful to point out that there are libertarian political theorists who would seriously disagree, and argue instead that if, say, socialism produced a better economic life for all, libertarianism would have to be considered undesirable in comparison.

   The natural rights libertarian does not, of course, argue that socialism will or is likely to promote economic well-being. But natural rights libertarianism holds, in part, that it is because of the nature of human life that this is so and that we can have, accordingly, confidence in libertarian politics as a matter of principle, not merely as a pragmatic tool.

44 Hayek, "The Moral Element in Free Enterprise."

45 I wish to thank Randall R. Dipert for his critical comments on an earlier draft of this paper.

5

LETTING PEOPLE BE PEOPLE AND THE RIGHT TO PROPERTY

Jan Narveson

In the minority view about property and income that I shall be generally defending here, most contemporary governments are pursuing the wrong policies, and we are all very much the worse off as a result. Those policies are very much influenced by the philosophy of equality and its entailed collective overseeing of our economic lives that is by far the majority view among contemporary philosophers, and notably by James P. Sterba. If, as I think, they are indeed wrong, it's obviously pretty important.[1]

The subject of justice is the right use of force against individuals: what do we get to *make* our fellows do, whether they like it or not? Libertarianism is the position that no one may use force (or fraud, which I take to be a special case of force) against anyone who has not himself initiated it against anyone else. So we are confined to using force to combat force, including, where needed, to correct previous wrongful uses of it. By extreme contrast, egalitarians tell us that force may be used to *equalize* people's fortunes and circumstances. The poor should be shored up with the money of the rich, the energetic and capable required to work for the incapable and less energetic, the healthy for the sick, and so on. On the face of it, it is difficult to see how anyone can think to be talking of "reconciliation" between such opposite views, and quite clear that that is not what Sterba does. Instead, he thinks he can show that libertarians *should* be socialists after all; the reconciliation consists in declaring one of the parties to be wrong. Whether he is right about that, of course, is the basic question.

1 Liberty as the indicated choice

Choosing general altruism or egalitarianism or Rawls' maximin principle, as most people understand it, is not what we can expect from an appeal to the reason of all. What there *is* a general case for, though, is not doing things that worsen the situations of our interactees. We should all constrain our pursuit of our interests in such a way that we confine ourselves to behavior that does not leave the other fellow worse off, insofar as that is possible. And it almost always is possible. But this means that we must reject egalitarian and myopically altruistic principles, for those will often require agents to do what worsens their own situations, for the sake of others, and without compensation. Similarly for Rawls' Difference Principle, which apparently[2] requires the talented, energetic and productive to sacrifice their gains for the sake of improving the lot of the worse off. None of these makes rational sense to all the parties whose behavior we are attempting to direct by means of these principles.

The libertarian enters the discourse at this point by suggesting that there is one especially great problem in human relations, and one that is susceptible to solution at the hands of the sort of institution that morality is. That problem is the use of coercive force in human affairs, the tendency for A to get his way at the expense of B instead of with B's voluntary cooperation. The libertarian calls upon us to forego those advantages that we might try to gain by taking advantage of certain liberties which, viewed in isolation, may look good, but which, on reflection, we see to be the sources of more evil than good. If I am free to gain by inflicting damage on others, it appears at first that I can do better than if I lacked such freedom. But when I reflect that others can play this game as well as I, I had better think twice about it. Perhaps I can gain from killing you, yes; but then, you or someone else can gain from killing me, or my brother, and then where are we? The answer, in short, is that we are at war, and very much worse off than if instead we could be at peace. The rational thing to do is to swear off this liberty, provided others do so as well.

The special feature of the libertarian view lies in its assessment of precisely *how* those others count. Its concern is with the use of interpersonally administered force in human affairs. Force, used against otherwise innocent persons, defeats cooperation, makes enemies of us. But cooperation is the great engine of prosperity and secure good living for all. With cooperation we can have not only bread, but two hundred kinds of it, along with pizzas, computers, ballet productions, institutions of higher learning, and innumerable other goods that can exist only by the concerted effort of many people. Force cancels the good of these efforts. In being forced to do something, A no longer works for what A sees to be good. The stings of the whip, the deprivations of the thief and the taxman, diminish the value of effort in the eyes of those who exert it. That some others benefit from them, if they do, is no consolation to the individual subject to these incursions. If I liked those people that much, I would do things for them without being forced to. Multiply that by several billion, and the point is clear. Philosophies that impose burdens that are not also, on the whole, beneficial to those imposed on are antithetical to social life, and thus, it seems to me, of human life. But when they would be beneficial, why would they need to be *imposed*?

This brings us to the sort of views that Sterba and others friendly to equality have advocated. Such theories permit us to impose on millions and billions of people in order to shore up the prospects of the remainder. How can such views be reconciled with the philosophy of cooperation that is the essence of the social contract? "Reconciliation" seems out of the question – it seems like reconciling good and evil.

The libertarian's bold proposal, which I state in terminology due to David Gauthier,[3] is that we proscribe, across the board, all *and only* behavior that worsens, on balance, the situations of others in the course of trying to better the situation of the agent. There are two qualifications: first, the proscription applies provided that the others in question do not themselves fall afoul of it; and second, it applies, assuming that the agent can comply without substantially worsening his own situation in the process.

Note also that "on balance" does not mean that *we* add up the gains to some and weigh them against losses to others, à la utilitarianism, or à la conservatism. Instead, it means that each individual upon whom our behavior impinges must be such that on balance *she* reckons herself to be no worse off for our impingement.

If a general proscription on worsening of others' situations is envisaged, then there is a particular class of other-regarding interests that we can*not* count as a "good to others," morally speaking, however welcome it may be to its immediately intended recipient. This class consists of what we may call *negatively other-regarding interests*. If Sue is Sam's enemy, and she would be delighted at his having to endure certain evils, then we can satisfy this interest of Sue's only at the expense of Sam. Since our principle forbids all worsenings of others' situations, however, it also forbids this one. Malevolent interests are *non grata*.

It will be noted that the reach of this last restriction is profound. Consider, for example, moral egalitarianism, which requires us to bring it about that everyone has about the same amount of something. What if we only achieve this by taking it from some who already have it? The fact that we thereupon give it to others who do not have it makes no difference: we have acted at the expense, to the detriment, of the "haves," and our proposed principle proscribes such action. If the proposed general right to liberty is to be respected, we must pursue equality in some other way.

The principle advocated here is known as "libertarianism" because the infliction of evils on others are curtailments in their pursuit of their preferred values, hence of their liberty. Inflicted evils keep one from doing what one wants, which is to pursue the good life as one sees it. Given that our criterion for assessing good and evil is liberal, not conservative, Jones benefits, in the relevant sense, only if Jones prefers the putative benefit to its absence, in the circumstances. Jones is at liberty, socially speaking, insofar as others refrain from interfering with his intentionally adopted line of activity. Invading Jones' body counts as an interference with his "liberty" in that it goes against what he wants for himself: it imposes what he sees to be a cost.

Many things besides the actions of others can keep us from doing what we would like, but morality only concerns the actions of agents. There is no point issuing moral rules and proscriptions to mountains, trees, tigers, or amoebas. Now, some propose that Jones is not at liberty unless external things are in one condition rather than another – e.g. he is amoeba-free. But the reply to that is that such things are relevant to morals only if the implication is that somebody else is to do something about it. At that point, however, we run up against the fact that the somebody in question may not be inclined to do the thing in question. She may not care about Jones, or may find the cost more than she is willing to pay. If so, then forcing her to do it is imposing on her, and that is proscribed by our general proposal.

Why accept the general proposal? The answer is that we can all be certain that we will all gain from its general observance, as compared with the situation we can expect in its absence. This is not true of any other moral proposal. For example, it is not true of a proposal to the effect that "all needs must be satisfied." For those called upon to satisfy them may not want to do that, for they may find the cost excessive. It may be claimed by the theorist that Ms Smith needs x "less" than Mr Jones does, but that doesn't mean that she is happy to surrender x to minister to Jones. And if she finds the cost of ministering to Jones excessive, then it *is* excessive, given liberalism. Only if reciprocation is reasonably expected, at a level justifying the cost of catering to others' needs, is there a basis for expecting it from persons whose sympathies will not otherwise motivate them to cater to the needs in question. And it is reasonable to suppose that in many cases neither of those conditions will obtain. It is therefore unreasonable to insist that morality include very strong requirements of aid to others. If we seek a rational morality, it must be consistent with the facts.

2 Mutual aid

This is not to say that there is no basis for *any* amount of requirement to help others. There is, I think, a reasonable basis for some such principle as the following. If A can provide a very large benefit, X, to B, at very low cost to A, and X is a benefit of a general type such that (1) others could possibly provide it to A, (2) it is probable that at least occasionally A is likely to be in a position of not having X *and* that having X would be highly beneficial to A, and (3) in the circumstances A could only get X by the untransacted-for voluntary assistance of others, *then* A ought to provide X to B.[4] I shall call this the principle of "mutual aid." It is to be emphasized that this is not an across-the-board duty to help others, and not an enforceable duty of justice. But it is nontrivial, and I believe it states, in suitably imprecise terms, a principle that virtually everyone does actually accept in day-to-day encounters with other people.

It is to be emphasized that the mutual aid principle is not that A is to do good to B provided that B *himself* does a like good to *A*. It is, rather, a principle to enter into a general social net in which, though we may never again see the person we help on occasion O, yet we too will likely be the beneficiary of needed assistance from other strangers at other times. It is a principle of generalized social reciprocity, not a matter of at-the-time transactions. We should also be grateful to those who help us, and express our gratitude in some way if we can – if no more than by saying "thank you."

It is, I think, quite clear that we are justified in saying demeaning things about those who signally fail to observe the principle of mutual aid. But it is also quite clear that we are justified in normally doing rather little to help others, except on a basis of agreed exchange, as in commerce.

3 Sterba's scenario of rich and poor

Sterba argues that the well-off have an enforceable duty, a duty of justice, to allow "starving poor persons unable to find work" to take from their "surplus." He does this on the ground that otherwise, those people are being denied a *liberty*, namely "the liberty ... not to be interfered with in taking from the surplus possession of the rich what is necessary to satisfy their basic needs."[5] I have previously pointed out[6] that this goes against the plain meaning of the libertarian principle. The liberty to take, from any innocent person, simply is not an available liberty in the libertarian scheme, for it involves a violation of that principle in the first place. The poor, in taking from the rich, are commandeering the latter's energies to their own purposes, without compensation, which is plainly contrary to the requirement that all refrain from imposing on others.

Some might argue that the well-off *are* compensated by participating in a system in which they involuntarily support those who cannot support themselves. How would this be so, though? The most likely reply is that they thereby avoid a sort of war: feed 'em and they won't bother you! This appears to be exactly the same sort of reasoning that has motivated appeasement strategies down through the ages. And it arguably doesn't work. But whether it does or not, what is the basis for it? What anyone receives in return for his committing himself to peaceful relations with others is – peaceful relations with others. Why should anyone, rich or poor, be able to claim a higher price than that? To say that someone is entitled to such a claim is, of course, to incorporate exploitation in the relationship. The unable exploit the more able: "you feed us for free, or we hit you!" Why should anyone think that that constitutes justice?

There have, to be sure, been a few answers to that, of sorts. Most simply consist in an unconsidered assumption of "egalitarianism." But some think there is an argument for it, usually of the "there but for the grace of God go

119

I!" variety. The bright, talented, energetic, creative, and, in general, productive did not, it will be said, *deserve* to be such. No problem there. But what of it? Well, it is then said, therefore we don't deserve our talents any more than the untalented, etc., deserve the low level of talents they possess. Let us agree with that also. Still, what of it? It seems that egalitarians think that it somehow follows that the rich should share their good fortune with the poor. But it doesn't. All that follows is that nobody can be said to deserve to be the person he or she is. This being so, if we are to have some basis for "rewarding" some people, it's going to have to be something other than the fact that they deserve to be the people they are. No problem there, either. What we in fact reward people for is their contributions to whatever it is we think is valuable, and this might be easy or difficult for those who so contribute, but we don't basically care which it is. We prefer the more efficient, the more productive, because we are interested in what they produce, and not how it is that they are ultimately capable of producing it.

What motivates most of us to assist the poor, the helpless and the unfortunate is general human sympathy, which most of us have in appreciable quantities. Why should we get to exploit our fellow members of the productive class by exacting from them as a "duty" their assistance in catering to the unfortunate persons we decide to help?

To be sure, it would be quite otherwise if it was our *fault* that the poor are poor. Many theorists tend to talk as if poor people are people who have been done down and exploited by others, the "rich." And probably there are some cases in which something of the sort may have happened, though it is very far from typical. Much more likely, however, in the sort of cases Sterba may have had in mind, is that the persons in question lacked a combination of employable skills, enterprise in seeking work, the ability to make oneself presentable enough to induce employers to hire them, and the like. It is to these cases that Sterba's claim must be centrally addressed. In the case where A deliberately impoverishes B, A may owe B compensation. In the case where impoverished B is so due to sheer failure to exert himself when he could have done so, again Sterba is not insisting that we owe B the duty in question.

4 The right of private property

In all this, I have talked as if the ownership of various things, by some persons to the exclusion of others, is unproblematic. There are those who deny this, however. Some of these deniers would no doubt reject the idea of a foundation for morality. Among those who don't reject it, some succumb to bad arguments of the kind just noted. But the serious question is whether a general principle of the sort espoused does in fact uphold a right of private property. I claim that it does indeed do so. The general right to do as we will, provided only we not invade and worsen others, is all we need. From there to private property is a short step, given one assumption: that in acquiring some previously untouched bit of the world, the acquirer does not *ipso facto* relevantly worsen the situation of others who, perhaps, come historically later. The reply to this merits a lengthier discussion than can be undertaken here, but the short of it is this. First, there is, on the contractarian view, no basis whatever for the idea that other people have some kind of basic claim on the world, independently of what they actually do. Second, the claim that if A gets x, then B does not, is true but irrelevant, since it is true of everyone in relation to everything, always. Nothing follows, therefore. Zero-sum games, so far as they go, have no solutions acceptable to all parties, by definition. Finally, and perhaps most to the point, property for A, and more generally the systematic right to acquire it by working or by getting it voluntarily from someone else who in turn got it by work, etc., is beneficial to B, not merely to A.

This does bring us to a problem about real-world ethics versus abstract possibilities. I deny that in the abstractly characterized case, we have an enforceable duty to the poor. But I need also to point out that in the real world, especially that of North America today, the picture of ragged and starving persons unable to find work is essentially unreal. It has nothing to do with the present-day "poor" in contemporary America, or in any first-line country in the world. For one thing, there is a serious problem of definition here, since the officially poor are so by virtue of having earned incomes of less than some quite high amount (incomes in the high teens of thousands, for example) as specified by politicians and bureaucrats. Moreover, the criteria for poverty-level income are drawn narrowly, so that in fact the American poor manage to spend about twice what they allegedly earn. If you look at what they have, rather than what politicians say about them, the American poor are in fact better off in the usual "material" terms, as a group, than the citizenry *as a whole* in other countries – not just Third-World ones. They have more cars, TVs, electric ranges, housing space, and so on and on, than the average citizens of other first-line countries, not to mention those in the Second and Third Worlds. If this is "poverty," it is certainly not what Sterba is talking about in his examples.[7] If we substitute slogans for thought and research on these matters, of course, it is easy to see that we would have an argument in name only, and one not likely to be settled by such means. But welfare-state enthusiasts uninterested in the facts are living in a fool's limbo (hardly a "paradise," after all).

Since much of the real income of contemporary American "poor" people comes from the state, to be sure, there is the question how they would be doing if the state weren't so deeply involved in their lives. This is a question of economic analysis, with a considerable burden of proof. But if we allow a bit of common sense as well as reasonable familiarity with the current economic facts, the reader would not find it hard to believe that the lower-income groups in American and Canadian society, at least, would be better off, not worse off, if the welfare state had never existed at all. Such is the burden of many studies on the subject[8] – all of which will be rejected without further thought by most readers on the ground that they are "right-wing." But common sense is enough to discern that the cost of elevating the incomes of people who would otherwise be working by extracting money from the better-off and transferring it to them is very high. It includes not only the payment of middle-class salaries to the numerous administrators of the system, but the loss of production from those who would otherwise be working (almost certainly almost all of them, since most people prefer making a living).

Sterba is far from alone in thinking that the existence of people with relatively low incomes in affluent countries is symptomatic of injustice. But in order to think this, you have to assume that we all have a duty to see to it that everyone has not only "enough" to live on, but in fact a quite high income. That assumption, however, is one he does not espouse – happily, since it has nothing whatever to be said in its favor, if we insist on a morality derived from reason rather than the sentiments of academics. The situation is, in fact, quite entirely the reverse. Those with lower incomes in contemporary America and Canada have very high incomes by world standards, and they have them *because of*, not *despite*, the economic activities of the so-called "rich." There is no good reason to doubt that if the rich were allowed to get richer, the poor would likewise be richer.

Wealth comes from productivity. All wealth is due to somebody's efforts – no wealth literally consists in "natural resources," since they, *in situ*, are of no value whatever. They become valuable when someone works out ways to utilize them, someone else sets to work utilizing them in that way, and still others set to work marketing the results. Wealthy countries are countries in which the productivity of people is high, and that is due to their working in environments designed and produced by other hard-working and inventive people. One man produces several dozen varieties of wheat that withstand difficult conditions better and have enormously higher yields; this one set of discoveries enables literally hundreds of millions of people to eat better than ever before. One man invented the mechanical reaper, and others refined it, which enabled American, then European, and eventually all farmers to produce far more with far less work. And so on. We all ride on a road paved by the ingenuity of others. In the process, we utilize such effort and skill as we are able, yielding useful output that is acquired by others in exchange for purchasing power, which then goes to stimulate still other productive effort elsewhere. All this is elementary, but seems to be often overlooked in contemporary academic discussions.

Some will respond to reminders like the above with the thought that, seeing our general indebtedness to all those ingenious people, we should be the more ready to accept a general duty to attend to the needs of others. But it doesn't follow. For one thing, those inventors have, characteristically, been well paid for their efforts – such being the nature of free-market activity. Moreover, insofar as all are benefiting from them, there is for that very reason no occasion for insisting on still further benefits being supplied by one beneficiary to another. And in any case, the indigent and the untalented also benefit from all that past activity. The panhandler's affluent clientele are able to support him in much better style, the storefronts he hangs out in front of are much more attractive, and in general the unfortunate are very much more fortunate than their forerunners on modern American streets. Or at any rate, they would be if modern law-enforcement agencies were not at work harassing them more effectively than of old – but that is another story. Meanwhile, contemporary panhandlers have set new marks in their business. In Toronto, a newspaper reporter posing as one of the homeless in that city pocketed some $223 in a day's "work", all from ordinary well-meaning passers-by, observing that he, an amateur, could hardly suppose himself to be doing better than his seasoned colleagues among the homeless. He also toured the lodgings offered to such people by the many churches and other charities in town, passing on ratings by his more experienced compeers.[9] (I noted with some interest that an enterprising panhandler, assuming this poser's experiences to be typical and assuming that he paid no taxes on his income, actually had take-home pay somewhat exceeding this writer's – and I am a full professor!)

Under the circumstances, it is difficult to address with a straight face Sterba's scenarios of rich and poor, the latter in abject misery and facing starvation. Those things are from storybooks nowadays, in most parts of the world. If we seek victims in the modern world, we should be looking not at the affluent poor, but at the victims of police state violence, which are numerous and increasing yearly – or, perhaps, the hundreds of millions of people genuinely poor by American standards, and beyond the reach of welfare state policies as advocated by Sterba and most others. The millions of American officially "poor" do not compare, as cases for concern, with the millions of Americans imprisoned over the years because of its draconian enforcement of punitive and illiberal laws against the taking of recreational drugs. And the incomes even of comparatively wealthy Americans could be much higher but for the numerous regulatory incursions and huge tax bills of their governments. The list of impositions against ordinary people in the name of law and order and democracy dwarf by comparison those supposedly suffering from the activities of people making their livings from commerce.

Tired marxist "analyses" in which evil rich people exploit the virtuous poor should not be substituted for reality, though they characteristically are among today's legions of social philosophers. Most of all, they suffer from a phenomenally question-begging and irrelevant use of standards in appraising the situations of people around the world. Compared to Americans or Canadians, most people in the world are poor, and the less well paid people in Bolivia or Indonesia dismally so. But in those areas of the world in which international capitalism is allowed to flourish, working people are very much better off than they were in decades, let alone centuries, past.

> These improvements have not taken place because well-meaning people in the West have done anything to help – foreign aid, never large, has lately shrunk to virtually nothing. Nor is it the result of the benign policies of national governments, which are as callous and corrupt as ever. It is the indirect and unintended result of the actions of soulless multinationals and rapacious local entrepreneurs, whose only concern was to take advantage of the profit opportunities offered by cheap labor. It is not an edifying spectacle; but no matter how base the motives of those involved, the result has been to move hundreds of millions of people from abject poverty to something still awful but nonetheless significantly better.[10]

These observations make contemporary American academics' lips curl in disgust. If those academics had their way about it, commercial activities of that kind would be priced out of the market in those countries – and instead of substantial but slowly improving poverty, the world would be enjoying the spectacle of absolutely desperate poverty, total hopelessness, and a life expectancy of three or four decades instead of the five or six already being enjoyed in those places.

Redistributive taxation, which has been all the rage in democratic countries for many decades now, cannot be a cure for poverty. There is only one such cure: greater productivity and greater freedom in the economic realm. The idea that you can make meaningful, long-term improvements in the lives of millions by hiring armies of bureaucrats to harass the productive and "reallocate" their incomes to people who do nothing, and whose incentives are to do more of same, is not one that commends itself to the impartial intellect – especially when those same bureaucrats are seen by the poor as harassing them while they're at it. Why contemporary intellects are so characteristically not impartial on such points is an interesting question – but one we must leave for another time. Meanwhile, the case for impositions on productive activities in the supposed interests of "equity" does not emerge from a rational analysis of the foundations of morals. What does emerge is the wisdom of freedom, complete with property rights and protection of individuals against the violence of their neighbors, including those in uniform.

Finally, we should remember that Sterba himself has set the terms of reference for this discussion as follows:

this case for restricting the liberty of the rich depends upon the willingness of the poor to take advantage of whatever opportunities are available to them to engage in mutually beneficial work.[11]

I take this to mean that political methods for feeding the poor out of taxation are not justified unless all private methods of doing so fail. Between private soup-kitchens, private handouts by sympathetic passers-by in the streets, private hostels for the homeless, and so on, it is simply obvious that private methods are very much more than adequate to deal with any situation that could reasonably be described in terms of genuine, desperate-type need. Thus on Sterba's own grounds, the case for the welfare state is actually nil – a not unimportant result, if our focus is really on justice "here and now."

NOTES

1 This essay is drawn from a longer essay which also considers Sterba's argument from rationality to morality.

2 I have argued, however, that it probably proves nothing of the sort. See "A Puzzle About Economic Justice in Rawls' Theory," *Social Theory and Practice*, vol. 4, no. 1, fall 1976, pp. 1–28.

3 David Gauthier, *Morals by Agreement* (New York: Oxford University Press, 1986) lays down essentially the same principle, calling it the "Lockean Proviso." It requires us to refrain from pursuing our own utility *by* imposing disutility on our interactees, relative to the baseline of noninteraction, except when this is necessary in order to avoid an even greater disutility being imposed on ourselves. See p. 203.

4 See my discussion in "Morality, Affluence and Distant People," presented at the APA Pacific, 2 April 1999; forthcoming in Deen Chatterlee (ed.) (title tba).

5 Sterba, *op. cit.*, p. 45.

6 "Sterba's Program of Philosophical Reconciliation," *Journal of Social Philosophy*, XXX.3, winter 1999, pp. 402 ff.

7 For figures already a decade old, see Robert Record, "How 'poor' are America's poor?" in Julian Simon (ed.) *The State of Humanity* (Oxford: Blackwell, 1995). Even at that time, the situation was striking; it is in general still better today. Here are some summaries: 1987: 38% of officially poor Americans owned their own houses; the median value of their homes was $39,205 – 60% of the median value of all owner-occupied housing. Only 7.5% of this housing had more than one person per room. They were less crowded than average West European households of 1980. At 0.56 persons per room, this puts them ahead of the average Japanese (at 0.8). They enjoyed an average living space per capita that was twice the Japanese standard, and four times the Soviet. Only 1.8% of American poor households lacked indoor flush toilets in 1980. This compares with 6% in the UK, 7% in West Germany, 17% in France, and 54% in Japan – for *all* households, not just their "poor". By 1987 virtually 100% of American "poor" households had running water, flush toilets, showers, electric lights, etc. 62% own at least one car, truck, or van; 14% owned two or more, a third had microwaves, and 29% owned two or more color TVs. 49% had air-conditioning (56% among those who owned their own homes). Fewer than 1% lack a refrigerator. 17% have automatic dishwashers; 95% own at least one TV. A poor American household is much

more likely to own a color TV than the average household in France, West Germany or Italy. The official US "poverty" threshold in the 1960s was about thirty times greater than the world median per capita income. In 1987 the welfare spending ignored in the official poverty report came to $9,058 per poor household, on average.

8 The classic study is, of course, that of Charles Murray in *Losing Ground* (New York: Basic Books, 1984).

9 See the Toronto *Globe and Mail* for 16–23 December 1999.

10 Paul Krugman, "In Praise of Cheap Labor," *Slate*, 20 March 2000. [http://slate.msn.com/Dismal/97–03–20/Dismal.asp]

11 Sterba, *op. cit.*, p. 51.

Welfare liberalism

6

WHAT (WELFARE) JUSTICE OWES CARE

Eva Feder Kittay

From libertarianism to welfarism – maybe, maybe not

James P. Sterba offers us a conception of philosophy as cooperation rather than conflict – as peacemaking rather than war-making. Being a peace-loving person myself, I find this notion very congenial. Philosophy is too often based on an antagonist/agonistic model where the winner in a philosophical debate is she who proffers the most devastating argument against her opponent. However, in the philosophical war games, or peace games, the only real victor should be truth – and, in this context, the truth of justice – or better still, what can truly and justly be established here and now.

I would like to engage with Sterba in the spirit of his peacemaking. But if I seem to be more conflictual than conciliatory, it is because I want the outcome to be what is most true and useful. My sense is, however, that although I believe I disagree with Sterba, he will nonetheless show that, in fact, our views are entirely compatible, and perhaps even identical. In fact, where I want to begin questioning his position with respect to "welfare justice" is precisely the point at which Sterba demonstrates his uncanny ability to reconcile what seem, at first at least, to be diametrically opposed views.

To those who have not followed the dialogue that Sterba has carried on with libertarians, Sterba seems to make a surprising claim, namely that the position of what he calls "welfare liberals" (among whom he counts himself) can be reconciled with that of libertarians.[1] Proponents of a "welfare state" hold the view that the only way that a democratic market-based state can adequately dispense justice to all is to protect us from, and to compensate us for, the extreme inequalities an unfettered capitalism is likely to produce. The welfare state is intended to address the needs we have when we are most vulnerable – when we are too old for gainful employment, too weak due to illness or disability, too young or otherwise incapable of competing in the marketplace. It is meant to help protect us from disaster when the economy shrinks or collapses, or when our own marketable skills are no longer

129

needed. The welfare state is a response to a particular economic and political system. It is with this sort of welfare justice that I am concerned, because it is this sort of welfarism that I believe pertains to "justice here and now," to borrow a phrase familiar to Sterba's readers

The standard argument between libertarians, who resist arguments for state provision of most sorts, and welfare liberals, who insist on state provision of many goods and services, is generally cast as a conflict between liberty and equality, with libertarians espousing liberty and welfare liberals championing equality. Libertarians argue that as long as the means by which wealth was first obtained, and was subsequently transmitted, accords with just laws, there is nothing unjust in the resulting pattern of distribution, no matter how unequal the resulting pattern of distribution. Attempting to alter that pattern by taxing the rich to subsidize the poor, or otherwise redistribute wealth, is an unwarranted interference by the state into the lives of its citizens, violating fundamental rights to property. The goal of equalizing resources must give way to the primary goal of the state, which is to insure the liberty of its citizens and to protect their rights to property.

Sterba wants to show us that what looks like a conflict between two traditional values of liberalism, and so a conflict between libertarians and a welfare liberal like himself, is really a conflict between the liberty or liberty rights of one group of persons (those with wealth) and that of another group (those who are poor). The exercise of the liberty of the wealthy to dispose of their wealth is, according to libertarians, justified as long as doing so will not interfere with the liberty of another to lead their life according to their own lights. But, says Sterba, where there exist people so poor that they cannot satisfy their most basic needs, the liberty of the wealthy to dispose of their surplus wealth as they see fit does interfere with the liberty of the poor to appropriate that surplus to meet their basic needs. The claims on the part of the poor can be cast in terms of liberty no less than can the claims on the part of the rich. Therefore, even if we grant that liberty rights trump all other rights, the libertarian is mistaken in holding that the claims of the wealthy are liberty claims, while those of the poor are merely claims for equality. But in that case, a libertarian could just as well champion the rights of the poor not to be interfered with in their efforts to avail themselves of surplus wealth, as to champion the right of the wealthy not to be interfered with in disposing of their surplus as they desire. Note that Sterba is not only casting the conflict as a conflict between two liberties, but that he also succeeds in finding a formulation that casts the conflict as one of competing *negative* liberties, so using the only liberties and rights most libertarians recognize (negative liberties and negative rights).[2]

An obvious objection to Sterba's argument would be that he apparently does not weigh property rights in the same way most libertarians do. But Sterba points out that even libertarians do not privilege liberty rights over all other rights, and so we need not worry ourselves about the claim of the wealthy to property rights. It is apparent that the wealthy will not suffer nearly as much by losing some of their surplus wealth as the poor will by being prevented from appropriating the surplus of the wealthy. The state therefore needs to protect the negative welfare rights of the poor more strenuously than protecting property rights of the wealthy. Using Sterba's principle of morality, we can conclude that the wealthy who horde their resources in face of the grave needs of others, and the state which protects their surplus, behave immorally; while the poor act within the bounds of morality (providing, that is, that they have made every effort to meet their needs by means of their own efforts, that they confine their appropriations to wealth that can reasonably be thought to be surplus, and that they do not take more than they need for subsistence). Arguing that if we have the capability to do what we ought to do, we then have the duty to do it, Sterba can maintain that those who can prevent such life-threatening hardships have the duty to do so. Thus not only do the poor have a negative right to welfare, but we have an obligation to provide welfare, or at least, we can say that the state has a right to protect the negative right of the poor to appropriate what they require to survive.

What would such protection amount to, short of having different laws for when it is and is not permissible for someone to help oneself to what is otherwise legally another's? A reasonable answer would be taxation of surplus wealth. Sterba's claim, then, is not only that libertarianism is compatible with a welfare liberalism, but that welfare justice can just as well be derived from a minimalist libertarianism as from a robust liberalism.

Furthermore, since this need is shared by many throughout the world, and since their need is as great, if not greater than those who are proximate, they too would have the right to the liberty to appropriate the surplus of the wealthy. Our obligation then continues until there is no more surplus to give to other needy persons. As there are so many more needy than wealthy, the effect of this redistribution is to achieve a near equality of wealth among all. Hence, we go from liberty to equality.

Here I will not attempt to examine the details of the argument. It appears that the argument has been picked apart and objections have been responded to often enough.[3] Nor will I look at the argument as a libertarian might. However, I do want to note that although Sterba's is a minimalist welfare – the needy are only entitled to what will keep them from starvation and other life-threatening ills – given the sheer numbers of the "have nots," it is so demanding on the "haves" that one could charge his view with exacting an "overload of obligations." Furthermore, one may argue that when wealth would be so severely reduced through welfare obligations, the motivation to produce the wealth may not be strong. In that case, less wealth will be produced and everyone may be worse off than under the less egalitarian scheme.

But as Alan Gewirth (1996) has argued, welfare, even of a more generous sort, need not result in such overload if a proper distinction is made between what is owed by one individual to another individual, and what a government owes to individuals. One problem with the account Sterba gives is that there is no accounting for the role of institutions in providing welfare. As Oxfam and other aid organizations have increasingly come to see, aid that enables and encourages governments to provide the means by which its residents can produce for themselves can be more effective than direct aid. In fact, direct aid in the form of cash transferred from the wealthy directly to poor populations can, in fact, perpetuate the very problems it is meant to solve.

However, this is not my main point. I am more concerned with the minimalism of the welfare provided, both the minimal amount that the poor are entitled to, and the fact that only some poor are entitled to aid. These strictures, I'll show, are directly related to Sterba's attempt to reconcile welfare liberalism with libertarianism.

From liberty to welfare$_s$

Welfare is a form of public provision, and as Michael Walzer has taught us, every society determines its own form of public provision, as well as its own justification for the form of public provision it chooses. The justifications for welfare need to address not only our obligation to provide for others, but also the sort of social goods we are obliged to provide and for whom they are to be provided.

Sterba, in *Justice for Here and Now*, says little directly about the sort of welfare he envisions and attempts to justify. We can, however, extrapolate from his remarks. Welfare, as he understands it, is provision to the poorest citizens and fellow human beings; particularly those among them who make every effort to provide for themselves and nonetheless don't succeed. These provisions, which are minimal and bare, are then confined to the *deserving* poor.

The notion of the deserving poor already reveals something important about this understanding of the welfare. The justification for welfare, on Sterba's account (and on many accounts), relies on two assumptions, neither of which is thought sufficient, but which together are necessary and jointly sufficient to warrant the aid we know as welfare. The first is that need, when it is urgent or concerns basic necessities, ought to be addressed by those who are in a position to provide relief. The second is that an individual's entitlement to resources is proportional to the willingness (or ability) of the individual to assume burdens and obligations associated with being the recipient of the benefits of social cooperation.

The second assumption, or condition of aid, is frequently cashed out in terms of an individual's contribution (potential or actual, past or current) to the production of wealth, as indicated by income-producing labor. At the very least, it is assumed that the willingness to so contribute must be sincere and actively pursued to the degree possible, given the individual's capabilities.

In a money-based economy, an important collorary of the second assumption is that non-income-producing activity is not "work." Its products or consequences are not included in reckoning the wealth of a nation.

Welfare, as understood here, is limited to those who are the poor. Furthermore, it is restricted to the deserving poor. For if an individual fails to meet the second condition, evidence of that person's need does not in and of itself obligate others to respond to those needs. In this way, the deserving poor or needy are distinguished from the undeserving poor or needy.

Where entitlement to public provision is connected to the willingness (and sometimes ability) to be "productive," that is, engaging in income-producing activities, the provision for the "undeserving poor" is, at best, a very debased and frequently even punitive welfare. Its purpose is as much to control the behavior of the "undeserving" poor (and often the "deserving" poor as well – for how do you really tell the difference?) as to relieve need.[4]

Those who see welfare as based on the two assumptions above worry about welfare becoming a "drug" or "crutch" or legitimated way of existing and therefore a disincentive to work. Consequently, this welfare, even when doled out to the "deserving poor," is frequently carried out with significant state intrusion into the lives of its recipients, and it is never generous. I will call the form of welfare doled out the deserving poor welfare$_S$ ("S" standing for stigmatized, stingy and subject to state surveillance). What's provided for those thought to be the "undeserving" we could dub welfare$_{S2}$ (the same but worse). It's worth noting that welfare$_{S2}$ exerts a downward pressure on welfare$_S$.

From welfare$_S$ to welfare$_E$

Welfare, understood as public provision, is not only and always understood in the sense of what is provided to the poor and needy, deserving or undeserving. It is also understood as that which gives a worker and citizen a source of dignity and maintains a level of well-being thought to be commensurate with the affluence of the society in which one lives. On this view, welfare is a social right, which raises citizens *above* subsistence levels of existence, providing security and a good degree of well-being, as well as protection from the deprivations of poverty. It does not merely save the poor from starvation. It aims to *prevent or end* poverty.

T. H. Marshall speaks of welfare in this sense as marking the rights of "social citizenship." Here welfare continues to depend on the second condition above, but rather than basing provision only on "need," provision is based on "rights" – positive rights to freedom and well-being. Citizens have a right to demand that the government step in to protect them from falling into poverty when, through either market failures or personal impediments, they are not in a position to compete in the marketplace, and also to fulfill roles and functions that are ill served by the market. In this more expansive sense of welfare, which I'll call welfare$_E$, the state serves as an insurer and provider of certain social goods thought to be essential for a good life. Walzer characterizes welfare in this sense thus:

> Certain key social goods have been taken out of private control or out of exclusive private control and are now provided by law to all (or to some subset of citizens and residents). The distribution is paid for with public funds and organized by public officials. Social Security is an easy example.
>
> (Walzer 1983, 13)

Universal healthcare, unemployment insurance and workers' compensation plans are also good examples. The welfare$_E$ state justifies the redistribution of resources inherent in social insurance schemes. It notes that under capitalism the distribution of resources is not necessarily well aligned with either the contributions or the needs of its members; that capitalism, with its capacity to produce great wealth, also produces great poverty; and that the market is either an inadequate or an imperfect way in which to arrange the distribution of certain critical resources and services. Furthermore, welfare$_E$ is based on the premise that all who have contributed to the production of wealth should not need to be reduced to poverty before they benefit from that wealth, even if the wealth has been accumulated in private hands. That is, that a mode of redistribution is justified, where the benefits of contributing to the production of wealth are very unevenly distributed.

Welfare$_E$ still carves out a category of the undeserving poor, namely those who could but do not contribute. Generally, a stigmatized welfare is available serving only the most basic needs for those individuals, on the grounds that need, in and of itself, ought to be addressed by those in a position to do so. Just as we do not condition the medical treatment of motorcyclists who have been injured on whether or not they were wearing helmets at the time of accident,[5] the proponent of welfare$_E$ argues that we should not demand that those who haven't shown sufficient motivation to earn their bread ought not to eat, especially when food is plentiful. Still, individuals who do not contribute, or make the effort to, may get some provision, but they do not become full citizens of the welfare state – they have a pariah status.

From welfare$_E$ to welfare$_C$: the demands of dependency

Where entitlement to welfare$_E$ (1) depends upon an individual's productivity; (2) assumes women to be primarily wives, mothers, and daughters, not workers, and presumes the worker to be male, we have a patriarchal welfare state. Women's entitlement to welfare appears to be conditioned by her tie to a "productive worker". But, Carole Pateman asks, how can women be citizens of the patriarchal welfare state? For citizenship depends on making a contribution to the welfare state. "What," she asks, "could, or did women contribute?" And she replies: "The paradoxical answer is that women contributed – welfare" (Pateman 1988, 247). That is to say, the patriarchal welfare state is itself dependent on the free labor of women doing the work of providing welfare, but in a privatized form. For Pateman, the problem manifests itself in what she calls "Wollstonecraft's Dilemma"[6] (1988, 252). The dilemma is found where citizenship has been modeled on and defined by the male wage earner, and arises from two incompatible demands: the demand to be accorded equal citizenship and the demand that women's special responsibilities *as women* be recognized.

At the heart of Wollstonecraft's Dilemma, I believe, lies the failure to include within political theory the concerns of fundamental human dependency and the gender-specific way in which concerns of dependency have been allocated. Liberal theory begins with the assumption that society is an association of equals, of those who can function independently, and who are equally situated with respect to power. It thereby excludes those persons whose dependency is the result of inevitable conditions related to age, ability and health, and in so doing makes invisible the contributions of those labors devoted to caring for dependents. Those who care for dependents, I have called "dependency workers" (Kittay 1999).

In the remainder of this paper, I wish to argue for and defend a sense of welfare that is stronger still than welfare$_E$. Welfare$_E$ is not adequate to resolving Wollstonecraft's Dilemma, even where employment opportunities are opened to women, because women continue to be the wives, mothers, caregiving daughters, and paid and unpaid care providers. This stronger sense of welfare, which I will call welfare$_C$, centers on the rights as well as the provisions that enable one to give and receive care. It is care, or rather the provision of care, that is, if you will, "welfarized" – that is, taken out of exclusive private control, provided by law to all, and paid for by public funds.

We need welfare$_C$ to address what I call dependency concerns, the needs and interests of those

1   who are dependent by virtue of youth, frail old age, illness and severe disability (these I call *inevitable dependencies*)[7] and
2   dependency workers, that is, those who attend to and have prime responsibility for the care of dependents.

By "welfarized care" I mean the right of caregivers and dependents alike to public provision that enables caregivers to provide care without

1   compromising their ability to care for their own needs,
2   sacrificing the needs of the dependents, or
3   failing to respect the nonfungible nature of most significant caregiving relations.

Insofar as women are still, in large part, dependency workers, assuring women's economic security and full equality requires enlarging welfare$_E$ to incorporate welfare$_C$.

Reconciling welfare$_C$ and libertarian principles

Sterba's aim to reconcile the welfare liberal with the libertarian, and to insist that from the primacy of the right to (negative) freedom we can derive the right to welfare, limits him to a right (and its correlate duty) to welfare$_S$. Only urgent need gives us any right to take property that is another's. Otherwise, all cases of theft that didn't leave the victim worse off than the thief would be justified. But in that case, all property rights are jeopardized, and we have a sort of Hobbesian war of all against all. The only way to distinguish welfare rights from robbery (the libertarian generally sounds as if he takes this to be a distinction without a difference) is by insisting that only the deserving poor have a claim to appropriate the property of the wealthy, and that they only have such a claim when it rescues them from a desperate state.

If we admit liberty rights to include not only a negative conception of freedom and rights, but also rights to positive freedom, what Gewirth calls additive rights (as opposed to subtractive rights) or the right to well-being, we can defend the right to welfare$_E$. However, to do so may mean not granting the premises of, at least, most libertarian positions.

The problem, I believe, is with a libertarian position that insists that the only (or primary) reason for government is to protect (negative) freedom. Even if, as Sterba claims, some conception of welfare can be derived from such negative freedom alone, that conception is limited to welfare$_S$. But why grant, even for the sake of argument, such a limited view of the reason for society or political association? Why not say that the most (or at least *a* most) fundamental reason for social and political association is to make possible the survival and thriving of dependent persons? This is a reason for social organization as basic as the protection of negative freedom and property (even when the term 'property' includes our own person). From recognizing the fundamental importance of making possible and supporting relations of dependency, we can derive a right to welfare$_C$ and a correlative duty to provide welfare$_C$.

I will develop and argue for a strong conception of welfare, welfare$_C$, one which cannot be reconciled with libertarian principles, even if libertarian principles can be reconciled with the weak sense of welfare that I have called welfare$_s$. However, I do not take this to be a weakness. Rather I take the libertarian conception of political association to be fundamentally flawed, and it is flawed in such a way that women, in particular, fail to be included in its understanding of justice.

Welfare$_c$, "welfarizing" care

Following Walzer, I use the term "welfarize" to denote the process of taking certain key social goods out of exclusively private control by making these goods available to all by law, where the distribution is paid for by public funds. I am arguing for the welfarizing of care, or more exactly, I want to advocate the welfarization of *provision* for care.

In my book, *Love's Labor* (Kittay 1999), I argue that the care of dependents renders the dependency worker "derivatively dependent". The care and attention, the investment of time and one's interests needed to allow a dependent person to survive and thrive makes the dependency worker necessarily neglectful of her own interests. As every parent who has gotten up in the middle of the night to care for a sick child knows, one's own condition, desires, needs are subordinated to attending to the child. To neglect a child's illness can be disastrous – the child can lose important capacities, or life itself. This is especially the case where the child is vulnerable to its caretaker alone, and where the child is too young or ill to help herself.

In nonagrarian societies, caring for a dependent is not compatible with the labor that provides income. To give care to a vulnerable dependent, especially hands-on care, can mean significant sacrifices in employment opportunities, prospects of leisure, health, and so forth. In some contexts, it can mean the full inability to provide even subsistence for oneself and one's dependent. Therefore, the dependency worker is dependent – to some degree or another – on "a provider," that is, on someone, or some institution that will provide income, respite, and attention to the well-being of the caregiver.

As long as women are largely dependency workers and dependency work remains privatized, the progress toward a world shared by men and women in both freedom and equality will elude us. Privatized provision for care keeps women who do dependency work within the power of those (usually men, husbands, fathers, lovers) who serve as providers, giving dependency workers poor exit options and a worse bargaining position in what Amartya Sen calls a "cooperative conflict." Those who attempt to serve both roles, provider and dependency worker, enter the competitive economic arena with a distinct disadvantage. And while highly educated and trained women whose skills command a hefty salary can delegate dependency work to others, those others are generally poor women, often poor women of color, who themselves have familial dependency responsibilities. The burden falls most heavily on women who are poor, lack a good education or highly valued skills, are disabled, and are nonwhite. Given the normative hetero-sexuality presumed in these privatized arrangements, lesbians, transsexuals and gay men pay a heavy price when they undertake dependency responsi-bilities. They garner no benefits of those institutional structures that do support dependency work (family leave, health insurance for family members, etc.). They frequently lack emotional and financial supports from family, understanding from co-workers, legal protections for the relation-ships in which they care for dependents. But even women who are middle class, well educated, and not subject to racism or other forms of exclusion, find that their economic well-being and professional success are impacted by dependency responsibilities.[8]

One of the few programs that did allow care to be publicly funded is the now defunct AFDC. However, it had all the trademarks of welfare$_s$. It was stigmatized, stingy and intrusive. It was dispensed only to destitute persons with dependents. Still, it was guaranteed as an entitlement,[9] and so permitted, to a small degree, the social good of care to escape exclusively private control.[10] The program that replaced it ended the entitlement and added (more) punitive practices.

In what sense is the public provision of care, the welfarization of care, a solution to women's poverty, inequality, and diminished freedom? Can we justify the public expenditures for such care? First, we should notice that care as such cannot be dispensed by a government, a state or any impersonal association. Care has to be given by those who are carers – who have, or have forged, a relationship with those in need of the care. What a nation can do is assure that those who give care and their dependents are provided for and have the full social citizenship of the independent citizen and worker.

Welfarizing care and women's equality

Despite their profound impact on women's freedom and equality,[11] political philosophies rarely concern themselves with the social organization of dependency work and what a just organization of such work might look like. Instead, ideals of self-sufficiency and independence are not only prized, but are taken as the starting point of all inquiry into just social institutions. The liberty that libertarians take to be the primary value takes no note of the essential dependency relations that allow us to bind into a society. In our dependency we need to be cared for by one who, willingly or not so willingly, puts their own liberty on hold in order to tend to our needs. (Think of the adult son or daughter of an ageing parent who falls ill and must be taken care of. Surely, they have a duty to see to it that their parent is taken care of, regardless of whether they wish to have this responsibility. Or consider a person whose long-time spouse or lover has an accident that leaves them brain-injured, develops Alzheimer's disease, or contracts another serious, chronic disease requiring long-term care. Even the spouse who refuses to do the daily care has the responsibility to ensure that their partner is cared for – whether or not they want the responsibility. And in each case, the persons involved have to forego certain liberties in assuming these responsibilities.)

By beginning with our dependency, and recognizing the derived dependency of the dependency worker, we come to see society not as an association of free and equal independent persons who associate to protect their liberty and property, but as a means by which to facilitate the care of vulnerable dependents. The justification of welfare, and even a robust understanding of welfare, grows quite naturally from such a starting point.

To justify welfare means to answer the question, "Why am I obligated to provide for the needs (of a certain sort) for another?" Alternatively, it is to answer the correlative question, "Why do (certain) others have a claim on my resources to meet their needs (of a certain sort)?" The reciprocity of social cooperation is frequently used as an answer to such questions. Hence the requirement that only those who make a *bona fide* effort to contribute to the productivity of a community (at times broadly conceived as the community of human beings) have a legitimate call on its resources. Yet this response supposes the parties involved are symmetrically situated to reciprocate.[12] Not so for the dependency worker and her charge.

In *Love's Labor* I suggest a notion of reciprocity better suited to dependency relations. I term this form of social cooperation *doulia*. I adopt the term from the postpartum caretaker, the doula, who assists the mother who has just given birth, not by caring for the infant as much as by caring for the mother so that the mother can herself care for the infant. The idea is that those persons whose attention and resources are directed to aiding others, those who cannot fend for themselves, also need to be tended to and supported by others. I argue for a *public* conception of doulia (service) by which we acknowledge the social responsibility to care for the caretaker.

In the case of the newborn, this is necessitated by the newborn's need and the mother's neediness in her own care while she devotes her physical and emotional energy – already somewhat depleted in the dependency work that is the nurturing of the fetus in her womb and the delivering of the infant in childbirth – to tending to the utterly helpless newborn. The newborn cannot reciprocate – she cannot say "Mom, take a break, I'll cook up a meal for us while you take a nap." Similarly, during periods of dependency in later life, when we need to be cared for, we are unable to reciprocate at the moment when the caretaker needs sustenance, needs to fetch material resources, etc. Another – those who benefit from the dependency workers' care of dependents, society at large, as well as those more intimately involved – is morally obligated to attend to the caretaker, because, I want to insist, at the heart of our notion of equality is the idea that we are "all some mother's child" – we are each persons who have benefited from the care of another, who have been seen as worthy of the care and attention we require merely to survive, much less thrive as we grow into adults. If another is worthy of my care, it is because I too am worthy of care. This is a notion of fairness and reciprocity that is not, as one commentator has pointed out, dyadic, but involves – at least – a third party, in fact an infinite spiral of relationships that reaches both into our past and projects into future generations. This argues for a collective, social responsibility for the provision of care.

This understanding contrasts to the traditional liberal contractarian position, such as that of Rawls,[13] who writes: "Those who can take part in social cooperation over a complete life, and who are willing to honor the appropriate fair terms of agreement are regarded as equal citizens" (Rawls 1992, 302). Political theorist Mary Shanley (Shanley 1999) writes, "Recognizing how and why contract is inadequate to characterize the ties that bind either family members or citizens to one another and to the state may be the first step in establishing both family (and political) life on firmer and more satisfying ground." Rather than a founding contract, care of dependents has to be seen as sitting at the very center of the relationships that forms not only the family but social order generally, because no society can exist beyond one generation unless its youngest dependents are to survive and mature into adulthood, and no decent society can neglect those who become dependent during the years that intervene between birth and death. Even if we take liberty or autonomy or agency as the hallmarks of personhood, we recognize that the development of free persons, persons who are autonomous and who can be agents, not only will have periods of dependency, but will have had to be nurtured through their first dependency.[14] While women remained within the "private sphere," where dependents were cared for, their hidden labor kept dependency from the purview of political concerns. As women move out into the public arena, the dependency hidden from public view becomes visible and is revealed as having the social dimension it has in fact always had.

Justifying the welfarization of care

Dependency work is work

However, even as dependency concerns become visible, dependency work takes on a new sort of invisibility. The fact that so many women with dependent children are employed, and manage employment and responsibility to dependents, has only reaffirmed the notion that care of dependents is not *work*, and as such does not constitute a social contribution that has the status or legitimacy of paid employment. And dependency work that is paid retains the aspect of what Ivan Illich has called "shadow work" (Illich 1981). That this shadow work is marginal and poorly paid is, I suggest, importantly connected to the fact that it competes with a large pool of unpaid dependency workers.

There is little doubt that the increase of women in paid employment fueled the fires of a welfare reform that eviscerated support for poor women with dependent children. The reigning presumption of welfare reform has been that paid employment and marriage offer women with dependents two acceptable ways of providing for their dependents and themselves. In that case there is no need for Aid to Families with Dependent Children (AFDC), only Temporary Aid for Needy Families (TANF). The new emphasis on workfare sometimes seems as if conservative critics of welfare are in cahoots with old-fashioned feminism which insisted that women's liberation depends on women's entrance into the paid workforce. Yet workfare,[15] as Rickie Solinger (Solinger 1999) has argued, is only really punitive: punishing women for their *in*dependence and for "bad choices," the "choice" to be poor and yet have a child; to be unwed and have a child.[16]

These points bring us to the presumption that familial dependency care is not "work." But why is it not work? It takes time and energy away from activities one might otherwise engage in. It may be done out of love, but so are a host of jobs: being an artist, an athlete, a writer, a professor (all the good jobs). It is socially useful – in fact, indispensable. It is activity that, when paid, is called work. How is it to become recognized as work? The answer seems all too obvious. By paying all who engage in dependency work – whether in a private setting or public setting (we pay educators who educate whether in public schools or private, whether in classrooms or in tutorial settings) – whether it is done by the poor or by the wealthy, and whether it is done out of necessity, duty or love (we continue to pay athletes no matter how wealthy they become and no matter how much they love playing the game).

But who is to pay? The child normally has no resources to remunerate her caretaker; nor often does an adult who is dependent due to illness, disability or the frailty of old age. Yet even in a market economy not all services are subject to market forces. Children who are being educated do not pay their teachers – nor even directly do their parents. (Of course, we should note that libertarians are generally opposed to public education as well.) The education of children, for instance, is understood as a social imperative, whose utility is shared by the entire society; and the responsibility for the provision of education is understood (by all but libertarians) to be as such a social responsibility. How could this be any less true for the care of (inevitable) dependents?

Societal obligations imposed by dependency work

If dependency care is work, it is work where the obligation to do the work derives not from the one who pays the tab, but from one who requires our care. Hence, (1) if the dependency worker is obligated to the dependent, and the dependent is not poised to reciprocate, the compensation due the dependency worker is owed from a provider. And (2) when relationships between the dependency worker, a provider and dependents fracture, the fault line divides the provider from dependency worker and dependent. Too frequently, the dependency worker is left stranded with a dependent and without provision. It is not merely women's perverse socialization, nor their inevitable biology, that makes women cling – often fiercely – to their dependents and their dependency responsibilities, even in the face of economic hardship and social stigma. It is rather the expectations and demands of dependency work that form bonds and obligations strong enough to endure the punishment. Nor would we want dependency work to be done without such relationship.

Dietmut Bubeck (1995) asks us to envision a fully automated society where "sick, old-aged, and disabled people are put into fully automated hospitals and asylums, and where children are brought up by robots." This is "a dystopia" (Bubeck 1995, 28) not only because we don't want to be cared for this way. Even though no-one enjoys cleaning bedpans, the relationship of caring for someone who requires our assistance is deeply fulfilling, and the work develops important human capacities which are basic and foundational.[17]

Moreover, the notion of self-sufficiency and independence derived from paid employment is a chimera. All employment involves some dependency.[18] Waged workers are themselves involved in nested dependencies – they are dependent on an employer who, in turn, is dependent on a market and on a particular configuration of economic structures and forces, such as interest rates, global competition, etc.[19]

Integrating care into a scheme of social cooperation

All the above considerations argue for a social obligation to the dependency worker that extends beyond the private provision to a social obligation for the provision of care. But if privatized provision makes the dependency worker (and, in turn, the dependent) vulnerable to the good will, nonviolence, industry and good fortune of an individual provider (usually a man), why doesn't publicly supported provision simply make the dependency worker beholden to the state – replacing "a man" with "the man", justifying all the intrusions (and maybe more) and surveillance which women currently participating in the welfare system now decry? Indeed, isn't such control and oversight simply the right, even the duty, of an employer?

Using the following diagram (Figure 6.1) may help explain why public provision gives the state no such right, although assuring the well-being of the charge remains a duty of the state.

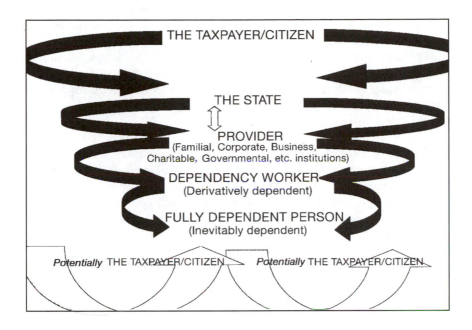

Figure 6.1 Nested dependency: reciprocity as doulia

The innermost core is the fully dependent individual, who may or may not be able to reciprocate at a later time in her life. The contingencies of human vulnerability are such that we can never know if the same individual we assist now will reciprocate our assistance at some point when they are fully functioning, for that time may never come. The obligation to that fully dependent individual sits nested within the scope of responsibilities of the person to whom she is most vulnerable – be it a parent, an adult child, a friend or a paid dependency worker. But the vulnerabilities incurred by the care of a fully vulnerable person create a set of obligations which, in turn, sits nested within the scope of responsibilities of another to whom the dependency worker is most vulnerable. Again, this may be a familial or an institutional relationship. Eventually the responsibility spills out to the larger social order of which the dependent and dependency worker are a part. The taxpayer pays for social programs that reimburse families and dependents; the citizen obligates the state to assure rights and responsibilities to see that care is adequately provided and compensated. But the lines of responsibility or accountability follow the lines of obligation. That is, the dependency worker is both obligated to care for the dependent, and her responsibility is to the dependent – not to the provider. In this respect it differs from ordinary employment. All forms of dependency care have this structure.

Rather than understand social cooperation as reciprocation between equal independent actors, the principle of a public ethic of care, doulia, is a principle that takes reciprocity to involve such nested sets of obligations. Such a principle asserts that insofar as each individual requires a caring relationship with significant others in order to grow, flourish, and survive or endure illness, disability, and frailty, the following hold:

> First, it is a social responsibility to support those relations in which individuals can be cared for while in a state of dependency that is inevitable by virtue of age, disability or illness.
>
> Second, social institutions must foster an attitude of caring and a respect for care by enabling caregivers to do the job of caretaking. Such enabling requires provision of the material conditions needed to sustain the caregiver and the dependent and/or by enabling the caregiver, to compete fairly within the marketplace by making available high-quality care for dependents, so that entrance into that competition does not jeopardize the caregiver or the caregiving.

What such a principle does *not* say is that each and every one of us must be engaged in dependency work. However, it does require that each and every one of us must share the responsibility for the cost (in the larger sense of the term) of dependency work, now too often borne by those who engage in it. And it also requires that both those who are dependents and those who engage in dependency work be ensured rights aimed at protecting carers from harm as they fulfill their obligations to care.

The vision: what would a welfarized care and a caring welfare look like?

In this paper, I have sketched a theoretical framework that justifies a robust conception of welfare, one which entitles each of us to care for our dependents both as a fundamental societal interest and as a fundamental social right. Such an interest and right requires both legal protection and conditions that enable one to fulfill one's responsibilities to care. Not only do these arguments justify public expenditure for poor women to raise their children, but they justify de-privatizing the provision of care for all who care for dependents. Basic to such a conception of welfare is the remuneration (both just and adequate) for all forms of dependency work, as well as high-quality substitute arrangements that can be purchased in lieu of doing the dependency work oneself. Equally central is a respect for dependency work that is evinced by properly training citizens for dependency work, and acknowledging the special skills involved in doing such work extrafamilially.

We need protections against the special vulnerabilities of dependency work. For example: income sufficient to leave abusive relations, retraining when familial dependency care is no longer needed, time off in the case of caring for severely and profoundly disabled family members, a recognition of the importance and nonfungible nature of those who stand in a relation of dependency to one another, a workplace more adapted to workers' familial dependency concerns, and the assurance that if we are unable to provide care to one who depends on it, that care will still be provided.[20]

Care of dependents not only needs to be valued as work, but as highly valued work. No other human activity expresses so well or so completely the imperatives of social cooperation that draw us into social and political association. Justice can only be realized if those who attend to such vulnerabilities are not excluded from the sharing of power, where we understand power to include political, economic and social resources. Throughout our history, such exclusion has been standard practice. Such exclusion goes unnoticed in political theories in which inevitable human dependency is not highlighted.

Libertarian theories cannot put dependence at the center, for dependents and dependency workers are poor exemplars of the negative right to liberty. When you are a dependency worker and the life or fundamental well-being of your charge rests with you, the exercise of liberty is only as useful as it enables you to carry on your duties to your charge. Many other social goods seem at least as significant. In addition, your own liberty is highly constrained by an urgent moral obligation to another. When you are too ill or too frail to survive, much less thrive without the offices of another to satisfy even the most basic of needs, many rights appear to trump liberty rights. John Hospers writes that we have no right to enlist others to our aid (Hospers 1982). Yet if the dependent had no such claim on another, dependents would not survive, and the world would have no humans in its future. Perhaps Hospers supposes that all caring labor is done "voluntarily." But how many persons who do familial caring, when asked why they do it (especially when it seems above and beyond what the dependent could demand) respond with the reply: "What choice do I have?" The moral obligation that makes the claim on those who are close at hand, who as Goodin (Goodin 1985) says, are vulnerable to your actions, overrides claims to liberty and property for everyone who has the requisite moral sensibility. When society has carefully taught girls and women, but not boys and men, to heed moral promptings of this sort, the collective obligation society has to its dependent persons is discharged through the free or poorly recompensed labor of women, and often men and women of color. Libertarians ignore such matters at the expense of nearly half the population. Women, who have been excluded from the concerns of so many theories of justice, not only the libertarian's, need to claim not only the right to work, but the right to care and to care in such a way that we do damage neither to ourselves nor to those in our charge.

To argue for such a robust sense of welfare may seem to be beside the point when others are trying to convince opponents and skeptics of even a minimal welfare that directs itself to the urgent needs of world hunger and poverty. Yet much of the poverty worldwide, as well as within our own borders, is that of women – women and their dependent children. If welfare$_S$, and the minimal welfare$_E$ that the US serves up, has done such a poor job of eliminating poverty and hunger among its own women and children (most of the adult poverty in the US is that of women, and between one fourth and one fifth of children in the US are poor) how well will it help in nations much poorer than our own? To alleviate poverty, we need to look at who is poor and why they are poor. The poverty of different groups requires different approaches. Looking at the particular needs of the elderly, and so altering social security provision to accommodate their circumstances, significantly alleviated poverty among the elderly. The same must be done for the poverty of women. Women, underrepresented in government, boardrooms, the professorate, and so forth, are overrepresented among the poor. And child poverty is largely a consequence of maternal poverty. Without an appropriate conception of welfare and of who is poor, we cannot begin to address adequately world poverty. Even if we convince our libertarian opponents of the justification for welfare, if we are only arguing for a stingy and stigmatized welfare, we will not make significant headway in bringing about welfare justice. Only a caring welfare can do so.

NOTES

1 Sterba is not alone among philosophers who have made an effort to show that welfare liberalism may be derived from libertarian principles. See Buchanan (1981), who argues for the case on different grounds.

2 This brief rehearsal of Sterba's argument is a bit crude, for Sterba himself distinguishes Spencerian libertarians, who derive all rights from the right to liberty, from Lockean libertarians, for whom liberty is the absence of constraints in the exercise of a fundamental set of rights. My argument against Sterba's accommodation of libertarianism to welfarist claims applies equally and in the same way to both arguments, and so I have taken the liberty of presenting them in this undifferentiated form.

3 The interchange between Sterba and libertarians is cited in Sterba (1998; see notes to chapter 3). For an excellent discussion of the difficulties of reconciling welfarist and libertarian views, including an argument against an earlier version of Sterba's argument, see Sample (1998).

4 See for example Piven and Cloward (1973); Abramovitz (1996).

5 I borrow this example from Goodin (Schmidtz and Goodin 1997).

6 Pateman posits Wollstonecraft's Dilemma as the complement to what Donald Moon (1988) has called "Hegel's Dilemma," that is, that while the redistribution of wealth can mitigate the poverty, such redistribution (through cash transfers or the provision of goods and services in kind) may, on the one hand, undermine a

citizen's sense of participation in community and so undermine the citizen's sense of self-worth. If, on the other hand, the state steps in to create jobs, such action interferes with the autonomous functioning of the market, and so disrupts the machine that generates wealth.

7 See also Fineman (1995).

8 For an account of how the wage gap importantly correlates with having childcare responsibilities more significantly than with gender, see Hewlett (2000). Sylvia Ann Hewlett, a fellow at Harvard's Center for the Study of Values in Public Life, is chairman of the National Parenting Association.

9 TANF still provides cash assistance to destitute persons with dependents, but not as a guarantee to anyone who meets the criteria of need. Time limits, workfare requirements and restrictions regarding citizenship mean that all those in the position of having to care for dependents are no longer guaranteed an income (however stingy). The welfarization of care that was stingily, restrictively, and often punitively meted out to poor women needed to be revamped, but not in the direction of the more restrictive, more stingy and still more punitive legislation that passed as welfare reform. The reform we need moves entirely in the opposite direction.

10 This has, for example, enabled women in abusive relations to leave and know that they will not subject themselves and their children to starvation and utter destitution. The high incidence of domestic abuse among AFDC participants is documented by the McCormack Institute and the Center for Survey Research, who found that among a representative sample of the Massachusetts Transitional Aid to Families with Dependent Children (TAFDC) caseload, 65% would be considered victims of domestic violence by a current or former boyfriend or husband using Massachusetts state law definition of abuse.

11 Notice that I am including not only economic inequality as a consequence of women's major responsibility for dependency work, but am also pointing to the constraint on women's freedom, a point developed in Kittay (1996) and again in Kittay (1999).

12 See Gewirth (1996) for an interesting discussion of the difference between "reciprocity" and "mutuality." Gewirth argues that the concept of mutuality is a better way to understand the relation between rights-bearing persons, and it is this notion, not reciprocity, that he employs in his discussion of welfare rights. While I agree that "mutuality" is the better concept to employ, it too suffers from the symmetry of reciprocity – a symmetry that does not pertain in the case of dependency relations.

13 In *A Theory of Justice*, social cooperation is characterized in the following way:

> The main idea is that when a number of persons engage in a mutually advantageous cooperative venture according to rules, and thus restrict their liberty in ways necessary to yield advantages for all, those who have submitted to the restrictions have a right to a similar acquiescence on the part of those who have benefited from their submission.
>
> (Rawls 1971, 112)

14 See MacIntyre (1999) for a discussion of a similar point, namely that to become rational moral agents we will have had to pass through a period of dependency when another assumed the virtue of caring for dependents.

15 However, we should not forget that the Personal Responsibility and Work Opportunity Act had as one of its major aims: "strengthening the family." The very first part of the bill is "Title 1 – Reducing Illegitimacy." It begins:

It is the sense of the Congress that:

1   marriage is the foundation of a successful society;

2   marriage is an essential social institution which promotes the interests of children and society as large;

3   the negative consequences of an out-of-wedlock birth on child, the mother, and society are well documented as follows: ...
(104th Congress, *HR. 4*, "The Personal Responsibility Act")

16 In fact, with beautiful irony, some conservative critics even worry that were workfare to really succeed in making women with dependents self-sufficient, it would undermine the goal of strengthening the family. Horn and Bush (1997), for example, state:

Rather than simply helping single-parent households figure out a way to generate earnings in the absence of a father, state reforms must find ways to bring more fathers back into (or into for the first time) the lives of their children.

They continue:

The problem is that strategies for promoting fatherhood and marriage are, to a very large extent, in conflict with those that seek to help single mothers achieve self-sufficiency through work. Indeed, a welfare system that helps single mothers become employed, but ignores the need to promote fatherhood and marriage, may serve only to enable unmarried women to rear children without the presence of the father.

I do not mean to ignore the importance of men in the lives of young persons growing up, nor the importance of men engaging in nurturing work. However, to think that the only way to achieve this end is for women to marry, and to do so to avoid impoverishment, is a failure of imagination and political will.

17 Mary L. Shanley, "Comments on Love's Labor," delivered at the Working Group on Law, Culture and the Humanities, Wake Forest Law School, Winston-Salem, North Carolina, March 1999.

18 Even Locke, in the *Second Treatise of Government*, acknowledges our inextricable interdependency when he adduces the extent and variety of the labor that goes into even a humble loaf of bread:

For it is not barely the ploughman's pains, the reaper's and thresher's toil, and the baker's sweat [that] is to be counted into the bread we eat; the labor of those who broke the oxen, who digged and wrought the iron and stones, who felled and framed the timber employed about the plough, mill, oven, or any other utensils, which are a vast number requisite to this corn. ... It would be a "strange catalogue of things that industry provided and made use of, about every loaf of bread" before it came to our use, if we could trace them: iron, wood, leather, bark, timber, stone, bricks, coals, lime, cloth, dyeing drugs, pitch, tar, masts, ropes, and all the materials made use of in the ship that brought any of these commodities used by any workmen to any part of the work; it would be almost impossible, at least too long, to reckon up.

(Locke 1976 [1690] p. 26)

19 Even the possibility of wages that are sufficient to meet the needs of families depends on the establishment of a floor on wages, which is importantly maintained by the existence of welfare benefits that assure potential workers that they do not have to sell their wages below a certain price in order to survive. Therefore, the very possibility of maintaining wages at a level where a family can be self-supporting depends on structures whereby some persons are not self-supporting in this sense.

20 More can be said, but I refer you to a document produced by feminist academics and activists, WC100/Project 2002 entitled "An Immodest Proposal for Ending Women's Poverty," in *Sojourner: The Women's Forum*, May, vol. 25, no. 9, and found on http:www.welfare2002.org.

References

Abramovitz, M. (1996) *Regulating the Lives of Women*, Boston MA: South End Press.

Bubeck, D. (1995) *Care, Gender, and Justice*, Oxford: Clarendon Press.

Buchanan, A. (1981) "Deriving Welfare Rights from Libertarian Rights," in P. G. Brown, C. Johnson and P. Vernier (eds) *Income Support: Conceptual and Policy Issues*, Totowa NJ: Rowman & Littlefield.

Fineman, M. A. (1995) *The Neutered Mother, the Sexual Family and other Twentieth Century Tragedies*, New York: Routledge.

Gewirth, A. (1996) *The Community of Rights*, Chicago: University of Chicago Press.

Goodin, R. (1985) *Protecting the Vulnerable*, Chicago: University of Chicago Press.

Hewlett, S. A. (2000) "Have a Child, and Experience the Wage Gap," *New York Times*, 16 May, p. 23.

Horn, W. and Bush, A. (1997) "Fathers, Marriage, and Welfare Reform," Hudson Institute Report, March 1997.

Hospers, J. (1982) "Libertarianism and Legal Paternalism," in T. R. Machan (ed.) *The Libertarian Reader*, Totowa NJ: Rowman & Littlefield, 135–44.

Illich, I. (1981) *Shadow Work*, Boston MA: Marion Boyars.

Kittay, E. F. (1996) "Human Dependency and Rawlsian Equality," in D. T. Meyers (ed.) *Feminists Rethink the Self*, Boulder CO: Westview Press.

——(1999) *Love's Labor: Essays on Women, Equality and Dependency*, New York: Routledge.

Locke, J. (1976) [1690] *The Second Treatise of Government*, Indianapolis: Bobbs-Merrill.

MacIntyre, A. (1999) *Dependent Rational Animals: Why Human Beings Need the Virtues* (Paul Carus Lectures, 20th series), LaSalle IL: Open Court Publishing Company.

Moon, D. J. (1988) "The Moral Basis of the Democratic Welfare State," in A. Gutman (ed.) *Democracy and the Welfare State*, Princeton NJ: Princeton University Press, 27–53.

Pateman, C. (1988) in A. Gutman (ed.) *Democracy and the Welfare State*, Princeton NJ: Princeton University Press, 231–60.

Piven, F. F. and Cloward, R. A. (1973) *Regulating the Poor: The Function of Public Welfare*, New York: Pantheon.

Rawls, J. (1971) *A Theory of Justice*, Cambridge MA: Harvard University Press.

——(1992) *Political Liberalism*, New York: Columbia University Press.

Sample, R. (1998) "Libertarian Rights and Welfare Rights," *Social Theory and Practice*, 24, 3, fall, 393–418.

Schmidtz, D. and Goodin, R. E. (1997) *Social Welfare as an Individual Responsibility: For and Against*, New York: Cambridge University Press.

Shanley, M. L. (1999) "Revisiting 'Marriage Contract and Social Contract,' " unpublished manuscript, New York.

Solinger, R. (1999) "Dependency and Choice," in G. Mink (ed.) *Whose Welfare?*, Ithaca and London: Cornell University Press, 7–35.

Sterba, J. P. (1998) *Justice for Here and Now*, New York: Cambridge University Press.

Walzer, M. (1983) *Spheres of Justice*, New York: Basic Books.

7

LIBERALISM AND FREEDOM

John Deigh

I

It is a commonplace of intellectual history that what chiefly separates the political thought of the moderns from that of the ancients and the medievals is a concern with individual freedom. Rousseau, in the most famous line from the *Social Contract*, expressed this concern brilliantly when he wrote, "L'homme est né libre et partout il est dans les fers."[1] One can only marvel at how much of modern political philosophy Rousseau crystallized in these twelve words. It is the birthright of every human being to be free, and it is the task of political philosophy to find an arrangement of the institutions and practices of political society that will secure this right for each of its members. A society that falls short of this ideal is an unjust society. It denies some of its members this right. It keeps them in chains.

Liberalism is the tradition that we most closely identify with the search for this ideal. Its hallmark is the defense of individual liberty against various forms of tyranny that are justified and prosecuted in the name of some other, allegedly higher ideal: higher, its proponents will argue, because it is of greater importance in the grand scheme of things than the life of an individual, or because it is of greater importance than liberty to an individual's life. Liberalism opposes all such claims, and it has been the primary bulwark against the authoritarian, totalitarian, and supremacist programs to which they give rise. At the same time, though liberalism is first among movements and theories of modern political thought in its concern with individual liberty, the concern is not exclusive to it. Anarchism too, in some of its forms, springs from this concern. And it is also a principal theme in Marx's early writings, the essay "On the Jewish Question," the *Economic and Philosophical Manuscripts of 1844*, and *The German Ideology*.

Of course, there are large disagreements across these movements and theories, not only about what interferences with action count as violations of individual liberty, but also about the very notion of individual liberty: whether it is an essentially negative notion, as Hobbes argued, or has some positive element in it, as Rousseau thought. What is more, large disagreements on these questions exist within liberalism itself. The dispute between libertarians and welfare state liberals that resurfaced a quarter century ago in the United States and Britain with the return to popularity of anti-government politics is perhaps the foremost example.[2] It defined one of the major splits within the British Liberal party in the late nineteenth and early twentieth centuries, divided as the party was between its traditional and radical wings. The former contained the classical or *laissez-faire* liberals for whom, following Locke, individual liberty was secured for all by instituting limits on the powers of government so as to protect private, voluntary transactions from government interference. The latter contained the reform liberals for whom, following T. H. Green, individual liberty was secured for the members of the weaker classes by protecting them from falling into servitude and wage slavery as a result of their poverty and ignorance. The reform liberals' program called for the government to interfere with contracts between workers and owners of private businesses in the interests of the former, and it thus put the reform liberals at loggerheads with the traditional wing. The earliest legislation that the reform liberals successfully got enacted included restrictions on the hours that a business owner could employ women and children, and requirements that a business owner maintain a safe and sanitary workplace. It also included compulsory education laws, which at the time were seen as interfering with the freedom of parents to contract with business owners for the labor of their children.

The reform liberals, it is important to keep in mind, endorsed such legislation on the grounds that it was necessary for securing individual liberty for the workers and their children in whose interests these laws were enacted. They could not have advocated it as part of a liberal program otherwise. That it was necessary for meeting these people's basic needs, for instance, would not have been a distinctly liberal basis for the laws, since that would be consistent with the illiberal regime of *noblesse oblige*. How they saw the laws as securing individual liberty for these workers and their children is therefore crucial to understanding the grounds of welfare state liberalism, since later reforms that are even more distinctive of this political program, reforms such as those achieved through laws establishing a minimum wage, entitlement to compensation for on-the-job injuries, and unemployment and old age insurance, had a similar justification.

Green's important lecture on liberal legislation supplies the key argument.[3] In brief, Green's argument was that individual liberty is realized only through the development of those human faculties by whose exercise men and women could "make the best of themselves," and such development is not possible in the conditions of poverty and ignorance to which British factory workers, railway workers, miners and their families seemed condemned as a result of being left on their own to sell their labor to the owners of private businesses. In these conditions, Green argued, workers were ruled by their primitive desires and inclinations. They lacked the maturity of judgment and strength of character essential to realizing a fully human existence, and consequently their actions were closer to mere animal behavior than to the conduct of a truly free agent. Merely removing legal constraints on their conduct so that they might act on their desires and inclinations as they pleased, Green pointed out, would not enable them to advance beyond such an impoverished life and limited selfhood. Rather, such advancement required positive action by the state. It required the state to create the conditions necessary for their developing those faculties without which a human being could not enjoy the blessings of individual liberty.[4]

J. S. Mill's influence on Green's thought is apparent in this argument. The argument's appeal to the development of our distinctively human faculties echoes Mill's own appeal to self-development in chapter 3 of *On Liberty*. Mill, of course, was concerned with how custom and popular opinion worked to stunt such development and crush its expression in a man or woman's individual personality, and the argument at the heart of *On Liberty* is an argument for absolute freedom of purely personal conduct, freedom to live one's life by one's own lights and plans, as a necessary condition for self-development and the individuality that results from it. He was not then concerned with how economic forces could work to prevent people from developing their intellectual and moral powers. In particular, he was not concerned with how such forces could keep people who lacked independent means – manual laborers, tenant farmers, their families, and the like – indigent and without hope of bettering themselves or improving the lives of their children. Nonetheless, there is no reason to suppose that one could not remake Mill's argument into one that applied to the circumstances of the indigent, or that doing so would violate its spirit. There is nothing, that is, in Mill's argument that opposes an analogous argument in support of state regulation of economic forces for the purpose of creating conditions in which people otherwise at the mercy of those forces, and thus reduced to a cruel and brutish existence, could develop their intellectual and moral powers and realize a more distinctively human life. In this way, one can see Green's argument as just such an extension of Mill's.

Unlike the original, however, Green's argument was meant to support political action that collided directly with the politics of classical liberalism. Green, that is, unlike Mill, had this clash in mind in developing the argument of his lecture, and to emphasize it, he explicitly defined a notion of individual liberty in contradistinction to the notion favored by the classical liberals. True freedom, Green declared, was a positive power or capacity to act in pursuit of morally and socially worthy ends.[5] It was not merely freedom from constraint or compulsion, not merely freedom to do as one pleased. Accordingly, in presenting his argument, Green set the positive liberty whose conditions were forwarded by the reform liberals' political program in opposition to the merely negative liberty whose security was the uppermost concern of classical liberal thought, and having set up this opposition, he then maintained that only the former met the ideal of human freedom.

Does this show that Green in fact did more than merely extend Mill's argument? Does it show that he went beyond its terms? It would be easy to think that he did, since the principle of liberty that Mill defended in his essay plainly concerns negative liberty. Yet this thought would be a mistake. While it is true that the principle Mill defended concerns negative liberty, the argument he gave in its defense is that its realization in society is a necessary condition of the development and exercise by individuals of powers and capacities of the kind Green identified with positive liberty. Hence, Mill too can be read as making the advancement of positive liberty the ultimate appeal in his argument.[6] To be sure, Mill himself did not speak of positive liberty or identify liberty with any set of powers or capacities. But his reliance on a similar ideal of human freedom as the one Green endorsed is unmistakable. It is evident, for instance, in such theses and remarks from chapter 3 of *On Liberty* as that human well-being requires the development and exercise of capacities for making choices that express one's individuality, that "the proper condition of a human being, arrived at the maturity of his faculties, [is] to use and interpret experience in his own way," and that "individual spontaneity" must be seen "as having intrinsic worth ... and deserving ... regard on its own account."[7] As several recent commentators have noted, the ideal to which Mill appeals is what we now commonly refer to as autonomy, and autonomy on our common understanding of it is a form of self-command or self-determination and therefore a form of positive liberty.[8]

Green's argument, by invoking a distinction between positive and negative liberty, thus explains how the reform liberals kept individual liberty at the forefront of their politics while rejecting the doctrines of classical liberalism that called for the immunity of private, voluntary transactions from state interference. The explanation, though, is open to being misunderstood. The language of positive and negative liberty is notoriously imprecise and cannot alone serve to capture the difference between the notion of individual liberty that gave impetus to the reform liberals' political program, and the notion that defined these core doctrines of classical liberalism. After all, even Locke, whose political philosophy is the most authoritative source of these doctrines, did not consider individual liberty to be merely negative. He neither took it to be the absence of compulsion and constraint, nor identified it with freedom to do as one pleased. Liberty, Locke declared early in the *Second Treatise*, is not license.[9] One does not exercise it simply by doing what one wants or desires. To the contrary, its exercise requires that one act under the direction of reason, which Locke understood to be the direction of laws that one can know only through reason.[10] The point of course is not that Locke too should be read as a theorist of positive liberty. It is rather that the disagreement between reform and classical liberals over the ideal of human freedom is much richer than the simple opposition between positive and negative liberty suggests.

Classical liberals are concerned with the distribution of individual liberty under the rule of law. Locke's distinction between liberty and license reflects this concern. For Locke, the rule of law is in the first instance the rule of reason as informed by the Natural Law. Accordingly, Locke connected liberty with actions done in the light of reason, for he understood liberty as something only people who are capable of acting under the guidance of law can enjoy. Specifically, his view was that liberty is something one exercises in voluntary actions, actions that proceed from one's volitions, and volitions are formed through rational thought about one's circumstances. Actions done, unthinkingly, on impulse or from some overwhelming desire, do not proceed from the actor's volitions and therefore, no matter how happily the actor does them, are not exercises of liberty. Locke likened such actions instead to the actions of beasts, who, because they lack reason, are incapable of acting under the guidance of law and are thus incapable of acting voluntarily. The general idea, which his theory presents and which other strands of classical liberalism endorse, is that the enjoyment of liberty is the special privilege of human beings who qualify as legally competent actors by virtue of their capacity for voluntary action. They, then, enjoy liberty to the extent that they exercise this capacity and are not coerced by others. The main agent of such coercion is of course the state, and hence the enjoyment of liberty chiefly depends on the reasonableness and justice of the state's laws. Here, then, is the nub of the classical liberals' defense of liberty: the voluntary actions of individuals must be protected from the state's use of its coercive power in ways that are neither reasonable nor just.

The reform liberals, by contrast, did not regard all voluntary actions as exercises of individual liberty. They did not think the enjoyment of liberty consisted in acting from volitions formed in uncoercive circumstances. In their view, it depended on how those volitions or, as they would say, choices, were formed. To be sure, a person is not free if their actions are coerced. But in addition, they maintained, a person is not free if their actions proceed from choices they make as a result of general ignorance, weak-mindedness, uncritical or naive beliefs, addictions to crude or infantile pleasures, or the steady undercurrent of fear and anxiety that comes with living in severely deprived or hostile circumstances.[11] Thus the reform liberals, by taking a person's enjoyment of individual liberty to depend on how the choices from which their actions proceed are formed, advanced a notion of individual liberty that presupposed complexity and depth to human psychology significantly greater than what the classical liberals' notion implied or what classical liberals, in their defense of liberty, entertained.

In this respect, the simple, seventeenth-century faculty psychology that informs Locke's theory is telling. On this basically Cartesian psychology, the human mind is constituted by two principal faculties, understanding and will, which operate on the sensory and affective experiences to which it is subject, transforming them into opinion and action.[12] One exercises one's understanding in interpreting the experiences and judging their practical import, and then, on the basis of these judgments, one exercises one's will in forming the volitions from which one's actions proceed. What is missing from this psychology is any mention of character or individual personality as a factor in the formation of volitions. And the reason why is clear. The psychology is too simple. It lacks the conceptual resources necessary for understanding a person's volitions as determined, at least in part, by their character or personality. *A fortiori*, it lacks the conceptual resources necessary for understanding a person's voluntary actions as reflections of strengths or weaknesses in their character or as reflections of their having a more or less well-ordered personality. Hence, any notion of individual liberty that includes the idea that a person is freer to the degree that their character is sound, their personality well ordered, which is to say, to the degree that they are in command of their opinions and actions, entirely escapes its grasp. What it supports is a notion that makes acting at the direction of one's volitions and in the absence of coercion the test of liberty, and thus suits a political philosophy that takes the reach of the state's coercive laws as the main measure of individual liberty. On such a philosophy, the degree to which a person exercises self-command in the formation of their volitions never enters the picture. The classical liberals' unconcern with how a person's volitions are formed is well expressed by Locke's famous assertion that "person" is a forensic term.[13]

The difference, then, between the notion of individual liberty that gave impetus to the reform liberals' political program, and the notion that supports the core doctrines of classical liberalism, is traceable to a difference in the way an individual's will is conceived. The latter notion is supported by a conception of the will as a basic human faculty distinct from other basic human faculties such as understanding and feeling. The former, by contrast, follows from a conception of the will as a synthesis of various faculties and capacities that a person exercises in making choices and that help to constitute their personality. This difference in conception of the will corresponds, then, to a difference in how particular exercises of the will are understood. On the conception of it as a basic faculty distinct from other basic faculties, particular exercises are likewise understood as distinct, basic mental acts, and the term "volition" is the appropriate quasi-technical one for such acts. On the conception of the will as a synthesis of various faculties and capacities, particular exercises are understood as mental processes that combine a number of different mental operations, rather than as individual mental acts. Accordingly, the use of the word "volition" as a quasi-technical term ceases to be appropriate, and the language of choice and decision-making, which is better suited to the idea of a process involving the exercise of various faculties, is favored instead. The point rings clearly in Mill's emphatic description of the faculties that are called upon in making a personal choice of a life plan.

> He who lets the world, or his own portion of it, choose his plan of life for him has no need of any other faculty than the ape like one of imitation. He who chooses his plan for himself employs all his faculties. He must use observation to see, reasoning and judgment to foresee, activity to gather materials for decision, discrimination for decision, and when he has decided firmness and self-control to hold to his deliberate decision.[14]

This shift from the language of volitions to that of choices and decisions marks a recovery of Aristotelian ideas about human psychology. For Aristotle's psychology, unlike the Cartesian psychology that Locke had adopted, does not include a basic faculty of the will whose exercise is the source of all voluntary actions. Rather, on Aristotle's psychology, voluntary actions – more exactly, those actions that would count as voluntary on a Cartesian psychology – follow from the actor's deliberative choices, and the actor comes to these choices through the exercise of various intellectual and moral capacities.[15] In this psychology, unlike Locke's Cartesian psychology, a person's deliberative choices issue from the complex of intellectual and moral capacities that forms his character. They do not issue from a separate, basic faculty for producing voluntary actions. There is no such faculty. The complexity of the human soul, on Aristotle's psychology, contrasts strikingly with its simplicity on that of Descartes.

The recovery of Aristotelian ideas in the philosophy that inspired the reform liberals' program is evident in another way as well. For the necessity of the development of the intellectual and moral capacities to the realization of one's humanity is also a central theme in Aristotle's thought. On his theory, the development of these capacities, when full and balanced, yields the moral and intellectual excellences that constitute the ideal the theory seeks to establish, and this ideal is entirely consonant with the ideal of human freedom expressed in the arguments from which the reform liberals drew inspiration. The influence of Aristotle's ideas about human psychology on the argument of chapter 3 of *On Liberty*, though perhaps not direct, is nonetheless substantial. Their influence on Green's thought is no less profound. The understanding of individual liberty that these thinkers advanced and that gave impetus to the reform liberals' program, the program on which welfare state liberalism was founded, arises out of these Aristotelian ideas. And in contemporary political thought, the same understanding has now resurfaced in the capabilities approaches of Amartya

Sen and Martha Nussbaum, each of whom has pressed it in the service of advocating liberal reforms to economic and political policies in international development.[16]

II

Contrary, then, to popular belief, the philosophical dispute between classical and welfare state liberalism did not originate in the Harvard Philosophy Department in the 1970s. This belief or something like it has contributed to the misconception of the dispute as a quarrel between liberals who love liberty and liberals who love equality. It is a misconception because, as Sen has instructively pointed out, the opposition between liberty and equality it assumes is a false dichotomy.[17] Classical liberals, no less than welfare state liberals, value equality in the possession of liberty, just as welfare state liberals, no less than classical liberals, value individual liberty. Both are champions of equal freedom; both maintain that everyone has an equal right to be free. They differ, as our review of the arguments of the political program on which welfare state liberalism was founded makes clear, in how they conceive of individual liberty and in what they count as its violation. And they do not necessarily differ in their support for equality in the distribution of other social goods, except insofar as such distribution is necessary for securing equal individual liberty. Or in other words, any difference in their support for equality in the distribution of other social goods, except insofar as such distribution is necessary for securing equal individual liberty, is inessential to understanding the difference between them.

The essential difference between them, therefore, is not reflected in disputes, such as that between Rawls and Nozick, over whether distributions of wealth in a society must, to be just, conform to some egalitarian standard like Rawls's difference principle. To be sure, welfare state liberalism, because its conception of individual liberty presupposes self-development – the acquisition of the central human capabilities, to use Nussbaum's helpful term – supports government-enforced transfers of wealth for the purpose of securing for everyone who needs them the goods necessary for developing and exercising these capabilities. But such transfers are consistent with huge disparities in the distribution of wealth. Hence, they are not undertaken to achieve and maintain some egalitarian pattern in this distribution, and transfers of wealth that are undertaken for that purpose should have no place in a liberal political program if they entail loss of individual liberty by those whose estates are reduced by these transfers.

Indeed, one can construct, following Sen's well known criticism of Rawls's account of primary goods, examples supporting this point. Sen's criticism is that Rawls's concern with achieving an egalitarian distribution of primary goods, and so wealth and income in particular, is insensitive to human diversity.[18] The value of those goods varies with the needs and abilities of those who possess them, and thus a transfer of wealth, as required by the difference principle, from someone, A, who was better off as measured by the bundle of primary goods they possessed to someone, B, who was worse off by the same measure, could turn out to impair A's ability to function physically or mentally while merely improving B's bottom line. Hence the transfer would achieve its aim of greater equality in the distribution of wealth at the cost of A's liberty, and no liberal theory of justice should endorse this.

This last point, to be sure, does not immediately apply to Rawls's theory. Rawls, after all, did not follow Green and other reform liberals in rejecting the notion of individual liberty contained in the core doctrines of classical liberalism. To the contrary, he accepted it, and as a result could, by pointing to his doctrine of the priority of liberty, deny that his theory called for imposing losses of individual liberty on some in order to increase the wealth of others.[19] But what this response would do was bring out Rawls's understanding of his theory as one that supports the institutions of the welfare state and at the same time retains, as the sole notion of individual liberty, the notion that is central to doctrines that such liberalism opposes.[20] What it shows, then, is that Rawls, having excluded the possibility of appealing to an ideal of individual liberty to justify the institutions of the welfare state, must turn instead for their justification to an ideal of equality in the distribution of social goods. Thus his theory comes to represent a conception of welfare state liberalism that, in opposition to classical liberalism, endorses an ideal of equality in the distribution of such goods, income and wealth, in particular. And it is reasonable to suppose that the now common understanding of welfare state liberalism, as differing from classical liberalism in being committed to an ideal of equality that comes into conflict with that of individual liberty, arises for the same reason. That is, it arises because of an assumption that the notion of individual liberty informing the latter ideal is the notion contained in the core doctrines of classical liberalism, for given this assumption, one then naturally supposes that to justify the institutions of the welfare state, appeal to the former ideal is necessary.

This understanding of welfare state liberalism, as the discussion of Section I makes clear, departs from the ideas on which the reform liberals grounded their political program. It departs from them, moreover, in two ways. Not only does it incorporate the classical liberals' notion of individual liberty and not the notion the reform liberals favored, it also elevates the ideal of equality in the distribution of social goods to an ideal worth realizing for its own sake. It treats this ideal as a separate standard from that of individual liberty. This separation of the two represents a revision of liberal thought. To be sure, liberalism, whether classical or reform, is an egalitarian philosophy. It bows to no other tradition in its commitment to promoting equal individual liberty for all. At its core is the doctrine that every man or woman has an equal right to freedom. What is more, it promotes equality in the distribution of other social goods wherever inequalities in their distribution threaten some with loss or curtailment of this right. But until recently, liberal thinkers did not regard inequalities in the distribution of such social goods as income and wealth, as injustices independently of their being a threat to human freedom. They did not support measures to make the distribution of wealth in a society more equal simply for the sake of achieving greater equality in its distribution. Liberalism is self-identified as a progressive philosophy. The aim of expanding people's individual liberty is a progressive aim. It is an article of liberal faith that humanity advances through the promotion of freedom for all. The aim of making the distribution of wealth more equal is not, as a final aim, obviously a progressive one. It is not obvious that realizing this aim in itself makes human life better.

The distinction between promoting greater equality in the distribution of wealth as an ideal worth realizing for its own sake and promoting it as necessary for protecting people – the poorer members of society in particular – from loss or curtailment of their right of freedom, is crucial to seeing why the now common understanding of welfare state liberalism represents a fundamental change in liberal thought from the ideas on which the reform liberals grounded their political program. For the distinction explains how the reform liberals could be strong supporters of greater equality in the distribution of wealth without ever regarding contingent inequalities in its distribution as in themselves unjust. It explains, in other words, how the strength of one's commitment to reducing such inequalities need not depend on one's regarding them as inherently bad. One might see them instead as conditions that threaten people's liberty, particularly those whose share of this good is the least bountiful. Hence the crux of the difference between the now common egalitarian understanding of welfare state liberalism and the understanding of the reform liberals, lies in the place in a liberal theory of the ideal of equality in the distribution of wealth, and not in the strength of the commitment to that ideal. The former understanding, because it incorporates the classical liberals' notion of individual liberty, places the ideal in competition with that of securing equal individual liberty for all. The latter, by contrast, places it in a position of support. On the reform liberals' understanding, promoting greater equality in the distribution of wealth advances the cause of freedom.

The key concept in the argument on which reform liberals based this view is the concept of the common good. Human beings, they held, are essentially social. Political societies are not, as some theorists suppose, organizations humans form to escape the dangers and deprivations of a solitary life, and theorists who start with this supposition misconceive political phenomena from the get-go. Conceiving human beings as social, then, the reform liberals understood the intellectual and moral capacities whose development was necessary to enjoying liberty as primarily, though not exclusively, capacities for engaging in social life. Such engagement consists in acting in concert with other members of one's society for the promotion of a common good, a good in which everyone shares, and consequently one's enjoyment of liberty is conditioned on one's living a life in which such activities are prominent, or in which one can see the activities that are prominent as contributing to social good. Green, for instance, identified the objects of such activities with the morally and socially worthy ends in the pursuit of which, he maintained, people developed the powers to make the best of themselves and so achieve freedom. "When we measure the progress of a society by its growth in freedom," he wrote,

> we measure it by the increasing development and exercise on the whole of those powers of contributing to social good with which we believe the members of the society to be endowed; in short, by the greater power on the part of the citizens as a body to make the most and best of themselves.[21]

And again, at the beginning of the next paragraph, he asserted, "Freedom ... [is] the liberation of powers of all men equally for contributions to a common good."[22]

The common good, as the reform liberals conceived of it, comprises the interests of every member of society. In addition, each member's interests contribute equally to its composition. The interests of each, in other words, are equal in weight and worth to those of everyone else. They all count the same, though of course in any given situation the best means to advancing the common good may entail benefiting some members more than others. To live in a society, therefore, in which some members' interests count less than others, in which the laws and customs treat the honor and well-being of some as less worthy of protection and promotion than the honor and well-being of others, and in which the institutions and practices mostly operate for the benefit of some and not others, would be to live in a society in which social engagements did not offer opportunity to act in concert with others in the promotion of the common good. It would be to live under social conditions that were unconducive to one's developing the moral and intellectual powers one needs to engage wholeheartedly in such activities. Hence, on the reform liberals' notion of individual liberty, it would be to live under social conditions unsuited to the enjoyment of such liberty.

Worse still, these conditions would foster types of personality in which the moral and intellectual faculties were arrested in their development, or distorted in ways that crippled their possessors for engagement in social life. The types are well known from history and literature. On the one hand, when a sense of superiority is bred into people as a result of their enjoying from birth institutional privileges from which others are excluded, the upshot often is to create in them an inner need to see those they regard as beneath them supplicate and suffer. Having a sense of superiority, they need to have it confirmed in the behavior of their "inferiors," and under the pressures of this need they develop dependencies that leave them excessively self-involved and unfree. On the other, when people come to see themselves as inferior to others as a result of being excluded from institutional privileges that those others enjoy, they can easily fall into states of humility and subservience that leave them without initiative, and prey to the control and manipulativeness of others. Alternatively, though, if they retain a sense of their own worth, they may then be consumed by an anger that, because it would be imprudent to vent it on the distant keepers and beneficiaries of the institutions that oppress them, is displaced onto local objects in destructive and self-destructive ways. In either case, the conditions of caste and exclusion give the members of the lower caste little chance of developing the energetic and balanced personalities on which the enjoyment of individual liberty depends.

The reform liberals' program thus included legislation intended to root out entrenched privilege from society's institutions and practices. Male privilege and class privilege, in particular, were both objects of reforms eliminating barriers to the participation in public life by women and the lowborn, and to their occupation of positions of advantage and influence in social and economic affairs. And efforts at establishing state provision of free, universal education were likewise aimed at eliminating the entrenched privileges of sex and class. All of these efforts were backed by the analyses of such privilege as creating conditions hostile to freedom, as denying those condemned to social and political inferiority the opportunities necessary for self-development, and as also productive of disordered personalities that left their possessors unhappy and unfree. Thus Hobhouse, writing about liberalism's dismantling of "those restraints on the individual which flow from the hierarchic organization of society, and reserve certain offices, certain forms of occupation, and perhaps the right or at least the opportunity of education generally, to people of a certain rank or class," could declare, "Once more the struggle for liberty is also, when pushed through, a struggle for equality."[23]

By extension, then, the same analysis can apply to large disparities in the distribution of wealth within a society. Because such disparities can take on the character of class divisions, they too can be a threat to individual liberty. Where wealth so influences the operations of society's institutions as to cause them to deliver disproportionately more benefits to those with large estates than to those with modest ones, and where it so influences legislation and social convention as to have the laws and customs of society tailored to treat wealthier people as worthy of greater protection of their honor and promotion of their well-being than the less wealthy, the same conditions deleterious to individual liberty arise as are created by entrenched privileges of sex and class. And where, as a result of these distortions in the workings of the society's institutions and practices, laws and customs, the wealthier members are encouraged to see their good fortune as a badge of superiority and the poorer ones to see their comparative lack of wealth as a social stigma, the same types of disordered personality, the same social pathologies, arise within these populations. Consequently, efforts at curbing disparities in the distribution of wealth so as to keep them from becoming so large or pronounced as to create social conditions unsuitable to the enjoyment of individual liberty, became part of the reform liberals' program. A prime example, precisely because of the privileged character of inherited wealth, was legislation imposing stiff inheritance taxes on large estates.

It is the corruptive power of wealth when amassed by private individuals, therefore, the tendency of concentrations of great wealth in private hands to take on the trappings of aristocracy, that justify, on the reform liberals' theory of the welfare state, efforts at curbing large disparities in the distribution of wealth. This threat of corruption is most serious when it centers on public institutions, a point of particular importance on the reform liberals' theory. On their theory, public institutions, above all, must work and be seen to work in ways that count everyone's interests as equal, for these institutions, more than any others, afford citizens the most direct and fundamental opportunities for acting in concert with other citizens in the promotion of their common good. These institutions, that is, more than any others, afford citizens with the most direct and fundamental opportunities for engaging in the kind of activities through which individual liberty is realized. Thus disparities of wealth must not be allowed to become so large as to enable wealthier citizens to use their greater wealth to influence the workings of these institutions, in ways that tilt the results to their advantage and to disadvantage of poorer citizens. They cannot be allowed to become so large as to enable them to use their wealth to increase significantly the prospects of electing officials who will act in their special interests, to induce lawmakers directly to shape legislation in ways more favorable to those special interests, or to harness the power of the courts in the service of those interests. Such uses of wealth, the tendency to which is perhaps inevitable in its amassing, destroys the common good as an end, toward the promotion of which citizens can see themselves acting through their participation in these institutions.

Rousseau, in the *Social Contract*, offered that wealth should not become so unequal in its distribution as to enable a wealthy citizen to buy a poor one.[24] He did not object to such inequality as unjust in itself. He saw it instead as destructive of the General Will and so of the liberty that depends on it. Equality, he said, is an object of legislative interest not because it is good in itself but because liberty cannot exist without it.[25] The reform liberals did not endorse Rousseau's peculiar test for when inequality in the distribution of wealth has become too great to be allowed. They did not make it part of their program. But their ideas and sentiments on the question of how much inequality in the distribution of wealth to allow were otherwise the same.[26]

NOTES

1 "Man is born free and everywhere he is in chains," *Social Contract and Discourses*, trans. G. D. H. Cole (New York: E. P. Dutton & Co., 1950) p. 3.
2 For a deft treatment of this dispute, see James P. Sterba, *Justice for Here and Now* (Cambridge: Cambridge University Press, 1998) pp. 41–76.
3 Lecture on "Liberal Legislation and Freedom of Contract," in T. H. Green, *Lectures on the Principles of Political Obligation*, eds P. Harris and H. Murrow (Cambridge: Cambridge University Press, 1986) pp. 194–212.
4 *Ibid.*
5 *Ibid.*
6 Of course, Mill said that the utility was the ultimate appeal of his argument. But he quickly added, "it must be utility in the largest sense, grounded on the permanent interests of man as a progressive being," and utility in this largest sense can encompass positive liberty. *On Liberty*, ed. David Spitz (New York: W. W. Norton, 1975) p. 12. On this point see Richard Wollheim, "The Ends of Life and the Preliminaries of Morality: John Stuart Mill and Isaiah Berlin," in his *The Mind and Its Depths* (Cambridge MA: Harvard University Press, 1993) pp. 22–38.
7 *On Liberty*, pp. 54–5.
8 See for example Gerald Dworkin, "Paternalism," in *Morality and the Law*, ed. R. Wasserstrom (Belmont CA: Wadsworth, 1971) pp. 107–26; Fred R. Berger, *Happiness, Justice and Freedom: The Moral and Political Philosophy of John Stuart Mill* (Berkeley: University of California Press, 1984) pp. 232–7.
9 *Second Treatise*, §6.
10 *Ibid.*, §57.
11 Perhaps the boldest statement of this idea is found in L. T. Hobhouse's *Liberalism* (Oxford: Oxford University Press, 1964), where he writes,

> It is also possible ... to foster the development of will, of personality, of self-control, or whatever we please to call the central harmonizing power which makes us capable of directing our own lives. Liberalism is the belief that society can be safely founded on this self-directing power of personality.
>
> (p. 66)

12 See Locke, *An Essay Concerning Human Understanding*, book II, chapter 21.
13 *Ibid.*, book II, chapter 27, §26.
14 *On Liberty*, p. 56.
15 On Aristotle's views of voluntary action, see Martha Nussbaum, *The Fragility of Goodness* (Cambridge: Cambridge University Press, 1986) pp. 264–89.
16 See, for example, Amartya Sen, *Inequality Reexamined* (Cambridge, MA: Harvard University Press, 1992) and Martha Nussbaum, *Women and Human Development: The Capabilities Approach* (Cambridge: Cambridge University Press, 2000).
17 *Ibid.* pp. 21–3.
18 *Ibid.*, pp. 79–84.

19 *A Theory of Justice* (Cambridge, MA: Harvard University Press, 1971) pp. 201–5, 243–51. Note that Rawls implicitly repudiates the reform liberals' notion of liberty when he writes (p. 204) that poverty and ignorance reduce the value of their sufferers' liberty but not their liberty itself.

20 Rawls nonetheless avoids a direct clash between the ideal of individual liberty and that of equality in the distribution of social goods, by limiting the former to what he calls basic liberties. These include freedom of speech and assembly, freedom of conscience and thought, the right to vote and hold public office, and so forth. He does not explicitly include freedom of contract among these basic liberties. He mentions "the right to hold (personal) property" but leaves what this right entails unspecified. Nonetheless, his theory as a whole makes it plain that he does not think this right precludes the state's interfering with a person's control over his estate or his labor for the purpose of achieving greater equality in the distribution of wealth and income. His doctrine of the priority of liberty, in other words, does not protect freedom of contract from being interfered with by the state for the purpose of promoting greater equality in the distribution of wealth, and it therefore follows that freedom of contract is not one of the basic liberties. See *ibid.*, p. 61.

21 "Liberal Legislation," p. 199.

22 *Ibid.*, p. 200. See also Hobhouse, *Liberalism*, pp. 67–9.

23 *Liberalism*, p. 21.

24 *Social Contract and Discourses*, p. 50.

25 *Ibid.*, pp. 49–50.

26 I am grateful to Dan Brudney, Eva Kittay, Martha Nussbaum, and Jim Sterba for comments on an earlier draft of this essay.

Virtue ethics and community

8

JUSTICE AS A VIRTUE

Robert C. Solomon

In this essay, I am concerned with justice as a personal virtue. Talking about justice by way of the virtues and moral psychology has two considerable benefits: first, it embeds justice in concrete practices and personalities, rather than leaving it in the abstract as just so much "theory" (accordingly, virtue ethics has sometimes been called a " 'no theory' theory"). And second, it makes justice into something personal, as I think it was for the great thinkers in the history of the subject, beginning with Socrates and Plato and certainly including Aristotle, David Hume, Adam Smith and, looking back and towards Asia, Confucius (I would also add Nietzsche, although what he has to say about justice would be much too complicated for me to get into here).

One might say that justice is one of, or akin to, the moral sentiments. Which is not to say that justice is, as our undergraduates would say, merely "subjective." It is rather to insist that it is inextricable from people and community. It is in this sense "communitarian," and virtue ethics and communitarianism are often considered strongly linked, if not (sometimes) identical. This is easy to understand in the light of Aristotle, and my thesis here might well be called an "Aristotelian" conception of justice. But I don't want to wed myself to Aristotle's particular concerns. Nor do I want to accept his rather antiquated objections to commerce. Nor do I want to suggest any sympathy whatever for the Athenian slave-state social structure in which Aristotle elaborated his *Politics*. Aristotle, of course, is sometimes considered the paragon communitarian, in the innocent sense that his conception of justice simply assumes the role of community in justice. Furthermore, although this is a point that is more often made in criticizing Aristotle, it is the community that determines what sorts of things *count* as just and unjust. But rather than join this attenuated effort to re-classify Aristotle in modern ideological garb, I want to limit myself to his general conception of ethics in terms of the virtues, and of justice in particular as a *social* virtue.

As for communitarianism, I want to distance myself as much as possible from many of the views that parade under this banner, a stance that Alasdair MacIntyre, perhaps the most respected proponent of this kind of view, has also taken. As he puts it, "there are good communities and there are bad communities."[1] To be sure, insofar as communitarian justice is conceived just as the emphasis on "the common good" and traced back to Aristotle, as Jim Sterba conceived of it in his previous work,[2] the notion seems innocent enough. But communitarian justice, insofar as it accepts the primacy of the community over the individual and to that extent undermines the significance of the individual and individual rights, is a conception of justice about which I have grave reservations. It makes no sense except in connection with other people. You might say that justice is a *communal* virtue, but the move I want to resist is the move to predicate justice of communities or societies or, more to the point of my paper, to abstract social systems or schemas, rather than of people and their actions.

To say that justice is a social virtue is to insist, as Confucius says, that as a virtue (*jen*, or humanity) it only makes sense in the context of two or more people. And it is a social virtue for the deeper Confucian reason that it is a virtue that is constituted by social norms, expectations, and practices (*li*, or ritual). It is what Hegel, in opposition to Kant, emphasized as *Sittlichkeit*, an ethics of actual customs and practices as opposed to an ethics of *a priori* rational principles. Where I disagree with Hegel (and agree rather with his critics Schopenhauer and Nietzsche) is in his minimizing the role of what they called "personality" in his conception of justice, or what I am highlighting as the central role of personal virtue. I also think that this is where I disagree most with Sterba and any number of other theorists of justice who would give primacy to impersonal talk over the personal.[3]

Let me very clear about the limits of my claim that justice is a virtue. Kurt Baier, several years ago,[4] distinguished between "strong" or "radical" virtue ethical positions on the one hand, and "weak" positions on the other. Although the Nietzschean in me bristles at the thought of it, my claim here is only of the "weak" variety. That is, I do not, like Michael Slote, for example, take virtue ethics to encompass the whole of ethics, much less the whole of social philosophy. I only claim that considerations of virtue and character are indispensable in discussions of justice, and supplement (not replace) considerations of the public good, obligation, and the like. To be sure, such considerations can and should be built into the conception of a social virtue, but I would not want to put too much weight on that sort of analysis. I do not by any means deny a role for Kantian or Millian considerations. In fact, one might well argue (and it has been well argued) that both Kant and Mill are not-so-closeted virtue ethicists.

My thesis therefore has a complex and not entirely antagonistic relationship to what Sterba has argued in *Justice Here and Now* and many of his other works. I applaud his defense of an anti-gladiatorial way of doing social philosophy, what he calls "peacemaking," but I would add that the peacemaking process can be greatly enhanced if personal feelings and practices are put on the table instead of being veiled in the abstractions of pure theory. Of course, philosophical prejudice goes in exactly the opposite direction, but this suggests several unappreciated intellectual and social virtues, which I would be the first to praise if not always to practice. I also applaud Jim's career-long ambition to establish what he calls "common ground." But is there any such common ground, as Jim tries to argue? I share the doubt that the notion of liberty (as opposed to the notion of rights) of the poor would have much impact on a diehard libertarian, and this isn't because Jim fails to make his case for trans-ideological translation. My doubt consists rather of my thinking that there are real incommensurabilities, and not only on a theoretical or ideological level.

Nevertheless, the real benefit of the virtue approach to justice is that it does not see the field of justice mainly in terms of debates and dilemmas. This was a point well defended by my colleague, the late Edmund Pincoffs, in one of the seminal books on virtue ethics.[5] He argued that too much of the discussions of ethics had focused on ethical dilemmas and bitter disputes, and what was left out was the less dramatic day-to-day behavior of people just going about their jobs and their lives. There need be no conflict in order for a discussion of justice to be perfectly appropriate. And when there are genuine and difficult disputes it is not insignificant to look at the everyday practices and personalities involved, as well as any abstract principles that may have bearing on the issue. The incommensurabilities and seemingly irresolvable conflicts that continue to rivet our attention may depend not just on a clash of principles and conflicts ("rights," "liberty," etc.) but on deeper and more personal considerations and determinations.

David Miller has written an impressive but under-appreciated book about how various "theories" of justice are based on differing social practices.[6] I would only add that they may also be based on different temperaments, both personal and cultural. I suggest that most of us have noticed, however much we resist stereotyping, that folks who pursue one or another of the standard social-political agendas share more than just an ideology, a vocabulary, and a set of philosophical assumptions. To take a familiar example, some anarchists tend to be rebels with an authority problem. I think it is safe, in such cases, to suggest that neither their rebellious temperament nor their anti-authoritarianism has been acquired by way of philosophical argument. Of course, philosophical conversions are of special interest here, and again, if I can appeal to our common experience, the now familiar transformation of late 1960s hippies into right-wing conservatives is something that all of us, whether out of approval or disgust, have tried to explain. What usually underlies such explanations is something along the lines of "he or she was that way all along," where "that way" specifies some personality trait that is continuous through such a socio-political *Bildungsroman*.

I do not intend these brief reflections as any sort of reductionist approach to justice as merely a matter of psychology. My point is rather that justice is grounded (although I have trouble with that metaphor for various reasons) not in reason or in the murky crucible of "highest values" but in particular social and personal practices, circumstances and the second-nature responses and feelings they engender. One of these often neglected ingredients in our various conceptions and practices of justice is *trust*. Trust plays an often unacknowledged role in how we conceive of justice. To put the matter in terms of a blunt hypothesis, the more that one trusts one's fellow citizens, the less important abstract schemes of justice become. The less one trusts one's fellow citizens, the more important abstract schemes of justice become. This, I suspect, might be a revealing optic from which to read many philosophical theories of justice. It will be, I am sure, an important consideration as we build the so-called global economy. But, to reiterate my main point here, a virtue, the virtue of justice in particular, is a manifestation of the confluence of such social and personal practices, circumstances, second-nature responses and feelings, and these are not irrelevant to our higher-level reflections of justice.

Justice as a personal virtue

> As my grandfather taught, it is not necessary for everyone to sacrifice our lives for others. We [just] need to take a little time from our lives to help.
>
> Arun Gandhi (*Newsweek*, 4 March 1989)

Looking back over the Western tradition in social philosophy, one might well object to calling justice a virtue. Bernard Williams, for example, who has many affinities with Aristotle, has claimed that the very idea of justice as a personal virtue – such as one finds in Aristotle – is a category mistake, an incoherence if not actually an oxymoron or a contradiction in terms. John Rawls, of course, says at the very beginning of his great *Theory of Justice* that justice is "the first virtue of social institutions as truth is of systems of thought." But a virtue of institutions, like the virtue of beta-carotene and vitamin C, isn't what I have in mind. Without getting into the large question about agency in organizations, let me just say that the virtues in question are the virtues of persons, and in *that* sense personal.

There is also a further sense, less obvious but equally central to my thesis, that the virtues are personal insofar as it is necessary for people to *care*, both about their being virtuous and about the situation and circumstances in which their virtues are appropriate. As for Rawls' own considerable virtues, I am afraid that the "virtue" part of his message is too easily lost in the theoretical rigmarole of the Veil of Ignorance and the debate over minimax preferences. This isn't just a matter of distraction. For all of his debt to Rousseau – and I believe that it is a heavy debt indeed and often unacknow-ledged by Rawls' followers – the sense in which justice is a virtue either of institutions or of persons is canceled out, on the one hand, by the blocking of particularities behind the Veil of Ignorance (for what is a virtue if it is not a particularity?) and on the other by Rawls' heavy emphasis on what has often been recognized as the Kantian aspects of his theory (the intimate relation between Rousseau and Kant notwithstanding). We don't get to what Rawls calls "the sense of justice" until page 453, and not surprisingly that sense has more to do with the internalization of the theory that has preceded this belated discussion than it has to do with what Rousseau would have clearly seen as personal virtue.

Nevertheless, none of this is to deny that reason and deliberation are essential to our sense of justice. To put the matter simply and bluntly, the ability and willingness to deliberate and debate is as central to the workings of justice as caring and the right sorts of feelings and practices. Caring can too easily degenerate into that pointless form of pity that Nietzsche so despised, and the moral sentiments without broader understanding can too easily manifest themselves in that obnoxious form commented on by William James, in which a wealthy matron weeps at an Italian opera about the horrors of poverty while her footman freezes to death outside in the snow. Deliberation and reflection are virtues of justice, as Aristotle saw so clearly. It is the synthesis of feeling, habit, thought and conversation (not necessarily debate) that constitutes a just life.

Since Socrates asked "What is justice?" twenty-five centuries ago, philosophical discussions of justice have emphasized the supremacy of rules, reason and rationality, and there has been too little appreciation of the role of the virtues. Plato insists on "harmony" between passions and reason as the hallmark of virtue, although I think that Nietzsche is ultimately right when he accuses Socrates, and with him Plato, of making a "tyrant" out of reason. Rawls, as I said, tends to think of the sentiments as dispositions to act on rational principles, and to this extent seems to view them as inessential in the determination of justice.[7] Of course, such sentiments may enter into the "reflective equilibrium" through which we evaluate our various theories against pre-theoretical intuitions (which Rawls variously describes as "intuitively appealing accounts," "various reasonable and natural presumptions" and "initial convictions"). But Rawls rarely describes these as sentiments as such, and seems to take their affective character simply for granted.

Many other authors, of course, have simply dismissed all such talk of the virtues and the sentiments as mere "sentimentality" and insisted that our personal feelings, such as compassion, only confuse and distort the rational deliberations of justice. Kant famously degrades the various "inclinations" as at best secondary to morality, and sarcastically dismisses "melting compassion" or "tender sympathy" in an infamous passage on the injunction to "love thy neighbor," just as he vigorously rejects any role for vengeance in his retributive account of justice.[8] Nevertheless, Kant had earlier referred to compassion as "beautiful," albeit without "moral worth." I have elsewhere argued that there can be no adequate understanding of justice without an appreciation and understanding of the role of the emotions in general and the moral sentiments in particular, but this stance doesn't make much sense unless one thinks of justice as a personal virtue. In this I am clearly in league with Hume and Smith, both of whom counted justice among the moral sentiments (though they gave them very different status). But I would add that this essential role for the emotions must make room for not only those benign moral sentiments such as sympathy, care and compassion and other "fellow-feelings" but also the nastier emotions of envy, jealousy, resentment and, especially, vengeance. (As much as I enjoy talking about these, I will not do so here.)

One problem with virtue talk is that it tends to be overly individualistic, its origins in philosophers like Aristotle and Confucius notwithstanding. Some of this, no doubt, comes from the moral sentiment theorists of the eighteenth century. Some of it is a spill-over from Kant, who despite his indifference to virtue talk (that is, in the sense of "virtue" intended here), was radically individualist in his ethics, the "Kingdom of Ends" notwithstanding. Much of it, needless to say, comes from our own American obsession with individuality, libertarianism being just one of the more dramatic versions of an ontology that deeply infects every ethical and political position in the United States (and especially in Texas). But to talk about justice as a personal virtue is necessarily to talk about justice as a social virtue and to insist that justice is necessarily two-sided: it is personal in that it is a virtue had and practiced by a person, but it is essentially social in that it has necessarily to do with our responses to and interaction with other people. Aristotle, despite his anti-commercial bias, was clear about this insofar as he insisted that justice is all about fair exchange. To juxtapose justice as a personal virtue against justice as a feature of abstract systems leaves out the central feature of justice, and that is human interaction, including, not least of all, the virtue of *listening* to other people.

I think that Confucius is especially good on this. He distinguishes *jen* or "humanity" and *li* or "ritual," which we (not he) might identify as the "internal" and the "external" aspects of one and the same virtue. The classic Confucian example is filial piety which (*contra* Aristotle) has many affinities with justice. To have the right sorts of feelings for your parents is praiseworthy, but only insofar as those feelings get expressed in actions, in practices that exemplify respect and reverence. But such actions and practices are worthy of praise only insofar as they are "filled" with the right kinds of feelings (not just "putting on a show"). But even to talk in terms of feelings and their outward expression is to distort the phenomenon. Thus Confucius argues that filial piety is not only an attitude, nor even an attitude plus action. It is ontologically a function of two (or more) people, an example of "co-humanity" or "shared humanity" (according to Confucian scholar

Wing-sit Chan).[9] So, too, I want to argue that justice as a personal virtue should not for a moment be considered in terms of some disposition, the "inside" of which is appropriately manifested on the "outside," in behavior. It is both personal and social insofar as the individual is defined and constituted by their role and relationships in the community with other people.

Thus we should not confuse justice with benevolence, nor even with beneficence. In this, I think, Hume was right and Smith wrong (in his description of justice in terms of being pained at the suffering of others). So, to this extent, I would admit that we should resist the temptation to talk about the virtue of justice in terms of feelings, even "compassion" and "benevolence."[10] It is perhaps instructive that Arthur Schopenhauer, no exemplar of the virtues, managed to rest the whole of ethics – in opposition to Kant – on the sentiment of compassion, which he simply characterized as the realization that we're all in the same shit. But Schopenhauer didn't feel compelled to do anything whatever, which he justified on the basis of his *ersatz* Buddhism. If he had studied Confucianism, or Chinese philosophy more generally, it might have been a very different ballgame (I would say the same – in fact, even more so – for Nietzsche). To summarize my position in Chinese, justice requires both *jen* and *li*. That is what makes it a virtue.

Is justice as a virtue "relative"?

Virtue is always and necessarily "relative to" some set of social and personal practices, the circumstances, the culture, and, I would argue, personal and cultural temperaments and experiences. This raises the specter, although its nature is by no means clear, of *relativism*. The not-so-innocent implication is that there may be no ultimate way of adjudicating differences between conceptions of justice, writ large, but, more important in my book, there may be no ultimate way of adjudicating differences in the street-level disagreements over specific acts and practices concerning justice and injustice. Sterba, like almost every other writer on the topic, dismisses relativism as, if not absurd, difficult and implausible,[11] to which my response is, "not so fast." I am often amazed that thinkers like Richard Rorty, for instance, who would seem to be drawn to relativism like the proverbial duck to water, given what else he has argued, nevertheless distances himself from it as much as possible, giving it an interpretation that no-one would want to defend. I am not so amazed that Alasdair MacIntyre similarly distances himself from relativism, given what else he has argued, but nevertheless I think that his argument poking some fun at Donald Davidson's bland Tarskiism (" 'snow is white is true' *iff* snow is white") and his use of the telling example of the different meanings of Londonderry/Doire Columcille (or Al-Quds and Yerusalayim) (*Whose Justice? Which Rationality?*, p. 378) is the best argument for relativism and incommensurability I have ever heard or read.[12]

But relativism, or perhaps just the word, rubs a raw nerve in philosophers (and in some politicians too). I have always tried to understand why. To be sure, the "any view is as good as any other" interpretation is one that no-one could hold for long. And it is indeed a very real question, as Jim asks, "relative to what?" and indeed a person stuck in a conflicted situation – the archetypal example is Huck with Jim in Mark Twain's *Huckleberry Finn* – in which the question of "relative to what?" is by no means a philosopher's challenge but a real-life existential dilemma.[13] Perhaps we, like Twain, can read of Huck's perplexity with a certain amusement, certain as we are that slavery is just plain dead wrong and the subculture in which it was an essential practice and considered legitimate was just plain wrong. But there are all sorts of cases where the moral considerations are not so one-sided, and I do not mean only those over-stressed "contemporary moral problems" such as abortion, euthanasia, the death penalty, and so on.

The question of "human rights" in China is one such case that I would bring up for consideration, in part because it so badly fits into the liberal-libertarian-socialist trichotomy that dominates so much of our discussion. The fact that the Chinese, under considerable international pressure (mainly from the US), have learned to adapt the language of rights in the debate just makes the very real incommensurability of positions all the more trouble-some. To be a relativist is not to conclude *a priori* that such disputes are irresolvable, but to try to understand such confrontations in very different terms without prejudging the inevitability of one side turning out to be right and the other wrong. To demonize relativism is too often a quick step toward insisting on a single "absolute" sense of values and a conclusion, without even for a moment bothering to listen to the other side. I guess I just don't see what's so "moral" about such an absolutist stance. Nor do I see what is so wrong with relativism, so conceived. Again I applaud Jim Sterba's attempt at peacemaking, but I question his ecumenical optimism. Making peace may sometimes consist in just "calling it a draw."

Thus I would argue that because the conception of justice as a social virtue is dependent on communal conceptions and social context, I am (relatively) a relativist on justice. Fairness is not first of all a matter of logic or proportion or equality. It is a function of local expectations, conversation and consensus. This is not to deny the obvious, that in pluralistic cultures (or even in supposedly homogeneous cultures) people seriously disagree, but the disagreements themselves are the product of the culture and its often divergent expectations and conversations. Nor is this to deny – what Martha Nussbaum has been tirelessly campaigning about in recent years – that there are universal values and virtues, not in an *a priori* sense but on the basis of the universal contingencies of the human condition. Nevertheless, what *counts* as justice or injustice and what counts as a serious issue or debate about justice and injustice depends very much on the local situation, the economy, the sociology, the religion(s), the philosophy.

Consider this rather *au courant* example: with the wave of IPO internet stocks and such, there are now a great many twenty-eight-year-old multimillionaires. (Michael Kinsley has coined the phrase "internet envy" to describe the social effects of this.) Is this unjust? Fifty years ago, indeed even twenty-five years ago, it would have been thought so by most Americans. Today? I doubt it. One may lament or celebrate the change in attitudes toward luck, risk, hard work, merit and the vicissitudes of wealth, but it is evident that attitudes have changed, and with that a critical perception of fairness has changed with the culture. Some of this, of course, has to do with scope and perspective. What's wrong with a twenty-eight-year-old multimillionaire by luck? Perhaps nothing, or so the argument goes, if the multimillionaire in question has profited from his own rather ingenious insight or invention (although I am hesitant to include those many small internet fortunes that are based on nothing other than buying up marketable website names).

But even the most avid free marketeer should be somewhat concerned with the lottery aspect of the modern economy, and when one adds to this the fact that nearly a quarter of Americans – and more than 3 billion people worldwide – are living in poverty, the question of justice painfully surfaces. Of course it soon founders on the questions of government intervention and control. What is to be done? Tax the rich? Regulate investing? Eliminate the stock market? Crush capitalism? Urge the poor to invest in start-up companies and IPOs? I don't expect much agreement here, but I just want to note how significantly feelings about justice have changed in only a few years, and that is within an already heavily if not obsessively free market culture.

But what does this have to do with perceptions of justice *as a virtue*? Doesn't this suggest, to the contrary, that justice and injustice are functions of society and its attitudes? Well, no. Society and its attitudes (that is *our* attitudes) do determine what will count as justice and injustice. But the object of our judgments is not so much the overall portrait of the society and its statistics as the behavior of the individuals within that society, and, in particular, the behavior of those twenty-eight-year-old multimillionaires. What is more to the point than the fact of gross inequality and the charges of dubious merit is the shameful fact that most of these young millionaires give virtually *nothing* to charity and have no thought of any obligation to do so. Here is where I want to focus my attention, not on the justice and injustice of institutions or the society as a whole, but on the moral intuitions and practices of people. One might say that the concept of justice has not caught up with the new economics and the new sociology that goes along with it. But I would say that the injustice lies not so much in a new world in which what used to be derided as "speculation" pays off so well and so

177

quickly as it lies in the insensitivity and lack of response of those who enormously profit in that world. This is not to deny that there are unjust social arrangements, of course, but I want to be very very cautious about making them *a priori* so. Were the societies of Nebuchadnezzar and Assurbanipal (better known in the guise of the mythologized Sardanapalus) unjust? Let's not jump to middle-class liberal conclusions.

The same conceptual drama is being enacted on the global stage. Our collective concepts of justice have not caught up with the new economic and technological realities and the new social world. Platonists of all stripes may prefer to think of justice as something that *precedes* any particular social situation, but I would suggest that conceptions of justice and social situations are co-evolving. What is it that remains the same? Nothing but that sentiment of fellow-feeling, and with it the sensitivity to the pain and suffering of others and social practices that reflect (and bring about) the particularities of fellow-feeling and sensitivity in each and every particular culture. The Confucian Chinese have a very different conception of the nature of society and the place of the individual within it than did Scottish industrial society in the eighteenth century. And yet it is remarkable that we find passages in Mencius that could have come right out of Adam Smith, and vice-versa. Concern and caring and the social practices that express them are where any conception of justice starts, and without them, justice is just an empty philosopher's scheme.

Of course, other people's envy is also a sort of suffering, and lest we jump too quickly into an overly saccharine portrait of human nature, let us remind ourselves how hard we work both to cultivate and to defuse envy in others. Communities are not just social arenas of cooperation. They also involve competition and are thereby breeding grounds for envy. One of the problems with so-called communitarianism is its tendency to whitewash communal relations, but justice, surely, means coping with envy just as much as it means sharing with others or having a right to one's own wealth. And how we cope with envy, including our readiness to provoke it in others, has a great deal to do with the virtue of justice. What one envies, however, is almost entirely determined by the particular relations and expectations of the society or culture. Justice, to put the matter overly bluntly, is "relative to" envy, to the particular social and cultural constructions of competition and interpersonal comparison.

Morality versus self-interest: an untenable dualism

One of the main virtues of the virtue approach to justice and to ethics in general is that it pretty much by-passes the opposition that is central to Sterba's concerns, between moral and self-interested conceptions of the good. Jim suggests that the opposition reappears as "different aspects of the self" in Aristotelian ethics, but I think this understates what is most important about the concept of virtue. To be sure, a virtue approach such as Aristotle's does not preclude the possibility of self-interested motivation, which at its most vulgar and anti-social appears as vice. One can still talk of "more or less" as a measure of self-interest along several dimensions (e.g. is it profitable? does it make you feel good? Does it increase your status in the community? Does it increase your power? Does it provide insight or otherwise improve your contemplative understanding?). But in the cases that count for most in discussions of social justice, for instance, giving some of one's goods to others and wielding power over them, the breakdown of the opposition between moral and self-interested conceptions of the good is surely welcome news.

The opposition between morals and self-interest lends itself to enormous abuse, both in philosophy (where it raises all sorts of dilemmas which distract us from worrying about justice) and on the proverbial street, where it inspires much mischief and misunderstanding. How much injustice is due to the rationalization "Well, it was either them or me!" as if the dichotomy of self and others is absolute? How much cheap moralizing has gathered under the banner of "Well, it also served his own self-interest" (e.g. when Ted Turner gave a billion bucks to the United Nations, and his critics only pointed to the clever tax advantages structured into the gift). Generosity, if it really is generosity, is not a rational moral duty, nor is it tainted by the pleasure and possibly even the tax deductions one gets out of it. As Aristotle and Confucius both so wisely pointed out, it gives one pleasure to be generous, which is not to either suggest or deny that a reason for being generous is to obtain that pleasure.

I recently opened up an endowment at the University of Texas for creative honors students. As they say these days, I felt that "it was time to give something back." What surprised me, in fact almost overwhelmed me, was the joy I got from doing it. Yes, I did get a hefty tax deduction. And yes, it is an on-going process to which I have committed more money in the immediate and continuing future. And, yes, I do hope to recapture some of that pleasure which I enjoyed on the first round of giving. But do any of these admittedly self-interested (or at any rate self-satisfying) reasons compromise my generosity? I do not think so. Why should we insist on "giving until it hurts" as the sign of the true virtue? Why should we expect corporations to sacrifice their self-interest (or, more accurately, compromise their fiduciary obligation to the stockholders) in the name of some other value or concern? But to leap from this to the Friedmanian argument that corporate charity is "stealing from the stockholders" (not to mention "pure, unadulterated socialism") is just to show the invidiousness and the destructiveness of the moral versus self-interest dichotomy. We can continue to condemn outright selfishness, and we can continue to praise saint-like sacrifice, but let's not make them the poles of the debate to which everyone must commit themselves, one way or the other.

I want to reject the supposed opposition between egoism and morality on the grounds that a good deal of our behavior is neither self-interested nor principled, but *participatory*, motivated by our membership in this or that community and participating in its rituals. I went to a conference a month or so ago and heard Russell Hardin, always brilliant, always perverse, argue (and most of the political scientists agreed) that voting is irrational as the costs almost always outweigh any possible impact one might have on the election.[14] I was, as usual, aghast. To understand why people vote is to understand that people value participation over so-called "utility functions," and I would say that any notion of rationality that fails to appreciate this is degenerate. In this sense, I am a communitarian, and I hold that the virtues of civic-mindedness are more basic to justice than principles or conceptions.

Back to basics?

I am not the only one who has latched onto the virtue approach to ethics because I think that the roles of deliberation, the use of moral principles, the abstractions of ethical theory, and centrality of rationality are often overstated in philosophy. We do not usually deliberate before doing the right thing. We do not normally have a principle "in mind" when we act morally. Of course one *can* deliberate and entertain such a principle in the way that philosophers argue, although I would suggest that it is mainly philosophers who do this. But most people are utterly incompetent when called upon to justify or even explain what they are doing when they act rightly, although to be sure they will usually parrot some principle ("It's wrong to lie") when provoked. Their actions are neither motivated by, nor are they to be explained in terms of, rational principles. The quasi-articulate, virtuous phrases, "because I just felt it was right" or "because that's the kind of person I am" are what we expect from most non-philosophers, and it's not because they don't understand what they are doing or why.

There is considerable slipperiness between the appearance of principles in ordinary deliberation and the use of such principles in the justification of ethical behavior in philosophy. I don't want to cast aspersions on the philosophical quest for justification (although I think that the philosophical quest for a justification *of morality*, that is, of morality *überhaupt*, is ill conceived). Nor do I think that it is a mistake to look for philosophical justifications of one or another conceptions of justice (though, again, I think that the philosophical quest for a justification *of justice*, that is, of justice *überhaupt*, is ill conceived). Such philosophical deliberations sharpen our focus and clarify our conversation. I think that conflict and confrontation in moral matters is a good thing – except perhaps at the dinner table and in bed. Peacemaking, as Sterba conceives of it, should not be confused with slurring over the differences, or with lazy relativism, which responds with an indifferent shrug of the shoulders, which is very different from any sort of defensible relativism. But so, too, peacemaking should not conceive of its success only in terms of overcoming all conflict and controversy, or finding basic principles upon which opposing philosophers can agree. Peacemaking may be no more than urging tolerance, making it possible to live together, if not harmoniously then at least without hostility. The philosophical emphasis on basic principles, I am afraid, more often exacerbates conflict rather than encouraging mutual tolerance.

I think that the ultimate virtue of the virtue approach to justice (and ethics more generally) is, in my view, the fact that it is a "bottom-up" approach, as opposed to most philosophers' "top-down" way of thinking about these things. That image, of course, goes straight back to Plato (although Socrates, I would argue, is much more subtle). It is this top-down way of thinking that insists on non-question-begging arguments and on basic principles ("norms of rationality"). I don't think that this is what goes on much in the street (thus the amusement with which the formulation of most philosophical arguments are greeted in practical contexts). Charles Taylor, addressing the serious multicultural issues in his native Quebec, encourages what he calls "ingenious adhoccery." This is not only opposed to the employment of general principles. It constitutes an admission that, in the cases that really count as matters for serious debate, there are no such principles, nor useful arguments to or from such principles, and so no such major concern over begging the question or not doing so. More generally, I would suspect that when Sterba argues that "a libertarian's idea of liberty has the same practical requirements as a welfare liberal's ideal of fairness and a socialist's ideal of equality,"[15] even if this is true, the street-level arguments between them – whether to cut or raise taxes, whether to expand or contract state welfare systems – would not be resolved. Perhaps the language would shift. Perhaps the liberal would start arguing in terms of "liberty" for the poor instead of the traditional liberal language of "rights." But I suspect that a broad incommensurability would remain. But then, Sterba is an optimist. I suspect that he has to be. I am not. But this, I think, says a lot more about the terms of our debate than the traditional discussions about justice would care to explore.

Which raises the more general question of rationality and its relation to morality ("morality grounded in rationality"). Sterba rehearses a number of arguments for rationally favoring morality over egoism. I have already questioned that dichotomy (as Sterba does very briefly, in passing, on page 23 of *Justice Here and Now*), but I would also want to raise some similar questions about the nature of rationality. The question "Why be rational?" is one that has always stuck in the philosopher's craw. Out of irritation, the query gets a rapid and dismissive response: "What kind of answer do you want? If a rational answer, then you have already accepted blah, blah, blah. And if you won't accept any answer at all, then blah, blah, blah." It's not a very convincing performance. A more honest way of putting it would be, "If you don't want to play the game, then get out of the seminar room." But I want to ask a Nietzschean question, which might be stated, "Why must we have rationality at any cost, anyway?" or "What's the value of rationality?" Since justice is often equated with rationality (in the social sphere, as is morality in the more personal sphere), this is not an irrelevant or merely rude question.

Sterba takes non-question-beggingness as one of the touchstones of rationality. But I am not sure that there is a non-question-begging answer to the very question "What is rationality?" Exactly what is the rationality that is at stake in socio-political debates? Obviously, I won't pursue this at length here, although I have tried to do so in a recent book of mine, which also talks about justice, called *The Joy of Philosophy*. Let me just say that, first, whatever else it may be, justice is not, as in many recent game-theoretical and economic treatments, the maximization of self-interests, whether or not this involves considerations of optimization or other people's interests as well as one's own. In other words, it is not the degenerate notion of rationality that I dismissed at the end of the preceding section. And second, it is not, as in the legacy left from Kant, a matter of impersonality, a feature that is variously suggested in such criteria as "universalizability" and "never treating yourself as an exception to the rule." To the contrary, the self is deeply involved, though not necessarily in a self-interested way, in even distant cases of justice and injustice.

I think there is a good deal to be said against even the most minimal constraints of such Kantian criteria, which might be summarized as "consistency." (Don [not John] Locke, many years ago, argued quite nicely that universalizability, despite all the fuss, came down to no more than a demand for consistency.) But as often noted, one can always find *some* difference between any two cases such that a moral judgment applies to one and not the other, even if that difference is no more than one situation follows the other. Specifying the *relevance* of such reasons is, as also often noted, not a formal matter. It involves a heavy dose of contextualism, and, I would argue, a consideration of local practices.

Mere consistency is not only the hobgoblin of little minds. It is also a philosophical dead end. As is universalizability. As is any conception of reason that pretends to be itself value-free. In my book and elsewhere, I suggest that rationality – that is, the version of rationality that is at stake in these debates – comes down to this: *caring about the right sorts of things*. I do not pretend that this is non-question-begging. And of course, it leaves quite open what the right sorts of things might be. But the shift I am suggesting, none too subtly, is that rationality is not impersonal. This should not be confused with any defense of that degenerate sense of rationality that is equated with self-interest. Rather, rationality is caring, and caring intelligently. The upshot of this, of course, is that we should care about justice and justice is thereby rational (as opposed to the other way around: justice is rational and we should therefore care about it). Again, I am aware of the question-begging nature of this response: "How do you know it is the right thing to care about other than the fact that it is rational to care about it?" but I suspect that this may be the best that we can do where such global human issues as the well-being of other people is involved. (In particular cases, of course, the "why should you care?" question almost always has some sort of answer, namely, fitting into a larger framework that is the appropriate context for caring.) The more probing question is how any such suggestion helps resolve the debate among competing conceptions of justice or, on a larger scale, competing practices of rationality. My answer is that it doesn't, nor do I think that any non-question-begging conception of rationality can do so.

As I read through Jim Sterba's book, the strong temptation, naturally, was to meet him on common ground, consider the strongest statement of his position, and I am sure that that is what many of the other discussants have been doing. But my objection is that this would leave something essential out of the discussion. Abstractions about "liberty" and "equality," though they provide grist for the philosopher's mill as well as banners and slogans for political pundits, demagogues and sacrificial lambs alike, do not capture the way we think about justice or, just as important, have only secondarily to do with how we *feel* about justice. Far more basic are the personal practices that we learn from our culture, the attitudes we form accordingly, and the virtues we come to develop by pursuing those practices and cultivating those attitudes. Needless to say, I am not saying that we should eliminate the language of "liberty" and "equality" from our debates about justice. But insofar as we do speak on that level, I hope that we all learn something from Sterba's efforts to be a "peacemaker" and reconcile opposing positions using some shared vocabulary. But my nagging lament is that such debates too easily leave out the "heart" of justice, and this is what the virtue conception of ethics tries to correct. It is not a substitute but a supplement to what is so vigorously articulated and debated in our high-falootin' philosophical language of justice. It reminds us that it is not what we think, nor even what we do, that makes us just. It is also what we feel, how we respond, and what sort of persons we are.

Conclusion

Socrates, it seems, had two very different kinds of lessons to teach us.[16] The first, exemplified in his character as well as his discussions, is the importance of justice – admittedly in a broader sense than our use of the term – as a personal virtue, a way of responding to the world and other people. So conceived, justice is highly personal and always situated in a particular social context. Indeed, the political vision of *The Republic* can be viewed as an attempt to schematize just that social context which will most effectively manifest and cultivate that virtue in each and every citizen. The second lesson has to do with the more philosophical vision of a singular ideal Form of justice, which today translates into the search for an all-embracing philosophical theory. The two lessons are not all that obviously compatible, but in any case, they certainly urge us in two very different directions. There is no question in which direction Anglo-American philosophy has gone. Justice, we are reminded again and again and again, is a matter of abstract, dispassionate, impersonal, rational principles and concepts.

The result, I'm afraid, is that we are losing our vocabulary of virtue. Because of our love of leaping from the particular context – in which our sense of justice is keen and healthy – to what the French postmodernist Lyotard calls "totalizations," empty but dangerous generalizations about "communism" and "national security." My argument is that we should be humble and suspicious of these grand generalizations and theories and remember that justice is not some grand ideal or abstraction, but a personal virtue, an open and receptive mind toward the world. In fact, the pluralism and unprecedented international awareness of our own society makes us particularly keen to understand the legitimacy of differences and ready to share with other societies. Our unique sense of power and affluence, even as it encourages arrogance, also provokes in us a deep sense of concern.

My activist friends will no doubt complain that I do not actually tell people what to do, and radicals will complain that I too readily accept our status quo without advocating its overthrow. Conservatives have complained that I am far too liberal, and liberals have argued that I have given far too much away to the conservatives. That makes me think I have it just about right. Choosing between ideologies is not my worry, and advocating some bold, grand scheme of action would once again turn the pursuit of justice into a specialized career instead of a personal concern which everyone ought to have and practice in their everyday lives. It is just that gap between the personal and the impersonal that I wish to fill here, and my argument is that, if justice isn't personally felt and practiced, then there can be no justice at all.

NOTES

1 In conversation, at some American Philosophical Association meeting or other, about 1985.
2 James P. Sterba, *How to Make People Just* (Lanham MD: Rowman & Littlefield, 1988). The communitarian conception seems to have lost status in the present book, Sterba's *Justice Here and Now* (Cambridge and New York: Cambridge University Press, 1998).
3 Sterba, *Justice Here and Now*, especially chapter 2.
4 Kurt Baier, "Radical Virtue Ethics," in *Midwest Studies in Philosophy XIII* (Notre Dame IN: Notre Dame University Press, 1988) pp. 126ff.
5 Edmund Pincoffs, *Quandries and Virtues* (Lawrence: University of Kansas Press, 1986).
6 David Miller, *Social Justice* (Oxford: Oxford University Press, 1976).

7 Rawls 1971, pp. 479, 481, 489, 540.
8 "Schmelzender Theilnehmung," Kant, *Grundlegung* (in *Werke*, Band IV, p. 399). Kant, *Grounding of the Metaphysics of Morals*, trans. J. W. Ellington (Indianapolis: Hackett, 1980) pp. 12, 399. "Melting compassion" is Paton's translation, "tender sympathy" Lewis White Beck's and Elliston's); Kant's account of retribution is in his *Philosophy of Law*, trans. W. Hastie (Edinburgh: Clark, 1889). I have commented at length on Kant's distinction between retribution and vengeance, a distinction he shares with Robert Nozick and a great many other theorists, in my *A Passion for Justice* (Addison-Wesley, 1990, Rowman & Littlefield, 1994), especially chapter 6.
9 Wing-sit Chan, *A Source Book in Chinese Philosophy* (Princeton: Princeton University Press, 1963).
10 This is something of a retreat from my argument in *A Passion for Justice*, which is mainly concerned with the role of feelings in justice rather than with justice as a virtue.
11 Sterba, *Justice Here and Now*, pp. 14–17.
12 Alasdair MacIntyre, *Whose Justice? Which Rationality?* (Notre Dame IN: Notre Dame University Press, 1988) pp. 378ff.
13 Jonathan Bennett, "The Conscience of Huck Finn," *Philosophy*, 1976.
14 Russell Hardin, "Street Level Epistemology and Democratic Participation," a paper given at the "Deliberating Deliberative Democracy" conference at the University of Texas at Austin, 4–5 February 2000.
15 Sterba, *Justice Here and Now*, p. 7.
16 Alexander Nehamas, *The Art of Living* (University of California Press, 1999).

References

Aristotle, *Nichomachean Ethics* (T. Irwin, trans.) (Indianapolis: Hackett, 1985).

Augustine, *The City of God* (Philip Levine, trans.) (Cambridge MA: Harvard University Press, 1956).

Bennett, Jonathan, "The Conscience of Huck Finn," *Philosophy*, 1976.

Calhoun, Cheshire H., "Justice, Care and Gender Bias," *Journal of Philosophy*, 85 (September 1988).

Chan, Wing-sit, *A Source Book in Chinese Philosophy* (Princeton: Princeton University Press, 1963).

Hume, David, *A Treatise of Human Nature* (Oxford: Oxford University Press, 1978).

Kant, Immanuel, *The Metaphysical Elements of Justice* (J. Ladd, trans.) (Indianapolis: Bobbs-Merrill, 1965).

——*The Grounding of the Metaphysics of Morals* (J.W. Ellington, trans.) (Indianapolis: Hackett, 1980).

MacIntyre, Alasdair, *Whose Justice? Which Rationality?* (Notre Dame, IN: Notre Dame University Press, 1988).

Miller, David, *Social Justice* (Oxford: Oxford University Press, 1976).

Nehamas, Alexander, *The Art of Living* (University of California Press, 1999).

Pincoffs, Edmund, *Quandries and Virtues* (Lawrence: University of Kansas Press, 1986).

Plato, *The Republic* (Grube, trans.) (Indianapolis: Hackett, 1985).

Rawls, John, *A Theory of Justice* (Cambridge MA: Harvard University Press, 1971).

Rousseau, Jean-Jacques, *Discourse on the Origin of Inequality* (D. Cress, trans.) (Indianapolis: Hackett, 1983).

Schopenhauer, Arthur, *The Basis of Morality* (Payne, trans.) (Indianapolis: Bobbs-Merrill, 1965).

Smith, Adam, *The Theory of Moral Sentiments* (London: George Bell & Sons, 1880).

Solomon, Robert C., *The Joy of Philosophy* (Oxford: Oxford University Press, 1999).

——*A Passion for Justice* (Reading MA: Addison-Wesley, 1990).

Sterba, James P., *How to Make People Just* (Lanham MD: Rowman & Littlefield, 1988).

——*Justice for Here and Now* (Cambridge and New York: Cambridge University Press, 1998).

Walzer, Michael, *Spheres of Justice* (New York: Basic Books, 1983).

Young, Iris, *Justice and the Politics of Difference* (Princeton: Princeton University Press, 1991).

9

JUSTICE, COMMUNITY, AND THE LIMITS TO AUTONOMY

Michael Boylan

One of the central issues involved in the debate about the limits of human autonomy is the role of the community and traditional authority as a check upon what the agent may or may not do. As a case study to bring this issue into sharp relief, I will examine a position of James P. Sterba from his book, *Justice for Here and Now*. Arising from this analysis will be the outlines of a position of public philosophy that will offer suggestions on how this parameter ought to be demarcated.

My strategy in this essay will be first to examine the case study of Gretchen (presented by Sterba in his book). Next, I will introduce the interpretative framework of justice. Finally, I will offer a solution to the problem that involves limitations on individual autonomy due to a community's conception of the public good.

1 The case of Gretchen

Let me begin by citing Sterba's case of Gretchen.[1]

> Gretchen, who is morally entitled to a $8,000 income, receives only a $5,000 income through legal channels. Suppose further that every means of correcting this injustice, save criminal disobedience, has been tried so as to be reasonably judged to be ineffective, or that using such means is reasonably judged too personally costly for Gretchen. If this is the case, it would be morally permissible for her to be criminally disobedient, provided that her criminal activity is directed at appropriating surplus goods from people who have more than a fair share of opportunities to lead a good life, and at appropriating such goods with a minimum of physical force. Of course, Gretchen will normally engage in such criminal acts only if there is some likelihood that she will be successful at appropriating the $3,000 income to which she has a basic right.
>
> Suppose, however, that Gretchen is caught by the legal authorities. Should they punish her? In a basically just society, the grounds

for punishing a person is the judgment that the criminal, unlike the victim of crime, would have been reasonably (i.e., morally) expected to act otherwise. But while this comparative opportunity judgment generally holds in a basically just society, it does not hold in the unjust society in which Gretchen lives. She could not be reasonably expected to act differently. In the society in which Gretchen lives (which appears to be strikingly similar to our own), there would be no grounds for punishing Gretchen's criminal activity.

Before offering an analysis of this case, there are several details that we will have to fill in or at least speculate about. First, it is not stated whether a $5,000 a year income (from a presumably minimum wage job-paying $2.50 per hour for a forty-hour week, fifty weeks a year)[2] is adequate to provide for the basic goods of existence: food, shelter, clothing. In the United States (we are encouraged to think that this example occurs in the United States),[3] the minimum wage was around this level in 1977.[4]

In 1977 my wife and I had a combined income of $3,500 a year. It was very tight, but we could afford rent (in a poor neighborhood), food (just the basics), utilities, and clothing. We didn't go out to eat or have enough money for entertainment, but we had a telephone (only sixty calls per month, local), a television (black and white), and access to a major research library. You might think these biographical details are irrelevant, but my point is to situate Gretchen. Was she like me, who could meet the necessities of life but not the little niceties that our society tells us are so important – such as being able to order out for pizza, or being able to afford movies, or buying new shoes when you get a hole in the sole instead of having them patched (some of my friends used cardboard instead)?

This is an important issue. First, if Gretchen were denied one of the basic necessities of life such that she might die were she to continue in that state, then we might be involved in an "ought implies can" sort of problem. In other words, Gretchen might have a moral ought to obey the law, but because of her life-threatening poverty, she might have to steal the proverbial loaf of bread.[5] This sort of case we shall call breaking the law due to a lack of the basic goods of life (food, clothing and shelter). Cases like this are rather special, since without the basic goods of action, one cannot be said to be a fully functioning purposive agent.[6] Thus, since being a fully functioning purposive agent is a necessary condition for moral culpability, the individual who steals a loaf of bread (or its equivalent) in order to keep from starving is not, *ceteris paribus*, fully responsible for her action, and any compassionate judge should show her every leniency.

However, the case becomes more complicated when Gretchen already possesses these first-order basic goods. In this case the additional monies will be for the acquisition of goods that go beyond first-order basic agency. These goods are of two varieties. First, there are goods that though they are not first-order basic goods of agency, they nevertheless promote more effective fundamental agency. These include education, access to books, and specific job skills. Whereas these second-order basic goods are beyond first-order basic goods, nevertheless, they are fundamental in order to compete within the society effectively. It is my opinion that Gretchen has a rights claim against society for these second-order basic goods. Part of the nature of these goods is that they are often culturally situated so that one must accept the community perspective in order to profit from them. For example, if one were receiving job training it is for the sake of improving one's job prospects in an actual job offered in the society. One is not learning these skills simply to pass a course or to pursue nefarious designs. Therefore, it would seem peculiar for Gretchen to break the law in order to obtain *these* sorts of goods. However, if Gretchen were denied access to these second-order basic goods because of discrimination, then I would be sympathetic to her being able to sneak into the library to read a book or to pop into a class at a public university and listen to lectures tuition-free.

The next sort of goods is designed to provide pleasure to the agent, but is superfluous to fundamental action (acting in order to provide one's self with first- or second-order basic goods). These are additive goods. Sports equipment, fancy clothes, restaurant dinners, fast cars, etc., fall into this category. It is certainly possible that what Gretchen desires (in the case presented) is further enjoyment of additive goods. But if this is the case, then it is difficult to understand the moral justification of her action. How can Gretchen claim a moral right to a VCR or a *color* television? Neither of these items is necessary for basic action or enhanced effective action. It seems clearly a case of one person seeing things that others have (that are supposed to yield pleasure), and that person's resulting desire that grows within the agent to possess those things for herself.

If we read the case this way, then there are problems. We could emend the case to read, "If William G. is the richest person in the world, and if we define the class of all the rest of the people as phi, then let John and Gretchen be members of phi. Both John and Gretchen believe that whatever their salaries are, they are morally entitled to more. They look to William G. as having a surplus, therefore; John and Gretchen get a job at William G.'s company and (using the private disobedience theory) proceed to embezzle William G.'s money from him."

What makes this second version of the case a plausible companion to the first is that when the *moral* basis of deserts is based upon one's desire to acquire additive goods (because they have been unequally distributed in favor of another), then there is no limit to desires for all members of phi. Since phi is defined as everyone save for the richest person, all members of phi have something to be covetous of, namely William G.

This is, of course, untenable because anarchy would result. The basis of the difficulty lies in:

(a) the definition of economic justice (hence the basis of the moral claims right for more), and

(b) the definition of moral agency and how we are to demarcate the limits of autonomy.

Let's examine each of these in order.

2 Justice

First is the definition of economic justice. If we hold to the principle that I have enunciated elsewhere that, all things being equal, we must always begin with egalitarianism,[7] then this means that one ought to distribute goods in a like manner to all. The problem is that things are rarely equal. There are countless instances in which some sort of merit-based compensation system will benefit everyone concerned.

There are many theories of distributive justice.[8] Each makes different recommendations pertaining to resource allocation. One of the difficulties in theories of justice is that different situations seem to require different theories. This complicates the issue of "how to choose a theory of justice." Such an exercise is beyond the scope of this essay; however, I will set out a selected sample of theories to make my intended point.

Some major theories of justice that are relevant in this context include *capitalism* (to each according to their work), *socialism* (to each according to their need), *egalitarianism* (to each equally), *aristocracy* (to each according to their "inherited station") and *kraterism* (to each according to their power to grasp what they want).

I would contend that the fairest situation is egalitarianism, unless situations warrant otherwise.[9] This would mean that the default system of allocation is always to give to each party equally unless there is a good reason to deviate.

If one were to deviate (on the principle of economic efficiency, for example), then I would advocate some sort of mixture of capitalism and socialism (as defined above). The way to put this in a very condensed fashion is that egalitarianism should be adopted unless compelling reasons indicate that another theory (or mix of theories) is more appropriate. What would count as a compelling reason? I would say that it would be a practical need that makes its case in the context of a moral theory. In my case that would mean a deontological theory that emphasized rights and duties.[10]

Since egalitarianism has proved (in a macro sense) to be a very inefficient system upon which to base an economy, we would turn to capitalism (modified by socialism). As a matter of fact, this is the direction that all the industrialized countries in the world have taken. The balance between capitalism and socialism is what is at issue. Various countries lean toward rewarding work while others emphasize meeting essential human needs (the so-called "cradle to grave" ideal).

Why do I advocate egalitarianism as the "default" system of justice? The reason for this lies at the micro level. At the micro level one has many sorts of allocation decisions. For example, in a family one must decide how to divide the chocolate cake for dessert. Given that everyone likes chocolate cake equally and that there are no other health considerations to think about, the fairest[11] distribution is to give everyone an equal slice. It is my opinion that this is (or should be) the driving principle of distribution among families. If we are allocating clothes, food, or any other desirable good within the family, then it is my opinion that it should be done equally. Birthday presents, parents' time – everything seems best distributed equally.

If the family is the basic social unit of society, then the principles of justice that hold there, ought to hold upwards until there is a principle that trumps it.

Certainly this thesis is a very ambitious one. It should encompass a monograph in itself. But if this brief treatment can be taken as suggestive, then I would put forth the following process whereby we can link these ruminations to the case of Gretchen (on the last interpretation, i.e. her quest for additive goods by criminal disobedience).

Step 1 We begin with egalitarianism. If we were to allocate in this fashion, then surely under-represented groups (including Gretchen) would be compensated (through enhanced access to jobs, schooling and government contracts) since the strategy is to allocate "to each equally."

Step 2 Egalitarianism is not the most efficient macro-allocation strategy. Therefore, in macro cases it should be replaced with a system of capitalism/socialism (the mixture to be argued for in another venue).

Step 3 The capitalism side of the equation could argue that if Gretchen wants more money she should get a job that society values, and earn more that way, e.g. as a computer programmer.

Under this scenario, institutions in the society invest in individuals of disadvantaged groups that are not presently producing at what one might expect (in order to get qualified labor that will make the owners more money). "To each according to their work" here must be understood in an Aristotelian *potentiality* sense. We will, as a society, invest in that which is potentially a lucrative market, namely our own people who are under-represented in the workplace. It is not unusual for capitalism to invest in potential markets. At the writing of this essay very few IT (information technology) stocks are showing anything close to a profit on Wall Street, yet they are besieged with offers to finance them. People see *actualized* earnings down the road even though some particular company – right now – has never shown a profit.

If we are willing to gamble in this way on IT and internet stocks, then why can't we gamble on our own people?

Now obviously, the depiction of capitalism's acceptance of helping people such as Gretchen succeed in the system may not be accepted by everyone. One of the most prominent critics of my view here might say that a true capitalist would deny any consideration to those who violate the basic formula: "to each according to their work."[12] But this begs the question of what the society is to do with such individuals (under a capitalist mind-set). For these people will not simply vanish. They won't starve to death because they have no employment. At the very least (that should be recognized by even the most ardent free marketer), the disadvantaged will pose a threat to the advantaged because as the gap widens between the groups, anger and frustration will accelerate. All of those "well deserved" possessions acquired by those who have flourished under the conditions of the present system are in jeopardy if a significant segment of the population decides that they have nothing, and therefore "nothing to lose." Such people are dangerous to those invested in the *status quo*. From the macro perspective, societies work best when everyone is brought into the economic picture. The advantaged who ignore the disadvantaged ("let them eat cake!") do so at their peril.

Thus, even from a non-moral prudential calculation, it makes no sense to disenfranchise any substantial disadvantaged group. Society needs these people to take a positive role, or society may face severe civil unrest.

The second half of my distribution formula includes socialism, "to each according to their needs." As we have seen above, "needs" must be related to goods that are basic to human action (either in the primary or the secondary sense) and goods that are not basic to action but represent an individual's desire satisfaction (additive goods).[13] It seems to me that the capitalism/socialism amalgam will not be able effectively to deal with this problem except through the management of income differentials between classes of population.

What I mean by this is the differential between the lowest 20% and the highest 20%. This gap describes the disparity in income distribution in a given community. Ideally, under egalitarianism there would be no gap at all. But as communities grow in size, this ideal seems practically impossible to achieve. Thus we are thrown into an efficiency/productivity v. income equity equation. As we reward the most productive more and more, productivity increases and the gap between the richest and the poorest increases. The Gretchens of the world look to those who are basking in material luxuries that they themselves have trouble even imagining, and feel resentment, jealousy, and covetousness. These are powerful emotions of the soul, and will incline Gretchen to want to steal her portion of the pie.

How does Gretchen react to her desire to steal her portion of the eco-nomic pie of additive goods? This will depend upon the vision of the good that Gretchen holds, and whether Gretchen herself should modify her conception of the good in light of the community in which she lives. Should the society be value-neutral, allowing all of its citizens full expression of developing their own view of the good – no matter what it is – or should the society endorse a view of the good that may guide decisions of justice such as we are discussing?

James P. Sterba addresses these questions by contending that there is a way rationally to view practical and moral situations with a similar cost/benefit lens.[14] Sterba's analysis here is one that I share in many respects. His table of ranking the importance of practical v. moral issues is compati-ble with my own "theory of embeddedness."[15] I agree with Sterba that when one can adequately judge the level of embeddedness of a problem (between moral and practical considerations) then the highest level of embeddedness ought to rule the decision-making process. Thus a problem that has a high degree of embeddedness at the practical, prudential level will trump a moral principle that has a low level of embeddedness (i.e. is relatively trivial).

This model (either Sterba's or mine) is in Sterba's terms "a non-question-begging" method for rational choice that utilizes assumptions from prudential decision theory and applies it to moral matters also.

However, Sterba and I differ on our evaluation of cases in which moral and practical problems are equally embedded. Sterba calls these "lifeboat cases" and brackets them aside. This is because he thinks that they are quite rare in occurrence. I feel that these sorts of cases occur regularly. It is my contention that in situations such as this ethics should trump practical considerations. But why?

This is the question that is *not* "non-question-begging." It involves the query of why someone should relinquish a possibility of self-satisfaction at the price of doing something that is *morally right*. Why should the agent care?

This leads us into the final section of the paper, which discusses the limits of autonomy.

3 The limits of autonomy

The only way in which the problem raised at the end of the previous section can be solved, is by providing to Gretchen (or other such agents) a compelling reason why she should *not* steal goods from others in order to provide her with additive goods that she desires. This reason must be consonant with Gretchen's worldview if it is to be compelling to her.

Sterba address this issue in two ways. The first is to refer to rational ethical theorists Alan Gewirth and Kurt Baier, who have made such arguments the cornerstone of their philosophies.[16] This is one of the central problems of ethics and may never be resolved to everyone's satisfaction, but these two proponents have valuable arguments (though I am partial to Gewirth).

The second appeal is toward the philosophy of reconciliation that lies at the heart of Sterba's philosophy.[17] In this case, the moral philosopher tries to enter into a negotiation of sorts in order to discover a way of accommodating (as much as possible) most of the central concerns each holds.

The way I favor for evaluating this process is by appealing first to a person's worldview.[18] A person's worldview contains her view of the good. It is my view that the values that constitute one's worldview (ethics, aesthetics and religion) ought to be worked out in concert with each other so that "All people must develop a single comprehensive and internally coherent worldview that is good and that we strive to act out in our daily lives."[19]

In questions of public philosophy (that includes justice), this view of the good must be seen in relation to others' view of the good in order to create a community's view of the good. I depict this process this way.

Each agent (after he has created his personal worldview) must also engage other agents with whom he lives in his community[20] in creating a shared community worldview. This is dictated by the *Shared Community Worldview Imperative*, "Each agent must strive to create a common body of knowledge that supports the creation of a shared community worldview (that is complete, coherent and good) through which social institutions and their resulting policies might flourish within the constraints of the essential core commonly held values (ethics, aesthetics and religion)." There are several key elements to this imperative. First, there is the exhortation to create a common body of knowledge (discussed below).[21] This is an essential element in order for positive group discussion to proceed. Second, there is a dialectical process of discussion among members of a single community and between members of various single communities that are united in a larger heterogeneous community. This discussion (which is similar to Sterba's concept of philosophical reconciliation) should seek to form an understanding about the mission of the community within the context of the common body of knowledge and the commonly held core values held by members of the community. These values will include ethical maxims, aesthetic values and religious values. Of course there will be disagreements, but a process that is enjoined in good faith will create a shared worldview that is complete, coherent and good.[22]

Third, the result of this dialectical creation of a shared community worldview is to employ it in the creation (or revision) of social institutions that are responsible for setting policy within the community/social unit. It should be clear that this tenet seems highly inclined toward democracy. It is. However, it is not restricted to this. Even in totalitarian states the influence of the shared community worldview is significant. One can, for example, point to the great differences among communist states in Eastern Europe, the Soviet Union, China, North Korea, and Cuba during the 1960s–1980s.

All were communist; yet there were great differences in the way the totalitarian regimes operated in each instance. This is because, even without the vote, the shared community worldview casts a strong influence upon the operation of society's institutions and their resultant policies.

Finally, it should be noted that the actions of those institutions must always be framed within the core values of the people who make up the society. Whenever the society veers too far away in its implementation of the social worldview from the personal worldviews of its members, then a realignment must occur. In responsive democracies this takes the form of "throwing the bums out" in the next election. In totalitarian regimes, change will also occur, but generally by *coup d'état* or armed revolution.[23]

The next principle to consider is the *Common Body of Knowledge* that is a set of factual and normative principles about which there is general agreement among a community or between communities of people. This includes (but is not limited to) agreement on what constitutes objective facts and how to measure them. It also includes (but is not limited to) what counts as acceptable values that will be recognized as valid in the realms of ethics, aesthetics and religion.[24]

At first glance, many would hold that the creation of the common body of knowledge is a very simple thing. But in our contentious world these points are not to be taken for granted. By engaging the issue head on, there is a much greater chance at meaningful dialogue among those involved in serious disputation.

The import of these distinctions in private and public morality is clear. It is a command that each of us individually examine our own lives and strive to create coherence, completeness and goodness among the myriad value maxims that we hold. In the social sphere it demands that we seek to do the same with others.

The force behind the community imperative is the fact that our lives as humans on the earth are increasingly interdependent. This may have always been true (as per John Donne's "No man is an island unto himself"), but in the twenty-first century it is a practical reality as well. At the very least (a minimalist position) this can be verified by interaction between the environments in which we live.

From a biological point of view, however, even this minimalist position contains some strong duties.[25] None of us lives in some sort of hermetically sealed bubble with all we need inside. We are social animals. We live with other humans. We also live in community with all of nature. We cannot confine this concern to the immediate environments in which we live, but must extend this to the entire world (and perhaps, by extension, the solar system, the galaxy, and beyond). Within our own world, warm waters off of Peru called the *El Niño* affect the weather and the well-being of ecosystems from eastern Asia to North America to Europe. It may be a stretch to say that a butterfly suddenly falling from the sky in Brazil affects a farmer in

Canada (as some of the purveyors of popular chaos theory have said), but it is a meteorological commonplace that regional and even global weathers are intricately connected.[26] The weather is an important component of the well-being of the ecosphere (the combined ecosystems of the world). Therefore, at the very least, everyone must acknowledge that one does not act in isolation. Almost every action that we commit has personal, social and ecological consequences.

What is the *result* of such a process of discussion in an attempt to find an adequate reconciliation that will constitute the shared community world-view? First, all participants in the discussion are committed as members of the community to furthering the view of the good that such a process engenders. This means that there will be cases in which a person is limited in the exercise of their autonomy. Since our discussion is about additive goods, our examples will only reflect these.

In example 1, let us say there is a rural town that is small enough so that there might be a town meeting that acts as a committee of the whole. In the town meeting it is agreed that there will be no hunting within certain clearly defined parameters. The reason for the town's decision is that there have been several hunting accidents in the past few years, and the town holds the safety of its citizens as a shared community value. Even if you (as a member of the town) love to hunt and are irritated that you have to hike or drive another ten miles to satisfy the new limits, you must follow the dictates of the shared community worldview.

The hunter's personal convenience and view of a personal good (to be able to hunt within yards of where he lived in his rural village) is trumped by a tenet of the shared community worldview, namely that the safety of the group demands that hunters go to spots of much lower population density.

In example 2 let us say there is a situation in which there has been vandalism and broken bottles around a community playground that is one of the sole areas of green open space in the neighborhood. The community association meets and decides that the only remedy is to take things into its own hands. Ten people are delegated the task of assigning people to cover the playground – especially in the evening hours of 8 p.m. to midnight. At first many of the citizens in the neighborhood complain. "Say, I didn't go to no meeting of yours. Why should I have to do this?" said one young man who was approached by the canvasser.

"Do you want us to call another meeting so that we can revisit the issue?"

"Yeah."

"Will you attend?"

"Sure."

"The meeting is Friday at DeSable High at 7 p.m."

"Okay."

"You understand that if you don't attend, I'll be back on Saturday morning."

This causes some consternation. "Say what?"

"You heard me."

"But I don't even got no kids."

"You live here. You don't like it, get a place down in Wentworth."

The young man was *mad*. Yet that man went to the meeting and headed a team that supervised the playground. The crazy thing was that as soon as enough people were involved in the *solution*, the *problem* disappeared.[27]

In example 2 the young man's ability to live life just the way he wanted to according to his personal view of the good was limited. It was limited by his having to devote one day a month to supervising the playground and to being on a phone tree that made sure that every night was covered. This meant that he could not pursue his personal view of the good during these intervals, but had to work for the shared view of the good.

It is of interest that in example 2, the point is made that even those who do not actively participate in democracy must bear the duties of community citizenship. The meeting was open to all. If there were enough people who wanted to create another vision of the community good, then they were free to express their views.[28] In the case presented, the non-participants were given a second opportunity to do so. This is a key principle that Saul Alinksky (the man who founded this neighborhood association) believed in.

The crucial problem for those advocating community values is that they do not become "exclusive" or "coercive."[29] In these situations, the value of free and open democratic dialogue is lost. But when the process is open and free, then people must follow the results (regardless of whether they participated personally in the process).

Thus, when we return to the case of Gretchen and her quandary of whether to pursue by criminal disobedience additive goods that she thinks are owed to her by a system she judges to be immoral (perhaps because it is more capitalist than socialist), we can say she should not break the law. Gretchen should abide by the decision of the shared community values (because they were arrived at in a democratic manner). Though Gretchen might feel that what she does ought to be economically valued by her community, the fact is that her existing community does not. Since Gretchen lives in a democracy she can travel about the country to find other communities in which she might feel better situated. She might also travel to Canada or Mexico and explore whether these communities might coincide more completely with her core personal worldview values.

The shared community values must be respected or changed. If they cannot be changed (and one lives in a democracy – even an imperfect one), then the agent should accept the limitations placed on her ability to garner additive goods, or else adopt the community's vision of the good and try to compete according to those rules, or else leave and find another community more consonant with her own personal worldview.

In any event, it is my view that the answer to the question of why a person should limit her own view of the good and its implementation is because of the community in which she lives. Each of us lives in numerous communities of ascending sizes. We are social animals and must take that into account. We are not and should not be completely empowered, self-absorbed autonomous agents seeking only our own path to our personal good. We must also be self- and other-regarding,[30] and as a result we are enjoined to actively engage our fellow community members in an ongoing dialogue that will determine the policies by which we may all live. The common vision of a shared good that follows from this process, binds every individual in the community. It is in this way that the shared community worldview limits personal autonomy. Without this community authority over the individual, the ideal of a participatory democracy will become a fiction. And when that happens, we will all be diminished.

NOTES

1 James P. Sterba, *Justice for Here and Now* (Cambridge: Cambridge University Press, 1998) pp. 179ff.

2 I have come up with these figures by assuming Gretchen works fifty weeks a year ($5,000 divided by 50 = $100 per week). Then I assumed Gretchen works a forty-hour week ($100 divided by 40 = $2.50 per hour.

3 Of course, all of these deliberations are skewed if we are considering a country that is totalitarian. In such a situation a person might react differently to an unmet duty of the state because the state is unresponsive and there are few alternatives. For simplicity, we will consider the United States (or a similar democracy).

4 It was actually moving from $2.30 to $2.60 in this year, but the point is essentially correct. For the history of the minimum wage since 1954 see *Statistical Abstract of the United States – 1999* (Springfield VA: National Technical Information Service, 1999).

5 Since we are talking about the United States, I would note that the Butternut Company, at this time, put all their stale bread into a special bin outside their 55th Street outlet store. That bread was never picked up by garbage men, whenever I went past. Those in the neighborhood whose food stamps did not cover their food costs picked it up and used it as a filler along with a thirty-five-cent can of meat.

6 I believe that Sterba intends his Gretchen case to refer to one of the two levels of basic goods and not to additive goods. If I am right, then Gretchen will not be fully culpable for her actions because she lacks the basic goods of agency. For a fuller discussion on the basic goods of agency see Alan Gewirth, *Reason and Morality* (Chicago: University of Chicago Press, 1978); cf. my commentary on Gewirth in "Choosing an Ethical Theory," in *Gewirth: Critical Essays on Action, Rationality, and Community* (Lanham MD, Boulder and Oxford: Rowman & Littlefield, 1999).

7 "Affirmative Action," *Journal of Social Philosophy* (forthcoming).

8 A brief survey of positions relevant to this essay include: A. W. H. Adkins, *Merit and Responsibility* (Oxford: Oxford University Press, 1960); Claudia Card, "On Mercy," *Philosophical Review*, 81 (1972): 182–207; Joel Feinburg, *Doing and Deserving* (Princeton: Princeton University Press, 1970); Lloyd Fields, "Parfit on

Personal Identity and Desert," *Philosophical Quarterly*, 37 (1987): 432–40; Alan Goldman, "Real People: Natural Differences and the Scope of Justice," *Canadian Journal of Philosophy*, 17 (June 1987): 377–94; Friedrich A. Hayek, *The Constitution of Liberty* (Chicago: University of Chicago Press, 1960); Kai Nielsen, *Equality and Liberty* (Totowa NJ: Rowman and Allenheld, 1985); C. Perleman, *Justice, Law and Argument* (Dordrecht: D. Reidel, 1980); Nicholas Rescher, *Distributive Justice* (Indianapolis: Bobbs-Merrill, 1966); George Sher, *Desert* (Princeton: Princeton University Press, 1987); Michael Walzer, *Spheres of Justice* (New York: Basic Books, 1983); Iris Young, *Justice and the Politics of Difference* (Princeton: Princeton University Press, 1990); James P. Sterba (ed.) *Justice: Alternative Political Perspectives* (Belmont CA: Wadsworth Publishing Company, 1980).

9 The reason for this choice comes from a "micro to macro" orientation. Like Plato, who in the *Republic* looked first toward the dynamics of the individual in his familial and interpersonal levels to ground his understanding of the *polis*, I also believe that this is the place to start. Barring any other changes in normal operating rules (such as giving one's children a piecework system in which the family members who do some particular task will get the largest slice of cake or whatever) we should allocate according equally. Everyone gets the same helping of dinner unless there are extenuating circumstances such as John is on a diet or Jane must gain weight for lacrosse. This point of view asserts that (on the micro level) the natural system of distribution (justice) is egalitarianism.

10 What I am saying here is that a practical need *per se* is not enough. Of course, though some moral theories such as utilitarianism might make the practical and moral calculations seamless, the broader point is that one must present a compelling moral justification for moving away from the default, egalitarian distribution formula. In most macro-economic situations, this is easily presented. But in individual, micro interactions, this is most often not the best way to allocate goods. Families, small organizations and community groups are better off beginning with egalitarianism and then arguing for a different allocation method if it is absolutely necessary.

11 Here I am following a conventional way of describing a value judgment between theories of justice. The normative term "fairest" really means "the best" which presupposes a theory of what constitutes "the best." In this instance (since such a discussion is beyond the scope of this essay), I will simply invoke a Kantian notion of Kingdom of Ends. The duty to treat others as ends and never as means only is grounded in a theory that counts each person equally and distributes basic rights *equally*. There is some fundamental sense, therefore, that egalitarianism is true with respect to basic moral rights and duties. The further step is into the realm of well-being. This includes distribution of tangible goods. It is my opinion that this sense of egalitarianism carries over here, as well. For an argument on how basic human goods of well-being must also be distributed according to egalitarianism, one need only look to such neo-Kantians as Alan Gewirth, *Reason and Morality* (Chicago: University of Chicago Press, 1978).

12 There is, of course, the unexamined issue of the value of work itself. Is all work on a par? Is the "invisible hand" of the marketplace the only indicator of what is good or bad? Are there no other "prescriptive" standards in capitalism? This is an important question that I hope to be able to address in another venue.

13 I also like to add a class of goods that represents those goods we already possess. This class can be called "personal property."

14 Sterba explicates this view in "Liberalism and a Non-Question-Begging Conception of the Good," in *The Liberalism/Communitarianism Debate*, ed. C. F. Delaney (Lanham MD: Rowman & Littlefield, 1994) pp. 227–44; cf. James P.

Sterba, *Justice for Here and Now* (Cambridge: Cambridge University Press, 1998) pp. 24–32.

15 For a discussion of my theory, see Michael Boylan, *Ethical Issues in Business* (New York: Harcourt Brace, 1995) and *Medical Ethics* (Upper Saddle River NJ: Prentice Hall, 2000).

16 I am very sympathetic to this move in Sterba's argument – both in its invocation and in the acceptance that there might be difficulties in its justification. See Alan Gewirth, *Reason and Morality* (Chicago: University of Chicago Press, 1978); Kurt Baier, *From a Moral Point of View* (Ithaca NY: Cornell University Press, 1958); cf. Sterba (1998) pp. 17–21.

17 For an example of this reconciliation procedure in the venue of liberalism, communitarianism and a view of the good, see James P. Sterba, *How to Make People Just: A Practical Reconciliation of Alternative Conceptions of Justice* (Totowa NJ: Rowman & Littlefield, 1988) pp. 74–84, 132–43. I would also like to note that the philosophy of reconciliation goes much deeper than any one particular issue; it is a peaceful, sincere striving toward truth (in the tradition of Socrates). This is not always the goal of many contemporary philosophers. For a discussion of these issues, see *Justice for Here and Now*, chapter 1.

18 For a discussion of my views of worldview, see Michael Boylan, *Basic Ethics* (Upper Saddle River NJ: Prentice Hall, 2000) introduction.

19 I call these conditions the Personal Worldview Imperative. I justify these in some detail in *Basic Ethics*, Introduction and Chapter 8.

20 By community here I mean (in ascending order) the family; the neighbors in his geographical region – some natural unit of a mile or so; his city, township, or county; his state; his country, and the world itself. All are in communities that we cannot ignore. I believe that one should begin in the order I have listed because that order allows the most interaction of individuals in the political process.

21 I discuss the common body of knowledge in greater detail as it pertains to logical argument in *The Process of Argument* (Englewood Cliffs NJ: Prentice Hall, 1988) chapter 1.

22 I discuss an example of how this shared community worldview might arise in my essay, "Affirmative Action: Strategies for the Future," *Journal of Social Philosophy* (forthcoming).

23 In cases of revolution against totalitarian states, private acts of criminal disobedience may be considered part of the revolution, provided that they are directed against the offending state or individuals who are symbols of the totalitarian state.

24 This is not to suggest that I am arguing for a sharp distinction between analytic and synthetic truths; I agree with Quine's insistence that analytic and synthetic truths don't easily segregate. See "Two Dogmas of Empiricism," in *From a Logical Point of View* (Cambridge MA: Harvard University Press, 1953) however; the structure of deontic truths and other propositions do form a natural classification.

25 It is not the purpose of this essay to argue that *only* the minimalist position ought to be adopted, but rather that this position is so basic that all rational agents must accept its authority. By adopting such a strategy, it is hoped that a wider range of assent can be achieved (cf. Common Body of Knowledge).

26 One accessible overview of these relations can be found in Marcel Leroux, *Dynamic Analysis of Weather and Climate: Atmospheric Circulation, Perturbations, Climatic Evolution* (New York: John Wiley & Sons, 1998) especially part III.

27 This is a fictionalized account of an actual event that occurred in the city neighborhood in which I lived.

28 This is *not* an expression of utilitarianism *per se* but only *per aliud*, since democratic decisions operate on such principles. What makes it different from utilitarianism is that in the meeting a person may bring up a value from her personal worldview that convinces others toward policy x even when policy x is against the community's aggregate or average pleasure.

29 For a discussion of these two drawbacks toward the establishment of a vision of good for the community (along with replies), see Michael Sandel, *Democracy's Discontent: America in Search of a Public Philosophy* (Cambridge MA: Harvard University Press, 1996), especially the argument from pages 205–321 that asserts that our society must promote community and work against too much centralization of power and the erosion of traditional forms of authority.

30 For a discussion of self-regarding v. other-regarding dispositions, see Michael Slote, *From Morality to Virtue* (Oxford and New York: Oxford University Press, 1992) pp. 126–44.

Socialism

10

SOCIALISM AND EGALITARIAN JUSTICE

Kai Nielsen

I

I shall first set out what socialism is and what it hopes to achieve. I shall then weave this account in with a critical examination of James P. Sterba's *Justice for Here and Now*. My central effort there will be to show – its genuine insights, generosity of spirit and well-meaning initiatives notwithstanding – what Sterba's account leaves out in saying what a decent and just world would be and, independently of Sterba, to articulate the conditions necessary for its realization or approximation. I will end by arguing what must be done if we are to have such a world. The prospects for it are pretty dim and seem at least to be growing dimmer. But let us remind ourselves of Antonio Gramsci's slogan about the pessimism of the intellect and the optimism of the will.

II

First, for socialism and its discontents. Socialism and leftism generally have come on bad days. From being a powerful social force feared and hated by the right and by centrist liberals alike, it has, particularly in North America, become something of a joke. It has no militant mass nor even a broadly sympathetic mass attuned to it. There is little by way of a socialist egalitarian ethos in the rich capitalist democracies. In North America there are no leftish parties, not even social democratic parties, with any standing (the NDP in Canada, dwindling away as it is, is a weak exception). And in the United States the "left wing" of the Democratic Party has practically disappeared. It is true that social democratic parties have recently (1998–2000) won victories in Western Europe. France, Germany, Italy, Sweden, Denmark, the United Kingdom and Greece have governments so formed. But with the major players at least – France, Germany, Italy and the United Kingdom – we have social democratic governments that, once in power, a bit of rhetoric and some band-aid policies aside, look pretty much like their neo-liberal right-wing predecessors. The Blair/Schroeder Manifesto sounds very much like, some vapid remarks about social responsibility aside, Thatcherism recycled (Blair and Schroeder 2000). And similar things can be said of the present (2000) governments of France and Italy. They sparked some hope when they were elected, but now that hope is dashed. The prospects for the left seem now very bleak. Cynicism and hopelessness about the public sphere are very widespread.

This is exacerbated by the so-called lessons of 1989. Many of us on the left – some with a little ambivalence – welcomed the tumbling down of the old Soviet empire. We hoped that with Thermidor gone a socialist/social democratic social order, providing a thoroughly democratic middle ground, would come into being in those countries that had formerly been part of that empire: a way that was neither Soviet authoritarian statism nor capitalism. But nothing like that was wanted by most of the people in these countries. Once liberated from Soviet domination they went straight for capitalism. And in the former Soviet Union itself, capitalism of the crudest sort. There was for them no "middle way."

Among intellectuals in those countries the belief remained that socialism was not only inherently undemocratic but grossly inefficient as well. Remember, Hayek is a hero in those countries. You can't, it was widely believed, run an efficient economy answering to people's needs on a socialist model. In the capitalist democracies many liberals and leftists, perfectly aware that there is nothing inherently undemocratic about socialism, and some of them (Sidney Hook, Irving Howe and Richard Rorty) convinced that a genuine socialism could not but be democratic, thought that we had now come to see, as clearly as could be, that in complex modern societies a socialist organization of the *economy* would not work. It wasn't that socialism couldn't be democratic – it could not be efficient. We would, they argued, if we would be reasonable, have to settle for as egalitarian a form of liberal egalitarian welfare statism as is compatible with capitalism. There is simply no rational alternative to capitalism (Rorty 1998a; 1998b).

This view, as we shall see, is not without its critics. Still, culturally and politically speaking, particularly in North America, and most particularly in the United States, the countervailing forces are politically speaking very weak. Given the mass media, given the political parties in power, in reach of power or influential, the near worldwide victory of neo-liberalism seems close to being total. Even with a large number of educated people aware of the evils of globalization – the rich getting richer and the poor poorer and increasingly many people living lives of greater insecurity, greater stress and in many instances a diminished ability to meet their needs – there is little in the way of a movement to the left. The rich, with increasing vigor and success, are ripping off the poor in the rich capitalist democracies and, when these societies are compared with the Second and Third Worlds, the rip-off is even greater. The disparity of life-conditions is simply staggering between the First World and the Third. In the Third World widespread starvation and malnutrition are rampant. The conditions of life for vast numbers of the world's population can only be accurately described as swinish. Thirty million people die of hunger every year and more than 800 million live in extreme poverty. Fifty million people are unemployed in Europe, one billion are unemployed or underemployed in the world as a whole. And those that do work are often savagely exploited, including 300 million children working in conditions of stark brutality. All of this goes on while the productive wealth of the society, rooted in the development of its productive forces, grows and the rich get richer and the poor get poorer, with more people becoming impoverished. The richest quintile of the world population has well over 90% of the world's income, and the poorest quintile holds 0.25%. This yields a quintile income inequality ratio of around 400:1. If wealth is taken into consideration the inequality is even greater (Pogge 1996). With capitalist globalization steadily marching on, things are getting worse. In 1960 the richest 20% of the world's population had an income thirty times higher than the poorest 20%. The wealth of that richest 20% is eighty-two times higher now (1999). Of the 6 billion inhabitants of this planet, barely 500 million live in comfort or something approaching comfort – leaving 5.5 billion in need. "In need" puts too nice a face on it. Many of them live in truly hellish conditions with little possibility of escape. Moreover, given these disparities and the world's productive forces, it is clear enough that transfers could be made to the poor without impoverishing the rich. It is not the lack of developed productive powers that keeps us from so meeting needs. It is the way we organize social life, along with the utterly uncaring attitudes and short-sightedness of the wealthy and powerful of this world. It is capitalism and the attitudes that go with it and not the world that is the problem.

That these conditions obtain is not a "necessary fact" or law of nature or of human nature, but a result of the design of the neo-liberal capitalist order that we have created and sustain. But given the power and pervasiveness of this order, it is likely to *feel* to most of us like something to which there is no alternative. This, I believe, accounts in part for the sense of helplessness and hopelessness that many of our students feel – often the most sensitive and reflective among them. It causes political inactivity and probably does much to generate and sustain postmodernism. Moreover, and more importantly, generally in the population there is this sense of powerlessness and helplessness. There is just this big political machine out there we can do nothing about. This is how many have become attuned to the world.

Richard Rorty is right in saying that the left is the party of hope. Without it there is no reasonable hope for justice here and now or ever or even for a decent society (Rorty 1998b). But it also seems like there is no hope for the left and so, unless we can play religious tricks on ourselves, we are left

207

without hope. In the last pages of his book, James Sterba shows some awareness of this (Sterba 1998, 174–81).

III

I will set out a normative-descriptive interpretive scenario which considers some of the possibilities for, in the face of all this, a just social order – a just world – and takes a shot at a characterization of what it would look like. In this context I will consider how well Sterba's account satisfies this and how well his distinctive methodology works here. But first, I will portray a little more fully the dismal state of affairs for socialism, and say something about what socialism, and more broadly of what the left, can and should be.

Richard Rorty – while regarding socialism, as shown by "the lessons of 1989," to be impossible – opts for a reformist non-socialist left position (he calls it "Old Left") (Rorty 1998a). He usefully distinguishes between the old left, the new left and the cultural left. In the following typology (Table 10.1) I expand and modify his typology and characterization into what I think yields a useful typology of the left. Like any typology it will have some blurred edges and leave some contestable classifications and require clarifications. Yet I believe it provides a useful classification of socialism and the left more generally, and a map for spotting vital options and non-vital options for the left.

Table 10.1 Typology of the left

I OLD LEFT	II NEW LEFT	III CULTURAL LEFT	IV ANALYTICAL LEFT
A. *Reformist* 1. Social democrats (Hook, Howe, Rorty) 2. Socialists (Bernstein, Thomas, Dewey)	C. *Neo-marxists* (Hayden, Callinicos)	F. *Existentialist Marxists* (Beauvoir, Merleau-Ponty, Sartre)	H. *Analytical Marxists* 5. Rational choice theorists (Elster, Roemer) 6. Non-rational choice theorists (G.A. Cohen, E.O. Wright, Levine)
B. *Revolutionary* 3. Marxists 4. Anarchist socialists (Bakunin, Malatesta)	D. *Neo-anarchist* (Chomsky)	G. *Cultural critics* (Jameson, Eagleton)	
	E. *Anti-theorist* (Foucault, Baudrillard)		I. *Analytical socialists/social democrats* (Joshua Cohen, Stuart Hampshire)

By a socialist of any sort I am going to mean someone who favors the public ownership of at least the principal means of production in a world which is to become a world (if it becomes socialist) in which there are only workers or retired workers or children who in due course will become workers when they grow up, and in a world in which, among able-bodied people, generally these people are committed to a democratic ordering of society. Some people (in some forms of socialism) may own small enterprises of various sorts, but to do so they must also be workers, typically working in their own enterprises. No able-bodied mentally stable adult person can be sustained by the society without work. And there must be made available to every non-retired adult person work if they choose to work (childcare and housework also count as work and should in some way be remunerated as any other work in society). We will in short have a social order of full employment. A person may choose not to work, but if they do so choose, work being available to everyone, they can expect no aid from the society if they are able-bodied, adult, of sound mind, and have not reached whatever society fixes as the retirement age.

There will, of course, be individual private property (clothes, tooth-brushes, cars, houses, tools, etc.), but *productive* property will be publicly owned except perhaps – and no doubt desirably – for some small businesses, e.g. family restaurants, shops, small plots of land producing vegetables, and the like. But, without extensive public ownership we do not have socialism. This *could* mean for this public property to be state-owned, but public property could also be worker-owned and controlled with various schemes of worker ownership and control. So Rorty's linking of socialism with nationalization confuses a particular type of socialism (and a problematic one at that) with socialism *sans phrase*. The key here is *public* ownership, public control and democratic governance, where public ownership need not at all mean state ownership and control. It may just be that workers jointly own and control the enterprises they work in or once worked in where they are retired.

In capitalism there are two principal classes: capitalists, who own and, directly or indirectly, control at least the principal means of production and who may or may not, as they choose, also work for a wage (a wage even in their own firms, after all their entrepreneurial work is work); and workers (proletarians, if you will) who work for a wage and typically own no means of production, but if they do, they do not own sufficient means of production to sustain themselves just with that.[1] This status leads to Marxists classifying workers in capitalist societies as wage slaves. They are dependent, unless they can break out of their class and become small capitalists themselves, on capitalists or on the state (and thus in a capitalist society indirectly on capitalists) for their sustenance and the sustenance of their families. Moreover, only a few could break out of their proletarian condition, for if a few break out they will block the exits for others. There is no reasonable choice under capitalism but for the great mass of workers to remain workers (G. A. Cohen 1983).

In socialism, by contrast, there would be no class divisions, for all able-bodied persons would be workers, potential workers (i.e. children) or retired workers. In this important way it would be a classless society, although since work in a complex society will often be very different, there will be distinctions and perhaps strata distinctions between different workers (Marx in his mature thought gave up the ideal of an end to any division of labor). Though these divisions of labor will exist in a properly functioning democratic socialist society, it will not be the case, where these societies are properly functioning socialist societies, that some types of workers (intellectual workers or bureaucratic workers) will be able to gain control over other types of workers such that they will gain political or economic power over them, or such that some types of workers will have much greater wealth or much better life conditions than others. (Ideally, there will be no better life conditions for any group of workers than for others, but if some do arise they will be small and not inherited.) A socialist society and a socialist world (by definition, if you will) must be thoroughly egalitarian, where everyone has equal moral standing in society, and where there are no systematic differences in wealth or control of society. It must have, to be socialist, a thoroughly egalitarian ethos.

Returning to my typology, it is important to recognize that socialists are always on the left (again, by definition if you will) but also that not all leftists are socialists. The most significant exceptions are A1 old-left reformist social democrats (e.g. Richard Rorty, Irving Howe and Sidney Hook), E new left anti-theorists (e.g. Michel Foucault) and I analytical social democrats (e.g. Joshua Cohen and Stuart Hampshire).

I shall argue that the most fundamental choices to be made on the left are between A1, A2 and I (taken as one rather differentiated group) and H5 and H6 (taken as another such group) (B3 and B4 are traditional revolutionary socialisms but H5 or H6 *may* also be analytical Marxist *revolutionary* socialisms. My own socialism is of that sort). The only other serious choice is between H5 and H6 and D and E (taken together) or E by itself as represented (though differently) in the work of Noam Chomsky and Michel Foucault.

Richard Rorty has made a powerful case for A1, as did Sidney Hook before him (Rorty 1998a; 1998b). Hook's case is clouded by his role in the Cold War – by what became his obsession with anti-communism – but Rorty, though he goes firmly on record as supporting the Cold War and commends Hook for his Cold War campaign, is not so compromised by his anti-communism, nor does it seriously mar his left-wing credentials (Rorty 1998a). All the left positions in the typology (with the possible exception of some G, i.e. some cultural critics) are members in good standing of the party of hope. But in my view the most serious choices are between some forms of D and/or E, A1 and A2, on one side, and H5 and H6 and I on the other.

I shall with *apparent* dogmatism set aside B3 (classical Marxism) and B4 (classical socialist anarchism). For some of the reasons that even some people on the left are attracted to libertarianism, a reading of Mikhail Bakunin's *State and Anarchy* cannot but attract one to its vision of liberty and a stateless classless society. But, viewed more soberly, it is too utopian a vision. There is no just smashing the state anywhere, anytime and then moving directly to a classless stateless society. There is, first, the inescapability of what Marxists call the transition period; and second, the fact that revolutions can be successfully made and socialism successfully established (if it can be established at all) only under certain conditions. Moreover, revolutions are not just overnight happenings (Nielsen 1971). And that we could ever move, in complex societies, to a stateless society is very problematical. Marx and Engels and the other classical Marxists thought we could, but it is very doubtful if a proper understanding of historical materialism or anything else would make that plausible (Moore 1993). It is Marx the young utopian who thought that we could eventually live in a stateless society. Sustained by his early *philosophical* anthropology, he continued to have that hope while he should have seen that his own work in historical materialism made such a belief utterly utopian (Moore 1993). Such a belief is, that is, as unjustified in Marx as in Bakunin, though Marx saw that we could not directly leap to statelessness after a successful revolutionary seizure of power. The point is that there is no reason to think that in complex societies we can get to statelessness at all.

Classical revolutionary Marxism should also not be taken as church. Indeed it needs extensive modification. I am an analytical Marxian and a revolutionary one at that. I regard Marx and Engels, and Rosa Luxemburg as well, as master thinkers of modernity. Much of my thinking has been formed and sustained by them. But I use "analytical *Marxian*" advisedly, on analogy with "Darwinian" rather than "Darwinist". Modern biologists are overwhelmingly Darwinian, but they are not "Darwinists". They realize – and how could it be otherwise with a broad-ranging scientific account – that Darwin was wrong about many things. But their very way of thinking was deeply formed by Darwin and they regard him as a scientific giant. I feel exactly the same about Marx. Moreover, I regard his account as a social scientific one and not (*pace* Kolakowski and Rorty) as philosophy, and most firmly not a speculative Hegelian teleological philosophy of history. I take historical materialism to be a scientific theory of epochal social change which, unfortunately, has probably been disconfirmed (Joshua Cohen 1992). But it is a perfectly proper empirical theory for all of that (Nielsen 1983; 1989c; G. A. Cohen 1978; Joshua Cohen 1982; Levine and Wright 1980).

The above notwithstanding, present-day classical Marxism has become a fundamentalist Marxism rigidly holding on to the labor theory of value, the idea of a command economy, and dialectical materialism. It has become a metaphysical theory and not the attempt at the large-scale and systematic scientific theory that it was in the hands of Marx.

I turn now, referring back again to my typology, to the new left. The new left did some fine practical things. It brought an end to the Vietnam War, helped us to view human relations in a new way and took an insouciantly dismissive attitude to capitalist society. Rorty maintains that the cultural left, a continuation of the new left, after it retreated into the academy, abandoned (for the most part) political contestation for cultural critique. Still it did, in a strikingly useful way, some important things (Rorty 1998a; 1998b).[2] It helped us spotlight the life conditions of people who are marginalized in various ways and usefully (if in some instances problematically) challenged the ways things are done in universities. But the cultural left tends, some more so than others, to be conceptually incoherent and naïve. They do not provide a new rationale for socialism or any other kind of plausible leftism. And, in effect, if not in intention, the new academics among them (G rather than F) are deeply apolitical. They are probably, at least to some extent, responsible for turning many serious social thinkers, including activists, away from socialism and Marxism.

IV

Taking socialism or at least leftism seriously, the serious options are between various forms of the reformist left (A) and analytical social democracy and reformist socialism (I) (e.g. Joshua Cohen 2000), on the one hand, and various forms of analytical Marxism (e.g. G. A. Cohen, John Roemer, Andrew Levine) on the other. Let us, to even further pinpoint matters, contrast old-left social democracy with analytical Marxism to see if we can ascertain which gives us the best model of what a just and otherwise desirable socialist/social democratic world would look like.

Social democrats such as Richard Rorty reject socialism, and particularly socialism, analytical or otherwise, with a Marxian flavor. They do so on three principal grounds.

1   The Soviet experiment has abundantly shown us that, in a modern dynamic economy answering to people's needs, a socialism without markets will not work. It is inefficient, and features a stifling bureaucracy. It cannot obtain goods and services when they are needed and where they are needed. It cannot be innovative and produce things that people want. People in such a world will not adequately get either what they need or want.

2   There is a strong tendency for a socialist society to either not be democratic at all or to be minimally and insecurely democratic. Historically speaking they are not societies (to put it minimally) with a firm

track record of respecting human rights. The Marxist tradition, as Rorty puts it, is a tradition "that is covered with filth because of the marks of the governments that have called themselves Marxist" (Rorty 1998a, 21). (However, we should carefully note and not forget that with respect to capitalism, this is the pot calling the kettle black.) Marx, Engels and Luxemburg had good intentions alright, but they assumed too easily and naively that after such a class-based revolution, with the struggle, discipline and control this would require, that with a workers' victory, no doubt in the beginning an insecure victory, democracy would eventually obtain. We could, and would, they thought, move from a socialist society victorious in a class-based civil war to a fully democratic society. But that is very unrealistic and it did not happen.

3   Marxists and Marxians, both classical and analytical, put too much trust in theory, and particularly in grand social theory: a theory that would make plain the underlying structure and necessary development of society. There is no such "science of society," and belief in one leads not infrequently to arbitrariness and to dogmatism and, when things go badly, sometimes even to fanaticism. The intellectual left generally, and Marxists in particular, are, Rorty puts it, "dominated by the notion that we need a theoretical understanding of our historical situation, a social theory which reveals the keys to the future development, and a strategy which integrates everything with everything" (Rorty 1998a, 45).

The Marxist idea is not just to have a bunch of disparate concrete proposals for reform with a minimal ordering, but to reject such piecemeal solutions unless they are integrated into a general theoretical package, theoretically sustained. Marxians, for example, aim at achieving a certain sort of society. They want in the course of doing so to see exactly how it is that the rich are ripping off the poor, what the underlying mechanisms and structures are and how it can be permanently so that we just don't clear up one local problem – make one local solution – only to create another local problem (perhaps even a worse problem) elsewhere. They want, working holistically, to achieve a rational ordering of society. To do that we need intelligent, general, integrated plans, but this requires some sophisticated general theory. It is natural to believe that to know which initiatives to press forward with and in what order and how to integrate them, we need to step back one remove from the situation in order to gain a clearer view so as to see what the more specific initiatives should be and how to prioritize them.

Rorty, as were Karl Popper and Friedrich Hayek, is utterly skeptical about this. He remarks, "It never worked before. Why should it work now?" (Rorty 1998a, 43). We have no "science of society" or (which is something else again) general moral theory which will give us a fix here (here he is at loggerheads with Sterba). All we can do, Rorty has it, is, as reflectively and concretely as we can, introduce specific initiatives – specific proposals backed up by specific campaigns – that might relieve some specific suffering without attempting some overall theoretical understanding and integration (Rorty 1998b, 111–24). Rorty remarks, taking a resolute anti-theoretical stance, in what he takes to be a good pragmatist spirit, "All social initiatives have unforeseen, and often bad, side effects. The idea that you can step back and fix it so that your initiative won't interfere with anybody else's initiative is crazy" (Rorty 1998a, 47).

The first objection to analytical Marxism is perhaps the most tractable. Rorty utterly ignores the possibility of market socialism. Command economies, he stresses, as have many others, do not work, at least in complex industrial societies. We cannot in a modern society and in a modern interdependent world have a *market-free* planned economy – even one planned with the considerable intelligence and the best will in the world to maximally and equitably meet human needs. They work staggeringly badly. Even if we had had conscientious socially committed egalitarian planners at the top steering society, instead of thugs or indifferent bureaucrats out to fill their own pockets, it could not be done. Allocations, if they are to be sufficiently sensitive, for a complex society, cannot be made this way. It is not, as in extreme forms of *laissez faire*, that there is no need for planning. A complex capitalist society will have both market and plan. Yet markets remain absolutely essential (Nove 1983).

However, market socialism recognizes, and indeed stresses, this. Market socialists have worked out, sometimes with great sophistication and with attention to feasibility considerations, models for a market socialist society that would be both socialist, in the sense I characterized, and have markets as well. John Roemer's and David Schweickart's models are well known and carefully articulated examples (Roemer 1994; Schweickart 1993).[3]

Most surely, as with any scientific enterprise, they can be improved on and they will need to be revised. But they have been worked out with great care and economic sophistication. Neither Rorty, nor anyone else who claims that there is no feasible and attractive alternative to capitalism, will have much credibility in that claim until they have carefully considered such models and shown how market socialism is not viable as a model that, if given a chance, could work.

Reformist social democratic leftists might respond that it is not the reasonability of such market socialist models that bothers them, but their *political impossibility*. Given the political forms that are in play, there is no chance that in any of the rich capitalist democracies – the places where, if they could be put in practice, they might work – that market socialism will be given a try. Capitalists and the politicians in their service will not allow this to happen. They will not willingly transform their societies into something which is not capitalist, even if a very strong case, considering the needs of people generally, is made for it. And democracy and the media are sufficiently hijacked by them for it to be non-utopian to think there are forces in such societies – that is in our societies – to bring market socialism onto the economic and political agenda. However good it may look on paper to a few intellectuals, there are no evident political mechanisms in our societies to get it on the agenda. We simply do not know how to get from here to there.

This is a powerful argument against any form of socialism, and perhaps it cannot be met. But, for all that, it is not as decisive as many think. Neo-liberalism, as its harsh globalizing face is becoming ever more evident, is working very badly – is hurting many people and not yielding its rosy promises. And it is generating increasing opposition, some of it radical, most of it liberal: a clamor on the radical side for the overthrow of capitalism, and on the liberal side for a rather more socially responsible capitalism. But there is a considerable reluctance on the part of the multinationals to become socially responsible. For example, the big GM producers such as Monsanto claim that their products are safe and that it is just ignorance for anyone to think otherwise. But they refuse to put their money where their mouth is. By fierce lobbying they have successfully blocked the passage of a bill in the European Parliament which would hold them legally liable if their food turned out to be harmful to humans or the environment. This is just one instance of repeated occurrences where multinationals in conjunction with conservative politicians make things worse for human beings – not just a few human beings but many human beings in different conditions in different countries and in different walks of life.

The natural thing, after this, in Europe (but not North America) is to vote in social democrats, sometimes in coalition with greens or socialists. But when it is seen that these parties do not develop policies that improve things, there is considerable disillusion (in the UK, for example, the gap between the rich and poor has actually increased under the current Labour government). *Perhaps*, after repeated such bumps, the electorate may be willing to give socialism a try, where for the socialists' part they present an intelligent plan for market socialism. This might produce a right-wing coup, but this is unlikely in countries such as Britain, France, Germany, Holland and the Scandinavian bloc. Again, we should remember Gramsci's slogan. Moreover, there will be no achieving anything without engaging in struggle.

There is also the bad name that socialist societies have acquired from their tendency in some instances to become (to understate it) undemocratic. More than that, some societies, running under the banner of socialism and Marxism, have been soaked in blood. This must be acknowledged and not forgotten. But it is also important to keep in mind that not everything calling itself socialist and Marxist is indeed so. We must see clearly what Marx and Engels stood for, and also understand that these tyrannical and bloodthirsty regimes have nothing in common with what Marx and Engels were about. And we must never forget how the nascent socialist countries had their backs driven to the wall by the capitalist countries. There is, to be sure, vanguardism. But there are also Marxist claims about the ill effects of the pervasiveness of bourgeois ideology, and how bourgeois attitudes affect our social lives in a way that runs against the attainment of community among us. This leads to subtle, and sometimes not-so-subtle, ways in which workers are dominated. The militancy of socialists comes from the recognition of the need to fight back here. We cannot, as Rorty is, reasonably be dismissive about this. Recognizing of the need for vigilance and militancy, vanguardism became an integral part of Lenin's thought, and has led away from democratic ways of doing things. But the vanguardism is Lenin, not Marx and Engels. They recognized the need for vigilance and militancy, but this is a different matter. Marx, in his seething rage (not unjustified) at the way people are treated under capitalism, sometimes became a bit fanatical. But that is not at all central to his thought, and it certainly has no place in analytical Marxism or socialism properly understood.

Socialists have been in capitalist societies subject to all kinds of repression, and deliberate disinformation concerning them has been and still is widespread. Think, for example, of the fate of Paul Robeson.[4] So it is natural for socialists to distrust the bourgeoisie and to worry about how they infiltrate socialist ranks. But socialism does not rest on that distrust of bourgeois intellectuals and related phenomena. And certainly analytical Marxism and the socialism that goes with it is non-vanguardist and democratic through and through. Moreover, where socialist revolutions have turned sour they occurred in societies lacking in two features essential for the development and sustaining of socialism: first, developed economic forces; and second, a tradition of liberal democracy.[5] Marx clearly saw that socialism develops on the back of capitalism while transforming it. It didn't have a chance in Russia or China, where there was little capitalist development. For it to work it must arise in the rich (economically developed) capitalist democracies which are, for reasons Marx well explained, also liberal democracies. They would remain such democracies with the transformation to socialism. Indeed, with a transition to socialism in such conditions, the democracy would actually even deepen, for two reasons: first, it would then be also some form of economic democracy and not *just* a political democracy; and second, the political democracy would be fuller, for finally ordinary people would have a say in how their society is ordered. What John Rawls calls constitutional essentials would remain in place, but it would also be so that people, given the end of class domination, would have a greater control over their lives. *Pace* libertarianism, there would be more liberty with socialism, not less (Nielsen 1985).

I turn now to the third old-left social democratic point against analytical Marxism and Marxism more generally – a point stressed particularly by Rorty – namely its alleged overtheoreticism. When Rorty thinks of theory in the context of Marxist social theory he thinks of grand *philosophical* theory seeking to integrate everything: a dialectical and historical materialism that will show us how societies *must* develop and, with this teleology of historical inevitability, what the end of history and the destiny of human beings must be. While most analytical Marxists are historical materialists, their historical materialism is not such a grand philosophical teleological theory replete with a philosophical anthropology. It is not a philosophical theory, grand or ungrand, at all, and it is not a teleological theory. It is rather an integrated cluster of empirical – and thus falsifiable – hypotheses about epochal social change (G. A. Cohen 1988; Satz 1989; Nielsen 1983, 1989c). So here we have Rorty versus strawman.

However, this does not end the matter about overtheoriticism. That grand "meta-narratives" are blather is tolerably evident. What is crucial, even when taking Marxist social theory in such a non-teleological, non-metaphysical way, as analytical Marxists rightly do, is to determine whether we can have warrantedly assertable and useful theories of such *general scope* as analytical Marxists (and Marxists generally) believe we can, and as Durkheim and Weber and contemporary Durkheimians and Weberians believe we can as well, or whether with Rorty and Peter Winch we must, or at least should, stick with contextual, practice-dependent, more piecemeal approaches to social life and to social problems. The anti-Marxian claim is, whether philosophical, empirical, normative or some amalgam, that we should not trust in general theories. We should (*pace* Sterba) no more trust in general ethical theories than in general empirically oriented interpretative-empirical theories. They (*pace* Marxists) are of no use in guiding practice; they are not warrantedly assertable and their very coherence is problematic. We are not going to get such a theoretical understanding of our historical situation or indeed any historical understanding; we are not going to get in any way such a systematic integrated understanding. Leftism, the argument goes, to be defendable must be a pragmatic, atheoretical, piecemeal, reformist social democracy, or perhaps a pragmatic socialism without theoretical danglers – at least the grand theoretical danglers of the classical sociological tradition (Nielsen 1999, 513–16).

I do not want or need in my articulation and defense of socialism here, and particularly with my juxtaposition of it with Sterba's account of justice, to take sides on this issue, though it is, I believe, a very important and very contestable issue. But for my purposes here, even a rather atheoretical socialism will do. What we do need to do is to see that without it at least Rorty is not going to be able to realize his utopian hopes for a *classless*, casteless, non-sexist, non-homophobic, non-racist egalitarian world. He cannot possibly realize it in a capitalist world, no matter how social democratic. A capitalist society without classes is a contradiction in terms. If there were no capitalists there would be no capitalism. And where, as in capitalism, there are capitalists and workers, there will be at least some inequalities; *perhaps* justifiable or at least unavoidable inequalities, but inequalities all the same. If, as Rorty thinks – and as social democrats generally think – some form of capitalism is functionally or rationally inescapable in complex modern societies, then he cannot have his classless egalitarian society or a classless egalitarian world unless perchance he would have us *per impossible* return to a situation where we live in stateless hunter-gatherer societies. He cannot have it even as a utopian hope, for it makes no sense to hope for what one firmly believes not to be achievable. If we are stuck with capitalism, as Rorty believes we are, and indeed reasonably so, then we cannot coherently hope for a classless egalitarian society. I do not think such a hope is unreasonable, but then I do not think that socialism is unreasonable, undesirable or impossible.

V

I turn now to consideration of a case that could be made for this in the context of comparing it with the account Sterba gives of justice.

I want to say initially that I am in strong agreement with Sterba's conception of "a peacemaking way of doing philosophy." Philosophers too often go around like game cocks spoiling for a fight. They see themselves as engaging in a philosophical battle in which the aim is to demolish their opponents, to shoot down their arguments and to destroy their conceptions. But that is infantile. The model should not be that of the Lone Ranger out to gun down "the errants," but C. S. Peirce's image of philosophy as an impartial cooperative inquiry where philosophers, assuming a fallibilistic orientation, seek to learn from each other and together to construct the best account they can make of whatever is at issue and to be prepared, indeed even in most cases to expect, to modify or even to abandon their account as inquiry proceeds. The cases of such macho-childish behavior on the part of philosophers that Sterba cites in his first chapter are, unfortunately, perfectly accurate and bring shame on our profession. "Philosophy as warmaking" is not philosophy – to engage in justified *persuasive* definition – but something like a silly verbal battle. *If* that is what philosophy is, philosophy surely should come to an end. I would only add that avoiding and detesting that is perfectly compatible with a philosopher of integrity sticking with something that she genuinely and reflectively thinks is so and is of central importance even in the face of universal opposition. She surely in such a circumstance should think twice (to very much understate it) about that opposition and to honestly consider and take to heart their objections. In the face of universal opposition, if she is reasonable, she will think that it is very likely – indeed almost certain – that she is mistaken. She must, that is, take their opposing views, with such a massive opposition to her own, as something that is very likely well taken. But after non-evasively doing that she still might believe that her views are a telling-it-like-it-is and not crazy, and thus stick with them, trying to articulate them more adequately so that they might fairly answer the objections directed at them.[6] In the process of doing this she might come to agree with her critics, but still she might instead stick with her views. But what she cannot do and still be acting reasonably and indeed still be doing philosophy, is to persist in her views "at the expense of fairmindedness, openness or self-criticism" (Sterba 1998, 10). To not proceed in a deliberately biased manner just goes with the job, or at least with a genuine sense of one's vocation as a philosopher and intellectual. Sterba is right in claiming that we should do philosophy in such a way that we maximize the possibility of coming up with genuinely justified views (Sterba 1998, 3–9).

Sterba not only argues that a commitment to morality is rationally acceptable – one can act rationally in acting in accordance with the moral point of view – but more than that that morality is rationally *required* of us. There is, he believes, no rational alternative to acting from the moral point of view. There must be some failure in rationality if a person does not act on moral principle. Hobbes's "foole" is indeed a fool. It is not only immoral (or at least amoral) not to so act (or at least sincerely strive to so act), but irrational as well. I have argued at length against Kurt Baier, David Gauthier, Alan Gewirth and others that such a moral rationalism cannot be sustained. What can be sustained instead is that it is rational to be committed to the moral point of view, but it can be rational as well to be an egoist or amoralist. Reason does not decide things here. It is permissive (Nielsen 1989a; 1996a, 207–71; 2001).

Sterba's articulation and defense of what I shall call moral rationalism – the view that rationality requires a commitment to morality – is developed, sophisticated and original, and well aware of the pitfalls of such accounts. And, if he is right, it is a very important claim in moral philosophy. I am, perhaps, not seeing the mote in my own eye, but inclined to think that this part of his view has not been made out. Where others have failed, from Plato to Gauthier, he fails too. I wish it were my mandate to examine his account here. But it is not, and in setting out his relation to socialism I shall *assume* (what I actually do not believe) that this part of his account – his morality as compromise – is basically sound, and I will limit myself to examining his claim that

> even when Morality as Compromise is given the minimal interpretation of a libertarian ideal of liberty, it leads, not as libertarians claim to the practical requirements of a minimal or night-watchperson state, but to the practical requirements of a welfare state and beyond.
>
> (Sterba 1998, 40)

I shall particularly be concerned with the "beyond" and whether his account leads us to socialism and, if so, to what kind of socialism and, independently of Sterba, to a consideration of whether socialism of any kind can be sustained.

Libertarianism appears at least to have minimal practical requirements, and so he reasonably starts there in articulating his theory of justice (Sterba 1998, 7). He believes that he has established that the libertarians' ideal of liberty has the "same practical requirements as the welfare liberals' ideal of fairness" (Sterba 1998, 7). The claim is that, despite what libertarians claim, the same rights to welfare and equal opportunity that are usually associated with a welfare liberal ideal are actually entailed by libertarianism (Sterba 1998, 8). He further argues that "these two rights lead to something like the equality that socialists endorse" (Sterba 1998, 8).

Libertarians operate with a pared-down conception of liberty and rights as negative liberties and negative rights only. Liberty is center stage for libertarians of any sort. But it is a negative liberty. People are unfree, on their account, when they are kept from doing what they want to do or are entitled to do by the *positive* actions of others. Their rights are violated when they are prevented from doing by the positive acts of others what they are entitled (legitimately free) to do. They take it as a fundamental political ideal that each person should have the greatest amount of liberty commensurate with the same liberty for all. If a starving stranger to whom I owe nothing – or at least I in libertarian terms owe nothing – comes to my door begging for food when I have more than enough and am in fact enjoying a sumptuous feast, if I am a kind and charitable person I will give him something. But if I turn him away without giving him anything I have, libertarians maintain, not wronged him. I have not violated his rights or limited his liberty or kept from him anything to which he is entitled. I have done him no wrong, though I have certainly not been kind or charitable. This remains true even if as a result of my omission he dies a few hours later. I may not make him worse off than he already is, but I am in no way required to aid him. Nice people, of course, will help him, but I am in no way morally required to be nice. People, of course, may contract to engage in mutual aid, but there is no antecedent duty or obligation to mutual aid.

Sterba thinks that libertarians fail to understand the logic of their own position. People in such circumstances (e.g. such as a starving person) implicitly, the self-understanding of libertarians to the contrary notwithstanding, given the very logic of the libertarians' own account, have legitimate claims on others. Consider conflict situations between the rich and the poor where the poor, through no fault of their own, lack the goods and resources to meet even their most basic needs while the rich have more than enough goods and resources to satisfy their basic needs. Libertarians argue, as we have seen, that the rich are at liberty to ignore the poor and to use their own goods and resources to satisfy their desires for various luxuries if that is what they want to do. This liberty can be rightly enjoyed by the rich even at the expense of the meeting by the poor of their most basic needs.

Liberty, libertarians believe, always has priority over other political ideals. The liberty of the poor – it is claimed – is not at stake here. Nobody is depriving them of their liberty. Nothing that is theirs is being taken from them; they are not prevented from exercising any of their own liberties. It would be a kind thing to help them, but such charitable acts cannot be morally, or otherwise, required because the poor have not been prevented from doing anything they are free to do.

However, Sterba responds, their liberty has been affected. It is affected in this way: the poor are not free to take from the surplus of the rich what is needed to satisfy their own basic needs. Libertarians will, of course, say they have no such liberty. But on what grounds? The poor need not be appealing to a positive liberty, but only to the very same negative liberty that libertarians are appealing to; the liberty of the poor is not being treated as a "positive right to receive something but a negative right of noninterference" (Sterba 1998, 45). We have here a genuine conflict of liberties – negative liberties – between the rich and the poor. Either

> the rich should have the liberty not to be interfered with in using their surplus goods and resources for luxury purposes or … the poor should have the liberty not to be interfered with in taking from the rich what they require to meet their basic needs. If we choose one liberty, we must reject the other. What needs to be determined, therefore, is which liberty is morally preferable: the liberty of the rich or the liberty of the poor.
>
> (Sterba 1998, 45–6)

We could, of course, say that there is no moral resolution possible in such circumstances and we just have to fight it out. We are simply faced with a naked power struggle. But that is hardly a desirable course to take if there is any reasonable resolution in sight. And, Sterba claims, there is something reasonable that can be said. We moral agents have two very fundamental principles of morality which are widely shared and are reasonable, and they can be reasonably used in such conflict situations. They are the "Ought Implies Can" Principle and its contrapositive, the "Conflict Resolution Principle" (Sterba 1998, 46–8). The first principle reads

> People are not morally required to do what they lack the power to do or what would involve so great a sacrifice that it would be unreasonable to ask them to perform such an action and/or, in the case of severe conflicts of interest, unreasonable to require them to perform such an action.
>
> (Sterba 1998, 46)

The second principle reads

What people are morally required to do is what is either reasonable
to ask them to do or, in the case of severe conflicts of interest, reasonable to require them to do.

(Sterba 1998, 48)[7]

The situation here – the conflict described between the rich and the poor – is
an extreme conflict-of-interest situation and, given the above principles, it is
clearly more reasonable, Sterba has it, for the rich to relinquish their liberty
here than for the poor to do so. For the poor to relinquish their liberty here
is to allow themselves to starve to death or something very close to that. We
cannot reasonably expect them to do that while for the rich no such dire
prospect obtains. If the conflict is resolved in the other way, the rich will lose
some opportunities to acquire luxury goods, goods which they would like
very much to have. But the Conflict Resolution Principle is a reasonable
principle to invoke here. It requires everyone affected to accept it and it
favors, in situations of the type described, the liberty of the poor over the
rich. But, Sterba claims, the Conflict Resolution Principle as well as the
Ought Implies Can Principle are principles libertarians must accept if they
would be *reasonable*, and these principles require libertarians to have moral
commitments, e.g. to accept negative welfare rights that they did not think
they were committed to (Sterba 1998, 49–50).

Sterba also argues that libertarians, if they think things through reasonably,
will be led from purely negative welfare rights (as in considering the poor) to
the richer positive liberal welfare rights espoused by welfare liberals and
socialists. Sterba argues:

in recognizing the legitimacy of negative welfare rights, libertarians
will come to see that virtually any of their surplus possessions is
likely to violate the negative rights of the poor by preventing the
poor from rightfully appropriating (some part of) their surplus
goods and resources. So, in order to ensure that they will not be engaging in such wrongful actions, it will be incumbent on them to set
up institutions guaranteeing adequate positive welfare rights for the
poor. Only then will they be able to use legitimately any remaining
surplus possessions to meet their own nonbasic needs.

(Sterba 1998, 55–6)

The reasonable thing to do, he claims, is to "set up institutions guaranteeing
adequate positive welfare rights. For these reasons, recognizing negative
welfare rights of the poor will ultimately lead libertarians to endorse the
same sort of welfare institutions favored by welfare liberals and socialists"
(Sterba 1998, 56).

Sterba extends what he says about how a reasonable libertarian would
come to accept not only negative welfare rights but positive welfare rights as

well to a conception of equality of opportunity (Sterba 1998, 63–4). We have a right to welfare and a right to equal opportunity, for both are required for meeting people's basic needs, and without the meeting of basic needs liberty is undermined (Sterba 1998, 64). "What these arguments show," claims Sterba, "is that libertarianism or a libertarian conception of justice supports the same practical requirements as welfare liberalism or a welfare conception of justice" (Sterba 1998, 65).

Further in pursuit of his reconciliation project, Sterba argues that the equal welfare rights and equal opportunity rights usually "associated with a welfare liberal ideal lead to something like the equality that socialists endorse, once distant peoples and future generations are taken into account" (Sterba 1998, 172–3).

Sterba has summarized his own basic argument well in the following passage:

> In sum, pursuing peacemaking as a model for doing philosophy, I have argued that, not only does rationality require morality, but even a minimal morality like libertarianism requires rights to welfare and equal opportunity that lead to socialist equality and feminist androgyny. In this way, I have brought together the moral ideals of libertarianism, welfare liberalism, socialism and feminism into what could be called a reconciliationist conception of justice. In addition, I have argued that the pursuit of this reconciliationist conception of justice, especially in its feminist dimensions, is theoretically and practically connected to the pursuit of racial justice, homosexual justice, and multicultural justice and is further constrained by specific principles of environmental justice and just war pacifism.
>
> (Sterba 1998, 174)

VI

I applaud Sterba's reconciliation project as far as it can be plausibly carried out without blurring the edges between different conceptions and positions which may well need, for the very justified view he rightly seeks, sharper articulation and differentiation. But when this sharper articulation has been carried out we may have lost our reconciliation. I further think that a good case can be made that morality – (*pace* Gauthier) the very fullbodied morality that Sterba believes is crucial for an adequate social and moral life – is in *accordance* with rationality, but I believe (*pace* Sterba) that it is not *required* by the norms of rationality (Nielsen 1989, 269–83). I further believe, like Rawls, that we should distinguish between reasonability and rationality (Nielsen 1996a, 427–50; 1998a; Rawls 1993). Sterba repeatedly makes great play with reasonability, which he unfortunately does not clearly distinguish from rationality. His criticism of libertarianism, taken on its own terms, is that it commits us to things which are unreasonable. But in many situations – and particularly in situations where Sterba uses "reasonable" and "unreasonable" – it is itself a moral notion, often meaning roughly "fair" or "impartial" and (for "unreasonable") "unfair" or "not impartial." There is, of course, no deriving morality from it, for we are already in the moral domain. Moreover, "reasonably," if not "essentially contested," is a deeply contested notion. And it is not clear that, in appealing to it in arguing against Hobbesian libertarians such as Jan Narveson, he has not begged the question (Sterba 1998, 72–6).

Because of these difficulties, Sterba's reconciliationist project would be better served, particularly over distinctively moral and political matters, if he would drop trying to derive moral norms from the norms of rationality; distinguish clearly between reasonability and rationality; and, recognizing that reasonability is itself in many of its contexts a moral notion, abandon what is in effect his ethical rationalism and utilize instead a coherentist approach like that of Rawls, deploying the methodology of appealing to considered convictions in wide reflective equilibrium.[8]

I do not argue this here, though I have argued for such a methodology elsewhere (Nielsen 1996a, 12–19, 159–272). I hope that somewhere in this volume someone will in some way take these issues up. However, to repeat what I said earlier, in what follows I shall *assume* that Sterba is right about deriving morality from "the norms of rationality," that indeed there are such norms, that there is nothing problematic about his appeal to reasonability and that he is right in thinking that libertarianism, properly understood, leads to welfare liberalism and perhaps even to something like a socialist equality.

"Perhaps" is too wishy-washy. Part of the trouble is that Sterba does not say what he means by "socialism" or "the equality that socialists endorse." I think he is in reality talking about social democracy and of the egalitarianism of social liberals such as Brian Barry and John Rawls. What they say is for the most part socialism-friendly, but they do not endorse socialism and, though their egalitarianism is robust, it is not distinctively socialist and does not take us beyond welfare and fair-equal opportunity liberalism. Socialist equality, rightly or wrongly, is still more robust (Nielsen 1985, 1996b; G. A. Cohen 1992, 1996, 2000). I shall specify something of what this comes to. Beyond what Sterba argues for, though starting there, socialists want, where this can be had, not only the setting of conditions for a genuine equal opportunity for an equal meeting of basic needs but, as well, for the meeting of all needs. Moreover, they also want to see a world where everyone will be able as fully as possible to satisfy those of their wants that they would continue to want on reflection, and with a good understanding of the causes and consequences of their satisfying them, that are also wants compatible with everyone else being able to satisfy their wants where they meet the same conditions. In short, they want a world where everyone could satisfy those compossible wants that they as individuals would reflectively and informedly endorse. The aspiration of socialist egalitarians is for there to be a world in which it is possible for everyone to have the best life that is possible for human beings to have. That is the equality of condition that socialists take to be a heuristic ideal. This goes a long way beyond, though of course it involves, a commitment to seeking equality in the meeting of the basic needs for everyone.

This should have a further filling-in and specification. We should ask what are socialist egalitarian aspirations? What are the utopian hopes of socialists? What sort of world would socialists ideally like to see? It is to have a world of equals – a world without any bowing and scraping – where the life of everyone matters and matters equally. We socialist egalitarians want a classless, casteless, genderless, non-racist, non-homophobic world where an egalitarian ethos prevails (G. A. Cohen 1992 and 2000). Socialist egalitarians aspire to a world of equals, people with equal effective human rights, equal (in so far as this is feasible) in power, equal in access to advantage, equal in whole-life prospects. But we also want a world in which people have a sense of community, with the common commitments that go with it. Socialist egalitarians want, as well, as far as that is possible, that well-being be something that everyone has at the highest level it is possible for them to attain. Such an egalitarian hope is not just to make the badly off well off, or, if that is not possible, to make them as close to being well off as possible, but to have a world in which there are no badly off individuals or groups of people, a world that is not hierarchically stratified (if that is not a pleonasm) along the lines of "the worst off," "the next worse off," "the middlingly situated," "the well off," "the better off" and "the best off" (Nielsen 1996b). Put in political terms, socialist egalitarians are socialists and not welfare state social democrats.

In practical terms (and aside from ideal theory), in societies situated as even the better off and more progressive of our societies are (e.g. Denmark, Holland, Finland, Iceland, Norway, Sweden), socialist egalitarians will, *vis-à-vis* equality in such a world, opt for very much the same things that social democrats will opt for: to make the worst off strata of society as well off as they can be. We should redistribute until no further redistribution would leave the worst off better off. But their underlying aim, utopian though it may be, is to cause to come into existence and to be sustained a world of equals: a classless, genderless, non-racist world where the necessary strata hierarchies (if such there must be) are as minimal as they possibly can be compatible with a reasonably efficient ordering of society. (This is not to say that efficiency trumps justice, but it is to say that efficiency remains an important consideration in the proper ordering of our social world.) Most essentially, any strata differentiations that may remain or arise must not be such as to be a source of some people having power over others. Perhaps that is an ideal impossible to even reasonably approximate, as the radical historian Eugene Genovese, along with many others, would insist, but for socialist egalitarians it is there as at least a heuristic.

This is the ideal for a perfectly good and just world. It is, of course, wildly utopian, but it gives us a standard against which to measure our actual societies and actual world.[9] Our world is indeed very distant from that. In our world, to speak of global justice is such a joke as to make one want to cry and sneeringly laugh at the same time (Nielsen 1998b). Even the best of our societies (say Sweden or Iceland) are very distant from "the socialist ideal." But measured against its standard, Iceland and Sweden come off much better than the United States or the United Kingdom. And they, in turn, come off much better than Burma and Saudi Arabia. So the standard, however utopian, helps us in some way to guide conduct.

Should Sterba extend his welfare state equal opportunity liberalism to such a socialist egalitarianism? He should, for without it he cannot get, as he wishes, to a classless society, let alone a classless world that both he and socialists want. Moreover, given his commitment to moral equality (the life of everyone matters and matters equally) and to a world of equals (equal moral standing), he cannot get either without socialism, for without it, as we have seen, there will be classes and power differentials rooted in the very structure of our social world. And these undermine moral equality and commitment to a world of equals. It makes an egalitarian ethos and the sense of community that goes with it very hard to attain and sustain.

It might be responded that I am ignoring Sterba's Ought Implies Can Principle. If socialism is impossible period, or impossible as a reasonable option, then the fact that a classless or hierarchically unstratified society cannot be achieved in a capitalist society is not a legitimate criticism of capitalism, or of an egalitarian conception of justice compatible with liberal social democratic capitalism. If socialism (as Rorty, for example, believes) cannot be had, or cannot be reasonably had, it is irrational to keep going on about it. Sterba, if this criticism stands, should not endorse socialist egalitarianism.

I shall argue that it does not stand. This takes us back to the first part of this essay. A socialism without markets is not a feasible option, but there remain market socialist alternatives. Here we have well worked out and feasible models for market socialism – models that could be applied in our actually existing developed societies and eventually could have worldwide application. The crucial problem, as we have seen, is not socio-economic coherence and plausibility, but baldly *political*. People in the developed capitalist societies where it arguably could work are not willing to give it a try; and in poor societies where people are willing to give it a try, their modes of production are not sufficiently developed to make socialism possible. But this is a weak "impossibility." For sometimes things – important big things – change very rapidly and unexpectedly. Think, for example, of the sudden collapse of the Soviet empire or the end of the apartheid regime in South Africa. Socialism is a non-starter now, but a decade down the road, with neo-liberalism and globalization taking their toll in all sorts of ugly and really harmful ways in the First, Second and Third Worlds (though somewhat differently in each), socialism may well become a reasonable possibility. This may be wishful thinking on my part, but again it may not be. There is obviously work for socialist intellectuals and activists here (they sometimes are the same).

Centrally, for them, it will be a matter of making clear and compelling arguments that socialism can work, that the horrible world we live in now is not inevitable and forever, that there is an alternative that will yield the possibility of a decent life for everyone. Social democracy, if it can continue to exist with globalization, and if it can be applied globally, will carry us part of the way. Imagine Sweden being the world. (There are also some reasons to think that that may not be a feasible possibility. The Swedish condition of life is not causally independent of what goes on in the rest of the world.) But, even if it is a feasible possibility, it cannot carry us all the way. It cannot give us as egalitarian and free a social world as it is possible and desirable to have, for it cannot give us a classless society, economic as well as political democracy, and it cannot equalize power as fully as can obtain in (to be pleonastic) a democratic socialist society (Nielsen 1985). Socialist intellectuals need to make this plain, not only to the academy but more generally. The opportunities to do this in our societies are limited, but there are enough cracks in the wall to give us some opportunities. If truth is on our side here, we, if we seize the day, if we throw ourselves into the task with vigor, integrity and all the intelligence we can muster, we can perhaps have some effect. If we have any sense of our vocation here, we must set out the case for socialism clearly, informedly, compellingly and repeatedly. It may not be a spitting into the wind. And remember we are agents and not just neutral observers, for we are involved in the very practices we describe.

To gain the thoroughly just world that we egalitarians seek, we must replace capitalism with socialism (we may do this and still not gain it, but it is a necessary condition for gaining it). A very real worry for people is over the manner of its replacement. It would, of course, be desirable if the replacement could come by the ballot box. But given the way things have gone historically, and how reasonably – from the capitalist point of view – it is to try to make them go thus, it is very unlikely that capitalists would so relinquish power (remember Chile). That means somehow toppling capitalists from power, and that means some sort of revolution.

Some people might pull back here, not because they think revolution in such a circumstance is morally wrong in itself, but because they fear all the death and destruction that a protracted war would bring about. The forces supporting capitalism have awesome means of control, repression and destruction and would clearly use it, if necessary, to protect their turf.

However, we must gain some perspective here. We must remember there are revolutions and revolutions. Some are short and decisive with minimal amounts of killing and destruction (Nielsen 1971). It is also important to recognize that the military and the police too are people capable of seeing the situation for what it is and changing sides. The rank and file here and the lower ranking officers suffer like everyone else, and they have people near and dear to them who suffer from repression. Why assume it is impossible for them to see through the ideology and change sides? They also know that if they act together they have a considerable amount of power.

At least two things are involved here. First, to make a clear and compelling case for an egalitarian socialist conception of justice. Sterba has nudged us in this direction and I, as has G. A. Cohen, have here tried to indicate something of what it would take to complete that task. Second, we must show that socialism is not *just* a utopian moral ideal – mere pie in the sky – but could be, and reasonably so, a way of organizing our social life. That is by far the more demanding task. I have gestured at what needs to be done here. But Sterba has done nothing in this respect. Here he sticks close to the standard philosophical preoccupations. But without engaging in this task there can be no serious talk about socialist justice. It would be just the self-indulgent or self-deceptive moralizing that Marx repeatedly inveighed against (Nielsen 1989b). Marx famously said, "The philosophers have only *interpreted* the world; the point is to change it." As his life's work makes abundantly clear, he did not think we could sensibly change it – or indeed successfully change it – without understanding it. We need all the understanding we can get, but what we very much need now as well – particularly in the rich capitalist democracies – is a new revolutionary militancy.

NOTES

1   It is their ownership and control of productive property that makes people capitalists. Their entrepreneurship may remain if (for example) they were specialized workers – workers doing entrepreneurial work – in socialist firms. Their being entrepreneurs does not make them capitalists.

2   This is largely true of the academic cultural left, but there are thousands of activist cultural leftists, some with their distinctive organizations, outside the academy, who do engage in political contestation (Cohen and Rogers 1998).

3   See also Nove (1983) for an important, carefully and empirically researched, and more historically oriented argument than Roemer's or Schweikart's for market socialism.

4   Paul Robeson was an African-American. He was a lawyer, a famous opera and spiritual singer and an equally famous actor. His work in all these domains was destroyed by blacklisting and other forms of harassment as a result of his principled commitment to socialism. He refused to back down or compromise in his defense of the Soviet Union, even in the most difficult McCarthy years. His persecution was so intense and so continuous that he was finally, toward the end of his life, physically and emotionally destroyed (Williston 1999).

5   Czechoslovakia might be thought to be an exception. Prior to the imposition from the outside of socialism, it was both economically developed and liberal. But it is not an exception, for its socialism was imposed on it from the outside. And its socialism ended when that pressure came to an end.

6 Given Rorty's anti-representationalism and perspectivism, both of which I am partial to, how do I get off talking about telling it like it is? Since I believe that there can be no one true description of the world or a way the world is in itself, then (the claim goes) I cannot coherently talk about telling it like it is. But just as Rorty can and does speak of truth without thinking truth is correspondence, so he and I can speak of telling it like it is without believing there is a one true description of the world. Telling it like it is is having what for the time is the best justified cluster of beliefs that we can obtain. And that is certainly possible. There is nothing more compelling that we can obtain. Here the "we" does not refer just to Rorty and myself but to people more generally (Nielsen 1999).

7 It seems to me plainly false to say that whatever it is reasonable to ask me to do is morally required of me. It is reasonable to ask me to have better table manners, but this is not morally required of me. Only a manners fanatic would think it so.

8 How, on such an approach, do we deal with libertarians? Quite shortly and bluntly. An approach which entails saying that if I let a child drown in a shallow pool when I can easily save him I have not wronged him, have not done anything that I ought not to do, can be just rejected out of hand. That we do not let a child drown whom we can easily save is a deeply ingrained considered conviction (judgment) of ours that fits well in a wide reflective equilibrium. We cannot find our feet with someone who thinks we have no obligation here. For an argument that we cannot, either in moral reflection or in doing moral philosophy, bypass considered convictions, see Nielsen (1996a, 261–72). It is hard to see how a reconciliation project can work here.

9 There are legitimate Deweyian worries here about the necessity of a means/ends continuum. I cannot pursue it here, but I believe Dewey's sound sense about the entanglement of means and ends can be made compatible with what I say here. If it can't then I have to go back to the drawing board.

References

Blair, Tony and Schroeder, Gerhard (2000) "The Third Way/*Die Neue Mitte*: A Manifesto," *Dissent* (Spring 2000) 51–65.

Cohen, G. A. (1978) *Karl Marx's Theory of History: A Defense*, Oxford: Clarendon Press.

——(1983) "The Structure of Proletarian Unfreedom," *Philosophy and Public Affairs*, vol. 12, 3–33.

——(1988) *History, Labour and Freedom*, Oxford: Clarendon Press.

——(1992) "Incentives, Inequality and Community," in G. B. Peterson (ed.) *The Tanner Lectures on Human Values*, Salt Lake City: University of Utah Press, 262–329.

——(1996) "Self-Ownership, History and Socialism: An Interview with G. A. Cohen," *Imprints*, vol. 1, no. 1, 7–25.

——(2000) *If You're an Egalitarian, How Come You're So Rich?*, Cambridge MA: Harvard University Press.

Cohen, Joshua (1982) "G. A. Cohen, Marx's Theory of History," *The Journal of Philosophy*, vol. 79/5, 253–73.

——(1992) "Minimalist Historical Materialism," in Rodger Beehler *et al.* (eds) *On the Track of Reason*, Boulder CO: Westview Press, 155–74.

——(1999–2000) "Equality, Justice and Democracy: An Interview with Joshua Cohen," *Imprints*, vol. 4, no. 2, 103–18.

Cohen, Joshua and Rogers, Joel (1998) "Review of Rorty's *Truth and Progress* and *Achieving Our Country*," *Lingua Franca*.

Levine, A. and Wright, E. O. (1980) "History and the Forces of Production," *New Left Review*, vol. 123, 47–69.

Moore, Stanley (1993) *Marx Versus Markets*, University Park PA: Pennsylvania State University Press.

Nielsen, Kai (1971) "On the Choice Between Reform and Revolution," *Inquiry*, vol. 14, 271–95.

——(1983) "Taking Historical Materialism Seriously," *Dialogue*, vol. XXII, 319–38.

——(1985) *Equality and Liberty: A Defense of Radical Egalitarianism*, Totowa NJ: Rowman & Allanheld.

——(1989a) *Why Be Moral?*, Buffalo NY: Prometheus Books.

——(1989b) *Marxism and the Moral Point of View*, Boulder CO: Westview Press.

——(1989c) "Afterword" in Robert Ware and Kai Nielsen (eds) *Analyzing Marxism*, Calgary: University of Calgary Press, 497–539.

——(1996a) *Naturalism Without Foundations*, Amherst NY: Prometheus Books.

——(1996b) "Radical Egalitarianism Revisited: On Going Beyond the Difference Principle," in Marcia Valiante (ed.) *The Windsor Yearbook of Access to Justice*, vol. 15, 121–58.

——(1998a) "Liberal Reasonability a Critical Tool? Reflections After Rawls," *Dialogue*, 739–59.

——(1998b) "Is Global Justice Impossible?", *Res Publica*, vol. IV, no. 2, 131–66.

——(1999) "Taking Rorty seriously," *Dialogue*, vol. XXXVIII, no. 3, 503–18.

——(2001) "Moral Point of View Theories," in Lawrence C. Becker and Charlotte B. Becker (eds) *Encyclopedia of Ethics, Second Edition*, New York: Garland Publishing Inc.

Nove, Alec (1983) *The Economics of Feasible Socialism*, London: George Allen & Unwin.

Pogge, Thomas (1996) "The Bounds of Nationalism," in Jocelyne Couture *et al.* (eds) *Rethinking Nationalism*, Calgary: University of Calgary Press, 463–504.

Rawls, John (1993) *Political Liberalism*, New York: Columbia University Press.

Roemer, John E. (1994) *A Future for Socialism*, Cambridge MA: Harvard University Press.

Rorty, Richard (1998a) *Against Bosses, Against Oligarchies: A Conversation With Richard Rorty*, Charlottesville VA: Prickly Pear Pamphlets.

——(1998b) *Achieving Our Country: Leftist Thought in Twentieth Century America*, Cambridge MA: Harvard University Press.

Satz, Debra (1989) "Marxism, Materialism and Historical Progress," in Robert Ware and Kai Nielsen (eds) *Analyzing Marxism*, Calgary: University of Calgary Press, 393–424.

Schweickart, David (1993) *Against Capitalism*, Cambridge: Cambridge University Press.

Sterba, James P. (1998) *Justice for Here and Now*, Cambridge: Cambridge University Press.

Williston, Floyd (1999) "Paul Robeson, 1898–1998," *Socialist Studies Bulletin*, no. 56, 32–45.

11

DEMOCRATIC EGALITARIANISM

Carol C. Gould

Is the concept of socialism and, more generally, socialist theory, any longer relevant, given the current dominance of global corporations and markets, as well as increasing worldwide democratization, at least of a formal sort? Is there any point in attempting to rescue the old-fashioned idea of socialism from its ignominious association with various repressive and authoritarian regimes of the twentieth century? Certainly there are strands in socialist theory that are still of interest, and many of these have been explored and developed by numerous philosophers and political theorists in recent decades. Among these are the concept of positive freedom, the requirement for greater equality and mutuality in social and economic life, the importance of economic democracy, and of course the critiques of alienation, exploitation and imperialism. Increasingly, self-identified socialists have also taken themselves to be feminists, multiculturalists, and anti-colonialists, and have integrated an emphasis on differences beyond those of class into their diverse approaches.

Crucial disagreements persist, however, no longer about forms of government – there is uniform commitment to democracy – but about globalization and trade, in their implications for labor standards and workers' rights. Do economic globalization and the world market simply represent the predictable course of capitalist development, opening opportunities for increasing labor solidarity worldwide and necessary economic development in the Third World? Or do they instead represent the triumph of global corporations, concerned only with profit at the expense of workers and of human needs more generally? Or perhaps both at the same time? On a more theoretical level, too, important differences persist in the interpretation and justification of equality, the role of rights, including the human rights, the nature and requirements of economic democracy, and the role of the state in facilitating greater economic and social equality.

These persisting questions set the framework for my considerations in this paper. I want to take up a few of the philosophical issues that arise from socialist theorizing, and its more current form of what I call democratic egalitarianism. It will be of interest to consider the import of this approach at this specific historical juncture, characterized by increasing globalization and international interdependence – economic, technological, social, and to a degree political – combined with democratization, and increasingly serious commitment to the idea of human rights. And if we are concerned with justice (and also freedom and democracy) for "here and now," it is relevant to begin with James P. Sterba's recent attempt to characterize the requirements of such justice in his masterful effort at reconciling a host of diverse social and political theories. In this paper, my discussion of current implications of a democratic and egalitarian approach will take off from an examination of Sterba's claims about socialism and the sense of justice that he suggests it entails. I will focus primarily on certain theoretical issues, but will conclude the paper with some more practical reflections about the import of these views for approaching current globalization processes.

In the introduction to *Justice for Here and Now*, Sterba provocatively states that while they may claim otherwise, "the libertarian's ideal of liberty ... actually supports the same rights to welfare and equal opportunity that are usually associated with a welfare liberal ideal," and that "these two rights lead to something like the equality that socialists endorse."[1] Likewise, in his conclusion, he summarizes his view on this matter by saying "I further argued that these two rights that usually are associated with a welfare liberal ideal lead to something like the equality that socialists endorse, once distant peoples and future generations are taken into account."[2] So here we have an interesting set of claims for our consideration, but how shall we interpret the phrase "the equality that socialists endorse"? Unfortunately, if we look to the intervening chapters in Sterba's book, we find only a handful of references to socialism and no explicit argument for his assertions about it, so if we are to give meaning to his claims, we will have to read between the lines. In his explicit references, in the chapter "From liberty to equality," socialists are grouped with welfare liberals in interpreting the possible constraints on liberty "to include, in addition, negative acts (acts of omission) that prevent people from doing what they otherwise want or are able to do," and not only the "positive acts (acts of commission) that prevent people from acting as they choose" to which libertarians restrict these constraints. He further sees this distinction as one way of understanding the debate between negative and positive liberty.[3] Further expanding this notion of socialism a little, Sterba refers to "welfare institutions" to guarantee "adequate positive welfare rights," which, he argues, libertarians will themselves have to endorse (contrary to their own self-understanding), if they are to avoid having the poor use their own discretion in exercising their negative welfare rights (by taking what they need from the rich).[4]

The other references (of a total of six) include one in which Sterba suggests "borrowing an idea from socialist justice," in a future society where "few resources are available for directly meeting nonbasic needs." In order to "ensure that the most talented people occupy roles and positions commensurate with their abilities," he says that "we will need to make the roles and positions people occupy as intrinsically rewarding as possible."[5] Finally, there are two references in passing to a socialist principle of equal rights to self-development, which, at the outset of the discussion of feminist justice, is held to support Sterba's interpretation of the ideal of androgyny,[6] and at a later point is recognized as permitting some degree of self-preference, while requiring that everyone be provided "with something like the same resources."[7]

I am of course pleased with the last two references, to equal rights to self-development, since this is the version of a quasi-socialist principle that I have defended in my previous work, including *Marx's Social Ontology* and *Rethinking Democracy*.[8] But what can we say about Sterba's own account of socialism, as hinted at in these references? Can it provide us with suggestions for a revitalized socialist theory? And, more to the point of Sterba's own concerns, is he correct in claiming that libertarians, welfare liberals and socialists can agree on his two rights – to welfare and equal opportunity – which he calls "practical requirements" entailed by all three approaches (as well as other theories)? Is this in fact a correct example of a supposedly "peacemaking" method of philosophizing? How does it compare to the dialectical approach in philosophy that emerges in the Hegelian-Marxist tradition?

Before turning to these questions, we should consider whether there is in fact some further position on socialism in Sterba's work beyond these few references that seem to identify it primarily with a commitment to equality and rather extensive welfare requirements. Indeed, if we read between the lines, it seems possible that Sterba identifies his own view in which basic needs for "distant peoples and future generations" should be met with a socialist perspective, or at least one that owes a great deal to socialism. Clearly, none of the other approaches he discusses necessarily support this requirement in the way that he regards as implied by socialist perspectives. Further, in his comment on my paper in our jointly authored volume *Morality and Social Justice*, Sterba endorses the principle of equal positive freedom that I defend and claims to agree with the normative conclusions that I draw there, where these conclusions about the extent of democratic requirements may be considered broadly socialist and egalitarian.[9] His reservation is that I propose a principle of positive in addition to negative liberty, which makes my account less agreeable to libertarians than the one he proposes. Yet, because of his method of beginning with each social and political theory to show agreement on the two rights he favors (welfare and equal opportunity), Sterba unfortunately gives few arguments of his own for these rights and for his more demanding idea that they apply – seemingly without qualification – to distant peoples and future generations.

Without attempting to construct such arguments here, we can look first to the concept of basic needs that seems so central to Sterba's claims.

Commendably from a socialist perspective, Sterba holds that people's basic needs should be met, even those of "distant peoples," and that this normative requirement has priority over the meeting of nonbasic needs of the well off. But what are these basic needs? Whereas Sterba's prevalent example of basic nutritional needs suggests an austere interpretation of these, in another place he seems to enlarge the sphere of basic needs enormously. Thus at one point he writes, "Accordingly, recognizing a right to welfare applicable both to distant peoples and to future generations would lead to a state of affairs in which few resources would be available for directly meeting nonbasic needs."[10] But in a second place he writes, "Basic needs, if not satisfied, lead to significant lacks or deficiencies with respect to a standard of mental and physical well-being. Thus, a person's needs for food, shelter, medical care, protection, companionship, and self-development are, at least in part, needs of this sort."[11] What standard, we might ask? Still, it is clear that the latter suggests a considerably more expansive account of basic needs, and when defined this way, might not support the redistribution he otherwise seeks from relatively wealthy societies like the United States to less developed countries. After all, we are far from meeting the basic needs, in this sense, of everyone in the United States, and such a full view, coupled with a certain priority to compatriots or to members of one's own political or economic society, would seem to leave nothing for redistribution elsewhere.

But let us assume we can somehow settle this issue satisfactorily. In other respects as well, the right to welfare interpreted as requiring the meeting of basic needs worldwide, however enlightened this demand may be, has certain inadequacies from a socialist perspective. It seems at one time too weak and too strong. It is too weak in the first place because it does not speak to the need for democratic participation in economic life, or even in the political sphere. Let us assume that this welfare right in Sterba's analysis can be construed somewhat along the lines of a human right to means of subsistence. If so, it does not address most of the other human rights, even taken together with Sterba's right to equal opportunity. And especially noteworthy for its lack is any account of rights to democratic decision-making, which are clearly crucial in themselves and also for their contribution to preserving and advancing other rights and interests, including gaining means of subsistence.[12]

The sense in which his approach is too strong is perhaps less obvious, but it is indirectly related to the previous point. Sterba abstracts from any consideration of the production process and considers only redistributive principles of justice. However, as Nozick argued against the early Rawls, disregarding the production process and property rights in means of production is problematic. And here, socialist theory tends to side with Nozick, but with a very different interpretation of the nature of production. Where Nozick saw this as individual, socialists have emphasized the social and interdependent nature of economic production processes, which give rise to rights to social property along with rights to personal possessions.[13] The social character of this production supports claims of workers to the benefits of their work and, together with requirements of freedom in this process and to democratic participation, gives rise also to their rights to participate in controlling the production process. As members of an economic and not only a political community, people gain rights to work and to benefit from their work.[14] Sterba by contrast adopts a purely redistributive principle, whereas socialist theory is concerned with meeting basic needs by attending to the organization of economic and social institutions to permit this to happen in an effective and more universal way than at present.

As I also suggested in a previous published comment directed to an earlier, but very similar, statement of his view, Sterba's welfare principle supposes a complete abstraction from nation-states and diverse economic communities.[15] This makes it considerably more visionary than it might at first appear, and it isn't clear how he feels it can be implemented. Would it be through a Singer-like requirement of each person in affluent societies donating one fifth of their income to fight famine or more general poverty in less developed countries, or would it rather proceed through a new enforcement of human rights (and if so, how? through international law?)? What might seem to be a minimal requirement of justice now appears as a distant vision.

Sterba's abstraction from social production is mirrored also in his effort to derive "socialist" principles of equality from negative liberty alone, with its concomitant individualist premises. One of the strengths of socialist theory, in the Hegelian-Marxist tradition, has in fact been its emphasis on the sociality of individuals. While this has historically sometimes been given an unfortunate holistic interpretation, I (and others) have argued that it is possible to interpret this sociality or commonality in a way that gives scope, even priority, to strong principles of individuality and difference.[16] Yet Sterba tries to derive his welfarist principle from the conflict between the negative liberty of the rich and the negative liberty of the poor, and the idea that the poor have the right to take from the rich what they require to meet their basic needs. Specifically, he writes that "What is at stake is the liberty of the poor not to be interfered with in taking from the surplus possessions of the rich what is necessary to satisfy their basic needs."[17] This claim has puzzled me since its appearance in Sterba's earlier version of his present chapter "From liberty to equality."[18] Aside from its connotation of each against the others, does "taking" here include at gunpoint, for example, or other obvious harms or infringements on another, even directly on their person? Clearly the sort of constraint on others that this would entail would violate the principle of negative liberty (among other rights), inasmuch as this principle is understood as permitting liberty compatible with a like liberty for others; it is, as Sterba recognizes elsewhere, a principle of equal liberty.

While it is not my aim here to defend libertarianism against Sterba's arguments, I would suggest that he is tacitly appealing to a principle of positive liberty or freedom at this point of his analysis. The idea of positive freedom, which, as I argued elsewhere, can be found in Marx's analysis and has in part Aristotelian roots, emphasizes that choices, to be effective, require access to certain "enabling" material and social conditions, in addition to being free from the external constraints or impediments that are entailed in the idea of negative liberty. To use a somewhat simplistic example, while I am free to make the choice to travel to Tahiti, without the material means to do so (money, in this case), I am not really free to go. Although some theorists, even in the socialist tradition, have chosen to look at the absence of means of subsistence as an impediment to free choice,[19] it seems more adequate to retain the common sense distinction between freedom from constraint on one's choices and the access to the means necessary to effect them, between constraining and enabling conditions.[20]

In addition to focusing only on constraining conditions and neglecting the further positive conditions that are required if freedom is to be substantive and not merely formal, libertarians also narrow down constraints too much, by failing to include domination and exploitation among them, and focusing only on government interference or coercion from others. Further, while theorists have correctly observed that negative, as well as positive, liberty requires positive actions and rights for its enforcement (e.g. Shue on courts, prisons, etc.[21]), nonetheless we can still usefully distinguish between others not constraining us and our having the means for effecting our choices. The positive freedom tradition insists that material and social conditions, including means of subsistence and recognition by others, are also required if equal freedom is to be real and not merely a formal possibility.

Democratic egalitarianism, as I have proposed it, goes beyond this to emphasize the development or flourishing of people over time, rather than simply looking at their ability to perform a single action. On the grounds of the recognition of everyone's equal agency, where the expression of this agency requires access to conditions, it can be seen to follow that there are (*prima facie*) equal rights to the conditions of self-development. This is the principle of equal positive freedom as a principle of justice.[22] In this account, individuals are understood to be social beings, engaged in common or joint activities, as well as having individual projects and goals of their own, where participation in these common activities is among the conditions of self-development. But if individuals have equal rights to determine their own actions (entailed in their equal agency), then where their engagement in common activities is concerned, they have equal rights to participate in decision-making concerning them, that is, a right of co-determination of these activities. This right of democratic participation applies generally, not only to politics but to social and economic activities as well.[23] Hence equal positive freedom as understood here includes not only relatively egalitarian distributional requirements, but also the need for democratic forms of decision-making considerably more extensive than presently interpreted. In addition, inasmuch as the emphasis on freedom as not only free choice but as self-development gives this view an individualist focus, it requires also an account of human rights, and distinguishes between basic and nonbasic ones, where the basic rights concern conditions necessary for any human action whatever, and the nonbasic concern rights to conditions necessary for the fuller development of persons.[24] At the distributional level, the emphasis on self-development requires attention to people's differences and the conditions for their flourishing, and prevents any leveling-down interpretation of this egalitarian approach.[25]

Returning to Sterba's analysis, then, his idea that basic needs have to be met as a condition for liberty or freedom is tacitly an appeal to the positive liberty tradition, with its emphasis on access to the means, although it does not necessarily entail the fuller account of democratic egalitarianism that I have just sketched. Sterba's reliance on the terms "rich" and "poor" also leaves open the issue of the criteria for membership in these classes. Presumably, he regards as rich all those who have access to "luxuries" as he puts it, or to meeting their nonbasic needs. But aside from the issue mentioned earlier of what are to count as basic needs, this approach remains blind to issues of exploitation and domination, and to concerns that workers receive what they are due for their work. It isn't the use of luxuries by the rich that (classical) socialist theory found especially objectionable, but rather their control over capital – how money used for investment can give to some a disproportionate control over social production, including the productive activities of large numbers of working people. It is, I think, a strength of the socialist tradition to have placed emphasis on these factors of social production and their import for questions of distributive justice. Sterba's analysis of rich and poor regrettably obscures these significant issues.

Of course, from a human rights perspective, there is merit in focusing on rights to means of subsistence as a universal right. Nonetheless, in considering how societies can assume their shared responsibilities for providing for this right, we need to consider economic and social institutions and their actual functioning, as well as nation-states and international organizations, if these rights are to be realized at all, and if they are to be realized in a manner required by justice. Sterba's abstract approach, in terms of people having rights to take from each other, or to give to each other, does not yet address these central contemporary issues.

Before turning to Sterba's reconciliationist methodology, it is perhaps helpful to clarify how the democratic egalitarianism I have presented may at the same time be regarded as a sort of "libertarian socialism," while differing in crucial respects from libertarianism. It is libertarian in its emphasis on the centrality of the value of freedom, and on the insistence that this includes negative liberty, with its traditional requirements of maximal civil liberties and political rights. As noted, it adds to these the idea of freedom from domination and exploitation, and access to enabling conditions – material and social – for making one's choices effective and thus meaningful. In this respect, it differs from some liberal thinkers, like Berlin, who do not regard these as part of liberty itself, but only as conditions for it, as well as from the libertarian analysis.

Yet the approach here also differs significantly from many exponents of negative liberty and individual property right, who argue – mistakenly, I suggest – that liberty and equality are necessarily in conflict with each other, and in fact exist in inverse proportion – the more of one, the less of the other. Against this incompatibility thesis, it should be noted that even libertarians recognize the requirement of equal distributions (of liberty). But more to the point here, we can argue for the consistency of freedom and equality by showing that the ideal of equality can be derived from the ideal of liberty or freedom, understood as not only the bare capacity for choice, but also its exercise in developing capacities and realizing projects over time. The argument, in brief, is that since the capacity for choice, or agency, characterizes all humans, the recognition of all as human entails a recognition of their equal rights to the exercise of this capacity as an activity of self-development, and therefore a *prima facie* equal right to the conditions or means for making choices effective. This is in effect a principle of equality which is immanent in the nature of freedom. If so, the fundamental relation between the two is evident. However, as already suggested, the principle of equal positive freedom does not entail equal distribution of the means of action, but rather differential claims based on the variety of needs, wants and abilities that characterize different individuals. This point has sometimes been misconstrued as requiring an equal apportionment of resources. This mistaken kind of leveling of the concept of equality seems to be common among critics of egalitarianism.

One source of the idea of incompatibility between freedom and equality is the set of related arguments that proceed from the premise of the natural egoism of human nature or from a conception of negative liberty and property. The phenomenological observation on which such arguments may be based is that people naturally want to be free to pursue their own interests and satisfy their desires; and that they want to be free also to keep or dispose of what they acquire in this way as they see fit. Any constraint on their freedom of acquisition, retention and disposition of what is acquired that is introduced to benefit others less successful than themselves is then felt as a violation of their liberty. If such constraints are introduced on the grounds of a more equal apportionment of goods or resources then it will be plain that such equality is directly incompatible with liberty. The philosophical correlate of this professed observation is the theory discussed above, of abstract negative liberty as the right to do as one pleases without external interference and the related notion of unlimited entitlement to property acquired by one's own activity. Any tax or use of such acquisitions of wealth or resources in the interests of some normative principle of equality or of just distribution is seen to conflict with such liberty and property rights.

Yet, as already noted, the classical formulation of such liberty, e.g. by Hobbes, imposes the natural constraint of equal liberty, which means that one's freedom to do as one pleases is limited by the requirement not to infringe on another's equal right to do so. Again, on the classic liberal view, e.g. of Locke, the right of property and of entitlement is not unlimited, as is well known. Contemporary versions of these views sometimes reject or neglect these limits established by rights to equality in liberty and entitlement. But even where they are recognized, such views persist in seeing a conflict between freedom and equality, either because of a commitment to the priority of property entitlements, or to conceptions of liberty as simply a matter of free choice (without the requirement of access to the means that would make such choices effective); or finally, a commitment to abstract individualist conceptions of social life, which do not take into account cooperative and interactive modes of action and the correlative phenomena of altruism and social responsibility.

To the degree that libertarians do recognize the value of equal liberty but interpret it as negative liberty, while socialists generally emphasize equal freedom in a positive sense as well, the dispute between libertarians and socialists is not a dispute between the value of liberty as against that of equality, as Sterba himself has sometimes put it,[26] but between two conceptions of freedom. There is certainly shared agreement on the importance of the value of freedom, though each theoretical approach interprets it in importantly different ways. It serves no purpose, I think, to present this agreement as though each type of theorist already agrees with the other in any fuller sense, for example, on the practical requirements of their views, and simply fails to recognize it. This is what is entailed in Sterba's effort at peacemaking, and it is interesting to contrast this with dialectical or synthetic methods of philosophizing that emerge from the Hegelian-Marxist tradition.

In one sense it is not surprising that there should be a harmony between several of the views that Sterba discusses – in particular, the socialist, feminist, anti-racist and multicultural perspectives. After all, as philosophical approaches, many versions of these have in large measure come out of, or are indebted to, the same philosophical traditions, namely the critique of domination and exploitation in Marx, based on Hegel (e.g. the master/slave section of the *Phenomenology*) and the left-Hegelians. As is well known, while Marx and Engels focused on class, they were also attuned to women's subordination (as were the Mills, at about the same time). Simone de

Beauvoir's feminist theory,[27] and more recent ones in the United States, owed a great deal to this tradition as well, as did critical race theory,[28] multicultural emphases on recognition and inclusion,[29] and both older and more recent anticolonialist theories.[30] Thus it is to be expected that these very diverse approaches should nonetheless agree, at least on the critique of domination and oppression. Further, many exponents of one of these perspectives are also exponents of one or more of the others. The ecological approaches that Sterba discusses are less obviously connected to this tradition, because Marx and his followers sometimes tended to bring in older, perhaps "industrial," concepts of the domination or at least transformation of nature to meet human needs.[31] Nonetheless, there has been no shortage of persuasive efforts to critically relate the domination of nature to other types of domination, especially of women, where all of these sorts of domination are seen as socially constructed, and where the argument then is that new approaches to nature are required along the lines of social ecology or of ecofeminism.[32]

The more controversial claim regarding agreement that Sterba makes concerns the harmony between libertarian, welfare liberal and socialist views, and I would take issue with the version of peacemaking philosophy that he promotes in that context. I have already suggested that the conception of liberty importantly differs between libertarian and socialist approaches, and there is not in fact agreement on the practical requirements that flow from each approach (although a libertarian socialism is possible, along the lines sketched earlier). I see no advantage in attempting to convince libertarians that their view already entails Sterba's strong right to welfare, and wonder whether this is really what is entailed in showing due respect for their approach. It seems, by contrast, that respect in dialogue, as in interaction, centrally involves acknowledging differences. What can Sterba say to libertarian thinkers who adamantly reject his interpretation of their views and do not believe that their position entails requirements equivalent to his own? Is he committed to saying that they already in fact agree with him but simply don't realize it? I have proposed instead that there is agreement on a shared value but disagreement about its interpretation. Moreover, it needs to be acknowledged that the libertarian insistence on the requirement of negative liberty, including the central role of civil liberties, political rights, and rather limited state interference in individuals' activities, is of great importance for political philosophy. From a dialectical or dialogical standpoint, however, the libertarian approach appears as one-sided or partial, once it is put in interaction with other views that may be critical of it or that add new features to the discussion.

Such a dialectical conception of theoretical interaction and construction does not focus simply on compromise on a set of minimal requirements, where each theoretical perspective remains essentially unchanged in the confrontation. Such a move may indeed be important in political contexts to reach practical agreement, where there may sometimes be a need for compromise on the lowest common denominator. But when we are discussing social and political theories, a more dynamic dialectical approach aims at syntheses among theories that contribute important insights to a changing and hopefully more adequate and comprehensive overall theoretical framework. Given also that these are theories about society and politics, the changing understandings also can be expected to be responsive to newly emergent social-historical realities that introduce heretofore unanticipated factors into the analysis. An important element of such an approach is critique, both social and purely theoretical: the first involves a critique of views that may be partial because ideological, and the second involves considerations of consistency and adequacy to the phenomena. In such a dialectical or dialogical interaction among theorists, peacemaking has to be based on acknowledgement of the unique and divergent perspectives of the interlocutors. Whereas Sterba does recognize this factor in his original presentation of his version of peacemaking philosophy, I would suggest that he does not hew to it forcefully enough in his treatment of some of the perspectives he discusses.

The peacemaking approach briefly sketched here is, I would suggest, more theoretical, more social, and perhaps more encouraging of differences than Sterba's version. It is more theoretical because it does not abstract from the actual theoretical perspectives of interlocutors to achieve agreement on only practical requirements. As noted, while this may suffice in politics, it does not suffice in political philosophy. It is more social because it sees theories as in part socially constructed out of the historical and social practices in which theorists are grounded, although they may also transcend these practices in various ways through their theoretical activity. Finally, it recognizes differences as well as critique as central for the process of understanding itself, and for the revisions and syntheses that may result.

What then is the possible ground for agreement on the principles discussed here, for example, on equal rights to the conditions of development, or on the human rights themselves? Without going into this difficult issue with the seriousness it merits, I would suggest that it is not to be found in conceptual compromises, but in another direction. Here, the social ontology that underlies the analysis I have given plays an important role (though there is much disagreement within the broadly democratic-egalitarian tradition on this issue). When we speak of freedom as a value that people should respect in each other and that gives rise to equal rights to conditions for it, it is the character of people as free that is here proposed as the basis for agreement on the importance of this value. In this quasi-foundationalist but nonessentialist approach, what provides a common basis for equality and the human rights is the phenomenologically evident fact that people are transformative and self-transformative. This must not be interpreted as necessarily a matter of individual self-transformation; it may be social or cultural as well. The

241

conceptual framework is based on this "normative fact" of individual or socio-cultural self-transformation over time, i.e. freedom. In addition, people's shared needs and their common projects, increasingly universalist in nature, also support the possibilities of shared perspectives emerging over time.[33] On this view, then, the very general features of the freedom and sociality of persons provides the required basis for mutual recognition and common understandings.

But what about the cross-cultural dimension here, and the criticism that despite the open social interpretation of freedom given here that encompasses social as well as individual self-transformation, this value seems to have been articulated more fully within Western traditions, indeed rather recent ones at that? This difficult issue merits considerable discussion, and has not been attended to sufficiently by socialist or other theoreticians. But I would suggest that this grounding in human freedom has advantages over Sterba's proposal of rationality. Indeed, Sterba explicitly puts aside this issue of the possible cultural relativism of his approach. While he grants that "At other times and in other places, particularly in non-Western societies, the requirements of justice may be different,"[34] he nonetheless concludes that

> Once one considers that the reconciliationist conception of justice defended in this book is grounded in the norms of rationality, and that its very demanding requirements of a right to welfare and a right to equal opportunity follow from even a minimal morality like libertarianism, it is difficult to see how the most morally defensible requirements of justice for other times and places could significantly differ from the basic rights required by this reconciliationist conception of justice.[35]

This seems too strong a claim. Clearly, rationality itself, so important to Sterba's analysis, is not interpreted in the same way by the Taoist tradition, just to choose one example, and the latter is indubitably also far from recognizing a right to equal opportunity as he proposes! Perhaps this is unfair, and it might be suggested that similar criticisms could be made of the idea of freedom or shared human dignity in the analysis I give. But I think that the latter ideas are more susceptible of the required universality, given that the general human capacities of transformation that they refer to need not be taken in a purely individualist sense. Moreover, the actual interpretation of these values, together with the concomitant idea of human rights, can draw strength and enrichment from the diverse but interconnected interpretations that they receive from various traditions, including non-Western ones. Indeed, the way that human rights in their specific interpretation have arisen from the contributions not only of Western European and North American readings (the civil and political "first wave" rights), but also from Eastern European approaches ("second wave" economic and social

242

rights) as well as readings from developing countries or the Third World (the "third wave" cultural and developmental rights), lends plausibility to the more dialectical interpretation I have advanced here. While building on the human freedom/dignity core, the very idea of human rights (and not only its applications) have been altered and enriched by the interplay of these culturally diverse theoretical interpretations.

Coming to grips with the variety of cultural traditions that influence theoretical approaches is one of the outstanding issues facing both socialist theory and other perspectives in social and political philosophy. But there are others that arise especially from the current context, and in the final section of this paper I would like to sketch one set of new issues that are of practical significance that democratic egalitarianism seems especially well suited to address. These issues are posed for social and political theory by globalization, in its various dimensions – economic (global corporations and markets), technological (especially the internet and, more generally, information and communications technologies), socio-cultural (media, voluntary associations, the arts and music, etc.), and to a degree political (new regional organizations, e.g. the European Union, and some strengthening of international organizations and NGOs). In this context, if we are concerned with justice (and freedom and democracy) for here and now, then it is relevant to consider not only principles for global redistribution of wealth or resources, but also the question of what I would call democratic globalization.[36] This is not simply the issue of extending political democratization worldwide, where the current hope is that economic globalization will bring democratization and respect for human rights along with it, but also the question of democratizing decision-making in international organizations, including those that have effects on global distributive justice.

I indicated earlier that the principle of equal positive freedom supports a requirement of democratic decision-making concerning the common activities that one is engaged in, where these include not only political contexts of activity, but social and economic ones as well. The idea of economic democracy is thus an implication of this view, where this gives rise in the first instance to conceptions of worker self-management. Given the increasing scale of economic cooperation, however, the question arises of the applicability of economic democratization to this broader sphere. The idea of equal freedom in economic contexts would also lead to a concern in the global context, not only with the obvious requirement for the elimination of unfree (even slave) labor, but more generally with workers' rights and international labor standards, as well as greater equalization of healthcare, education, and so forth. The socialist perspective clarifies the ways in which increasingly global corporations, while employing new workers in many countries, understandably also tend to place profit-seeking above a concern with workers' freedom and well-being. It is by now a truism to observe that these corporations also have considerable influence on the organizations that seek to foster development and trade, the International Monetary Fund, the World Bank, and more recently the World Trade Organization. A democratic egalitarian framework of the sort I have sketched requires that we go beyond speaking of the responsibilities of global corporations (though this also has merit) to consider more fundamentally what the requirements are for democratizing the international organizations that are designed to foster trade and development, so that they can be more responsive both to workers and to people in the less developed countries.

If profit-maximizing corporations and trade alone cannot be counted on to achieve greater global distributive justice, and if these and other international organizations are to make decisions concerning development, trade and equalization, then there needs to be input from and accountability to those most directly involved. This suggests the need for representation of these affected groups within these bodies, perhaps by directly including representatives of unions, NGOs, and environmental and human rights groups, and by giving a more effective role to representatives of the less developed countries. It is apparent as well that the traditional democratic requirement of openness of deliberations would be helpful in these new organizations. In addition, to the degree that these organizations remain responsive primarily to corporate interests, they cannot be expected to support the needed health and welfare programs in developing countries, or the environmental protections and regulations, that are required by principles of global justice, whether of Sterba's sort or those of a more explicitly democratic egalitarianism.

Whereas democratizing decision-making within these international organizations, along with the more established political ones like the United Nations and its organs, seems a daunting task, and the practical details remain to be worked out, it is a direction clearly entailed by the social and political philosophy advanced here. It is perhaps worth adding, however, that this democratization could be expected not only to help realize some of the human rights (including Sterba's basic rights), but would also have to be constrained by respect for others of these rights themselves. Because the democracy discussed here is in the service of freedom and required by it, ways also have to be found to protect the basic liberties (and minority rights) from encroachment by majority decisions in these new contexts, as well as ways to use democratic decision-making to advance equal freedom. I would suggest that extending rights and democratic participation to this international domain is an issue that calls for new attention by social and political philosophers, democratic egalitarian and otherwise.

NOTES

1 James P. Sterba, *Justice for Here and Now* (Cambridge: Cambridge University Press, 1998) p. 8.
2 Sterba, *Justice for Here and Now*, p. 172.

3 Sterba, *Justice for Here and Now*, p. 42.
4 Sterba, *Justice for Here and Now*, p. 56.
5 Sterba, *Justice for Here and Now*, p. 63.
6 Sterba, *Justice for Here and Now*, p. 77.
7 Sterba, *Justice for Here and Now*, p. 130.
8 Carol C. Gould, *Marx's Social Ontology: Individuality and Community in Marx's Theory of Social Reality* (Cambridge MA: MIT Press, 1978); and *Rethinking Democracy: Freedom and Social Cooperation in Politics, Economy, and Society* (Cambridge: Cambridge University Press, 1988).
9 James P. Sterba, Tibor R. Machan, Alison Jaggar, William Galston, Carol Gould, Milton Fisk and Robert C. Solomon, *Morality and Social Justice* (Lanham MD: Rowman & Littlefield, 1995) pp. 216, 219.
10 Sterba, *Justice for Here and Now*, p. 63.
11 Sterba, *Justice for Here and Now*, p. 194 n5.
12 Cf. for example Henry Shue, *Basic Rights* (Princeton: Princeton University Press, 1980) esp. chapter 3. See also Gould, *Rethinking Democracy*, esp. pp. 209–10.
13 Cf. my discussion in Gould, *Rethinking Democracy*, chapter 6 (reprinted from "Contemporary Legal Conceptions of Property and their Implication for Democracy," *The Journal of Philosophy*, vol. LXXVII, no. 11, November 1980, pp. 716–29).
14 Cf. Ross Zucker, *Democratic Distributive Justice* (Cambridge: Cambridge University Press, forthcoming 2000).
15 "A Comment by Carol C. Gould," in Sterba *et al.*, *Morality and Social Justice*, pp. 53–7.
16 Cf. Gould, *Marx's Social Ontology*, esp. chapters 1 and 4; and *Rethinking Democracy*, esp. chapter 2.
17 Sterba, *Justice for Here and Now*, p. 45.
18 James P. Sterba, "Reconciling Conceptions of Justice," in Sterba *et al.*, *Morality and Social Justice*, esp. pp. 4–11. See my "Comments by Carol C. Gould" concerning that paper in Sterba *et al.*, *Morality and Social Justice*, pp. 53–7.
19 See for example C. B. Macpherson, *Democratic Theory: Essays in Retrieval* (Oxford: Oxford University Press, 1973) pp. 95–119.
20 See Gould, *Rethinking Democracy*, esp. pp. 35–60.
21 Shue, *Basic Rights*, pp. 37–8.
22 See Gould, *Rethinking Democracy*, esp. pp. 40–71.
23 For a fuller statement of this argument, see Gould, *Rethinking Democracy*, esp. pp. 71–90.
24 See Gould, *Rethinking Democracy*, chapter 7.
25 Gould, *Rethinking Democracy*, chapter 5, and Carol C. Gould, "Democracy and Diversity: Representing Differences," in Seyla Benhabib (ed.) *Democracy and Difference: Changing Boundaries of the Political* (Princeton: Princeton University Press, 1996) pp. 171–86.
26 Sterba, *Justice for Here and Now*, p. 7; see also Sterba, "Reconciling Conceptions of Justice," in Sterba *et al.*, *Morality and Social Justice*, pp. 1–2.
27 Simone de Beauvoir, *The Second Sex*, trans. H. M. Parshley (New York: Alfred A. Knopf, 1952 and 1980).
28 Cf. Anthony K. Appiah, *In my Father's House: Africa in the Philosophy of Culture* (New York: Oxford University Press, 1992); Cornel West, *Race Matters* (Boston MA: Beacon Press, 1993); Charles Mills, *The Racial Contract* (Ithaca NY: Cornell University Press, 1997).
29 See for example Charles Taylor, *Multiculturalism and the Politics of Recognition* (Princeton: Princeton University Press, 1992); Iris Marion Young, *Justice and the Politics of Difference* (Princeton: Princeton University Press, 1990).

30 See for example Franz Fanon, *The Wretched of the Earth* (New York: Grove Press, 1963).
31 Although Marx's 1844 manuscripts suggest a rather different direction, with the idea of the humanization of nature, but also the naturalism of human beings. See especially Karl Marx, "Private Property and Communism," in *Writings of the Young Marx on Philosophy and Society*, ed. Loyd D. Easton and Kurt H. Guddat (Garden City NY: Anchor Doubleday, 1967) pp. 301–14.
32 Cf. Murray Bookchin, "The Concept of Social Ecology," Val Plumwood, "Ecosocial Feminism as a General Theory of Oppression," and Vandana Shiva, "Development, Ecology, and Women," all in Carolyn Merchant (ed.) *Ecology* (Atlantic Highlands NJ: Humanities Press, 1994) pp. 152–62, 207–19, 272–80; and Carolyn Merchant, *Radical Ecology* (New York: Routledge, 1992).
33 This argument is developed in Carol C. Gould, "Two Concepts of Universality and the Problem of Cultural Relativism," forthcoming in C. Gould and P. Pasquino (eds) *Cultural Identity and the Nation-State* (Boulder: Rowman & Littlefield, 2001); originally presented at the Fifteenth International Social Philosophy Conference, North American Society for Social Philosophy, August, 1998.
34 Sterba, *Justice for Here and Now*, p. 174.
35 Sterba, *Justice for Here and Now*, pp. 174–5.
36 Cf. also David Held, Anthony McGrew, David Goldblatt and Jonathan Perraton, *Global Transformations* (Stanford: Stanford University Press, 1999).

Part IV

CHALLENGES TO SOCIAL
AND POLITICAL
PHILOSOPHY

Feminism

12

FEMINISM AND THE OBJECTS OF JUSTICE

Alison M. Jaggar

In this paper, I explain what I take to be one of the most significant contributions made by feminism to Western understandings of social justice. This is feminism's disclosure of objects of justice ignored by most other mainstream philosophers.[1] I also consider whether a feminist approach to social justice is usefully described as a way of fleshing out the ideal of androgyny.

Central to justice is the notion of moral balance. Philosophers often express this idea in terms of giving each her due, meaning that goods and evils should be distributed in quantities and qualities proportionate to the desert of the recipients. Saying that the punishment should "fit" the crime is one way of expressing this intuition. Justice as a social ideal thus invokes a condition of morally appropriate balance within a system of social relationships.

Contemporary accounts of social justice usually divide it into two branches, distributive and corrective justice, and they typically present theories of justice as proposing rival answers to the question:

1 *What should count as just deserts? That is to say, according to what principle should goods and evils be distributed in a just social system?*
   In discussions of so-called distributive justice, this question is generally interpreted as asking for moral grounds capable of justifying state intervention to redistribute material goods.[2] In terms of corrective justice, the question is often interpreted as one about which principles should determine the kinds of behavior that deserve to be punished by law and the kinds of legal penalties that are appropriate or "fitting." Feminists have proposed a variety of answers to these questions, but they have also raised several additional questions about justice, one of which is the following:
2 *What are the kinds or categories of things that should be distributed in a just manner?*
   I call this the question of the proper objects of justice and, in the present paper, I show how recent work by feminist philosophers has challenged some widely accepted answers to this question.

251

John Rawls famously defines justice as a fair distribution of the burdens and benefits of social cooperation (Rawls 1971). Contemporary theories of justice recognize various types or categories of such burdens and benefits, which may be used to distinguish several kinds or categories of justice:

1   Political justice is concerned with the proper distribution of legally guaranteed authorities, powers and liberties, and of legally required obligations, such as military service, jury duty and, most generally, obedience to the law.
2   Economic justice is concerned with the proper distribution of material goods and the human labor needed to produce them.
3   Recent discussions of justice increasingly have raised questions concerning the proper distribution of intangible benefits and burdens. Such goods include "Honor, respect, esteem, praise, prestige, status, reputation, dignity, rank, regard, admiration, worth, distinction, deference, homage, appreciation, glory, fame, celebrity" (Walzer 1983, 252). The evils include dishonor, contempt, disgrace, discredit, insult, degradation, shame, stigma, scorn, and humiliation. These goods and evils are often institutionalized in symbolic systems such as forms of language, ranks, titles, rituals, and public holidays. The branch of justice concerned with the distribution of such goods and evils could be called justice in the distribution of "social recognition." Nancy Fraser calls it cultural or symbolic justice (Fraser 1997, 14).
4   Finally, corrective justice is concerned with the proper distribution of rewards, punishments and compensations for behavior that is legally required, permitted or prohibited.

Many feminists argue that the Western philosophical tradition has tended to identify the various objects of justice in ways that on the surface are gender-neutral but which, on a deeper level, are gender-biased. Specifically, they contend that many Western philosophers have failed to acknowledge the full range of privileges enjoyed by some, especially by many men, or to appreciate the full range of burdens imposed on others, especially on most women. They also argue that Western philosophers typically have failed to credit the full range of contributions made by some groups, especially though not exclusively by women. Finally, feminists argue that Western philosophers have failed to recognize that the disproportion between the privileges, burdens and contributions of men and women respectively often results from choices by men and women made in the context of social institutions that impose on them constraints that are systematically unequal and unjust. In what follows, I illustrate these feminist claims with examples drawn from the realms of political, economic and cultural justice; because of space limitations, I do not address feminist work on corrective justice.

1 Feminism and the objects of political justice

Feminist work on political justice highlights distinct political privileges enjoyed by many men and injuries suffered by many women that have been ignored by most mainstream political theory. It also draws attention to political contributions made by women that mainstream theory has generally disregarded. Finally, feminist work identifies unjust and also largely neglected social constraints that influence the gender distribution of political privileges, burdens and contributions. I'll sketch these points quite briefly, beginning with questions of formal electoral politics.

It is often forgotten that women in Western Europe and North America won the vote only in the lifetimes of many people alive today (1920 in US; 1947 in France; 1971 in Switzerland). Moreover, it is not widely known that women's fight for suffrage often had to be followed by separate struggles for other citizen rights that are widely assumed to accompany the suffrage. These included women's rights to pass their citizenship on to their children, to retain their citizenship on marriage based on their own nationality and place of residence rather than their spouse's, to run for and hold political office and to serve on juries. Women still have not gained quite all of these rights in all of the advanced industrial democracies but, in most of them, women's political rights and responsibilities are fairly close to those of men. Thus Western women are now able to vote and run for public office on the same terms as men, at least as far as the law is concerned.

Despite their formal political equality, women remain strikingly under-represented in electoral politics, especially at the national and international levels. For example, eighty years after women won the vote in the United States, white men constitute 80% of the House of Representatives, 90% of the Senate, and 100% of all presidents and vice-presidents. News photographs of top political leaders invariably show a row of suited white and occasionally brown men, against which the few women leaders, such as Margaret Thatcher and Madeleine Albright, stand out in striking contrast. Female faces rarely appear in photographs of political leaders in the North Atlantic democracies. Systematic inequality in the political standing of members of groups that are formally equal calls for explanation in liberal democratic societies, because it is a *prima facie* sign of injustice.

How can the sexual, as well as racial/ethnic, disproportion between public officials and their electorates be explained? Does it result from free and rational citizen choices, or do women, especially poor women and women of color, currently have disproportionately limited opportunities to exercise their formal rights to assume political office? Feminists have identified a number of mutually reinforcing ways in which systematic inequalities based on class, sex and race/ethnicity restrict the political opportunities of women, especially poor women and women of color.[3] For example, the vast majority of successful candidates come from a handful of elite professions such as law, which require high levels of education, yet many women, especially women of color, enjoy fewer educational opportunities than do most white men. A record of military service is also helpful in establishing a political career, but it is more difficult for women to achieve such a record, as we shall see. In addition, running successfully for the US Congress costs a great deal of money and few women, especially women of color, have the financial resources necessary to mount a successful campaign. Studies show that party activists are typically less willing to raise funds for the campaigns of promising women candidates than they are for those of white men.[4] When women do manage to get elected, they are likely to be excluded from the informal political relationships that are crucial to a successful political career. Finally, some voters regularly reject women candidates, especially women of color, solely on the basis of their sex and ethnicity. Studies show that even those voters who consider themselves to be "open-minded toward women candidates" are less likely to vote for women with small children. Thus, even when women's formal political rights are equal with those of men, women's socially available opportunities to exercise those rights are systematically unequal to those of men.

Differential liability for military service remains the most conspicuous difference between the formal rights and responsibilities of men and women respectively in some liberal democracies, including the United States. Women in the United States, unlike men, have never been subject to conscription, and today, still unlike men, they are not required to register for the draft; moreover, although women may now serve in the military in most capacities, they are still excluded from some combat positions. Women's exemption from compulsory military service and the limits on the positions they may occupy might be construed as an unjust benefit to women rather than a burden on them, but some feminists argue that the limits on women's opportunities for military service constitute an unjust burden on them. For instance, not only do they withhold from women the career opportunities provided by military service, but they also deprive women political candidates of credibility on military matters. More generally, these limits reinforce a public perception that women (like gay men) are less than full citizens insofar as they need the protection of (presumed heterosexual) men (Carter 1996; Allen 2000).

In addition to formal political inequities, second-wave feminists have identified other forms of political injustice to women that have been invisible in mainstream philosophy. The problems that most women experience as especially acute in their daily lives include: problems regarding bodily appearance and self-presentation, which sometimes lead to life-threatening eating disorders; problems regarding sexuality, including sexual harassment and the absence of orgasm in heterosexual relations; problems with violence, including incest, rape and domestic violence; and problems regarding the domestic division of labor and responsibility for the care of dependent family members. Most of these problems fall into the realm that liberal political theory categorizes as personal and they are still usually addressed by urging women to "cope" better, for instance, by adopting various self-help methods. For women of my generation, however, much of the inspirational force of second-wave feminism derived from its slogan, "The personal is political," which suggested that, on the most basic level, women were not individually to blame for many of their so-called personal problems. The slogan reflected the insight that these problems did not arise primarily from women's laziness, selfishness, weakness of the will, poor coping skills or any other individual defect – even though most women, like most men, are certainly lazy, selfish, weak-willed and lacking in coping skills on occasion. Rather than rooting women's so-called personal problems in individual deficiencies, the slogan "The personal is political" implied that many of these problems had systemic causes, rooted in institutional arrangements that were systematically male-dominated and compounded by racism and poverty. The slogan also hinted that justice required addressing these problems by changing institutional arrangements, rather than by asking individual women to develop better coping skills.

Feminists do not contend that women bear no individual responsibility for creating or addressing any of the problems they face. However, they do argue that mainstream political theory fails to recognize that many of women's so-called personal problems are systematically generated by social institutions. For instance, there is a reason why the vast majority of those with health- and life-threatening eating disorders, as well as the vast majority of those who undergo cosmetic surgery, are women, and that reason goes beyond personal greed or vanity. The reason, in a nutshell, is that a woman's face (and her figure) still constitutes much of her fortune today, just as in the time of the nursery rhyme. Women's appearance influences their opportunities for political and career advancement to a much greater extent than men's appearence. It also influences their opportunities for marriage, which is still most women's best chance for economic security.

Marriage offers a good example of a social institution that often creates problems for women that mainstream theory construes as "personal." Marriage is a relationship of formal equality and at least one philosopher has taken the wedding, with its smiling bridegroom, as a paradigm case of freewill (Flew 1956). Most brides as well as grooms smile at their weddings, yet feminists have pointed to the economic and social pressures that make marriage more imperative for women than for men (Okin 1989). Feminists have also noted that the same pressures often compel many women to remain married, even after they find that they are unhappy in their marital relationship. For instance, many women stay married because they fear that, if they divorced, they would not be able to support themselves and their children, and other women stay married because they fear physical harm if they leave.

Women's fears for their physical safety are often well founded, as Sterba convincingly documents (Sterba 1998, 89–90). Many women are subjected to sexual assault by strangers who break into their homes or attack them on the street, and many times more women are beaten and killed by present and previous boyfriends and husbands. Yet despite these high rates of violence against women, contemporary states seem curiously indifferent to women's physical safety. To the extent that their bodily integrity is not guaranteed, women surely lack one of the basic rights of citizenship. Some feminists argue that women are subjected to systematic political terrorism, and Sterba asserts that "the condition of women in our society is actually that of being subordinate to men by force" (Sterba 1998, 80).

When women's problems are generated by institutional structures that assign women systematically less power than men, feminists contend that the redesign of those structures should be seen as a matter of political justice rather than of private morality. Building on the insight expressed in the slogan, "The personal is political," many feminist political philosophers have argued that the public/private distinction, so central to Western political theory, in fact has often operated ideologically to exclude many harms to women from the realm of political justice. For instance, in the work of liberal political philosophers such as John Rawls and Jürgen Habermas, the public/private distinction divides matters of ethics or the good life, determined by subjective preference, from matters of morality or justice, determined by impartial and objective reason (Benhabib 1992). However, even when it is acknowledged that addressing women's problems requires some social changes, liberal political theory does not usually categorize these as changes in what Rawls calls the "basic structure" or "basic institutions" of society. Even if women are not directly blamed for their "personal" problems, placing them within the domain of private morality means that tackling these problems is not a matter of justice and therefore not among a state's first priorities.

If social institutions systematically promote harm to women, then work addressed to changing those institutions is necessarily a form of political activism. Yet women's relative absence from formal politics is often taken as evidence that they are passive or apathetic rather than active citizens, living "their lives in a private sphere protected ... from the mainstream of 'public' life and politics" (Ackelsberg 1988, 297). Martha Ackelsberg challenges this view by pointing out that women have been extremely active in community life at local or grassroots level. Women have been "leaders and activists in 'bread riots' and tenant organizations ... participated in factory-based strikes that engendered, and depended on, local community support ... they have led struggles for new and better schools" (Ackelsberg 1988, 303). Women, especially poor women of color, have also been leaders in struggles for environmental justice. In addition, women have also led explicitly feminist struggles against rape, sexual harassment, domestic violence, and so on. There are at least two reasons why mainstream political theory has often failed to recognize the extent and value of women's political contributions. First, women in, for instance, the African American civil rights movement and in trades unions have often avoided high-profile roles and instead supported male spokespersons (Sacks 1988). Thus women's leadership style has often made their contributions less visible. Second, women's activities are often distinguished from politics proper by being called community organizing, a tendency that has been reinforced with the recent advent of a theoretical discourse emphasizing the distinction between civil society and the state. Feminists argue that a broader and less gender-biased under-standing of political activity would enable women's political contributions to be recognized more adequately.

Feminists thus argue that mainstream theories have offered inadequate and gender-biased accounts of the objects of political justice. These theories have ignored not only unjust constraints on women's abilities to exercise their political rights, but also serious violations of such basic liberties as the right to bodily integrity. Mainstream theorists have also failed to recognize many political benefits enjoyed by men, including disproportionate power and authority in both public and private spheres. Finally, mainstream theorists have disregarded the numerous and substantive political contribu-tions made by women.

2 Feminism and the objects of economic justice

Feminist work on economic justice includes several claims that are parallel to those made by feminist theorists of political justice. That is to say, feminists argue that most contemporary theories define economic benefits, burdens and contributions in ways that exclude many of the benefits enjoyed by men, the burdens carried by women and the contributions that women make.

The most egregious example of neglecting women's economic burdens and contributions is the practice, standard in mainstream economic theory and in systems of national accounting, of ignoring unpaid work in the family and the community.[5] Much feminist scholarship argues that subsistence, maintenance and reproductive labor – including sexual, emotional and sometimes even gestational labor – is "real work" in several senses. It takes a toll – often a heavy one – on the worker's time and energy; it requires skills that are often sophisticated; and it produces goods and services that are often socially indispensable and which would command a high price if purchased on the market (Anderson 1993; Folbre 1994; Waring 1988).

Not all unpaid labor is performed by women, of course. It is also per-formed by indigenous people (men as well as women), most of whose life activities occur outside the market; by poor people (men as well as women), who cannot afford the goods and services available on the market; and by people with plenty of time and money (men as well as women), who simply enjoy exercising the skills necessary for this kind of production. However, feminists contend that, in contemporary societies, unpaid work for families is performed disproportionately (though not exclusively) by women, that the benefits of this family labor are enjoyed disproportionately by men and by larger social institutions, and that the same men and institutions withhold reciprocal economic benefits from the women who do this work. Feminists also argue that the gendered division of labor assigning this unpaid work is not freely chosen.

Those who benefit from women's unpaid labor are, in the first instance, their children and the male members of their immediate families. Leaving aside children, who are not expected to engage in fair economic exchanges, it is often argued that men more than repay women's domestic labor, including sexual and emotional labor, by their larger monetary contribution to the family budget; indeed, many women and children are saved from poverty only by a man's wage. However, feminists respond that this economic exchange is quite unequal when it is measured in terms of time and energy rather than money. Studies have shown that adult males across the world tend to enjoy benefits that the women in their families enjoy to a much lesser extent. For instance, male family members tend to have more leisure time than female members and they have higher levels of sexual satisfaction and self-esteem. Marriage lengthens a man's life but shortens a woman's. Moreover, because women take on the bulk of the necessary domestic labor, men have more time and energy for paid work and thus are enabled to advance their careers, whereas women's career options are limited. Men's relatively stronger position in the market then gives them greater exit options from marriage than women, and this in turn supplies them with more power in the family (Okin 1989). Thus a woman's unpaid labor in the family tends to strengthen her husband's position at the expense of her own – just as, according to the Marxist analysis of alienation, wage earners' labor strengthens the position of capitalists *vis-à-vis* their employees.

Women's unpaid labor also carries benefits for those beyond their immediate families because it provides goods and services that then need not be paid for either by private industry or by public funds. Companies can pay wages that do not cover the cost of buying many goods and services, such as prepared food, laundry and housecleaning, and they can require their male employees to work long hours on the assumption that someone else is taking care of children and household maintenance. It becomes possible to avoid making public provision for the disabled, the infirm or the elderly, and healthcare services can discharge sick patients from hospitals or mental health facilities on the assumption that they will be cared for at home. In debtor nations worldwide, policies of structural adjustment can shift many social responsibilities from the state onto women. Thus women's unpaid work provides a hidden subsidy both to private industry and to public coffers.

Despite its enormous monetary as well as social value, women's unpaid labor is not seen as entitling those who perform it to public recompense, such as pensions or social security. On the contrary, women who work without pay are portrayed as not being self-supporting or self-sufficient, and their use of social services is stigmatized as dependent (Fraser and Gordon 1997). Feminists argue that the conventionally accepted definitions of economic concepts such as self-sufficiency, independence and dependence are arbitrary and gender biased. For instance, they ignore the facts that women's caring work makes an indispensable social contribution and that paid work may often be socially counterproductive, even though it raises the GNP. Iris M. Young's example of such socially counterproductive work is designing junk food commercials for children's television (Young 1997). The use of "dependency" as an epithet misleadingly suggests that women who find it difficult to take on well paid jobs because of their unpaid family responsibilities are undeserving, in the sense of being lazy or inept. However, feminists argue that it is far more likely that such women are disadvantaged by institutional sexism, often compounded by classism and racism, including employment discrimination, lower pay for jobs that are of comparable value to men's, and the assignment of primary care-taking responsibilities for children, spouses, or parents.

The distinction between "entitlement" benefits, which do not position their recipients ideologically as dependents, and "charity" benefits, which do so position them, rests on assumptions about social contribution and desert that are gender-biased. For instance, government payments from which men are more likely to benefit, such as agricultural subsidies, corporate tax concessions and military expenditures, do not stigmatize their recipients as dependent. Nancy Fraser argues that, in the US economy, the system's real free-riders are men who shirk care work and domestic labor and corporations who free-ride on the labor of working people, both underpaid and unpaid (Fraser 1997, 62). Gender-biased definitions of economic contributions are extremely unjust to women, since they shape public perceptions of what women are entitled to receive, especially women who have few marketable skills, who are women of color, and/or who have assumed primary responsibility for care work.

Some feminists contend that no individual is economically independent in the sense of not needing to rely on the contributions of others. Socialists and anarchists have pointed out for over a hundred years that everyone's knowledge and skills are derived from the stock created by the species, and that we all need the help of others in acquiring a share of it; moreover, most people's economic contributions are made possible only by their participation in a larger economic system that coordinates the contributions of many others (Kropotkin 1987). For this reason, some feminists argue that the notion of economic self-sufficiency is an ideological fiction or illusion, what Eva Kittay calls a "conceptual chimera," serving primarily to rationalize the privilege of those whose good fortune has placed them in a position to receive economic benefits in a market economy (Kittay 1999, 141).

Economic justice does not require that all individuals or groups should make quantitatively equal contributions to a given system of cooperation, nor that all should reap quantitatively equal benefits. As Marx noted long ago, assessing justice also requires considering people's differing abilities and needs. Thus it would not necessarily be unjust for women to make disproportionately large contributions to men's economic well-being if women's abilities were typically greater than men's or if men's needs were typically greater than women's. However, it is hard to imagine how either of these claims might be argued. It would also not be unjust for women to make a disproportionately large contribution to men's economic well-being if women freely chose lower-paid occupations or freely chose to make a gift of their time and energy. However, feminists have argued that women's occupational choices in fact are often constrained by institutional factors, such as employment opportunities and cultural norms, in ways that most men's choices are not (Folbre 1994). The paid labor force is still largely sex segregated, "female" occupations are devalued, and it is still typically women who find themselves required to care for children and other family members who cannot care for themselves. Most women's actions are constrained by these institutional factors to such an extent that they are often virtually forced into traditionally female occupations and to engage in a disproportionate amount of unpaid labor. It is the presence of these elements of coercion that has encouraged some feminist theorists to argue that women are exploited both by the men in their families and by the larger society (Holmstrom 1981).[6]

To summarize, feminists do not argue that so-called women's work, either paid or unpaid, is inherently unpleasant or degrading. Instead, they contend that the present social organization of this work is unjust for several reasons. First, this work is performed disproportionately by women, who are coerced to perform it by gender-specific social constraints that do not similarly coerce men. Yet men reap disproportionate benefits from this work, both as individual family members and as participants in male-biased institutions. Finally, the men and institutions that benefit from women's unpaid family labor do not reciprocate, reward or even recognize the women who perform it. On the contrary, this work is unfairly devalued as menial and unskilled and the women who perform it are often despised precisely on that account. Those who perform the socially indispensable work of caring for dependent others, become themselves stigmatized as "dependent."

Thus do feminists contribute to our understanding of the objects of economic justice by offering expanded conceptions of economic burdens and benefits, costs and contributions, as well as by drawing attention to structures of social constraint that hitherto were unacknowledged. Feminists have made visible what was previously invisible in traditional theories of economic justice – despite being quite visible to most women.

3 Feminism and the objects of cultural justice

With a few exceptions, such as the United Kingdom, present-day liberal societies have largely abolished hereditary distinctions of rank. For this reason, theories of justice in the twentieth century (unlike earlier theories) have usually ignored matters of public respect or dishonor, and restricted their focus to politics and economics. In the closing decades of the twentieth century, however, theorists of justice once again began to address questions of social honor and shame, recognition and misrecognition. The new attention to these questions emerged as part of a more general concern with matters of cultural representation, which in turn was linked both with postcolonial resistance to Eurocentrism and with the ever-increasing cultural diversity in the populations of most states, due to unprecedented political and economic migrations.

In the sphere of culture, just as in the spheres of politics and economics, feminists have drawn attention to injuries to women that have been ignored by mainstream theories of justice. For instance, they have complained that many everyday social practices reflect a cultural climate of masculine dominance, in which women regularly experience shame, embarrassment and vulnerability. Well known examples of such practices include men's touching or commenting on women's bodies in professional or work settings, staring at women's body parts, and using styles of address that are inappropriately affectionate or intimate ("honey," "dear"), or that define women by their family rather than professional relationships (using Miss or Mrs rather than Doctor or Professor). Other examples include conversational interactions in which men interrupt, ignore or misrepresent what women say or tell jokes that ridicule or sexualize women. At my own university, female faculty and teaching assistants, especially junior faculty, have recently reported many cases of what they call "gender harassment" by disruptive and disrespectful students. A cultural injury of whose extent I have become aware only recently is that of voyeurism, which now involves not only the familiar phenomenon of peeping toms outside women's bedroom windows but cameras hidden in homes, under office desks, in women's bathrooms, and so on.

People who are unsympathetic to feminist concerns about cultural androcentrism often accuse feminists of being overly sensitive, looking for trouble, unable to take a joke or to deal with normal sexual attraction – even of seeking to impose artificial standards of "political correctness." Such critics fail to recognize that cultural norms and standards that are covertly masculine, coupled with offensive stereotypes of femininity, operate to rationalize political and economic harms to women. They make the exclusion of women from politics appear to be chosen, sexual harassment and assaults on women appear to be normal, and the sexual division of labor appear to be natural.

Beyond its role in rationalizing political and economic injustice, cultural contempt for women and the feminine also constitutes a harm in its own right. Insult may be an injury in itself, especially when offensive views are widely shared. Sterba rightly observes that women are humiliated by sexual harassment, whether or not it culminates in job loss, and they are deeply traumatized by rape, even if they suffer little physical injury. Sexual harassment and assault humiliate and degrade women in ways that are distinctively gendered, which explains why women who have been harassed or assaulted are typically reluctant to report such incidents and even go to great lengths to conceal them, when they would not hesitate to report a theft.[7]

John Rawls asserts that self-respect is the primary social good, but it is difficult for women to maintain their self-respect in a culture in which women and everything associated with the feminine are systematically scorned, mocked, belittled and disparaged.[8] Even Western philosophy has participated in the cultural devaluation of women and the feminine by contrasting mind with body, reason with emotion, public with private, the sublime with the beautiful, and culture with nature and then associating the first and superior term of each opposition with the masculine and the second, inferior, term with the feminine.

Feminists have responded to the cultural devaluation of women and the feminine in a variety of ways. Some have contended that women are as capable as men of realizing values culturally coded as masculine; others have embraced the hitherto devalued "feminine" pole of the binaries; yet others have tried somehow to combine "masculine" and "feminine" values, while others still have sought to de-gender these symbolic oppositions. Finally, some feminists are working to deconstruct many of the conceptual dichotomies. Thus feminism tends to revalue both the culturally masculine and the culturally feminine, and feminist work in this direction can be observed not only in political and economic theory, as we have seen, but also in art, literature and sports. Rejecting the pre-eminence of masculine standards of value accords with the liberal ideal of accepting diversity in conceptions of the good, and is likely to benefit not only women but also large numbers of men, who are unable or unwilling to meet rigid, unrealistic and often abhorrent masculine norms and standards.

Feminist reflections on the objects of cultural justice run parallel to feminist work in political and economic justice, by revealing injuries to women that mainstream theorists of justice have ignored and by pointing to aspects of the culturally feminine that deserve to be revalued. The devaluation of women and the feminine is so deep-rooted in Western culture that it is often invisible to its members, with the result that feminists often appear to be challenging the natural order of things. For this reason, the struggle for cultural justice is in some respects the most difficult feminist struggle of all.

4 Feminism and the objects of social justice

Several linked themes run through feminist thinking about the objects of social justice. First is the theme of making visible those burdens and benefits of social cooperation that have been largely ignored in mainstream social theory, and related to this is the theme of gender blindness as gender bias. A second theme is that of the need to challenge masculine norms in every domain, and a final theme is that all the various dimensions or aspects of justice are inter-related and mutually reinforcing. For instance, just as the cultural devaluation of femininity rationalizes political and economic discrimination against women, so political and economic injustices to women also inflict psychological and emotional damage.[9] It has often been observed that people of color suffer not only from various forms of disenfranchisement and discrimination, but also from racist stigmatization, and that working-class people suffer not only from poverty but also from what have been called the hidden injuries of class. In the same sorts of ways, political and economic injustices to women not only reinforce each other but also make it difficult for women to maintain their self-respect.

5 Androgyny

James P. Sterba's recent book, *Justice for Here and Now*, echoes the reconciliationist project of his 1988 book, *How to Make People Just*, insofar as it seeks to demonstrate that the policies generated by several conceptions of justice are largely compatible with each other on the practical level. In addition to its substantive arguments, *Justice for Here and Now* models an approach to doing philosophy which Sterba presents as an alternative to the dominant approach. Sterba calls the dominant approach the "warmaking" model, and the examples of this that he offers in his opening chapter all involve philosophers seeking by fair means or foul to refute other philosophers, whom they position as adversaries or opponents. In opposition to the warmaking approach, Sterba recommends what he calls a peacemaking model of doing philosophy. The peacemaking model positions other philosophers as co-learners or collaborators, and requires that they be fair, open and self-critical. Sterba's examples of the warmaking approach are sadly familiar, while something like the peacemaking model has long been associated with feminist philosophy (Moulton 1983). I shall therefore approach Sterba's account of feminist justice in a peacemaking spirit.

I'd like to begin by saying how much I appreciate Sterba's sustained and serious engagement with feminist philosophy. Feminist and mainstream philosophy both stand to benefit from direct interaction with each other, as

Sterba rightly points out, yet feminist contributions too often are ignored in the mainstream. I'd also like to compliment Sterba on his knowledge of the feminist public policy literature. I think his discussions of the need to change the social organization of paid work and to end violence are excellent and his discussion of sexual harassment is superb. Indeed, I find little with which to disagree in the policy section of Sterba's chapter on feminist justice. However, I do have some concern with the theoretical sections of his chapter, which raise an old debate between Sterba and myself as to whether feminist justice is best characterized as androgyny.

The last time that Sterba and I discussed this was in 1992 on a panel at the American Philosophical Association. At that time, I resisted character-izing feminism as androgyny for several reasons:

1　I thought that the term suggested a mix of conventionally masculine and feminine characteristics within a single individual. When Sterba explained that instead he meant the elimination of gender norms in society at large – i.e. the elimination of social expectations and practices designed to ensure that males were masculine and females feminine – I suggested that it would be less misleading to refer to this ideal by the same term as that used by other feminists, namely, genderlessness.

2　I also disliked the term "androgyny" because I thought it focused attention on changing people rather than on changing social institu-tions.

3　Strategically, I thought that talking about "androgyny" would scare people away from feminism because it would seem to require a radical reconstruction of their personal identities.

4　I pointed out that the substantive ideal to which "androgyny" referred was incompatible with the views of some feminists.

5　I worried that defining feminism as a commitment to androgyny would draw too sharp a line between feminism and other political intellectual traditions, obscuring continuities and interconnections. For instance, it would make it more difficult to see that feminists are not proposing an ideal that is completely different from the ideals that Sterba assigns to other theories of justice, ideals such as equality, freedom, democracy and community, but rather proposing re-interpretations of these tradi-tional ideals.

6　Finally, my conclusion expressed some resentment about Sterba's insistence on defining feminism in terms of androgyny, even though few contemporary feminists accepted that term. I explained that I thought it was presumptuous in general to label people in terms that not only were not their own but which they even rejected explicitly. Moreover, I wor-ried that imposing the label "androgyny" on feminism would tend to reduce its richness and diversity and to suppress dissident voices within the feminist tradition. Of course, this final objection would have collapsed if Sterba had asserted that androgyny was simply his own personal ideal of feminism.

My reasons for opposing the use of the term "androgyny" to characterize feminist justice did not persuade Sterba, since he continues to use this term today, but he does address my concerns in a section of *Justice for Here and Now* entitled "Feminist objections." Here, he acknowledges that some feminists do oppose the ideal of androgyny but he argues that I should not do so, despite my criticism of his use of the term, since my practical views on sexual equality are very close to his. After comparing a passage from my work to a passage in his, Sterba concludes that, "there is very little separating the ideal that Jaggar endorses from the ideal of androgyny that I endorse" (Sterba 1998, 86). Several questions can be raised about this argument:

1   Is Sterba justified in inferring substantive agreement between his practical views and mine?
2   Even if he and I agree on most practical policies, what do other feminists think?
3   If feminists agree on most practical policies, does this mean that disagreement on how to characterize this cluster of views is "only" verbal and thus trivial and unimportant? In other words, does labelling matter?

With respect to the first question, I think Sterba is correct that he and I share substantive agreement regarding many practical questions of feminist justice – though I suspect that we may differ on some issues, such as pornography, abortion and the need to abolish social class. I do not know whether or not Sterba accepts all of my views on the objects of justice, but I have no reason to suppose that he rejects them and I shall therefore assume that he and I share a wide range of practical agreements.

With respect to the second question, Sterba knows that he and I do not represent all feminists, but he seems to believe that, if one studies their work, one can see that it too points toward what he calls androgyny. Let us assume for the sake of argument that he is correct about this, so that Sterba, I and most other feminists are in general agreement about the need to abolish gender norms. Does this mean that our disagreement over whether feminist justice should be called "androgyny" is "only" a verbal disagreement and therefore trivial and unimportant? Let us once more consider what might be gained and lost if feminist justice is defined as a commitment to androgyny.

The advantages that I see in characterizing feminist justice as androgyny are as follows:

1   "Androgyny" is a handy label, which defines feminism in terms of a positive social vision rather than simply in negative or reactive terms.

2   It suggests that the social changes required by feminism go very deep, requiring change not only in social institutions but also in what is often taken to be human nature.

3   The ideal of androgyny is thin, open and flexible. Like other social ideals, such as freedom, equality and certainly justice, it is susceptible to multiple interpretations and thus can be adapted to new circumstances.

Some of the disadvantages that I see in characterizing feminist justice as androgyny are the inverse of the advantages.

1   First, a negative definition of feminist justice may be easier for many people to accept than a positive one. There are several reasons why I usually choose to define feminism in minimalist terms as a commitment to ending women's subordination. One reason is that this definition is non-controversial; few feminists disagree with it. In addition, this definition helps people to accept that feminism is not a wildly unreasonable doctrine, since most people oppose the systematic subordination of any group. Finally, this definition leaves open – properly, in my view – the question of what a society would be like in which women were no longer subordinated.

2   "Androgyny" is an unsuitable characterization for a theory of social justice, because, etymologically and in its historical associations, it is a character ideal rather than a social ideal. Defining feminism in terms of a character ideal distinguishes it from all the other theories of justice that Sterba discusses, since liberty, equality, community and the opportunity for self-development are all social ideals. Although I agree with Sterba's assertion that character types are integrally related to social institutions, not everyone holds this view and I worry that highlighting a character ideal will encourage the belief that feminism focuses primarily on personal rather than institutional change. Since it is common to speak of individual men or women as androgynous, taking androgyny as the defining feminist ideal might even be thought to imply the possibility of individual liberation in the absence of systemic social change. This runs counter to another favorite slogan of second-wave feminism, namely "There are no individual solutions."

3   If the openness or vagueness of "androgyny" is its strength, it is also its weakness. The term does not even hint at many of the deepest contributions that feminists have made to Western understandings of justice. Even if "androgyny" is understood in social rather than individual terms (namely as a recommendation that the burdens and benefits of social cooperation should be distributed without regard to sex or gender), it does not indicate that feminists have raised fundamental ques-

tions about how to identify those benefits and burdens. Nor does it point toward other theoretical contributions made by feminists, which I have not raised here, regarding the domain of justice and even its ultimate value.

For all these reasons, as well as for some of those that I listed in 1992, I continue to resist Sterba's recommendation to define feminist justice as a commitment to androgyny. However, I do share his sincere and substantive commitments both to feminist justice and to a peacemaking model of doing philosophy.

NOTES

1 This paper was written for a conference on Alternative Conceptions of Justice at the University of Notre Dame. The conference was organized to discuss James P. Sterba's *Justice for Here and Now* (Sterba 1998), and I'd like to thank Jim Sterba and the University of Notre Dame for giving me this opportunity to think about feminist views on justice.

2 For example, James Sterba's classic textbook, *Justice: Alternative Political Perspectives* (Sterba 1980), takes this to be the central question of justice.

3 The following points are drawn from an unpublished paper, "Preferring Women: Increasing Women's Participation in Market and State," by Alison Jaggar and Michelle Wilcox.

4 Thus it may not be coincidental that the ninety-year-old citizen who walked across the country in 1999–2000 advocating campaign finance reform was a woman, Dolores Haddock, a.k.a. "Granny D."

5 In the late 1960s and early 1970s, a long and acrimonious feminist debate took place over the Marxist practice of categorizing women's production of "use values," including goods for domestic consumption and the services involved in maintaining the home and its inhabitants, as "unproductive," in contrast to men's supposedly "productive" generation of "exchange values" for the market.

6 A different example of gender-bias in assessing economic contribution is the systematically varying valuation placed on traditionally male and female occupations. As Sterba explains, "men's" jobs, such as trucking or tree-cutting, are paid more highly than "women's" occupations, such as clerk-typist or nursing, despite being comparable in terms of skill, responsibility, effort and working conditions (Sterba 1998, 86). The feminist movement for comparable worth seeks to reassess the value of "men's" and "women's" occupations by reference to criteria such as those listed above.

7 This is not to deny that men too can be sexually assaulted and raped – but part of the shame of such assaults for men is that they have been made symbolically feminine.

8 This is not to assert that it is easy for most men to maintain their self-respect in contemporary societies whose norms of masculinity are simultaneously racist, classist and heterosexist.

9 For instance, a recent report on sex discrimination by the US Information Agency and its one-time broadcasting agency, the Voice of America, was headlined "At the heart of a long legal battle: not just jobs but self-esteem" (*New York Times*, 24 March 2000, p. A11).

Bibliography

Ackelsberg, Martha A. (1988) "Communities, resistance, and women's activism: some implications for a democratic polity," in *Women and the Politics of Empowerment*, eds Ann Bookman and Sandra Morgen, Philadelphia: Temple University Press.

Allen, Holly (2000) "Gender, sexuality and the military model of US national community," in *Gender Ironies of Nationalism: Sexing the Nation*, ed. Tamar Mayer, New York and London: Routledge.

Anderson, Elizabeth (1993) *Value in Ethics and Economics*, Cambridge MA and London: Harvard University Press.

Benhabib, Seyla (1992) *Situating the Self: Gender, Community and Postmodernism in Contemporary Ethics*, New York: Routledge.

Carter, April (1996) "Women, military service and citizenship," in *Gender, Politics and Citizenship in the 1990s*, eds Barbara Sullivan and Gillian Whitehouse, Sydney: University of New South Wales Press.

Flew, Antony (1956) "Philosophy and language," in *Essays in Conceptual Analysis*, ed. Antony Flew, London: Macmillan.

Folbre, Nancy (1994) *Who Pays for the Kids? Gender and the Structures of Constraint*, New York: Routledge.

Fraser, Nancy (ed.) (1997) *Justice Interruptus: Critical Reflections on the "Postsocialist" Condition*, New York: Routledge.

Fraser, Nancy and Gordon, Linda (1997) "A genealogy of 'dependency': tracing a keyword of the US welfare state," in Nancy Fraser (ed.) *Justice Interruptus: Critical Reflections on the "Postsocialist" Condition*, New York: Routledge.

Holmstrom, Nancy (1981) " 'Women's work,' the family and capitalism," *Science and Society*, XLV:2 (summer) pp. 186–211.

Kittay, Eva Feder (1999) *Love's Labor: Essays on Women, Equality and Dependency*, New York and London: Routledge.

Kropotkin, Peter (1987) "Anarchist communism: its basis and principles," in *Peter Kropotkin: Two Essays*, ed. Nicolas Walter, London: Freedom Press.

Moulton, Janice (1983) "A paradigm of philosophy: the adversary method," in *Discovering Reality*, eds Sandra Harding and Merrill B. Hintikka, Dordrecht: Reidel, pp. 149–64.

Okin, Susan (1989) *Justice, Gender and the Family*, New York: Basic Books.

Rawls, John (1971) *A Theory of Justice*, Cambridge MA: Harvard University Press.

Sacks, Karen (1988) "Gender and grassroots leadership," in *Women and the Politics of Empowerment*, eds Ann Bookman and Sandra Morgen, Philadelphia: Temple University Press.

Sterba, James P. (1980) *Justice: Alternative Political Perspectives*, Belmont CA: Wadsworth Publishing Co.

——(1988) *How to Make People Just*, Totowa NJ: Rowman & Littlefield.

——(1998) *Justice for Here and Now*, Cambridge: Cambridge University Press.

Walzer, Michael (1983) *Spheres of Justice: A Defense of Pluralism and Equality*, New York: Basic Books.

Waring, Marilyn (1988) *Counting for Nothing: What Men Value and What Women are Worth*, Wellington: Allen & Unwin.

Young, Iris M. (1997) "Mothers, citizenship and independence: a critique of pure family values," in *Intersecting Voices: Dilemmas of Gender, Political Philosophy and Policy*, Princeton NJ: Princeton University Press.

13

JUSTICE FOR HERE AND NOW
OR THERE AND THEN?

Rosemarie Tong

James P. Sterba's latest book on justice, *Justice for Here and Now*, represents a significant improvement over his earlier book, *How to Make People Just*. Always eager to respond to his critics, Sterba has addressed virtually every concern that was raised against his previous efforts to provide a theory of justice broad enough to accommodate all rational persons happily. More than any other philosopher I know, Sterba strives to practice what he preaches; namely, "a peacemaking way of doing philosophy."[1] He assesses his opponents' arguments fairly; he tries to understand positions with which he is unfamiliar or with which he disagrees; he tries to undo his own objections to others' arguments; and he willingly modifies or abandons his own views whenever other persons' views appear more compelling.[2] Nevertheless, despite the fact that Sterba's position on justice is in principle always open to revision, it has remained essentially the same over the years.

The basic argument of *Justice for Here and Now* is very similar to the basic argument of *How to Make People Just*. In both of his major works on justice, Sterba bravely insists that if it is possible to demonstrate that the libertarian ideal of *liberty* has the same practical requirements as the welfare liberal ideal of *equality*, then it is also possible to show that all the major (Western?) theories of justice have these same practical requirements. After all, if the lion of libertarianism can rest beside the lamb of welfare liberalism, then the less diametrically opposed creatures in the kingdom of justice theories can also find common ground. Not wanting to keep his readers in suspense, Sterba quickly lets us know that what unifies libertarians, welfare liberals, socialists, feminists, and exponents of racial justice, homosexual justice, multicultural justice and environmental justice is their supposed shared commitment to a set of welfare rights and equal opportunity rights, the enforcement of which will eliminate the unjustified disparities which plague us here and now.

In many ways, Sterba's latest effort to do philosophy peacefully is a *tour de force* in which he brings together and relates all the issues typically covered in one of the many "social justice" anthologies currently on the market. I can easily imagine myself using one of these textbooks in conjunction with *Justice for Here and Now* to show my students how issues such as environmental biodegradation, hunger and poverty, war and violence, gender discrimination, racial and ethnic discrimination, and healthcare reform can each be classified either as a "welfare" or "equality of opportunity" issue. (Note that Sterba has moved from claiming that all major (Western?) theories of justice support welfare rights and *affirmative action* rights, to instead claiming that they all support welfare rights and *equality of opportunity* rights. There is, after all, an argument to be made that insofar as affirmative action is understood as a compensatory right to preferential treatment, it exceeds the scope of an equality of opportunity right.) Nevertheless, despite my support for Sterba's general line of reasoning, I find certain aspects of his revised theory of justice unsatisfactory. First, I am specifically dissatisfied that Sterba continues to identify "androgyny" as his preferred ideal for feminist justice; to present as uncontroversial among feminists a range of issues that remain contested; and to downplay certain topics in his discussion of men's and women's reproductive rights and responsibilities. Second, I am generally worried that Sterba's theory of justice might, after all, be somewhat dated – a justice theory not for here and now, the year 2000, but for there and then, the United States in the 1960s and 1970s.

I Specific concerns

According to Sterba, androgyny is the goal of feminist justice. To his credit, Sterba's definition of androgyny is better than most. As he sees it, androgyny requires "no more than that the traits that are truly desirable in society be equally open to both women and men, or in the case of virtues, equally expected of both women and men, other things being equal."[3] Sterba realizes that many of the masculine and feminine traits which society currently views as desirable are not, from a feminist point of view, *truly* desirable. For example, since supposedly feminine traits such as "gullibility" and supposedly masculine traits such as "brutality" are not truly desirable from a feminist point of view, they are not open to Sterba's androgyne.[4] So far so good, but what Sterba fails to see is how prescriptive and limiting his ideal of androgyny is, despite the fact that he requires monoandrogyny only in so far as *bona fide* "feminine" and "masculine" *virtues* are concerned, permitting polyandrogyny with respect to acceptable "feminine" and "masculine" psychological traits.[5] In other words, although every man and woman must, according to Sterba, display the supposedly feminine virtue of care and the supposedly masculine virtue of justice, each man and woman is free to develop a totally "feminine" personality, a totally "masculine" personality, or some combination thereof.

Arguing that androgyny is not necessarily the best or the only way for feminists to break down sexual polarization, Kathryn Pauley Morgan notes

271

that there might be even better (i.e. *more* feminist) ways to end male/female opposition. She notes, for example, that

> we might expand the number of sexes that we recognize, for example, through the category of intersexes ... [or] we might advocate a stage of theory of Sex-role Transcendence which posits a three stage process of sexual development. This theory necessitates a second stage of learned, polarized, oppositional sex-roles. It then proposes a third, final stage of completely individualized responses, in which assigned gender is irrelevant in the individual's decision-making process. (The proponents of this theory sharply distinguish it from androgyny) ... [or we might] call for institutionalized degenderization of behavior, personality traits, forms of labor and so on. This process would leave completely open the question of what human beings should be like in such a society.[6]

As Morgan sees it, these alternatives (if operationalized) would lead to the breakdown of sexual dichotomization, but none of them would result in the kind of androgynous individuals Sterba envisions.

Since the alternatives to androgyny Morgan suggests are all viable feminist ideals, I see no reason to privilege androgyny over any one of them. In fact, I see some reasons to prefer Morgan's ideals over Sterba's ideal of androgyny, for the former ways to break down the male/female divide have the advantage of not introducing a vague distinction between desirable traits and expected virtues. Sterba provides neither a set of criteria for distinguishing between desirable traits and expected virtues, nor a set of conditions under which desirable traits might earn the status of expected virtues. For example, is "being compassionate" a desirable feminine *trait* or an expected feminine *virtue*? Is it a *psychological* feature of one's personality or a *moral* feature of one's character? I think Sterba views "being compassionate" as an expected feminine virtue to be cultivated by men and women equally. But there is a case to be made that society in general might view "being compassionate" simply as a desirable feminine trait rather than an expected feminine virtue. Moreover, from the perspective of some feminists, there is a case to be made that "being compassionate" is not really a *desirable* feminine trait – let alone a virtue – because what the larger society understands by "being compassionate" requires too much self-sacrifice and not enough self-affirmation and self-care on the part of the compassionate individual, who, more often than not, is a woman.[7] Finally, even if it is possible to distinguish between desirable traits and expected virtues, and to establish that "being compassionate" is indeed an expected feminine *virtue*, Sterba fails to explain how a totally masculine personality (exhibited by either a male or female person) is capable of cultivating the expected feminine virtue of "being compassionate." Is there no relationship between traits and virtues; between our psychological personalities and our moral characters?

But even if I am wrong, and Sterba's ideal of androgyny is indeed better than any of the other feminist ideals Morgan proposes, I still think it is misleading to describe androgyny as the *goal* of feminist justice. I agree with Alison Jaggar that the task of feminist justice is to reform society, not to reform individuals.[8] In other words, the essential work of feminists is to eliminate those structures, systems, ideologies, and so forth that perpetuate male domination and female subordination so that women and men can have equal (though not necessarily the same) freedom and well-being (material, psychological, spiritual and social). It is not to impose an abstract conception of full personhood on the bodies and psyches of concrete men and women.

Over and beyond rejecting Sterba's insistence on upholding the ideal of androgyny as feminists' *pièce de résistance*, there is much that concerns me about his presentation of the practical applications of feminist justice. He presents as universal feminist dogma what amounts to a very mainstream liberal position on the family, the workplace, and sexual relationships. Although Sterba claims he is interested in justice for both racial and ethnic minorities and homosexuals and lesbians, he presents as idyllically "feminist" a dual-parent, dual-career, child-centered heterosexual family. This ideal of the family works well enough for relatively privileged couples both of whom have meaningful careers and a desire to include children in their lives. However, it does not work nearly so well for working-class couples whose workplace (how about a chicken factory, a textile mill, or a fast-food restaurant?) is not likely to foster either the production of desirable traits or the cultivation of expected virtues, and whose home is not a haven of tranquillity but a place in which to collapse at the end of an exhausting day. Can Sterba's recommendations for flex-time, maternity leaves, and dad and mom taking turns cooking solve what is wrong with the latter scenario?

Furthermore, the dual-parent, dual-career, child-centered heterosexual family ideal does not fit single-parent households, a certain proportion of which are *deliberately* one-parented; lesbian or homosexual households; childless by choice households; and households in which one member, with the other's wholehearted consent, chooses not to work outside of the home. Are we to conclude that the adults and children in such households are likely to have fewer desirable traits and expected virtues than the adults and children in dual-career, dual-parent, child-centered heterosexual households? If not, Sterba needs to consider the possibility that his ideal of androgyny is far from universal, combining as it does primarily those masculine and feminist traits and virtues that mainstream liberals, including liberal feminists, find respectively desirable and expected.

In addition to proposing what he, but not all feminists, would regard as a "radical" modification of the wage structure,[9] Sterba claims that women's and men's economic status needs to be equalized. As he sees it, the best way to achieve this goal is through required programs of affirmative action and comparable worth. Not once, however, does Sterba mention or consider how divided feminists are, for example, about the desirability of comparable worth programs.

Like Sterba, *liberal* feminists want to use comparable worth as a means to end gender discrimination by proving that women are indeed men's equals since they can do and do do men's work. In the State of Washington study Sterba cites, liberal feminists argued that in terms of "worth points" for the four components found in most jobs – "knowledge and skills," "mental demands," "accountability" and "working conditions" – many low-paying female-dominated jobs were actually worth more in points than many high-paying male-dominated jobs.[10] Thus they concluded that, for example, nurse practitioners (mostly female) who scored 385 worth points should earn more and not the same as boiler operators (all male) with only 144 points to their credit.[11]

Initially, *radical* cultural feminists, who affirm women's values and virtues over men's, were also attracted to the comparable worth movement. They viewed it as a way for society to properly reward women's traditional "caring" work. Over time, however, radical cultural feminists came to suspect that the standards and measures developed to assess comparable worth were no more gender neutral than the schema Lawrence Kohlberg devised to measure "human" moral development.[12] Kohlberg's scale recognized persons as morally developed if they spoke the language of abstract principles and rules rather than the language of concrete responsibilities for and attachments to human persons. Since men are more inclined to speak the former language than the latter, men consistently scored higher than women on Kohlberg's moral development scale, with the implication that women are less morally developed than men. Like Kohlberg's scale, many comparable worth schemes use male standards and measures to add and subtract "worth points." Thus radical cultural feminists gradually concluded that comparable worth schemes reward women for the wrong reasons; namely, for doing "manly" activities.

Consider, for example, Helen Remick's analysis of comparable worth initiatives, particularly in the field of nursing.

> Nursing, like most other areas in the health care field, has changed drastically over time. Nursing specialties, for example, can make extensive use of electronic monitors, involve significant amounts of teaching, and/or require sophisticated diagnostic work. Unfortunately, the work of nurses is not always visible to the patient, in part because of stereotypes about nurses and women in general. In a well-publicized example, after the attempted assassination of President Reagan, he recalled the nurse who had been so comforting to

him while he was in the intensive care unit and conducted a search to thank her. Giving comfort was one of her *least* important duties in terms of his survival; she was constantly monitoring his vital signs for change and was fully competent to initiate emergency procedures should the situation have called for it.

(my italics)[13]

Remick concludes that there is a tendency to undervalue and underestimate what women do, even though women's jobs require just as much in the way of knowledge and skills, mental demands, accountability and working conditions as men's jobs. Although Remick's conclusion seems "pro-woman," one can easily see why radical cultural feminists found her analysis ultimately disappointing. They accused Remick of undervaluing and underestimating the female or feminine *value of nurturance*. Why seek to justify higher wages for a nurse on the grounds that she exhibits "doctor-like" characteristics? Why not instead seek to justify lower wages for a doctor on the grounds that he fails to exhibit enough "nurse-like" characteristics? Thus, if comparable worth is to satisfy radical cultural feminists' concerns, new measures and standards must be developed to select for and to reward characteristics traditionally associated with women. This is like asking Lawrence Kohlberg to reconstruct his scale of moral development to favor those who are enmeshed in the world of concrete particulars rather than those who are committed to the pursuit of abstract universals. Or, even more difficult, it is like asking Kohlberg to get together with his most perceptive critic, Carol Gilligan,[14] to construct a unitary scale of moral development that measures women's and men's morality equally well.

Although it pleases me that Sterba now realizes that if men and women are to become equal, we must not only transform family structures and pay women the kind of wages we pay men, but also eliminate sexual violence against women, I am nonetheless disappointed that his discussion of pornography glosses over the profound disagreements feminists have had about sexually-explicit depictions of women. Although many feminists view pornography, particularly violent pornography, as contributing to men's tendency to view women as mere sexual objects rather than full human persons, other feminists view pornography more positively.[15] This latter group of feminists claim that women need to explore the darker as well as lighter sides of their sexuality, and to experiment with rough, even violent, sex as well as the kind of gentle sex that links one body to another in a comforting embrace.[16] They maintain that many feminists enjoy all sorts of pornography and use it to fuel their sexual fantasies.

Contributing to my disappointment with Sterba's discussion of sexuality is the additional fact that he makes no mention of the so-called beauty trap which, in my estimation, does more harm to more women than the pornography he singles out for special condemnation. To be sure, when it is understood not as an opportunity for women to explore the full range of human sexuality, but as part of a series of related actions, all of which demean women, pornography is certainly not something for women to applaud. The images of women portrayed in most pornography are, as Catharine MacKinnon has argued, ones that create a frame of reference in which women are viewed as less human and therefore less deserving of respect, good treatment and rewards than men.[17] But since the *worst* types of pornography tend to be hidden and purchased relatively infrequently by men, I do not worry about the images of women in pornography nearly as much as I worry about the images of women on television, in the movies, and in popular fashion magazines. Images of rail-thin women with perfect skin, teeth and facial features have produced more in the way of anorexic, bulimic, weight-preoccupied and exercise-obsessed women than anything else I can think of in our society. Women are far more focused on their bodies than men are in our society; and to the degree that a woman is preoccupied with her physical appearance, she cannot focus on thinking the kind of ideas and generating the kind of actions that have the power to transform an unjust society into a just society.

Finally, it utterly bewilders me why Sterba does not include any *substantial* discussion of women's reproductive role and the ways in which it affects women's equality with men. When he does bring up the issue of women's reproductive role, Sterba trivializes it. He comments that:

> now some feminists would want to pursue various possible technological transformations of human biology in order to achieve equal opportunity. For example, they would like to make it possible for women to inseminate other women and for men to lactate and even bring fertilized ova to term.[18]

To be sure, in all fairness to Sterba, some feminists have argued that in order to achieve gender equity, artificial reproduction would have to be introduced. For example, Marge Piercy envisions a feminist utopia called Mattapoisett in which babies are born from what is termed the "brooder." Female ova, fertilized *in vitro* with male sperm selected for a full range of racial, ethnic, and personality types, are gestated within an artificial placenta.

Piercy explains that the women of Mattapoisett did not casually give up biological reproduction for technological reproduction. They did so only when they concluded that the loss of biological reproduction was the price they had to pay to eliminate racism and classism as well as sexism.

> It was part of women's long revolution. When we were breaking all the old hierarchies. Finally there was one thing we had to give up too, the only power we ever had, in return for no power for anyone.

276

The original production: the power to give birth. Cause as long as we were biologically enchanted, we'd never be equal. And males never would be humanized to be loving and tender. So we all became mothers. Every child has three. To break the nuclear bonding.[19]

Piercy suggests, in other words, that as a result of women giving up their monopoly on the power to give birth, the supposed paradigm for power relations was destroyed, and everyone in Mattapoisett was in a position to reconstitute human relations in ways that defy the hierarchical ideas of better/worse, higher/lower, stronger/weaker, and especially dominant/submissive.

Whatever the merits of Piercy's views, I do not think that most feminists think that women have to give up biological reproduction in order to be men's equals. Rather I think they believe, as I do, that provided women can control their reproductive capacities through contraception, sterilization and abortion, women can achieve parity with men. A program serious about gender justice begins with the provision of contraceptive services. Men (and women) must reject the belief that an unwanted pregnancy is the *woman's* problem. Men, no less than women, are morally obligated to protect themselves from unwanted pregnancies. Indeed, feminist Mary Mahowald goes so far as to suggest that, at present, men may be *more* obligated than women to use contraceptives. She claims that:

> From an egalitarian perspective, responsibility for contraception should be shared by sexual partners in a manner that respects the values and preferences of each, and the disproportionate burdens and benefits that pregnancy involves for each. It may be argued, for example, that men have a stronger obligation to practice (accept the burden of) contraception because the burden of pregnancy falls on women rather than men. If pregnancy is seen as a benefit mainly to women, the opposite claim could legitimately be made.[20]

Even if Mahowald is wrong about men's purported reproductive obligations, most feminists still think it is time for society to shift the burden of responsibility for contraception off of women and onto both sexes. It is not fair that women should have to shoulder the risks of using sometimes unsafe contraceptives as well as the risks associated with bearing a child, when more contraceptives other than the condom could be and are in fact already being developed for men.

Increasingly, feminists also think that the right to have an abortion – the issue that Sterba seems most reluctant to discuss – should be viewed as an "equality" right rather than a "privacy" right. For example, according to Catharine A. MacKinnon, the right to privacy works far better for men than for women since it helps men keep women hidden, subjected, and dominated in the so-called personal realm. It is in this realm that men get women pregnant and then tell them to "handle" the situation by getting an abortion. Comments MacKinnon:

> The meaning of abortion in the context of a sexual critique of gender inequality is its promise to women of sex with men on the same terms as promised to men – that is, "without consequences." Under conditions in which women do not control access to our sexuality, this facilitates women's heterosexual availability. In other words, under conditions of gender inequality, sexual liberation in this sense does not free women, it frees male sexual aggression. The availability of abortion thus removes the one remaining legitimized reason that women have had for refusing sex beside the headache. As Andrea Dworkin puts it, analyzing male ideology on abortion: "Getting laid was at stake." The Playboy Foundation has supported abortion rights from day one; it continues to, even with shrinking disposable funds, on a level of priority comparable to its opposition to censorship.[21]

In short, according to MacKinnon, women must understand that their right to abortion is dependent not on their having more privacy, but on their having more equality with men.

One of MacKinnons's interpreters, philosopher Russell McIntyre, restates her view on abortion rights very strongly. He claims that:

> the only way in which a woman can truly compete equally with men in this society is if she is truly equal both in opportunity and protection under the law. ... Because women – and not men – get pregnant and have to interrupt their lives (personal and private) to be mothers, they have unequal opportunities unless women are as free as men not to be under the burden of an unplanned or unwanted pregnancy.[22]

If the law truly viewed women's abortion rights as a matter of equality rather than of privacy, says McIntyre, it would have to permit women to terminate their pregnancies at any point in time and for any reason. Realizing that this interpretation of women's abortion rights entirely undermines any claim to life that a fetus might have, McIntyre adds that women should have their abortions as soon as possible – ideally, before the fetus is viable. In his estimation, there is no need for women to assert their abortion rights by deliberately timing their abortions as late as possible in their pregnancy.[23]

The fact that Sterba pays but slight attention to reproductive issues is a major problem for his discussion of feminist justice. Indeed, unless Sterba takes reproductive issues as seriously as he apparently takes sexuality, socialization of children, and workplace issues, he will continue to present, as "feminist" justice, a version of justice that resembles welfare liberal justice dressed in a skirt. Years ago, feminist Juliet Mitchell abandoned the traditional Marxist feminist position, according to which woman's condition is simply a function of her relation to capital, of whether or not she is part of the productive workforce. In place of this monocausal explanation of woman's oppression, Mitchell suggested that woman's status and function are multiply determined by her role in production, *reproduction*, the socialization of children, and sexuality.

> The error of the old Marxist was to see the other three elements as reductible to the economic; hence the call for the entry into production was accompanied by the purely abstract slogan of the abolition of the family. Economic demands are still primary, but must be accompanied by coherent policies for the other three elements (reproduction, sexuality and socialization), policies which at particular junctures may take over the primary role in immediate action.[24]

Sterba has coherent, though admittedly contestable policies for not only women and production, but also for women and sexuality and the socialization of children. But where is his policy for women and reproduction? Until he tells us how a just society should handle women's *reproductive* rights and responsibilities, what Mitchell called the causal chain of "maternity – family – absence from production and public life – sexual inequality"[25] will continue to bind women to their subordinate status to men.

II General concerns

As real as my specific concerns about Sterba's theory of justice are, my major worry about it is far more serious. The more I reflect on *Justice for Here and Now*, the more I think that Sterba's view of justice is the *old* liberal welfare theory of justice – a theory of justice that has seen better times and might be ready for retirement. In recent years a significant group of political theorists, some of whom happen to be feminists, have claimed that discussions of justice focus too much on issues of economic redistribution. Theories of justice preoccupied with the redistribution of rights and resources find it difficult to accommodate key components of gender injustice – e.g. violence against women (including rape and domestic battery), the sexual "double standard," the reduction of women to bodies that must be disciplined to fit the narrow contours of an unrealistic ideal of beauty. Similarly, theories of justice preoccupied with the distribution of rights and resources also find it difficult to capture feminists' attempts to recognize the value of "feminine" traits and virtues as much as "masculine" traits and virtues. Not unaware of these developments, Sterba has, as noted above, sought to respond to them. Yet, despite important women-centered revisions in Sterba's thinking, Sterba's theory of justice remains a *traditional* theory of distributive justice, increasingly ill suited to handle the complexities of the new world that is taking shape around us. In my estimation, redistributive theories of justice need to be replaced by more recent theories of justice that attend to the non-economic causes and consequences of injustice with the same intensity that they attend to the economic causes and consequences of injustice.

As it so happens, two of these more complete theories of justice are those of feminists Iris Marion Young and Nancy Fraser respectively. According to Young, oppression can take one of five forms depending on which sort of human capacities it inhibits: exploitation, marginalization, powerlessness, cultural imperialism or violence. Exploitation occurs when some people live under the control of others, according to the purposes and for the benefit of others, thereby systematically increasing the power of others. Marginalization is the process by which people whom society regards as virtually useless – e.g. the old, the young, the disabled, the underclass – are excluded from gainful employment and the responsibilities and rights of full citizenship. Powerlessness consists in always being told what to do by others but never having the opportunity to be the person in charge. Cultural imperialism is the universalization and establishment of the dominant group's experience and ethos as the gold standard for all groups, which has the result of rendering inaudible and invisible the so-called Other. Violence is susceptibility to systematic attacks on one's person and/or property at random and for no reason other than the fact that one belongs to a disfavored social group.[26]

Although each of the five forms of oppression is unique in Young's mind, they appear to fall into two categories, according to Nancy Fraser. Exploitation, marginalization and powerlessness seem to be the direct products of economic disadvantage. In contrast, cultural imperialism and violence seem to be the direct products of social disadvantage – of being silenced, put in one's place, disregarded, shown who's "boss," and the like. Thus Young's prescription for justice is twofold: eliminate economic disadvantage by restructuring the division of labor, and eliminate social disadvantage by affirming the value of difference.[27] However, if this is Young's remedy for injustice, perhaps her theory is not really that new after all. In all fairness to Sterba, he repeatedly comments in *Justice for Here and Now* that equal advantages in the marketplace cannot achieve justice for all unless they are accompanied by major social changes that acknowledge people's differences. But even if Young's theory of justice is in the end similar to Sterba's, Fraser's theory of justice clearly departs from both of their efforts.

Commenting on Young's theory of justice in particular, Fraser claims that in contrast to a quarter of a century ago when the only paradigm of justice was a redistributive paradigm (think here of Rawls and Nozick), we now have two paradigms of justice equal in strength: a redistributive paradigm and a recognition paradigm.[28] The problem, says Fraser, is that these two paradigms do not work in tandem in a liberal welfare state, not even in a liberal welfare state that doffs its hat to multiculturalism. In fact, the redistributive and recognition paradigms often pull in two different directions. The redistribution paradigm pulls us in the direction of viewing men and women as the same – as being entitled to (because capable of) the same kinds of job, for example. In contrast, the recognition paradigm pulls us in the direction of viewing men and women as different – as enjoying different kinds of work because of different biological and psychological differences. Moreover, to the extent that these paradigms are mixed, and women are given the same jobs as men but with allowances made for women's biological and psychological differences from men (e.g. women's [supposed] need for maternity leave), resentment will be directed against women. The only way to avoid this state of affairs, says Fraser, is to recognize that Sterba's solution for injustice – combining the liberal welfare state agenda with a mainstream multiculturalism agenda – will not permit us to escape the "vicious circles of mutually reinforcing cultural and economic subordination."[29] What will help us out of this dizzying vortex is instead "socialism in the economy and deconstruction in the culture."[30] We have to figure out the ways in which we want to be treated the same, and the ways in which we want to be treated differently.

Clearly, Fraser's theory of justice is new compared to Sterba's. Whether it is better than Sterba's theory of justice is, of course, a matter for debate. Certainly, Fraser's theory is far less "peaceful" than Sterba's. I very much doubt that libertarians, welfare liberals, socialists, feminists, and advocates of racial justice, homosexual justice and multicultural justice can each be interpreted to support deep restructuring of relations of production and relations of recognition. Nevertheless, I suspect that Fraser is right: that justice demands no less than the transformation she has in mind. Unfortunately, I very much doubt that "peaceful" types are in the mood for a revolution.

Toward the end of *Justice for Here and Now* Sterba asks why more of the have-nots in the US are not rebelling against their lot in life. He speculates that the reason rebellion is not in the air, despite the fact that things are getting worse for the have-nots relative to the haves, is that the have-nots do not have powerful allies among the haves; and that since revolutionary success is unlikely without the support of some of the haves, it is not reasonable for the have-nots to risk life and limb for nothing or very little.[31] Not only do I find it problematic to suggest that the have-nots are in need of saviors from the class of the haves, I also find it odd that Sterba fails to consider another possibility; namely, that the welfare liberal state has given the have-nots just enough in the way of welfare and equality of opportunity rights to take the edge off their misery. Furthermore, as I see it, Sterba underestimates the power of co-optation when he claims that

> Because women are found at all economic levels of society, the feminist movement may more easily be able to generate the kind of political power necessary to rid society of the lack of equal opportunity for women. It may also happen that, in the process of securing justice for women, other forms of justice will be recurred as well.[32]

In the first place, not all women are feminists. Second, like all human beings, even feminist women are imperfect. It is not clear that women, including feminist women in the higher economic brackets of society, are really ready to defend as morally justified those poor women who would appropriate from them their surplus goods – their treasured "luxuries." Perhaps some privileged feminist women might be willing to do this, but my guess is that their number would be relatively small.

III Conclusion

Since I am by nature a peacemaking person, I have to admit that it was not easy for me to find fault with Sterba's theory of justice. It is one thing to find the motes in a colleague's eyes and quite another to offer a perspective on justice that has fewer flaws than the perspective one has been invited – indeed encouraged – to critique. Unlike Sterba, I cannot present a complete theory of justice, but I can suggest a view of feminist justice that is not based on the concept of androgyny. For me, feminist justice is not so much about permitting and/or requiring men and women to develop certain traits, as it is about giving women the same opportunities men have to develop two sets of what Martha Nussbaum terms "functional human capabilities"[33] – those which, if left undeveloped, render a life not human at all; and those which, if left undeveloped, render a human life less than a *good* human life. Nussbaum's full list of capabilities includes

1 life
2 bodily health
3 bodily integrity
4 senses, imagination and thought
5 emotions
6 practical reason
7 affiliation
8 other species
9 play
10 control over one's environment[34]

To be sure, Nussbaum's list is the product of her own mind, and as such it is contestable on the grounds that once again, a self-appointed Western expert has decided what it is to be fully human. But this objection is surmountable, for Nussbaum's definition of a human being is very similar to the definitions typically produced whenever and wherever people have the opportunity and means to express their deepest desires for themselves and their children freely.

Before we endorse the norms of a society, we must determine whether those who say they espouse them genuinely accept them. In order to make this determination we must, says Jürgen Habermas, ask whether under conditions of undistorted communication, everyone who is currently abiding by these norms would continue to embrace them as rational standards for appropriate human behavior. If the answer to this question is "no," we should, in his estimation, conclude that the members of the community in question have been tricked, mystified or otherwise manipulated into internalizing its norms.[35] In other words, we should not assume that simply because a woman or a group of women defends cultural practices that subordinate women to men, that a woman or a group of women would, upon reflection and given certain opportunities, continue to endorse such practices.

Defending her capabilities approach to constructing a globally just ethics, Martha Nussbaum comments:

> The capabilities approach insists that a woman's affiliation with a certain group or culture should not be taken as normative for her unless, on due consideration, with all the capabilities at her disposal, she makes that norm her own. We should take care to extend to each individual full capabilities to pursue the items on the list and then see whether they want to avail themselves of these opportunities. Usually they do, even when tradition says they should not. Martha Chen's work with [Indian] widows like Metha Bai reveals that they are already deeply critical of the cultural norms that determine their life quality. One week at a widows' conference in Bangalore was sufficient to cause these formerly secluded widows to put on forbidden colors and to apply for loans; one elderly woman, "widowed" at the age of seventy, danced for the first time in her life, whirling wildly in the center of the floor. ... Why should women cling to a tradition, indeed, when it is usually not their voice that speaks or their interests that are served?[36]

The image of Nussbaum's dancing septuagenarian brings a smile to my face in a way that the image of Sterba's virtuous androgyne does not. Feminist justice is not about *making* women and men rightly ordered and well balanced; rather, it is about providing women and men with equal capabilities for leading a full human life. In the feminist utopia I envision, society will not have to require people to be virtuous, for people will want to be virtuous, having recognized that unless they treat each other with equal respect and consideration, rejoicing in each other's differences, they will not only fail to flourish but fail to survive as a society.

NOTES

1 James P. Sterba, *Justice for Here and Now* (New York: Cambridge University Press, 1998) pp. 1–13.
2 *Ibid.*, p. 13.
3 *Ibid.*, p. 78.
4 *Ibid.*, p. 79.
5 Joyce Trebilcot, "Two Forms of Androgynism," in Mary Vetterling-Braggin (ed.) *"Femininity," "Masculinity," and "Androgyny"* (Totowa NJ: Littlefield, Adams, and Co., 1982) pp. 71–3.
6 Kathryn Pauley Morgan, "Androgyny: A Conceptual Critique," *Social Theory and Practice*, no. 3 (fall 1982) p. 255.
7 Sarah Lucia Hoagland, "Some Thoughts About *Caring*," in Claudia Card (ed.) *Feminist Ethics* (Lawrence: University Press of Kansas, 1991) p. 255.
8 Alison Jaggar, "Comments on James P. Sterba," in James P. Sterba, Tibor R. Machan, Alison Jaggar, William Galston, Carol Gould, Milton Fisk and Robert C. Solomon, *Morality and Social Justice* (Lanham MD: Rowman & Littlefield, 1995) pp. 45–52.
9 Sterba, *Justice for Here and Now*, p. 86.
10 Helen Remick, "Major Issues in *a priori* Applications," in Helen Remick (ed.) *Comparable Worth and Wage Discrimination: Technical Possibilities and Political Realities* (Philadelphia: Temple University Press, 1984) p. 102.
11 *Ibid.*, p. 103.
12 Lawrence Kohlberg, "From Is to Ought: How to Commit the Naturalistic Fallacy and Get Away with It in the Study of Moral Development," in T. Mischel (ed.) *Cognitive Development and Epistemology* (New York: Academic Press, 1971) pp. 164–5.
13 Helen Remick and Bonnie J. Steinberg, "Technical Possibilities and Political Realities: Concluding Remarks," in Remick (ed.) *Comparable Worth and Wage Discrimination*, p. 289.
14 Carol Gilligan, "Concepts of the Self and of Morality," *Harvard Education Review*, 47, no. 4 (November 1977) pp. 481–517.
15 Ann Ferguson, "Sex Wars: The Debate Between Radical and Libertarian Feminists," *Signs: Journal of Women in Culture and Society*, 10, no. 1 (autumn 1984) pp. 108–10.
16 Deirdre English, Amber Hollibaugh and Gayle Rubin, "Talking Sex: A Conversation on Sexuality and Feminism," *Socialist Review*, 13, no. 4 (July/August 1981).
17 Catharine A. MacKinnon, "Francis Biddle's Sister: Pornography, Civil Rights, and Speech," in Catharine A. MacKinnon, *Feminism Unmodified: Disclosures on Life and Law* (Cambridge: Harvard University Press, 1987) p. 176.
18 Sterba, *Justice for Here and Now*, p. 82.
19 Marge Piercy, *Woman on the Edge of Time* (New York: Fawcett Crest Books, 1976) pp. 105–6.
20 Mary Mahowald, *Women and Children in Health Care: An Unequal Majority* (New York: Oxford University Press, 1992) p. 79.

21 Catharine A. MacKinnon, "Roe v. Wade: A Study in Male Ideology," in Lewis M. Schwartz (ed.), *Arguing About Abortion* (Belmont CA: Wadsworth, 1993) p. 223.

22 Russell L. McIntyre, "Abortion and the Search for Public Policy," *Health Care, Law and Ethics*, 8, no. 3 (Summer 1993) p. 15.

23 *Ibid.*

24 Juliet Mitchell, *Woman's Estate* (New York: Pantheon Books, 1971) pp. 100–1.

25 *Ibid.*, p. 107.

26 Iris Marion Young, *Justice and the Politics of Difference* (Princeton: Princeton University Press, 1990) pp. 47–63.

27 Nancy Fraser, *Justice Interruptus: Critical Reflections on the "Postsocialist" Condition* (New York: Routledge, 1997).

28 *Ibid.*, pp. 11–40.

29 *Ibid.*, p. 33.

30 *Ibid.*

31 Sterba, *Justice for Here and Now*, pp. 177–8.

32 *Ibid.*, p. 178.

33 Martha Nussbaum, *Sex and Social Justice* (New York: Oxford University Press, 1999) p. 41.

34 *Ibid.*

35 Jürgen Habermas, *Communication and the Evolution of Society*, trans. T. McCarthy (Boston: Beacon Press, 1979) p. 75.

36 Nussbaum, *Sex and Social Justice*, pp. 146–7.

Lesbian and gay perspectives

14

ROUTES TO
LAKE WOBEGON

Claudia Card

Garrison Keillor, narrator of the popular radio show *A Prairie Home Companion*, reports that in Lake Wobegon all the women are strong, all the men are good looking, and all the children are above average. Presumably, the men are strong, too, and the women also good looking, and how could the children of such parents fail to be above average? The Lake Wobegon self-image is not only idealized but, in a sense, androgynous. Whatever the realities, this ideal remains compelling, especially if we expand it to include and emphasize traits of character. But how to make such an ideal a reality? James P. Sterba has some suggestions, for here and now. I have some alternative suggestions.

In *Justice for Here and Now* Sterba offers a refreshing and attractive "peacemaking" way of doing philosophy.[1] He seeks practical reconciliations of alternative moral and political perspectives by drawing on positions held in common by those who have those perspectives, exploring the implications of their positions with a view to locating a compromise that honors something important, equally, in each position. He argues creatively that libertarians' minimal interpretation of morality commits them, for all practical purposes, to acknowledging rights to welfare and equal opportunity and even to something like the equality that socialists endorse. He then applies this libertarian/welfare-liberal morality to the cases of feminist, racial, homosexual and ethnic justice.

Throughout *Justice for Here and Now*, philosophical argumentation is conducted in a peacemaking spirit of compromise. But Sterba also recognizes that not everything should be up for compromise. Morality, for example, is not to be compromised, although both egoism and altruism are, and morality represents the compromise between them. Feminism, likewise, is not compromisable. It is presented as the application of morality (justice) to certain kinds of issues. Yet the feminism also defended in this book is presented as itself a compromise – or intermediate – between two extreme views about women, a different sort of compromise from that of morality. One of the extremes between which it is a compromise is the view of women as merely victims. The other is the view of women as superior beings. Both views have been associated by anti-feminists, and even by some liberal feminist critics, with radical feminist separatism, although Sterba does not explicitly make that association himself. In this chapter, I offer a feminist separatist vision that I find compatible with Sterba's ideal of feminist justice for here and now. Although it takes very seriously the fact that women in misogynist society have been victims of hostile practices, it presents women as much more than victims, but without claiming the superiority of females to males in native endowment.

Sterba's feminist ideal is that of an "androgynous" society in the sense of a society that is "genderfree." Androgyny as he understands it requires that "truly desirable traits in society be equally available to both women and men or, in the case of virtues, be equally expected of both women and men" (p. 173). He considers in some detail what social changes might be required to implement this ideal, and he argues for several fairly specific and practicable changes. In order to give children of both sexes the same type of upbringing and to give mothers and fathers the same opportunities for education and employment, he proposes that employers institute more flexible work schedules to allow all parents to spend more time with their children without sacrificing career or educational opportunities. He defends certain programs of affirmative action and of comparable worth and the implementation of programs against sexual harassment as means to change the distribution of economic power in society, so as to remove structural violence against women. He takes seriously the idea of banning violent pornography as one strategy for addressing the overt violence of rape, domestic battery and sexual abuse that forcibly keeps women and girls in subordinate positions.

Sterba's chapter on feminist justice is remarkable for its appreciation of the pervasiveness and seriousness of violence against women and girls and for its will to propose constructive measures to reduce and eventually eliminate that violence. It contains detailed statistical documentation of the impact on women and girls of both structural and overt violence. The challenge of justice for here and now with respect to such violence is to come up with plans of action that are likely to move us toward what Sterba calls the androgynous ideal.

The phrase "justice for here and now" calls to mind justice for what John Rawls would call a nonideal society. A nonideal society is one in which there does not exist perfect, or even nearly perfect, compliance among its members with institutions whose defining norms satisfy basic principles of justice. In such a society people cannot count on most others being moved most of the time by an effective sense of justice. But they can count on most people knowing this very fact about each other. Achieving anything like justice in deeply unjust societies is one of the most difficult of moral challenges. In societies like that of the United States today, which have legacies of profound injustice against racial and ethnic minorities, lesbians and gay men, the elderly and disabled, and against females of all groups, no course of action may be available that does not violate anyone's just claims. Any remedy we seek may be less than just to at least some of those who are affected by it. The challenge is then to identify which alternative policies or courses of action would minimize injustice while at the same time moving us closer than we were to the ideal of perfect justice. This means that we should be prepared, regarding any remedy we propose, for rationally grounded claims to the effect that our proposal would be unjust to some parties. Justification will need to take the form of arguing that the most realistic alternatives to the proposed change are even more unjust, or that they would even more greatly impede progress toward a just society, or both.

Affirmative action is a good example. There may be no way to implement affirmative action so as to fulfill everyone's just claims. Arguments in favor of affirmative action (including Sterba's) tend to point out the even greater injustices in the alternative of implementing equal treatment here and now as it would be implemented in a perfectly just society. They argue that to implement such equality now would impede progress toward a just society in that it would simply preserve the status quo. The most compelling way to criticize affirmative action would be to propose an alternative that would also move social practice toward ideals of justice, and at the same time be less unjust than affirmative action. It is not enough simply to point out the likely injustices of affirmative action.

In that spirit I propose some alternatives to some of Sterba's family restructuring proposals for implementing his androgynous ideal. As he has characterized it, I find the androgynous ideal itself entirely unobjectionable. It is compatible with great variety of personal styles, but insists only that when it comes to moral character traits, differences of sex are irrelevant. All human beings should have equally the opportunity to develop all human traits that are truly and fundamentally desirable, and the truly human virtues should be equally expected of all human beings, at least in the sense that no one is excluded in advance simply because of their sex.

I would not call this ideal "androgynous," however, because of a history in feminist theory that associates the "andro" and the "gyn" with the gender concepts of "masculine" and "feminine" rather than with the more biological concepts of "male" and "female." If we understand "masculine" and "feminine" in their current meanings as not just accidentally incorporating the perspectives of dominator and dominated, the resulting "androgyne" would be something like an incoherent or schizophrenic "master-slave," whereas the intention behind Sterba's ideal is a perspective that is neither that of a master nor that of a slave.

Sterba understands "androgynous" as "genderfree," a concept which, on a psycho-social understanding of "gender," may be just right for an aim of feminist justice. The combination he favors is of the best human traits that have been historically more available to *men* with the best human traits that have been historically more available to *women*. This idea also seems to me entirely unobjectionable. More concretely, in his genderfree society – reminiscent of Lake Wobegon – women as well as men would be independent, decisive, and strong, and men as well as women would be cooperative, open, and nurturing (if not good-looking). And we might expect the children raised by such women and such men to be definitely above average (that is, the average of here and now).

It might appear at first that transgendered people would object to the idea of a genderfree society, and prefer instead a greater variety of socially accepted genders with individual freedom to choose, or to own, whichever one (or ones) feels right. If genders, as transgendered people understand them, could be defined independently of moral character traits and considered simply matters of personal style, however, there need be no incompatibility between the society that Sterba calls "genderfree" and the transgender ideal of gender multiplicity. Presumably, the transgender ideal would not include genders that were defined in part by unacceptable moral character traits or by the absence of morally important ones.

From a pragmatic point of view, the question then is, "How can we get from where we are, with a minimum of injustice, to a society that produces people like that, people who have all the basic morally desirable traits of character?" Sterba begins by citing the family as a locus for radical restructuring. The radical restructuring that he proposes is that men do their fair share of the housework and childcare and that both female and male parents have flexible work schedules to make it possible for each to do their fair share of childcare and housework. Lest anyone find this not such a radical restructuring, in view of the trend of the past several decades for men to take on household and childcare tasks, I would point out that legal scholar Joan Williams, in her work on conflicts between family and paid labor, has documented that in the 1990s women in the US still do the lion's share of housework and childcare, and that women's jobs tend to be part-time, underpaid because part-time, and lacking in benefits and opportunities for advancement.[2] Her proposals, which mesh well with Sterba's, include paying part-time workers at the same rate as full-time workers and offering them proportional benefits and opportunities for advancement.

Something like the family is actually a very good place to begin, considering that it is where women and girls suffer so much of the violence that Sterba documents. However, I would go further than he does in radical restructuring. I would begin, more specifically, with *households*. Heterosexual *cohabitation* is an extremely important, influential, and pervasive practice that deserves to be re-evaluated from a feminist perspective.

What many people understand today by their "family" is actually a household of people, often including members who are not biological kin, sometimes entirely members who are not biological kin, who live together for an extended period of time, people who are intimately interdependent in a variety of ways (economic, sexual, emotional – it varies). So understood, "families," or households, may be either heterosexual (mixed) or same-sex. Thus lesbians today speak of "families we choose" by contrast with their "families of origin."

Sterba's discussion of changes to be made in families seems to take for granted the context of a heterosexual (mixed) household. His references to parents seem likewise to assume that a child's parents will consist of one male and one female. Yet households can also be same-sex, and parenting (understood as "raising children") can be done by persons of the same sex.

In what kind of household is it most likely that women and girls will learn to be independent, decisive, and strong? In what kind of household is it most likely that men and boys will learn to be cooperative, open, and nurturing? In an all-female household, women are less likely to depend on men for decision-making, income, physical defense, household repairs or social status. They may be more likely to cultivate in themselves and in each other some of the valuable traits and skills that a heterosexual society encourages a woman to seek in a man. Likewise, in an all-male household, men may be less likely to depend on women for the day-to-day emotional support and nurturance that most people need, for someone to listen to their ideas or stories and offer constructive or sympathetic responses, and for housework, laundry, and meal preparation. Consequently, men also may be more likely to cultivate in themselves and in each other the truly desirable traits and skills that a heterosexual society encourages a man to seek in a woman.

Of course, there is no guarantee. People of the same sex can certainly take up masculine and feminine roles in the same household. Many have done so. Even when they do, however, at least *some* members of such households are likely to develop valuable traits and skills that a heterosexual society encourages only in members of the other sex. Although it is possible for a woman who has learned to depend on men simply to transfer that dependence to another woman, same-sex households may be a better bet for bringing about the desired character traits and skills, rather than simply trying to reform heterosexual households in the context of a misogynist society with a laundry list of new rules reapportioning tasks.

I use the terms "heterosexual" and "same-sex" here to describe only the sexes of household members, not the activities in which they engage with each other (which may or may not include sexual activities). A same-sex household could include members who had heterosexual relationships with people outside the household or who became the biological parents of children with them. Still, I draw, in this thought experiment, on what I have observed of lesbian households and gay male households over the past few decades. Contrary to popular myth, it is not unusual for a lesbian household to consist of adult females, all of whom have been raised to depend on men, nor for a gay male household to consist of adult males, all of whom have been raised to seek emotional nurturance from women. Same-sex cohabitation in such circumstances is a powerful learning experience.

only might same-sex cohabitation be more likely to be effective for
ng about the character transformations that the androgynous ideal
res, but it might also be fairer to children. The one aspect of Sterba's
posal for restructuring the family that I find truly disturbing is the
ggestion that men would *learn* to be cooperative, open and nurturing by
caring for children. He notes that "the traits of openness, cooperativeness,
and nurturance that promote peaceful solutions to conflicts tend to be
fostered exclusively in women, who are effectively excluded from positions of
power in a society characterized by widespread overt and structural violence
against women" (pp. 91–2). He then argues, plausibly, that only if our
leaders develop these traits can we expect peace in the international arena.
This reasoning provides a good argument for putting more women, here and
now, into positions of leadership. But Sterba's only proposal for male
leadership is that "men will acquire these traits through equal sharing of
child-rearing and housekeeping tasks" (p. 92).

It sounds as though the idea is that men who are not already cooperative,
open and nurturing would be given major childcare responsibilities and that
children would pay the price of the learning experiences of their male care-
takers. The proposal is even more disturbing if we understand it to imply
that men who have already been socialized to find children sexy, to think
that rape is natural, and to express anger violently would also be given
childcare responsibilities as a means to educate them out of such attitudes.
The latter idea, which Sterba does not explicitly consider, reminds me of the
proposal made spontaneously (and with genuine goodwill) by a male student
in my feminism and sexual politics course many years ago – that men who
are found guilty of rape or battery should be sentenced to work in shelters
for battered women. Even were it true that such male perpetrators would
learn valuable lessons by serving such a sentence, how could we inflict such
"care-takers" on women who had sought shelter from other men guilty of
similar crimes? The student who made this proposal, of course, quickly
realized that he was taking only the men's perspective, that is, thinking only
of what would be good for the men, what they needed to learn. In the case
of Sterba's proposal, we need to include the children's perspectives as well,
not just those of adults who might benefit by having the responsibilities of
caring for them.

And what *would* be good for the children? Who *should* pay the price of
men's learning to be good care-takers? The question of who should pay the
price seems to me the easier one. It is not only that men need to learn how to
give care. Care giving requires skills that females are not born with either,
and those skills are naturally developed through practice. But there are
attitudes that stand in the way of acquiring those skills, attitudes that
women are not as encouraged to develop as are men in a misogynist society.
The problem for men raised in such a society is that they are encouraged
toward violent displays of anger and toward the eroticizing of those who are

vulnerable. They can often incorporate these attitudes into their behavior without actually falling foul of laws that prohibit assault, and without ordinarily getting caught even when they do so. They need to unlearn that socialization, as well as to acquire care giving skills. In the spirit of poetic justice, I think men, those who do need to unlearn these things, should practice on each other. Younger men, for example, could begin by caring for older men and for sick men who have been socialized to the same violent and erotic attitudes. Men who are not already good care givers should pay the price of the relevant learning and unlearning experiences of other men. It would not address the problem if men were to identify some socially disfavored minority group of men to be care givers, as has been done all too often in the history of racism.

What would be good for children, however, is far from obvious. Sterba's androgynous ideal includes the idea that all children would have the same kind of upbringing, in the sense that both girls and boys would be encouraged equally to develop all of the human virtues and all humanly desirable traits. I would point out that this goal, however, need not require that both boys and girls be parented by both women and men, especially in an ideal society in which women and men had the same traits. Nor need it require even that each child be parented by exactly two people or by parents who are of the same generation. Parenting (child-rearing) can be shared not only by parents of the same sex but also by grandparents and other older members of the household, by aunts and uncles, friends, and many members of larger communities. Heterosexual parenting might be fine, although not necessarily the most usual form, in a perfectly just society. But for here and now, it is highly problematic in relation to just those forms of violence that Sterba acknowledges. Children are especially vulnerable. They require not just caretakers who have skills, but caretakers whose attitudes are nurturing, nonviolent and nonexploitative. Few men have been encouraged to develop these attitudes here and now. I therefore conclude that endorsing widespread heterosexual coparenting ought not to be among the *first* steps taken in a program for moving from where we are toward an androgynous society. Other steps ought to be taken first toward undoing what is problematic and too often dangerous to children in the prevalent misogynist and violent socialization of men.

It may be pointed out that much is also problematic in women's socialization, and that is surely true. But when we compare the likely injustices of parenting by sexist women and parenting by sexist men, the danger to children from overt violence seems to me to tip the balance toward tolerating parenting by women as the lesser of likely injustices to children. At any rate, girls are probably in general more at risk from male parenting by sexist men than from parenting by women, and more at risk than male children would be from parenting by either sex. An experiment worth trying might be to resurrect the ancient Amazon custom of women raising girls and men raising boys.

As with affirmative action, my proposal that people choose on principle to cohabit and coparent only with members of the same sex, is conceived not as an end in itself (although for many individuals the choice might well last a lifetime) but as a practical step for moving toward an androgynous society. With the achievement of androgynous society, there would presumably be no need for individuals to rule out the possibility of heterosexual cohabitation and coparenting, although there would presumably also be no reason to expect that these would be the dominant forms. The task for here and now is to create a setting in which both women and men would be more likely than at present to develop as whole persons, morally speaking, with the eventual goal being sustainable development of androgynous characters.

It might be protested that prohibiting heterosexual households would be unfair to individual men and women who have already transcended the stereotypes of masculinity and femininity that the androgynous ideal requires be overcome. There are, here and now, individual men who are open, cooperative and nurturing, more so than some individual women. Prohibiting men generally from raising daughters, for example, would be unfair to men who do not (and perhaps never did) find little girls sexy, who can control their anger, and so forth.

There are several things I would point out in response. One is that I am not recommending a legal prohibition of heterosexual households. The existing sexist distribution of power that Sterba describes so well in the realm of economics also applies in the realm of law. This distribution of power makes it unlikely that such laws would find support, given the history of sexist exploitation of heterosexual households. But even if they did find support, such prohibitions might well encourage more rebellion than anything else. It is important that households be maintained voluntarily. I am thinking extra-legally of choices that people could make, although a society could take many steps to encourage same-sex households and make them more attractive to people than they are at present. I would at least recommend and encourage individuals in the voluntary experiment of principled same-sex households. That is, although I do not here and now recommend a legal ban on heterosexual households, I recommend that individuals reject them as a matter of principle for here and now.

Second, it is true that not everyone in a sexist society fits the stereotypes that such a society encourages and rewards, and that there is a certain unfairness in a practice, or even in the principled decision on the part of an individual, that treats all members of the other sex as though they did fit the stereotype. There is a certain unfairness to trustworthy men, for example, in the practice of a women's transit service designed to offer women safe rides at night, that excludes men from being drivers. However, this unfairness needs to be compared with that risked in alternative policies. It is not unreasonable in a rape culture for women not to trust men who appear to be quite ordinary. It may be unfair, even in a rape culture, for women to distrust even men whose individual trustworthiness they have had or could have ample opportunity to ascertain. That unfairness needs to be weighed in the balance in evaluating social policies that exclude men from certain positions of trust. However, women might reject heterosexual cohabitation here and now without assuming the untrustworthiness of all individual men, and do so as a step toward making same-sex options eventually at least as socially eligible as heterosexual ones, thus making possible generally safer environments for women and children. The progress in justice to women and children might well outweigh the injustice to men.

Third, the observation that not everyone fits sexist stereotypes also suggests certain more modest policies that might be implemented and even enacted in law, regardless of the sexual identity constitution of households. For example, as long as the institution of marriage exists and married partners become guardians of children, there could be elementary restrictions on who is permitted to marry (or even become a domestic partner) that would make more fundamental good sense than the current prohibition on marrying close biological kin. Anyone found guilty of domestic violence or child abuse might be denied a license for future marriages (or be denied future domestic partnership status), their current partners be granted immediate divorce upon request, and children be removed from the guardianship of the violent or abusive parent. It could be legally required, at least, that information about one's history as an abuser (reports, arrests, convictions) be supplied to prospective spouses or partners, as a matter of course or on request. As I have argued elsewhere, the dangers of bad driving are generally taken more seriously here and now than those of domestic abuse.[3] One can automatically lose a driver's license as a result of flagrantly abusing driver privileges. Yet domestic abusers do not have marital privileges revoked by the license grantor (the state). It is up to the abused partner to seek an injunction or divorce, which can be highly dangerous for them to do. The upshot is that usually abusers retain intimate access to their victims. And if divorced, abusers can generally and readily obtain a license to marry again whenever they please.

Sterba presents his androgynous ideal as, if not a compromise, then at least intermediate between two extreme views, which he rejects. One extreme is the negative view of feminism as simply an emancipation of women from traditional roles in order that they may be free to develop in ways hitherto encouraged only in men. The other is the positive view of feminism as basically a celebration of female superiority. On Sterba's view there are genuinely bad things to be escaped by women, but also good things in women to be preserved and shared more widely. This is a sensible view. However, it should also be clear (though it has not always been to critics of feminism or even to feminist theorists) that female separatism need not be based on a belief in female superiority, in the sense of superior native endowment. One can hold that females and males are born with roughly similar potentialities for character development and yet acknowledge that a sexist society encourages the development of dangerous potentialities in men that women are not generally encouraged to develop.

But further, the separatist practice of same-sex households that I have here proposed does not presuppose even generally superior character development in females, or that women's characters in sexist society are not seriously flawed, although I have suggested that in a sexist society, men are generally more dangerous to children, especially to girls. The vices that women learn in a sexist society, such as deviousness, tend to differ from those that men learn. The argument that women in same-sex households (at least, households where the adults are women) may be more likely to develop the desirable traits that a heterosexual society encourages a woman to seek in a man simply entertains the hypothesis that here and now women may be better for women (and girls) in fundamental ways than men are for women, an opinion that was also held by Margaret Fuller in *Woman in the Nineteenth Century*.[4] A parallel argument applies for same-sex male households. In the context of a sexist society, men may well be in some ways better for men than women are for men, as women's attitudes toward men are bound to be deeply ambivalent in any society that has a history of making women dependent on men for protection against men.

But yet another argument for male same-sex households comes from the point of view of fairness: it should not be women's responsibility, even if they could, to improve the characters of adult men who have already had more than their fair share of privilege. Thus the separatism that I propose need not view women in sexist society only as victims, either.

If separatism is a good idea for cohabitation, it may also be a good idea, for some of the same reasons, in the areas of economics and education. For example, instead of seeking to integrate women into an existing labor force by affirmative action, comparable worth, and programs to address sexual harassment, women might do better to organize female businesses, female credit unions, and so forth. The rationale would be that doing so would more effectively promote the androgynous (genderfree) ideal and do so with less injustice than alternatives. At any rate, such experiments ought to be tried by some and encouraged by everyone concerned, even if others are working on affirmative action and so forth.

The reform of heterosexual families is a common liberal feminist proposal. The spirit of compromise that characterizes Sterba's peacemaking way of doing philosophy suggests bringing opposing parties together, not driving them apart. In the case of feminism, that spirit is apt to suggest bringing women and men together, not separating them. However, I have argued that a liberal, as Sterba understands her, need not be such a reformist. What he wants to bring together are traits, not necessarily the sexes. It may be that separating the sexes in the context of a sexist society is the most effective and least unjust way to bring those traits together. The form that women's oppression has taken, which some 1970s feminists called "interior colonization," has produced an alienation of women from other women that has no parallel among men. It has mandated a one-on-one bonding of women to men, who are encouraged to become more bonded to other men than to any woman, and it has encouraged a more lopsided development of traits in women than in men by way of that combination hothouse-and-refrigerator environment that John Stuart Mill famously deplored in his 1869 essay *The Subjection of Women*.[5] The disastrous relationships that women have had with men may not be changeable, as a social pattern, without a radical break that makes possible and socially eligible women's bonding with other women. Abandoning heterosexual cohabitation, rather than trying to reform it in the context of a misogynous society, might be a more effective and less unjust way to further the androgynous ideal.

This idea might have presented itself naturally had Sterba discussed "homosexual justice" in the same chapter with feminist justice, rather than in the chapter on racial and multicultural justice. "Homosexual justice," as Sterba understands it, is concerned with how people are treated when they are known or believed to engage in (or perhaps to want to engage in) *sexual acts* with people of the same sex. It would seem natural to treat homosexual justice as analogous to racial and ethnic justice if one assumed that regardless of whether people acquire or inherit homosexual desires, a homosexual orientation is no more of a choice than one's race or ethnicity. However, contemporary lesbian and gay liberation movements have been conceived much more broadly than as a concern with the liberty to engage in sexual acts with partners of one's choice. They have been concerned with orientations that are as much social as they are sexual – with domestic partnerships, for example, which (like marriages) are ordinarily much more than sexual contracts. Far more radical than engaging in homosexual sexual acts may be the choice to live homosexually throughout one's social life insofar as one can – to maintain a same-sex household, for example, and to foreswear heterosexual cohabitation as long as one lives in a rape culture.

NOTES

1 James P. Sterba, *Justice for Here and Now* (Cambridge: Cambridge University Press, 1998).
2 Joan Williams, *Unbending Gender: Why Family and Work Conflict and What To Do About It* (New York: Oxford University Press, 1999).
3 Claudia Card, "Against Marriage and Motherhood," *Hypatia*, 11:3 (summer 1996) pp. 1–23.
4 Margaret Fuller, *Woman in the Nineteenth Century* (New York: Norton, 1971).
5 John Stuart Mill, *The Subjection of Women* (Indianapolis: Hackett, 1988) p. 23.

15

JUSTICE FOR GLENN AND STACY

On gender, morality, and gay rights

John Corvino

During a recent commencement ceremony at the university where I teach, an award was presented to "the outstanding man and the outstanding woman" in the graduating class. This award, which is given annually, struck me as rather odd. There is nothing odd, of course, about recognizing outstanding students – indeed, the award, as well as the exuberant speeches given by the respective recipients, reminded me of the familiar high school tradition of selecting a class valedictorian. But unless the recipients were expected to make a baby after the ceremony, I could not fathom why it was important to select one man and one woman. We would not think to grant an award to the outstanding white student and outstanding non-white student in the class – even though, given current social conditions where I teach, race is likely to affect the educational experience at least as much as gender. Nor would we consider granting an award to the outstanding student over 5'8" and the outstanding student under 5'8", or the outstanding student who had suffered through Corvino's Intro to Philosophy class and the outstanding student who had not. Yet the audience – a majority of whom were college graduates, at least by the end of the ceremony – showed no signs of puzzlement at the gender division.

We live in a gendered society – not merely in the obvious sense that people have genders, but in the less obvious sense that we act as if a great deal more hinges on this fact than actually does. I am not suggesting that gender is an unimportant or irrelevant feature of human beings. Rather, I am asking *where* and *why* it is relevant. Plato illustrates this point about relevance nicely in the *Republic*, when he argues that although women and men have opposite natures, that difference is irrelevant to the question of whether women should be rulers:

> We might therefore just as well, it seems, ask ourselves whether the nature of bald men and long-haired men is the same and not opposite, and then, agreeing that they are opposite, if we allow bald men

to be cobblers, not allow long-haired men to be, or again if long-haired men are cobblers, not allow the others to be.[1]

Like Plato, I am prepared to grant that men and women are different in important ways. The question is to what ends such differences are relevant. Are they relevant to who should rule the state? Are they relevant to who should receive a graduation award? The tendency to think of men and women as opposite – as when we refer to "the opposite sex" – may lead us to a number of conclusions unjustified by their differences. (This tendency doubtless explains the difficulty many people have with understanding bisexuality: they conceive of the sexes as opposite and then invalidly infer the false conclusion that insofar as a person is attracted to one they must not be attracted to the other.)

The subject of homosexuality is a paradigmatic case of gender playing a far more influential role than its effects merit – or so I shall argue in this paper. Consider the following scenario: Glenn and Stacy love each other very much and have chosen to commit themselves to a monogamous relationship. They do not plan to have children – indeed, Stacy is sterile as a result of a childhood accident – although they might consider adopting someday. But even without children, their relationship is a source of meaning and growth in their lives. To put it simply, Glenn and Stacy believe – and the evidence suggests – that their relationship with each other makes them better people. Glenn's outgoing nature has broken through Stacy's shyness; Stacy's even-temperedness has softened Glenn's impatience. The physical affection that they share with each other is an important element of that relationship, enabling them to express and create feelings for which mere words would be inadequate. In sum, their relationship – including its physical component – realizes a variety of concrete goods that are evident to both them and those who know them.

I have deliberately chosen the names "Glenn" and "Stacy" because both are somewhat gender-ambiguous (cf. Glenn Close and Stacy Keach). Many people – perhaps a majority in our society – would read the above paragraph quite differently in the homosexual case than in the heterosexual one. They might argue that whatever benefits came from such a relationship, they would be in spite of the homosexuality, and besides, that the harms or evils brought about by the homosexuality would outweigh any such benefits. What seemed at first glance to be an obvious good becomes at best controversial and at worst a moral abomination simply by changing the gender of one of the parties.

In contemporary American society, the homosexual Glenn and Stacy would be treated quite differently from the heterosexual Glenn and Stacy – morally, socially and politically. Morally, they would be subject to censure; socially, they would be subject to ostracism and ridicule, and politically, they would be subject to prosecution (in states with anti-sodomy laws) and would be denied the protections afforded by legal marriage to the heterosexual Glenn and Stacy. The homosexual Glenn and Stacy would lack certain hospital visitation rights, inheritance rights, tax benefits, and a host of other privileges afforded to the heterosexual Glenn and Stacy. If one of them were a foreigner, the other could not secure citizenship status for him or her. Moreover, each could be forced to testify against the other in court, robbing them of a kind of marital privacy the heterosexual Glenn and Stacy would likely take for granted – along with scores of other legal benefits. All because of a difference in gender.

In his important work *Justice for Here and Now*, James Sterba argues that a just society must be an androgynous, or genderfree, society. By an androgynous society he means one in which basic rights and duties are not assigned on the basis of gender. More generally, an androgynous society is one that substitutes "a socialization based on natural ability, reasonable expectation, and choice for a socialization based on sexual difference."[2] Thus put, the ideal of an androgynous society sounds desirable, and for the purposes of this paper I will assume that Sterba is correct in advocating it. The question I wish to explore is whether the ideal of an androgynous society has implications for homosexual justice, as Sterba suggests. For many would agree with Sterba that rights and duties be assigned on the basis of "natural ability, reasonable expectation, and choice" while maintaining that society is nevertheless justified in treating the homosexual Glenn and Stacy rather differently from the heterosexual Glenn and Stacy.

In this paper I develop the connection between gender justice and homosexual justice by arguing that gender is irrelevant to the moral character of romantic and sexual relationships, and thus to the rights and duties associated with such relationships. The paper proceeds as follows. In the first section, I define gender and argue that, despite initial appearances, neither gender nor gender discrimination is *necessarily* inconsistent with Sterba's androgynous ideal. I also situate discrimination against homosexuals within the context of gender discrimination and ask whether discrimination against homosexuals is justified with respect to some good. In the second section, I attempt to answer that question by developing a *prima facie* case for the moral equivalence of homosexual and heterosexual relationships, and then considering three important attempts to rebut that *prima facie* case. In general, my aim is to buttress Sterba's claim that discrimination against homosexuals is incompatible with the androgynous ideal.

Gender and the androgynous society

Let me begin by distinguishing gender from biological sex. I define biological sex – for which I shall use the terms "male," "female," and "intersexed" – in terms of chromosomal structure: females are XX, males are XY, and intersexed persons are those with any other combination.[3]

Gender – for which I shall use the terms "man" and "woman"[4] – is much more difficult to define. Consider the case of Brandon Teena, whose story was recently popularized in the critically acclaimed film *Boys Don't Cry*. Brandon Teena was biologically female (born Teena Brandon) but conceived of himself as man and successfully presented himself as such for a time. Such persons, whose biological sex differs from their gender identity, are considered "transgendered". More broadly, the term "transgender" is sometimes used to refer to anyone whose gender identity challenges traditional notions of gender. ("Transsexual" is sometimes used to refer to those whose sex characteristics have been surgically or hormonally altered.)

But to say what gender is not (biological sex) is not to demonstrate what it is. Some have attempted to define gender identity in terms of self-perception – that is, a person is a woman if and only if she conceives of herself as a woman. But first, this definition fails to explain what it *is* to conceive of oneself as a woman; and second, more important, the condition seems too weak. Just as thinking that I am a millionaire doesn't make me a millionaire, thinking that I am female does not (by itself) make me female. A person who had all of my other properties – including my physical and mental history, my public presentation, and my various preferences – but conceived of himself as a woman would not be a woman; he would simply be confused.

What, then, is gender? I submit that it is a mistake to try to capture gender in terms of necessary and sufficient conditions. Rather, being a woman and being a man are family resemblance concepts.[5] To be a woman or a man is to possess a substantial portion of a cluster of characteristics, none of which is necessary but some of which must be present in order for the term to apply correctly. Such characteristics would include, but are not limited to

- being biologically male or female
- having (or wanting to have) a certain kind of bodily structure (e.g. broad or narrow shoulders or hips, body hair, and so on)
- having (or wanting to have) male or female genitalia
- conceiving of oneself as a man or a woman
- presenting oneself as a man or a woman
- exhibiting certain masculine or feminine characteristics (many of which may be culturally bound)
- relating (or desiring to relate) to other persons sexually in a particular way (e.g. penetrating or being penetrated)

I have listed these in no particular order, although it may be the case that some (notably self-conception) have priority over others. It is crucial to remember, first, that this list is by no means exhaustive, and second, that none of these characteristics individually is a necessary determinant of gender. Biological sex aside, a person might present himself as a woman (perhaps for theatrical purposes), exhibit certain stereotypically feminine traits, and enjoy being penetrated by men (or women), yet still be a man; and a person might present herself as a man, exhibit certain characteristically masculine traits, and enjoy penetrating women (or men), yet still be a woman.

On the other hand, if a person lacked *all* of the characteristics typically associated with being of a particular gender (except perhaps biological sex) but still claimed to be of that gender, something would be amiss. Suppose Jack tells me, "I want to conceive of myself as a woman, and I want breasts, a narrow waist, and broad hips, and I want to wear make-up and dresses and long hair," and so on, including all of the non-biological characteristics commonly associated with being a woman in our society. It would be natural for me to reply, "You mean you want to be a woman." If he were to respond, "Actually, I want to be a man who has all of those things," I would be confused about what being a man means to Jack. Surely, it must mean more than having Y chromosomes: Teena Brandon wanted to be a man but presumably did not want Y chromosomes (for their own sake). At the very least, I would expect that I had missed some relevant background information: perhaps Jack is a spy who needs the transformation for espionage purposes. But barring such background, it seems that Jack is simply confused about what it is to be a man or a woman.

Again, none of this is to say that a person could not be of a particular gender but lack (and desire to lack) several features typically associated with that gender. Compare the paradigmatic case of a family resemblance concept: games. A person might want to play a game that involves no other people (e.g. solitaire) even though the presence of others is a typical feature of games. Similarly, a person might want to be a woman but not want to wear clothing culturally designated as feminine, even though wearing such clothing is typical of women. Or she might want to have certain typically male bodily parts without wanting to be a man (perhaps for the convenience of being able to pee while standing).

I define a homosexual relationship as one between two people of the same gender. Thus, a relationship between a man and a female-to-male transgendered person (such as Brandon Teena) is a homosexual relationship, but a relationship between a man and a male-to-female transgendered person is not. It follows that discrimination against homosexuals is on its face a form of gender discrimination. Among the interesting implications of my definition of gender are that a person may be more-or-less a member of a particular gender and thus that a relationship may be more-or-less homosexual (for example, all else being equal, a butch-femme lesbian relationship would appear to be less homosexual than a "plain" lesbian relationship).

Sterba conceives of gender (as opposed to biological sex) as being essentially connected with oppressive social roles; thus he conceives of the genderfree society as literally that – without gender. For him, a society with gender is one that unjustly restricts the opportunities available to men or women in virtue of their being men or women. By contrast, I wish to advocate a broader, value-neutral conception of gender, such that the presence of gender is compatible with egalitarian social structures. To eliminate it would be to eliminate an interesting and valuable element of human diversity. It is true that on my view, *one* of the defining characteristics of gender is social sex role – having masculine or feminine characteristics – and that such roles have tended to limit opportunities for both genders, especially women. But this need not be so: we could acknowledge that a role is typical of women while still permitting and even encouraging men to pursue it. Moreover, on my family-resemblance view, social sex role is not a necessary determinant of gender (since none of the characteristics are of themselves necessary), and many of the other characteristics associated with gender (e.g. biological sex, bodily structure, sexual preference) are clearly value-neutral in themselves.

Suppose, then, that we were to achieve the androgynous ideal that Sterba and I both advocate, one where rights and duties are based on "natural ability, reasonable expectation, and choice." In such a society, it is possible (and perhaps likely) that there would be much less of a correlation between biological sex and gender than in our own society. It is also possible (and perhaps likely) that there would be many fewer gendered persons or persons of an unambiguous gender. But it does not follow that gender would necessarily disappear. One might ask what the point of making gender distinctions would be in such a society: after all, no one is restricted from pursuing any characteristic or role (save certain biological ones) on the basis of either gender or sex. The answer, I think, is that in such a society gender would be thought of in a more positive way: not as a limitation indicating what people cannot do, but as a convenient shorthand for clusters of characteristics each of which (except for the biological) is in theory open to everyone.[6] Again, in an androgynous society there might be fewer people falling neatly into such clusters. But that does not mean that the clusters are incompatible with such a society: they can indicate difference without indicating hierarchy. And the differences that they indicate might be very useful for a number of benign purposes.

Dating strikes me as one obvious example. Suppose Phyllis, a woman, likes to date men. This does not entail, of course, that she likes to date men who are aggressive, or wear masculine clothing, or have broad shoulders, narrow hips and chest hair – all of which are typical but non-essential defining characteristics of men. Nor does it entail that she likes to date biological males, for indeed, she might be quite indifferent to her partners' chromosomal structures provided that a sufficient number of the other typical characteristics of males are present (as they were in the case of Brandon Teena). So Phyllis, who is herself gendered, has a gender preference in partners. Because she likes to date men, she might frequent places (e.g. straight singles bars) attended by men who like to date women; moreover, she might make her friends aware of this (as well as other) preferences so that they might suggest suitable partners for her. Phyllis' expressed preference for and pursuit of men strikes me as morally unproblematic of itself – especially in an ideal society where the evil of sexism has been overcome. But this preference and pursuit make ample use of gender distinctions, and would be far more complicated without such distinctions.

Let us here distinguish between two different senses of "discrimination." In one sense, to discriminate is simply to treat things differently. We discriminate in this sense all the time – when we choose ripe produce over unripe or overripe produce, flattering clothing over unflattering, good books over bad. In all of these cases, the differential treatment is justified with respect to some good. But in another sense, to discriminate is to treat things differently *for irrelevant or unjust reasons*. Most of what we call "racial discrimination," for example, falls into this latter category. Phyllis' preference for men is a case of discrimination in the former, benign sense. It is justified with respect to some good – namely, the good of her being able to enjoy fulfilling relationships. It follows that gender discrimination (in the sense of differential treatment) may be compatible with the androgynous society, provided that it is justified with respect to some good.

Discrimination against homosexuals is one form of gender discrimination. Could it be justified? There are some cases where it would be obviously so: for example, if we were conducting a survey of homosexual people for the purpose of better understanding diversity on campus. Such a survey would in some sense discriminate against heterosexual people, though arguably for an overriding good. But the cases I have in mind are the more controversial ones: is it possible, for example, that the discrimination against the homosexual Glenn and Stacy in terms of the various marriage rights I have discussed is compatible with the androgynous ideal? I turn now to some arguments regarding this type of discrimination.

The moral equivalence of homosexuality and heterosexuality

At first glance, the ideal of androgynous society might seem inconsistent with such discrimination. Consider one of the more blatant forms of such discrimination: anti-sodomy laws. At the time of writing, anti-sodomy laws are officially on the books in eighteen states plus Puerto Rico and the US military. Five of these states – Arkansas, Kansas, Missouri, Oklahoma and Texas – prohibit only homosexual sodomy.[7] The laws in these latter states seem clearly to discriminate on the basis of gender: they allow women to perform certain acts that men cannot and vice-versa. As such, they assign a legal right on the basis of gender rather than "natural ability, reasonable expectation, and choice" – as the androgynous ideal requires.

But the issue is not so simple. First, many people see *all* anti-sodomy laws – and not just those that specify homosexual sodomy – as discriminatory. It is by no means clear how the ideal of androgyny implies anything about the gender-nonspecific sodomy laws in the other thirteen states. Second, even in the states with gender-specific sodomy laws the traditionalists can make the following argument: no individual – male or female – is permitted to engage in homosexual sodomy; ergo, the laws do not unjustly discriminate on the basis of gender. It is not enough to respond to this argument by pointing out that the concept of *homosexual* sodomy depends upon gender distinctions, since, as I have just argued, not all gender distinctions are invidious. The issue is the following: are there good *reasons* for the prohibition of homosexual sodomy? Even an androgynous society could allow for gender distinctions in cases where such distinctions are justified with respect to some good.

The central reason offered for the prohibition of homosexual sodomy – and indeed, for most opposition to gay rights – is that homosexuality is morally wrong. Not all political opposition to gay rights presupposes this moral claim. For example, opponents of gays in the military often claim that regardless of the moral status of homosexuality, there are concerns about unit cohesion that justify exclusionary policies.[8] Nevertheless, even when moral opposition is not an explicit rationale, it is often lurking in the background. Consider the gay marriage debate. Some opponents of gay marriage argue that this debate is not about the moral status of relationships at all. Rather, the state chooses, for the purpose of protecting children, to support those relationships that can produce them; homosexual relationships cannot produce children; therefore, homosexual relationships do not merit state support. But this argument is not entirely convincing, since it is by no means clear that this is the state's primary justification for being in the marriage business. For one thing, neither all nor only heterosexual partners have children, and it would seem that the children of lesbian mothers (for example) are as deserving of a secure home as any other children. Moreover, the state permits couples past childbearing age to marry, as well as couples whom it wishes to discourage from having children – for example, couples where one or both partners is incarcerated, or partners with certain inheritable diseases – not to mention those who have been convicted of domestic abuse.[9] Note that our heterosexual Glenn and Stacy can be married even though they are no more capable of producing children than our homosexual Glenn and Stacy (recall that Stacy is sterile). Since the capacity for bearing children is not a necessary condition for marriage, its absence seems shaky ground for denying marriage to the homosexual Glenn and Stacy.[10]

The more ingenuous approach for opponents of gay marriage to take is to acknowledge that opposition to gay marriage is grounded in the belief that homosexual relationships are morally inferior to heterosexual relationships, and thus undeserving of social and legal sanction. I contend that this belief is the primary rationale for most forms of anti-gay discrimination – including anti-sodomy laws, denial of legal marriage, and housing and job discrimination, among others. Therefore, in what follows I will focus on the moral evaluation of homosexuality. In attacking the moral opposition I hope to undercut much of the political and social opposition as well. Since I am ultimately interested in a question of public policy, I will focus on the secular moral arguments.[11]

Many defenses of homosexuality focus exclusively on rebutting the arguments against homosexuality. I wish to begin somewhat differently, by developing an argument *for* homosexuality. The case of Glenn and Stacy suggests an argument from analogy. Arguments from analogy attempt to show that because A and B are similar in some relevant respects, they are likely similar in other respects as well. For example, if Bruce's car gets good gas mileage, then Susan's car – which has a similar engine and a similar weight – is likely to get good gas mileage as well. The key here is "relevant respects." If Bruce's car and Susan's car were similar in certain other respects – for example, being the same color or being American-made – the conclusion would be far less probable. Engine design and weight are directly relevant to gas mileage; color and national origin are not. Thus A and B must be similar in ways that are relevant to the conclusion that one wants to establish.

The conclusion I want to establish is that the homosexual Glenn and Stacy have a relationship that is morally equivalent to that of the heterosexual Glenn and Stacy – or more broadly, that gender is irrelevant to the moral character of relationships. My *prima facie* argument for the equivalence is quite simple. Consider the case of the heterosexual Glenn and Stacy. Virtually everyone would agree that their relationship is morally good, or at least morally permissible. Why? I have already observed that it brings them happiness, and helps them grow, and expresses and facilitates their long-term commitment. These are good reasons for regarding the relationship as good. Yet these reasons are all present in the case of the homosexual Glenn and Stacy as well.

Here I wish to stave off a likely objection. Opponents of homosexuality might retort that my *prima facie* argument equivocates on the term "relationships." It is not the fact that the homosexual Glenn and Stacy offer emotional support to each other, or share a household, or shop at IKEA, that is morally troublesome – it is the fact that they have genital sexual contact. These other things might be morally neutral or even morally good, my opponents might concede, but they are entirely separable from the relationship's sexual aspect.

It is precisely this last contention that I wish to deny. There is no reason to assume – and indeed, there are good reasons to doubt – that one can remove the sexual aspect of the relationship and have all others remain the same. Sex can be a powerful and unique way of building, celebrating, and replenishing intimacy in a relationship. This is one important reason why heterosexual people have sex even if they don't want children, don't want children yet, or don't want any more children. It is a reason why sexless marriages are typically cause for concern. To assume that one can subtract sex without affecting the rest of the equation is to take a naive and reductionistic view of sexual relationships. This is not to say that physical intimacy is *always* connected with other forms of intimacy: sex is sometimes impersonal, mechanical, or fleeting. But in the cases that I'm considering, sex is much more than that. The physical union of the partners manifests and contributes to a much larger union.

Virtually everyone would agree that the sexual relationship between the heterosexual Glenn and Stacy is good – even though it cannot produce children. It realizes, of itself and through its effects, a variety of concrete benefits. Pleasure is one of these benefits, but (as I have argued) it is not the only one. But what about the homosexual Glenn and Stacy? At first glance, the only difference between the two cases appears to be the gender of one of the parties. All of the other factors – the mutual regard, the long-term commitment, the personal growth – are present. This constitutes a strong *prima facie* case for treating the two relationships equally – morally, socially and politically. The burden of proof is now on those who would treat them differently.

My claim about burden of proof deserves elaboration. In offering a *prima facie* argument in favor of homosexuality I intend to correct what I perceive to be a rhetorical miscalculation on the part of some gay rights advocates. These advocates hold that no argument in favor of homosexual relationships is necessary: the burden of proof is always on those who would condemn people or restrict their relationship options. Their opponents, by contrast, claim that the burden of proof is always on those who would alter established tradition. In a sense they're both wrong: the burden of proof is on whoever wants to prove something. Thus, in line with what Sterba calls "a peacemaking way of doing philosophy,"[12] I begin my argument with gay rights opponents on a point of agreement. We agree that the heterosexual Glenn and Stacy's relationship is good and worthy of approval. My next move is to point out that, at first glance, the only intrinsic difference between them and the homosexual Glenn and Stacy is the gender of one of the parties. Why is that difference morally significant?

In response to my *prima facie* argument from analogy, opponents of homosexuality have three options (assuming that they wish to be consistent). They can extend their opposition to non-procreative heterosexual relationships. For obvious reasons, few will do this. They can renounce their opposition to homosexual relationships. Or, finally, they can explain why gender constitutes a morally relevant difference, either of itself or through its effects. Most opponents choose this third option. I turn now to three representative attempts: John Finnis' natural law argument, Michael Levin's abnormality argument, and what I call "the PIB reductio." Since the first two arguments have received considerable attention elsewhere, I shall keep my remarks about them somewhat brief and instead focus on the third.[13]

Finnis' argument is especially relevant for two reasons. First, Finnis has explicitly addressed the question of why the homosexual couple should be evaluated differently from the sterile heterosexual couple, who seem at first glance to resemble their homosexual counterparts in every respect but one. Second, Finnis has explicitly connected his moral argument to public policy considerations, including not only gay marriage but also civil rights protections as well.[14]

Understanding Finnis' argument requires understanding his natural law theory. As one of the "new natural lawyers," Finnis holds that there are certain basic goods that are intrinsically worthy of pursuit. By "basic," he means that they are irreducible to other goods (e.g. happiness). One of these goods is what Finnis calls "the marital good." The marital good is the two-in-one flesh union of a husband and wife. This union realizes two important values (though it is not reducible to either): procreation and friendship. Even in cases where procreation is impossible – as in the case of the sterile heterosexual couple – a sexual act can still be of "the reproductive kind" – that is, of the sort normally suitable for reproduction. Such an act actualizes the two-in-one-flesh biological union of the partners in a way that homosexual acts cannot. The problem with homosexuality, as Finnis sees it, is that it turns away from a basic good and puts a counterfeit in its place. Instead of realizing the marital good through bodily union, the homosexual couple treat their bodies as mere instruments of pleasure. Homosexual conduct is therefore unnatural, immoral, and worthy of condemnation.

Suppose, for the sake of argument, we were to grant that homosexual intercourse cannot achieve "the marital good." Finnis' argument nevertheless seems to depend on a false dichotomy: either sexual acts achieve the marital good or they fail to achieve any goods at all, instead counterfeiting the marital good and treating the body as a mere object. But what about the various concrete goods we described in the case of Glenn and Stacy? Their sexual acts are a way of generating, replenishing and enhancing emotional intimacy. They are an avenue of communication for which words would be inadequate. More generally, they make Glenn and Stacy happy – not merely in a short-term, hedonistic sense, but in a long-term, "big picture" way. Such goods are at least as intelligible – and valuable – as Finnis' somewhat nebulous "marital good." Indeed, on closer inspection, "the marital good" appears to be an *ad hoc* construction for distinguishing between the sterile heterosexual couple and the homosexual couple, who are otherwise essentially similar.

Michael Levin's argument depends upon the concept of "normality" rather than "naturalness." For Levin, the difference between the heterosexual Glenn and Stacy and the homosexual Glenn and Stacy is that the latter's behavior is abnormal and thus likely to lead to unhappiness.[15] It is abnormal because the homosexual Glenn and Stacy are not using their sexual organs for what they are *for*. Penises are for inserting into vaginas, not for inserting into mouths or other orifices; vaginas are for receiving penises, not for rubbing up against other vaginas. An organ is *for* some function if and only if that function explains its existence (i.e. why it was selected through evolution). Our teeth are *for* chewing: we have teeth because our ancestors who used their teeth for chewing tended to survive and reproduce, creating progeny who also had teeth and used them for chewing. Levin illustrates with an analogy:

> Shark teeth are for tearing flesh, since primeval sharks with sharp teeth devoured prey more efficiently than less well-endowed competitors, and were thereby fitter. Thus, their ability to tear flesh explains why there are shark teeth. Shark teeth also impress aquarium visitors, but that is not what shark teeth are *for* because impressing aquarium visitors is not why today's sharks have sharp teeth.[16]

Simply put, we have penises and vaginas because our ancestors who put their penises into vaginas (or put their vaginas around penises) tended to reproduce, passing along the tendency to have penises and vaginas and to use them in this way.

According to Levin, abnormal behavior in humans tends to cause unhappiness because evolution reinforces (makes us enjoy) normal or adaptive behaviors. Our ancestors who enjoyed using their teeth for chewing tended to use their teeth in this way and thus live longer and create more offspring, who in turn enjoyed using their teeth in this way. In a sense, we are "programmed" through evolution to enjoy using our organs in evolutionarily adaptive (i.e. normal) ways. Correspondingly, we are likely to be unhappy when we use them in abnormal ways. Because of the connection between abnormality and unhappiness, it is reasonable for society to discourage abnormal behaviors through legal and social sanctions.

Herein lies Levin's justification for treating the homosexual Glenn and Stacy differently from the heterosexual Glenn and Stacy. The homosexual Glenn and Stacy, insofar as they are engaging in abnormal behavior, are likely to be less happy than their heterosexual counterparts. Society has an interest in maintaining and promoting the happiness of its members. Therefore, society is justified in using legal and social sanctions to discourage the homosexual Glenn and Stacy from pursuing their relationship. I should note that Levin does not see his argument as establishing a *moral* difference between the two cases. Rather, he claims that homosexuality is intrinsically bad in a prudential sense.

There is much to say about Levin's argument, and in particular about his account of evolution, but I shall focus on two brief points.[17] First, Levin's argument depends on the implausible premise that there is one and only one purpose that the genital organs are *for*. Given Levin's sense of "for" – in which a thing is for whatever purpose explains its continued existence through evolution – it is not surprising that Levin identifies procreation as what genital organs are for. But it is also plausible, given Levin's account, to hold that the genitals are for experiencing pleasure and intimacy. Our ancestors who used their genitals for experiencing pleasure and intimacy in a variety of situations – both procreative and non-procreative – would likely be happier, live longer and produce more offspring than those who did not (all else being equal). Pleasure and intimacy are conducive to emotional health, which is in turn conducive to physical health, and both are conducive to longevity, which is conducive to procreation. Homosexual intercourse would not have prevented our ancestors from procreating any more than my writing philosophy papers prevents me from procreating – they are simply non-procreative activities. Levin's argument thus has the absurd implication that the homosexual Glenn and Stacy would cease being abnormal as long as they began using their genitals in procreative ways from time to time (perhaps with opposite-sex lovers on the side). Or, to put the point another way, Levin's account seems to entail that even if homosexual behavior is abnormal, bisexual behavior is not.

My second response has to do with the connection between normality and happiness. Here Levin's argument seems blatantly to ignore the evidence. Most homosexuals are in homosexual relationships precisely because such relationships make them *happier* than heterosexual relationships would. Levin seems to think that if heterosexuality is normal and if normal behaviors make people happier than abnormal behaviors, then heterosexuality should make people happier than non-heterosexuality. But that conclusion is at best a prediction regarding what to expect, not an account of what in fact occurs. And even if, contrary to the best available evidence, heterosexuals were on average happier than homosexuals, and even if that supposed disparity had nothing to do with society's treatment of the groups in question, Levin's conclusion about how to treat the homosexual Glenn and Stacy wouldn't follow. For if the point is to encourage a happy society, the question to ask is not, "Who is happier – heterosexuals or homosexuals?" The question to ask is "Is society better off (i.e. happier overall) by supporting or discouraging the homosexual Glenn and Stacy?" Given that Glenn and Stacy's relationship not only enhances their own happiness but also makes them more cheerful, stable, and productive members of society, supporting the relationship (and others like them) produces a net gain in overall happiness. Conversely, condemning the relationship fails to make them or anyone else happier.

The final argument I wish to consider is quite different from that of Finnis or Levin. According to this argument, if we accept homosexuality, then there is no principled reason for not accepting polygamy, incest and bestiality (PIB for short). As Dr Laura Schlessinger of radio fame put it, in response to the Vermont decision granting statewide domestic-partner benefits:

> If two men can be sanctified in this country as marriage, then what is your logical or justifiable reason to exclude adult incest? A man and a woman – consensual, 25 years old, who are brother and sister – should not be discriminated against because they have a genetic relationship.[18]

Although there are several ways of parsing the argument, the general form seems to be that of a *reductio ad absurdum*: the reasons in favor of homosexual relationships constitute reasons in favor of the clearly objectionable PIB relationships; if the latter are worthy of condemnation, then so are the former.

Why do opponents of homosexuality think that the reasons in favor of homosexual relationships constitute reasons in favor of PIB relationships? The answer, I think, is that they misunderstand – or mischaracterize – the argument in favor of homosexual relationships. They take the argument to be, "It feels good and it's consensual, so it must be permissible." If that were all there were to the argument in favor of homosexual relationships, it would indeed offer support to many PIB relationships.[19] But that argument is a strawman. The better argument for homosexual relationships is the argument from analogy developed above: homosexual relationships offer all of the significant benefits of non-procreative heterosexual relationships without any apparent drawbacks.

"But wait," object the traditionalists. "Can't you make the same argument for PIB relationships?" Not exactly. It is true that you can use the same *form* of argument for PIB relationships: PIB relationships have benefits X, Y and Z and no relevant drawbacks. But whether PIB relationships do in fact have such benefits and lack such drawbacks is an empirical matter, one that will not be settled by looking to homosexual relationships. To put the point more directly: to observe that many people flourish in homosexual relationships is not to prove that others might flourish in incestuous, bestial or polygamous relationships. Whether they would or not is a *separate question* – one that requires a whole new set of data.

So my answer to the PIB challenge is to argue that there is no reason to assume that concrete benefits realized in homosexual relationships can be realized in PIB relationships. (This is not to prove that there are *no* benefits sufficient to justify PIB relationships; exploring that issue would take me too far afield here.) But there is another way to understand the PIB *reductio*, one that escapes the argument I have given. On this approach, the point of the PIB argument is to prove that not all of our moral judgments can be captured in terms of flourishing and harm considerations. This claim is controversial. Sterba, for instance, explicitly contradicts it in *Justice for Here and Now*:

> Now it might be objected here that what is wrong with contraception, masturbation, and homosexuality is that they all violate the principle that one should never (intentionally) do evil that good may come of it, where it is claimed that the evil involved in these acts is that of interfering with or frustrating the human procreative process. But if interfering with or frustrating the human procreative process is always evil, whom does it harm? Surely if evil is done, someone is harmed, and if no one is harmed then the actions in question cannot be evil.[20]

Many traditionalists would deny this last contention. One such traditionalist is David Bradshaw, who uses the "Why not bestiality?" objection in his response to my defense of homosexual relationships in the book *Same Sex*.[21] According to Bradshaw, what is wrong with homosexuality is not (necessarily) that it produces harm, or that it fails to promote flourishing, but that it fails to respect what he calls "the body's moral space." Consider the following two distinctions:

1   male/female
2   animal/human

Bradshaw argues that just as bestiality is wrong because it fails to respect the second distinction, homosexuality is wrong because it fails to respect the first. (Set aside for a moment the obvious question about how homosexuality "fails to respect" the male/female distinction. Clearly, in one sense, it *presupposes* this distinction.) There's something intuitively appealing to many people about the claim that homosexuality fails to respect distinction 1 and bestiality fails to respect distinction 2, and that both are wrong for precisely those reasons. This argument fits with a larger point Bradshaw wants to make about how much of our moral understanding cannot be understood in terms of flourishing and harm. Thus the question I have raised about potential benefits of PIB relationships is beside the point, according to Bradshaw. Bestiality and homosexuality are wrong, not because they're harmful (though they may be in many cases), or because they're not conducive to flourishing, but for a quite different reason.

On Bradshaw's view, the PIB *reductio* applies not merely to an argument about homosexuality, but to the larger attempt to ground moral claims purely on considerations of flourishing and harm. If we restrict our moral discussions to considerations of flourishing and harm, he argues, then we will have to embrace paradigmatically immoral activities like bestiality. In what remains I respond to this argument.

Consider another distinction:

3   caucasian/non-caucasian

One can easily imagine someone arguing (people did it not very long ago) that interracial relationships are wrong because they fail to respect distinction 3. Most of us today would respond "Why is that morally relevant?" Keep in mind that the Bradshaw-type traditionalist could not deny the moral relevance of 3 on consequentialist (or more broadly, flourishing/harm) grounds, since he has already abandoned that perspective. Nor would an appeal to tradition work, since just a few decades ago one could make the same appeal in both cases. Rather, we have reached an impasse: either you draw the line of moral relevance before 3 or after 3. And there doesn't seem to me to be any principled reason for drawing it one way or the other without appealing to flourishing/harm considerations.

One might retort that while 1 and 2 both involve bodily structure, 3 does not, and that might be a reason for drawing a sharp line between 2 and 3. But this response is circular. I grant that 1 and 2 deal with bodily structure and 3 doesn't, but the question at hand is why draw the line at bodily structure? Why is that a morally relevant fact? Why not draw the line at general appearance (below 3) or merely at species (between 1 and 2) or somewhere else? I don't see that the traditionalist has much of an answer at this point, except to say, "That's just the way things are." But as I argued above, the opponent of interracial relationships can say the same thing. Such an answer is insufficient to justify treating the homosexual Glenn and Stacy substantially differently from the heterosexual Glenn and Stacy.

This raises, I think, a more general lesson about how to proceed in applied ethics – particularly when using arguments from analogy, which are almost unavoidable in that area. My argument in this paper begins with an analogy between

(a) something widely approved (non-procreative heterosexual relationships) and
(b) something controversial (homosexual relationships).

Bradshaw's argument begins with an analogy between

(b) something controversial (homosexual relationships) and

(c) something widely condemned (PIB relationships).

My argument proceeds by showing that (a) and (b) are similar in morally relevant respects and that they lack any morally relevant differences. Bradshaw's argument, by contrast, does not begin by showing that (b) and (c) are similar in morally relevant respects, since the reasons for condemning (b) (namely that it fails to respect the male/female distinction) are different from the reasons for condemning (c) (namely that it fails to respect the human/non-human distinction).[22] As such, the moral distinctions drawn by Bradshaw smack of arbitrariness.

Conclusion

I have argued that the best moral arguments against homosexual relationships fail to rebut the *prima facie* case in their favor. It is possible that better arguments might surface. But in the absence of such arguments, the case for treating heterosexual and homosexual relationships as morally equivalent stands. And insofar as the justifications offered for treating them differently socially or politically depend upon the moral arguments, the case for treating them the same socially and politically also stands. I conclude that the controversial forms of discrimination against the homosexual Glenn and Stacy are incompatible with the androgynous ideal.

We are a long way from that ideal, particularly with respect to homosexual justice. As noted above, there are scores of legal benefits denied to the homosexual Glenn and Stacy that the heterosexual Glenn and Stacy take for granted. But there is some reason for optimism. While the Vermont decision extending domestic-partner benefits to gay and lesbian citizens has not met with universal acclaim, it has furthered a national discussion on the rights of homosexual persons. Moreover, a state appeals court in Houston has just ruled (in June 2000) that the Texas sodomy law is unconstitutional under the state's Equal Rights Amendment; various other states face similar challenges.[23] It is worth noting that both the Vermont decision and the Texas decision are based on premises regarding sex (or, more broadly, gender) discrimination: they argue that the existing laws treat men and women differently in ways that are unjustified with respect to any compelling state interest.[24] The connections between gender justice and homosexual justice merit further exploration.[25]

NOTES

1 Plato, *Republic*, 454c, trans. G. M. A. Grube (Indianapolis: Hackett, 1974) p. 116.
2 James P. Sterba, *Justice for Here and Now* (Cambridge: Cambridge University Press, 1998) p. 80.
3 This is not to deny that there are other plausible definitions of biological sex or that there are difficult, vague or borderline cases.

4 I do not mean to preclude the possibility of additional genders; perhaps we should add the category of "intergendered"?

5 I am indebted to Jacob Hale for enlightening exchanges on this issue, as well as to Adriane Friedl, Herbert Granger, Lawrence B. Lombard, Bruce Russell, Susan Vineberg and Robert J. Yanal.

6 It may happen that because of natural ability some characteristics are more difficult for some individuals to attain. The point is that, in an androgynous society, one's biological sex will never constitute an absolute bar to any desirable characteristic.

7 The remaining thirteen states, which have gender-nonspecific sodomy laws, are Alabama, Arizona, Florida, Idaho, Louisiana, Massachusetts, Michigan, Minnesota, Mississippi, North Carolina, South Carolina, Utah and Virginia. Several of the eighteen states currently face court challenges that could overturn their anti-sodomy laws.

8 For a defense of this view see John Luddy, "Make War, Not Love: The Pentagon's Ban is Wise and Just," in John Corvino (ed.) *Same Sex: Debating the Ethics, Science, and Culture of Homosexuality* (Lanham MD: Rowman & Littlefield, 1997) pp. 267–73. For a response see Paul Siegel, "Dry-Cleaning the Troops and Other Matters: A Critique of 'Don't Ask, Don't Tell'," in the same volume, pp. 274–80.

9 In *Turner v. Safely* 482 U.S. 78 (1987), the US Supreme Court affirmed the right of prisoners to marry on the grounds that the emotional and legal benefits of marriage were sufficient justifications for marriage despite the limitations of prison life. For a discussion of this point, see William N. Eskridge Jr, *The Case for Same-Sex Marriage* (New York: Free Press, 1996) chapter 5.

10 In fairness, there may be more complex indirect arguments connecting legal marriage with the nurturing of children. But I would argue (given more space than I have here) that these are less successful than arguments connecting marriage to the nurturing of human beings more generally.

11 For discussion of some religious arguments, see Daniel Helminiak, *What the Bible Really Says About Homosexuality* (San Francisco: Alamo Square Press, 1994); and John Corvino, "The Bible Condemned Usurers, Too," *The Harvard Gay and Lesbian Review*, vol. III, no. 4 (fall 1996) pp. 11–12.

12 *Op. cit.*, chapter 1.

13 For fuller responses to Finnis see Stephen Macedo, "Homosexuality and the Conservative Mind," *Georgetown Law Journal*, vol. 84, no. 2 (December 1995); and Andrew Koppelman, "Homosexual Conduct: A Reply to the New Natural Lawyers," *Same Sex, op. cit.* For fuller responses to Levin, see Timothy F. Murphy, "Homosexuality and Nature: Happiness and the Law at Stake," *Journal of Applied Philosophy*, 4 (1987) pp. 195–205; Laurence M. Thomas, "Preferences and Equality: A Response to Levin," in Laurence M. Thomas and Michael E. Levin, *Sexual Orientation and Human Rights* (Lanham MD: Rowman & Littlefield, 1999) pp. 159–68. For a discussion of both see Andrew Koppelman, "Is Marriage Inherently Heterosexual?", 42 Am. J. Juris. 51 (1997).

14 Finnis testified in *Romer v. Evans*, a case in which the Supreme Court ultimately invalidated Colorado voters' attempt through referendum to repeal various city ordinances banning discrimination on the basis of sexual orientation. Finnis argued that such discrimination was reasonable given the moral status of homosexuality. See John Finnis, "Law, Morality, and 'Sexual Orientation'," in *Same Sex, op. cit.* The article grew out of Finnis' affidavit in the *Romer v. Evans* case.

15 See Michael Levin, "Why Homosexuality is Abnormal," *Monist*, vol. 67 (1984) pp. 251–83; and "Homosexuality, Abnormality, and Civil Rights," *Public Affairs Quarterly*, vol. 10, no. 1 (January 1996) pp. 31–48.

16 "Homosexuality, Abnormality, and Civil Rights," *op. cit.*, p. 32.
17 For a fuller discussion see the articles cited in note 13.
18 Quoted in the *Advocate*, 15 February 2000, p. 35.
19 Sex with animals occurs without the animals' consent; on the other hand, so do all of our other dealings with animals. Adult–child incest is non-consensual but peer incest may be consensual.
20 Sterba, *Justice for Here and Now*, p. 113.
21 See John Corvino, "Why Shouldn't Tommy and Jim Have Sex?," and David Bradshaw, "A Reply to Corvino," in John Corvino (ed.) *Same Sex: Debating the Ethics, Science and Culture of Homosexuality* (Lanham MD: Rowman & Littlefield, 1997).
22 Bradshaw might reply that (b) and (c) *are* wrong for similar reasons: both fail to respect the body's moral space. But why is the same not true of interracial relationships? It seems to me that the only salient similarity between (b) and (c) is that they've traditionally been condemned. But that consideration is question-begging: the issue at hand is *why* should (b) be condemned?
23 *John Geddes Lawrence and Tyron Garner v. The State of Texas*, Fourteenth Court of Appeals, 8 June 2000.
24 I would argue that what they call "sex discrimination" is better termed "gender discrimination," since it is based on external characteristics rather than chromosomes.
25 I am indebted to numerous people for discussions that aided the development of this paper, especially Lawrence B. Lombard, Brad Roth, Bruce Russell, James P. Sterba, Susan Vineberg, Thomas Williams and Robert J. Yanal.

Racial and multicultural
perspectives

16

WHITE SUPREMACY
AND RACIAL JUSTICE,
HERE AND NOW[1]

Charles W. Mills

In the ever-expanding, impossible-to-keep-up-with philosophical literature on justice, James P. Sterba's *Justice for Here and Now*[2] is distinguished by many virtues: the accessibility and clarity of the writing; the self-conscious attempt to be comprehensive in his coverage of contemporary issues; the constant recourse to crucial empirical data; and the provocative "reconciliationist" program. If I am critical of Sterba on certain points, as I will be, this should not be taken to imply that I do not think the book has considerable merit. Indeed, there is an ironic sense in which Sterba opens himself up to criticism by this very meritoriousness, in that his ambition to be comprehensive raises more issues than can possibly be dealt with adequately in a 250-page book. Even the single topic of racial justice, I will suggest, has more dimensions than Sterba addresses.

1 Challenging the orthodox framework

My contribution in this present volume is located under the umbrella heading, "Challenges to social and political philosophy." In some sense, then, it is supposed to be radical, unconventional. Take a minute to think about this. What exactly is the "challenge" posed by the idea of racial justice?

One way to answer this question might be to ask ourselves what a racially just society would be like. A straightforward response is that it would be a society in which people's life-chances would be independent of race; that nobody would be unfairly advantaged or disadvantaged because of race. Articulating norms of *racial* justice, then, is not the same as propounding all-encompassing criteria for justice as a whole. In this respect, racial justice differs from socialist justice, and those varieties of feminist justice which do have such pretensions (feminism as a comprehensive and self-sufficient world-view). Some Afrocentrists might argue that an African-centered ethical outlook, drawing on pre-colonial communitarian values, *would* be able to provide such a framework to compete with the more familiar Western ones – for example, through being predicated on a different model of the self than that familiar from liberal theory. But interesting though this challenge might be, I am not seeking to develop it here. For me, then, racial justice is only a *part* of justice, and one could have a society which is racially just but unjust in other ways. Racial justice is best seen as corrective justice, remedial justice, addressing the legacy of the past and the ongoing practices of the present.

So part of the philosophical work that has to be done in determining what racial justice requires is getting straight on this legacy. Political philosophy is sometimes represented as a purely normative subject, but in fact it also has a crucial descriptive/explanatory component. Indeed, we can regard moral judgments in general, including judgments about justice, as based on a combination of factual and value claims, as expressed in the following simple equation: FACTS (what happened, what is happening, what is likely to happen, what is the case) + VALUES (what is good/right) = OVERALL MORAL JUDGMENT. (I am using "facts" broadly enough to cover both empirically more discrete, localizable events, and larger ongoing states-of-affairs that would need to be characterized in systemic terms.) People can, of course, disagree about both, but usually in ethics and mainstream political philosophy, the focus is on divergence in *values*, e.g. debates among utilitarians, Kantians, and libertarians about the most defensible axiology, and what its implications would be.

It is not that *no* attention at all is paid to the facts. Utilitarians, for example, will typically argue that once we take likely future consequences into account, we will be able to see why their recommended policy is the better one. Libertarians will be concerned, among other things, to trace the past factual history which, according to them, gives people normative entitlement to certain property holdings. And all parties may, from time to time, appeal to empirical features of the world, whether natural or social. So facts do play some role in these debates. But because there will be, or will be presumed to be, a high degree of commonsensical or scientific consensus on the factual picture (the description of natural and social reality), it tends to drop out as a major factor. In other words, even when utilitarians and libertarians are tracing future consequences or past causal chains, they are doing so within a framework on which "we" can agree – they are reminding us of things we (putatively) already know, or spelling out in greater detail what that picture implies. So the factual component of the equation is taken to be – not exactly, but more or less – relatively uncontroversial between the different parties, and the real fight is then over what follows when different conceptions of the right and the good are linked with these facts, and how well, in some coherentist process of cognitive equilibrium, the outcome matches our moral intuitions.

But for those judged to be politically "radical" – for example, socialists and feminists – the agenda is different. Usually it is precisely the factual, or allegedly factual, picture of the social world that comes under challenge. What is seen as an uncontroversial, largely consensual characterization of sociopolitical reality by mainstream figures is exactly what is contested by the heterodox.[3] The radical nature of their challenge, then, often inheres not in a startling new axiology, but in a startling new picture of the world, which overturns the conventional wisdom and the orthodox consensus on what "we" know about social reality. Indeed, it puts into question the idea of an uncontested "we" as cognizing agent by arguing that the "consensus" is more likely to reflect the perspective of the socially privileged (bourgeois, male) than a classless, genderless "ideal observer." Marxists claim that even what seem to be inclusivist and egalitarian liberal democracies are structured by oppressive relations of class exploitation. Feminists claim that male domination, patriarchy, has been so ubiquitous that it has been naturalized, ignored at best, when not overtly justified, by the (male) political philosopher.[4]

So it will often be the case that the heart of the matter – or, to switch metaphors, what does most of the work in the "challenge" to mainstream theorizing on justice – really lies here. Once this divergent factual picture has been sketched, once a case has been made for the pervasiveness of class and gender domination, and the mechanisms by which they reproduce themselves, thus perpetuating systemic unfairness, even ethicists with fairly divergent value-commitments should be able to agree that a given society is unjust. Susan Moller Okin's *Justice, Gender, and the Family*, for example, does a highly effective feminist job simply by going through a range of different male theorists with quite divergent axiological assumptions – Michael Sandel, Alasdair MacIntyre, Michael Walzer, Robert Nozick, John Rawls; communitarianism, libertarianism, welfare liberalism – and showing how their prescriptions would all have to be radically revised once the real-life (as against the mythical idealized) family and its gender-structuring is examined.[5]

In this spirit, Iris Marion Young argues that from the perspective of left-wing "critical theory":

> Normative reflection must begin from historically specific circumstances. ... Reflecting from within a particular social context, good normative theorizing cannot avoid social and political description and explanation. ... Unlike positivist social theory, however ... critical theory denies that social theory must accede to the given. Social description and explanation must be critical, that is, aim to evaluate the given in normative terms. Without such a critical stance, many questions about what occurs in a society and why, who benefits and who is harmed, will not be asked, and social theory is liable to reaffirm and reify the given social reality.[6]

From the somewhat different viewpoint of mainstream analytic political philosophy, Jean Hampton strikes a similar note. She criticizes those conceptions of political philosophy that would restrict it purely to normative theorizing, and points out that descriptive/explanatory claims, though at a different level of abstraction than political science, are also crucial:

> The task of political philosophy is not any surface description of particular political societies. Instead, the political philosopher wants to understand at the deepest level the foundations of states and their ethical justification. ... [the] political and social "deep structure" which generates not only forms of interaction that make certain kinds of distributions [of resources] inevitable but also moral theories that justify those distributions.[7]

Both theorists agree, then, that the prescriptive needs to be anchored in the descriptive as well as the axiological: we need to understand how the polity works, and in particular how systemic unjust disadvantage may be continuously reproduced, in order to make well informed judgments about justice and what it requires of us in the way of social reform or transformation. And on the reflexive, meta-theoretical level – where we self-consciously theorize about our theories – we need to be particularly watchful that our moral reflection does not in crucial respects simply adapt to existing background "deep structures," "given social realities," of injustice instead of putting them into question also, since such adaptation is precisely what these structures and realities promote.

So to summarize: here, and elsewhere in radical political theory, it is often really the facts that are doing the revisionary work rather than the values. And one can mount a challenge to mainstream orthodoxy simply by contesting hegemonic, but misleading, pictures of social reality and bringing the underlying deep structures of injustice to light.

2 Critical race theory

Let us now turn to race, which, I am claiming, is one of Hampton's "deep structures." Socialism and feminism are well established viewpoints in political philosophy. But because of the whiteness of the profession, demographic and conceptual, race is still a very new and unfamiliar perspective to most philosophers. So I want to provide a brief background sketch before I go any further.

There is a body of work emerging across a number of different disciplines that is beginning to be known as "critical race theory." The provenance of the term is legal theory: "critical race theorists" was the designation of racial minorities within the critical legal studies movement (CLS) who, while applauding the "crits'" critique of mainstream conceptions of the functioning of the law, were in turn critical of them for their neglect of racial issues.[8] But the term is increasingly being used in a much broader sense to refer to theory that takes race to be central to the making of the modern world, and tries to elucidate and unravel its complicated implications in various areas – cultural studies, film theory, gender studies, labor history, even (dare one say it?) philosophy.[9]

The adjective "critical" signifies several different things.

(i)   It self-consciously distances critical race theory from the *un*critical "race theory" of the past, for example nineteenth- and twentieth-century Social Darwinism, or Nazi *Rassenwissenschaft*. Unlike these theoretical outlooks, critical race theory is explicitly anti-racist.

(ii) Indeed, in a sense it self-consciously distances itself from "race" also, by putting the word in scare-quotes to indicate its constructed rather than biological character.

(iii) Finally, it links critical race theory with the older left idea of a "critical theory" that seeks to understand structures of social oppression for the emancipatory purpose of transforming them.

What would critical race theory mean in political philosophy? I have argued elsewhere that it would mean following the feminist, and, before that, the Marxist example, and looking at society as a system of group domination.[10] Marxists talk about class society in general, and, for the modern period, capitalism. Feminists use the term "patriarchy." The equivalent theoretical move for critical race theorists in political philosophy, I suggest, would be to revive the term "white supremacy." On the rare occasions the term is used nowadays in mainstream discourse, it is employed to refer to the values and beliefs of racist fringe groups, for example skinheads, the Ku Klux Klan, Aryan Nations, etc. So the sense intended is really ideational and attitudinal: the individual's subjective beliefs. The usage I am recommending, by contrast, which can be found in the black radical tradition, is objective. "White supremacy" is meant to refer to a certain politico-economic system which is founded on white racial domination. So race would be seen as a "deep structure," that generates not only disadvantageous and unjust patterns of social interaction and resource transfer, but moral theories that naturalize/justify/obfuscate this systemic inequity.

Now the interesting thing about this term is that – however oddly it might strike people today – originally there was nothing in the least controversial about it. By contrast with the oppositional Marxist characterization of "class society," or the feminist "patriarchy," which were originally, and for many still are, quite controversial, "white supremacy" was a description that the dominant group, i.e. the white population, originally embraced quite matter-of-factly. There was little pretense, in other words, that the society was supposed to be racially inclusive: rather, the United States was explicitly thought of as a "white man's country." In his recent book *Trouble in Mind*, which seems likely to be the definitive history of Jim Crow for years to come, Pulitzer Prize-winning historian Leon Litwack writes: "America was founded on white supremacy and the notion of black inferiority and black unfreedom. ... The ideology of white supremacy always rested on the arrogant assumption that white people owned the country, that this was essentially their domain."[11] Similarly, in what is regarded as a classic work of comparative history, George Fredrickson's *White Supremacy*, the author argues that the phrase "applies with particular force" to South Africa and the United States, since they, more than other multi-racial societies, "have manifested over long periods of time a tendency to push the principle of differentiation by race to its logical outcome – a kind of *Herrenvolk* society in which people of color ... are treated as permanent outsiders."[12]

So the historical reality here is well documented (if a closed book to contemporary white political philosophers). That the phrase now strikes us as radical, perhaps even extremist, is a tribute to a remarkably successful engineered amnesia about a now-embarrassing past. Penny von Eschen pinpoints the ideological transition in the postwar, Cold-War concern of the American governing elite about necessary strategies for winning over a colored Third World, and the need for distancing from the ideas of the defeated Third Reich. In the interwar years, and into the 1940s, "racism had been widely portrayed not only by African American intellectuals but also in popular discourse as located in the history of slavery, colonialism, and imperialism," the product of "global processes."[13] So race was explicitly seen in terms of political economy, the systemic domination and exploitation of one group by another brought about through European expansionism and racial capitalism. But the postwar ideological "consensus," recoiling from left-wing analyses, undertook a "retreat from explanations grounded in political economy." Race was now framed in terms of "prejudice," the problematic attitudes of individual personalities, having no connection with the broader social structure: "The eclipse of historical analysis ... in the 1950s reconstructed 'race' and 'racism' from something rooted in the history of slavery and colonialism to something seen as a psychological problem and an aberration in American life."[14] (This, it will be appreciated, is how "white supremacist" gets its current transformed usage.) So it is important to understand that what I am doing here is *not* conceptual innovation: this is not a new paradigm, but a resurrected old one. Rather, it is the recovery of what used to be a standard usage which, for political reasons, and the need to whitewash and sanitize the past, was deliberately dropped.[15] Racial domination as a *system* vanishes, and we are left with atomic individuals, some of whom have bad attitudes.

The reality is, then, that white racial domination – white supremacy – has been central to US history. Whether one wants to date the republic from 1776, or go all the way back to 1607, we have had hundreds of years of *de jure* discrimination, that is, discrimination backed by the force of the law and the state, followed by decades of *de facto* discrimination. The crucial legal decisions formally ending these practices – *Brown v. Board of Education* in 1954, the Civil Rights Act in 1964, the Voting Rights Act in 1965, the Fair Housing Act in 1968 – are all comparatively recent, and in some cases the practices have continued. After a brief period of (partial) desegregation in education, the country is segregating again, as the Harvard Civil Rights Project has documented.[16] In fact, in a 2000 *New York Times* article decrying "The lost promise of school integration," some commentators predict that "the central premise of the Brown decision – that integrated public schools are the most important institutions in a pluralistic society – will not survive the 21st century."[17] Residentially, the country is more segregated today than a century ago, as the authors of *American Apartheid* have demonstrated.[18] And the white backlash against affirmative action, anti-discrimination laws, congressional redistricting, and other race-conscious policies has imperiled those gains earlier made. Indeed, Philip Klinkner and Rogers Smith argue that substantive racial progress in US history has been confined narrowly to three periods (the Revolutionary War, the Civil War and its aftermath, and the Cold War), has been motivated by contingent historical circumstances and perceived white benefit rather than white moral transformation, and has always been followed by a period of rollback and retrenchment – such as, in their opinion, the period we are living through now.[19]

These political truths have, of course, long been recognized in the black radical political tradition. From David Walker and Martin Delaney, through Marcus Garvey and W. E. B. Du Bois, to Malcolm X and Stokely Carmichael, blacks have had little difficulty in perceiving the central reality of white racial domination.[20] But these figures and their views were not, of course, seen as academically respectable. Within mainstream political science, as Rogers Smith has recently massively documented, the orthodox conception of the American polity – as represented by the classic texts of Alexis de Tocqueville, Gunnar Myrdal and Louis Hartz – has been that of a flawed (where flaws are conceded) liberal democracy: the "anomaly" view of American racism. It is admitted (when it is admitted) that there was some racism, but this is at best an offhand or *sotto voce* concession that does not affect the dominant conceptualizations of the polity itself. In a remarkable evasion of the facts, the systemic subordination of people of color by both law and custom is theoretically ignored. Thus instead of the "anomaly" view, Smith advocates what he calls the "multiple traditions" view, which recognizes that alongside the tradition of liberal inclusiveness, there is also the long-standing tradition of white-supremacist exclusion.[21] (An older position, more radical than Smith's, is the "symbiosis" view, which would claim that the divergent "traditions" are not in any necessary tension, as Smith supposes, since liberalism develops as a racial liberalism so that its crucial terms are really only meant to extend fully to whites, i.e. the human population.)[22]

In deciding how to conceptualize the American polity in its present period, then, one would at the very least have to utilize, and work out the implications of, the concept of a "white privilege" that rests on the legacy of white supremacy. And some theorists would argue that – admittedly in a weaker sense – we are still living under white supremacy, though of a *de facto* rather than *de jure* form. But in either case, white domination in its various manifestations would need to be recognized and be taken seriously by the political philosopher concerned about justice.

3 White supremacy and racial justice

This has been a long background discussion, but it is necessary to set the stage for my critique of Sterba. I would suggest that most white social and political philosophers work with the philosophical version of the anomaly view. If you think this is unfair, just reflect on the most important works in political philosophy of the past few decades, and ask yourself in which of them the fact of systemic racial subordination, and what is needed to correct for it, gets any sustained discussion. Can it be found in Rawls, Nozick, Walzer, Sandel? The answer is, of course, no. It is a rare piece by a white author that begins, as Amy Gutmann's recent article does, "Racial injustice may be the most morally and intellectually vexing problem in the public life of this country."[23] In this respect, most white political philosophy reflects its racial origins, its "whiteness" – not in the sense of overtly advocating the racial suppression of people of color, but in the weaker sense of being written from the perspective of white racial privilege, so that certain realities, certain structures of oppression, do not come into view at all, or do so only distantly, non-urgently, so that no recommendations are made for their elimination. (Compare the pejorative Marxist term "bourgeois" theory, the feminist "androcentric" theory.) If the facts were conceded, their recommendations for justice – given their *own* value-commitments – would have to be radically different.

The strategy of my critique should now be obvious. What I will claim is that Sterba's recommendations, though praiseworthy, are inadequate because they do not appreciate the multi-dimensionality of white supremacy. Nominally, he rejects the anomaly view, since he says explicitly (e.g. p. 102) that whites have dominated blacks. But because the details are not spelled out, we do not get enough of a sense of what this means in practice – the whole discussion, especially when compared with his discussion of feminism, is somewhat cursory. In fact, a useful contrast can be drawn between Sterba's treatment of gender and his treatment of race, starting with the formal allocation of a whole chapter to the former (and part of a second chapter too) and merely a subsection of a chapter to the latter. (I should emphasize that I do not mean to single Sterba out as a *bad* example – on the contrary, he is more conscientious than most. The lack of attention here is one that pervades the field.) His treatment of gender draws extensively on the impressive body of work by feminist philosophers, which has transformed the way we think about political philosophy. But there is a conspicuous lack of citation of black philosophers, with only one – Bernard Boxill – even being mentioned (though to be fair, other black thinkers are cited). And while the family as a main site of gender injustice, the need to reform domestic structures, the role of rape and domestic violence in forcibly subordinating women, the ideal of androgyny, all get extensive discussion in Sterba's text, the material on race is brief and under-theorized. There is no sense of white supremacy as a pervasive system of entrenched racial advantage with interlocking manifestations in numerous spheres that tends to reproduce itself, and whose elimination is a requirement for racial justice.

(It should be noted that Boxill's classic *Blacks and Social Justice* has been out since 1984, and has been re-issued in a revised edition.[24] Howard McGary's *Race and Social Justice* was only published last year, but the essays collected there have been around for much longer.[25] Bill Lawson has an important edited collection on the underclass, *The Underclass Question*, that has obvious implications for issues of social justice, and has also co-authored an essay collection with McGary, *Between Slavery and Freedom*.[26] These books are all more or less in the analytic tradition, and deal explicitly with normative issues. There are also many other black philosophers who work on race and racism from somewhat different perspectives and who are well known – Cornel West, Lucius Outlaw, Anthony Appiah, Laurence Thomas, Lewis Gordon – as well as white philosophers such as David Theo Goldberg, whose work would be relevant.)

In a forthcoming piece in the *Blackwell Companion to African-American Philosophy* – you know a field is in danger of becoming respectable when they start to publish companions, guides, etc. – I suggest that white supremacy has at least six dimensions: economic, juridico-political, somatic, cultural, cognitive-evaluative, and "ontological."[27] Complete racial justice would thus require eliminating white privilege/advantage in all these areas. But because of shortage of space, I will have to confine myself to the economic dimension, which is Sterba's main focus.

Sterba defends affirmative action and policies of "comparable worth" against their critics. In the present period of national rollback of the former in particular, this is certainly a stand to be applauded. I do not have much to add or to criticize in what he says in response to the five objections he considers (pp. 105–9), though I *do* think that more could be said in response to the identity objection raised by people like Christopher Morris.[28] But setting that aside, I am, as one would expect, in favor of Sterba's overall strategy. The problem, however, is that because of his inadequate framing of the full dimensions of black economic disadvantage, this measure, even if it were strengthened and retained, can only go a limited way to remedying the situation.

To begin with, there is no discussion of a training program for blacks without the skills to be eligible for affirmative action; for example, those in the so-called underclass.[29] Sterba wants to defeat the conservative objection that affirmative action will mean giving jobs to the unqualified, so his focus is on those qualified blacks who are, or are likely to be, the victims of discrimination. But nothing is said about the large number of blacks who don't have the skills, not because of personal irresponsibility but because of an unjust educational system. Historically, for example, in the South fewer resources were allocated to black schools. So children who graduated from such a program were underprepared, and not able to compete adequately on equal terms. But if we ask the question of why they lacked the requisite skills, we do not come up against bedrock, or something impermeable to issues of justice, but rather a conscious public policy decision. Today, schools continue to be segregated – there is, as mentioned, a pattern of resegregation occurring – and schools in the inner city are generally inferior to those in the suburbs.[30] And again, if we ask why this is so – why, for example, the suburban tax base is higher – we encounter facts that are not remotely neutral, but the legacy of decades of white supremacist policies.

Moreover, segregation has broader ramifications that need to be examined. It is noteworthy that the word "segregation" does not even appear in Sterba's book. That is not to say that it makes much of an appearance in the books of other white political philosophers. Indeed, as Douglas Massey and Nancy Denton point out, in the 1970s and 1980s the term "disappeared from the American vocabulary," a vanishing act all the more startling since "it once figured prominently in theories of racial inequality."[31] But segregation today, at the start of the twenty-first century, remains a principal feature of the topography of the United States. And segregation is a key factor in the perpetuation of racial inequality, through poor housing, lack of an equal chance to acquire a good home and build wealth, sub-standard education, inferior access to new economic opportunities and the jobs in the new "edge cities," etc. In fact, Massey and Denton argue that though there are various processes of racial domination,

> Residential segregation is the institutional apparatus that supports other racially discriminatory processes and binds them together into a coherent and uniquely effective system of racial subordination. Until the black ghetto is dismantled as a basic institution of American urban life, progress ameliorating racial inequality in other areas will be slow, fitful, and incomplete.[32]

330

Why have whites been so reluctant to integrate society? We need, I suggest – as part of the reconceptualization of the polity – to focus on the benefits whites as a group derive from the present order, and to start talking about *racial* exploitation. There is an interesting comparison here with Marxism's view of group domination. For Marxist theory, the central societal relationship is class exploitation, and this – for those who do take a normative position – is what makes capitalism unjust. So the Marxist challenge inheres in the claim that what seem to be equal consensual relations between wage-laborer and employer are really structured by domination and exploitation. Now the Marxist claim is, of course, not taken seriously these days, for various reasons – the rejection of the labor theory of value, the controversy over the thesis about economic constraint narrowing proletarian choice, the seeming non-viability of socialist alternatives underlined by the collapse of the former Soviet Union and the Eastern European states. But the point is that we can all see how the argument would go through, if the premises were in fact defensible. The fact of class exploitation pervades society; because of class exploitation, the worker is always at a disadvantage; and the result of class exploitation is an unfair net transfer of assets from the workers to the capitalists.

Now what I want to argue is that a straightforward case can be made – far more easily and uncontroversially than the Marxist case – that racial exploitation has been central to US history, and that it structures society as a whole, so that unjust economic transfers from the black to the white population are going on all the time. There are a number of illuminating contrasts to be drawn with class exploitation. First, racial exploitation takes place far more broadly than at the point of production. It certainly includes inequitable economic arrangements like slavery and the debt servitude of sharecropping which succeeded it. But I am also using the term broadly to cover things like the denial of equal opportunity to homestead the West, differential allocation of educational resources, job discrimination, promotion discrimination, blocking of union membership, segregation in housing, inequitable transfer payments by the state, etc. So there is a constellation of different factors whose net effect is to systematically deprive blacks of an equal chance to accumulate material and human capital, and which benefit whites as a group. But the second illuminating contrast is that whereas class exploitation is the subject of a huge body of literature, racial exploitation – which should be quite uncontroversial by conventional liberal bourgeois standards, and thus condemned by a philosophical audience much broader than the political left – is a topic on which there is virtual silence. One recent anthology on exploitation in a left-wing series has only one chapter out of twenty-one on the subject, and it is squeezed into a Marxist framework.[33] And a recent, highly praised liberal treatment by Alan Wertheimer does not even have "race" in the index.[34] Finally, whereas, given Marx's conceptualization, class exploitation can only be eliminated by moving beyond capitalism to communism, racial exploitation can – in theory anyway – be ended within a capitalist framework.[35]

Though undiscussed by philosophers, a growing body of literature elsewhere is beginning to map these processes in their different dimensions. There is older work that is still valuable – Boris Bittker's *The Case for Black Reparations* and Lester Thurow's *Poverty and Discrimination*. But there are also many more recent books: *The Wealth of Races, Black Labor, White Wealth, Race, Money, and the American Welfare State, The Possessive Investment in Whiteness*, and, perhaps most importantly, and most widely read, the prizewinning *Black Wealth/White Wealth* by Melvin Oliver and Thomas Shapiro.[36]

The last undertakes a systematic survey of households and an analysis of statistics on wealth to track the processes by which wealth is accumulated, the racial disparities in white and black chances at obtaining it, and the consequent overall differential impact on people's lives. What the authors conclude is that wealth is far more important than income in determining the long-term prospects for racial equality. Wealth furnishes a cushion in times of layoffs and medical emergencies, enables one to start a small business, can be invested, used to influence the political process, and to provide a head start for one's children through better education and inheritance. So wealth represents past history, and in the case of race it represents a past history of accumulated illicit advantage and disadvantage. The standard practice is to use white/black income differentials as the measure of racial inequality, and these figures are somewhere (depending on the time period and social class being considered) in the 50–70% range. But the figures on the wealth differential are much greater: the median white household has more than *ten times* the wealth of the median black household. This is not because white people are ten times as smart as blacks (even the *Bell Curve* authors limit it to one standard deviation on IQ curves), and it is certainly not because they have worked ten times as hard! What this differential reflects is systemic illicit advantage, carried out at the personal, institutional, state and federal level, in pursuance of a policy of privileging the white population at the expense of the black population.

So original injustice is compounded by further injustice – it's not just slavery, it's not just that the freed slaves never got their forty acres and a mule, and were promptly resubordinated through debt servitude, it's also Jim Crow, the denial of access to white markets, the blocking from better jobs, the denial of promotions, the differential in educational funding, the diminished opportunity as a result of discriminatory Federal Housing Authority policy for blacks to own their own home, the burning down, in some cases, of successful black businesses by white mobs, as with the 1921 Tulsa Riot, where the Greenwood business district (known as the "Black Wall Street") was destroyed in the worst US race riot of the twentieth century, with perhaps as many as 300 deaths, and details of the incident suppressed until very recently, and so forth. So there's a whole set of mechanisms, which an adequate theory of racial justice would need to track down and show the workings of, drawing, obviously, on research in political science, economics and sociology. The fairy stories that white political philosophers tell each other would be blown away.

So the facts, as I emphasized at the start, would be doing the real work in the argument. These would constitute the equivalent, for race, of the kinds of sociological points that, for gender, Sterba *does* talk about. The basic idea would be to show how systemic racial advantage is produced and reproduced, through mechanisms of racial exploitation that continue in somewhat different forms today. And the implication would be that these facts, put into conjunction with most mainstream values, have radical implications for how we think about justice and what our moral priorities should be. Oliver and Shapiro sum up their findings:

> This book [*Black Wealth/White Wealth*] develops a perspective on racial inequality that is based on the analysis of private wealth. ... Private wealth ... captures inequality that is the product of the past, often passed down from generation to generation. ... We argue that, materially, whites and blacks constitute two nations. ... To take these findings seriously, as we do, means not shirking the responsibility of seeking alternative policy ideas with which to address issues of inequality. *We might even need to think about social justice in new ways.*[37]
>
> (my emphasis)

Note that the claim is not that they have come up with a revolutionary new set of values – after all, they are sociologists, not philosophers. Rather, the point is that simply by documenting, tracking and analyzing the different mechanisms that have affected the respective fates of blacks and whites, a case can be made for radical conclusions even within a conventional normative framework. As they point out later:

> The sedimentation of inequality occurred because blacks had barriers thrown up against them in their quest for material self-sufficiency. Whites in general, but well-off whites in particular, were able to amass assets and use their secure economic status to pass their wealth from generation to generation. What is often not acknowledged is that the accumulation of wealth for some whites is intimately tied to the poverty of wealth for most blacks. Just as blacks have had "cumulative disadvantages," whites have had "cumulative advantages." Practically, every circumstance of bias and discrimination against blacks has produced a circumstance and opportunity of positive gain for whites. When black workers were paid

less than white workers, white workers gained a benefit; when black businesses were confined to the segregated black market, white businesses received the benefit of diminished competition; when FHA [Federal Housing Authority] policies denied loans to blacks, whites were the beneficiaries of the spectacular growth of good housing and housing equity in the suburbs. The cumulative effect of such a process has been to sediment blacks at the bottom of the social hierarchy and to artificially raise the relative position of some whites in society.[38]

I apologize for the length of this quotation, but I would argue that it vindicates my point about where the real challenge posed by theories of racial justice lies. In which book on justice that you have read in the last three decades do facts such as these appear? Here we have vividly illustrated the thematic/conceptual whiteness of political philosophy – a process of massive injustice carried out over decades is all but ignored in the most prestigious publications on the subject.

And this brings me to another way in which Sterba's treatment of racial justice needs supplementation. There is no discussion at all of reparations. This issue has never gone away in the black community, and in recent years it has gained renewed vigor because of the precedents in dealing with Native Americans and the Japanese-Americans interned during World War II, the Canadian government's treaty with native peoples, German reparations to Israel, and, earlier this year, the publication of the well known TransAfrica activist Randall Robinson's *The Debt*, which has been getting a lot of publicity in the black media.[39] Since 1989, Rep. John Conyers (D-MI) has been introducing in Congress H.R. 3745, the "Commission to Study Reparation Proposals for African Americans Act." So far it has yet to make it out of committee, but it has the endorsement of many mainstream black organizations, such as the National Association for the Advancement of Colored People and the Southern Christian Leadership Conference.[40] There is also a national umbrella group focused specifically on this question, the National Coalition of Blacks for Reparations in America (N'COBRA), and various prominent black intellectuals have called for a public discussion of the issue (at least one prominent white conservative, Charles Krauthammer, has endorsed the idea). The argument would be that blacks have been systematically deprived of an equal opportunity to accumulate material and human capital, and that whites in general have illicitly benefited from this, so that reparations are owed on respectable Lockean grounds.

There is no extensive opposing literature on this subject by white philosophers, since it is seen as so off-the-wall (when it is seen at all) as not even to merit a reply. But the basic counter-argument would probably be the point that the same persons are not involved, since the original victims of slavery are long since dead. There are two replies here. The first is to argue that the descendants of the victims are still suffering the long-term consequences of these processes, even if it is just slavery that is considered. Moreover, if the indictment is directed against white supremacy more broadly, and not just slavery, then in most cases it *will* be people still living who have been directly affected. And certainly the "paper trail" by which subsequent generations have been disadvantaged is far easier to document here, since these are twentieth-century practices. One would talk about the massive disadvantage blacks suffer today in terms of inferior education, lower life expectancies, differential incarceration rates, worse jobs, confinement to unsafe neighborhoods, etc., which, with the help of fact-finding books like Oliver and Shapiro's, can plausibly be traced to the legacy of white supremacy. Moreover, it is not as if we are talking about reducing whites to penury, but rather following some policy of progressive taxation, especially with the budgetary surpluses that the recent Wall Street boom has created. Overall, then, I think that the issue of reparations deserves to be taken far more seriously by mainstream political philosophy than it has been.

4 Conclusion

Obviously, there is a great deal more that would need to be said, on the economic question alone, quite apart from all the other dimensions of racial injustice I have suggested we also need to consider (juridico-political, somatic, cultural, cognitive-evaluative, "ontological"). The unwhitening of mainstream political philosophy has barely begun. A prerequisite is an end to the pattern of theoretical evasion by white philosophers, and their acknowledgment – at the *conceptual* level – of the historical reality and continuing significance of white supremacy.

NOTES

1 An earlier version of this paper was presented at the conference on "Alternative Conceptions of Justice," University of Notre Dame, 14–16 April 2000.

2 James P. Sterba, *Justice for Here and Now* (New York: Cambridge University Press, 1998). All page references will be to this book.

3 Sometimes, of course, there is an axiological challenge also. Many theorists have seen Marxism as being anti-moralist, but among those who have sought to extract an ethical commitment from his work, it has sometimes been argued that he implicitly advocated a left-wing communitarianism. Marxists sympathetic to this line of argument would then critique the mainstream discourse of rights and justice as the contaminated superstructure of alienated bourgeois class society, and represent communism as a utopia beyond justice and rights (such claims have obviously not worn very well … !). Somewhat similarly, some feminists have argued for a distinctive feminist "ethic of care," which allegedly arises out of the peculiar moral standpoint of women, and its difference from the perspective of brittle male egos maintaining their distance from each other in the masculinist public sphere. But the point is that many socialists, and many feminists, have simply relied on mainstream moral values to indict capitalism and male domination. (This is admittedly less the case for deep ecologists as "radical" theorists,

where the value shift away from an anthropocentric normative system is what is really crucial.)

4 See, for example, Susan Moller Okin, *Women in Western Philosophy* (Princeton: Princeton University Press, 1979), and *Justice, Gender, and the Family* (New York: Basic Books, 1989).

5 Okin, *Justice, Gender, and the Family*.

6 Iris Marion Young, *Justice and the Politics of Difference* (Princeton: Princeton University Press, 1990) p. 5.

7 Jean Hampton, *Political Philosophy* (Boulder CO: Westview Press, 1997), pp. xiii–xv.

8 Allan C. Hutchinson (ed.) *Critical Legal Studies* (Totowa NJ: Rowman & Littlefield, 1989); Richard Delgado (ed.) *Critical Race Theory: The Cutting Edge* (Philadelphia: Temple University Press, 1995); Kimberlé Crenshaw, Neil Gotanda, Gary Peller and Kendall Thomas (eds) *Critical Race Theory: The Key Writings* (New York: New Press, 1995).

9 For an important pioneering article, see Lucius Outlaw Jr's "Toward a Critical Theory of 'Race'," in *Anatomy of Racism*, ed. David Theo Goldberg (Minneapolis: University of Minnesota Press, 1990) pp. 58–82.

10 See my *The Racial Contract* (Ithaca NY: Cornell University Press, 1997), and *Blackness Visible: Essays on Philosophy and Race* (Ithaca NY: Cornell University Press, 1998) esp. chapter 6, "The Racial Polity."

11 Leon F. Litwack, *Trouble in Mind: Black Southerners in the Age of Jim Crow* (New York: Knopf, 1998) pp. xvi, 205.

12 George Fredrickson, *White Supremacy: A Comparative Study in American and South African History* (New York: Oxford University Press, 1981) pp. xi–xii.

13 Penny M. von Eschen, *Race Against Empire: Black Americans and Anticolonialism, 1937–1957* (Ithaca: Cornell University Press, 1997) pp. 22, 155.

14 *Ibid.*, pp. 6, 155.

15 Obviously there is no room to explore this issue here, but it needs to be recognized that the American case is just part of a broader process of the rewriting and reconceptualization of "race" that took place in the West in the period of postwar decolonization. For a discussion, see Frank Füredi, *The Silent War: Imperialism and the Changing Perception of Race* (New Brunswick NJ: Rutgers University Press, 1998).

16 The Harvard Civil Rights Project has mapped a pattern of *resegregation* in education. The number of black students in schools where at least half the students were minorities was 76.6% in 1966–7, fell to 62.9% in 1980–1, but has risen to 68.8% in 1996–7. For Latino students, the figures were 54.8% in 1968–9 and have risen to 74.8% in 1996–7. Most white American students today go to nearly all-white schools (*New York Times*, 18 July 1999).

17 "The Lost Promise of School Integration," *New York Times*, 2 April 2000, section 4, pp. 1, 5.

18 Douglas S. Massey and Nancy A. Denton, *American Apartheid: Segregation and the Making of the Underclass* (Cambridge: Harvard University Press, 1993).

19 Philip A. Klinkner with Rogers M. Smith, *The Unsteady March: The Rise and Decline of Racial Equality in America* (Chicago: University of Chicago Press, 1999).

20 See for example Wilson Jeremiah Moses (ed.) *Classical Black Nationalism: From the American Revolution to Marcus Garvey* (New York: New York University Press, 1996); William L. Van Deburg (ed.) *Modern Black Nationalism: From Marcus Garvey to Louis Farrakhan* (New York: New York University Press, 1997).

21 Rogers M. Smith, *Civic Ideals: Conflicting Visions of Citizenship in U.S. History* (New Haven CT: Yale University Press, 1997).

22 For a discussion, see Jennifer L. Hochschild, *The New American Dilemma: Liberal Democracy and School Desegregation* (New Haven CT: Yale University Press, 1984) chapter 1.

23 Amy Gutmann, "Responding to Racial Injustice," in K. Anthony Appiah and Amy Gutmann, *Color Conscious: The Political Morality of Race* (Princeton: Princeton University Press, 1996) p. 107.

24 Bernard R. Boxill, *Blacks and Social Justice* (1984) revised edn (Lanham MD: Rowman & Littlefield, 1992).

25 Howard McGary, *Race and Social Justice* (Malden MA: Blackwell, 1999).

26 Bill E. Lawson (ed.) *The Underclass Question* (Philadelphia: Temple University Press, 1992); Howard McGary and Bill E. Lawson, *Between Slavery and Freedom: Philosophy and American Slavery* (Bloomington: Indiana University Press, 1992).

27 Charles Mills, "White Supremacy," in John Pittman and Tommy Lott (eds) *The Blackwell Companion to African-American Philosophy* (forthcoming).

28 Christopher Morris, "Existential Limits to the Rectification of Past Wrongs," *American Philosophical Quarterly*, vol. 21 (1984) pp. 175–82.

29 See the Lawson collection, *The Underclass Question*.

30 See for example Jonathan Kozol, *Savage Inequalities: Children in America's Schools* (New York: Crown, 1991).

31 Massey and Denton, *American Apartheid*, pp. 1, 3.

32 *Ibid.*, p. 8.

33 See Gary A. Dymski, "Racial Inequality and Capitalist Exploitation," in Kai Nielsen and Robert Ware (eds) *Exploitation* (Atlantic Highlands NJ: Humanities Press, 1997).

34 Alan Wertheimer, *Exploitation* (Princeton: Princeton University Press, 1996).

35 The qualification is necessary since some left theorists have argued that the racial nature of American capitalism, originally contingent, is now an *integral* part of it, and so too deeply embedded to be eliminated without disrupting the class system itself.

36 Boris Bittker, *The Case for Black Reparations* (New York: Random House, 1973); Lester C. Thurow, *Poverty and Discrimination* (Washington: Brookings Institution, 1969); Richard F. America (ed.) *The Wealth of Races: The Present Value of Benefits from Past Injustices* (New York: Greenwood Press, 1990); Claud Anderson, *Black Labor, White Wealth: The Search for Power and Economic Justice* (Englewood MD: Duncan & Duncan, 1994); Melvin L. Oliver and Thomas M. Shapiro, *Black Wealth/White Wealth: A New Perspective on Racial Inequality* (New York: Routledge, 1995); George Lipsitz, *The Possessive Investment in Whiteness: How White People Profit from Identity Politics* (Philadelphia: Temple University Press, 1998); Michael K. Brown, *Race, Money, and the American Welfare State* (Ithaca NY: Cornell University Press, 1999).

37 Oliver and Shapiro, *Black Wealth/White Wealth*, pp. 2–9.

38 *Ibid.*, pp. 50–1.

39 Randall Robinson, *The Debt: What America Owes to Blacks* (New York: Dutton, 2000).

40 See the cover story in *Emerge* magazine (February 1997) "Righting a Wrong," by Lori Robinson, pp. 43–9.

17

THE RELATIONSHIP BETWEEN THE JUSTICE OF THE STATE AND THE JUSTICE OF PERSONS

Chung-ying Cheng

John Rawls' theory of justice is primarily a theory of political justice which applies to the system of society as a whole. His key notion of justice as fairness seems to imply a wider range of application, as indicated in his wish to study rightness as fairness in regard to interpersonal relationships.[1] We may infer from this that fairness could apply equally to a whole system and to individual persons, and thus in this sense we can speak of both just society and just persons. But the real question is whether a just society must imply the existence of just persons. It might be suggested that a just society must have some just persons so that it could be called just, in the same way a just person must perform some just actions so that he could be called a just person. We may agree to such a suggestion and yet we are unclear how a just society must produce just persons, or just citizens for that matter.

When a just society is merely defined in Rawls' theory of justice as fairness, we see no mechanism or process of transformation which would transfer the quality of fairness of a system to a person in the system, so that the person can be said to be equally as fair or just in an independent sense of justice. This is because there are two levels of reference, namely the level of the state and the level of individual persons, which require a difference and stratification principle of specification and explanation. How these two levels are related, on the other hand, requires a principle of composition and synthesis for explaining the natural interaction between the two levels, in light of historical experience and prescriptions for normative interaction in light of rational reflection. In both processes of interaction we might be able to develop a new enriched sense of justice, to be posited as a condition for demanding satisfaction at both the level of state justice and of personal justice.

Perhaps we may conceive a just person in a Rawlsian just society as one fully consenting to Rawls' two principles of justice, and also as one devoted to vigorously practicing them. Thus such a person claims his rights, respects others' rights, seeks out equal opportunities to benefit or develop himself, and agrees to any strategy of structural arrangement as he sees fit according to the second principle of justice. Will these make this person just or will this match our sense of justice, whether within a cultural tradition or across different cultural traditions? This appears to be a difficult question to answer, and the difficulty consists in that we may have different senses of justice, particularly when we reflect on the fact that some traditions, which may include traditions from the West, do not readily identify justice with lawfulness as in the modern West. Thus we could have a cold-minded, calculating individual who has no care nor charity toward his fellow citizens, but who may follow the law in a meticulous manner and yet manipulate the law and the system of jurisprudence and justice to advance his interests at every available opportunity. This would be a person whom the Confucian sage would not call just, nor the Platonic philosopher, nor the Christian believer. This problem arises with respect to James P. Sterba's work on justice, particularly his books *How To Make People Just* and *Justice for Here and Now*, because he clearly identifies more with the Rawlsian than with the Confucian tradition in political philosophy.

On the other hand, from the Confucian point of view, a just person is a benevolent and righteous (dutiful) person, who respects the proper relationships in society and relates to them in propriety; yet it is totally conceivable that he may have no sense of law in the modern sense at all. For example, he may judge others by his moral standard and may not be aware that his attitudes, language, decisions and behavior might be biased and cause great harm to the fair process of law, and thus damage the rights and equal chances of advancement of other individuals in the same system. In other words, a Confucian just person who is aware of his elitist status can be self-righteous, yet lack knowledge or rational perspective to provide a fair judgement regarding his own rights and interests, the rights and interests of others, and the rights and interests of the whole community.[2] Confucianism insists on the distinction between righteousness and profits, but there is no objective standard on how the distinction can be always effectively made. It often becomes a matter of trust and a matter of attribution. Hence it is totally conceivable that one may have justice at the personal level without necessarily entailing justice at the level of state.

In fact, this is the permanent predicament of Confucian idealism in political philosophy: to realize outer kingliness on the basis of inner sageliness (*neisheng-waiwan*).[3] But history has inevitably left the Confucian-ist in the middle of an unrealistic hope of the converse: to realize inner sageliness on the basis of outer kingliness. Not only may the ideal Confucian government not be a just state in the modern sense, but even when there is some beneficial influence of its sagely learning on the ruler it can be very limited, and there is no guarantee that it will continue or even be self-correcting. This is the Confucian predicament and this is the Confucian irony. When we come to modern times, the question becomes how the justice of a system can guarantee the justice of a person, since personal justice is regarded as the goal of society.

The logic of virtue and the logic of political power or interest are simply different logics, just as the state and the person are different entities. Each must have its range of application, and each needs to perform well in order that the entirety of humankind as realized on these two levels may function well, and its individuals feel satisfied. There should be no unrealistic hope of substituting one for the other, or insistence on the self-sufficiency of one for the well-being of humanity entire, or of the whole individual for a citizen of the nation-state. It is in this sense that the two levels can be mutually supportive and capable of mutual harmonization, and this sense of mutual support and harmonization is premised on realizing the distinction between person and state and the distinction between their distinct logics of self-realization.

In the light of the above I do not wish to argue for incommensurability between justice in one tradition and justice in another, in the narrow sense of finding a common denominator. What we need for both, from the depth of heart and mind of human existence, and above both levels, is the ideal harmony for the fulfilment of the logics of both levels, to which the holistic existence of humanity – whether in an individual or a community – again aspires. It gives rise to both, and needs to develop both; and it also needs to see both work and function in mutual support and harmony, not in mutual cancellation or conflict. In this sense we already have a common ground, and therefore a common measure in the common existence of humanity, to compose the stratified wisdom and ideal values as embodied in the modern and classical traditions, or in the rationality of the system and the humanity of the individual.

My concern is not to contrast rationality from the Greek tradition or the West with humanity or co-humanity (ren) from the Chinese Confucian tradition; it is rather to contrast rationality on the state level with co-humanity on the personal level. To contrast these is to see the possibilities of mutual complementarity. There could be co-humanity to complement rationality on the state level, just as there could also be rationality to complement co-humanity on the personal level. It is necessary in fact to see how the Greek tradition merges with the Confucian tradition on the personal level to make a more rationally conscious just *junzi* (the superior man) on the Confucian side, as well as to make a more humanely conscious and less self-interest-driven citizen on the modern Western side. Since justices and rationalities can be contested, as MacIntyre explains,[4] they can also be synthesized once we recognize the distinctions between different levels and functions. We have counted on functional correspondences to translate one concept of justice into another. Do we not also need to explore the concept of a potential "universal human nature in the making" in order to harmonize the two levels of justice (state and personal) and harmonize various traditions of justice on these two levels?

We may now see that the justice of persons does not guarantee justice of society or state, nor does the justice of state or society guarantee the justice of persons. One may argue that since Confucius and Mencius extended their notion of a moral person to that of a moral ruler, and then to that of a moral community, there must be some structural and causal interdependence between society and the individual. In the case of Xunzi, it is the moral sage-king who would transform society into a community of propriety (*li*) because he believed that human nature is fundamentally bad and needs guidance from above. We have seen historically that in the formation of the Confucian state there can be just people and even a just society (family and community) and yet not necessarily just rulers or just political systems. As we know, the historical Confucian state is not the ideal Confucian state that a genuine Confucianist would dream of.[5] The discrepancy, of course, could be explained and understood, but this explanation and understanding in no way alleviates the difficulty of the transformation of individual and interpersonal justice into the morality of a state. Similarly, how to transform the morality of state justice into the morality of personal justice proves an equally difficult task. The net result is that there need not be full commensurability between justice at system level (as projected) and justice at individual level (as actual): they belong to different categories, and it is a mistake to mix them up.

We could of course argue that the reason why Rawls could develop his notion of justice is that we as individuals have already developed a partial understanding of the contractrian position, and Rawls' theory of justice as fairness is merely a formal articulation of a combination of the best of the proprietarian tradition of Locke and the best of the utilitarian tradition of Mill from a historical and theoretical point of view. In this sense we can see that we must have the just person before pushing for the founding of the just state and the just society. It may even be that the founding of the USA represents such a process of transformation. Consequently there may be both a just man and a just state in the same sense of justice as characterized by Rawls.

However, as a pragmatic test we have also to mention that social and political issues such as abortion, drugs, racism and, not least, bureaucratic inefficiencies in contemporary America, have all suggested the actuality, not simply the possibility, of the co-existence of a just system as far as laws are concerned with unjust individuals as far as practice is concerned.[6] Of course it may be that the actual system of justice does not fully incorporate the Rawlsian ideal of justice as fairness. But then there is nothing in the Rawlsian theory of justice which guarantees or even suggests that the justice of a state system must give rise to individuals who are bound to be just persons doing just actions.

As the justice of the Confucian state may not harmonize with the justice of the Confucian person, and the justice of a modern liberal state may not harmonize with the justice of the modern liberal individualist in regard to optimum fulfillment of justice, we may therefore suggest that we separate the level of system from the level of individuals, and consider their separate standards of justice as belonging to two different categories, each reflecting a different historical tradition, and each requiring different values to satisfy its different deep needs of humanity. In this sense we could combine the Confucian concept of justice as virtue for individual persons with the Rawlsian concept of justice as fairness for the state, to achieve a combination of just persons and just state. There is no intrinsic incompatibility between the social ethics of justice for the person in Confucianism and the political theory of justice for the state in modern political liberalism. Any conflict arising from a combination of the two has to be resolved in favor of the interest of mutual support and mutual enrichment, which should take place in the direction of introducing more rationality on the personal level, and introducing more consideration of equality and benevolence on the state level.

But in order to make a successful combination of the two as a matter of imaginative experiment, apart from making a clear distinction between the two levels, one has also to ask the person to play two different roles, namely as a citizen of the state and as an individual human in a network of interpersonal and social relationships. He has to resolve conflicts of interest and values by obeying laws, and yet he has also to be a morally cultivated or virtuous person in himself so that he may use his wisdom and understanding to resolve social and moral problems, with or without the benefit of law.

With regard to the need of a balanced unity between laws and virtues in promoting a benevolent government (*renzheng*), Mencius says something very instructive: "By mere virtues one cannot conduct government; by mere laws the government will not move by itself."[7] Mencius argued that a ruler may have the heart of *ren*, but if he does not use proven laws and norms from the past, he will not make a good ruler. Notice that Mencius requires the ruler to be a good person first and then urges him to use good method of rule in order to become a ruler. This can be interpreted as requiring a just ruler to be a just person first, before he devises or uses just laws for rule. This means that although in practice Mencius sees a priority order of two levels of justice, the justice of persons first, followed by the justice of the state, he stresses both the interdependence and the mutual indispensability of the justice of the state in the form of *fa* (laws and norms) and the justice of persons in the form of virtues.

It is interesting to note that Confucius can be said to have also recognized the need to distinguish two levels of justice, and to have called instead for the recognition of the primordial importance and indispensability of *ren* at the personal level as the foundation for justice at state level. Confucius

342

distinguishes between the virtue of *ren* as whole virtue on the one hand and *zhi* (knowledge) on the other hand. Although knowledge can be also regarded as a virtue, the special value of knowledge for Confucius is to enable men to establish themselves in society and relate to other people, and in a broader sense could be said to imply understanding of the ways of government.[8] With this understanding, we may see how Confucius focused on the sustaining importance of *ren* for *zhi*. He says:

> If one has knowledge, but cannot preserve it with benevolence, even if one has acquired the knowledge, one must lose it. If one has knowledge, and can preserve it with benevolence, but does not approach it with solemnity, then people will not show respect. If one has knowledge and can preserve it with benevolence and further is able to approach it in solemnity, and yet act without following the propriety (*li*), this cannot be said to be good.[9]

Confucius' message is very clear: even if we have the best kind of justice system, and even if we know it thoroughly, yet if we do not have the whole virtue and whole heart to cherish it and practice it correctly, the knowledge will lose its value or its meaning. If we interpret *ren* as pertaining to justice on the personal level and *zhi* as pertaining to justice on the state level, it is clear that for Confucius, justice on the personal level is not only a starting point for justice on the state level, it is the constant guard and moving (not merely motivating) force for the justice of the state based on knowledge. Hence a just society cannot be just without just persons who will not abandon justice for a single moment.

Logically speaking, the distinction of the levels of laws (*fa*) and virtues (*shan*) in Mencius, and the distinction of the levels of knowledge (*zhi*) and whole humanity (*ren*) in Confucius, provides us with a clue to perceiving the relationship between the two levels of justice. For the Confucianist, personal justice is absolutely fundamental. But even so, the classical Confucianist also always recognizes the necessity of state justice which can be acquired by knowledge and which is to be expressed in norms and laws. Therefore there is no reason why a Confucian theory of justice as virtue on the personal level may not be integrated with a liberal and democratic theory of justice as fairness on the state level.

As laws do not regulate everything, and justice as fairness cannot be expected to cover everything, it is also fair that we developed different useful traditions of justice to their utmost to see if it could enhance our practical wisdom (or *phronesis*) and help us to reach a concrete universality by common experience and rational interchange. In this way we may expect to integrate them where possible in a framework of harmonization of *ren* and *zhi* which allows full peaceful interaction among all traditions, while preserving the basic rights and liberties of people as equal participants capable of rational dialogue and discourse.

The development of a framework of harmonization may take some time, but its goal of achieving an inter-group and inter-tradition recognition of justice as an overall system of human cooperation and mutual learning and support cannot be doubted. It is not only possible and just that following the paradigm of interpreting justice as fairness we can explain and interpret all virtues as fairness, it is equally possible and just to start at the other end and interpret fairness as justice but all other virtues as justice also. Rawls has made an important and successful step toward integrating the European traditions of natural rights and utilitarianism in a contractarian unity in the best rational Greek spirit of logos, and Sterba's work has added to this project as well. Perhaps the next significant step will be a theoretical attempt to unify the modern liberal political tradition of human rights and democracy with the humanistic traditions of *renyi* and *dikaiosyne* in classical China and Greece. What I have done in distinguishing the two levels of state and individual, and in arguing for their mutual dependence, should be an example of such an attempt. It can be said that the rationalistic spirit of modern justice as lawfulness and equity is already a manifestation of the heritage of the Greek; what therefore needs to be stressed in reality is the incorporation of the moral humanism of *ren* and the humane spirit at the interpersonal and social level from the Confucian tradition. This is a great challenge for philosophers and non-philosophers alike.

NOTES

1   *Analects*, 17.
2   In modern and in recent Chinese history there have been many actual personages befitting this type, particularly in light of the tortuous process of late-Qing reforms, dealing with foreign people, revolutions and modernization.
3   The phrase is derived from *tianxiapian* of the Zhuangzi. One can see the chapter called *Daxue* in Liji as an illustration and presentation of the thesis of *neisheng-waiwan*, which also becomes one of the main themes of neo-Confucianism in the Sung Period.
4   Alasdair MacIntyre, *Whose Justice, Which Rationality?* (Notre Dame IN: University of Notre Dame Press, 1988).
5   There is no indication in the Confucian system that just persons in the Confucian sense make the just system of the Rawlsian type. Neither does the Confucianist vision of a just or even perfect society on the basis of virtuous persons and perhaps a perfectly virtuous sage-king match the liberal political society which Rawls has implicitly assumed in his theory.
6   In a speech following the elections of November 1994, Representative Newt Gingrich, the newly elected Republican leader in the House, claimed that contemporary American society had lost its morality and had no culture. See also the essay by Lance Morrow, "Yin and Yang, Sleaze and Moralizing," in *Time* magazine, 26 December 1994, p. 158. A typical case of just system and unjust man is well illustrated in the case of Anita Hill v. Clarence Thomas.

7   See the *Mencius*, 4A-1. Of course the laws (*fa*) which Mencius has in mind are not laws in the modern sense, but norms and ways of government as practiced by early sage-kings.

8   There is a rich repertoire of Confucius' statements on knowledge, whether practical or theoretical or even metaphysical, in the *Analects*. I have discussed these in various articles of mine: cf. "Theory and Practice in Confucianism," *Journal of Chinese Philosophy*, I:2, 1974, pp. 179–98; "Lun Gongzi zhi zhi yu Zhuzi zhi li (On Knowledge in Confucius and Principle in Zhuxi)," in my book *Zhishi Yu Jiazhi* (*Knowledge and Value*) (Taipei: Linking Press, 1986) pp. 141–72.

9   See the *Analects*, 15–33.

Environmentalism

18

ENFORCING ENVIRONMENTAL ETHICS

Civic law and natural value

Holmes Rolston III

How much environmental ethics should we write into law? Care for our environment is something on which we must gain minimal consensus, but also something that will require considerable enforcement. Not all duties are matters of justice, but many are. If you doubt that, try stealing. Or killing. Or raping. Or dumping hazardous wastes (maybe a kind of killing, stealing, or raping). Our inquiry is how far such enforcement is and ought to be so, how far environmental ethics is, in this larger sense, environmental justice.

Politically, "command and control" solutions are out of vogue; what we need instead, many cry, are "incentives." Even incentives, such as pollution permits, operate against a background of required compliance. They sweeten the obedience to environmental law, and introduce some voluntary choices, but the insistent command is still there. We dangle carrots up front, but at the rear we hold a stick.

Ethically, law-like forms of ethics are also out of vogue; what we need instead, many cry, is "caring." Others emphasize "virtues." Caring, virtuous persons need no rules. That may be true in later stages of personal moral development; but in public life, caring in concert needs regulation. The virtuous ahead, up front, may need no laws; but those at the rear, and most of us along the way, need enforcement, reinforcement – which helps us move along. Rules channel caring and discipline virtuous intentions. To this issue we will return.

1 Legislating environmental care

You may be surprised how much is enforced, and at how many levels, from Acts of Congress to lighting campfires. Starting at the top, recall a dozen examples from over one hundred Acts of the US Congress.

*   Clean Air Act (1955), Amendments (1963, 1965, 1969, 1977, renewed 1970, 1990)

- Wild and Scenic Rivers Act (1968)
- Wilderness Act (1964)
- National Environmental Policy Act (1969)
- Marine Mammal Protection Act (1972)
- Endangered Species Act (1973, 1982), Amendments (1976, 1977, 1978, 1979, 1980)
- National Forest Management Act (1976)
- Federal Land Policy and Management Act (1976)
- International Environmental Protection Act (1983)
- Comprehensive Environmental Response, Compensation, and Liability Act (Superfund) (1980), Amendments (1986)
- Clean Water Act (1987)
- Emergency Wetlands Resources Act (1986)

With agency and court interpretation, these acts enforce much environmental behavior. If you doubt this, try shooting a bald eagle, or filling a wetland, or riding a motorbike in a designated wilderness. Following the last quarter century of environmental law and regulation, enforced by the Environmental Protection Agency, no-one in the United States today can do business legally in the manner in which our parents and grandparents routinely conducted business.

Internationally, there are over 150 international environmental agreements registered with the United Nations, and these are often enforced by the participating nations (United Nations Environment Programme, 1991; and see below). Two examples are the *Convention on International Trade in Endangered Species of Wild Fauna and Flora* (CITES) (1973) and the United Nations *Convention on Biological Diversity* (1992). If you are caught trying to bring a snow leopard skin into the United States, you will find yourself in prison with a fine of tens of thousands of dollars.

More locally, with state and local governments, court decisions, actions of regulatory agencies, such as the US Fish and Wildlife Service, or even decisions of the district rangers, this enforcement enlarges, ramifies, and becomes quite detailed. Go elk hunting a day early, and you may end up in jail with your weapon confiscated. Do you want to do a master's thesis in wildlife biology? Your project is to find out among antelopes what proportion of males and females survive the winter, with a view to changing the hunting season for better survival of the herd. Fail to fill in a permit form detailing whether you have used the most humane method of capture, and the Animal Welfare Committee for the Colorado Division of Wildlife, on which I sit, will cancel your project.

Anyone who backpacks in Colorado wilderness is prohibited from camping within 100 feet of lakes, streams, trails. That zone is often where nearly all the desirable campsites are. Two years back, in the Rawah Wilderness, after a hard day's climb, partly because there was more snow at the treeline lakes than expected, I took extra effort to find a legal site. I pitched a late camp, only to find the next day, alas, behind my tent, half buried yet in the snow, a trail that I had not seen.

Sure enough, the backcountry ranger came through, and asked me to move my tent. Fortunately he appeared late the second day; I was leaving the next morning, so he relented. But he had the legal power, and if I had insisted on staying on there despite his orders, I would have been taken to court. I spent the evening without the campfire I wished, since fires are prohibited in the subalpine zones. Add up these enforcements, great and small, and one could probably conclude that, far from environmental ethics being optional and voluntary, to the contrary, most of it is enforced.

Environmental ethics is a personal ethic, or it is no ethic at all. But it is equally true that environmental ethics must go public or, likewise, it will be no ethic at all. Enforcement is more appropriate in communal space, and the environment is communal space.

2 Concern and concert; cheating and coercion

The environment, a public good, cannot be a private matter only; how we act must be collective, institutional, coordinated, corporate. In a community, there are things we cannot do unless we do them together. Let us analyse ways in which this requires civic law protecting natural value.

Many environmental problems result from the incremental aggregation of actions that are individually beneficial. A person may be doing what would be, taken individually, a perfectly good thing, a thing they have a right to do, were they alone, but which, taken in collection with thousands of others doing the same thing, becomes a harmful thing. These actions must be regulated when aggregated. This is Garrett Hardin's tragedy of the commons (1968). Pursuit of individual advantage destroys the commons.

Here, contrary to Adam Smith, there is no invisible hand. Hardin found that solutions will often require "mutual coercion, mutually agreed upon." A community nearing the carrying capacity of its resource base will have to curb short-term self-interest for the long-term good of all. Long-term sustainability requires suppressing short-term desires. Humans can and often do the wrong thing – "by nature" we might say – and law needs to "civilize" these instincts.

Our evolutionary history shaped us for short-range tribal survival, seldom asking us to consider future generations beyond children and grandchildren, never figuring in the welfare of others thousands of miles away or the incremental build-up of heavy metals. Perhaps a commons ethics could work for tribes, but for nations and global commerce, we need regulation of the common good. Often we humans are not so much evil as thoughtless. Social powers external to the self, such as government or business, cause even well intended persons to act against their individual wishes. Those powers can work against environmental ethics; but we wish to turn governmental powers toward the building of an environmental ethics.

The communal good is mutual and requires broad social agreement on environmental policy. But it also requires enforcement, for some will be tempted to exceed the limits set by policy. This is the problem of "cheaters," persons who will in self-interest take advantage of cooperating others. Nor is this always consciously intended; individuals may act as they have been accustomed to over many decades, without waking up to how these customary individual goods are aggregating to bring communal evils to which we are unaccustomed. Environmental law will be needed to curb prevailing practices. The social contract must be policed. Civic law protects natural value.

This ethic will be voluntary, an enlightened and democratically achieved consensus, with the willing support of millions of citizens (as we hope and outline in the next section). But this voluntary compliance depends on the expectation that even those who do not wish to obey will be required to do so. No laws can be enforced without the widespread voluntary compliance of citizens; there are never enough enforcement officers to compel everybody. But even if 99% of citizens are glad to behave in a certain way, provided that all others do, 1% of the citizens will be pressed to freeload, and this will trigger bad faith. Minority rights and the right to dissent have also to be considered – and enforced! But no-one has the right to harm others, without justified cause. Where some destroy public goods entwined with biotic community, enforcement can be justified.

One rotten apple spoils a barrel. The corruption is contagious. Unless a society polices out the polluters, the rot will spread. Maybe that is not the way it ought to be, had we human nature ideally; but, with human nature realistically, this is the way it is. This is especially true when: "New occasions teach new duties; Time makes ancient good uncouth" (Lowell 1844, 1966, p. 191).

Environmental goods have long been assumed as nature's gift. Only in the last century did these goods come under jeopardy and threat. Now tacit goods have to be made explicit; assumed goods have to be guaranteed by legal enforcement. This is going to require nudging people along, where they do not wish to go – not yet at least, though they may, in retrospect, be quite glad when they get there. Vested interests, often with much inertia, have to be divested. Habits have to be de-habituated. Self-interest is easy enough to rationalize under the old rationale. This is the way we have been doing it for decades; can what was right yesterday be wrong tomorrow?

Such established self-interest, combining with established and tacit goods, will quickly be asserted as individual rights. "My water rights go back to 1890! What do you mean I can't irrigate with it like I used to because the selenium from the return flow is building up and is toxic downstream? That's not fair!" But we cannot leave old decisions in place when new information comes on line, without in effect making new and different decisions.

Nudging people out of their old habits and privileges, shifting patterns of right and wrong at shifting levels of scale and scope, is going to require enforcement.

Consider changed attitudes toward smoking and the long effort to mix incentive and regulation. Our forefathers did not know what we now know about tobacco, any more than they knew about selenium. We require tobacco warnings on packages; we prohibit the sale of tobacco to minors. In public, you must smoke outside and in the cold. Every cigarette smoker has felt pushed around. But it would not have been possible to achieve a smoke-free environment without enforcement. *Mutatis mutandis*, apply this to clean air and environmental health. Or to clean water, despite 1890 rights.

"Liberty" is a virtue word; everybody wants it. "Enforce," the seeming contrast, is often pejorative; nobody wants to be forced. But this is superficial. In fact one cannot have the freedom one desires without law enforcement. Unless thieves are restrained and property laws enforced I am not free to own my home. One has more options in a decently ordered society. My right to free speech and action requires policing of those who would curtail it. Environmental ethics needs to learn to extrapolate and innovate these classical arguments into the domain of environmental goods.

Many of the liberties that we protect are quite precious. I am not even free to breathe unless toxic air emissions are enforced. The Clean Air Act of 1970 turns thirty years of age this year, one of the most successful environmental laws ever. According to the Environmental Protection Agency, air pollution has been cut by a third and acid rain by 25%. Cars are 95% cleaner. The ozone layer is projected to recover by mid-century. Emissions of the six worst air pollutants dropped 33% from 1970–97 despite a 31% increase in US population, a 114% rise in productivity and a 127% jump in the number of miles driven by Americans in their automobiles. All this would not have been possible without enforcing environmental ethics. As much could be said for clean water, or environmental health.

There are useful analogies with the US civil rights movement (I speak, let it be noted, as a Southerner, whose great grandparents were slaveowners). The US South (often also the North and West) did not desegregate voluntarily. Typically, compliance was forced by civil rights legislation. But neither was the enforcement unconstitutional, nor was it often violent. Many Southerners had a deep sense that it was right, although not something they particularly wanted to do. Today, no Southerners would return to the segregated South. They are proud of what they have done.

Environmental enforcement will often be similar. The fluorocarbons were removed from refrigerators, mandated by law. The forest industry moved to plantations and sustainable forestry, and decried government interference locking up too much wilderness. Wolves were returned to Yellowstone, with sheep ranchers muttering "Shoot, shovel, and shut up." But refrigerator makers, foresters and ranchers (or at least their children) are going to be proud of their environmental success.

Enforcement covers a wide spectrum of occasions when an agent acts contrary to that agent's own wishes, owing to forces brought to bear from the outside. The main idea is of external restraints counter to internal desires. These may involve boycotts, tariffs, fines, prohibition of access, impounded equipment and funds, or jail. Enforcement need not be violent; indeed it will seldom be.

Unfortunately, enforcement can be in the interests of injustice as well as justice, and this is as true environmentally as socially. Enforcement is often used to maintain undesirable practices in the service of privilege and vested interests. Enforcement can settle issues the wrong way, and it often has. But few social issues have been settled the right way without enforcement – not slavery, not child labor, not women's suffrage, not workplace safety, not minimum wage, not civil rights.

I concede that an enforced ethic is incomplete. I do not murder, or pollute, for fear of punishment. If so, my ethics is not autonomous; it is nominal. Enforced ethics is necessary but not sufficient for environmental ethics. But with enforcement, we can perhaps change habits, and once habituated, the behavior may be internalized. There is enforcement initially, when the actors have as yet no will; but, having done it, afterward the actors come to make up the former deficiency of will. The automobile industry was forced to clean up, but there are no auto makers who now wish to return to the cars of the sixties. I agree that, where there is frequent use, one ought not camp near lakes, or build fires in alpine country; and I do not need a backcountry ranger to make me behave this way.

Enforcement will tend to be for the status quo, when what is as often needed is enforcement to produce change. Enforcement will be part of the establishment, and environmental ethics is often anti-establishment, that is, reformatory. Enforcement will have a certain prestige. "That's the law!" with the suppressed premise that it's a good law and ought to be obeyed. Then we must assert that enforcement does not carry its own credentials, but needs its own authorization and justification. Enforcement is no substitute for argument. We do not want coercion to substitute for intelligence, but we also recognize that intelligent action will need enforcement on those not so enlightened. Meanwhile, there always underlies such action the prior question of whether enforcement is just. Lawyers have to argue, even if policemen do not. Philosophers have no powers of enforcement; they can only argue. They question authority. That is why I am arguing for the legitimate and rational use of enforcement.

A general moral principle is that the excessive use of force is unwarranted, and that applies here. There will be debate about appropriate means and degrees of enforcement. Also, we will hope for arguments that while the enforced behavior may be contrary to the actor's desires, it is not contrary to that actor's welfare. My concern is whether enforcement is moral, compared with caring, and I conclude only halfway so. Here, as elsewhere in ethics, one wants enforcement in the service of desirable ends, appropriate caring, regulated by consitutional processes, preferably those of democracy.

3 Democratic environmental ethics

Hardin's "mutual coercion, mutually agreed upon" leads to the question of how far an environmental ethic can be democratic. The answer is complex. We recall, amused and chastened, Winston Churchill's quip that "Democracy is the worst form of government, except for all the others." Democracy, though the best alternative we have, is not entirely well suited for environmental protection. If environmental policy is to be just, and also enforced, such law ought be enacted and policed through democratic process. This requires some thinking through. A non-democratic government might enforce a just environmental policy, but it would be better to have a democratic environmental ethics.

Two places where humans pursue their values most zealously are in politics and economics. Other domains of value, such as school and church, are no less important, for these also critically help us to form a concept of natural value. Still, in the modern world humans intensely value democracy and capitalism. In business we are consumers; in politics we are citizens. These concerns are allies but they are also in tension. Capitalism can be indifferent to values outside the economic domain (political, religious, aesthetic, ecological). Capitalism has produced wealth, but it has distributed it rather inequitably, while often claiming that it allots wealth meritoriously to those who work hard, efficiently and intelligently. Here we typically think that government is needed to regulate business on matters such as worker safety, minimum wage, or minority hiring, or the rights of labor and dangers of unfair competition. Law is needed to preserve those domains of value that cannot safely be left to the open marketplace.

This ought to extend to environmental concerns – so the democrats (and republicans too!) now argue. For this superintending of commerce we turn to government (aided by school and church) to forge a community bound by ties of mutual service, rather than mere commercial exchange. Natural resource decisions have been long considered primarily economic decisions. Lands under private ownership were bought and sold in markets and cared for under economic incentives. Even public lands, in the commons, could best be managed with a cost/benefit approach; we were interested in what goods we could collectively harvest from them.

Shifting concepts of natural value, however, now mean that many, even most, of the values carried by natural systems cannot be safely left to unregulated capitalist markets. We no longer want a purely economic conception of the natural good, any more than we want a purely economic conception of the social good. Hence we look to democracy to insure that these kinds of natural values are sufficiently protected by the regulation of economics, by removing some natural values from economic access, or, where we do consume resources, by creating incentives or prohibitions to obtain the balance of other natural and social goods that we value as citizens.

Regulation polices these interconnections to see that the economic ones stay in their legitimate domain. Environmental regulation has arisen to protect by national will environmental values whose protection cannot be left to economic interests alone. A democracy places the constraint of the general will on those who would degrade the commons. We sometimes legislate morality, at least in minimum essential or common denominator areas. In environmental policy, there must be a management ethic for the commons – about soil, air, water, pollution, environmental quality, the ozone layer, mutagens, wildlife, the eagle as a national symbol, endangered species, future generations.

Not only is the environment a public good, but further, most remaining wildlands are public lands – national forests, parks, wilderness areas, seashores, grasslands, wildlife refuges, lands under the Bureau of Land Management, state or county parks and forests. These areas are largely managed for multiple use and only semiwild; still they constitute a major component of the natural environment. They also contain most of the relict pristine wildlands, as nearly as these anywhere remain. One cannot look to the market to produce or protect the multiple values that citizens enjoy in general on public lands, much less in wilderness areas, since many of the values sought here are not, or not simply, economic ones. A nation needs collective choices producing a public land ethic.

Democracy, though more admired than is capitalism, is no more perfect. The humans who gather to do business together are the same humans who gather to form government. They do not leave behind one human nature and take on another when they move from marketplace to courthouse – even though the values at stake differ. If human nature is sometimes flawed, these flaws will as soon turn up in government as in business. We have largely thought that democracy is the form of government best able to combine individual freedoms and mutual cooperation with checks on these flaws in human nature. With its more comprehensive sense of the public good, with all the citizens cross-checking each other, democracy can put checks on the flaws in human nature that will make the unregulated market inhumane.

But we have also to realize that democracy can itself be a flawed institution. A tough question is whether democracy can discipline itself enough to be environmentally rational. A test of a democracy is whether its citizens can learn to practice enlightened constraint, developing an ethic for the use of the environment, and more, developing ethical concern for the whole commonwealth of a human society set in its ecosystems. One thing that democracy can produce is debate, discussion about values (though, alas, it does not always do so); and we are more likely to uncover and conserve all of the natural values at stake when issues have been well debated.

In this debate, an initial problem is that ordinary people often lack the needed expertise. Popular desires are not always a useful guide to environmentally wise or just decisions, especially about complicated matters that involve judging risks or balancing tradeoffs. Selenium is as necessary for human health as it is toxic. At how many parts per million of selenium in the drinking water, or in the ducks shot on the marsh, or the fish caught in the river, do we pass from the healthy to the tolerable and then to the toxic? One needs to trust experts.

Experts may concede that their knowledge is incomplete, and what then? Apply the precautionary principle. But then one needs experts to know where the precautionary thresholds lie, if such there are. One needs time to realize the results, although the actors are impatient for decisions. Just how much old-growth forest is required for those spotted owls? That is not the kind of question one puts to popular vote. Who is competent to decide? That is not the kind of question one puts to popular vote either. To the contrary, politically popular answers are as likely to be wrong as right.

The Endangered Species Act requires consultation when a project involving federal funds is likely to place an endangered species in jeopardy. Permitting depends on what is called a "biological opinion." There has been a fight to keep these opinions strictly "biological," meaning not "economic" or "political," certainly not "democratic." Such biological opinions, rendered by biologists and their supervisors, will be enforced. The laws that require and enforce such opinions are democratically achieved, perhaps also politically biased, and they could be changed, if there were sufficient social pressures. Meanwhile, those who cherish democracy must turn over some decisions to experts.

Environmental concern tests the popular will for long-term decisions. There are lag times for effects, as with aerosol sprays and carbon dioxide emissions. Future generations are not here to vote today. One is tempted to discount the future environmentally. Although environmentalism has increasingly become popular, it is also true that what environmentalists want is usually out of step with the immediately prevailing majority. Environmentalists are frequently nudging the majority where it does not yet quite want to go. Another way of putting this is that environmentalists make explicit what is as yet latent in the public mind. Environmentalists use law to do this, because otherwise people wake up too late. "You never miss the water until the well runs dry."

Most people are anthropocentric. Only people vote. But the most seminal environmental laws push further than concern for civic values. They recognize how civic values are entwined with natural values. People need to vote with a concern for endangered species, for humane hunting, for marine mammals, for wilderness. The scale and scope of environmental affairs is typically decades, even centuries. The scale and scope of Congress can sometimes match that, but the scale is often two years, or even the election three months away. If citizens insist on short-sighted, immediate, humanistic values, then Congressional representatives, who have to be re-elected every two years, and Senators, who have to be elected every six, will not be in a much better position than corporate executives whose stockholders insist on maximum dividends every quarter, without regard for the long-range health of the business. We can be tempted to vote for the legislator who promises rewards now; those who do not will be out of office next election.

This can mean decisions that are not really sustainable over the generations of our children and grandchildren. The half-life of a politician is about four years; the half-life of a corporate director is twice that. The half-life of a forest is about a century. The half-life of a species is several million years. The half-life of a plutonium dump is almost forever. All this means that democracies need to seek longer-term views, and more appropriate supporting laws, than voting citizens are inclined naturally to supply.

One way we do this is with checks and balances. The judiciary is not that branch of government placed under immediate democratic control; to the contrary it is relatively free of it. Judges do not have any more environmental expertise than ordinary people, but they have the power and legal obligation to consult experts and to take longer-range views. They must apply laws that they do not make; our democratically elected representatives make them. Such laws must also be constitutional. But judges do not answer directly to democratic will. They listen to argument. They rather consider what is just, or right, what optimizes the greatest good for the greatest number – and that means, environmentally, what combines civic law with the greatest protection of environmental value.

4 Human rights, responsibilities, and caring for nature

Perhaps one will conclude that the only enforceable environmental ethics is the sort that protects humans from harms. Anthropocentric caring for what humans have at stake in nature will be the most persuasive part, politically correct, and readily enforceable, because it builds on a classical humanistic legacy, enforcing justice where persons threaten other persons. One ought not to harm other persons, and this can be readily extrapolated to environmental harms. We might call this a right to normal living, where "normal" becomes "normative" about the natural givens – air, soil, water, living space – when such traditional givens are jeopardized by encroaching human activities. One ought to have "sustainability"; this sustainability enters as an ingredient of environmental health.

If one has a right to national security and hence the Department of Defense, one has a right to environmental security and hence the Environmental Protection Agency. If one has a right to civic security, and hence the sheriffs, one has a right to environmental security, and hence the police lock up the illegal dumpster or shut down the nonconforming industrial plant. Protection against undue harms has long been the province of judicial power. Rights, legally claimed and enforced, must be coordinated with responsibilities. Thus your right to clean water is my responsibility not to pollute the streams, and one cannot be enforced without the other. If social security can be mandated, so can environmental security.

In these environmental laws, however, humans do not always have themselves at the focus of every evaluation, as for example with laws about cockfighting, bullfighting or leghold traps. Over most of the nation, hunters are now required, many against their will, to use steel shot when hunting water fowl. Ducks feed on spent shot that falls into their ponds, needing grit for their gizzards, and afterward die slowly from lead poisoning. Two or three million ducks and geese were dying this way, until law required the steel shot – against a long struggle of resistance by hunters and munitions manufacturers.

In 1992, Coloradoans prohibited spring bear hunting, as well as bear hunting by dogs or over bait. Hunted in the spring, a sow is taken and her cubs starve. Hunted spring or fall, dogs chased a bear relentlessly, a cruel and unfair hunt. The prohibition was made by state referendum, a majority decision, with 70% of voters rejecting the hunt. This is a fully democratic decision. It is also enforced, unwillingly, on those who wish to hunt bears.

A sign in Rocky Mountain National Park urges visitors not to harass the bighorn sheep: "Respect their right to life." Park visitors are prohibited from stopping their cars, or walking, along a half mile of road, so as to give the sheep freedom to pass at will. The hiking trail up Specimen Mountain, a favorite one, is closed during lambing season, several months in the spring. The general park ethic is that if you are interfering with any animal's behavior, you are too close. Back off. One ought to give animals their freedom, no matter how much you wish to get up closer for that marvelous take-home photograph. All such regulations are enforced.

A Wyoming rancher built a wire mesh fence, twenty-eight miles long and five feet high, to protect his cattle-grazing land from antelope. He also hoped to scatter or destroy the herd, because there was a likelihood that wildlife authorities would declare the area critical habitat, and this would make difficult or impossible stripmining the area for coal. An early, severe winter (1983–4) followed; snows prevented the antelope from foraging elsewhere; and the fence blocked their migration to snow-free areas. About 1,500 antelope were threatened with starvation. The fence was put up and taken down over several winters, and finally, in a series of appeals which went all the way to the US Supreme Court, the courts ordered the fence removed or rebuilt. The case was complex, turning on wildlife as a public good more than on animal cruelty, but concern for animal welfare was an important factor. Again, civic law protected natural value.

That we can at times be legally required to be "humane" is a revealing choice of words. We are treating humanely something that is not human. Such an ethic is often persuasive, because we obviously share with animals the capacity to suffer. Inflicting pain requires justification. If the infraction is serious enough, you will have to answer for it in court. Notice, however, that environmental regulation can enforce what some consider to be inhumane, as when Yellowstone Park regulations forbade the rescue of a drowning bison, insisting that "nature should take its course."

Some laws extend to species and ecosystems. The US Congress has lamented, in the Endangered Species Act (1973), the lack of "adequate concern (for) and conservation (of)" species, which have "esthetic, ecological, educational, historical, recreational, and scientific value to the Nation and its people" (Sec. 2), and mandated species protection. The Act was tougher than first realized. It has stood over a quarter century, protecting endangered species beyond any reasonable expectation of benefits, interpreted in the usual medical, industrial, agricultural, or even recreational senses, as for example with saving the snail darter or spotted owl. The National Forest Management Act (1976), the Federal Land Policy and Management Act (1976) and the Wilderness Act (1964) are interpreted in terms of "ecosystem management," and the US Forest Service can prefer to say that it manages for the "multiple values" on public lands, rather than for the traditional "multiple uses."

5 Humans versus nature

Can and ought we enforce environmental ethics if this benefits nature over against humans? We use "versus" provocatively, in the legal court-case sense: Humans v. Nature.

Some will immediately claim that this need not be "versus"; that is too adversarial. What one seeks is humans "with" nature, "in" nature, humans "and" nature, "caring for" nature; or some more complementary and inclusive conjoining of the two. The central problem is precisely this dualist "versus"; and so – critics will lament – I phrase the problem the wrong way. Look for harmony, not opposition; and write laws that way.

So let me hasten to state that one ought to legislate win-win solutions, where this is possible. Culture and nature have entwined destinies. People cannot be healthy in a sick environment. Faced with a dilemma, we try to find a way out by showing that no hard choices need to be made. Make the laws so that there is the greatest good for the greatest number, and include the fauna and flora in the cost/benefit analysis. Look for multiple values, natural and cultural, as does the Forest Service and the EPA. My critics will twist and turn to show that the "versus" can be eliminated.

Consider poverty in developing nations. The *Rio Declaration* insists, "All States and all people shall cooperate in the essential task of eradicating poverty as an indispensable requirement" (United Nations Environment Programme, *Rio Declaration*, Principle 5), presumably using legislation to do so. It also declares, rather piously: "Human beings are at the centre of concerns for sustainable development" and that these humans "are entitled to a healthy and productive life in harmony with nature" (Principle 1). Typically, it turns out that humans are not really winning, if they are sacrificing the nature that is their life-support system. Humans win by conserving nature – and these winners include the poor and the hungry. "In order to achieve sustainable development, environmental protection shall constitute an integral part of the development process and cannot be considered in isolation from it" (Principle 4).

But I remain to claim, with equal insistence, that daily the decisions we face are "versus" in the win-lose sense. We face disjunctions as often as conjunctions. Just as typically, nature is sacrificed for human development; most development is of this kind. Conservation dilemmas are very much with us in developing countries. My analysis is not of some ideal but of the real world. As much as anyone else, I will convert such situations into win-win if I can. Only I face the reality that they do not so easily or so soon convert.

Not all development is justified, but that which gets people feed seems basic and urgent. Then nature should lose. Surely that is just. James P. Sterba formulates this as "a principle of human preservation."

> Actions that are necessary for meeting one's basic needs or the basic needs of other human beings are permissible even when they re-quire aggressing against the basic needs of individual animals and plants or even of whole species or ecosystems.
>
> (Sterba 2000, p. 34; cf. Sterba 1998, p. 128)

On that principle, any laws protecting species, ecosystems, animals, or plants, when this thwarts meeting the basic needs of humans, will be unjust. Sterba desires, he claims, a "peacemaking model" for his ethic (1998, pp. 1–13); but he here becomes quite "aggressive."

Two words in this principle, "necessary" and "basic," will prove elastic enough that various debaters can shrink and stretch them to their liking. Perhaps they can thereby make the principle effectively cover a wide range of cases. But I am now arguing that environmental ethics and law ought, at times, to run counter to this principle. Let us move through a spectrum of cases building this argument.

Members of the Hopi tribe, native Americans in Arizona, wish to engage in a ceremony that requires killing golden eagles. The eagle is captured as a chick, kept well, even reverenced, for months, then ritually suffocated, sending the spirit of the eagle to fly to the world of their Hopi ancestors, informing the ancestors of what the Hopis need in today's world – no doubt including their basic needs, since many of the Hopis are poor. The ancestors engage powers that ensure that these needs are met. The eagle chicks are taken from Hopi sacred lands, but these are now often in national parks and monuments. Although the Hopis received permission from the US Fish and Wildlife to take up to forty eaglets, they were refused by National Park Service officials, on grounds of wildlife conservation. In particular, they were refused admission to Wupatki National Monument, outside Flagstaff, Arizona. The tribe has protested (Stevens and Velushi 1999; Shaffer 1999).

By Sterba's principle, if, in their culture, this is a necessary way of meeting their basic needs, this refusal is unjust and should not be enforced. So much the worse for the eagles. I argue to the contrary that the Hopis were justifiably refused admission; and, should they persist, should be forcibly prevented. In our Western view, of course, this ceremony is not "necessary" to meet their "basic" needs. To retain Sterba's principle we must become "Eurocentric," though he dislikes this (1998, pp. 116–21), and impose our view on theirs. Meanwhile those who engage in the ceremony believe that it is "necessary" to have this eagle contact their ancestors to supply their needs.

This view, I maintain, is false. There is no scientific, ethical, social, religious, or other evidence that the sacrificed eaglet improves their lives. Probably one could find psychosomatic evidence; that those who believe so are reinforced in their resolution, courage, thrift, ingenuity, and might indeed manage to meet their basic needs better in result. We ought to impose our view on theirs, and the imposition couples our Western world-view with a valuing of what eagles are in themselves.

Ethicists would certainly prohibit the Hopis if they were sacrificing their children. In that case, you would appeal to human rights, and to the obligation of the government to protect the rights of the would-be sacrificed child. My argument is by extension. I do not claim, however, that the eagle has rights, but that the eagle has intrinsic value, intensified in this case by concern for a threatened species, and that such value overrides protection of the false beliefs of the Hopis. One need not wait to persuade the Hopis of this; one ought enforce this ethic. Even if, in multicultural tolerance, you wish to remain agnostic about the Hopi belief, one ought not to "agress against" eagles to protect a doubtful human belief about ways to meet basic needs. Surely native Americans, though thwarted by the white man's law, have a venerable tradition of respect for animals, and they can find some way of revising their belief system so as to spare the eagles.

In the United Kingdom, as elsewhere, Orthodox Jews have long practiced kosher slaughter. This is "necessary" in their view for the proper service of God. Are not religious needs quite "basic"? The slaughterer, or *shohet*, slits the throat; butchering is designed to remove as much blood as possible. Jews have been commanded not to eat the blood, out of respect for life and in reminder that life belongs to God. Also, rabbis have long argued that this is humane slaughter.

Times change, and today there is a stun gun available that instantly paralyzes the animal with an electric shock, after which it is killed. The British government has considered legislation to require the use of such stun guns, on grounds that this is now the most humane method of slaughter. Some Orthodox rabbis have objected, since this prevents the maximal removal of blood, and the meat is not kosher (Linzey and Cohn-Sherbok 1997, pp. 54–6; Farm Animal Welfare Council, 1985, pp. 19–20, 24–5). Should this law be enacted and enforced?

I argue that such enforcement is justified. I can concede that Jews worship God with their observances (as I cannot concede that the eagle contacts Hopi ancestors). I concede that religious needs are basic. But I cannot bring myself to believe that the Jewish God commands continuing traditional kosher slaughter, if this causes the animal more suffering. I would plead the case on the strength of their own premises, as well as mine, out of reverence for life and of compassion for sentient animals. Nevertheless, should they insist on their orthodoxy, I am prepared to resist it by enforcing civic law.

In twenty years Africa's black rhinoceros population declined from 65,000 to 2,500, a loss of 97%; the species faces imminent extinction. There has been loss of habitat due to human population growth; but the primary direct cause is poaching for horns. People cannot eat horns; but they can buy food with the money from selling them. Zimbabwe has a hard-line shoot-to-kill policy for poachers, and over 150 poachers have been killed (Berger and Cunningham 1994).

Lest I seem callous, let me insert caveats to guard against inhumanity. One ought to take much care to see that poachers have other alternatives for overcoming their poverty. Such obligations equal any obligations we have to protect the rhinos. If we were zealous, we could make poaching unnecessary. Still, when I face facts in the pressing context in which these Zimbabwean poachers are today caught up, it is highly probable that some of these poachers have no feasible alternative available to them for meeting their basic needs.

I also maintain that such policy is right. Given the fact that rhinos have been so precipitously reduced, given that the Zimbabwean population is escalating – the average married woman there *desires* to have six children (Bongaarts 1994) – one ought to put the black rhino as a species first and make poaching illegal, even if basic human needs thereby go unmet. Anyone familiar with sub-Saharan Africa will realize that, otherwise, there will be no rhinos, or elephants, or lions, or gorillas. Sterba's principle is aggressive indeed. Always putting human basic needs first guarantees, sooner or later, the extinction of every jeopardized species that cannot be preserved as a food animal. Nature co-opted to feed people is seldom wild nature saved.

Royal Chitwan National Park in Nepal is a primary sanctuary for Bengal tigers and the Asian rhinoceros, both extremely endangered species. Other species protected in the area are the sloth bear, the pygmy hog, the swamp deer, the black buck, the Asian rock python, and the gharial crocodile (the most endangered crocodile). The region, in lowland Nepal, was too malarious to live in year-round until the 1950s. In earlier years, what is now the park area was kept as a hunting preserve for the Rana rulers of Nepal in the dry season. Oddly, the tigers and rhinos survived because of the mosquitoes.

Following a mosquito eradication campaign in mid-century, Nepalis began to move into the region. The migrants cleared the forests and started cultivating crops, also poaching. In 1973, to increase protection, the hunting preserve was designated a national park. Nepalis were surrounding it. The population of the Terai (lowland) region was 36,000 in 1950; in less than a decade it was one million. With one of the highest birthrates in the world, and with the influx continuing, the population in 1991 was 8.6 million, 90% of them poor, 50% of them desperately poor (Nepal and Weber 1993; Shrestha 1997).

No-one is allowed to live in the park. People complain that they cannot cut grasses, graze cattle and buffalo, or timber the park at will. They are allowed to cut thatch grasses several days a year, and 30% of park income is given to Village Development Committees. The Royal Nepalese Army, with 800 soldiers, is responsible for preventing poaching, grazing, cutting grasses, pilfering timber, and permanent habitation of the land. Enforcement is quite rigorous. In 1985, 554 violations were fined and 1,306 cattle were impounded. In 1993 thirty-seven rhino poachers were apprehended. The soldiers also do what they can to improve the lot of the people. But being hungry is not a sufficient reason to sacrifice the park, and this is legally enforced, no matter that human needs go unmet.

Again, my caveats. One needs to fix this problem by attacking its root social causes. But, alas, in a recent visit to Nepal, I did not find any answers in sight. You can stretch the word "necessary" to make it unnecessary for the Nepalis to sacrifice the park – had they a different kind of society, had they more foreign aid than they do. (Even now about one half of the government's revenue depends on foreign aid and borrowing; one third of the hard currency entering the country is aid.) Yes, there are other options in principle, and the destruction is unnecessary – logically, ideally, eventually. But fact of the matter again is that, practically, no such options are viable for most of these nine million Nepalis. "Justice for here and now," Sterba's emphasis, requires decisions in law enforcement that save nature and leave basic human needs unmet.

But by Sterba's principle, these millions will be justified in destroying Royal Chitwan National Park, the last refuge in Nepal of the tigers and rhino, also of a dozen other species. Unless civic law can protect natural value, long before their needs are met, most of the biodiversity in Nepal will be gone. Humans ought not always and everywhere dump their mistakes, mismanagements and misfortunes onto jeopardized wildlife; and basic needs unmet is no unchallengeable exception. We might not make this argument for every endangered beetle or nematode worm, but the lithe, supple cat, epitome of feline power, joined with the other charismatic species, displays richness in value that one ought not to sacrifice for a temporary and ultimately futile solution to these deep human problems.

6 Global enforcement: nature and the nations

Enforcement requires government; there is no world government. But environmental ethics has gone global in scale: climate change and global warming, fishing in the deep seas, population control, developed/developing nations, inequitable distribution of wealth driving environmental degradation, trade in ivory, tiger skins and rhino horns. Can and ought there be enforcement on this scale? Or will we stay adrift in a multicultural and pluralist morass? On national scales, enforcement is possible, but on international scales, there is anarchy. At least there is only incentive, never command and control. Internationally – at least short of war – there are only carrots, never sticks.

One possibility is that in the burgeoning nations, whether escalating in numbers or appetites, enforcement sufficient to provide quality environments may be impossible, because it is too demanding on human capacities. Quality environments would be desirable, ideally; but realistically, it is already too late. In 1970 in only one nation (Chad) was the average person, on balance, becoming poorer, with population growth overwhelming economic advance. By 1980, the number of such nations had risen to thirty-five; by 1990 the number was ninety! (Westing 1993, p. 100). One shudders when waiting for the 2000 figure. Under such pressures, civic law is unlikely to be able to protect natural values – certainly not tiger habitat, and hardly even soil and water quality.

Escalating populations and consumerism are likely to escalate the need for enforcement, at the same time that they escalate its difficulty. Indeed, given the human nature about which we earlier worried, even decent environments are likely to become uncommon. Perhaps the most we can hope for is environmental justice, more or less, in more fortunate regions of the globe.

When it comes to nature, the nations are often as much part of the problem as part of the answer. The divisive troubles that arise among the world states, with their competing national sovereignties, are not well adapted for harmonious relations with the Earth commons. The "rights" of nations, and "rights" as claimed by citizens of these political states are not well aligned with the ecology and geography of the planet. The shapes of the continents are the result of natural forces, and natural resources lie where they lie by nature. On these continents, national boundaries were drawn for political reasons and often with minimal attention to natural resources – nearly all were drawn before many of the modern essential resources were resources at all: coal, electric power, uranium, copper or iron ore.

People assert their need for a productive and quality environment as citizens of nations that have economic policies, political agendas, and laws demanding loyalties in support. Their access to natural resources comes filtered through political units that are not formed, or continued, with these ecologies in mind. They want resources, but the political alignments can often mean suboptimal and unjust solutions to the problems of resource distribution. *Natural* resources have to become *national* resources, and "nationalizing" natural resources can be as much part of the problem as part of the answer, especially when the sovereign independence of nations is asserted without regard for the ecological and social interdependencies of these nations.

But it is a mistake to conclude that nothing is enforceable because, on this one Earth, there are 178 sovereign nations. Although there is no world government nations can and do enforce, on their own nationals and on other parties, the provisions of treaties into which they have entered. The number of international treaties that generate environmental law is considerable (Kiss 1983; Rummel-Bulska and Osafo 1991; Weiss *et al.* 1992). Providing social security is a principal justification for nation-states, a principle of justice for both domestic and foreign policy. The transition now needs to extend to environmental security and justice, nationally and internationally.

Consider the possibility that most of these myriad nations could enter into a treaty guaranteeing a universal human right to a quality environment (Westing 1999). The United Nations General Assembly has decreed: "All individuals are entitled to live in an environment adequate for their health and well-being" (United Nations General Assembly 1990). A UN-related group, the InterAction Council, consisting of over two dozen former heads of state, prepared in 1997 a *Universal Declaration of Human Responsibilities* on the occasion of the fiftieth anniversary of the *Universal Declaration of Human Rights* (1948). Although that document has not been officially adopted by the UN, it does contain widely recognized principles. Of particular interest is one of its nineteen principles:

> Article 7: Every person is infinitely precious and must be protected unconditionally. The animals and the environment also demand protection. All people have a responsibility to protect the air, water and soil of the earth for the sake of present inhabitants and future generations.
>
> (InterAction Council 1997)

Such language is broad, and, like all international consensus documents, subject to interpretation. Still, there is the idea that humans in their environments, their biosphere, warrant protection, and all persons may be held so responsible. That does not guarantee enforcement; but again, the suggestion is that enforcement at some levels and degrees could be appropriate. Often such UN resolutions are only a rhetorical veil over power relations. But national powers can and do enter into various kinds of international relations, which can bring levels of enforcement.

What start out as hortatory ideals can, in due course, become formal international commitments, as happened with the *Universal Declaration of Human Rights*. This declaration was first promulgated in 1948, and it took eighteen years, but by 1966 there had been widely adopted international covenants, to which about three quarters of the states on Earth are now party. Something like this could be on the horizon for environmental concerns.

Could this ever extend to a more fundamental protection of nature? The *World Charter for Nature* (United Nations General Assembly 1982) is another aspirational declaration that might be deepened into formal international commitments, eventually guaranteeing appropriate respect for nature for what it is itself. That route would probably be by discovering that, in trying to assert human rights to and over the environment, the problem is deeper than we first thought. Asserting our rights and "aggressing against animals, plants, species, ecosystems" that stood in our way, demanding our human rights to a quality environment, we would be increasingly confronted by population growth and desires for economic advance.

By then the tigers and rhinos would long be gone, but we might begin to realize that both of these thwarting problems result from regarding nature as nothing but natural resources. Environmental justice, so we had thought, was a matter of settling conflicting human rights claims. Justice is for "just us" people. After all, only persons can be just; whooping cranes and sequoia trees cannot. Maybe we would realize that it does not follow that persons cannot behave rightly or wrongly with regard to animals, plants, nature. It might become clearer to us that to see nature and its conservation solely in terms of natural resources is as much part of the problem as the answer. There is no rule of ethics by which cultural values automatically and always trump natural values. Human systems and natural systems have entwined destinies; what we ought to seek, indeed what we must seek for any workable, or enforceable solution, is a complementary welfare.

We do not seek more intelligent and sustainable exploitation; when we seek that and that only, we overshoot. Maximizers always overshoot. We ought to seek, and enforce, harmony, sustainable development but equally a sustainable biosphere, human citizenship in a biotic community, civic law protecting natural value.

References

Berger, Joel and Cunningham, Carol (1994) "Active Intervention and Conservation: Africa's Pachyderm Problem," *Science*, 263, pp. 1241–2.

Bongaarts, John (1994) "Population Policy Options in the Developing World," *Science*, 263, pp. 771–6.

Convention on International Trade in Endangered Species of Wild Fauna and Flora (CITES) (1973) Washington: US Government Printing Office.

Farm Animal Welfare Council (1985) *Report on the Welfare of Livestock when Slaughtered by Religious Methods*, London: HMSO.

Hardin, Garrett (1968) "The Tragedy of the Commons," *Science*, 169, pp. 1243–8.

InterAction Council (IAC) (1997) *Universal Declaration of Human Responsibilities*, Tokyo: InterAction Council.

Kiss, A. C. (ed.) (1983) *Selected Multilateral Treaties in the Field of the Environment*, Nairobi: United Nations Environment Programme.

Linzey, Andrew and Cohn-Sherbok, Dan (1997) *After Noah: Animals and the Liberation of Theology*, London: Mowbray-Cassell.

Lowell, J. R. (1844, 1966) *The Present Crisis*, pp. 185–91 in *The Poetical Works of James Russell Lowell*, vol. 1, New York: AMS Press.

Nepal, Sanjay Kumar and Weber, Karl E. (1993) *Struggle for Existence: Park–People Conflict in the Royal Chitwan National Park, Nepal*, Bangkok: Asian Institute of Technology.

Rummel-Bulska, I. and Osafo, S. (eds) (1991) *Selected Multilateral Treaties in the Field of the Environment, II*, Cambridge: Grotius Publications.

Shaffer, Mark (1999) "Wupatki Won't Let Hopis Gather Golden Eagles," *Arizona Republic* (Phoenix) 31 July, pp. A1–A2.

Shrestha, Nabina (1997) *Protected Species of Nepal*, Kathmandu: IUCN Nepal.

Sterba, James P. (1998) *Justice for Here and Now*, New York: Cambridge University Press.

——(2000) *Three Challenges to Ethics*, New York: Oxford University Press.

Stevens, Jan and Velusii, Lukas (1999) "Hopi Eaglet Ceremonies Thwarted," *Arizona Daily Sun* (Flagstaff) 29 July, pp. 1, 11.

United Nations Environment Programme (1991) *Register of International Treaties and Other Agreements in the Field of the Environment*, UN Doc. EP/GC.16/Inf.4.

——(1992) *Convention on Biological Diversity*, UN Doc. UNEP/Bio.Div/N7-INC.54.

——*Rio Declaration on Environment and Development*, Principle 1, UNCED document A/CONF.151/26, vol. I.

United Nations General Assembly (1982) *World Charter for Nature*, New York: UN General Assembly Resolution no. 37/7, 28 October.

——(1990) *Need to Ensure a Healthy Environment for the Well-being of Individuals*, New York: UN General Assembly Resolution no. 45/94, 14 December.

United States Congress (1973) *Endangered Species Act of 1973*, 87 Stat. 884. Public Law 93–205.

Weiss, E. B., Magraw, D. B. and Szasz, P. C. (1992) *International Environmental Law: Basic Instruments and References*, Ardsley-on-Hudson NY: Transnational Publishers.

Westing, Arthur H. (1989) "Comprehensive Human Security and Ecological Realities," *Environmental Conservation*, 16, 4, winter, p. 295.

——(1993) "Human Rights and the Environment," *Environmental Conservation* 20, 2, summer, pp. 99–100.

——(1999) "Towards a Universal Recognition of Environmental Responsibilities," *Environmental Conservation*, 26, 3, September, pp. 157–8.

19

THE MORAL STATUS OF NONHUMAN LIFE

Mary Anne Warren

One of the most important debates in environmental ethics is that between proponents of anthropocentric (human-centered) and biocentric (life-centered) approaches. At one extreme, radically anthropocentric ethicists, such as John Passmore,[1] hold that we have moral obligations only toward human beings, and never toward nonhuman organisms. This view is sometimes expressed by saying that nonhuman life has no intrinsic value. On this view it cannot be morally wrong for human beings to harm organisms of other species unless doing this adversely affects other human beings. At the opposite extreme, radically biocentric ethicists, such as Albert Schweitzer[2] and Paul Taylor,[3] extend equal moral status to all living organisms, refusing to distinguish between the respect due to human beings and that due to animals, plants and microbes. This view is sometimes expressed by saying that all living organisms have the same intrinsic value.

In *Justice for Here and Now*, James P. Sterba seeks to bridge the gap between anthropocentric and biocentric forms of environmental ethics. His project is to outline an ethic for the adjudication of conflicts between human and nonhuman needs that is neither radically anthropocentric, nor so demanding of self-sacrifice that human beings could not reasonably be expected to adopt it. His compromise is to accord moral status to all living organisms, as well as to species and ecosystems, but to retain a limited preference for human over nonhuman interests. I agree with this strategy, but disagree with the way in which his principles treat all nonhuman organisms as having essentially the same moral status. I argue that organisms of different species often differ in moral status, both because of differences in their intrinsic value, and because of their different relationships to human beings and terrestrial ecosystems. I will begin with an explication of Sterba's view, and then explore some of the sources and implications of this disagreement. Finally, I will comment briefly on a common objection to the view that we have moral obligations to nonhuman life, namely the claim that human beings are psychologically incapable of accepting such obligations.

Sterba's rejection of anthropocentrism

Professor Sterba begins his chapter "From anthropocentrism to nonanthropocentrism" by arguing that there are no non-question-begging grounds for regarding human beings as superior to members of other biological species (p. 125).[4] There is, in other words, no noncircular argument for the claim that we are objectively better, or more admirable, than other organisms. To be sure, human beings have linguistic, artistic, technological, and other capacities that appear to be unique amongst terrestrial species. But this fact provides no evidence of human superiority, since every species possesses distinctive traits and adaptations. Our unique adaptations have served us fairly well; but those of other species have also been valuable to them, i.e. conducive to their survival. All living organisms can be harmed or benefited; they have a good of their own, which is independent of the uses we may wish to make of them. Consequently, they are moral subjects, i.e. entities deserving of moral consideration (p. 148). Sterba concludes that, because other organisms are moral subjects, and because they are not inferior to human beings, we are required to treat them as equals (pp. 126–7).

Nevertheless, Sterba says, we are entitled to give some degree of preference to human needs over the needs of other organisms. To do this is not to presuppose human superiority, because "regarding the members of all species as equals still allows for human preference in the same way that regarding all humans as equals still allows for self-preference" (p. 127). For instance, the principle of human moral equality does not prohibit us from defending ourselves or other human beings against wrongful human aggression, or from investing more effort to promote our own well-being and that of our family and friends than to promote the well-being of strangers.

The question, then, is: How much preference for human interests is compatible with treating other organisms as equals? Sterba proposes three principles which define and limit the extent of this preference. First, the Principle of Self-Defense permits us to kill or harm plants or animals (and presumably other nonhuman organisms) in order to defend ourselves or other human beings from harmful aggression. Second, the Principle of Human Preservation permits us to aggress against the basic needs of plants and animals to meet human basic needs. Basic needs are those which, "if not satisfied, lead to lacks or deficiencies with respect to a standard of a decent life" (p. 128). Sterba says that, although this is a vague standard, we can at least distinguish between needs that clearly are basic and those that clearly are not. Finally, the Principle of Disproportionality prohibits aggression against the basic needs of plants and animals in order to meet nonbasic or luxury needs of humans (p. 128). Together, these three principles represent a compromise between human and nonhuman needs, in which basic human needs trump the basic needs of other organisms, but nonbasic human needs are trumped by the basic needs of other organisms.

Sterba proposes a parallel compromise between human needs and the needs of biological species, and ecosystems. He argues that if individual organisms have a good of their own, then so do species, insofar as "they evolve, split, bud off new species, become endangered, go extinct, and have interests distinct from the interests of their members" (p. 148). Similarly, ecosystems can be harmed or benefited; they have a good of their own which is distinct from the good of their components. Thus it makes sense to give moral consideration not only to individual organisms, but also to species, ecosystems and the terrestrial biosphere. It would, Sterba says, be unreasonable to ask human moral agents to sacrifice their basic needs for the sake of nonhuman species or ecosystems. However, when basic human needs are not imperiled, "we would be justified in acting on holistic grounds to prevent serious harm to nonhuman individuals, or species, or ecosystems, or the whole biotic community" (p. 131). He therefore extends the three principles, to permit harms to species and ecosystems for the sake of human self-defense or human preservation, while prohibiting aggression against the basic needs of species and ecosystems for the sake of nonbasic human needs (p. 146).

This compromise view points toward a reconciliation between the individualistic ethic of animal liberation and the holistic environmentalist ethic. Animal liberationists value the interests of individual animals over environmental considerations, while environmental holists value the protection of species and ecosystems over the interests of individual plants and animals. Nevertheless, Sterba points out, both can support policies that benefit both individual animals and ecosystems. For instance, they can agree that a less meat-based diet would be desirable for most First World people, since it would be less ecologically destructive and would require the killing of fewer animals. However, Sterba says that his view does not require adherence to a strictly vegetarian or vegan diet. He argues that universal veganism would not serve the interests of domestic animals, since many breeds and species would no longer be worth rearing, and might cease to exist except in zoos (p. 133). It is more in the interests of domestic animals such as cattle and sheep that some of them be reared for food, under humane conditions.

Sterba's justification for human preference

Sterba denies that human beings are superior to other organisms, yet contends that they are entitled to protections that are denied to nonhumans. They are entitled, for example, to basic moral rights to life and liberty. We may not aggress against them except in self-defense, even to meet basic needs. But if human beings are in no way superior to other organisms, then why are we not permitted to aggress against fellow humans for the same reasons that justify aggression against nonhuman organisms? Why, for instance, may we not kill other human beings for food when we are starving? Sterba's answer is that human beings derive enormous benefits from "implicit nonaggression pacts based on a reasonable expectation of a comparable degree of altruistic forbearance from fellow humans" (p. 129). It would be unreasonable to require human beings to forego these benefits, which are probably essential to the survival of our species. Moreover, it is pragmatically impossible to extend the same benefits to all other living organisms. To require this "would, in effect, be to require humans to be saints, and surely morality is not in the business of requiring anyone to be a saint" (p. 129).

I think that this is at least part of a reasonable answer. There is no contradiction between the claim that all living organisms have intrinsic value, and the claim that human beings are entitled to stronger moral and legal protections than are most other organisms. However, I adopt a different strategy for justifying the second claim. Sterba argues that, given the benefits of mutual nonaggression, human beings have greater intrinsic value than other organisms, and thus a higher moral status (p. 146). I argue for a sharper distinction between intrinsic value and moral status. In my view, an organism's intrinsic value is only one of the factors that can determine its moral status; social and ecosystemic relationships can also alter what we owe it in the way of protection and assistance. Thus it is possible to claim special moral rights for human beings, without assuming that their intrinsic value is greater than that of organisms of all other species – a claim which would appear to be as difficult to prove in a non-question-begging way as the claim that human beings are superior to all other organisms.

Defining intrinsic value

Sterba describes his concept of intrinsic value as recipient-centered, rather than agent-centered. On the agent-centered concept of intrinsic value, he says, a thing has intrinsic value if its good is an end for some agent, rather than merely a means to other ends. This form of intrinsic value does not admit of degrees, since the condition is either met or not. On the recipient-centered concept, "to say that X *has intrinsic value* is to say that *the good of X ought to constrain the way that others use X in pursuing their own interests*" (p. 146). Recipient-centered intrinsic value admits of degrees, provided that there are good reasons for believing that the good of some entities should constrain our actions toward them more than the good of others. Thus if the good of human beings ought to constrain our actions more than the good of other organisms, then it follows that human beings have greater intrinsic value.

This recipient-centered concept of intrinsic value is very similar to what I call moral status. I define moral status in terms of human moral obligations. An entity has moral status if human beings can have moral obligations toward it, whether those obligations are based upon its intrinsic value, or on other morally relevant considerations. In my view, moral status is distinct from intrinsic value. I argue that an entity's intrinsic value depends upon the presence or absence of certain intrinsic properties, including life, sentience and mental sophistication; whereas its moral status depends not only on its intrinsic value, but also on certain of its relational properties, including its ecosystemic importance, and its social relationships (if any) to human beings.

The intrinsic value of life

Like Sterba, I believe that biological life is a sufficient condition for having intrinsic value, in part for the reasons that Paul Taylor has given.[5] Taylor points out that living organisms are teleologically organized systems, which function and behave in ways that tend to preserve the organism and enable it to reproduce its kind. Thus all organisms have a telos, or good of their own. This fact lends plausibility to the claim that all living organisms have intrinsic value. The life of an organism has value *to the organism*. Even if an organism is unable consciously to desire continued life, to kill it is (usually) to harm it, by defeating the goals that it naturally pursues. Deliberately to do this requires some moral justification.

Thus even very simple life forms, such as bacteria, have moral status, based upon their internal teleology. In contrast, most machines do not have moral status, because they do not have a good of their own. Their proper functioning may promote human ends, but it does not promote ends which are theirs, including their own survival and reproduction. On the other hand, a machine might be produced whose internal functions and behavior were organized to promote its own survival, and to enable it to reproduce itself. Such a machine could be regarded as a nonliving thing with a good of its own, and thus a claim to moral status. Alternatively, it could be regarded as an artificial life form, whose internal teleology makes it just as alive as any naturally evolved organism.

It does not follow from the claim that all living organisms have intrinsic value, that all of them have equal intrinsic value, or equal moral status. There are good reasons to believe that some organisms have lives that are of greater value, to them, than others. Sentience is one property that can increase the value of organic life.

Sentience and moral status

Sentience is the capacity to experience pleasure, pain and other conscious mental states. Although sentience is not a necessary condition for having moral status, it generates moral obligations that have no application to nonsentient organisms. When I pull crab grass plants from my garden, I need not fear that I am causing them pain, or depriving them of lives that they were consciously enjoying. The nonsentience of crab grass makes it easier to justify aggressing against it for less than compelling reasons. I would not poison moles or gophers to improve the appearance of the garden, because I think it wrong to subject sentient beings to a painful death without a more compelling reason. Sentient beings are vulnerable to cruelty, the unjustified infliction of suffering or death. Because they are capable of consciousness, they lose more that is of value to them when they are killed than do nonsentient organisms, which cannot consciously enjoy their own existence. I conclude that sentient beings should not be killed or caused to experience pain, except when there is no other way to meet significant human or ecosystemic needs. How great the need must be to warrant harm to a sentient being depends upon, first, how highly sentient it is; and second, the strength of the evidence that it is sentient.

It is a plausible hypothesis that sentience is subject to degrees, such that highly sentient animals experience greater pleasure and pain than do minimally sentient ones. Vertebrate animals, such as birds and mammals, have more complex central nervous systems and behavioral repertoires than do most invertebrates, and thus are apt to be more highly sentient. Moreover, we can be more confident of the sentience of some animals than others. Vertebrates are so similar to human beings in their sensory systems, neurophysiology and behavioral responses that there can be no real doubt of their sentience. There is more uncertainty about the sentience of many invertebrates, such as worms, arthropods and crustaceans. While I believe that the survival value which a capacity for pleasure and pain would have for such complex and mobile animals argues for their possessing some form of sentience, it is difficult to be fully confident that they do. I conclude that a greater need is required to warrant harming animals that are highly sentient, and whose sentience is empirically well established, than to warrant harming animals that are minimally sentient, or whose sentience is uncertain.

Mental complexity and sophistication

A being's mental complexity and sophistication also matter to the strength of our obligations toward it. I feel worse about accidentally running over a skunk than about accidentally stepping on an ant, even though both are probably sentient. One explanation of this apparent bias is that skunks are more like human beings in their physiology and behavior, and thus I find it easier to empathize with them. However, there are more pertinent reasons for making this distinction. The ant, while it may be sentient, is probably less highly sentient than the skunk. Furthermore, the ant seems not to possess a very sophisticated mind. Much of its behavior appears to be "hard-wired," rather than the result of learning, judgment and intention. Thus it is unlikely to be what Tom Regan calls a subject-of-a-life.

Regan defines a subject-of-a-life as a being who is not only sentient, but also capable of beliefs, desires, memory, anticipation of the future, emotion, intentional action, and a psychophysical identity over time.[6] Because of these additional abilities, subjects-of-lives lose more that is of value to them when they are killed or otherwise harmed than do sentient beings with less sophisticated minds. When a minimally sentient being dies, it loses only the continuation of a life that might have been pleasant to it. It does not have hopes for the future, or conscious commitments that will be defeated by premature death. Subjects-of-lives, on the other hand, have lives that can go better or worse for them from their own subjective perspective. They can be harmed, not just by pain or the loss of pleasure, but by the frustration of their conscious goals.

For these reasons, I think it appropriate to exercise special care to avoid harming creatures that possess the mental capacities constitutive of this kind of subjecthood. While Regan believes that only mammals over a year of age are clearly subjects,[7] I think that a good case can also be made for birds, many younger mammals, and possibly some other vertebrates. The difference between subjects and simpler sentient beings is not a sharp one. Subjecthood and mental complexity come in many types and degrees. Thus I think it futile to look for a sharp boundary between subjects and nonsubjects. Rather, we should recognize that the more mentally sophisticated a being, the greater its claim, other things being equal, to moral consideration.

Moral agency and basic moral rights

While I believe that subjects-of-lives deserve special consideration, I do not accept Regan's view that all nonhuman subjects-of-lives should have exactly the same basic moral rights as human beings. Human beings are a special case. One reason for according a special status to human beings is that most (though not all) human beings are capable of moral agency.

Moral agency is the capacity to regulate one's behavior by moral concepts, principles and ideals. Moral agency provides a basis for the extension of special moral rights to human beings, in part because it makes possible the implicit mutual nonaggression pacts that Sterba stresses – as well as such explicit pacts as laws and international human rights agreements. It also greatly expands the potential for cooperation and mutual assistance. Moral agents are not necessarily more intelligent than other subjects-of-lives. However, a capacity for linguistic communication – the great problem-solving tool – is probably essential to moral agency. Most animals, even those that are highly social, do not appear to act upon moral concepts, ideals or rules. Even if they do possess such concepts, we are unable to communicate with them well enough to converse with them about moral issues. Thus, when an intractable conflict occurs between our needs and theirs, we cannot negotiate compromises that require each species to respect the rights of the other. That is one reason why, when mice overrun our homes or granaries, we sometimes have no feasible option but to kill them.

376

Moral agency is the one capacity that Immanuel Kant considers intrinsically valuable. In his view only rational moral agents have intrinsic value, and they alone are entitled to be treated as ends in themselves.[8] In my view, Kant was right to treat moral agency as a sufficient condition for having full and equal basic moral rights, but wrong to treat it as a necessary condition. There are a number of cases in which we are justified in extending equal moral status to beings who are not moral agents.

First, there are compelling reasons for extending the same basic moral rights to human infants, young children, and mentally disabled persons as to mentally competent adults. Although they may not be capable of moral agency, and in some cases never will be, they are members of human social communities, and their welfare is important to those who care about them. Furthermore, all of us are vulnerable to physical or mental disabilities that can undermine our capacity for moral agency, or our ability to persuade others that we are moral agents. Thus all of us are more secure because of the protections extended to sentient human beings who are temporarily or permanently incapable of moral agency.[9]

Second, there are strong arguments for extending equal moral status to animals whose mental sophistication is exceptional. Chimpanzees and other great apes, cetaceans (dolphins and whales) and elephants possess mental abilities that are far more impressive than formerly believed.[10] It is not coincidental that these highly intelligent animals are also highly endangered by human activities. Highly intelligent animals are likely also to be relatively large and long-lived, and to produce few offspring. Consequently, these animal species are especially vulnerable to human-caused extinction. Their populations cannot withstand much pressure from human hunting or habitat destruction, and once decimated, they take a long time to recover. As I will argue in the next section, this vulnerability provides an additional argument for providing an unusually high level of protection to animals of these species.

Relational properties and moral status

I have argued that four intrinsic properties of organisms – life, sentience, mental sophistication and moral agency – establish a *prima facie* scale of moral status. Other things being equal, sentient beings are entitled to more consideration for their individual interests than are organisms that are nonsentient, such as microbes or plants. Similarly, subjects-of-lives are entitled to more consideration than are simpler sentient beings, such as worms or oysters. And moral agents (human or otherwise) are entitled to full and equal basic moral rights, because of the mutual benefits of nonaggression and cooperation.

But from an environmentalist perspective, it is equally important to recognize that relational properties can influence moral status. J. Baird

Callicott is a prominent interpreter of Aldo Leopold's land ethic. Callicott argues that an organism's moral status depends upon its importance to the social and/or biological communities of which it is part. On this view, we have especially strong moral obligations toward plants and animals of species that are rare and endangered by human activities, and those that are especially vital to the stability, integrity and beauty of the natural ecosystem. Callicott says that

> to hunt and kill a white-tailed deer in certain districts may not only be ethically permissible, it might actually be a moral requirement, necessary to protect the local environment, taken as a whole, from the disintegrating effects of a cervid population explosion. On the other hand, rare and endangered animals like the lynx should be especially nurtured and preserved.[11]

This is an important insight. The restoration of ecosystems which have been damaged by human activities requires that rare and endangered plant and animal species be protected with special care, while plant or animal populations that cause serious damage to the ecosystem may need to be reduced or locally eliminated. Although both deer and lynxes are sentient, and both are probably subjects-of-lives, protecting lynxes is at present a higher priority because they are rare and endangered, while deer are thriving to the point of sometimes endangering the health of the ecosystem.

Callicott argues that social relationships can also alter our moral obligations toward animals. As Mary Midgley points out, human social communities have usually been mixed communities, which include some animals of other species. She argues that animals who are members of our social communities, such as dogs, cats and horses, are entitled to special protections. We owe more to them, as individuals, than to most wild animals.[12] Animals who have been admitted into our social world, and with whom bonds of trust and affection have been established, are entitled to benefits to which wild animals usually are not entitled, including food, protection from predators, and veterinary care (when available and affordable).

I agree that social and ecosystemic relationships can alter our obligations toward nonhuman organisms. However, I do not agree with Callicott's stronger claim, that all of our moral obligations are derived from social and ecosystemic relationships. For instance, I argue that sentient animals which have no positive ecosystemic value, and no social relationships with human beings, still have moral status. For years, elephants in some South African parks have been periodically culled because there were (thought to be) too many for the available territory, and they were damaging acacias and other vegetation. On Callicott's view, the "excess" elephants have no moral status, because they are part of no human social community, and their effects on the ecosystem are predominantly negative. In my view, this does not follow.

Elephants are exceptionally sensitive, social and intelligent creatures, who value their lives and those of their companions. Thus it is important to find non-lethal ways of regulating their populations. There is now an experimental project to control elephant population increases through annual contraceptive injections. If this approach proves successful, then I would argue that it represents a morally better option. It is an option that is worth the sacrifice of some significant, though not basic, human interests – such as the interest in profiting from the sale of elephant hides and meat.

Callicott's skepticism about the moral relevance of sentience, and other intrinsic properties, springs from his denial that intrinsic value is "objective and independent of all valuing consciousness."[13] In his view, there is no such thing as the intrinsic value that an organism has, and would have *even if no-one (else) actually valued it*. If my arguments in the previous four sections are sound, then this skepticism is unnecessary. Living organisms have a good of their own, which represents an intrinsic value for them. Even nonsentient organisms benefit from survival, and are harmed by premature death. Similarly, species benefit from continuation, and are harmed by extinction; and ecosystems benefit from natural biological diversity, and are harmed by its loss. These benefits and harms are real, even when humans fail to treat them as morally significant.

Callicott rejects my approach, which permits both intrinsic and relational properties to influence moral status. He regards this approach as unsatisfactory, because it is more complex and less clear in its implications than a theory which traces all moral obligations to social and ecosystemic relationships. "Ethical eclecticism leads," he says, "to moral incommensurability in hard cases. So we are compelled to go back to the drawing board."[14] My response to this argument is that a theory that denies that life, sentience, mental sophistication and moral agency have any relevance to moral status is implausible. It contradicts a principle which is central to many (though not all) moral codes, i.e. that we may not be cruel to sentient beings, even those that are common and ecosystemically detrimental. It also renders problematic the basis for universal human rights, since it is only in fictional utopias that all human beings constitute a single social community. I think that these problems are serious enough to outweigh the value of increased simplicity.

Yet Callicott is surely right to insist that relational properties are relevant to moral status. We cannot give equal consideration to the interests of all sentient beings, as some animal liberation theories require,[15] because some sentient beings are members of rare and endangered species, while others are common, and dangerous to the lives and health of human beings. Rats are probably just as intelligent as giant pandas – perhaps more so – but it does not follow that their lives deserve equal protection. There are so few giant pandas that the species' survival is in question, despite captive breeding projects in China and elsewhere, and extensive international support. Rats, in contrast, are extremely numerous and possessed of a very high reproductive rate. When rats have been introduced to ecosystems to which they are not native, especially fragile island ecosystems, they have often contributed to the extinction or near-extinction of many indigenous birds and reptiles.[16] Moreover, they often carry pathogenic organisms that are lethal to humans; and they inevitably consume a substantial portion of our food supply, unless their numbers are kept in check. These are morally sound reasons for declining to protect the lives of rats as carefully as those of pandas.

While social and ecosystemic relationships can influence the moral status of nonhuman organisms, it is not clear that such relationships can alter their intrinsic value. I prefer to say that the intrinsic value of an organism depends on its intrinsic properties. I doubt that the intrinsic value of an organism's life – its value to the organism – automatically rises or falls in proportion to its importance to the ecosystem, or its social relationships to human beings. Its moral status, however, may be raised or lowered because of such relationships.

Revising Sterba's principles

If nonhuman organisms differ in moral status, then two of Sterba's three principles, the Self-Defense Principle and the Principle of Disproportionality, will need revision. The Self-Defense Principle permits us to harm nonhuman organisms to protect human beings from harmful aggression. Sterba says that the standard of justified self-defense is higher when the aggressor is human, because there are "more ways effectively to stop aggressive humans than there are to stop aggressive nonhumans" (p. 128). This is an important point, although this reason does not apply to all cases. A more basic reason for setting a higher standard for self-defense against human beings is the mutual value of the mutual restraint of which moral agents are capable.

However, Sterba's Self-Defense Principle neglects an equally important point: that the magnitude of the risk we should be prepared to tolerate in order to avoid harming an organism depends upon the sort of organism it is. For instance, I think it is often a legitimate form of self-defense to kill millions of bacteria, e.g. by washing one's hands. This is true even though the threat which these organisms pose to human well-being, on a given occasion, may be quite modest. Bacteria are nonsentient, ubiquitous, and in no danger of extinction. Consequently, the threat need not be severe and immediate to justify destroying them in large numbers.

The situation is different when the threatening organism is a highly sentient animal, and/or a vital part of the natural ecosystem. I think it would be wrong to kill the voles that have established an underground colony in my front yard, even though I am told that voles sometimes carry the Hanta virus, which can be lethal to human beings. The threat does not seem severe enough to justify killing highly sentient beings, who are probably subjects-of-lives. And I would fight to protect the mountain lions that inhabit the Point Reyes National Seashore next to my home, even though they pose a small threat to human lives, and a larger threat to cats, dogs and livestock. Mountain lions are a vital part of the integrity, stability and beauty of the ecosystem. Because in the past they were hunted to near extinction, there are very few of them in this part of California. For the health of the ecosystem, and for the pleasure of sharing the land with mountain lions, I think we should be willing to endure a modest danger to human beings and domestic animals.

At the same time, I do not believe that mountain lions are entitled to exactly the same right to life that human beings possess. They are not (as far as we can tell) moral agents. We cannot negotiate with them, arriving at mutually binding nonaggression pacts. Thus I think it appropriate to kill individual lions that have repeatedly attacked human beings, pets or livestock. Permanently imprisoning them is not a feasible option, nor one that is clearly more humane; and they cannot be left at large.

Sterba's Principle of Disproportionality also needs modification, to reflect differing human obligations to organisms of different species. As it stands, this principle subjects us to excessively strict restrictions in some cases, and in other cases to restrictions that are not strict enough. It permits us to aggress against the needs of individual organisms, species or ecosystems, to meet only those human needs that are basic. But if a species is common, not native to the ecosystem, unendangered, quick to reproduce, and nonsentient, then I do not think that there is a strong moral objection to harming some of its members for less compelling reasons. For instance, I think it morally permissible to pull common weeds from my garden, just for the pleasure of growing more decorative plants.

On the other hand, if a species is uncommon, vital to the ecosystem, slow to reproduce, and greatly endangered by human activities, then it is imperative to protect as many of its members as possible. If some people are accustomed to meeting their basic needs through exploiting that species, then they may be entitled to compensation for lost income, and assistance in finding other work. They are not, however, automatically entitled to continue exploiting the species at the risk of causing its extinction. We need to stop cutting old growth forests in the Pacific Northwest, even though preserving old growth forests can cost jobs in the short run. Similarly, the international ban on commercial whaling needs to remain in place, even though there are people who would like to earn a living by whaling.[17]

Six principles of moral status

I think that these suggested alterations to two of Sterba's principles are consistent with the spirit of his project. With suitable adjustments for species differences, the three principles make good moral sense. Nevertheless, it is often useful to view the same philosophical ground from several angles. In this spirit, I offer my own principles for the adjudication of conflicts between human and nonhuman interests.[18] These principles represent a summary of the points that I have been making in the previous five sections. The first three principles establish a *prima facie* scale of moral status, based upon morally significant intrinsic properties, while the last three appeal to social and ecosystemic relationships as additional criteria of moral status.

1   *The Respect for Life Principle*: Living organisms are not to be killed or otherwise harmed, without good reasons that do not violate other sound moral principles.

2   *The Avoidance of Cruelty Principle*: Sentient beings are not to be killed or subjected to pain or suffering, unless there is no other feasible way of furthering goals that are:

   (a) consistent with other sound moral principles; and
   (b) important to human beings, or other entities that have a stronger moral status than could be based upon sentience alone.

   The more certain we are of a being's sentience, and the more highly sentient and mentally sophisticated it is, the greater the need must be to warrant harming it.

3   *The Rights of Moral Agents Principle*: Moral agents have full and equal basic moral rights, including the rights to life and liberty.

4   *The Human Rights Principle*: Within the limits of their own capacities, human beings who are capable of sentience but not of moral agency have the same moral rights as do moral agents.

5   *The Interspecific Principle*: Within the limits of principles 1–4, nonhuman members of mixed social communities have a stronger moral status than could be based upon their intrinsic properties alone.

6   *The Ecosystemic Principle*: Living things belonging to species that are important to the ecosystems of which they are part, and that are endangered by human activities, have, within the limits of principles 1–5, a stronger moral status than could be based upon their intrinsic properties alone.

Altruism toward nonhuman life

Before closing, I want to respond to a common objection to the claim that human beings have moral obligations toward nonhuman organisms, species and ecosystems. As Sterba points out, anthropocentric and biocentric ethicists can agree about many specific goals. Because the human species is dependent upon the health of the terrestrial biosphere for its own survival, human interests and the health of the earth's ecosystems will tend to coincide in the long run. Thus, just as there are egoistic reasons for acting as though one cares about other human beings, even if one does not, so there are anthropocentric reasons for acting as if we believe that other living things have moral status, even if we do not. Nevertheless, there are compelling reasons for rejecting the strictly anthropocentric view. Unless we recognize moral obligations to nonhuman life forms, we will be too easily tempted to sacrifice irreplaceable species and habitats for the sake of such short-term goals as jobs, highways or dams.

The solution of local, regional, and global environmental problems requires altruism toward nonhuman life. But is genuine altruism toward nonhuman life possible for human beings? Human beings cannot be compelled by philosophical arguments to accept moral obligations toward entities for which they are psychologically incapable of caring. David Hume believed that, for this reason, we can have no moral obligations to plants, animals, species or ecosystems.[19] However, his own theory of the psychological basis of human morality ought to have led him to question that view.

In Hume's view, the human moral impulse originates in empathy, and other "social sentiments." He argues that it is natural for human beings to care about the people with whom they are socially connected; and that if it were not for these natural sentiments, no amount of rational argument could persuade them to adopt a genuinely moral attitude. But it is equally clear that human beings find it natural to care about the plants, animals, species and ecosystems with which they are acquainted. As E. O. Wilson argues, human beings are "biophilic": given the opportunity, they strongly prefer to live with a rich diversity of plant and animal species, and within healthy ecosystems.[20]

The worldviews of those indigenous peoples of North and South America, Africa, Australia and Asia who have maintained a hunting and gathering economy into modern times provide another argument for the possibility of altruism toward the nonhuman world. Almost invariably these worldviews include a recognition of moral obligations to animals, plants and other portions of the natural world.[21] Often these include entities which most of us would not regard as living, such as mountains, rivers, winds and stones. Although the nonanthropocentric elements of indigenous worldviews may not fit comfortably within our own conceptual frameworks, their ubiquity is powerful evidence that human altruism is capable of crossing the species boundary. If we are psychologically capable of accepting moral obligations to the nonhuman world, then the burden of proof is shifted to those who defend the radically anthropocentric position.

Conclusion

I agree with Sterba that all living organisms have moral status, as do species and ecosystems. I also agree that it is pragmatically necessary to give some preference to human interests over those of most other organisms. However, I think that it is a mistake to assign essentially the same moral status to all nonhuman organisms. Sentience, mental sophistication and moral agency make a difference to what we owe to organisms of diverse species. These intrinsic properties are the best guide that we have to an organism's intrinsic value, i.e. the value of its life to it.

An organism's relationships to its ecosystem, and to human beings, can also influence our obligations toward it. What we owe to organisms of a given species depends not only on their intrinsic properties, but also on their importance to the ecosystems in which they exist. It also depends, in some cases, upon the social relationships established between humans and animals of that species. Domestic dogs and cats may be no more highly sentient or mentally sophisticated than racoons, but we have special obligations to them, based upon the mutually beneficial relationships of trust and affection that link our species to theirs.

These arguments point to the need for a more nuanced theory of the moral status of nonhuman life than Sterba offers. However, the differences between his approach and mine are minor in comparison to the gulf that separates the radically anthropocentric approach characteristic of most Western philosophers from any of the biocentric approaches being developed by environmental ethicists. We need to welcome the proliferation of biocentric ethical theories, and to look, as Sterba advises, for basic points of agreement, as well as for interesting disagreements.

NOTES

1 John Passmore, *Man's Responsibility for Nature* (London: Charles Scribner's Sons, 1974).
2 Albert Schweitzer, *Out of My Life and Time: An Autobiography* (New York: Holt, Rinehart & Winston, 1933); and *The Teaching of Reverence for Life*, trans. Richard and Clara Winston (New York: Holt, Rinehart & Winston, 1965).
3 Paul Taylor, *Respect for Nature: A Theory of Environmental Ethics* (Princeton NJ: Princeton University Press, 1986).
4 All page numbers in the text are from James P. Sterba, *Justice for Here and Now* (Cambridge and New York: Cambridge University Press, 1998).
5 Taylor, pp. 121–3.
6 Tom Regan, *The Case for Animal Rights* (Berkeley: University of California Press, 1983) p. 243.
7 *The Case for Animal Rights*, p. 78.
8 Immanuel Kant, *The Moral Law: Kant's Groundwork of the Metaphysics of Morals*, trans. H. J. Paton (London: Hutchinson, 1948) pp. 96–7.
9 I argue that presentient human fetuses (those younger than about twenty-four weeks) should not have equal basic moral rights, both because they are nonsentient, and because according them equal rights would seriously conflict with the

basic moral rights of women. I also argue that the rights of sentient fetuses, although strong, are limited by women's moral rights to self-defense and physical integrity. See Mary Anne Warren, "The Moral Significance of Birth," *Hypatia*, vol. 4, no. 3 (fall 1989); and chapter 9 of *Moral Status: Our Obligations to Other Living Things* (Oxford: Oxford University Press, 1995).

10 See Mary Anne Warren, "The Moral Status of the Great Apes: Equality or Difference?", and other articles in *Great Apes and Humans at an Ethical Frontier*, edited by Peter Cannell (Washington DC: Smithsonian Institution Press, 2000).

11 J. Baird Callicott, "Animal Liberation: A Triangular Affair," in *In Defense of the Land Ethic: Essays in Environmental Philosophy* (Albany: State University of New York Press, 1989) p. 21.

12 Mary Midgley, *Animals and Why They Matter* (Athens GA: University of Georgia Press, 1983) pp. 112–24.

13 J. Baird Callicott, "Intrinsic Value, Quantum Theory, and Environmental Ethics," in *In Defense of the Land Ethic*, p. 161.

14 J. Baird Callicott, "Animal Liberation and Environmental Ethics: Back Together Again," in *In Defense of the Land Ethic*, p. 50.

15 See Peter Singer, "Animal Liberation," *New York Review of Books*, vol. 23, 1990.

16 See David Quammen, *The Song of the Dodo: Island Biogeography in an Age of Extinctions* (New York: Scribner, 1996).

17 However, there is a reasonable argument for permitting small-scale noncommercial whale hunting by some indigenous peoples who have hunted whales traditionally and consider the activity important to their cultural identity – provided, that is, that the particular species is clearly capable of withstanding this predation.

18 I discuss these principles more extensively in *Moral Status*.

19 David Hume, *Enquiries Concerning Human Understanding and Concerning the Principles of Morals*, edited by L. A. Selby-Bigge and P. H. Nidditch (Oxford: Oxford University Press, 1975) pp. 190–1.

20 Edward O. Wilson, "Biophilia and the Conservation Ethic," in *The Biophilia Hypothesis*, edited by Stephen R. Kellert and Edward O. Wilson (Washington DC: Island Press, 1993).

21 See J. Baird Callicott, *Earth's Insights: A Multicultural Survey of Ecological Ethics from the Mediterranean Basin to the Australian Outback* (Berkeley and Los Angeles: University of California Press, 1994).

Part V

THE APPLICATION OF SOCIAL AND POLITICAL PHILOSOPHY TO NONIDEAL CONDITIONS

Just war theory and pacifism

20

PACIFISM FOR NONPACIFISTS

Robert L. Holmes

With characteristic balance and fairness, James P. Sterba makes a compelling case for abandoning a confrontational and combative way of doing philosophy – the "warmaking" model as he calls it – in favor of a cooperative, "peacemaking" approach. Toward this end he undertakes to effect a reconciliation between pacifism (P) and just war theory (JWT).

I applaud the effort to encourage adoption of a peacemaking model of philosophy, and agree furthermore that, in some sense, it may be possible to reconcile P and JWT. I stress the words "in some sense," however, because it seems to me there are other senses in which that hasn't been shown to be the case, and the reconciliation hasn't in fact been achieved. So I welcome this opportunity to join with Sterba, so to speak, in exploring this issue further.

Let me say at the outset, however, that I shouldn't count a failure to achieve a reconciliation of the two as a failure of the peacemaking conception of philosophy. Part of the aim of peacemaking, if it is understood to include conflict resolution, is to make clear where there are differences and to confront them openly and directly in the hopes of cooperatively resolving whatever problems they generate. Indeed, in the Gandhian conception, conflict is valued for just this reason. So insofar as I point out differences between us on the issue of the relationship between P and JWT, I take that to be in the spirit of philosophical peacemaking rather than opposed to it.

I

Let's begin by asking what it would be to reconcile P and JWT. I assume it wouldn't constitute a reconciliation if one side were to convince the other to give up its position. That might reconcile pacifists and just war theorists as persons, but it would represent the victory, so to speak, of one theory over the other, not a reconciliation of the two. I take reconciliation to imply that the two remain intact (though perhaps modified) but with their differences minimized in some significant way. Another possibility is that P and JWT might be said to be reconciled if one could show that, despite their theoretical differences, the two yield the same conclusions when implemented. That is, one might try to show that they are, so to speak, extensionally equivalent, in that when applied correctly they show precisely the same wars to be permissible and impermissible (in the way, for example, that a realist and anti-realist in ethics, despite their different accounts of the nature of moral judgments, might as a matter of fact agree in their substantive moral judgments). It's not difficult to show how this might in principle be the case.

Let us take *absolute pacifism* (AP) to be the view that all wars, actual and hypothetical, are without exception impermissible, and *absolute warism* (AW)[1] to be the view that all wars, actual and hypothetical, are without exception permissible. Taking "hypothetical" to range over all conceivable wars, few if any persons hold AP or AW in these forms. In any event, AP and AW couldn't be reconciled in the sense of being shown to be extensionally equivalent. AP would judge every conceivable war to be wrong, AW would judge every conceivable war to be permissible. But if we distinguish *conditional pacifism* (CP) and *conditional warism* (CW), we can see that these two theories could be extensionally equivalent. Each will specify the conditions under which war is thought to be impermissible or permissible. The form of each might then be:

CP: All wars, actual and hypothetical, are impermissible under conditions——.

CW: All wars, actual and hypothetical, are permissible under conditions——.

So stated, CP and CW are formal theories that yield a variety of substantive theories depending upon how they are completed. Most of those theories – at least of the sort that have been most often defended – have radically different practical implications (virtually all pacifists think the Gulf War was wrong, at least some just war theorists think it was just, and so on). But with enough tinkering one could complete the blanks in such a way that CP and CW yield precisely the same conclusions. That is, one could design them so as to show the same wars to be permissible and impermissible. As an example (though not a particularly plausible one), CP might be understood to say that all wars that violate the UN Charter are impermissible, and CW might be understood to say that all wars that accord with the UN Charter are permissible. If it is understood in each case that all other wars are respectively permissible and impermissible, these two seemingly different theories – even if they were expressed elliptically as saying respectively "all wars are wrong" and "some wars are just" – would yield the same evaluations in particular cases. Yet on the surface they would seem radically different. Expressed elliptically, one would say "all wars are wrong" and the other would say "some wars are permissible." Such a "reconciliation," however, wouldn't have much practical significance. Most pacifists and just war theorists would simply take issue with the specification of the conditions. If those conditions had the effect of making most or all actual wars permissible, pacifists would object; if they had the effect of making most or all actual wars impermissible, probably just war theorists (at least many of them) would object. Their differences over the permissibility of war would simply shift to the level of the formulations of their respective theories. They would either reject those formulations or deny being pacifists or just war theorists in those senses.

If, however, there were a correct or preferred formulation of each theory, and if it could be shown that P and JWT are extensionally equivalent (or even nearly so) on those formulations, then that would be of importance. For then one could present each side with reasons why it should accept the preferred form. It should then be possible to point out to both that although one is opposed to war and the other in favor of war, the conditions defining P and JWT lead to the same practical evaluations of the justice or injustice of war. If I understand Sterba correctly, this is essentially his tack. He's saying, in effect, that whatever pacifists and just war theorists say in defense of their theories, the morally preferred versions of those theories are extensionally equivalent, or very nearly so. Once pacifists and just war theorists see this, and accept its implications, the reconciliation is achieved.

As it seems uncontroversial to assume that any given war is either permissible or impermissible, it should be possible to formulate a theory that enables us to decide which wars are which, or which at least explains why particular wars are one or the other. That is, it seems uncontroversial to assume that either P or JWT – when properly understood – is the correct theory about the permissibility of war. But now it would be remarkable if both theories were correct, in the sense of leading to virtually the same evaluations, even on their preferred versions. So Sterba's contention is an important one.

II

Sterba proceeds by distinguishing different forms of pacifism, "nonviolent pacifism," "nonlethal pacifism" and "anti-war pacifism," singling out anti-war pacifism (AWP) – the view that "[a]ny participation in the massive use of lethal force in warfare is morally prohibited" (p. 153) – as the preferred type. While I'm unconvinced that nonviolent pacifism has been shown to be incoherent, since he doesn't discuss the issue I won't take it up here. It should simply be noted that AWP hasn't been shown to be the preferred form of P unless it has been shown to be morally preferable to nonviolent pacifism.[2]

In arguing that JWT and AWP can be reconciled, Sterba focusses upon intended and foreseen harm to innocents. He contends that we can in practice distinguish between what is intended and what is foreseen, and that we should favor a differential restriction "that is more severe against the intentional infliction of harm upon innocents but less severe against the infliction of harm that is merely foreseen, over a uniform restriction against the infliction of harm upon innocents that ignores the intended/foreseen distinction" (p. 156). While I agree that we can make the distinction, I'm uneasy with the way in which he draws it. Partly for this reason, I'm unconvinced that a differential restriction is morally preferable to a uniform restriction. Let us consider his reasoning.

He considers the Counterfactual Test for distinguishing between intended and foreseen consequences and finds it wanting. The test asks two questions of acts that have both good and evil consequences:

1   Would you have performed the action if only the good consequences would have resulted and not the evil consequences?
2   Would you have performed the action if only the evil consequences resulted and not the good consequences?

A "yes" to question 1 and a "no" to question 2 supposedly would show that the good consequences are intended and the evil consequences merely foreseen. Following Douglas Lackey,[3] however, Sterba concludes that the test is inadequate in a case like the bombing of Hiroshima, in which the good is the shortening of the war, the evil the killing of civilians. The Counterfactual Test would seem to indicate that the killing of the civilians was merely foreseen, whereas in fact it was "self-evidently a means for shortening the war" (p. 155) (hence, presumably, intended). To remedy this, Sterba adds a Nonexplanation Test:

3   Does the bringing about of the evil consequences help explain why the agent undertook the action as a means to the good consequences?

If the answer is "no", then the evil consequence is merely foreseen; if it's "yes" then it's "an intended means to the good consequences." This supposedly gives the correct result in the Hiroshima case by showing the killing of civilians to have been intended.[4]

But let's now look at the use that's made of the distinction between intended and foreseen consequences. This brings us to Sterba's argument for a differential restriction (recognizing and attaching moral weight to the distinction between intended and foreseen consequences) rather than a uniform restriction (which presumably either doesn't recognize the distinction or doesn't attach moral weight to it).

From the standpoint of innocents suffering the harm, he asks: "Don't those who suffer harm have more reason to protest when the harm is done to them by agents who are directly engaged in causing harm to them than when it is done incidentally by agents whose ends and means are good?" (p. 156). And from the perspective of those causing the harm, he says

> it would seem that we have more reason to protest a restriction against foreseen harm than we do to protest a comparable restriction against intended harm. This is because a restriction against foreseen harm limits our actions when our ends and means are good, whereas a restriction against intended harm only limits our actions when our ends or means are evil or harmful.
>
> (p. 156)

He concludes:

> Consequently, because we have more reason to protest when we are being used by others than when we are being affected by them only incidentally, and because we have more reason to act when both our ends and means are good than when they are not, we should favor the foreseen/intended distinction that is incorporated into just means.
>
> (p. 156)

So the argument thus far is for placing a more severe restriction upon the intentional harming of innocents than upon the merely foreseeable harming of them.

But the more severe restriction isn't an absolute one. Sterba believes that consequentialist considerations hold sway here. Such harm is permissible when it's trivial ("stepping on someone's foot to get out of a crowded subway"), easily reparable ("lying to a temporarily depressed friend to keep her from committing suicide") or greatly offset by consequences, particularly to innocents ("shooting one of two hundred civilian hostages to prevent, in the only way possible, the execution of all two hundred") (p. 157). Notice that although Sterba usually uses the term "harm" when speaking of consequences for innocents, it's clear from some of his examples that his concern extends to the permissibility of both harming and killing. Thus the analysis of the intended/foreseen distinction, and the detailing of its bearing upon the relevant moral issues, is presumed to show – in a way that supposedly should be acceptable to advocates of both AWP and JWT – that:

1 There is a more severe restriction against intentionally harming or killing innocents than against merely doing so foreseeably.
2 It is sometimes morally permissible to foreseeably harm or kill innocents when it would be wrong to do so intentionally.

3   Despite the more severe restriction, it is also morally permissible to harm or kill innocents intentionally when that harm is greatly out-weighed by the consequences, especially to other innocents.

As a minor point, it should be noted that item 2 doesn't follow from item 1. There might be a less severe restriction against merely harming innocents foreseeably than against doing so intentionally, but one that is still suffi-ciently severe to prohibit the actual harming of innocents. All that clearly follows from 1 is that it's morally worse to kill innocents intentionally than to do so foreseeably. And one action can be morally worse than another even though both are wrong (torturing someone to death is worse than wrong-fully giving him a painless but lethal injection). Let us assume, however, that if 1 is true, then 2 is true also. Then it will presumably be easier to justify harming or killing innocents where that is a merely foreseen outcome of what one does. The consequentialist consideration in 3 is sufficient (and perhaps even necessary) to justify harming or killing them when one does so intentionally. Sterba apparently believes there is no reason to think that advocates of AWP would reject these conclusions.

III

As a pacifist who has argued against the moral permissibility of war precisely on the grounds that war inevitably kills innocent people and such killing hasn't been shown to be justified, I am troubled by theses 1 through 3, but I shall concentrate on 1. Granted there is a distinction between intended and foreseen consequences, the problem is with the differential as opposed to the uniform restriction.

The reasoning for favoring the differential restriction, once again, involves looking at the matter, first, from the standpoint of the innocents to be harmed and, second, from the standpoint of those doing the harming. Those harmed supposedly have more reason to protest "when the harm is done to them by agents who are directly engaged in causing harm to them than when it is done incidentally by agents whose ends and means are good" (I take it that being "directly engaged in causing harm" here means that the harm is intentional). Those causing the harm have more reason to protest the restriction against foreseen than against intended harm,

> because a restriction against foreseen harm limits our actions when our ends and means are good, whereas a restriction against in-tended harm only limits our actions when our ends or means are evil or harmful, and it would seem that we have stronger grounds for acting when both our ends and means are good than when they are not.
>
> (p. 156)

My first concern is with the apparently equal weight attached to the two alleged grounds for protest. Innocents are protesting being harmed or killed. Those proposing to cause the injury or death are protesting a limitation of their freedom to harm or kill innocents. These don't seem comparable. Surely innocent persons have far stronger grounds to protest being harmed (for the sake of simplicity, I'll speak for the most part of harm, taking it to include being killed) – whether intentionally or foreseeably – than perpetrators of injury or death have to protest being prevented from foreseeably harming innocent persons. Indeed, I would turn the matter around. Knowingly killing innocent persons against their will is presumptively wrong if anything is. If it can be justified at all – and I'm not sure that it can – it requires a compelling justification. On the other hand, having one's harmful or lethal conduct toward innocent persons restricted in the manner indicated (to include prohibiting foreseeable as well as intended harm), isn't presumptively wrong. In fact, such a restriction would seem presumptively right. In the absence of further assumptions, no-one has grounds to protest a moral restriction upon their infliction of harm upon innocents. But even in the absence of further assumptions, every innocent person has grounds to protest knowingly being harmed by others (and even for unknowingly being harmed where that is a result of negligence). In other words, there's a moral asymmetry between the considerations appealed to in deciding the issue of how to assess the relative weights of intended and foreseen harms to innocents.

Moreover, those suffering harm are said to have more reason to protest when the harm is done intentionally "than when it is done incidentally by agents whose ends and means are good." And regarding those protesting limitations of their maleficent actions it is said that "it would seem that we have stronger grounds for acting when both our ends and means are good than when they are not."

In both of these cases the means as well as the ends in question are described as good. Moreover, in the former case, the resultant harm – when merely foreseeable – is said to be only incidental. The supposed goodness of means and ends, and the incidental character of the harm, contributes to whatever plausibility the differential restriction may be thought to have. Leaving the postulated goodness of the end unchallenged, I should like to question the ascription of goodness to the means and the use of the label "incidental" to characterize the harm to innocents.

When you knowingly harm innocent persons in pursuit of a good end – even if the infliction of such harm isn't your intention – you're adopting means that cause harm, injury, or death. It's this which, by hypothesis, constitutes the evil consequence of acts in cases of the sort under consideration. The question, then, concerns what justification there is for calling the means in question good (unless one assumes that a good end somehow makes the means to it good as well). If one wanted to describe *bad* means to a good end, one could hardly do better than to describe means that involved harming innocent persons. My point is that there are obvious grounds for calling the means in question bad and no obvious grounds for calling them good. If we're to accept the characterization of them as good, there needs to be some compelling argument to that conclusion.

Let me turn now to the second element in the characterization. It holds that the foreseen harm or death to innocents is only incidental. This I take to be a separate point from the preceding one. Harms might be incidental whether or not the means with which they're associated are good. And I think it's plausible to say, as Sterba does, that sometimes such harms might be incidental. But are they incidental in the sorts of cases he describes? Is a foreseeable outcome incidental solely by virtue of the fact that it wasn't brought about intentionally? And if those harms are incidental, does that support the judgment that those harmed have fewer grounds for protest than they would if the harms were intended (if, as Sterba maintains, they have more grounds for protest if the harms are intended, then it follows that they have fewer grounds for protest if they're merely foreseeable)? Let us take these questions in turn.

Are the harms or deaths in question incidental in the sort of case Sterba describes? They certainly aren't incidental in the example to try to show that the prohibition against intentionally killing innocents isn't absolute. That example, recall, is the shooting of one of 200 (presumably innocent) civilian hostages to prevent, "in the only way possible," the execution of all 200. It looks here as though killing the one is the means to saving the remaining 199.[5] To be sure, Sterba uses this example to show the permissibility of sometimes intentionally killing innocent persons and not to argue for the differential restriction. But the example lends itself to the other sort of case as well. If the only way possible to prevent the execution of the 199 is to shoot a beer can off a fence post, and the designated hostage is strapped to the fence post, then one foreseeably kills the hostage even though the intention is only to save the 199. But it would strain credibility to call the killing either good or incidental.

Be that as it may, let us now look at some of the hypothetical cases Sterba cites to which the intended/foreseen distinction is directly relevant.

1   "only the intentioned or foreseen killing of an unjust aggressor would prevent one's own death" (p. 158).
2   "only the intentioned or foreseen killing of an unjust aggressor and the foreseen killing of one innocent bystander would prevent one's own death and that of five other innocent people."
3   "only the intentioned or foreseen killing of an unjust aggressor and the foreseen killing of one innocent bystander would prevent the death of five innocent people."

4   "only the intentioned or foreseen killing of an unjust aggressor and the foreseen killing of five innocent people would prevent the death of two innocent people."

5   "only the intentioned or foreseen killing of an unjust aggressor would prevent serious injury to oneself and/or five other innocent people" (p. 159).

6   "only the intentioned or foreseen infliction of serious harm upon an unjust aggressor and the foreseen infliction of serious harm upon one innocent bystander would prevent serious harm to oneself and five other innocent people."

7   "only the intentioned or foreseen infliction of serious harm upon an unjust aggressor and the foreseen infliction of serious harm upon one innocent bystander would prevent serious harm to five other innocent people."

8   "only the intentioned or foreseen killing of an unjust aggressor and the foreseen killing of one innocent bystander would prevent serious injuries to the members of a much larger group of innocent people."

Case 1 is one of personal self-defense, in which the infliction of harm or death upon an innocent person isn't at issue; and two others – 4 and 8 – are cases in which Sterba thinks, and I agree, that the killing of innocents wouldn't be justified.

In each of the remaining cases it's said that only the act against the aggressor *and* the foreseen harming or killing of innocents would prevent the harm in question. Anything less won't achieve one's end. If, knowing this, one then harms/kills the innocent person(s), it would seem as though the bringing about of those consequences "helps explain why the agent undertook the action as a means to the good consequences." But this, by the Nonexplanation Test, would render those consequences part of what is intended. If, to take case 3 above, you know that the only way to save five innocent people is to kill two people, one of them innocent, and you make it your end to save the five, then killing the innocent person is part of the explanation of why you performed the act you did. If asked to explain why you killed that person, you'd surely answer that you thought you had to in order to save the five. Had you done anything less you wouldn't have achieved your aim. It would appear, then, that by the Nonexplanation Test, the killing of the innocent person is intended. Now that may be a reason for re-examining the Nonexplanation Test as a way of sorting out intended from foreseen consequences. One might want to argue that the innocent death is still, as hypothesized, merely foreseen. Be that as it may, the death isn't incidental, even though it wasn't intended. It was inextricably bound up with the indispensable means to one's end and by hypothesis was known to be such.

But suppose there were a good argument to show that these harms or deaths are nonetheless, in some meaningful sense, incidental. Would that show that those harmed or killed have less reason to protest what is done to them than if it were intentional? It's hard to see why. If what's at issue is whether you have less reason to protest foreseen than intended harm to yourself, then it shouldn't make any difference what the intention is when the harm is merely foreseen. If it's something about an outcome's being merely foreseen that's relevant, then I should have less reason to protest being foreseeably harmed or killed even when the accompanying intention is bad. Consider three cases, in one of which the intention is bad, in two of which it's arguably good.

1   You're a student about to detonate a bomb in the car of a professor who gave you a bad grade, when I unexpectedly get in the car with the professor. Your intention is to avenge the bad grade but you foresee that in so doing you'll kill me as well.

Do I have less reason to protest your killing me simply by virtue of the fact that your intention isn't to kill me but to kill the other person? And would you have more reason to protest a restriction against harming me simply on the grounds that the harm is merely foreseen and not intended? I think not in either case.

2   You're about to detonate a bomb in the car of a person about to go steal candy from a baby, when I unexpectedly get in the car with the person. Your intention is to prevent the theft of candy but you foresee that you'll kill me in the process.

Here the intention is arguably good, even though both the chosen means and the foreseeable consequence are bad. Do I have less reason to protest your killing me simply by virtue of the fact that your intention isn't to kill me but to prevent a theft? And would you have more reason to protest a restriction against merely foreseeably harming me than one against intending to harm me? It's doubtful.

3   You're about to detonate a bomb in a car of a person about to assassinate the mayor, when I unexpectedly get in the car with the person. Your intention is to prevent the assassination, but you foresee that you'll kill me in the process.

Here again the intention is arguably good and of greater moment than in case 2. The means are at best problematic. But the foreseeable consequence of killing me is clearly bad. Again, I should maintain that I have as much grounds for protesting your killing me as I would if it were intentional, and that you have not one whit more grounds to protest a restriction against killing me simply because my death is merely foreseeable, than you would if it were intentional.

If we're accurately to assess the respective merits of a differential restriction as opposed to a uniform restriction – and if the matter is to be decided by abstract hypothetical cases – then we shouldn't limit our concern to cases in which the intended ends and means are as pure as snow and the resultant harm merely incidental. There are those cases, to be sure. But there are as many others in which that isn't the case. Indeed, for every hypothetical case one can design in which the intended means and ends in the foreseeable harming of innocents are good, one can design another in which they aren't. And if it's our "intuitions" about such cases that are thought to be relevant, they seem to go in one direction at least as often as in the other. If this is correct, then while there is certainly a distinction between intended and foreseen consequences, the moral weight Sterba and just war theorists would attach to it hasn't been established. This doesn't show that it can't be established, though I doubt that it can. It shows only that the considerations centering around grounds for protest on the part of perpetrators and victims of harm to innocents don't suffice to establish it.

Suppose, however, that the differential weights to intended and foreseen consequences in the sorts of cases Sterba characterizes could be established? Would that bolster the case for JWT? I want to suggest reasons for thinking it would not.

IV

The reasons center about the fact that the cases Sterba characterizes all appear to involve interpersonal relations and, by implication, to deal with the actions of one agent. Case 1 sets the tone. It's the case of personal self-defense in which "only the intentional or foreseen killing of an unjust aggressor would prevent one's own death." Case 2 likewise is one of personal self-defense enlarged to include defense of five others. In the remaining cases personal self-defense drops out, but in each case it sounds as though we're talking about the killing of *an* individual aggressor and doing so to prevent death or injury to varying numbers of other individuals (five at most, except in case 8 where reference is to a "much larger group"). Just as there is a major leap from the permissibility of personal self-defense to the permissibility of war, so there is a major leap from the affirmed conclusions (assuming they could be established) in each of the other cases to the permissibility of war. As Sterba characterizes AWP, its opposition is to "any participation in the massive use of lethal force in warfare." So, the question is whether we can make the transition from killing in the sorts of cases Sterba hypothesizes – even assuming such killing is permissible – to killing in the sorts of cases of concern to advocates of AWP. It's this transition that I want to question.

401

As this issue is more complex than I can deal with adequately here, I shall only focus upon two aspects of it. I shall argue that *even if* one were to concede Sterba's analysis regarding intended and foreseen consequences in the sorts of cases he describes, there would be compelling grounds for adopting pacifism. But this pacifism would be of a sort that nonpacifists in the other senses could embrace; hence, in a sense, what I shall present is a pacifism for nonpacifists. To give it a label, I shall call it liberal-democratic pacifism, or Liberal Pacifism (LP) for short.

The first aspect I want to focus upon is simply a conceptual point. It's one that's obvious once stated, but it's rarely stated directly so that it's implications become clear. It is

A1 War is a cooperative undertaking between warring parties.

This I take to be true of any war, actual or hypothetical. And by "war" I mean war in a standard sense, as the attempt by two or more states to achieve their objectives by the use of organized, systematic military violence. One would think that warring parties would be the last ones to cooperate, but that's not always so. Paradoxical as it seems, in every war it's as though a tacit agreement has been made by both sides to try to settle their conflict by violence. It follows from this

2   If either side refuses to fight, war cannot take place.

This again is obvious, once one thinks about it. One side can still assault the other and inflict death and destruction. That's aggression, to be sure. But it doesn't constitute war. Both sides have to fight in order for war to take place.[6] Now the following proposition doesn't apply to all conceivable wars; one could imagine a war in which all the fighters on both sides are equal in authority and all decision-making is by consensus or democratic vote (as, for example, it might be in some small guerrilla bands today). But it almost certainly applies to war in any standard sense, and to virtually every war that is waged in the modern period. It also arguably applies to virtually every war that is likely to be waged in future.

3   For both sides to cooperate in fighting:

(a) Some persons must *command* others to kill; and
(b) Some persons must *obey* those commands.

Armies are hierarchical, authoritarian institutions. Some persons have authority and control over others. Those persons issue commands and others obey commands. Indeed obedience is essential to the efficient operation of any army, even one made up of volunteers. From this we can conclude:

Therefore:

4 If enough people on either side refuse to kill on command, or to command others to kill, war cannot take place.

If this is correct, then starting from what I take to be incontrovertible conceptual points in 1 and 2, and an empirical claim in 3 that is almost certainly true of all – or virtually all – modern wars in any standard sense, we reach another empirical claim in 4 that has at least as much certainty as 3.

Now the point here is that Sterba's examples say nothing about armies, conscription, command structures and obedience, not to mention tanks, planes, bombs, missiles and nuclear weapons as the means by which to wage war, and weapons factories and militarized economies by which to support the whole enterprise. Yet these must be factored in if we are to make the transition from the sorts of cases he describes to the case of war as actually contemplated and waged. Why? Because they all introduce considerations that are morally relevant at the macro level that typically don't apply at the micro level.

So let us return to the moral issues, again with another conceptual point.

B1 For war to be *fully justified* morally, both sides would have to be justified in fighting.

If we compare war with other sorts of contests – from chess to bingo to basketball – we find that these other activities can be seen to be fully justified (granting a few relatively unproblematic assumptions) because it's perfectly permissible for both (or all) sides to be engaged in them. For war to have that kind of justification it would have to be the case that both sides are in the right. However,

2 Both sides cannot be morally justified in fighting.

By this I mean both sides can't be objectively justified – that is, can't be doing what is objectively permissible; not that both might not think they're justified (which often happens) and not even that both might not have good evidence that they're justified (which probably doesn't often happen but could happen). If this is correct, then:

3 War cannot be fully justified morally.

Standard JWT implicitly recognizes this when it says that a war cannot be just on both sides.

This means that when we talk about a "just war" we don't mean a war that is just throughout. We don't mean a war in which the whole of the activity that both sides are engaged in is just. We mean a war that is just on one side only and unjust on the other. Thus we can narrow our focus:

C1 For war to be *just*, one side must be justified in fighting, the other not.

The assumption here, which again underlies standard JWT, is that although a war can be unjust on both sides, it can't be just on both sides (though there can be degrees of justice on both sides). The very considerations that would render one side in the right would render the other in the wrong, and vice-versa.

Now here we can formulate a substantive difference between pacifists and just war theorists. Using just war categories, we may say that just war theorists typically think that there are some wars – perhaps many – in which one side is just and the other unjust; whereas the pacifists typically think (or would think, if putting it in just war theoretic terms) that virtually all wars (actual, not hypothetical) are unjust on both sides. Now can these views be reconciled? I think not. For if, now, we bring moral categories to bear upon the considerations brought out in A, we can say:

2   For one side to be justified in fighting:
     (a) Some persons must be justified in commanding others
          to kill; and
     (b) Some persons must be justified in killing on command.

That is, once we look at the inner structure of war systems – even in general outline, as in A – it seems clear that if one side is to be justified in the massive use of violence to achieve its ends, at the very least it must be possible to justify the command-and-obedience structure of the institution whose business it is to do the killing. This, again, I take to be relatively unproblematic. But the following isn't unproblematic:

3   No one has a right to command others to kill, and no one is justified in killing on command.

Before making a few points of clarification, let us note the continuation of the argument to the liberal pacifist conclusion.

Therefore:
4   Neither side is justified in fighting.

Therefore:
5   No war is just.

In the context of which I'm speaking (that is, of modern nation-states with armies waging war in a standard sense), those who are commanded to kill *typically* are put into that position involuntarily. Most nations draft young people for the military. Even a country like the United States cannot count on enough volunteers in wartime to provide it with the army thought necessary. There was a draft during the Civil War, World War I, World War II, the Korean War and the Vietnam War. While there is at present no draft in the US, the Selective Service System is in place, and draft notices reportedly would go out in a matter of days if it were deemed necessary in an emergency. But a draft by its nature represents involuntary servitude. And in the US and most (though not all) countries it's discriminatory as well, singling out young males to bear a disproportionate part of the burden of waging the government's wars.

Now while I think that C3 is correct, its defense would require more space than is available here. So I shall merely point out that *if* C3 is correct, then a liberal democratic society cannot wage war in the modern world. The social, political, and economic structures it must keep in place even to maintain readiness for war are incompatible with such a society. The toll that it takes of human liberty is simply too great. Any country that relies upon conscription is imposing involuntary servitude upon its young people, and, in a country like the US, discriminatory servitude as well. And this, I should maintain, is incompatible with a free and open democratic society. Thus I would say that even if one has no principled objection to killing, and even if one were to accept the permissibility of killing innocents in the sorts of cases Sterba describes – that is, even if one weren't a "pacifist" on these issues – it doesn't follow either that one is justified in compelling others to kill or that one is justified in killing at the command of others. If this is so, then if one seriously honors the principles of a free and open society, one has grounds, and I should say compelling grounds, for being a liberal pacifist.

Are there grounds here for yet saying that there is a reconciliation of P and JWT? Not many, perhaps. But there's one that may provide promising soil for attempting to achieve a reconciliation. It involves shifting the focus of the debate. If both have a commitment to the values of a liberal democratic society, then they can join together in tracing out the implications of that commitment for the issue of whether war in the modern world can be justified. If they should be led to the conclusion of argument C, then the just war theorist could cling to their convictions about the justifiability of killing – including killing innocents in some of the sorts of cases Sterba outlines – but would have to give up the central claim about the extension of such killing to the level of warfare; and the pacifist could settle for seeing war fade from the repertoire of free societies but without necessarily having convinced anyone of its inherent wrongness. If the pacifist seems to get the better of this "reconciliation," so be it. What's important is that they both end up with the correct position.

NOTES

1 Taking the term "warism" from Duane Cady. See his *From Warism to Pacifism* (Philadelphia: Temple University Press, 1989).
2 I concentrate on anti-war pacifism in my *On War and Morality* because it seems to me that war can be shown to be wrong without assuming a commitment to nonviolence, even though a commitment to nonviolence entails holding that war is wrong.
3 Douglas Lackey, "The Moral Irrelevance of the Counterforce/Countervalue Distinction," *The Monist*, vol. 70 (1987) pp. 255–76.
4 It's worth noting that Sterba's account is at variance with standard formulations of the Doctrine of Double Effect, which has a separate condition preventing one from doing evil, even if merely foreseen, so that good may come of it. The evil consequence can't, in other words, be causally necessary to the production of the good (which would, in Sterba's terms, make it part of the explanation of why the agent performed the act). Whereas traditional DDE allows that merely foreseen consequences can play this role, Sterba's account entails that any consequence playing that role (hence part of the explanation of why the act was performed) becomes part of what was intended, not merely foreseen.
5 Hair-splitters may want to note that killing the one hostage can't prevent all 200 from being executed because killing the one itself constitutes an execution. If, on the other hand, one were to say that it doesn't constitute an execution – or if one took "execution" to cover only execution at the hands of others – then it would no longer be true that killing the one is the only way possible to prevent the execution of the 200, since one could kill them all oneself. While relatively unimportant to this case, this point is of considerable importance in many of the problems centering around the distinction between killing and letting die.
6 I'm not talking about a legal state of war, which can exist without fighting once a declaration of war has been made, but war itself.

Civil disobedience and revolutionary action

21

THE MORAL SELF IN THE FACE OF INJUSTICE

Laurence Thomas

If I am to die by the bullet of a madman, I must do so smiling. There must be no anger within me. God must be in my heart and on my lips.

(Mahatma Gandhi)

The theoretical arguments for equality are most compelling. If respect can be, or could come to be, demanded of an individual, then surely that very same individual can be accorded respect. There is no biological feature of any human being which contravenes this consideration. Men and women cannot demand respect of one another and, with any justification, refuse to accord respect to one another simply on account of gender differences alone. Likewise for blacks and whites or, in general, any two ethnic or racial groups. Indeed, the same holds for sexual orientation, whether or not this has a biological basis. Heterosexuals cannot demand respect of homosexuals and then, with any justification, refuse to accord them respect, and conversely, where sexual orientation alone is the basis for the refusal to accord respect.

James Sterba has perhaps made the case for equality, across diversity, more forcefully and eloquently than any other contemporary philosopher. At the very least, justice demands equality with respect to the basic rights of society. There is no getting around this truth. Unfortunately, though, this truth does not address a very pressing question, to wit: What should be done if a society fails to accord the basic rights to a particular group of its citizens? Since the non-violent protests against the British by Mahatma Gandhi in India, and the Civil Rights Movement that took place in the United States in the late 1950s and early 1960s, civil disobedience has been widely recognized as an appropriate way for individuals to protest injustices which they must endure in their very own society. In his work *A Theory of Justice*, John Rawls appears to have adequately captured the moral significance of civil disobedience from a philosophical perspective when he noted that civil disobedience is an appeal to the moral conscience (or sense of justice, to use his terminology) of the fellow citizens of society. Surely, it seems that Martin Luther King Jr understood the civil disobedience that he advocated in precisely this way.

But there is something paradoxical here. If a society has systematically refused to accord the full complement of basic rights to a group of its citizens, why would protests of civil disobedience by members of this deprived group suffice to move the society to accord these citizens the full complement of rights? And if it takes no more than civil disobedience, then why is it needed in the first place? That is, if group X judges group Y not to be worthy of certain basic rights, why would acts of civil disobedience by Ys suffice to move Xs to regard Ys as now being worthy of the basic rights in question, as opposed to its happening, instead, that their opinion of Ys as moral low-life is mightily reinforced by the very acts of civil disobedience in which Ys engage? After all, the systematic violation of basic rights cannot be attributed to an oversight, but only to a willfulness to treat certain others as inferior. It is, for instance, never a surprised discovery among the citizens of a society that certain of its members are not allowed to vote. It does not seem that civil disobedience would suffice to change this willfulness if what that means is that civil disobedience succeeds by appealing to the moral conscience of society-at-large. When members of society are systematically denied some or all of the basic rights, precisely what seems to be absent, in the first place, is a sufficiently developed moral conscience toward the individuals in question which their acts of civil disobedience might awaken.

In *The Demands of Justice*, Sterba writes

> it should be clear that accepting an ideal of justice as fairness re-
> quires a person to make a considerable sacrifice for the sake of the
> basic welfare of others.

While I fully share Sterba's view, I believe that, barring certain conditions, people are not naturally disposed to make such sacrifices, and that the reason for this has to do with experiencing the other as a moral person; for, as the existence of evil behavior makes abundantly clear, we do not have the appropriate moral sentiments toward other individuals just because they are persons. This is especially so when the other is an individual who belongs to a group that (seemingly) can be defined in sharp contradistinction to our own and where we believe that our group is superior (it not being a given that we must believe that our group is superior).

Drawing upon both Plato and Aristotle, and then an insight from Kant regarding self-respect, the view that I shall defend here is that civil disobedience succeeds not so much by appealing to the moral conscience of society-at-large, but by forcing society to take the civil disobedient seriously. This they do by forcing society-at-large to bear witness to their dignity. I begin with a little history.

I History: morally noble behavior

In *The Jewish War*, the great historian Flavius Josephus reports the following:

> Thus Pilate declared to them [the Jews] that he would have them all slaughtered if they did not accept the flags of [Rome], and he commanded his soldiers to ready themselves by pulling their swords. Upon hearing these words, the Jews en masse threw themselves to the ground, as if this had been planned, and presented their throats to Pilate, crying better that we are killed than that we should violate our holy laws. Their moral stance and the ardent zeal for their religious convictions occasioned such admiration on Pilate's part that he ordered his soldiers to take the flags out of Jerusalem.

If any thing is true, it is true that in this situation, the Jews succeeded in commanding the respect of Pilate. How did they do that? The answer, quite simply, is that they made it unmistakably clear that they embraced values for which they were willing to die. Of course, Pilate could very well have regarded them as fools for being willing to take such a stance. Still, there is no getting around the fact that by the very action of offering their throats they thereby made it impossible for Pilate to hold the threat of death over them. They irrevocably diffused that threat.

The Jews displayed a moral power that Pilate could not ignore; though, to be sure, he need not have responded in the positive way that he did. For instance, he could have become absolutely livid over the fact that they had so effectively diffused his threat of death. And that he did not is surely to his credit. Just so, I think that it would be a mistake to regard Pilate's not becoming angry with them as merely an accident of history. Even if it is true that all sentient creatures naturally avoid circumstances that they sense will bring about their death, only human beings can both value life and, at the very same time, hold that it is worth adhering to some values even if this should mean a loss of their life. And I submit that when a person exhibits with grace behavior which starkly exemplifies the latter value, as Josephus informs us that these Jews did, then it is extremely difficult not to experience the individual's behavior as morally noble – and not merely quintessentially human. It seems to me that Hitler was well aware of this and strove hard to reduce the Jews to such a state of utter despair and fearfulness that it was very nearly impossible for Jews interned therein to exhibit any morally noble values.

It can be understandable that a person begs for mercy or pity – a form of behavior that is quintessentially human. Yet begging does not constitute morally noble behavior, no matter what the context. Not even a mother's begging that her child be spared an unjust death, as with Sophie in Styron's *Sophie's Choice*, stands as morally noble behavior. It is in this context that one must appreciate Pilate's reaction. It is true that he could have become angry; however, it is no mere accident that he did not. He was standing face-to-face with morally noble behavior; and this caught him quite by surprise, since he surely expected the fear of death to get the better of them.

I want now to look briefly at a display of morally noble behavior that comes from an entirely different direction. One of the great ironies of American history is that those who penned some of the greatest language of equality ever written were also slaveholders. Who better illustrates the Faustian doctrine of the divided self than the slaveholders who wrote the following words:

> We hold these Truths to be self-evident, that all Men are created equal, that they are endowed by their Creator with certain unalienable Rights, that among these are Life, Liberty, and the Pursuit of Happiness.
>
> (The Declaration of Independence)

My own view is that the obvious discrepancy between these words and the deeds of slavery is perhaps more explicable than one is initially inclined to suppose.

In the same document, these authors also noted there comes a time when people have suffered such egregious injustices that "it is their Right, it is their Duty, to throw off such Government, and to provide new Guards for their future Security." And the last paragraph includes the following words: "we solemnly Publish and Declare, That these United Colonies are, and of Right ought to be, Free and Independent States: that they are absolved from all Allegiance to the British Crown." When one considers that at the time the British Empire was the greatest military power on earth, this stance of the colonies can only be seen as sheer hubris. It also constitutes morally noble behavior. Why they might have ever thought that they would have prevailed against it is a mystery. But when a fledgling people is prepared to stand up to the greatest power on earth, it seems reasonable to suppose that they are rather besotted with the conviction that insofar as a people is worthy of liberty they must be prepared to die for liberty. And it is this morally noble behavior that the black slaves did not display.

It goes without saying, of course, that there is a perfectly good explanation for why blacks may not have been prepared to die for their freedom. They arrived entirely emaciated as a result of the most grueling and inhuman journeys a human being could be forced to take. Quite simply, the Middle Passage was an utterly traumatizing experience. And one does not reasonably expect morally noble behavior of traumatized individuals. The colonists could not have rightly expected morally noble behavior of slaves arriving off the ships; and subsequent treatment of slaves most certainly did not ameliorate matters. Besides, one naturally thinks, why should displays of morally noble behavior be a prerequisite for treating a person justly? After all, human beings should be treated justly in virtue of their humanity, and not in virtue of other things that they do.

Once again, the Holocaust is very illuminating in this regard. For what the concentration camps show quite poignantly is that if we can get human beings to act in so-called subhuman ways, then such subhuman behavior can itself be a powerful barrier to others being humanely responsive toward them in the absence of powerful independent considerations of commitment. Just as compassion is not called forth by any set of circumstances whatsoever, humaneness is not as well. If a person is lying unconscious in her own feces and blood, that may repulse me mightily, although I am painfully aware of the fact that rudimentary medical attention is what they need and that, moreover, I am a physician who can provide that attention. That is, rather than being moved by compassion to help such a person, bringing myself to help them may require overcoming enormous feelings of disgust.

From the outset, there were no independent considerations of commitment that inclined slavemasters to be humanely responsive to blacks. And the tormented condition in which blacks arrived upon American soil did nothing to arrest whites from their shameful attitude toward blacks. These remarks neither excuse slavemasters nor blame blacks. Had Jews accepted the flags of Rome, as Pilate had ordered them to do, they would not have been blameworthy for having done so, as they were in no position to withstand the might of Rome. From this, though, it does not follow that there would not have been any morally noble behavior in which they could have engaged which would have bettered their situation. For there was, namely the very behavior in which they in fact engaged. Likewise, had blacks resisted slavery in a morally noble way when they arrived, this might have very well have made a difference for the better, although it is ever so understandable why they did not.

One thing is clear: If in the name of justice the blacks brought over had in unison refused to work as slaves, even if this meant their death, then slavery would not have survived. An obstreperous slave does not make for a good slave; and this holds *a fortiori* for a dead slave. This is true although no blame whatsoever need accrue to blacks for failing to so behave. Still, and perhaps this is the more poignant point, had blacks en masse so behaved, then the white slaveholders would not have had an easy way of differentiating between themselves and blacks. Blackness and whiteness would not have come to be the asymmetrical moral markers that they came to be, with whiteness being regarded as morally superior to blackness. We must bear in mind that equality, as we now understand it, is in fact a very modern idea promoted by the Enlightenment thinkers, Rousseau and Kant in particular. It was the genius of Rousseau and Kant that removed the chains of natural inequality that Aristotle forged. Against this backdrop, the absence of a dramatic display of dignity may have been more of an impediment to appreciating the humanity of blacks arriving upon the soil of the United States than we would surely like to suppose or, given our present vantage point, can even appreciate. To suppose that rationality alone could have delivered the desired results, is to attach far more weight to rationality alone yielding the right moral results than the history of ideas warrants.

II The moral sentiments

In the spirit of Kantian moral philosophy, I believe that all human beings are owed justice in virtue of their humanity. However, the unvarnished truth is that individuals do not always get what they are owed and that, in some instances, they will get what they are owed only if they themselves seize the initiative to obtain it. Unfortunately, justice is not an exception to this truth. More specifically in this regard, I do not believe that ratiocination will always deliver the right moral attitude toward those whom we do not regard as being worthy of the basic moral rights. For having the right moral attitude toward others is itself often a reflection of the kinds of feelings that they can engage in our life. And the history of ideas would seem to support these remarks. Though surely there must be such a case, I am not aware of any instance where major injustices against a people, which had been in place over the years, were voluntarily corrected by those in power simply because they came to see the error of their ways after much reflection.

If, for example, compassion and shame are natural moral sentiments, history makes it abundantly clear that neither need be occasioned by witnessing egregious moral wrongs, though nothing is more clear than that the sufferer of these wrongs is a human being. Indeed, one can be the active moral agent in bringing about the suffering without experiencing any compassion or shame. After all, as I noted in *Vessels of Evil*, there is no recorded case where human beings thought that they were rounding up animals only to have it turn out, upon closer inspection, that the supposed animals were human beings, nor the other way around. The slavemasters wanted black women to serve as nannies for their children – not chimpanzees. And the slavemasters did not come to this conclusion via trial and error. Again, the Nazis wanted to make it the case that certain human beings, namely Jews, would exhibit subhuman behavior. They (the Nazis) were not at all interested in making (non-human) animals even more unruly in their behavior. And as I have already indicated, in subjecting Jews to such subhuman conditions, the very aim of the Nazis was to insure that shame and compassion with respect to the horrendous treatment of the Jews was not experienced.

I have not argued that rational reflection cannot result in people abandoning their morally objectionable ways. I have merely pointed out that rational reflection, alone, does not invariably have this result. Why? Because our rational reflections about others often has more to do with the sorts of feelings that they engage in us than philosophical theory is normally inclined to suppose. That is, contrary to philosophical theory: *our reflections often presuppose these feelings rather than regulate them.*

Philosophers typically commit what I shall call the just person fallacy. It seems reasonable enough to suppose that

1   if persons are wholly just, then they express the moral sentiments in all the right ways. Thus, if they are wholly just, then they feel compassion where compassion is appropriate, shame where shame is appropriate, resentment where resentment is appropriate, indignation where appropriate, and so on.

To this one adds that

2   the just life is a rational life.

And from these two premises, one infers that

3   the moral sentiments are regulated by rationality.

In so doing, however, one has made a fallacious inference. It is a basic truth of elementary logic that an argument is not valid just because its premises are true. Thus, suppose that a person asserted that all women are human beings and suppose it to be true that all women bear children. It would nonetheless be a mistake to infer that bearing children is an essential feature of being human.

It seems to me that precisely the lesson to be learnt from Plato is that although statements 1 and 2 are true, 3 is false. This is for two reasons. The first is that the moral sentiments are only an *ally* of rationality. Second, they are an ally of rationality only insofar as they have been properly developed in the first place. As is well known, Plato held that if persons are to experience the moral sentiments in the right way, then the foundation for this had to be laid long before rationality is operative in the life of persons. The wherewithal to live the just life as is required by rationality is not a result of the sentiments being regulated by rationality; rather, it is a result of the properly developed sentiments being established in the first place. Of course, human beings can change. But this, I have claimed, is rarely if ever a result of mere ratiocination. People who were moved by the moral eloquence and lack of bitterness on the part of Nelson Mandela changed as a result of a profound moral experience, and not simply as a result of a sustained act of ratiocination.

Once more, history is quite instructive here. Though Western culture is hardly free of sexism at this point in time, it is fair to say that male attitudes towards females are quite some distance from the sexist attitudes of merely fifty years ago. Many men have changed. But this change took lots of prodding and pain, and lots of re-habituation. Men did not simply come to their senses, and insist upon change on behalf of women. A male born fifty years ago did not, in his 20s, expect a woman to be an airline pilot or a man to be a flight attendant. So that male has had to adjust to these changes. By contrast, for a male born just twenty years ago, no such re-habituation has been necessary because having a woman as an airline pilot or a man as a flight attendant has been a part of that male's world from the very outset. Thus, for all the subtle forms of sexism that continue to exist, the moral sentiments of a male born twenty years ago *vis-à-vis* women will in many ways be superior to those of the male born fifty years ago, although the latter may very well be able to produce far more sophisticated arguments for gender equality than the former.

In *Justice for Here and Now*, Sterba speaks of a right to equal self-development. And the idea here is that minimally a just society is one that provides a social environment that is conducive to the self-development of all persons, regardless of their categorization with respect to gender, racial, sexual orientation or physical abilities. My own view is that in a society that, indeed, is basically just, the appropriate moral sentiments for carrying out such a project are already in place, but that in a society that is blemished with egregious injustices, precisely what is needed is the appropriate moral sentiments. More significantly, my view is that rational reflection alone will not suffice to produce these sentiments. Most poignantly, my view is that it is precisely those who deserve to be the object of the appropriate moral sentiments who often enough must act so as to engage the moral sentiments of those who treat them unjustly. It is, on my view, an aspect of the fragility of human beings that, in the absence of independent moral commitments toward others, we need to experience the humanity of others from time to time, especially across seemingly well defined phenotypical differences, in order for our moral sentiments toward others to be as they should be. It is easy to lose sight of this truth if we limit our sights to no more than what people know to be true rationally.

III A moral burden

One of the obvious difficulties with my view is that it places an obvious burden upon the victims of injustice. And that seems to be: well, yet another injustice. This concern confuses the reality with the ideal. The ideal, to be sure, is that those who are guilty of perpetrating the injustice of egregious social inequality should do what is necessary to raise their victims to the level of social equality. I do not deny that this should be the ideal. My claim is that unfortunately this ideal is just that – an ideal. The reality is that victims of egregious social inequality must themselves be instrumental in effecting change among those who are perpetrating this inequality. This is because it is an aspect of the fragility of human beings that if they have been socialized to believe that a group of people is morally inferior, then they do not come to have the appropriate moral sentiments toward members of that group simply in virtue of witnessing such individuals being the object of egregious inequality.

Recall here Aristotle's claim that no one is just or unjust by nature, but only as a result of how they have been trained. I am suggesting how we might understand Aristotle's claim in a modern context. Justice is not an all-or-nothing matter; and members of any society may very well be trained to be just toward some groups of persons in society and not others.

In this regard it will be useful to look at a lovely example introduced by Bernard Boxill in his essay "Dignity, Slavery, and the Thirteenth Amendment." He argues with great ingenuity that when the slavemaster asked the slave to make the case that he (the slave) is indeed a human being, there really is nothing that the slave could have done to satisfy this demand of the slavemaster – no action the slave could have taken or words he could have uttered. More importantly, Boxill's point is that there is nothing that the slave should, morally speaking, have to do. While right in the second instance, Boxill is, I believe, mistaken in the first. The slave could have engaged in morally noble behavior. Moreover, the burden to do so fell upon him.

No doubt one reason why many are mightily inclined to resist the idea that this burden fell upon the slave is that this would seem to entail that the slavemaster was not morally obligated to treat the slave justly. But not so. The obligation to treat a person justly is not conditional upon whether a person is in the position to insist upon being treated justly. The fact, though, that this obligation is unconditional does not settle at all what a person should do if it turns out that others will not fulfill their obligation to treat her justly.

Suppose John treats Rachel rather unjustly; and Rachel knows that by performing a certain series of actions she could bring it about that John will come to have the appropriate moral sentiments toward her, and so be moved to treat her justly. Suppose, further, that Rachel realizes that John is rather intransigent in his moral attitude toward her. Should John treat Rachel justly? Absolutely! But given that John is not about to behave in this way of his own accord, what should Rachel do? Surely, the answer is not that Rachel should just wait until someone else comes along and deliver her from John's unjust behavior. Surely, it is incumbent upon her to perform the series of actions in question, as a result of which John will be moved to treat her justly. And if she does not, then she may very well be open to moral criticism for failing to do so. To be sure, she will not be open to the same severity of moral criticism that can be leveled against John. After all, it is John – and not she – who is guilty of treating someone unjustly. But from this truth, it does not follow that she is not open to any moral criticism at all. Arguably, precisely what the Kantian idea of self-respect demands of her is that she act so as to invite John to treat her justly. This it demands of her without at all relieving John of his moral obligation to treat her justly.

To avoid any misunderstanding, let me state explicitly that the case of John and Rachel is not strictly parallel to the case of slavery. In Rachel's case, I have claimed that, on pain of being open to moral criticism, there is something that she should do to bring it about that she is treated justly by John. However, I do not hold that in all cases a person is open to moral criticism for failing to do what, at least in principle, she could have done to bring it about that she is treated justly by another. There can be excusing conditions, surely. What I want to make very clear, though, is that we distort the moral landscape if we suppose that whenever a person is the victim of injustice there is nothing that they can do to bring it about that they are treated (more) justly.

Under conditions of egregious injustice, acting in accordance with self-respect is very likely to acquire morally noble behavior – behavior which poignantly engages the moral sentiments of the perpetrator of injustice, and so renders manifestly evident a person's dignity. And one consequence of the failure of a people to have self-respect is that their very own behavior – that is, their lack of noble behavior – may be a factor in its being the case that they are continually treated in an egregiously unjust way. On the view that I hold, how we act toward another is much more likely to be a function of the sentiments that we feel toward that person than any considerations which rational reflection yields. In fact, as I noted earlier, the sentiments that we feel often function as a part of the justificatory argument that we give unless we already embrace independent reasons for reaching a different conclusion. Accordingly, if a group of people displays considerable servile behavior, then far from inspiring others to take them seriously as full-fledged moral agents, and so treat them justly, their very own behavior invites others not to do so. By contrast, if a group of people displays noble moral behavior in the face of egregious injustices as required by self-respect, then their behavior most certainly does not invite others not to take them seriously as full-fledged moral agents, even if it fails to move others to take them seriously, and so to treat them justly. It is generally recognized that our own behavior can have an impact upon how others behave toward us. It would be a mistake to think that matters of justice are the exception to this truth.

IV The demands of justice: bearing witness to dignity

One of the very notable features of Sterba's work is his insistence that justice is very demanding. This is very much in keeping with Annette Baier's extraordinary essay "Why Honesty Is a Hard Virtue." Doing the right thing by others is not easy precisely because what constitutes the right action in a particular case can be so very much tied to the circumstances of a person's life. Likewise, justice without sacrifice seems to amount to no more than paying lip service to an ideal.

Arguing for a something of a welfare state, much of the impetus of Sterba's writings is tied to articulating the claims that a society's disadvantaged, variously described, can make against the advantaged members of society. This a most important moral exercise. Still, the view that I hold is that universal justice is not possible until people are able to make with force their own demands. For it is not enough that people, the advantaged in this case, want equality for the disadvantaged, it is absolutely necessary that the advantaged experience the disadvantaged as equals, lest the former should unwittingly come to think it their proper place to speak on behalf of the latter. In this respect, interestingly, justice is quite unlike love. It is perhaps possible, and useful, to think of love as a gift from one person to another. By contrast, it is a mistake to think of justice in this way. One adult may or may not have a claim to being loved by another adult; whereas one adult always has a claim to being treated justly by another adult. Because justice should not be understood as a moral gift, it is, on my view, of the utmost importance that the advantaged in society experience the disadvantaged as equals; and this, needless to say, is something that in the end only the disadvantaged can make happen. Otherwise, the result is what we may refer to as moralistic paternalism.

It has been become fashionable to note that we cannot speak on behalf of others because we hardly know their point of view. The considerations I have advanced in the preceding paragraphs, while compatible with that claim, make a different point, namely that in speaking on behalf of others being treated as equal we can deprive ourselves of the opportunity to experience them fully as equals. There is a moral deference that we have toward others only when we experience them as equals.

The aim of civil disobedience in the face of egregious injustice is not to appeal to an extant moral conscience; for with respect to the egregious injustice in question none exists. Rather, its aim is to be taken seriously by the perpetrators of the injustices – to be experienced fully as equals – engaging in behavior that engages their moral sentiments and causing them to bear witness, if you will, to one's dignity. I would imagine that one reason why many have assumed that the aim of civil disobedience is to appeal to the conscience of society is that they have taken this to be the best way to account for the emphasis upon non-violence in actions of civil disobedience. Not so, however. If its aim is to cause others to bear witness to one's dignity, then we can account for the emphasis upon non-violence just as well. Indeed, this approach has even greater explanatory power.

If the aim of civil disobedience is to obtain justice by appealing to the moral conscience of others, then history shows that civil disobedience most certainly turns out to be a failure in many, many instances. If the police force of the state should force the participants in a march of civil disobedience to retreat or otherwise disband, then what have the participants gained? Have their actions been for naught, since the march had no impact upon the moral conscience of the perpetrators of injustice? If we focus simply upon changing the behavior of the unjust, it looks as if this is what must be said.

If, on the other hand, we focus upon the importance of bringing others to bear witness to one's dignity, then we get an entirely different picture. This is because it is often the case that either adversity or defeat provides the greatest opportunity for showcasing dignity, and not letting one's spirit be broken. Even in the face of defeat, there can be a defiance that reminds the other of one's humanity. As a response to defeat, viciousness and hostility tend only to beget more viciousness and hostility, and so to blind one's oppressors to one's humanity, often enabling them to excuse their horrific behavior in the name of self-defense. Violence inevitably gives rise to an excuse to be violent. This, I believe, is the insight that Gandhi recognized, and King after him. By contrast, in forcing others to bear witness to one's dignity, one confronts them with the reality of one's moral personhood; for dignity, unlike happiness or fear or anger or even anxiousness, is something that only a human being can have.

As I have just said, an animal can show fear. However, only a human being can show fearlessness in the face of wrongdoing, and make it unquestionably clear to the wrongdoer that this is precisely what is being done. This is a display of dignity. It can be disarming.

Hannah Arendt, for instance, was alarmed by the number of Jews who went silently and without disturbance to their deaths. She saw this as cowardice. No doubt this was true of sufficiently many. Yet we need not hold this to have been true of everyone. Certainly, some Jews could have thought to themselves that they would prefer to walk quietly to their death, which was inevitable in one way or the other, rather than display any fear or beg for their life, thereby giving the Nazis pleasure in their power over the Jews. In so doing, such Jews displayed dignity. But one might very well ask: To what end, since they died anyway?

In *Vessels of Evil*, I noted that no voice, however mellifluous, constitutes a choir; likewise no conviction, no matter how firmly held, constitutes a consensus. In both cases, the whole is more than just the sum of its parts. While it may very well be true that the relatively few Jews who marched to their deaths with dignity failed to move the Nazis to respect the Jews, it does not follow from this that had all Jews so behaved the Nazis would nonetheless not have been so moved. It will be remembered that the Nazis did not just slaughter Jews, but that they went to great lengths to first do all that they could to strip the Jews of their humanity. Dignity in the face of inevitable death is perhaps the most profound form of defiance possible, invariably touching those who bear witness to it in spite of themselves. The truly evil rejoice in the exercise of power that they manifest over others, generally supposing that the capricious threat of death is the ultimate exercise of power over others. Thus, as a response to evil, dignity is disarming precisely because it disempowers the evil agent by making it clear to the agent that his threat is inefficacious, regardless of the amount of coercive force that he can bring to bear.

This, for example, is precisely what made the early Christians so extraordinarily influential. In many cases, the threat of death, far from terrorizing the early Christians, was welcomed by them as liberating. Thus, in his essay "Martyrs et Fiers de l'être," Jean-Marc Prieur reports that Bishop Ignace of Antioch insisted that no-one intervene on his behalf as he was being carried to his execution by a Roman convoy. The threat of death was diffused by the very dignity which the martyrs displayed in the face of every conceivable threat. It was not by might but by masterful displays of dignity that the early Christians conquered mighty Rome.

Understood as a display of dignity, then, the civilly disobedient violate the law in order to bring attention to a grave injustice. This, however, is not to appeal to a moral conscience that has already proven itself to be indifferent to the wrong that is being perpetrated. Rather, it is an awakening of that moral conscience by displaying dignity in their acts of civil disobedience, and so making it manifestly clear that the threat of evil is inefficacious.

V The moral self

In the face of injustice, the most precious moral good that the morally wronged have is their dignity. From this it does not follow that violence can never be justified. Rather, what does follow is that violence cannot replace dignity. If we lose sight of this, we may yet gain power, but power in the absence of dignity is a most Pyrrhic victory. And it is a sublime moral truth that in terms of bringing about change for the better, a manifest display of dignity can achieve what brute force cannot. If, in the struggle for equality, we should lose sight of this moral truth, then we unwittingly disempower those who live in the hopes of being treated equally by others.

Rousseau thought it clear that it was not the ability of human beings to provide for themselves that distinguished them from other animals. Indeed, while many have supposed that his contractarian doctrine is based upon the struggle among human beings to meet their basic needs, this reading is not supported by Rousseau's observation that I have just noted, nor his claim that it is in the family that we have the very first society. Rousseau thought that human beings have a nobility in living in concert with one another that they could not have living in isolation from one another. In this regard, he said nothing about dignity in the face of evil. Yet it is the very power of dignity displayed en masse in the face of evil that provides such a profound moral echo to his words; for dignity en masse provides a moral resonance against evil that not even death can extinguish.

References

Boxill, Bernard (1992) "Dignity, Slavery, and the Thirteenth Amendment," in Michael J. Meyer and W. A. Parent (eds) *The Constitution of Rights* (Ithaca NY: Cornell University Press, 1992).

Harris, George W. (1999) *Agent-Centered Morality: Aristotelian Alternative to Kantian Internalism* (Berkeley: University of California Press).

Hill Jr, Thomas (1973) "Servility and Self-Respect," *The Monist*, 57.

Prieur, Jean-Marc (2000) "Martyrs et Fiers de l'être," *Historia*, no. 64 (Mars–Avril). Theme of this issue: The impact of the first Christians upon the world (Premiers Chrétians: ces aventuriers qui ont changé le monde).

Sterba, James P. (1980) *The Demands of Justice* (Notre Dame IN: The University of Notre Dame Press).

——(1998) *Justice for Here and Now* (New York: Cambridge University Press).

Thomas, Laurence (1989) *Living Morally: A Psychology of Moral Character* (Philadelphia PA: Temple University Press).

——(1993) *Vessels of Evil: American Slavery and the Holocaust* (Philadelphia PA: Temple University Press).

Part VI

CONCLUSION

TOWARD RECONCILIATION IN SOCIAL AND POLITICAL PHILOSOPHY

James P. Sterba

To have a justified social and political philosophy, one must attend carefully to the views of others, and particularly to the objections they might raise to one's own views. By attending to the philosophical views of others, and especially to the objections they might raise to one's own view, one can come to see the need to modify one's own view, or to develop it in new ways, or at least how to present it in a better fashion so as to be better understood.

Moral methodology

In her contribution to this volume, Eve Browning Cole significantly adds to my discussion of warmaking philosophy by commenting on its history, nature and disadvantages, as well as its attractions. Unfortunately, the warmaking, which Cole laments, dominates not only philosophy and academia generally, but also the media, politics, and the practice of law.

There was a joke going around during Bill Clinton's first term in office. The president went on a fishing trip with members of the press. After their boat left the dock, the president realized he didn't have his tackle so he stepped off the boat and walked to shore, picked up his tackle, and walked back over the surface of the water to the boat. The next day's headline read "CLINTON CAN'T SWIM." This joke pokes fun at the tendency of the press to give everything a negative slant, to ignore accomplishments and to focus on failures. But the tendency is there.

If we turn from the media to politics, we find, at least in the US, a similar emphasis on negativity and conflict rather than on compromise and governance. For example, Speaker Newt Gingrich opposed Clinton's healthcare plan, reasoning that if the Democrats succeeded in reforming the healthcare system, they would then be unbeatable. Not surprisingly, a similarly motivated opposition defeated Gingrich's own plan for restructuring Medicare and Medicaid.

In the law, there is the question of how far one should go in defense of one's client or to build or prosecute a case against someone. In a lawsuit in California, one side requested tax returns from the other side, which objected on grounds of privacy. There followed a year and a half of costly litigation going all the way up to the California Supreme Court and back. In the end, the lawyer was compelled to produce the returns, at which time he revealed what he had known all along – his client had no returns for that year.[1] The lawyer had judged that this delaying action was in the interest of his client. On the prosecutorial side, surely the excesses that Kenneth Starr went to in order to build a case against President Clinton, far removed from his initially mandated Whitewater investigation, did not serve well the interests of American people in having a government focussed on solving their important political, economic and social problems. What this shows is that the need for peacemaking extends far beyond the social and political philosophy with which we are primarily concerned, but its need there is clearly evident.

Rationality

My argument from rationality to morality is a central part of my social and political philosophy. I was motivated to develop the argument because I perceived difficulties in earlier arguments advanced by Alan Gewirth and Kurt Baier. In his contribution to this volume, however, Gewirth claims that my failure to recognize the strength of his particular argument is rooted in our different accounts of prudential and moral rights. For Gewirth, prudential rights aim to support the interests of the agent or speaker, whereas moral rights aim to support or take favorable account of the interests of at least some persons other than the speaker or the agent. For me, prudential rights are asymmetrically action-guiding in that they are action-guiding for the rightholder only and not for others, and so they do not imply that others ought not to interfere with the exercise of those rights. I also think that these rights are analogous to the asymmetrical "oughts" found in most ordinary cases of competitive games. Thus in football a defensive player may think that the opposing team's quarterback ought to pass on a third down with five yards to go, while not wanting the quarterback to do so and indeed hoping to foil any such attempt the quarterback makes. By contrast, moral rights, I claim, are symmetically action-guiding. Thus if I have a moral right to my life then that right should guide both my actions and the actions of others, in particular, it should lead others not to unreasonably interfere with my life.

Gewirth thinks that these two accounts of moral and prudential rights do not coincide because, on his account, a (moral) right may guide a person's actions with the aim of supporting both his own interests and the interests of others. But this is true on my account as well. This is because in claiming that moral rights are symmetically action-guiding, guiding both oneself and others, I never held that the reasons why they are action-guiding for oneself are always just self-interested. For example, I can exercise my right to life, and typically do, for the benefit of others as well as myself. Nevertheless, it still holds that my right to life, unlike prudential rights and the oughts of competitive games, is action-guiding for others as well as myself because others have at least a *prima facie* duty not to interfere with my life. So contrary to what Gewirth claims, our accounts of moral and prudential rights do coincide after all.

Now, Gewirth thinks his argument from rationality to morality works because when an agent universalizes a prudential claim that she ought (prudentially) to have – or (prudentially) has a right to – freedom and well-being, and thus asserts that *everyone* ought to have (or has a right to) freedom and well-being, the agent is thereby committed to "upholding the interests of other persons as well as herself." But while an agent, through universalization, does certainly make a claim *about* others as well as herself (the claim clearly refers to everyone), the claim still does not commit the agent to "upholding the interests of other persons as well as herself," as long as the ought or right in the universalized claim is interpreted as asymmeti-cally action-guiding, in a manner analogous to the oughts of competitive games. What this shows is that while consistency and universalizability do require an egoist to admit, at least to herself, that everyone else has the same justification as she has for behaving egoistically, they do not require her, in my terms, to endorse symmetically action-guiding oughts or rights or, in Gewirth's terms, to "uphold the interests of other persons as well as herself." But while consistency and universalizability alone cannot logically require the egoist to endorse morality, my argument shows that we can achieve that result by fully utilizing a standard of non-question-beggingness.[2]

With respect to my own argument from rationality to morality, Gewirth correctly perceives that it requires a non-question-begging way of deter-mining both what is in a person's self-interest and what is in the interests of others, and a non-question-begging way of ranking these interests on their respective scales, from the most important to the least important in each case. Yet the possibility of determining and ranking such interests on their respective scales in a non-question-begging way, is something that is taken for granted by those who think that egoism is the most rationally defensible view – the main opponents of morality. In addition, Gewirth himself must think that there is a non-question-begging way to determine and rank such interests, otherwise he could not hold that there is a non-question-begging way of defending morality over egoism, as he does. So the assumption that in a non-question-begging way we can determine what is in a person's self-interest and what is in the interests of others, and rank these interests on their respective scales, is actually shared by both Gewirth and myself and by other defenders of morality, as well as by our main opponents, those who think that egoism is rationally required.

In his contribution to this volume, Bernard Gert concedes that my argument from rationality to morality may well succeed as an argument of theoretical reason, which is concerned with true beliefs, valid arguments and acceptable modes of argumentation, but he claims it fails as an argument of practical reason, which is concerned with harms and benefits.

But it is unclear here how we are supposed to understand this distinction that Gert makes between theoretical and practical reason. Can't the defender of theoretical reason be concerned with those true beliefs, valid arguments and acceptable modes of argumentation that are also about harms and benefits? And isn't the defender of practical reason concerned with the same? Surely, the defender of practical reason does not think that false beliefs about harms and benefits will always do just as well as true ones. Surely, if one is concerned about harms and benefits, one should be generally concerned to ascertain what is true or false about those harms and benefits. Of course, as Gert points out, there are cases where we don't want to know certain truths or cases where knowing certain truths will not be good for us to know, as in the case of Oedipus. But surely this does not show that true beliefs, valid arguments, and acceptable modes of argumentation are not relevant to a concern for harms and benefits. It only shows that certain true beliefs, valid arguments, and acceptable modes of argumentation may get in the way of securing particular benefits and avoiding particular harms.

But which particular harms and benefits is practical reason, as opposed to theoretical reason, primarily concerned with according to Gert? They would seem to be those harms and benefits that all normal persons would either want to avoid or to pursue. The harms would be those of uncompensated-for death, non-trivial pain, loss of ability, loss of freedom or loss of pleasure, and the benefits would be the necessary means of avoiding these harms. Clearly, Gert wants to employ a notion of rationality such that it wouldn't make sense to ask: Why should I avoid acting irrationally? Accordingly, he defines irrational action in terms of failing to avoid these basic harms. So understood, the irrational person is simply crazy, and so it doesn't make much sense for any one of us to ask: Why should I avoid acting in a crazy fashion? Surely, acting in a crazy fashion is a way I shouldn't want to act.

Of course, we can explain why some people do, in fact, act in a crazy fashion. We can, for example, provide a biological explanation or postulate a chemical imbalance. Yet, as Gert rightly maintains, he is concerned with justification not explanation, and surely crazy people cannot really justify their crazy actions: that is, in part, why they are crazy.

But can egoists justify their egoistic behavior? Can immoralists justify their immoral behavior? Oddly, Gert seems unconcerned with these further questions of justification. Having established that there is no justification for acting in a crazy fashion, despite the fact that some people do act in that way, Gert does not pursue whether there might also be no justification, or no adequate justification, for people's acting simply egoistically or acting immorally, although clearly some people act in these ways as well.

Of course, pursuing these broader questions of justification might require us to be more concerned with determining true beliefs and using valid arguments and acceptable modes of argumentation, the concerns that Gert has linked to theoretical reason rather than to practical reason. Nevertheless, if one is concerned with the questions of justification, as Gert clearly is, it would seem that one should also be interested in these so-called theoretical concerns, which in this context I would judge to be eminently practical as well.

Gert goes on to argue that even if Gewirth and I were successful in answering our broader questions of justification, that is, even if Gewirth had succeeded in showing that immoral people act inconsistently or I had succeeded in showing that they beg the question, we would not have provided answers of the right sort. Now, in *Justice for Here and Now* I responded to a similar objection raised by Reiman.[3] Reiman had objected that a justification of morality, like my own, does not succeed even in its own terms, that is, it does not succeed in justifying morality. According to Reiman, avoiding inconsistency (as in Gewirth's justification) or avoiding question-beggingness (as in mine) are only logical requirements, whereas the offense of being immoral is something more than a logical offense. Reiman claims that a justification of morality, like my own, only succeeds in showing that the egoist or immoralist is guilty of a logical mistake, and that is not enough. Reiman asks us to imagine a murderer who says, "Yes, I've been inconsistent (or begged the question) but that is *all* I've done." Reiman claims that morality requires something more, it requires that we recognize the reality of other people, and immorality denies that reality.[4]

But notice that if Reiman's view of morality were sound, egoists and immoralists, by denying the reality of other people, would be solipsists, but clearly they are not.[5] Nevertheless, there is something to Reiman's objection. Putting a defense of morality in terms of a non-question-begging compromise between relevant self-interested and altruistic reasons for action can obscure the fact that what is at stake is the prohibition of the infliction of basic harm on others for the sake of nonbasic benefit to oneself, given that the infliction of such harm is what egoism would require. Thus what needs to be made clear is that the failure to be moral involves both a logical and a material mistake. The logical mistake is that of begging the question or acting contrary to reason. The material mistake is the infliction of basic harm for the sake of nonbasic benefit. Both of these mistakes characterize any failure to be moral, and they mutually entail each other.[6] They are simply two different aspects of the same act.

But does this response to Reiman suffice as a reply to Gert? What if people claim not to be moved by the fact that their immoral actions involved inflicting basic harm on others for the sake of nonbasic benefit to themselves? Clearly, the task of justifying morality to everyone is not the same as the task of providing everyone with sufficient motivation to be moral. Accordingly, success with respect to the former task should not be judged by whether or not one has succeeded with respect to the latter. After all, Gert himself claims to have the correct answer to the question why we should not act irrationally, even though he allows that his answer will not succeed in motivating everyone to act rationally. What I have been trying to show is that morality is justified over egoism and pure altruism. I did not hope, nor would it be reasonable for me to expect, that I would succeed in providing everyone with a sufficient motivation to be moral.

Gert, however, has still other objections to my justification for morality. He notes that my argument for morality is directed at the egoist and the pure altruist, or rather that it is directed at ourselves insofar as we are capable of behaving egoistically or altruistically. Gert has no problem with my directing my argument for morality at the egoist, or rather at ourselves insofar as we are capable of behaving egoistically or self-interestedly, but he thinks that it is inappropriate for me to direct my argument at the pure altruist, or possibly even at ourselves insofar as we are capable of behaving altruistically. Why does he think this? Gert says: "Anyone who chooses his own total ruin to prevent the least uneasiness to an Indian, or person wholly unknown to him, contrary to Hume, is acting irrationally." But surely even a pure altruist would agree that this sort of behavior was irrational because it is certainly a poor use of one's personal resources in the service of others. Of course, pure altruists would be willing to sacrifice themselves for others far beyond what many of us think is appropriate. Yet so too would egoists be willing to sacrifice others for the sake of some small benefit to themselves far beyond what many of us think is appropriate. Egoism and pure altruism are, after all, mirror images of each other, and for that reason the egoist cannot disregard the pure altruist's perspective without begging the question. Furthermore, I have argued that once egoism and pure altruism are looked at from a non-question-begging standpoint, it turns out that it is neither of these two perspectives, but rather the perspective of morality, understood as a nonarbitrary compromise between egoism and pure altruism, that emerges as the rationally preferable alternative.[7]

Apart from my argument for the justification of morality, Gert also has some difficulties with my account of morality as a compromise between egoism and altruism, requiring high-ranking self-interested reasons over low-ranking altruistic reasons, and high-ranking altruistic reasons over low-ranking self-interested reasons. In particular, Gert finds it difficult to read off from this account of morality what we would be required to do in certain troublesome cases. Yet an account of morality that is useful for some purposes may not be useful for others, and the account of morality I have defended was not intended to be useful as a decision-procedure for churning out the particular requirements of morality. If I had thought that my account was useful as a decision-procedure, I would not have gone on, in subsequent chapters of the book, to evaluate particular moral and political ideals such as libertarianism, welfare liberalism, socialism, feminism and multiculturalism, in order to arrive at particular moral requirements. Rather, I would have simply used my account of morality as a compromise between self-interested and altruistic reasons to churn out those requirements. Instead, in subsequent chapters of *Justice for Here and Now*, I have argued not from "morality as compromise" but from a minimal libertarian morality, claiming that this morality requires rights to welfare and equal opportunity that lead to socialist equality and feminist androgyny, and I have further argued that this conception of morality requires racial justice, homosexual justice and multicultural justice, and is constrained by specific principles of environmental justice and just war pacifism.

As I see it, morality as compromise is, for the most part, a useful way of thinking about morality for the purposes of showing that morality is rationally preferable to both egoism and pure altruism. I don't think the account is useful for other purposes such as deriving particular moral requirements, especially for troublesome cases. Of course, once we have reached a resolution concerning what is morally required in a troublesome case, it should normally be possible to read that resolution back into my account of morality by showing that the resolution implies that some particular altruistic reason ranks higher than some particular self-interested reason, or vice-versa. And I have done this for a number of cases that Gert has discussed. Gert's suggestion here that my account of morality makes "no distinction between hurting someone to avoid a lesser harm to oneself and not helping someone because doing so would result in harm to oneself, even though it is a lesser harm," ignores my defense of the intended/foreseen distinction in chapter 7 of *Justice for Here and Now*, which in turn can be read back into my account of morality as compromise.

Libertarianism

According to Tibor Machan, libertarian justice "consists in establishing and maintaining a political system in which the respect and protection of the right to life, liberty and property of the human individual are of primary legal significance." With this, I am in full agreement. Where Machan and I disagree is how these rights are to be interpreted as negative rights of noninterference. I have argued that when these rights are interpreted in the most morally defensible way, they lead to a right to welfare and a right to equal opportunity. In his contribution, Machan denies that a right to welfare and a right to equal opportunity can be so derived on the grounds that "there is no justification for even a good person to deprive another from what belongs to another merely because he may need sustenance." But, in fact, a right to welfare and a right to equal opportunity do not violate Machan's restriction; they do not require us to regard a need for sustenance as overriding property rights. Rather, these rights are based on the moral superiority of the negative liberty of the poor over the negative liberty of the rich which, in turn, rules out the possibility of there being any conflicting property rights.[8]

Machan goes on to argue that by denying the poor a right to welfare the rich would not be doing violence to them (that is, unjustly interfering with them), because the poor would still be in need if the rich did not exist. But, of course, this is not true for just any particular group of rich people. A particular group of rich people's hoarding of resources may be exactly why other people are poor. Moreover, consider a case where the claim holds. Suppose you and I would still be very needy even if certain rich people did not exist. Does this show that we do not have a right not to be interfered with in taking from the surplus resources of those same rich people when they do exist? Suppose you and I are drowning in a pond. Even when others did not cause our plight, they may still be required not to interfere with our attempts to save ourselves, even when these attempts involve using their surplus resources.

Machan thinks that cases where the poor are in need through no fault of their own are quite rare and so laws are not required to deal with them. But I have argued that even in the US, and certainly in the Third World, there are large numbers of people, particularly children, who are needy through no fault of their own. Machan claims that there may be other ways to meet the needs of the poor, for example, by obtaining wealth from the punishment of rich citizens or from resources not owned by anyone. It stands to reason that I am all in favor of utilizing these means for meeting the needs of the poor. I just don't see how these means will suffice to meet the basic needs of all those who are poor without also having recourse to a right to welfare and a right to equal opportunity.

In his contribution to this volume, Jan Narveson maintains his libertarian view rests on the "general right to do as we will, provided only we do not invade or worsen others." This means, Narveson elaborates, "that each individual upon whom our behavior impinges must be such that, on balance, she reckons herself to be no worse off for our impingement." What Narveson fails to see, however, is that his own view, if it favors anything at all, favors the liberty of the poor over the liberty of the rich. To see this, consider a typical conflict situation between the rich and the poor. In this situation the rich, of course, have more than enough resources to satisfy their basic needs. By contrast, the poor lack the resources to meet their most basic needs, even though they have tried all the means available to them that libertarians regard as legitimate for acquiring such resources. Now, in this situation there is a conflict between the liberty of the poor not to be interfered with in taking from the surplus possessions of the rich what is necessary to satisfy their basic needs, and the liberty of the rich not to be interfered with in using their surplus resources for luxury purposes. If we favor one liberty, we must reject the other. Moreover, if we favor the liberty of the rich over the liberty of the poor, then the poor would be clearly worse off as a consequence. Likewise, if we favor the liberty of the poor over the liberty of the rich then the rich would be clearly worse off as a consequence. Consequently, Narveson should admit either that his own view has no resolution at all in these typical conflict situations, or that it favors the liberty of the poor over the liberty of the rich because only that resolution provides for the basic needs of the deserving poor, does not violate the "Ought" Implies "Can" Principle, and is reasonable for all parties to accept.

Narveson points out that persons living below the poverty line in the United States (a standard which is based on a food plan that was developed for "temporary or emergency use" and is inadequate for a permanent diet) have a monetary income that is quite high – in fact, many times the median income of people in Third World countries. Of course, what Narveson ignores here is that the costs of meeting basic needs can vary between different societies and within the same society at different times. This is due to the way that the means most readily available for satisfying basic needs are produced. For example, in more affluent societies, the most readily available means for satisfying a person's basic needs are usually processed so as to satisfy nonbasic needs at the same time as they satisfy basic needs. This processing is carried out to make the means more attractive to persons in higher income brackets who can easily afford the extra cost. As a result, the most readily available means for satisfying basic needs are much more costly in more affluent societies than in less affluent societies, thus requiring a higher welfare minimum in more affluent societies than in less affluent societies. Over time, however, this can and should be changed, as more and more efficient ways of meeting people's basic needs worldwide are developed.[9]

Citing data about how the American poor fare with respect to the number of persons per room (.56) and with respect to the number who lack indoor flush toilets (1.8%), Narveson suggests that "the American poor are in fact better off in the usual 'material' terms as a group than the citizenry as a whole in (some) other ... front-line countries, not to mention those in the Second and Third Worlds." Unfortunately, there are other data which I think suggest a less rosy picture.[10] For example, 22.4% of children live below the poverty line in the US as compared to 4.9% in Germany, 5% in Sweden, and 7.8% in Switzerland, and the US shares with Italy the highest infant mortality rate of the major industrialized nations. The US also ranks sixty-seventh among all nations in the percentage of national income received by the poorest 20% of its population, ranking it the absolute lowest among industrialized nations.[11]

Narveson also claims, citing Charles Murray, that the poor in the US and Canada would have been better off if the welfare state had never existed. According to Murray,

Basic indicators of well-being took a turn for the worse in the 1960s, most consistently and most drastically for the poor. ... We tried to provide more for the poor and produced more poor instead. We tried to remove the barriers to escape from poverty, and inadvertently built a trap.[12]

Yet while Murray's work has been widely hailed in certain quarters, critics have argued that the relevant data do not support his argument.

For example, Michael Harrington points out that while black male labor force participation did drop 7% between 1969 and 1981 (thus fitting nicely with Murray's thesis that welfare programs are the villain) there was a drop of 7.4% between 1955 and 1968.[13] So the drop in employment was actually greater before welfare programs came on line than it was after, just the opposite of what Murray's thesis would lead us to expect.

Or consider black women. Supposedly, they are even more exposed than men to the supposed work disincentives of welfare programs, since as mothers they could have qualified for Aid to Families of Dependent Children. But, as Harrington shows, their labor force participation rate increased between 1955 and 1981 by 7.5%, and more than half of that progress occurred after 1968.

And on the question of whether welfare programs did any good, Christopher Jencks claims that the relevant data tell a story that is quite different from the one Murray tells in *Losing Ground*. He writes:

First, contrary to what Murray claims, "net" poverty declined almost as fast after 1965 as it had before. Second, the decline in poverty after 1965, unlike the decline before 1965, occurred despite unfavorable economic conditions, and depended to a great extent on government efforts to help the poor. Third, the groups that benefited from this "generous revolution," as Murray rightly calls it, were precisely the groups that legislators hoped would benefit, notably the aged and the disabled. The groups that did not benefit were the ones that legislators did not especially want to help. Fourth, these improvements took place despite demographic changes that would ordinarily have made things worse. Given the difficulties, legislators should, I think, look back on their efforts to improve the material conditions of poor people's lives with some pride.[14]

So much then for the claim that the poor, at least in the US, would have been better off if the welfare state had never existed.

Narveson also cites Paul Krugman with respect to the benefits that international capitalism has brought to poor people in Third World countries like Indonesia and throughout the Pacific Rim. However,

Krugman himself notes that for twenty years international capitalism did very little for these countries, keeping them as exporters of raw materials and importers of manufactures. Only recently, through a combination of factors, have industries been willing to take advantage of very low wages in these countries (sixty cents an hour), and, as a consequence, they have improved somewhat the situation of the poor in these countries.[15] Nevertheless, the situation of the poor would clearly be improved much more if Narveson and others were to recognize that what I have argued is the logical consequence of his own libertarian moral view – a basic needs minimum guaranteed to all those who are willing to take advantage of whatever opportunities are available to them to engage in mutually beneficial work.

Welfare liberalism

In her contribution to this volume, Eva Kittay distinguishes three different kinds of welfare: a stingy welfare that only keeps the poor from starving and from other life-threatening ills, an expansive welfare that provides the social goods necessary for a good life, and a caring welfare that makes possible the survival and thriving of dependent persons, frequently by providing for those who, in turn, provide for the dependent persons themselves. She rightly argues that a morally defensible welfare liberal ideal would not stop at either a stingy welfare or even an expansive welfare, but would have to include a caring welfare as well. She further argues that from the libertarian's ideal of negative liberty one can only succeed in deriving a stingy welfare, and not the expansive welfare or the caring welfare that are also needed.

One way to support something like Kittay's view here but on libertarian premises (obviously not the approach that Kittay herself takes) is to point out that no one is, in fact, interfering with many of those who are dependent or are severely in need. Rather, people just seem to be simply leaving them alone, ignoring them. How then could this be in violation of the libertarian ideal of noninterference?

In *Justice for Here and Now*, however, I recognized that there will be cases in which the poor fail to satisfy their basic needs, not because of any direct restriction of liberty on the part of the rich, but because the poor are in such dire need that they are unable even to attempt to take from the rich what they require to meet their basic needs. In such cases, the rich would not be performing any act of commission that would prevent the poor from taking what they require. Yet even in such cases, I argued that the rich would normally be performing acts of commission that would prevent other persons from taking part of the rich's own surplus possessions and using it to aid the poor. And when assessed from a moral point of view, restricting the liberty of these allies or agents of the poor would not be morally justified for the very same reason that restricting the liberty of the poor to meet their own basic needs would not be morally justified: it would not be reasonable to require all of those affected to accept such a restriction of liberty. So I think that it is possible in this way to derive not only a stingy welfare, but also an expansive and a caring welfare from the libertarian's ideal of negative liberty.

Kittay also thinks that since the rich will be providing welfare, to others and not themselves, they will tend to be stingy in determining the amount of welfare to be provided. That is why she wants to pay both the rich and the poor for doing dependency work, to insure that the stipends for everyone will be sufficiently generous. But in my argument from liberty to equality, there is another consideration that has a similar effect. It is the fact that the provision of an adequate welfare to all those in need leads to equality. Kittay notes this feature of my view, but she doesn't appreciate its significance.[16] If the provision of welfare leads to equality, however, then the rich, or should we say those who start out rich, have good reason to want the welfare minimum to be an adequate one, because that welfare minimum will be all that they are allowed to keep for themselves. So if I am right that the libertarian ideal of liberty leads to equality, as Kittay seems to grant, then it should lead to the kind of welfare that Kittay favors.

In his contribution to this volume, John Deigh, drawing on the reform liberalism of T. H. Green, raises an interesting challenge to contemporary welfare liberalism. Contemporary welfare liberals, like John Rawls, have sought to defend their political agenda by appealing to both liberty and equality, in effect defending a compromise between the two ideals. The problem with this defense of welfare liberalism is that it can leave the defenders of either ideal unsatisfied. Why should one sacrifice one's ultimate political ideal for the sake of an ideal that one does not recognize, or at least does not recognize as having priority over one's favored ideal? Or in contemporary terms, why should libertarians sacrifice their ideal of liberty when it comes into conflict with the ideal of equality endorsed by welfare liberals?

John Deigh thinks that that reform liberals such as T. H. Green have a persuasive answer to this question that has been neglected by contemporary welfare liberals. The answer is that the ideal of liberty itself, when correctly understood, requires the equality endorsed by welfare liberals. Of course, that is my view as well, although my argument is quite different from Green's.

Green argues that the most adequate notion of liberty has both positive and negative dimensions. On this view, liberty is not simply an ideal of noninterference; it is also a positive ideal which provides the capacity to act in pursuit of morally and socially worthy ends.[17]

According to Green, persons are not free if their actions proceed from choices made under conditions of poverty or ignorance which result from the necessity of having to sell their labor for whatever wages are offered by owners of capital. When the ideal of liberty is so understood, it alone suffices to justify the institutions of a welfare state. Thus there is no need to pit the ideal of liberty against the ideal of equality to justify the welfare state; liberty by itself will do the job. But while Green's ideal of liberty does provide a sure justification for the welfare state, contemporary libertarians, like Tibor Machan and Jan Narveson, have yet to endorse its positive dimension, because while contemporary libertarians grant that poverty and ignorance are bad things, they still maintain that liberty as noninterference is the only ideal that the state can coercively support.

This is where my liberty to welfare argument has an advantage over Green's because it utilizes only a strictly negative liberty ideal of noninterference. The way my argument proceeds is by showing that in virtually all those situations where Green would see a lack of positive liberty, there is also a lack of negative liberty, or noninterference, and, moreover, the lack of positive liberty is, in fact, due to the lack of negative liberty. For example, consider wherever people around the world are living in conditions of poverty. Surely, these conditions would not obtain except for the enforcement of the property rights of the rich and the powerful here and elsewhere. Absent this interference, either the poor themselves would be able to remedy their condition, or other people, concerned about the welfare of the poor, would be able to use the resources of the rich and powerful to remedy it. This could be done either by arranging immediate transfers in the particular society where the poverty exists or by arranging transfers from other societies worldwide. In this way, I argue that even according to a strictly negative ideal of liberty, the liberty of the poor trumps the liberty of the rich and powerful, and thereby supports the requirements of a welfare state.

Of course, I have no objection to Deigh's appropriation of Green's ideal of positive liberty to defend those same requirements. In fact, I welcome Deigh's defense. It is just that I think my approach will be more successful in winning over our libertarian opponents.

Virtue ethics and community

Robert C. Solomon in his contribution to this volume provides an account of justice as a virtue. He wants his account to be Aristotelian, but an account that is still considerably different from the historical Aristotle. The virtue of justice is for him both "personal and social insofar as the individual is defined and constituted by their role and relationships in the community and with other people." He defends, as a form of relativism, the view that we should look at disputes, such as the dispute concerning human rights in China, without thinking that one side must be right and the other wrong. This seems to be a perfectly sensible position to take since it may be that the right view requires combining elements from perspectives that are, in fact, opposed. Fortunately, this is not what people usually object to when they object to relativism. Solomon also points out that people's judgments of what is just change over time, but this is also something with which people generally agree.

Solomon questions my focus on conflicts between morality and self-interest because he thinks that in the cases that count most in discussions of social justice, there is a breakdown of the opposition between morality and self-interest. As examples of such a breakdown, he cites Ted Turner's, and his own presumably mixed reasons, for making substantial bequests to good causes.

Yet are these examples really typical of the cases where justice makes demands on us? Isn't it far more likely for justice or morality to make demands on us that conflict with our self-interest at least to some degree? In any case, it is only where there are such conflicts that we need a justification for acting morally rather than self-interestedly. And it is for just such cases that I have tried to show that rationality understood as non-question-beggingness does favor morality over self-interest.

It is just here that Solomon wants to raise a further question: Why accept a standard of non-question-beggingness? To this question, I could, of course, reply that the standard of non-question-beggingness is required for good argumentation. But what if Solomon were to persist and ask: Why do you want to give good arguments for your views? At that point, I think our discussion would have to come to an end. This is because Solomon would then be challenging the basic presupposition of our discussion, which is that we were trying to reach agreement through an appeal to good arguments. Without that presupposition, we would just be playing verbal games.

I now turn to a more practical question. Can one be morally justified in engaging in criminal disobedience against fellow members of one's community? This is the question on which Michael Boylan focuses in his contribution to this volume, drawing upon and developing an example that I discuss in the last chapter of *Justice for Here and Now*.

Boylan offers three interpretations of my example of Gretchen, who commits a criminally disobedient act to secure certain goods that she is denied. In the first interpretation, the goods that Gretchen is denied are basic necessities of life. In the second interpretation, they are necessary for her to compete in her society. In the third interpretation, they are luxury goods that she has not been able to earn. Now, as I understood the example, it accords with the first two of Boylan's interpretations. And, with respect to these two interpretations, Boylan and I agree that Gretchen would be morally justified in engaging in criminal disobedience provided certain conditions are met.[18] With respect to the third interpretation, however, Boylan argues that if agreed-upon community practices result in Gretchen not securing certain luxury goods, she would not be morally justified in engaging in criminal disobedience to secure such goods. Although this is not an interpretation of the example that I have considered before, I am in complete agreement with Boylan's account of it. In this respect, Boylan and I are both communitarians.

Socialism

In his contribution to this volume, Kai Nielsen provides a very useful discussion of various forms of socialism, distinguishing the analytical Marxist form of socialism which he favors. Nielsen also comments on the socialist equality which I claim to derive from libertarian premises.[19] While the socialist equality that I defend aims to meet everyone's basic needs, the socialism that Nielsen defends aims to meet not only people's basic needs, but all their needs and all their wants too insofar as these can be possibly satisfied. But I really don't think that Nielsen wants to satisfy all the needs that people might have. For example, he surely would not want to satisfy a robber's need for a gun. Moreover, once distant people and future generations are taken into account, I argue that it is not clear that we can do anything more than directly meet everyone's basic needs, interpreted in a fairly substantial way. This is, in fact, how my defense of a basic needs minimum leads to equality.

According to Nielsen, to achieve a just world we must replace capitalism with socialism, but in my earlier book, *How to Make People Just*, I argued that a suitably constrained capitalism will be practically indistinguishable from a morally defensible socialism.

At the very end of his essay, Nielsen laments that I have not done more to prepare the way for a revolutionary future. But if I have succeeded in showing that rationality leads to morality and that even the most minimal morality, libertarianism, leads to the equality that socialists defend, then I would have succeeded in showing that a revolutionary socialist future is built into the norms that virtually everyone endorses. Surely, that should make it somewhat easier to begin to realize that revolutionary socialist future even now from within present-day capitalism.

In her contribution to this volume, Carol Gould defends a form of socialist equality which she calls democratic egalitarianism, by deriving it from an ideal of positive liberty. She goes on to challenge my own attempt to defend a similar form of socialist equality by deriving it from an ideal of negative liberty. She argues that the basic needs minimum which I derive from the libertarian's ideal of negative liberty does not support a right to democratic decision-making or a right to participate in controlling the productive process. But in earlier published work with which Gould is unfortunately unfamiliar, I argue that these rights are included in my understanding of a basic needs minimum.[20] Gould also claims that my argument from liberty to equality must be "tacitly appealing to a principle of positive liberty" if it is to get to socialist equality. This is a plausible claim to make about my view, at least at first blush, but if you then look at the considerable number of libertarian responses to my argument that have been published over the years, you find that not one libertarian has ever raised this objection to my argument, and surely libertarians would be the first to raise this objection to my argument if there were any grounds for doing so.[21]

At the very end of her essay, Gould argues that we need to consider the actual way social and economic institutions, including nation-states and international organizations, function if we are going to succeed in adequately realizing rights to welfare and equal opportunity. Here Gould and I are in complete agreement. Moreover, the need to examine actual institutions, particularly nation-states and international organizations, making specific recommendations for change will be even more appropriate if I have succeeded in showing that rationality leads to morality and that even the most minimal morality, libertarianism, leads to the equality that socialists defend, because when specific recommendations are so grounded in such a view, it will be virtually impossible to rationally oppose them.[22]

Feminism

In her contribution to this volume, Alison Jaggar provides an excellent discussion of the objects of justice from a feminist standpoint. In several places throughout her discussion she cites my work approvingly, noting that she has very little to disagree with in respect to the policy implications of my view. Where she does disagree, as does Rosemarie Tong in her contribution to this book, is with respect to my defense of an ideal of androgyny as a feminist ideal. The ideal of androgyny, as I define it, requires that the traits that are truly desirable in society be equally open to both women and men or, in the case of virtues, be equally expected of both women and men.

Actually, this debate that I have been having with Jaggar and Tong has extended over ten years![23] So it is a little difficult to know what I am supposed to say or do at this point. As I have indicated, very little is at stake in this debate at the practical level. We all three are feminists who share much the same practical agenda. So what are we disagreeing about? At the most basic level it concerns whether I and other feminists should endorse an ideal of androgyny as I have characterized it. Some other feminists who have similarly endorsed this ideal are Claudia Card, Marilyn Friedman, Carol Gould, Martha Nussbaum, and Mary Anne Warren.[24] Note, too, that philosophers who endorse the ideal are not claiming that all other feminists must also endorse this ideal, nor are they claiming that this is the only way to conceive of feminist justice. Rather, what is being claimed is simply that this way of conceiving of feminist justice can be easily linked to other social and political ideals, like equal opportunity, welfare liberal justice, and socialist justice. What, then, are the objections to conceiving of feminist justice in this way? Both Jaggar and Tong have quite a few.

Jaggar thinks that a negative definition of feminist justice as simply a commitment to ending women's subordination would be easier for many people to accept. But if we were to abide by a similar consideration elsewhere in social and political philosophy, very little would get done. Much of social and political philosophy attempts to move people beyond where they already are, with the expectation that change will not occur overnight, and that it will take time and more discussion before many people come to accept the views that are being proposed. So I think that it would be a mistake in feminist philosophy and elsewhere to limit our discussion to what many people are already willing to accept. Moreover, traditional conceptions of justice, like welfare liberal justice, libertarian justice and communitarian justice, which Jaggar wants an account of feminist justice to parallel, are almost always presented in positive terms, quite different from the negative definition to which Jaggar proposes to restrict feminist justice.

Both Jaggar and Tong also object to characterizing feminist justice in terms of androgyny because they think androgyny is a character ideal rather than a social ideal. On several occasions I have responded to this objection by claiming that the ideal of androgyny, as I define it, closely resembles the ideal of equal opportunity, and since the ideal of equal opportunity is thought to be a social ideal or an ideal for reforming social structures, the same should hold of the ideal of androgyny, as I define it. But since this response of mine has yet to be addressed, let me try another tack. Jaggar in this essay says

> For women of my generation ... much of the inspirational force of second-wave feminism derived from its slogan, "The personal is the political."

Yet surprisingly, when it comes to the ideal of androgyny, Jaggar appears to be going against this very basic slogan of feminism, failing to recognize that the ideal of androgyny is not just a personal but also a political ideal, and that its general realization would clearly transform society, allowing both women and men to be the best that they can be.

Jaggar has also suggested that if one must go beyond the characterization of feminist justice as simply a commitment to ending women's subordination, it is preferably to endorse the ideal of genderlessness. Androgyny, she thinks, will scare people away from feminism. But it is hard to see how androgyny will be any less scary than genderlessness. In fact, genderlessness seems a bit more scary because it only tells us what we need to get rid of, not what we need to put in its place. Moreover, probably the most well known defender of a genderfree society, Susan Okin, has no trouble also endorsing the ideal of androgyny as I define it.[25]

Finally, Jaggar has "expressed some resentment about [my] insistence on defining feminism in terms of androgyny, even though few contemporary feminists accepted that term." The first thing to note here is that we are talking about defining or characterizing feminist justice, not feminism. The second thing to note here is that it is not as though large numbers of contemporary feminists are flocking to any other positive conception of feminist justice. The field is wide open here, and only a few contemporary feminists, such as Jaggar, Tong, and Kathryn Morgan, whom Tong cites, have explicitly rejected it, although in the case of Jaggar her rejection is complicated by the fact that she endorses an ideal that at least verbally is hard to distinguish from androgyny as I define it.

Furthermore, I don't see the problem here. Why shouldn't I, and other feminists who feel inclined to do so, develop and defend a characterization of feminist justice in terms of the ideal of androgyny? Of course, we should be willing to address those who explicitly reject that characterization. But suppose we were to invite them to develop their objections in conferences and publications, and suppose we were to listen carefully to their objections and to provide replies which we thought were reasonable. Why, then, should it not be acceptable for us to continue to develop our views, and why should anyone resent our doing so?

Tong's main reason for objecting to androgyny, as I define it, is quite different from Jaggar's. She does not want to limit her characterization of feminist justice to a negative definition as Jaggar does. Rather she wants to defend a somewhat different positive definition of feminist justice. She begins by citing Kathryn Morgan as favoring three alternatives to "the kind of androgynous individuals Sterba envisions." But Morgan in her 1983 article does not discuss the form of androgyny I defend, focusing her attack primarily on the early psychological literature on this topic. At one point Morgan comes close to discussing the androgyny I favor, but then rejects it for a reason that is clearly at odds with thinking about androgyny as an ideal for achieving feminist justice. She writes,

> Suppose we ... arrive at something approximating consensus on a set of positively-valued characteristics, we would have very few left and certainly very few relative to the total set of sex-coded characteristics even in one culture. Moreover, if we engage in this process of elimination in hopes of reaching accord on positively-valued characteristics, we undercut one of the most powerful claims made on behalf of androgyny, namely, that it presents us with a model of the fully human individual. If, in fact, being an androgynous individual turns out to mean that one has, for example, fourteen out of possible sixty sex-coded characteristics, then the claim that such an individual represents full humanity is ludicrous.[26]

Clearly, if one is interested in androgyny as an ideal for feminist justice, as I am, then one is not particularly concerned that it capture our full humanity

– our human vices as well as our human virtues. Morgan is not thinking about androgyny as providing an ideal for just relations between women and men, nor does she consider what an account of androgyny would look like if it were designed for that purpose.

Fortunately, Tong does not rest her rejection of my account of androgyny on Morgan's views alone. She goes on to object to the distinction between truly desirable traits and expected virtues in my ideal of androgyny. Recall that my ideal of androgyny requires that the traits that are truly desirable in society be equally open to both women and men or, in the case of virtues, be equally expected of both women and men. What Tong specifically objects to here is my claim that there is a set of virtues which should be equally expected of both women and men.[27] Instead, Tong favors an ideal of feminist justice which will simply provide women and men with equal capabilities for leading a full human life. When I indicated to Tong that some virtues (like justice) will need to be enforced, and that is why, putting a feminist spin on this necessity, I proposed in my ideal of androgyny that we enforce the same virtues for everyone, Tong responded in the revised version of her paper, the one included in this volume, as follows:

> In the feminist utopia I envision, society will not have to require people to be virtuous for people will want to be virtuous, having recognized that unless they treat each other with equal respect and consideration, rejoicing in each other's differences, they will not only not flourish but not survive as a society.

I think that Tong's view here is far too utopian for an account of feminist justice for here and now, and that my account of feminist justice, which recognizes the need to require certain virtues of everyone, is preferable in the unjust world in which we live.

Unlike Jaggar, Tong goes on to criticize the practical requirements I derive from my ideal of feminist justice. With respect to family life, I argue for affordable, quality day-care, flex-time, and more equal sharing of childcare and housekeeping. With respect to the distribution of economic power in society, I argue for the end of the wage gap, affirmative action and comparable worth. With respect to the overt violence, I argue for stronger laws, and more enforcement of existing laws against rape, domestic violence and child abuse; for banning hard-core pornography, for de-emphasing violent sports like football and boxing, for teaching conflict resolution, childcare and the history of peacemaking in our schools, and for recognizing the interconnection between violence in international relations and violence in personal relations. Finally, after a lengthy discussion of the issue, I argue for new programs against sexual harassment.

Tong argues that the reforms I propose will not work well for working-class families, for single-parent families or for homosexual households. I think that this charge comes from failing to properly situate my chapter on feminist justice within the context of the chapters that come before and after. The argument from liberty to equality of the preceding chapter would basically equalize the economic resources of all families, and this would surely speak to the needs of middle-class and single-parent families. The chapter that follows takes up the topic of homosexual justice and defends as radical a view on that topic as I think Tong would want.

Tong also criticizes me for not discussing feminist criticisms of the implementation of comparable worth programs, for not discussing feminist arguments against the banning of hard-core pornography, and for not discussing the "beauty trap" and reproductive issues. In my defense, I have discussed some of these topics (e.g. reproductive issues and pornography) at length elsewhere, and it would have been difficult to include more material in this chapter while still maintaining parity with other discussions of justice in my book.[28]

At the very end of her essay, however, Tong makes a very serious criticism of my work. She claims that my work is not a theory of justice for here and now, "but for there and then, the United States in the 1960s and 1970s." Attempting to support this claim, Tong starts out with a discussion of Iris Young's and Nancy Fraser's recent work. But then her discussion of Young's work leads her to conclude that it is not that different from my own, and so she rests her claim on a contrast she perceives between Nancy Fraser's work and my own.

Now, Fraser puts forward a theory of social justice and a theory of cultural justice. Her theory of social justice, which she develops from Marx and Habermas, is not unlike the egalitarianism which I, maybe more usefully in the present political climate, derive from libertarian premises. In contrast, her theory of cultural justice combines feminism, anti-racism and anti-heterosexism. Her overall goal is to integrate her theory of social justice with her theory of cultural justice. But once we note the components of Fraser's theory of cultural justice, we see they are just the same components that I am trying to integrate, along with an account of economic justice, into my overall theory of justice. So if Fraser's overall theory of justice is appropriate for here and now, then so, it would seem, is mine.

Lesbian and gay perspectives

Claudia Card in her contribution to this volume agrees with many of the conclusions and arguments that I develop in my book, but she also seeks to draw out further implications of feminist justice for the nonideal conditions in which we work and live. I find her work here, as elsewhere, very helpful and insightful.

Feminist justice, with its ideal of genderfree or androgynous society, applies under both ideal and nonideal conditions. Under ideal conditions, children, irrespective of their sex, would be given the same type of upbringing and parents would have the same opportunities for education and employment. There would be equal pay for comparable work and the incidence of rape, battery, sexual abuse and sexual harassment would be extremely low or nonexistent. Under the nonideal conditions in which we live and work, none of this has been achieved, and we face the problem of determining what measures and programs are needed to move us toward a more just society, like those I discuss in *Justice for Here and Now*.

In her essay, Card proposes some additional measures that she thinks are also needed to move us toward a more just society. She suggests, and I agree, that anyone guilty of domestic violence or child abuse might be denied a license for future marriages or guardianship of children. She also suggests that "[a]bandoning heterosexual cohabitation, rather than trying to reform it in the context of a misogynous society, *might* be a more effective and less unjust way to further the androgynous ideal" (emphasis added). Here too I agree.[29]

Card then goes on to recommend that individuals reject heterosexual households "as a matter of principle" under existing nonideal conditions, although she does not favor a legal ban on such households. But an in-principle rejection of heterosexual households would not permit individuals to weigh the strengths and weaknesses of the various homosexual or heterosexual households that they might form. It would require that they automatically opt for a homosexual household whatever their particular circumstances. It seems to me that this would have disastrous consequences for particular individuals.[30] Nor do I think that such an uncompromising stance is required to move us to the androgynous ideal. In fact, that transformation would be better achieved if homosexual and heterosexual households were both considered open possibilities whose desirability depended on the particular individuals with whom one would be forming those households. Other things being equal, forming a household with a caring and insightful man would be preferable to forming a household with a selfish and obtuse woman.

One reason that Card is so critical of heterosexist households is that she thinks that men do not do very well as parents. In this context, she is disturbed by my suggestion that in nontraditional, better structured families, men would learn to be open, cooperative, and nurturant by equally sharing childrearing and housekeeping responsibilities. She compares my suggestion to a suggestion by one of her students to the effect that convicted rapists or batterers should be required to work in shelters for battered women. But I don't think this comparison holds, given that I agree with Card that men who are guilty of such offenses might be denied a license for future marriages or guardianship of children. Moreover, the basis for thinking that men would learn to be open, cooperative and nurturant by shouldering their childrearing and housekeeping responsibilities is that this is frequently how women learn these very same traits. Women today have frequently grown up in smaller families (and so have not been much involved in raising their brothers or sisters) and have gone through many years of schooling before deciding to establish a heterosexual household and have children. As a result, they are often as ignorant of what is required for good childrearing as are their male partners. Given this context, it is not unreasonable to assume that both women and men could learn the desired traits that they need through an equal sharing of childrearing and housekeeping responsibilities. Even assuming that women frequently have a head start over men with respect to certain desirable traits needed to form a good household, and that men frequently have a head start over women with respect to other desirable traits needed to form a good household, why would it not be reasonable for them to choose to form heterosexual households, under certain conditions, so as to learn from their partner's gentle coaxing and example how to acquire the desired traits they lack? If we look at today's society, many women have done amazingly well, given the hindrances they face, in acquiring just those desirable traits, like independence, decisiveness and strength, which are stereotypically associated with men. Yet while some of this success can be attributed to women helping women, some of it is also due to men helping women, both inside and outside of households. Accordingly, I think it would be a mistake, especially under the unjust conditions in which we live and work, to simply reject the support for feminist justice that men can provide within heterosexual households. So, rather than endorsing an in-principle rejection of heterosexual households, I think that we should treat homosexual and heterosexual households (and other relationships) as open possibilities whose desirability depends on the particular individuals with whom we would be forming those households (or relationships). This alternative, I think, is more likely to be beneficial to the particular individuals involved, and also more likely to advance us toward a more just society.

Nevertheless, the differences between Card's view here and what I now think would be my own view (since this is new terrain for me) are really quite small, and, for the most part, we share a common political agenda with respect to feminist justice and with respect to other issues as well.

In *Justice for Here and Now*, I argue that feminist justice which seeks to remedy the injustice of sexism is theoretically connected to homosexual justice, which seeks to remedy the injustice of heterosexism. The theoretical connection is that each of these injustices is supported by a similar argument. That argument begins by noting certain differences among either individuals or groups. It then claims that these differences are grounds for regarding some individuals or groups as superior to other individuals or groups. This superiority is then claimed to legitimate the domination of some individuals or groups by other individuals or groups. In each case, this argument moves from a claim of difference to a claim of superiority and then to a claim of domination. In the case of sexism, the biological differences between men and women, or other differences claimed to be linked to these biological differences, are said to be grounds for regarding men as superior to women; this superiority is then claimed to legitimate the domination of women by men. In the case of heterosexism, the biological or acquired differences between heterosexuals and homosexuals are said to be grounds for regarding heterosexuals as superior to homosexuals; this superiority is then claimed to legitimate the domination of homosexuals by heterosexuals. It is possible, of course, for someone to reject the argument for sexism but accept the argument for heterosexism, despite their similar structure. That is why I was concerned in my book to offer independent reasons for undercutting the general argument in each case.

John Corvino, in his contribution to this volume, assumes that my argument for feminist justice is successful, and is primarily concerned to buttress the case for homosexual justice. He too is concerned with the possibility that someone might grant the need for feminist justice, but reject the need for homosexual justice. Feminist justice, as I defend it, requires an androgynous or genderfree society, which, in turn, requires that the traits that are truly desirable in society be equally open to both women and men or, in the case of virtues, be equally expected of both women and men. This ideal of justice, I argue, substitutes a socialization based on natural ability, reasonable expectation and choice for a socialization based on sexual difference. Corvino is particularly concerned with those who might accept this argument for feminist justice but reject any argument for homosexual justice. Accordingly, most of his essay is concerned with developing a positive argument for homosexual justice and then rebutting three popular arguments that have been used to support restricting the rights of homosexuals. With all this, I am in perfect agreement.

In the course of developing his arguments for homosexual justice, however, Corvino does employ a different notion of gender from the one I used in my book, and I would like to consider how they are related.

A society which has realized feminist justice, as I define it, must be genderfree, that is, it must have a socialization that is based on natural ability, reasonable expectation and choice rather than a socialization that is based on sexual difference. Now, Corvino thinks that it is possible for a society to be genderfree in this sense, but also gendered in another sense. He writes:

> What, then, is gender? I submit that it is a mistake to try to capture gender in terms of necessary and sufficient conditions. Rather, being a woman and being a man are family resemblance concepts. To be a woman or a man is to possess a substantial portion of a cluster of characteristics, none of which is necessary but some of which

must be present in order for the term to apply correctly. Such characteristics would include, but are not limited to

- being biologically male or female

- having (or wanting to have) a certain kind of bodily structure (e.g. broad or narrow shoulders or hips, body hair, and so on)

- having (or wanting to have) male or female genitalia

- conceiving of oneself a man or a woman

- presenting oneself as a man or a woman

- exhibiting certain masculine or feminine characteristics (many of which may be culturally bound)

- relating (or desiring to relate) to other persons sexually in a particular way (e.g. penetrating or being penetrated)

One thing to note about this characterization is that in a society which is genderfree in my sense, such that where equal opportunity exists at all levels – early socialization, formal education, sports, work, dress and body language – it is not clear that there will be any "culturally bound masculine and feminine characteristics." Of course, if it turns out, for example, that under a system of equal opportunity for women and men, women turn out to constitute most of the fighter pilots, now a premier role in the military, because of the shorter distance, on average, between their head and heart, making them more capable of withstanding G-forces, and men turn out to make up more of the grunt soldiers needed primarily for hand-to-hand combat, because of their average larger body size, we may want to refer to such roles as feminine and masculine gender roles, but it is not clear that we would.[31]

Yet even if I am right that there would be few culturally determined feminine and masculine gender roles or traits that would survive the equal opportunity requirements of feminist justice, there would still exist gender roles or traits in Corvino's sense, as he explains:

Suppose Phyllis, a woman, likes to date men. ... Because she likes to date men, she might frequent places (e.g. straight singles bars) attended by men who like to date women; moreover, she might make her friends aware of this (as well as other) preferences so that they might suggest suitable partners for her. Phyllis' expressed preference for and pursuit of men strikes me as morally unproblematic of itself

448

– especially in an ideal society where the evil of sexism has been overcome.

Thus people's preferences for either heterosexual, homosexual, or bisexual relationships will lead to gender roles or traits in Corvino's sense, and I certainly agree with Corvino that these preferences are compatible with the achievement of feminist justice in my sense.

Racial and multicultural perspectives

In his contribution to this volume, Charles W. Mills takes up the topic of racial justice, a topic he rightly claims has not been given sufficient consideration in contemporary social and political philosophy. He argues that if contemporary social and political philosophers would only attend to the legacy and current practices of racism in the US, then even their own normative perspectives would require them to endorse fairly radical changes. In *Justice for Here and Now*, I did cite the following general data to support such changes:

> In the case of blacks in the United States, almost half of all black children live in poverty. Black unemployment is twice that of white. The infant mortality rate in many black communities is twice that of whites. Blacks are twice as likely as whites to be robbed, seven times more likely to be murdered or to die of tuberculosis. A male living in New York's Harlem is less likely to reach 65 than a resident of Bangladesh. Blacks comprise 50% of the maids and garbage collectors but only 4% of the managers and 3% of the physicians and lawyers.[32] While one study of the nation's ten largest cities showed that blacks and whites rarely interact outside the workplace, another revealed that about 86% of available jobs do not appear in classified advertisements and that 80% of executives find their jobs through networking, thus showing the importance for employment of contacts outside the workplace.[33]

According to another study, black children adopted by white middle-class families score significantly better on the Wechsler Intelligence Scale than black children adopted by black middle-class families, and the scoring difference is of the magnitude typically found between the average scores of black and white children.[34]

I also cited specific data on environmental racism:

1   Penalties under hazardous waste laws at sites having the greatest white population were 500% higher than penalties at sites with the greatest

minority population, averaging $335,566 for the white areas, compared with $55,318 for minority areas.[35]

2   The disparity under toxic waste law occurs by race and not by income. The average penalty in areas with the lowest median income is only 3% different from the average penalty in areas with the highest median income.[36]

3   For all the federal environmental laws aimed at protecting citizens from air, water and waste pollution, penalties in white communities were 46% higher than in minority communities.[37]

4   Under the giant Superfund cleanup program, abandoned hazardous waste sites in minority areas take 20% longer to be placed on the national priority action list than those in white areas.[38]

5   In Tacoma, Washington, where paper mills and other industrial polluters ruined the salmon streams and the way of life of a Native American tribe, the government never included the tribe in assessing the pollution's impact on residents' health.[39]

6   Three of every five black and Hispanic Americans live in a community with uncontrolled toxic waste sites.[40]

7   The developed countries ship an estimated 20 million tons of waste to the Third World each year. In 1987, dioxin-laden industrial ash from Philadelphia was dumped in Guinea and Haiti. In 1988, 4,000 tons of PCB-contaminated chemical waste from Italy was found in Nigeria, leaking from thousands of rusting and corroding drums, poisoning both soil and groundwater. In 1991 a Swiss broker negotiated on behalf of Italian companies a twenty-year deal with one faction in Somalia to ship toxic wastes into the country. According to the contract, the shipments – each of 100,000–150,000 tons – were to yield a profit of 8–10 million dollars per shipment, with 2–3 million dollars per shipment going to the Swiss broker.[41]

In his essay, however, Mills provides a much more detailed account that ties current practices to a history of racism in the US, and thus more convincingly supports the radical practical requirements that both of us favor. I now regret not having done something similar. Expanding my discussions of racial justice, homosexual justice and multicultural justice into separate chapters of their own would have certainly helped support the book's claim to convey "the breadth and interconnectedness of questions of justice – a rarity in social and political philosophy."[42]

As to radical practical requirements to deal with the history and current practice of racism in the United States, I argue for affirmative action, comparable worth, and allocating environmental risks by consumption, which would place most waste disposal sites in wealthy neighborhoods. Mills points out that training programs for unskilled blacks are also needed, as are reparations for past injustices. Now although I did not argue for training programs for unskilled blacks, I did assume their legitimacy in my argument for affirmative action. Reparations for past injustices to African Americans, however, is something I did not discuss. Nevertheless, I take up the similar question of reparations to American Indians in a recently published book, *Three Challenges to Ethics: Environmentalism, Feminism, and Multiculturalism* (Oxford University Press, 2001), and there I endorse a fairly specific plan for reparations as the appropriate response to what some have called "the American Holocaust."

In his contribution to this volume, Chung-ying Cheng explores the puzzling relationship between just states and just persons, drawing on insights found in both Western and Confucian philosophical works.[43] In the Confucian tradition, the just person is primary; nor does the just person always act in accord with the laws of a just state. In contemporary social and political philosophy, particularly John Rawls' work, it would seem that the justice of the state is primary. Still, Rawls recognized that there is more to being a just person than simply a person who obeys the laws of a just state. For example, Rawls recognized, at least in some of his later work, that a just person would also be just in their familial relationships.[44] Nor in Rawls' view would a just person always obey the law, even in a just state, because, even in a just state, the laws do not always secure just results.[45] Given the similarities and differences between these different perspectives, it seems reasonable to follow Cheng's approach of trying to combine them into a defensible account.

Environmentalism

There is much that I agree with in Holmes Rolston's contribution to this volume. He provides a sweeping overview of enforcement in environmental ethics, relating it to enforcement in ethics more generally. At one point, however, he challenges one of my principles of environmental ethics, specifically my Principle of Human Preservation. According to this principle,

> Actions that are necessary for meeting one's basic needs or the basic needs of other human beings are permissible even when they require aggressing against the basic needs of individual animals and plants or even of whole species or ecosystems.

Rolston objects to this principle on the grounds that it benefits humans too much at the expense of nonhuman nature, as he tries to show through a number of examples.

His first example is that of the Hopi Indians of Arizona, who claim that they need to capture and kill baby golden eagles in order to communicate with their ancestors. Rolston thinks that in our present circumstances, preserving golden eagles is more important than satisfying the Hopi's felt religious need. Although he thinks that given my Principle of Human Preservation, I would disagree with him. I actually agree with him. I think that capturing and killing baby golden eagles under present circumstances is arguably not a basic need, even when properly judged from the perspective of the Hopi themselves.

Rolston's second example involves whether to use the traditional method of kosher slaughter rather than a less painful contemporary method which utilizes a stun gun. Rolston thinks that the use of a stun gun is preferable, even when judged from an orthodox Jewish perspective. But here too I guess I surprise Rolston again by agreeing with him.

So while neither of these first two examples presents a challenge to my Principle of Human Preservation, Rolston's final example does appear to do so. In this example, thousands of Nepalese have cleared forests, cultivated crops, and raised cattle and buffalo on the land surrounding the Royal Chitwan National Park in Nepal, but they have also made incursions into the park to meet their own basic needs. In so doing, they are threatening the rhino, the Bengal tiger, and other endangered species in the park. Now this clearly is a case where basic human needs are in conflict with the survival of other species. Does this mean that if we want to favor the endangered species in this conflict, we would have to reject my Principle of Human Preservation? Not at all. This is because it is possible to redescribe this example as a conflict between two groups of Nepalese, each of whom is striving in different ways to meet basic needs. The Nepalese who want to preserve the park can be seen to want to maintain its tourist revenues to meet their own basic needs or the basic needs of other Nepalese. The Nepalese who want to use the resources of the park are similarly trying to meet their basic needs and the basic needs of other Nepalese. Accordingly, my particular Principle of Human Preservation does not even apply in this case, because its applications are limited to cases where meeting the basic needs of humans only requires aggressing against the basic needs of individual animals and plants, or even of entire species or ecosystems, but not when it also requires aggressing against the basic needs of other humans.

Nevertheless, it should not be that difficult to come up with a conflict case of the sort that Rolston envisions – a case where meeting the basic needs of humans is simply in conflict with protecting the needs of endangered species, especially if you think, as I do, that the best description of the relationship of the human population to the rest of the living world is that of a cancer on the biosphere, a species out of control, wreaking havoc on the rest of the biosphere. Even so, before we can justifiably use force to keep other humans from meeting their basic needs in order to preserve endangered species, I think that it is beholden on us to have first done all that we can, using whatever surplus we happen to have, to meet the basic needs of those people whom we propose to restrict. That would seem to me to be a difficult condition for most environmentalists to meet.

In her contribution to this volume, Mary Anne Warren defends an environmental ethics that is very similar, if not identical, to the one I defend. Warren thinks that it is a mistake to assign the same moral status to all nonhuman organisms. For her, sentience, mental sophistication, moral agency, their importance to species and ecosystems to which they belong, and their social relationships with us all, affect their moral status. In my account, these factors too have to be taken into account, because we clearly do more harm, other things being equal, when we harm sentient rather than nonsentient living beings, humans rather than animals, whole species or ecosystems rather than simply individuals who belong to those species or ecosystems, or animals with whom we have developed mutually beneficial social relationships rather than those with which we have no such relationships. On this account, these rankings would have to be taken into account in applying my principles.[46]

Warren also suggests one area for the application of these rankings that I did not explore. My Principle of Human Defense was focused on the permissibility of defending ourselves against aggression from nonhuman living beings. Warren takes up the question of to what degree we are justified in defending ourselves against simply risks to our well-being from other living beings, and she argues that the above rankings would affect what it is morally permissible for us to do in this regard. For example, she argues that she is morally justified in killing millions of bacteria to defend herself against a small risk, as in washing her hands, but not morally justified in killing an underground colony of voles in her front yard, even though they sometimes carry the Hanta virus which can be lethal to human beings; nor is she justified in eliminating mountain lions from the park near her home, even though they pose a small threat to human life. What these cases show is the relevance of whether living beings are sentient or not, and whether they are endangered species or not. Still, I think, given the possible threat to her life, she would be justified in removing the voles from her front yard, since voles are anything but an endangered species.

There is one place, however, where Warren clearly thinks that her account has different practical implications from my own. She thinks that on my account it would not be morally permissible to pull weeds from one's flower garden. However, if tending a flower garden were one of one's main forms of relaxation, then it would serve one's basic recreational interests, and so would be permissible according to my Principle of Human Preservation. The satisfaction of basic recreational needs is necessary for preservation. But suppose tending one's garden does not serve this purpose, but only serves to meet one's nonbasic or luxury interests. In that case, pulling weeds from one's garden could still be justified as a means of defending the basic interests of other plants in one's garden, again something that is permitted to do, but this time for the sake of the other plants in one's garden and not for oneself.

But let us consider still another case. Suppose one wants to enlarge one's already fairly large swimming pool. Suppose this is clearly a luxury interest and that it would require taking out a cluster of oak trees to satisfy it. Let us also suppose, probably contrary to fact, that the interests of no other living beings are at stake here. Applied to this case, my Principle of Disproportionality would clearly prohibit enlarging the pool.

But what would Warren's principles have to say about this case? The relevant principles from her account are principles 1 and 6. What is crucial to applying these principles is what counts as a good reason for killing nonsentient living things, a cluster of oak trees in this case, that do not belong to an endangered species. In her book *Moral Status: Our Obligations to Persons and Other Living Things*, Warren says: "That something is a living organism is a prima facie reason for not harming it, but one that is easily overridden when it has no other claim to moral status."[47] Since this cluster of oak trees would presumably not have any other claim to moral status, it would appear that enlarging the swimming pool would serve as a good enough reason to cut it down on Warren's account. On my account, it would not. So while there are many similarities between our accounts, it appears to be easier to take nonsentient life on Warren's view than it is on my own.

Pacifism and just war theory

In *Justice for Here and Now*, I argue that pacifism and just war theory, in their most morally defensible interpretations, can be substantially reconciled in both theory and practice. As I mention in the book, my work in this area draws upon the important work of Duane Cady and Robert L. Holmes in defense of anti-war pacifism.[48] In his contribution to this volume, Robert L. Holmes suggests that his arguments in favor of anti-war pacifism do not preclude a commitment to nonviolence. I agree. Anti-war pacifism is compatible with a general commitment to nonviolent strategies in dealing with conflict, which I endorse as well. But a commitment to nonviolent pacifism (or nonlethal pacifism) requires more than a general commitment to nonviolent strategies in dealing with conflict because it rules out ever using violence (or lethal violence), even if it were the only way to defend one's life from an unjust aggressor. This is a very uncompromising view that not even Gandhi endorsed.[49] Moreover, Holmes always limits his objections to war to the harming or killing of innocents; he does not argue that it would be wrong or impermissible to harm or kill an unjust aggressor if it were the only way to save one's own life or the lives of others.

What Holmes really objects to in this essay, however, is my argument for a differential restriction on harm that is more severe against the intentional infliction of harm upon innocents but less severe against the infliction of harm that is merely foreseen, leading to the conclusion that the foreseen killing of innocents can be morally justified in certain cases.

In my book, I argued for this differential restriction on harm because we have more reason to protest when we are being used by others than when we are being affected by them only incidentally, and because we have more reason to act when both our ends and means are good than when they are not. Initially, Holmes objects that these two grounds I offer in support of a differential restriction on harm are not comparable, that the first is far more significant than the second. Again, I agree, since I never claimed that they were comparable, only that they were two considerations that favored a differential restriction on harm.

I claim that in cases where the death of innocents is merely foreseen, one's end and means can still be good. Holmes argues that in such cases at least one's means is not good because it causes harm or death to innocents. But I think that it would be a mistake to call means bad whenever their intended use has such unintended harmful side effects. Consider a patient who dies from complications following necessary surgery that was competently performed. Surely, we would still say that the surgical means used were good and that they were used for a good purpose, despite their unintended lethal consequences for the patient. Of course, one's means can be bad when they cause harmful unintended consequences, if there are other means available for attaining one's end which do not cause such consequences. But this is not the sort of case that Holmes is envisioning. He wants unintended harmful side-effects to innocents to standardly rule out the pursuit of ends that we would otherwise think are morally justified, even when there are no other means available to pursue those ends that have less harmful unintended side-effects.

Holmes also questions my use of the term "incidental" to describe foreseen but unintended consequences of our actions. Yet given that the first meaning of "incidental" in *Webster's New World Dictionary* is "happening in connection with something more important," I think my use of this term is justified because one's end and means are more important to morally assessing one's actions than are the foreseen but unintended consequences of one's actions.

In my book, I consider a number of hypothetical cases for the purpose of assessing the anti-war pacifist critique of just war theory. Holmes argues that for many of these cases my Nonexplanation Test gives the result that what I call foreseen consequences are actually intended consequences. Now I am not entirely happy with the Nonexplanation Test, for reasons I indicated in the text, but I don't think it is defective in the way Holmes claims here.

According to the Nonexplanation Test, the relevant question to ask is:

Does the bringing about of the evil consequences help explain why the agent undertook the action as a means to the good consequences?

Suppose we apply this test to the hypothetical case where only the intentional or foreseen killing of an unjust aggressor and the foreseen killing of one innocent bystander would prevent the death of five innocent people.[50] To make this case easier to consider, imagine that it involves rushing a terrorist just as the terrorist is beginning to execute each of the hostages he has taken. The result of this action is that the terrorist and one hostage are killed but five hostages are saved. Now applying the Nonexplanation Test, we can ask: Does the death of one of the hostages in the crossfire help explain why the terrorist was rushed to save the other hostages, in the way that the civilian deaths at Hiroshima and Nagasaki due to their presumed effect on Japanese morale helped explain why Truman dropped atomic bombs on those two cities in order to end the war? I think the answer to this question is clearly no. The death of one of the hostages in the crossfire in no way explains why the terrorist was rushed in order to save the other hostages. It is simply an unintended but foreseen side-effect.

Arguing further against my use of the foreseen/intended distinction, Holmes considers a case where a student is about to detonate a bomb in the car of a professor who gave her a bad grade when another person unexpectedly gets into the car. Given that the death of the other person would only be foreseen, Holmes, in effect, asks: Would the student's action be any worse if the death of the other person was intended and not simply foreseen? Holmes thinks not. But I think that bad as the student's action already is, it would be significantly worse if the student intended to kill two innocent persons rather than just one, and that we have more reason to condemn the student if she intended to kill two innocent persons rather than just one, even though I agree that we already would have plenty of reason to condemn her if she just intends one of the killings.

In the last section of his essay, Holmes proposes an alternative way of bringing pacifists and nonpacifists together. He calls it liberal pacifism. Liberal pacifism begins with the observation that if modern wars are to be fought, those who are commanded to kill must be put into that position involuntarily, that is, they must be drafted into the society's armed forces. The key thesis of liberal pacifism is that the involuntary servitude required by compulsory armed forces is incompatible with the ideals of a liberal democratic society, even if (quoting Holmes) "one has no principled objection to killing, and even if one were to accept the permissibility of killing innocents in the sort of cases Sterba describes." Hence, Holmes thinks liberal pacifism can establish that modern wars cannot be fought by liberal democratic societies.

456

Now, much as I would like to endorse other ways of bringing pacifists and just war theorists together, beyond the approach I took in my book, I don't quite see how liberal pacifism can succeed in this endeavor. Assuming, as Holmes does here, that individuals can legitimately defend themselves against unjust aggressors in the ways that I have argued, it would be perfectly acceptable for the society to which they belong to set up an all-volunteer force to defend itself in analogous ways. Holmes allows that this would be acceptable, even though it would presumably require all citizens to pay their fair share for the upkeep of such a volunteer force.

But now let us assume that this volunteer force for some reason proves insufficient. Suppose it is because the society is flourishing economically and jobs in the volunteer army are not as desirable as those now available in the private sector. Under these circumstances, why would this society, through democratic procedures, not be justified in drafting a certain number of its citizens to fulfill vacancies in its military forces? Under exactly what circumstances the leaders of the armed forces would have "a right to command others to kill" is a separate question, but assuming that at least sometimes such commands are properly given by leaders of an all-volunteer force, it would seem that, in analogous circumstances, they could also be properly given by leaders of a partly conscripted force.

In *Justice for Here and Now*, I have argued that the few wars and large-scale conflicts that meet the stringent requirements of just war theory are the only wars and large-scale conflicts to which anti-war pacifists cannot justifiably object. I hope the above clarifications I have made regarding the way that I believe that this reconciliation can be achieved will bring us a step or two closer to its realization in practice.

Civil disobedience and revolutionary action

In the last chapter of *Justice for Here and Now*, I consider why particularly the have-nots are not resorting to civil disobedience or revolutionary action to secure the rights that they are denied in the US. In an earlier book, *Contemporary Social and Political Philosophy*, I spend more time describing legal protest, civil disobedience and revolutionary action, and in both works I discuss the possibility of morally justified criminal disobedience.[51] In his contribution to this volume, Laurence Thomas sets out a new account of how civil disobedience works, or should work, that fits nicely with my account of justice for here and now.

Traditionally, civil disobedience has been understood to be an illegal action whose purpose is to draw attention to what is believed to be a breach of a commonly accepted moral principle. But Thomas points to a paradox that surrounds this understanding of civil disobedience. If a society has refused to accord the full complement of rights to a group of its citizens, why would protests of civil disobedience by members of this deprived group suffice to move the society to accord those citizens the full complement of their rights? This leads Thomas to favor a different understanding of civil disobedience that avoids the paradox. According to Thomas, civil disobedience succeeds not so much by appealing to the moral conscience of society-at-large but by forcing society to take the civilly disobedient seriously. Moreover, it is those who are treated unjustly who have an obligation to assert themselves and demand that they be treated as equals. That is what Gandhi and King did; they forced their oppressors to bear witness to their dignity. Interestingly, Thomas' account of civil disobedience falls somewhere between traditional accounts of civil disobedience and revolutionary action. On the traditional accounts, the civilly disobedient appealed to moral standards commonly accepted in society, while the revolutionary justified their actions on the basis of moral principles not commonly accepted. On Thomas' account, civilly disobedient persons shock their fellow citizens into a new moral awareness, an awareness of them as their moral equals. Thus, if successful, the civilly disobedient, like Gandhi and King, bring about at least a moral revolution.

Working through the essays in this anthology will not always be an easy task. Some essays will be clear on the first reading, whereas others will require closer scrutiny. You should also make sure you give each selection a fair hearing, because although some will accord with your current views, others will not. It is important that you evaluate these latter with an open mind, allowing for the possibility that after sufficient reflection you may come to view them as the most morally defensible. Indeed, to approach the selections of this anthology in any other way would surely undermine your ability to reasonably resolve those disputes about justice in which our lives are inescapably involved.

NOTES

1 This case is discussed in Deborah Tannen, *The Argument Culture* (New York: Basic Books, 1998) pp. 152–3.

2 Gewirth himself appeals to a standard of non-question-beggingness but, for some reason, he doesn't fully utilize it to get beyond the egoistic presumptions of his discussion and introduce an altruistic perspective which can then be played off against an egoistic perspective.

3 Jeffrie Reiman, "What Ought ' "Ought" Implies "Can" ' Imply? Comments on James Sterba's *How To Make People Just*," *Journal of Social Philosophy* (1991) pp. 73–80. This objection was actually directed against Alan Gewirth's defense of morality, but in private correspondence, Reiman has directed it against my own view as well.

4 Jeffrie Reiman, *Justice and Modern Moral Philosophy* (New Haven: Yale University Press, 1990) pp. 112–29.

5 In private correspondence, Reiman claims that, as he understands the denial of the reality of other people, it does not require solipsism but only the failure to "recognize the first-person reality of other people" (2 August 1995). But even given this interpretation, it still seems that Reiman is making too strong a claim

about the egoist. For example, the egoist does not have to deny that other human beings are in pain, as would seemingly be the case if she failed to "recognize the first-person reality of other people."

6 The logical mistake of begging the question entails, in this context, preferring low-ranking self-interested reasons over high-ranking altruistic reasons or low-ranking altruistic reasons over high-ranking self-interested reasons, which, in turn, entails the material mistake of inflicting basic harm for the sake of nonbasic benefit. Likewise, the material mistake of inflicting basic harm for the sake of nonbasic benefit entails preferring low-ranking self-interested reasons over high-ranking altruistic reasons which, in turn, entails the logical mistake of begging the question.

7 On this point, Gert in a recent e-mail exchange seems to express considerable agreement with my view. He writes

> I am surprised that you claim that Morality as Compromise is simply useful to show that the egoist begs the question by ruling out altruistic reasons. We have no quarrel on that matter. ... I have much more trouble with your second point: your suggestion that Morality as Compromise is ... still useful for ... showing that something that has the form of morality is preferable to either egoism or altruism if we start from a standard of non-question-beggingness. Your conclusion seems to me correct in one sense, namely that a compromise between egoism and altruism is preferable to either egoism or altruism if we start from a standard of non-question-beggingness; however, that does not seem to me to be an interesting conclusion, it seems to be simply tautologous.

I take Gert's description of my argument here as "tautologous" as a backhanded way of saying: "It works!"

8 Machan goes on to buttress his claim with some examples. "No one has a right to my second kidney," he says, "even though I may not need it, or my second eye, even though I could see well enough without it." But these examples are clearly not just garden-variety examples of the general claim that Machan has endorsed. Nevertheless, even in these unusual cases, we still need to nonarbitrarily evaluate the competing liberties involved, which in cases of the sort that Machan cites may lead us to deny people the liberty to deny others in need the use of their bodily organs once they are dead.

9 I discuss these and other aspects of a welfare minimum in *How To Make People Just* (Totowa: Rowman & Littlefield, 1988) pp. 45ff, and footnote this discussion in *Justice for Here and Now* (New York: Cambridge University Press, 1998) p. 44.

10 Richard Rose and Rei Shiratori (eds) *The Welfare State East and West* (Oxford: Oxford University Press, 1986). In fact, the living standards of poor children in Switzerland, Sweden, Finland, Denmark, Belgium, Norway, Luxembourg, Germany, the Netherlands, Austria, Canada, France, Italy, the United Kingdom and Australia are all better than they are in the United States. See James Carville, *We're Right They're Wrong* (New York: Random House, 1996) pp. 31–2.

11 Michael Wolff, *Where We Stand* (New York: Bantam Books, 1992) pp. 23, 115; George Kurian, *The New Book of Work Rankings*, 3rd edn (New York: Facts on File, 1990) p. 73; *New York Times*, 17 April 1995.

12 Charles Murray, *Losing Ground* (New York: Basic Books, 1984) pp. 8–9.

13 Michael Harrington, "Crunched Numbers," *The New Republic*, vol. 193 (28 January 1985) p. 8.

14 Christopher Jencks, "How Poor are the Poor?" *New York Review of Books*, vol. 32 (9 May 1985) p. 44.

15 Paul Krugman, "In Praise of Cheap Labor," *Slate*, 20 March 2000 (http://slate.msn.com/Dismal/97–03–20/Dismal.asp).

16 Although I think Kittay did appreciate its significance in the public discussion we had on this topic at the Conference on Alternative Conceptions of Justice held at Notre Dame, 14–16 April 2000.

17 Lecture on "Liberal Legislation and Freedom of Contract" in T. H. Green, *Lectures on the Principles of Political Obligation*, P. Harris and H. Murrow (eds) (Cambridge: Cambridge University Press, 1986) pp. 194–212.

18 The conditions that I argue must be met are, first, that other options (e.g. normal politics, legal protest, civil disobedience, and revolutionary action) would have to be either ineffective for achieving reasonable progress toward a just society or reasonably judged too costly for those persons they are intended to benefit; and second, that there would only be minimal violations of the moral rights of others.

19 Although Nielsen thinks the argument does not work, he does not provide any specific criticism of it. Similarly, while he thinks that my argument from rationality (i.e. non-question-beggingness) to morality does not work, here too he does not note any specific defects in it.

20 Gould laments the limited number of references to socialism in *Justice for Here and Now*, finding only six (actually there are fourteen), but unfortunately she fails to take into account my book *How to Make People Just*, which has two chapters devoted to socialist justice.

21 Moreover, beyond simply raising the objection herself, Gould does nothing to show how my discussion of the libertarian ideal of negative liberty illicitly smuggles in some notion of positive liberty. In fact, I responded to this same objection at length some years ago in a book co-authored with Gould and others, a book to which Gould herself refers in this paper. Unfortunately, she has yet to address that response.

22 Near the end of her essay, Gould questions whether someone in the Taoist tradition would accept my account of rationality. Since as far as my argument is concerned, a commitment to rationality is simply a commitment to a standard of non-question-beggingness – part of the standard of good argumentation – it is hard for me to think that those in the Taoist tradition would not also be committed to a standard of non-question-beggingness in argumentation.

23 The debate began a bit earlier than Jaggar indicates. It actually began in 1991 with hers and Tong's contributions to the symposium issue of the *Journal of Social Philosophy* on my book *How To Make People Just*.

24 Claudia Card, "Routes to Lake Wobegon" (this volume); Marilyn Friedman, "Does Sommers like Women?", *Journal of Social Philosophy*, vol. 22 (1991) pp. 75–90. Carol Gould, "Privacy Rights and Public Virtues: Women, the Family and Democracy," in Carol Gould, *Beyond Domination* (Totowa: Rowman & Littlefield, 1983) pp. 3–18; Carol Gould, "Women and Freedom," *The Journal of Social Philosophy*, vol. 15 (1984) pp. 20–34; Martha Nussbaum (see her endorsement on the back cover of *Justice for Here and Now*); Mary Anne Warren, "Is Androgyny the Answer to Sexual Stereotyping?", in *"Femininity," "Masculinity," and "Androgyny"*, ed. Mary Vetterling-Braggin (Totowa: Rowman & Littlefield, 1982) pp. 170–86.

25 In a personal communication with Okin concerning the feminist chapters of *How To Make People Just*.

26 Kathryn Morgan, "Androgyny: A Conceptual Critique," *Social Theory and Practice* (1982) p. 268.

27 As she did in her contribution to the symposium issue of *the Journal of Social Philosophy* on my book *How To Make People Just* in 1991.

28 Moreover, none of the material that Tong would have wanted included would have affected the conclusions that I do endorse. Even the critical material on comparable worth simply argues only for a more refined program.

29 Card suggests that my discussion of families seems to take for granted a heterosexual household, and that my references to parents seem to assume that a child's parents will be one male and one female. Actually, I was thinking of families as being either homosexual or heterosexual, and while my reference to parents may have assumed that there were typically two parents in each family, I wasn't assuming anything else. Even in the one reference I make to mothers and fathers, I wasn't assuming that persons occupying these different roles had to be of different sexes.

30 I probably should say that the considerations that I am advancing here draw heavily on my own personal experiences and observations. From aged fourteen to twenty-six, I belonged to the Christian Brothers religious order, so I have had some experience of, as we are using the term here, a large homosexual household. For the last twenty years or so, however, I have been in a heterosexual household, where my partner, Janet Kourany, and I have raised one child, a daughter, who has just gone off to college. So I actually have some personal knowledge of what is achievable, and not achievable, in both homosexual and heterosexual households.

31 For more information on the natural advantage of women as fighter pilots, see Linda Bird Franke, *Ground Zero* (New York: Simon & Schuster, 1997) p. 236.

32 *New York Times* 12 July 1994; Gerald Jaynes and Robin Williams (eds) *A Common Destiny* (Washington DC: National Academy Press, 1989) p. 23; Andrew Hacker, *Two Nations* (New York: Ballantine Books, 1992) pp. 46, 231; Gertrude Ezorsky, *Racism and Justice* (Ithaca NY: Cornell University Press, 1991) p. 27. Actually, the homicide rate in poor black communities is 159 per 100,000 compared to 17 per 100,000 in middle-class white communities. See *Hunger 1995: Fifth Annual Report on the State of World Hunger* (Silver Spring: Bread for the World Institute, 1995) p. 43.

33 For a discussion of these studies, see Ezorsky, *Racism and Justice,* pp. 14–18.

34 *Ibid.,* p. 20. See also *New York Times,* 19 October 1994. It also turns out that the IQ gap between Protestants and Catholics in Northern Ireland is the same as the gap between whites and blacks in the US. See *New York Times,* 26 October 1994.

35 *National Law Journal,* 21 September 1992. See also B. J. Goldman, *Not Just Prosperity: Achieving Sustainability With Environmental Justice* (Washington DC: National Wildlife Federation, 1993).

36 *National Law Journal.*

37 *Ibid.*

38 *Ibid.*

39 *Ibid.*

40 Marcia Coyle, "When Movements Coalesce," *National Law Journal,* 21 September 1992.

41 John Bellamy Foster, " 'Let Them Eat Pollution': Capitalism and the World Environment," *Monthly Review,* vol. 44 (1993) p. 14; Hussein Adam, "Somalia: Environmental Degradation and Environmental Racism," in *Faces of Environmental Racism,* eds Laura Westra and Peter Wenz (Lanham MD: Rowman & Littlefield, 1995) pp. 195–6.

42 Of course, as the book stands, it is still probably the most wide-ranging discussion of justice to appear in decades.

43 This is a relationship to which I unfortunately paid little attention in my work.

44 John Rawls, "The Idea of Public Reason Revisited," *The University of Chicago Law Review* (1997) pp. 787–94.

45 John Rawls, *A Theory of Justice* (Cambridge MA: Harvard University Press, 1971) chapter 6.
46 This is why I argued that my Principle of Human Preservation must be implemented in a way that causes the least harm possible, which means that, other things being equal, our basic needs should be met by aggressing against nonsentient rather than against sentient living beings, so as to avoid the pain and suffering that would otherwise be inflicted on sentient beings (p. 128 n17), and we should favor culling elk herds in wolf-free ranges (p. 132).
47 Mary Anne Warren, *Moral Status: Our Obligations to Persons and Other Living Things* (New York: Oxford University Press, 1997) p. 178.
48 See Duane L. Cady, *From Warism to Pacifism* (Philadelphia: Temple University Press, 1989); Robert L. Holmes, *On War and Morality* (Princeton: Princeton University Press, 1989).
49 On the point, see Cady, p. 12.
50 Holmes' comments have convinced me that it would have been better if in the text I had initially described this case as "one where only the intentional or foreseen killing of an unjust aggressor would prevent the death of five innocent people and would result in the foreseen killing of one innocent bystander," and similarly for the seven other hypothetical cases I consider in the text. My rationale for describing the cases the way I did was to make it easier to assess the morality of the hypothetical action in each case by keeping separate each action's costs and benefits. But I now see this may give rise to the mistaken impression that the foreseen side-effects of the actions are somehow intentional.
51 James P. Sterba, *Contemporary Social and Political Philosophy* (Belmont: Wadsworth Publishing Co., 1994) chapter 8.

INDEX

entitlement 133–4, 136–7, 259;
Gewirth 132; institutions 232; justice
129, 146; libertarianism 222–3;
needs/rights 133–4; philosophy 67;
privatized provision 142; public
provision 132–3, 142–3; race 434;
single-parent households 148n16;
social right 133; stigma 133
welfare benefits 259, 434
welfare entitlement 135–6, 137, 138
welfare liberal state 281–2
welfare liberals 435–7; equal
opportunity 15–16, 17–18; equality
32, 270; justice 16; libertarianism
129–30, 152, 232; needs 54n105;
positive welfare rights 222–3; Rawls
159, 436; self-development 158
welfare programs 434; coercive 9;
libertarianism 9, 12–13, 129–32, 136–7
welfare rights: international
organizations 440; justice 271;
libertarianism 101–2, 222–3, 431–2;
nations 440; poor 100;
positive/negative 222–3, 232;
recognition of 14–15, 234–5; universal
16
welfare state: Canada 433–4; liberalism
158; Machan 437; multiculturalism
281; Narveson 437; patriarchy 135;
poverty 433–4; Sterba 226, 419
welfare state liberalism 152, 159
welfare statism 110n1, 121–2, 125, 129–30,
226
Wertheimer, Alan 331
West, Cornel 329
Westing, Arthur H. 365, 366
whale hunting 385n17
white supremacy 325–6, 328–35
Whitewater investigation 426
Wild and Scenic Rivers Act 350
wilderness 350–1, 356
Wilderness Act 350, 360

wildlife 360
will 156–7
Will, George 107, 108
Williams, Bernard 172
Williams, Joan 292
Wilson, E. O. 383
Winch, Peter 217
Wing-sit Chan 175
Wittgenstein, Ludwig 97
Wobegon, Lake 289
Wollstonecraft's Dilemma 135, 146–7n6
wolves 353–4
women: affirmative action 20, 290;
alienation 299; black 254, 257, 437;
civil rights 21; devaluation 262–3;
exclusion 145–6; labor force 19;
oppression 20–1; self-sufficiency
259–60; socialization 295–6;
subordination 239–40, 441; violence
against 20–1, 254, 256–7, 275, 290;
see also gender
work: hours 152; paid/unpaid 19, 142,
209, 257–9, 292; value 199n12; worth
points 273–4
workers: capitalism 209–10; domination
216; Marxism 209–10; rights 231,
243–4; self-management 243–4
workfare 141
World Bank 244
World Trade Organization 244
worldviews 194
worth see comparable worth policies
Wright, E. O. 208, 211
Wupatki National Monument 362

Xunzi 341

Yellowstone Park 360
Young, Iris M. 259, 280, 323, 444

zhi (knowledge) 343–4
Zimbabwe 363

481